Sixth Edition

THROUGH WOMEN'S EYES

An American History

WITH DOCUMENTS

Sixth Edition

THROUGH WOMEN'S EYES

An American History

WITH DOCUMENTS

Volume One: To 1900

Ellen Carol DuBois
UNIVERSITY OF CALIFORNIA,
LOS ANGELES

Brenda E. Stevenson
UNIVERSITY OF OXFORD AND
UNIVERSITY OF CALIFORNIA, LOS ANGELES

Lynn Dumenil
OCCIDENTAL COLLEGE

bedford/st.martin's
Macmillan Learning
Boston | New York

To Emma, Beverly, and Iris; to Gwen, Anna, and Sara

Senior Program Director: Erika Gutierrez
Senior Executive Program Manager: William J. Lombardo
Director of Content Development: Jane Knetzger
Executive Development Manager: Susan McLaughlin
Director of Media Editorial: Adam Whitehurst
Senior Development Editor: Cynthia Ward
Media Editor: Cara Kaufman
Assistant Editor: Kalinda Collins
Senior Marketing Manager: Melissa Rodriguez
Senior Director, Content Management Enhancement: Tracey Kuehn
Executive Managing Editor: Michael Granger
Senior Manager, Publishing Services: Andrea Cava
Executive Content Project Manager: Christina M. Horn
Senior Workflow Project Manager: Lisa McDowell
Production Supervisor: Jose Olivera
Director of Design, Content Management: Diana Blume
Cover Design: William Boardman
Cartographer: Mapping Specialists, Ltd.
Text Permissions Editor: Allison Ziebka-Viering
Text Permissions Researcher: Elaine Kosta, Lumina Datamatics, Inc.
Executive Permissions Editor: Sheena Goldstein
Photo Researcher: Cheryl Du Bois, Lumina Datamatics, Inc.
Senior Director of Digital Production: Keri deManigold
Assistant Director of Digital Production: Michelle Camisa
Copyeditor: Susan Zorn
Indexer: Rebecca McCorkle
Composition: Lumina Datamatics, Inc.
Printing and Binding: Lakeside Book Company

ISBN 978-1-319-24456-9 (Combined Edition)
ISBN 978-1-319-50753-4 (Volume 1)
ISBN 978-1-319-50752-7 (Volume 2)

Library of Congress Control Number: 2023942602

Printed in the United States of America.

1   2   3   4   5   6   28   27   26   25   24   23

Acknowledgments
Text acknowledgments and copyrights appear at the back of the book on page A-23, which constitutes an extension of the copyright page. Art acknowledgments and copyrights appear on the same page as the art selections they cover.

For information, write: Bedford/St. Martin's, 75 Arlington Street, Boston, MA 02116

PREFACE
FOR INSTRUCTORS

EACH NEW EDITION OF *Through Women's Eyes: An American History, with Documents* provides an opportunity to revisit and refine our vision for this textbook. Our original goal was to create a U.S. women's history that combined an inclusive and diverse narrative with primary source essays — a comprehensive resource to aid instructors and encourage student engagement and analysis. We have been thoroughly delighted that this book has resonated with instructors and students alike and were gratified to hear from one instructor that it is "the single best textbook in U.S. women's history." Our belief that U.S. women's history is U.S. history and vice versa continues to fuel our approach to this book, and we are pleased that *Through Women's Eyes* is the number one choice for U.S. women's history.

◆ NEW TO THIS EDITION

Brenda Stevenson joins *Through Women's Eyes* as coauthor of the new edition. She brings her expertise as a scholar of gender, race, slavery, family, and racial conflict to the revision, focusing on the period to 1900. Overall, the goal for the sixth edition has been to represent the diversity of women who have shaped and been shaped by U.S. history. We continue to decenter the existing historical narrative from an emphasis on white privileged women, instead providing an integrated analysis of the rich variety of women that includes racial and ethnic diversity and class, immigration status, geographical information, and sexual orientation difference. This also includes attending to the experiences of girls, young women, and seniors. These changes are in every chapter, but examples include new details on mothering under slavery; greater attention to the activism of Black, Native American, Puerto Rican, and Filipino women in the 1920s and 1930s; girls and young women in the civil rights movement; and LGBTQ+ rights and backlash in the twenty-first century. Chapter 12, on the contemporary period, has been extensively revised to cover the political, economic, cultural, and social events affecting women today. Included with the new content for Chapter 12 is a map showing the status of abortion access in the states.

Of the thirty-five Primary Source collections at the end of chapters, six are new or significantly revised:

- Voices from the Suffrage Movement
- Women Use Their Votes in the 1920s

- Girls and Young Women in the Civil Rights Movement
- Jane, the Underground Abortion Collective
- LGBTQ+ Lives in the Third Wave
- Gloria Steinem Reflects on a Life of Activism

In addition, many new textual and visual sources have been added within existing Primary Source collections, such as an antebellum photo of an enslaved girl and Jacob Riis's photo of an elderly woman immigrant.

Within chapters, ten of the "Reading into the Past" documents are new:

- Florence Hall's account of the slave trade
- "Thirteen Toasts" from the revolutionary era
- Charlotte Forten Grimké's story of teaching freedpeople on the Sea Islands
- The "Brandeis Brief"
- Meridel LeSueur's short story "Women on the Breadlines"
- Luisa Moreno's speech "Caravan of Sorrows"
- Betty Friedan's "The Sexual Sell"
- The Moynihan Report
- Pauli Murray and Mary Eastwood's "Jane Crow and the Law"
- Congressional testimony from "Dreamer" Maria Gabriela Pacheco

In the Appendix we have added *Dobbs v. Jackson Women's Health Organization* (2022) and *Students for Fair Admissions, Inc. v. President and Fellows of Harvard College* (2023) to the Supreme Court documents, and we have updated the historical tables to include data from 2020.

We have made some changes to the chapter review material: bolding key terms within the chapter and adding cross-references to these terms within the key terms list; and bringing the "Suggested Reading" list into the Chapter Review, so that students will see this list as a resource for their own research. The chapter Notes are now at the end of the book, before the Index.

For the first time, *Through Women's Eyes* is available with Macmillan Learning's Achieve**,** an intuitive and user-friendly online learning system that can be integrated with your learning management system. Achieve for *Through Women's Eyes* includes a full-color e-book, LearningCurve adaptive quizzes, summative quizzes for each chapter, metacognitive reflection activities, and chronology-based activities that guide students in identifying and understanding patterns of change.

Finally, with the sixth edition, we once again offer *Through Women's Eyes* as split volumes (Volume One, Chapters 1–7; Volume Two, Chapters 6–12) in addition to the combined comprehensive volume with all chapters. As with previous editions, instructors can choose to package *Through Women's Eyes* with titles from the Bedford Series in History and Culture and with trade books from other Macmillan imprints. For a complete list of titles, visit **bedfordstmartins.com/history/series** and **macmillanlearning.com/tradeup**.

◆ APPROACH AND FORMAT

Through Women's Eyes: An American History, with Documents challenges the separation of "women's history" from what students, in our experience, think of as "real history." We treat all central developments of American history always through women's eyes, so that students may experience the broad sweep of the nation's past from a new and illuminating perspective. *Through Women's Eyes* combines in-depth treatment of topics associated with women's history, such as the cult of true womanhood, the woman suffrage movement, and the rise of feminism, with developments in U.S. history not usually considered from the perspective of women, including the conquest of the Americas, the institution of slavery, war and the military, post–World War II anticommunism, the civil rights movement, and the outcome of recent presidential elections. Our goal of a **full integration of women's history and U.S. history** is pragmatic as well as principled. We recognize that there may be some students who read *Through Women's Eyes* who have little background in U.S. history and that they will be learning the nation's history as they follow women through it.

Just as many of our students hold preconceived notions of women's history as an intriguing adjunct to "real history," they often equate the historian's finished product with historical "truth." We remain determined to reveal the **relationship between historical scholarship and original sources** to show history as a dynamic process of investigation and interpretation rather than a set body of facts and figures. To this end, we divide each of our chapters into narrative text and primary source essays. Written sources range from diaries, letters, and memoirs to poems, newspaper accounts, and public testimony. Visual sources include artifacts, engravings, portraits, photographs, cartoons, and television screen shots. Instructors often tell us that these Primary Source collections are their favorite aspect of the book. "The primary source essays are an outstanding way for students to explore topics more in-depth," one instructor wrote, "and students really connect to the individual stories."

Together, the sources reveal to students the **wide variety of primary evidence** from which history is crafted. Our documentary and visual essays not only allow for focused treatment of many topics — for example, the experience of Indigenous women before and after European conquest, the higher education of women before 1900, women's use of cosmetics in the context of a commercialized beauty culture, women's roles in World War II, women's activism in the civil rights movement, and underground abortion services pre-*Roe* — but also provide ample guidance for students to analyze historical documents thoughtfully. Each essay offers advice about evaluating the sources presented and poses questions for analysis intended to foster students' ability to think independently and critically. Substantive headnotes to the sources and plentiful cross-references between the narrative and the essays further encourage students to appreciate the relationship between historical sources and historical writing.

◆ FEATURES AND PEDAGOGY

We are proud as well of the pedagogical features we provide to help students enter into and absorb the text. Each chapter opens with a **thematic introduction** that starts with a particular person or moment in time chosen to pique students' interest and segues into a clear statement of the central issues and ideas of the chapter. A **chapter chronology** alerts students to the main events covered in the narrative and relates women's experience to U.S. history by visually linking key developments. At the close of each narrative section, an **analytic conclusion** revisits central themes and provides a bridge to the next chapter. A chapter review contains a list of **key terms**, as well as **review questions** that will encourage students to reread and think about what they've learned throughout the chapter.

Beyond the visual sources presented in the essays, more than **100 historical images and 11 maps and charts** extend and enliven the narrative, accompanied by **substantive captions** that relate the illustration to the text and help students unlock the image. Also animating the narrative while complementing the documentary essays are **30 primary source excerpts, called Reading into the Past, drawn from classic texts** featuring women such as Anne Hutchinson, Charlotte Forten Grimké, Sojourner Truth, Emma Goldman, and Pauli Murray. At the end of each chapter, we provide a list of **suggested reading** that gives students a myriad of opportunities for reading and research beyond the boundaries of the textbook.

In addition, we open the book with an **Introduction to Women's History** that discusses the evolution of women's history as a field and the approach we took in capturing its exciting state today. An **extensive Appendix** includes not only tables and charts focused on U.S. women's experience over time but also the Seneca Falls Declaration of Sentiments and Resolutions and annotated extracts of Supreme Court cases of major relevance to U.S. history "through women's eyes."

◆ RESOURCES FOR INSTRUCTORS

Bedford/St. Martin's offers a wide variety of teaching resources for this book and for this course, including presentation materials, lecture strategies, and suggested in-class activities. All can be downloaded or ordered at **macmillanlearning.com /catalog/history**.

Guide to Changing Editions. Designed to facilitate an instructor's transition from the previous edition of *Through Women's Eyes* to this new edition, this guide presents an overview of major changes as well as changes in each chapter.

Online Test Bank. This test bank includes a mix of carefully crafted multiple-choice questions for each chapter.

Images and Maps as PowerPoints. Slides with all images and maps are available for download from Macmillan Learning's Achieve or from the online catalog at **macmillanlearning.com**.

◆ ACKNOWLEDGMENTS

Textbooks are for learning, and writing this one has taught us a great deal. We have learned from one another and have enjoyed the richness of the collaborative process. But we have also benefited immensely from the opportunity to read and assess the works of literally hundreds of scholars whose research and insights have made this book possible. Many colleagues and friends have helped with and are thanked in previous editions. Sharla Fett made major contributions to the previous edition. For this volume specifically, Ellen thanks Vicki Ruiz, the Pauli Murray Foundation, Gloria Steinem, Torie Osborn, Alix Kates Shulman, Heather Booth, Jane Mansbridge, Phillip Hoose, Ula Taylor, Lisa Souza, and *Ms.* magazine. Brenda would like to thank Ellen DuBois, Nancy Cott, Darlene Clark Hine, Deborah White, Rosalyn Terborg Penn, Sharon Harley, Sylvia A. Boone, Margaret Washington, and Angela Davis.

We have a great deal of admiration for the people at Bedford//St. Martins who worked so hard to bring all six editions of this book to fruition. For this edition, we would specifically like to thank editorial director Leasa Burton; senior program director Erika Gutierrez; senior executive program manager William Lombardo; senior development editors Rachel Goldberg and Cynthia Ward; media editor Cara Kaufman; executive content project manager Christina Horn; senior marketing manager Melissa Rodriguez; assistant editor Kalinda Collins; designers William Boardman and Diana Blume; and assistant director of digital production Michelle Camisa. Text and photo permission work was expertly handled by Hilary Newman, Cheryl Du Bois, Sheena Goldstein, Elaine Kosta, and Allison Ziebka-Viering.

The revisions for this new, sixth edition benefited significantly from the comments of instructors who have used the textbook in their classes. We'd like to thank the following reviewers:

Valerie Adams, Arizona State University

Daniel Ballentyne, Blue Ridge Community and Technical College

Aaron Berkowitz, Lincoln Land Community College

Elizabeth Chamberlain, Aquinas College

Sara Davis, Pima Community College

KateLynn Hibbard, Minneapolis Community and Technical College

Elizabeth Hohl, Fairfield University

Melissa M. Soto-Schwartz, Cuyahoga Community College

Angela Tharp, University of Houston

Cristina Zaccarini, Adelphi University

We continue to acknowledge the pioneering work of Mary Ritter Beard, *America Through Women's Eyes* (1933), and also note that this book would not have been possible without the dynamic developments and extraordinary output in the field of U.S. women's history since Beard's book appeared. In 1933 Beard acknowledged that the "collection, editing, sifting and cataloguing of sources dealing with women's work and thought in the making of civilization" was ground as yet uncultivated.[1] We have been fortunate to reap a rich harvest from the scholarly literature of the last forty years, a literature that has allowed us to express the diversity of women's lives and to conceive of U.S. history from a gendered perspective.

Ellen Carol DuBois
Brenda E. Stevenson
Lynn Dumenil

1. Mary Ritter Beard, ed., *America Through Women's Eyes* (New York: Macmillan, 1933), 9.

BRIEF CONTENTS

C O N T E N T S

photos: Chapter 1, Beinecke Rare Book and Manuscript Library, Yale University; Chapter 2, GRANGER — Historical Picture Archive

CHAPTER 3
**Mothers and
Daughters of the
Revolution,
1750–1810**   98

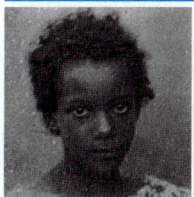

photo: National Archives file no. 12017/37232

PRIMARY SOURCE DOCUMENTS AND IMAGES

Reading into the Past

Reading into the Past boxes are embedded within chapters and contain shorter documents than the end-of-chapter Primary Source collections.

Primary Source Collections

Primary Source collections bring together written and visual historical sources focused on a theme.

INTRODUCTION TO WOMEN'S HISTORY

I N READING THIS TEXTBOOK, you will encounter a rich array of source materials and a narrative informed by a wealth of scholarship, so you may be surprised to learn that women's history is a comparatively new field. When Mary Ritter Beard, the founding mother of women's history in the United States, assembled *America Through Women's Eyes* in 1933, she argued that an accurate understanding of the nation's past required as much consideration of women's experience as of men's. But so limited were the sources available to her that she had no choice but to present the first women-centered American history as a spotty anthology of primary and secondary writings by a handful of women writers. Not until the 1970s, with the resurgence of feminism that you will read about in Chapter 11, did researchers start to give extensive attention to women's history. In that decade, history, along with other academic disciplines such as literature and sociology, underwent significant change as feminist scholars' desire to analyze as well as to protest women's unequal status fueled an extraordinary surge of investigation into women's experiences. Feminist theorists revived an obscure grammatical term, "gender," to distinguish the meaning that a particular society attaches to differences between men and women from "sex," or the unchanging biological differences between men and women. Because gender meaning varies over time and among societies, gender differences are both socially constructed and subject to change.

The concept of gender and the tools of history complement each other. If we are to move past the notion that what it means to be a woman never changes, we must look to the varying settings in which people assume female and male roles, with all their attendant expectations. Definitions of femininity and masculinity; family structures; what work is considered properly female or male; understandings of motherhood and of marriage; accepted, marginalized, and criminalized sexual behaviors; women's involvement in public affairs — all vary tremendously across time, are subject to large forces like economic development and warfare, and can themselves shape the direction of history. As historian Joan Scott forcefully argued, gender can be used as a tool of historical analysis, to explore not only how societies interpret differences between women and men but also how these distinctions can legitimize other hierarchical relations of power.[1]

This textbook draws on the rich theoretical and historical work of the past fifty years to present a synthesis of American women's experiences. We begin by

---

1. Joan Wallach Scott, "Gender: A Useful Category of Historical Analysis," *American Historical Review* 91, no. 5 (December 1986): 1067.

discussing the many meanings of "America" and end with a chapter that examines the issues women face in the twenty-first century. In between we highlight the broad patterns of change concerning women's political and legal status, their economic and family lives, and the diversity of American women's experiences.

As its title suggests, however, *Through Women's Eyes: An American History, with Documents* aims for more than an account of U.S. women's history. Beyond weaving together the wealth of scholarship available to U.S. women's historians, we seek to fulfill Mary Beard's vision of a text that covers the total range of the nation's history, placing women — their experiences, contributions, and observations — at the center. We examine major economic developments, such as the emergence of slavery as a labor system, the rise of factories in the early nineteenth century, the growth of an immigrant labor force, and the shift to corporate capitalism. We explore major political themes, from reform movements to political party realignments to the nation's many wars. We look at transformations in family and personal life, the rise of consumer and mass culture, the racial and ethnic heterogeneity of the nation's peoples, and shifting attitudes about sexuality and gender identity. And we analyze international developments, beginning with the interrelationship of the Americas, Europe, and Africa in the Atlantic world of the sixteenth and seventeenth centuries and ending with contemporary globalization. But as we do so, we analyze how women experienced these national developments and how they contributed to and shaped them.

◆ THE HISTORY OF WOMEN'S HISTORY: FROM SEPARATE SPHERES TO WOMEN'S DIVERSITY

When the field of U.S. women's history began to take off as a scholarly endeavor in the 1970s, one particular form of gender analysis was especially influential. The "separate spheres" paradigm, as historians termed it, focused on the nineteenth-century ideology that divided social life into two mutually exclusive arenas: the private world of home and family, identified with women, and the public world of business and politics, identified with men. In a subsequent phase, as scholarship on women of color increased, the primacy of the separate spheres interpretation gave way to a more nuanced interpretation of the diversity of women's experiences.

Separate Spheres and the Nineteenth-Century Gender System

Women's historians of the 1970s found in the nineteenth-century system of separate spheres the roots of the gender distinctions of their own time. They observed that although ideas about separate spheres had been of enormous importance in the nineteenth century, these ideas had received little to no attention in historical accounts. The approach that women's historians took was to re-vision this nineteenth-century gender system through women's eyes. They found that, although women's lives were tightly constricted by assumptions about their proper place within the family, expectations of female moral influence and a common sense of womanhood allowed women collectively to achieve a surprising degree of social authority.

The separate spheres paradigm proved a valuable approach, but it hid as much as it yielded about women's lives, particularly the lives of women of color and poor women. Early on, historian Gerda Lerner observed that it was no coincidence that the notion of white women's exclusive domesticity flourished just as factories were opening up and young women were going to work in them.[2] Because adherence to the ideology of separate spheres helped to distinguish the social standing of middle-class women from their factory-working contemporaries, Lerner urged that class relations and the growth of the female labor force be taken into account in understanding the influence that such ideas held. Subsequent historians have observed that the idealization of women within the domestic sphere coincided exactly with the decline of the economic importance of family production relative to factory production; and that just as class inequality began to challenge the nation's democratic self-understanding, American society came to define itself in terms of the separate spheres of men and women.

Additional problems emerged in the reliance on the separate spheres paradigm as the dominant basis for nineteenth-century U.S. women's history. Historian Nancy Hewitt contends that whatever sense of female community developed among nineteenth-century women rarely crossed class or race lines. On the contrary, hierarchical relationships — enslaved person to enslaver, immigrant factory worker to moneyed consumer, nanny to professional woman — have been central to the intricate tapestry of the historical female experience in America.[3] Even among the middle-class wives and mothers who did not work outside the home and whose family-based lives made them the central focus of separate spheres ideology, Linda Kerber urges historians not to confuse rhetoric with reality, ideological values with individual actions.[4] The lasting contribution of the historical exploration of separate spheres ideology is the recognition that gender differentiation had a vital impact on American history; the challenge posed by its critics is to develop a more complex set of portraits of women who lived in, around, and against these notions. As it matures, the field of women's history is able to move from appreciating the centrality of gender systems to accommodating and exploring conflicts and inequalities among women.

Toward a More Inclusive Women's History: Race and Ethnicity

The field of U.S. women's history has struggled to come to terms with the structures of racial inequality so central to the American national experience. As Peggy Pascoe

---

2. Gerda Lerner, "The Lady and the Mill Girl," *Midcontinent American Studies Journal* 10 (1969); 5–15.

3. Nancy Hewitt, "Beyond the Search for Sisterhood: American Women's History in the 1990s," in Vicki Ruiz and Ellen Carol DuBois, eds., *Unequal Sisters: A Multicultural Reader in U.S. Women's History*, 3rd ed. (New York: Routledge, 2000), 1–19.

4. Linda K. Kerber, "Separate Spheres, Female Worlds, Woman's Place: The Rhetoric of Women's History," *Journal of American History* 75, no. 1 (June 1988): 9–39.

observes, modern scholars have learned to think about race and gender in similar ways, no longer treating either as unchanging biological essences around which history forms but as social constructions that change meaning and content over time and place.[5] Building on a century-long scholarly tradition in African American history, in the 1980s Black women scholars — particularly Deborah Gray White, Angela Davis, Paula Giddings, Darlene Clark Hine, and Rosalyn Terborg Penn — started to chart new territory as they explored the interactions between systems of racial and gender inequality, or what came to be called "intersectionality." Analyzing the implications of the fact that late nineteenth-century Black women were denied the privileges granted white women, Evelyn Brooks Higginbotham observes that "gender identity is inextricably linked to and even determined by racial identity."[6]

Other scholars of color advanced this thinking about racial hierarchy and its intersections with the structures of gender. They made it clear that the history of other women of color could not be understood within the prevailing Black-white model of racial interaction. A multivocal narrative of U.S. women's history that acknowledges women's diversity in terms of race, class, ethnicity, and sexual orientation can be found in *Unequal Sisters: A Multicultural Reader in U.S. Women's History,* coedited by Vicki Ruiz and one of the authors of this text, Ellen Carol DuBois. This anthology of pathbreaking research pays particular attention to the historical experiences of western women, noting that "the confluence of many cultures and races in this region — Native American, Mexican, Asian, Black, and Anglo" — required "grappling with race" from a multicultural perspective.[7] By using her own southwestern experience, Gloria Anzaldúa added the influential metaphor of "borderlands" to this approach to suggest that the division between different communities and personal identities is somewhat arbitrary and sometimes shifting.[8] This new approach took the logic of the historical construction of gender, so important to the beginning of women's history, and pushed it further by emphasizing an even greater fluidity of social positioning.

◆ APPROACHING HISTORY THROUGH WOMEN'S EYES

How then to bring together a historical narrative told from such diverse and at times conflicting viewpoints? All written histories rely on unifying themes to organize what is otherwise a chaotic assembly of facts, observations, incidents, and

---

5. Peggy Pascoe, "Gender," in Richard Wightman Fox and James Kloppenberg, eds., *A Companion to American Thought* (Cambridge, MA: Blackwell, 1995), 273.

6. Evelyn Brooks Higginbotham, "African American Women's History and the Metalanguage of Race," *Signs* 17, no. 2 (Winter 1992): 254.

7. Ellen Carol DuBois and Vicki L. Ruiz, eds., *Unequal Sisters: A Multicultural Reader in U.S. Women's History* (New York: Routledge, 1990), xii. This reader has three later editions (1994, 2000, 2008) that include substantially different articles.

8. Gloria Anzaldúa, *La Frontera/Borderlands: The New Mestiza* (1987; repr., San Francisco: Aunt Lute Books, 1999).

people. Traditionally, American history employed a framework of steady national progress, from the colonial revolt against England to modern times. Starting in the 1960s, the writing of American history emphasized an alternative story line of the struggles of workers, enslaved people, Native Americans, and (to some degree) women to overcome enduring inequalities. Initially, women's history emphasized the rise and fall of the system of separate gender spheres, the limits of which we have already suggested. In organizing *Through Women's Eyes,* we employ another framework that emphasizes three major themes that shaped the diversity of women's lives in American history — work, politics, and family and personal life.

Work and the Sexual Division of Labor

The theme of women's work reveals both stubborn continuities and dramatic changes. Women have always labored, always contributed to the productive capacity of their communities. Throughout American history, women's work has taken three basic forms — unpaid labor within the home, chattel slavery, and paid labor. The steady growth of paid labor, from the beginning of American industrialization in the 1830s to the present day (women now constitute essentially half of America's workforce), is one of the fundamental developments in this history. As the female labor force grew, its composition changed, by age, race, ethnicity, and class. By the mid-twentieth century, the working mother had taken over where once the working girl had predominated. We have also followed the repeated efforts of wage-earning women to organize collectively in order to counter the power of their employers, doing so sometimes in conjunction with male workers and sometimes on their own. Historically a small percentage of union members compared to men, women exhibited unanticipated militancy and radicalism in their fight with employers over union recognition and fair wages and hours.

Most societies divide women's work from men's, and America has been no exception. Feminist scholars designate this gender distinction as the "sexual division of labor." Yet the content of the sexual division of labor varies from culture to culture, a point made beginning with the discussion of Native American communities in the precolonial and colonial eras and of African women's agricultural labor in their native lands. When women first began to take on paid labor in large numbers, they did so primarily as servants and seamstresses; the nature of their work thus generally followed the household sexual division of labor. The persistence of sex segregation in the workforce has had many sources of support: employers' desire to have a cheap, flexible supply of labor; male workers' control over better jobs and higher wages; and women's own assumptions about their proper place.

The division between male and female work continued, and with it the low wages and limited opportunities on the women's side of the line. This was true even as what counted as women's jobs began to expand and as teaching and secretarial labor, once securely on the male side of the line, crossed over to become "feminized" job categories. American feminism in the late twentieth century was committed to eroding this long-standing principle that work should be divided into male and female categories. As historian Alice Kessler-Harris puts it, feminists "introduced the language of sex discrimination onto the national stage, casting a new light on seemingly natural patterns of accommodating sex difference."[9] The degree to which the sexual division of labor has been substantially breached — whether it is half achieved or half undone — we leave to our readers, who are part of this process, to determine.

Gender and the Meaning of Politics

The theme of politics in women's historical experience presents a different sort of challenge, for it is the exclusion of women from formal politics that is the obvious development in U.S. women's history, at least until 1920, when the Nineteenth Amendment granting woman suffrage was ratified. While the story of women's campaign for the vote plays an important role in our historical account, we have not portrayed the suffrage movement as a monolithic effort. Rather, we have attended to the inequalities of class and race and the strategic and ideological conflicts that ran throughout the movement. We have also stressed the varying political contexts, ranging from Reconstruction in the 1860s to the Populist upsurge in the 1890s to Progressivism in the 1910s to the civil rights movement in the 1950s and 1960s, within which women fought for their voting rights. Finally, we have traced the significance of voting in U.S. women's history after the right to it was formally secured, following women's efforts to find their place — as voters and as officeholders — in the American political system.

U.S. women's historians have gone beyond the drama surrounding the vote, its denial and its uses, to a more expansive sense of the political dimension of women's historical experience. Feminist scholars have forged a definition of politics that looks beyond the formal electoral arena to other sorts of collective efforts to change society, alter the distribution of power between groups, create and govern important institutions, and shape public policy. Women's historians have given concrete substance to this broad approach to female political involvement by investigating the tremendous social activism and civic engagement that thrived among women, especially through the long period during which they lacked formal political rights. "In order to bring together the history of women and politics," writes Paula Baker, "we need a more inclusive definition of politics . . . to include any action, formal or informal, taken to affect the course or behavior of government or the community."[10]

From this perspective, the importance of women in the realm of politics reaches back to the Iroquois women who elected chiefs and participated in decisions to go to war and the European women colonists who provided the crucial support necessary to sustain prerevolutionary boycotts against British goods in the struggle for national independence. Just a small sampling of this rich tradition of women's civic

9. Alice Kessler-Harris, *In Pursuit of Equity: Women, Men, and the Quest for Economic Citizenship in 20th-Century America* (New York: Oxford University Press, 2001), 245–46.

10. Paula Baker, "The Domestication of Politics: Women and American Political Society, 1780–1920," *American Historical Review* 89 (June 1984): 622.

activity through the nineteenth century includes the thousands of New England women, Black and white, who before the Civil War signed petitions against slavery and Indian removal; the campaign begun by Ida B. Wells against the lynching of southern Blacks; the ambitious late nineteenth-century national reform agenda of Frances Willard's Woman's Christian Temperance Union; and Jane Addams's leadership in addressing problems of the urban immigrant poor and on behalf of international peace. "Women's organizations pioneered in, accepted and polished modern methods of pressure-group politics," observes historian Nancy Cott.[11]

Indeed, this sort of extra-electoral political activism extended into the twentieth century, incorporating women's challenges to the arms race of the post–World War II era and the civil rights leadership of women such as Ella Baker of the Southern Christian Leadership Conference in the 1950s and Dolores Huerta of the United Farm Workers union in the 1960s. This inclusive sense of what constitutes politics has not only enriched our understanding of women's history but has also generated a more complex understanding of the nature of political power and process within U.S. history in general.

Given the theme of politics as one of the major frames for this book, what is the place of the politics of feminism in the tale we tell? There are many definitions of feminism, but perhaps the clearest is the tradition of organized social change by which women challenge gender inequality. The term "feminism" itself arose just as the woman suffrage movement was nearing victory, but the tradition to which it refers reaches back to the women's rights movements of the nineteenth century. Historical research has unearthed a great deal of breadth and diversity in the many campaigns and protests through which women from different groups, in different times and places, dealing with different challenges, expressed their discontent with the social roles allotted to them and pursued their ambitions for wider options, more individual freedom, and greater social authority.

Feminism and women's history are mutually informing. Feminism is one of the important subjects of women's history, and history is one of feminism's best tools. Knowing what the past has been for women, doing the scholarship that Anne Firor Scott calls "making the invisible woman visible," is a necessary resource in pressing for further change.[12] But feminism is also a method by which historians examine the past in terms of women's efforts to challenge, struggle, make change, and sometimes achieve progress. Like so many of the scholars on whom the authors of this text rely, we have worked from such a perspective, and the passion we have brought to this work has its roots in a feminist commitment to highlighting—and encouraging—women's active social role and contribution to history. For us, however, a women's history informed by feminism is not a simple exercise of celebration, but a continuing and critical examination of what we choose to examine in the past and the methods we use to do so.

---

11. Nancy Cott, *The Grounding of American Feminism* (New Haven: Yale University Press, 1987), 95.

12. Anne Firor Scott, "Making the Invisible Woman Visible: An Essay Review," *Journal of Southern History* 38, no. 4 (November 1972): 629–38.

The Role of Family and Personal Life

The third integrating category of *Through Women's Eyes* is the theme of family and personal life. In contrast to the categories of labor and politics, which have been recognized in all narratives of the nation's past, women's historians took the lead in bringing family and personal life into the mainstream of American history. Indeed, one of the fundamental contributions of feminist scholarship has been to demonstrate that kinship and sexuality have been not static elements of human nature but elements with their own complex histories. We try to make this clear by discussing the variety of family patterns evident among Native Americans, immigrants, African Americans, white middle-class Americans, and other ethnic groups.

Over the span of American history, family life has gone from the very center of political power and economic production in the seventeenth and eighteenth centuries to a privileged arena of emotional life in the early twenty-first century. As we write this introduction, issues relating to family life — who can marry whom, what forms of sexuality and gender identity should be tolerated, who controls reproductive decisions, who should bear and care for children and how — have become topics of intense public contest and political positioning. Thus concepts and experiences of family and sexual life, once viewed as the essence of women's separate sphere, are increasingly understood as a major connection between private concerns and public issues.

The histories of both motherhood and female sexuality reveal this connection. Motherhood not only has been central to women's individual family lives but also has served larger functions. Within enslaved communities, mothers taught their children how to survive within and fight against their servitude. Among middle-class women in the nineteenth and early twentieth centuries, motherhood became an effective way to claim female public authority. In the 1950s, at the start of the Cold War between the United States and the Soviet Union, radical women subverted intense anti-Communist interrogations under the cloak of motherhood, thus trumping one of the decade's most dramatic themes with another. The social significance of motherhood has been used for conservative political purposes as well, with claims about the centrality of women's maternal role to social order providing the fuel of the antifeminist backlash of the 1970s and through it the emergence of a new political right wing.

When it comes to the subject of sexuality, historians have proved particularly innovative in learning to read through the euphemisms and silences that obscure women's sexual lives even more than men's. They have delved into documents left by guardians of sexual propriety about sex workers and by lascivious masters about enslaved women, in order to imagine how the objects of these judgments themselves experienced these encounters. When historians set aside modern attitudes toward sexuality and reexamined the lives of seemingly prudish nineteenth-century middle-class women, they found, as Linda Gordon demonstrates, the origins of the American birth control movement and all the radical changes in women's lives that flowed from it.[13] No longer content to portray the history of female sexuality as a simple move from repression to freedom, historians have examined the changing understandings of female sexuality and its shifting purposes in the twentieth century, as it played a major role in advancing new standards of consumerism and in modernizing — though not necessarily making more egalitarian — relations between men and women.

Perhaps historians of women have been most creative in learning to look beyond the heterosexual relations that traditionally have defined sexuality to explore the intimate, romantic, and ambiguously sexual relations among women themselves. Carroll Smith-Rosenberg pioneered in demonstrating how common romantic friendships among women were in the nineteenth century, describing them as "an intriguing and almost alien form of human relation, [which] flourished in a different social structure and amidst different sexual norms."[14] Historical work on what has come to be called "homosociality" has deepened understandings of sexuality overall. Thus, as with the concepts of gender and race, women's history has led us to view sexuality itself as socially constructed, not as biologically prescribed.

Sexuality has been an especially important site for historians to locate the intersections of race and gender. Middle-class white women's historical prominence rested in considerable part on the contrast between their reputed sexual innocence and propriety and the supposedly disreputable (and titillating) sexuality of women of color on the margins, such as enslaved Black women, so-called Indian squaws, and Asian sex workers. This intersection between sexuality and race has also been investigated from the position of women who found themselves on the other side of the vice–virtue divide. As historian Paula Giddings argues, the rising up of recently freed African American women against their reputation as sexually available and that of African American men as sexually predatory helped to create a Black middle class and "a distinctive mix which underlined Black women's activism for generations to come."[15]

These and other discoveries in the field of U.S. women's history have made this textbook possible. The rich body of scholarly literature developed over the past decades has also enabled us to achieve our goal of integrating women's history into U.S. history, of showing how material once separated as "women's history" contributes to a broader understanding of the nation's history. In *America Through Women's Eyes,* Mary Beard insisted that women be rendered not as the passive objects of men's actions but as makers of history themselves; and that their history not be removed from the historical flow into a separate narrative but be understood as part and parcel of the full range of national experience. This has been our guiding principle in writing this textbook — and the reason we have titled it an American history "through women's eyes."

---

13. Linda Gordon, *The Moral Property of Women: A History of Birth Control Politics in America* (1976; repr., Urbana: University of Illinois Press, 2004).

14. Carroll Smith-Rosenberg, "The Female World of Love and Ritual," *Signs* 1 (1979): 1–29.

15. Paula Giddings, *When and Where I Enter: The Impact of Black Women on Race and Sex in America* (New York: William Morrow, 1984), 50.

Sixth Edition

THROUGH WOMEN'S EYES

An American History

WITH DOCUMENTS

1

America in the World

TO 1650

PEOPLE WHO LIVE IN THE UNITED STATES OFTEN refer to themselves as Americans and to their nation as America. From this perspective, "America" includes the places, peoples, and economic systems that eventually became the single national entity of the United States. But there are other meanings of "America" to consider. "America" is the name given to the entire hemisphere by the Europeans who accidentally encountered it in the late fifteenth and early sixteenth centuries. "America" is also the term that eventually devolved on the northern continent of that hemisphere; there, many European empires vied for control before England prevailed. The Indigenous peoples of North America had many names for themselves that translated as "men" or "the people," but Europeans called them "Americans" or "American Indians." Finally, colonists of European descent came to refer to themselves as Americans, to distinguish themselves from their Old World predecessors. Modern Americans, even recent immigrants from other "American" locales, have inherited all of these meanings of "America."

To begin American history, more and more historians are looking beyond (or before) the English establishment of the thirteen Atlantic colonies. Using a lens of diverse peoples, we can reconfigure early American history as the intersection of and conflict between several distinct histories — Native American, European, and African. In addition, each of these groups contained many different ethnicities and societies. With this approach, we can reach back before the traditional starting events, the first English settlements that proved to be permanent on the North American continent — Jamestown in

1607 and Plymouth in 1620 — to important and shaping processes in the 1500s. These include the developments among Indigenous peoples; the impact of the initial sixteenth-century contact between Indigenous peoples and Europeans, including disease, trade, conquest, cultural exchange, enslavement, and resistance; the powerful Spanish empire in the New World that preceded, inspired, and competed with the later-arriving French, Dutch, and English; the development of transatlantic slavery and the emerging colonial economies that it served; and political, economic, and religious upheavals in Britain and Europe from the late Renaissance through the Protestant Reformation.

To view these beginnings of American history through women's eyes requires creativity. Although our revered national myths emphasize the family origins of seventeenth-century New England immigration, the first century of European incursions in the western hemisphere was overwhelmingly male. So was the introduction of African enslaved peoples to the Americas in the sixteenth century, because of both complementary and conflicting notions of the appropriate division of labor between men and women in Africa and Europe. But Indigenous women and European and African men encountered one another, willingly and unwillingly, across a divide of massive cultural difference that has been described as "an epochal cross-roads of gender."[1]

For much of their national history, many Americans have preferred to think of their country as exceptional, different from the other nations of the world, set apart by geography, democratic traditions, wealth of natural resources, and Christian heritage. Today, claims to American exceptionalism and superiority on these grounds seem outdated. North America in the twenty-first century is situated thoroughly in a global system of culture, economics, power relations, and human migration.

But America was in and of the world in other periods as well. From the 1500s on, people, ideas, natural materials, and manufactured goods went back and forth between the Old World and the New and across the globe. The horse, for example, was an animal that dramatically changed the culture of Native peoples, while the maize plant, first developed in what is now Mexico and then imported to Europe, became an important staple crop. As one historian has put it, "America was international before it was national."[2]

1540– 1542	Vásquez de Coronado marches into Zuñi lands in New Mexico
1542	Bartolomé de Las Casas publishes account of the devastation of the Indies
1550– 1600	Portuguese and Spanish sugar cultivation begun in Americas, first using bound Indigenous labor, later using bound African labor
1558– 1603	**Reign of Queen Elizabeth I**
1565	Spanish establish St. Augustine, Florida
c. 1585 –1587	Roanoke Colony
1587	**Birth of Virginia Dare**
1598	Spanish Franciscan friars come to New Mexico
1598	Acoma rebellion in New Mexico
c. 1600	Powhatan Confederacy established
1607	Jamestown founded
1607	John Smith taken captive and adopted by Powhatans
1608	Samuel de Champlain establishes Quebec
1614	**Pocahontas marries John Rolfe**
1616– 1617	**Pocahontas travels to England; dies the next year**
1619	**First record of enslaved Africans brought to British North America; among them are women from the Ndongo Kingdom**
1624	**Nzinga becomes ruler of Ndongo Kingdom**

◆ INDIGENOUS WOMEN

With at least two hundred languages spoken in North America on the eve of European contact, the world of Indigenous peoples defies simple generalization. Historians usually analyze Indigenous peoples in the context of region and economic activities. The Pueblos, who were agriculturalists, lived in the Southwest. The Chumash were hunter-gatherers in California. The fishing Nootkas resided in the Northwest, while the Great Plains were home to hunters such as the Crows, the Sioux, and the Blackfeet. In the Great Lakes region, groups such as the Ojibwas also emphasized hunting. In the eastern woodlands, the Iroquois lived inland west of the Hudson River; and Algonquian-speaking peoples populated the Atlantic Coast from what is today Maine to the present Carolinas. Both the Iroquois and coastal Algonquians were farmers (see Map 1.1).

The diversity of Indigenous peoples extended to their gender systems. Here, as in all of the history that went into creating America, this fundamental fact stands out: the divisions between the worlds of men and the worlds of women, the distinctions that we call gender, were omnipresent but infinitely varied. In horticultural societies, where people depended on corn and other crops, lineage was generally traced through the mother's line. In hunter-gatherer societies, patrilineal descent was dominant. Women's experiences after marriage depended on whether they were expected to live among their husband's people (patrilocal marriage) or whether their husbands came to live with them (matrilocal). Indigenous women's daily work varied according to where they lived and what foodstuffs were available. For example, women planted and tended corn in both the Northeast and the Southwest, but southwestern women spent more time irrigating their crops. Women also had different degrees of status and autonomy in their societies. No matter what specific tasks were included, roles related to economic activities and domesticity were a powerful determinant in Native women's lives.

Indigenous Peoples before 1492

Archaeological evidence indicates that at least 14,000 years ago (and probably much earlier), the ancestors of Native Americans migrated across a land bridge that once united Siberia and Alaska. Historians believe that by the fifteenth century, between 7 and 12 million people lived in the area that is now the United States. Although popular images of Indigenous peoples depict them primarily as hunter-gatherers or nomadic hunters, a significant number engaged in farming, fishing, or hunting. The Cahokia settlement in present-day Illinois, for instance, featured large cornfields around a residential and ceremonial center. In these agricultural communities, females fulfilled crucial roles in planting, harvesting, and processing food. Before the arrival of Europeans, some Indigenous groups hunted bison on the Great Plains by using fires to stampede the animals over cliffs. It was not until Indigenous peoples living on the borders of the Plains — like the Comanches, Arapahos, Cheyennes, and Sioux — had access

♦ Map 1.1 Indigenous Peoples of the Americas, 1492

By the time of Columbus's arrival, Indigenous peoples populated the entire western hemisphere. Among those groups who practiced intensive agriculture, both men and women farmed. Among groups who practiced both hunting and agriculture, men were primarily the hunters while women did most of the farming. Among tribes engaged primarily in hunting, women hunted smaller game, gathered wild plant foods, and processed the meat and skins of the larger animals killed by men.

◆ **Effigy Bottle from Cahokia Mound (c. 1200–1400)**
The people of Cahokia were part of a large group whom historians call Mississippians, who lived in the Mississippi and Ohio Rivers' watersheds from roughly 1000 to 1730. Distinguished by the large earthen mounds they built for ceremonial, political, and residential purposes, they apparently had a highly stratified social structure and complex culture. Artifacts recovered from the mounds reveal a wide variety of artisanal crafts, including pottery and stonework, some of which may have been produced by women. This meticulously carved ceramic bottle in the shape of a nursing mother was presumably not for everyday use but for ritualistic or symbolic purposes; perhaps it was placed in a grave for use in the afterlife. What insight into Mississippian women's lives and into the larger meanings of motherhood in their culture does the image offer? © *The Detroit Institute of Arts/Photo © The Detroit Institute of Arts/ Bridgeman Images.*

to horses that significant numbers migrated to the Great Plains and became nomadic bison hunters. In all groups that emphasized hunting, men killed big game while women skinned the animals and prepared the meat, providing essential protein and clothing sources for their children and other family members along with valuable skins for trade.

Wherever they lived, Indigenous Americans were not a static people, frozen in time waiting for Europeans to "discover" them. Historians have mapped out an amazing array of Indigenous trails that crisscrossed the continent. Trading in shells, furs, agricultural products, pottery, salt, and copper, as well as in captives, communities of Native Americans had contact with and knowledge of many other groups with whom they shared the continent. Although trade was peaceful, Indigenous peoples sometimes warred with one another over land and other resources. This violence had special meaning for women since they and children were often captured and forcibly integrated into enemy societies. Both warfare and ecological pressures such as drought prompted significant migration, the merging of communities, and the rise and fall of powerful Indigenous nations. Although we have virtually no documents written by the women themselves, material culture items such as pottery, clothing, and paintings, ritual translations, songs, poetry, and oral narratives, along with a cautious reading of European eyewitness accounts of Native American communities, provide historians with some insights into Indigenous peoples' lives. (See Primary Sources: "European Images of Indigenous Women.")

In many Indigenous peoples' nations, women had more power and sexual choices than most non-elite European women of their time did, albeit in the context of clear distinctions between the labor and responsibilities of men and women. In other words, in traditional Native American societies, relations between the sexes were characterized simultaneously by difference and by a degree of equality. The following examination of two well-documented groups reveals the diverse lives of Indigenous women and their cultures.

Pueblo Peoples

Perched on cliffs in present-day New Mexico and Colorado are the remains of prehistoric dwellings of Indigenous people called Anasazi, who settled in the area as early as 300 B.C.E. From their distinctive multistoried, mud-plastered buildings came the generic name "Pueblos," which the Spanish gave to Anasazi descendants such as the Zuñis, Hopis, Acomas, and similar peoples who were living in the American Southwest (New Mexico, Arizona, Colorado, and Utah) by 1250 C.E. When the Spanish arrived in the region in the mid-sixteenth century, there were close to 250,000 **Pueblo peoples** living in more than one hundred towns and villages. They encompassed seven language groups, and undoubtedly customs and rituals varied from group to group, despite many points of similarity. Like many other Indigenous peoples, the Pueblos apparently experienced some social disruption in the years preceding European arrival. The incursions of more nomadic Apaches from the Great Plains into their region may have been one of the causes for significant Pueblo migration and change during the thirteenth and fourteenth centuries.

By the 1500s, the Pueblos were already practicing intensive agriculture through growing corn, squash, and beans. As in other societies, labor was gendered. Men typically traded goods, provided defense, and tended the corn crop. They collected and placed the timbers for the construction of their homes, but women plastered the walls. Women's work centered on what went on "inside" of their communities. They crafted pottery; made moccasins, clothing, and blankets; and, most crucially, prepared the food and cared for children. Grinding the dried corn was women's work, a task that daughters and mothers shared. Women viewed their food production as vital to their people, as something spiritual, a point reinforced by the Acoma Pueblo origin story (see Reading into the Past: "Two Sisters and Acoma Origins").

In addition to its association with corn and the earth's fertility, women's spirituality—and men's—was tied to their sexuality. Intercourse often had ritualistic and religious meanings. It was not only the source of life, but also a means of taming bad spirits in nature and of integrating outsiders into the community. It also helped to maintain the cosmic balance. Pueblo ideology thus recognized women's sexual power, a factor that, like women's role in food production, contributed to relatively egalitarian relationships between the sexes.

The **matrilineal system**, tracing ancestry and control of land through the female line, consolidated women's position in their communities. As with most

READING INTO THE PAST

Two Sisters and Acoma Origins

According to the Acoma Pueblos' origin story, the first women in the world were two sisters, born underneath the ground and sent above by Tsichtinako (Thought Woman). She first taught them to plant corn, tend and harvest it, grind it for food, and use fire to cook it. What follows is an excerpt from one such story told in 1928 by residents of the Acoma and Santa Ana Pueblos to anthropologist Matthew W. Stirling. Indigenous peoples' oral traditions, recorded by ethnographers, have become the source of much knowledge of Indigenous history.

Tsichtinako spoke to them, "Now is the time you are to go out. You are able to take your baskets with you. In them you will find pollen and sacred corn meal. When you reach the top, you will wait for the sun to come up and that direction will be called ha'nami [east]. With the pollen and the sacred corn meal you will pray to the Sun. You will thank the Sun for bringing you to light, ask for a long life and happiness, and for success in the purpose for which you were created." Tsichtinako then taught them the prayers and the creation song, which they were to sing. . . .

They now prayed to the Sun as they had been taught by Tsichtinako, and sang the creation song. Their eyes hurt for they were not accustomed to the strong light. For the first time they asked Tsichtinako why they were on earth and why they were created. Tsichtinako replied, "I did not make you. Your father, Uchtsiti, made you, and it is he who has made the world, the sun which you have seen, the sky, and many other things which you will see. But Uchtsiti says the world is not yet completed, not yet satisfactory, as he wants it. This is the reason he has made you. You will rule and bring to life the rest of the things he has given you in the baskets." . . . Tsichtinako next said to them, "Now that you have your

Native American peoples, land and households among the Pueblos were occupied communally by particular families and, in their case, passed through the female line. Control of the land was tied to its use, not to some abstract concept of ownership. In addition to being matrilineal, Pueblos were **matrilocal**, meaning that men left their mothers' homes to marry and move in with their wives' families. In Pueblo society, men and women could leave their marriages and choose new partners without stigma, an arrangement in accord with the understanding that an individual's primary identity was defined by his or her mother's identity, not a names, you will pray with your names and your clan names so that the Sun will know you and recognize you." Tsichtinako asked Nautsiti which clan she wished to belong to. Nautsiti answered, "I wish to see the sun, that is the clan I will be." The spirit told Nautsiti to ask Iatiku what clan she wanted. Iatiku thought for a long time but finally she noticed that she had the seed from which sacred meal was made in her basket and no other kind of seeds. She thought, "With this name I shall be very proud, for it has been chosen for nourishment and it is sacred." So she said, "I will be Corn clan." . . .

When they had completed their prayers to the sun, Tsichtinako said, "You have done everything well and now you are both to take up your baskets and you must look to the north, west, south, and east, for you are now to pray to the Earth to accept the things in the basket and to give them life. First you must pray to the north, at the same time lift up your baskets in that direction. You will then do the same to the west, then to the south and east." They did as they were told and did it well. And Tsichtinako said to them, "From now on you will rule in every direction, north, west, south, and east."

SOURCE: Matthew W. Stirling, *Origin Myth of Acoma and Other Records* (Washington, DC: Smithsonian Institution, 1942), 3–5.

ANALYZING PRIMARY SOURCES

1. What are the advantages and disadvantages of oral traditions recorded by outsiders as a source of historical knowledge?

2. What does this origin story tell you about the importance of corn to Acoma Pueblo identity and to Pueblo gender roles, especially those of women?

marital bond. Older women were therefore particularly influential members of the community.

The Iroquois Confederacy

Far away from the southwestern Pueblos, the **Iroquois Confederacy** — initially consisting of the Seneca, Cayuga, Onondaga, Oneida, and Mohawk people — constructed another version of Indigenous life. In the forests of what became

◆ **Iroquois Longhouses**
Iroquois Confederacy longhouses were unique residential settings for the women and men
known as the Seneca, Cayuga, Onondaga, Oneida, and Mohawk located in modern-day
Ontario and New York State. In the seventeenth century, they numbered at least twenty
thousand. These were matrilineal societies, and women had distinct political, economic,
and social powers. The elderly women supervised life in the longhouses among the multiple
families who lived within, chose and deposed male chiefs, and influenced their clan's land use
privileges. *Stock Montage/Archive Photos/Getty Images.*

New York State and Ontario, Canada, an estimated twenty to thirty thousand
people lived in perhaps ten villages at the turn of the seventeenth century. The
Iroquois were unique among Indigenous peoples for their Great League of
Peace and Power, thought to have been founded in 1451, which linked them in
an elaborate confederation. The chiefs of the Iroquois Confederacy were always
men, but women chose them and could depose them. The distinctive political
power of Iroquois women also was reflected in how families were organized.
The Iroquois' matrilineal system emphasized women's importance for establishing identity and rights to the use of land in each clan. Several families lived
together in longhouses, large bark-and-log dwellings, which the clan's elder
women supervised.

The gendered division of labor reinforced women's dominance in the village.
Men prepared fields for planting, but their major duties took them to the forests,
where they hunted, conducted trade, and warred. Women's responsibilities centered in the village, where they raised crops (corn, beans, and squash); gathered
mushrooms, berries, and nuts; prepared food; distributed the results of men's hunting; reared children; and made baskets, pottery, and other utilitarian and ornamental implements. They worked hard and communally. This gendered division of
labor continued even after European arrivals. Mary Jemison, a British captive who

married and raised a family among the Senecas in the eighteenth century, later explained: "In order to expedite their business, and at the same time enjoy each other's company, they all work together in one field, or at whatever job they may have on hand." In the spring, Jemison continued, "they choose an older woman to be their driver and overseer, when at labor, for the ensuing year. She accepts the honor, and they consider themselves bound to obey her."[3]

Women also had a significant voice in religious activities. Seneca women formed Chanters of the Dead, a group that interpreted dreams and participated in numerous rituals. In other ways Iroquois women influenced what might be termed the political side of life. Because they controlled food supplies — both current crops and the food they had carefully preserved and stored — they provisioned warriors and thus had a say in plans for raids and wars. They also determined adoptions into a clan — a means of integrating captives and minimizing losses due to disease and warfare — and could call for the avenging of deaths in their own families, thus initiating raids and warfare. Iroquois women's political power impressed European observers. Father Joseph-François Lafitau, a French Jesuit missionary in Canada, noted as late as 1724 that "nothing, however, is more real than this superiority of the women. . . . The land, the fields and their harvest all belong to them. They are the souls of the Councils, the arbiters of peace and of war. They have charge of the public treasury. To them are given the slaves. They arrange marriages. The children are their domain, and it is through their blood that the order of succession is transmitted."[4]

Indigenous Women's Worlds

Pueblo and Iroquois women lived a great distance from one another. Their economic systems and their environments varied dramatically, as did their social structures. Iroquois women had more formal power than Pueblo women. But the similarities in their lives suggest a few broad generalizations about Indigenous women of North America in the era of European arrival and settlement. What were their social and economic roles? What can we know of their intimate lives? What political and religious influences did they exert within their communities?

Women's economic significance was a common denominator that most Indigenous peoples shared. Starting with a culturally biased Christopher Columbus, who observed in 1493 that "the women seem to work more than the men," the productive role of women was an object of much "commentary." European men, mired in the gender prescriptions of their places of origin and time, reacted as if their own women were entirely free from hard labor, which they certainly were not. Among the coastal Algonquians, women not only tended crops but also participated in the fishing vital to their people's survival. They fashioned mats and baskets and other essential artifacts of daily life. Among the groups that emphasized hunting, like the Ojibwas of the Great Lakes region or the Apaches of the southern Plains, men's role as hunters was complemented by women's labor of curing meat and dressing skins. Women also gathered feathers from birds, fashioned clothing and moccasins, and sometimes bartered in the increasingly important fur trade. In 1632 a French cleric, Paul Le Jeune, observed of the Iroquois: "The women know what they are to do, and the men also; and one never meddles with the work of the others." As one Iroquois man reported to Le Jeune, "To live among us without a wife . . . is to live without help, without home, and to be always wandering."[5]

All Indigenous peoples had strict moral codes within their own cultural norms. European observers tended to view Native American sexual practices through a pejorative lens, giving the impression that Indigenous women were promiscuous. It is also difficult to untangle the effects of intimate relations across cultural borders, notably in fur-trading regions, on sexual mores. In some cases, European men projected their own desires onto Indigenous women. In others, women entered into liaisons with fur traders so that these outsiders could be incorporated into the community. Europeans also were shocked by some groups' polygyny, whereby a man might have multiple wives who were often sisters. Another factor that seemed to give Indigenous women more sexual freedom than their European counterparts, especially in matrilineal societies, was that women did not need to stay in unhappy marriages for economic security. According to a French observer of a group of Algonquians, "A Young Woman, say they, is Master of her own Body, and by her Natural Right of Liberty is free to do what she pleases."[6]

To early Europeans, one of the most striking aspects of Native American sexuality was the existence of individuals who crossed what Europeans regarded as strict gender lines and lived as a member of the opposite sex. Later anthropologists used the word **berdache** for such a person. Male-to-female transgendering was present in virtually all Native American societies, but female-to-male crossing was by no means unknown. Modern feminist theory contends that the possibilities of gender extend beyond two categories, and evidence for this is striking in several traditional Native American societies. In the 1520s on Mexico's northern frontier, Cabeza de Vaca recorded, "I saw one man married to another . . . , and they go about dressed as women, and do women's tasks, and shoot with a bow, and carry great burdens . . . and they are huskier than the other men and taller."[7] The explanations of transgendering were multiple. Some men may have been responding to desires to play a female role, although there is evidence of male homosexuality in Indigenous cultures that took other forms. In some cases, the berdache was regarded as an especially spiritual person whose path across a set gender was dictated by a youthful vision quest.

Most Indigenous American women held no formal political power. The Iroquois matrons were one exception; another were the few Algonquian women — like Weetamoo, a sachem (chief) of the Wampanoag people of New England, or Cockacoeske, a sachem of the Pamunkey Indians of Virginia. Informally, however, women's influence was often significant, especially in the many Indigenous communities that emphasized consensus in decision making and allowed the voices of women, particularly older ones, to be heard. As one historian has noted of the Indigenous peoples of the East Coast, "The women's power normally operated more covertly, though often no less effectively than the men's, for they were the acknowledged guardians of tradition and peace in societies whose survival depended in large measure on both."[8] In religious matters, a female's access to high-status roles varied from group to group. In some, they might be healers, crucial to the well-being of their people, while in others they were religious leaders. Women always held social and cultural power as mothers and mates.

Whatever their roles in their societies, Native American women, like men, faced extraordinary challenges in the wake of the European invasion. Historians often describe the interaction of the two worlds of Indigenous peoples and Europeans in the context of a **Columbian exchange**. From the Americas, the Europeans took gold and silver, furs, fish, and crops such as corn, potatoes, and tobacco. To the Americas, they brought disease, slavery, Christianity, and different kinds of warfare and weaponry, along with new ways to exploit the land's natural resources. The meanings of this complex process of conflict and contact varied for Indigenous peoples. But overall these changes would have specific — and usually damaging — effects on Indigenous women.

◆ EUROPEANS ARRIVE

Europe in the sixteenth century was a continent undergoing dramatic change, not all of which constituted "progress" for European females, but much of which had an impact on American history. On the one hand, this was the age of powerful, educated, and politically savvy European queens, two of whom — Isabella of Castile and Elizabeth of England — presided over the beginnings of two major European empires in the Americas. The Protestant Reformation, starting with Martin Luther in Germany in 1517, challenged the hierarchical control of the Catholic clergy and eventually led to important changes in women's status. Yet processes that two centuries later would lead to enhanced education and greater independence for elite women had the immediate impact of limiting their possibilities. Conflict between Catholics and Protestants restrained and even eliminated female religious orders that had permitted some females education, spiritual authority, and alternatives to family life. One historian has called the sixteenth century "the zenith of the patriarchal family" in Europe, as women were newly confined to wifehood and motherhood.[9] Similarly, as the foundations of modern European capitalism unfolded, women found themselves in subordinate economic and social positions, rarely controlling the production of goods for market, confined to very limited posts in the economy, and always earning less than men for their labors.

Early Spanish Expansion

In the century before the English settlement of North America and the Caribbean began in earnest, Spanish America flourished. The Italian explorer Christopher Columbus mistakenly happened upon the Indies of the West, while traveling in search of the Indies of the East, under the sponsorship of King Ferdinand and Queen Isabella of Spain. However, the funds for Columbus's journey came not, as the story goes, from the queen's jewels, but from the confiscated wealth of the Jews, whom the royal pair was expelling from Spain and Portugal along with the Moors (Muslims), in an effort to "cleanse" the Iberian Peninsula of non-Christian influences. Queen Isabella was devoted to the triumph of the Catholic faith against all competitors. Her support for Columbus's oceanic adventure was also shaped by her desire to spread what she understood as the one true faith. When it became clear that the lands Columbus claimed in her name were not the East Indies but a "new" world, Isabella showed considerable concern for the "souls" of the Indigenous peoples there, rejecting, for instance, a gift of Native Americans who had been enslaved. Her death in 1504 removed one important obstacle to Spanish conquistadores' exploitation of Indigenous labor and the natural resources found on Indigenous peoples' lands. Forty years later, the Spanish Dominican priest Bartolomé de Las Casas passionately pleaded the case of Indigenous Americans, arguing that men and women alike were enslaved under horrific conditions, but by then their cause was virtually lost.

Las Casas documented the catastrophic collapse of Indigenous populations as European diseases ran rampant among peoples with no immunity to them. The first places to be devastated were the Caribbean islands of the Columbian expeditions, Hispaniola and Cuba especially. This process of disease, death, and conquest happened over and over in the New World, with European microbes often preceding European settlement. The first Spanish incursion into Florida in 1513, for example, failed to establish a permanent settlement, but the Spaniards' brief visit spread disease and by the time the next Spanish landed there, twenty-five years later, the population had already fallen precipitously; the pathogens had spread farther, all the way to the Mississippi River. Two and a half centuries later, when the Spanish finally settled northern California, the same process occurred again. As the population of Indigenous peoples plummeted, female fertility suffered in particular, leaving the very foundations of the community and culture in tatters and the way opened for occupation and conquest. Although historians are still debating the actual numbers of people living in the Americas in 1500, it is likely that the population losses during the first century after Columbus, which varied from group to group, ranged from 60 to 90 percent.[10]

In the initial phases, the Spanish invaders of the Americas were almost entirely male and focused on the wealth to be gained, first from the booty of existing cultures, then from the resources of the land, and finally from the labor and tribute of the Indigenous peoples, in a system known (in Spanish) as the ***encomienda***. In 1519, Hernán Cortés, who had participated in the Spanish conquest in the Caribbean, made his way to the east coast of Mexico. As he moved inland, the Indigenous Aztec empire he found there was notable not only for its incredible wealth but also for its high level of political organization. Cortés's success in subduing the Aztecs colored all subsequent Spanish exploration, including that into North America. Other adventurers followed rumors and legends of cities of gold and Indigenous peoples easily subjugated elsewhere on the continent.

◆ **Queen Isabella and King Ferdinand Reconquer Granada**

Many of the images of Queen Isabella show her at prayer or surrounded by religious icons that testify to her intense devotion to Catholicism. This 1520–1522 image, however, a carved relief of wood, depicts her in an explicitly political role. Here, with their army in the background, Isabella and her husband, King Ferdinand, are shown entering Granada after having reclaimed it from the Moors in 1492. The image speaks both to Isabella's militant defense of Catholicism and to her role in consolidating the power of Spain. *Capilla Real, Granada, Spain/Bridgeman Images.*

The virtually all-male character of the first phases of the Spanish invasion resulted in patterns of intimacy between Indigenous women and European men that shaped American history until European women began to appear later in the sixteenth century. As we shall see, this intimacy distinguished somewhat the gender relations of Spanish America from those of British America a century later, in which official, legitimate marriages across cultural, racial, and religious barriers were frowned upon and mostly outlawed. In Spanish America, cross-cultural conjugal relationships took various forms and have been the subject of much scholarly controversy, especially turning on the role and volition of the Indigenous females involved. Many of these relations were coercive, best described as rape and/or sexual and domestic enslavement. In others, Indigenous women determined that attaching themselves to European men would bring some relief to themselves, their children, and their people. Ambitious European men also sought out elite Indigenous women, as among the Aztecs for example, to secure a higher status and these women's diplomatic and economic resources. Some of these connections also involved genuine affection.

Many of the individual Indigenous women whose names we know from these early years were involved in such relationships and played important diplomatic and political roles as bridges between the Indigenous and European communities of the Americas. Of these, the first and most controversial was Malintzin, known to history as Malinche. Originally one of twenty female captives given to the Spaniards as a gift, she became Cortés's interpreter and the mother of his son. Her language skills aided Cortés in communicating with the Nahuatl-speaking Aztecs. After the conquest of Tenochtitlan, Malintzin took a lower-ranking Spanish husband and continued to work with Cortés. Among subsequent generations of Mexicans, Malintzin has been both revered as the mother of their race and reviled as the first to betray Indigenous peoples to Europeans. In the 1970s, Chicana feminists sought to understand her, not merely as a victim of Europe and of men, but as a woman seeking to act in a swiftly changing historical environment and to find a way between cultures and to the future. Regardless of her controversial legacy, these words from a translated sixteenth-century Nahuatl song offer insight into Malintzin's possible response to her difficult position as an enslaved concubine: "Hey mother, I am dying of sadness here in my life with a man. I can't make the spindle dance. I can't throw my weaver's stick."[11]

By the middle of the sixteenth century, Spanish women in the New World were increasing in number, although they never exceeded more than a third of the immigrants in any one decade. The pressure from crown and clergy to curb the violence of womanless men and to facilitate permanent settlement in the Americas encouraged wives to join their husbands and unmarried daughters to marry unattached male colonials. A pattern was for European women to marry men much older than they were, making widowhood a common experience. Spanish property law (in contrast to English) allowed widows to inherit easily, and this made widows attractive candidates for remarriage. Women immigrants congregated in the great cities of Mexico City and Lima. Throughout the Spanish colonial settler empire, the wealth that the Americas promised, plus the presence of Indigenous women

Xaltelolco.

◆ Malintzin and Cortés

Prior to the arrival of the Spanish, the Indigenous peoples of Mexico recorded their culture and history in pictorial form; they continued to do so after the conquest. This image comes from a painting on cloth that records the experience of the Tlaxcalan people, who remained independent of the Aztec empire and became Spain's most important Indigenous allies. Malintzin occupies the center of the frame, indicating the central importance of her role in the encounter and conquest. She is wearing Indigenous dress and is depicted as unmarried, with her hair unbraided. She is interpreting for Cortés, who sits beside her, in a conversation with people from a community called Xaltelolco, to whom she points. The name of the community is written in the Roman alphabet above the traditional place glyph, which depicts a sandy hill, the community's own name and representation for itself. The people from Xaltelolco are offering tribute to Cortés, his soldiers, and the Tlaxcalan warriors in the form of food. *Universal History Archive/UIG/Bridgeman Images.*

as servants to do most of the domestic labor, elevated Spanish women beyond the class from which they had come. Maria de Carranza encouraged her sister-in-law in Seville to give up "the poverty and need which people suffer in Spain" and hurry to immigrate to "a land where food is plenteous."[12] Life on the northern frontier of Spanish America was more difficult for women; amid continuing warfare between colonists and Indigenous peoples, the threats of kidnapping and captivity shadowed their sex. Fewer Spanish women immigrated to the northern frontier voluntarily, and more were recruited to strengthen settlement.

One unusual woman in Mexico about whom we know something is Marina de San Miguel, who came to Mexico from Spain as a child in 1547. After her father squandered his American riches, she dedicated herself to religious life, serving as a Christian teacher of Indigenous girls and a sort of freelance religious advisor and spiritual counsel to her community. She earned enough from her labors to buy her own home in Mexico City. Her spiritual independence and economic success, unusual for Spanish women outside of marriage, drew her to the attention of Spanish authorities. In these years, church and royal authority combined to bestow enormous power on the Inquisition, an institution for the detection and rooting out of all forms of heresy from the Catholic faith. In 1601, finding Marina de San Miguel guilty of spiritual arrogance and sexual misconduct, the Mexican wing of the Spanish Inquisition subjected her to community humiliation and the termination of her vocation.

The history of these European women in the New World points to their changing options in the context of Protestant/Catholic conflicts in Europe. Reformation-era pressures to cleanse the Catholic Church of corruption bore down particularly hard on females, whose allegedly unruly sexuality seemed to threaten religious purity. Starting in the middle of the century, the church placed religious sisterhoods under male supervision, strictly cloistered them, and prohibited their efforts in education and social service. In 1540, the first American convent, **Nuestra Señora de la Concepción**, opened under these conditions in Mexico City under Franciscan supervision. Most of the females who lived there were Spanish and of high birth, but Indigenous women, also of elite birth, were occasionally admitted: two of the granddaughters of Aztec ruler Montezuma became sisters of la Concepción.

In the sixteenth century, the Spanish made several incursions north, into what would eventually be the United States. These lands, much more sparsely populated than those of Mexico and Peru, offered fewer known empires to conquer and loot. The Spanish explored and mapped out the coast of northern California but did not settle there substantially until the eighteenth century. In 1565, the Spanish established St. Augustine in what is now Florida; formed to protect Spanish Cuba from British and French marauders and pirates, it is the longest continually occupied European colonial settlement in the United States, founded four decades before the English established permanent settlements to the north. None of these incursions, however, uncovered stores of gold or mountains of silver. Indeed, the only valuable commodity of these early frontier efforts was the Indigenous peoples, whom the Europeans seized and sold as enslaved captives. The overwhelmingly male population of European soldier-colonists regarded Indigenous women as valuable sexual partners (willing or not), as mothers of their children, as laborers, and as a bridge between Indigenous and European men.

Spain's Northern Frontier

The northern territories in which the Spanish were most active in the sixteenth century were the lands occupied by the Pueblo peoples. In 1540, a group of Spaniards from central Mexico led by Vásquez de Coronado ventured into the land of one of these peoples, the **Zuñis**. Frustrated at failing to find the gold they had expected, Coronado's men seized food, blankets, and women. The Spaniards' relationship to and treatment of Indigenous women lay at the root of this first and formative disastrous encounter on Mexico's northern frontier. Some Indigenous men traditionally exchanged women to cement treaties with former enemies. What the Pueblos saw as the gift of a marital alliance, Spanish men saw as their right as conquering patriarchs. When the Spanish kept demanding tributes and women's bodies without offering appropriate exchanges, the Pueblos' anger mounted. The Zuñis drove Coronado back to central Mexico. Evidence of his failure to find great wealth, his loss to the Zuñis, and news of his brutal treatment of them created such controversy that the Spanish made no further attempts to subdue the northern territories for another six decades.

In 1598, when the Spanish returned to the Pueblos' lands, they did so under another guise. Instead of soldiers in search of gold and tribute, Franciscan missionaries led the way, in search of souls to convert to Christianity. Less openly violent than the military men of the 1540s, Spanish Christians nonetheless wreaked their own kind of havoc on Indigenous cultures and peoples. Franciscan friars pressured the Pueblos to participate in Catholic rites and suppressed traditional religion. The church tried to impose a patriarchal system on Indigenous women by attempting to restructure a division of labor consistent with European notions of proper gender roles. They urged men to take over building and farming tasks that formerly had been women's work. The friars also called for Indigenous peoples to enter into monogamous, lifelong marriages and for women to emulate European notions of female modesty and reserve.

To ensure that the events of the 1540s were not repeated, the friars required that the soldier-settlers who accompanied them be married men. Even so, and although their purpose was to "pacify" Native peoples under Spanish and Catholic authority, violence soon broke out, as it had a half century earlier. Accounts differ. The Native men objected to the arrogance with which the soldiers seized their women. Not recognizing or respecting the complex rules and rituals surrounding Pueblo sexuality, the soldiers acted on their assumption that the women were making themselves sexually available. Modern scholars point to the very different ways in which Native peoples and the soldiers conducted their sexual relations and the violent turn that these differences could take under conditions of abrupt cultural clash and colonial oppression. We have little written evidence of what the women thought. In 1598, in response to the rape of one of their women, Native men killed a dozen soldiers. The Spanish massacred eight hundred Native peoples as retaliation. Most of those slaughtered were men. Then the Spanish rounded up and enslaved the survivors, who overwhelmingly were women and children.

Male priests were responsible for converting and educating Native Americans. How might the first contacts between Europeans and Native Americans have been affected if colonial women had also been representatives of the Christian faith? Would the sexual tensions and abuses that accompanied conversion efforts have been defused? Would the traditional sexual/spiritual role of Pueblo women have found more room to survive? Or would colonial women have been as oblivious to Native American concerns, even those of the females, as Spanish men were?

In New Mexico, Spanish rule proceeded along two lines: the physically violent, economically exploitative, military-led version of the conquistadores and the spiritually driven, culturally and morally coercive version of the priests. Both undermined and profoundly altered Pueblo societies. At the beginning of the seventeenth century, then, European invasions had already established a century-long legacy of invasion, disease, military conflict, religious coercion, and enslavement, contributing to a precipitous decline in the numbers and integrity of Indigenous cultures and the position of women in them.

Fish and Furs in the North

Spanish and Portuguese colonial dominance in Central and South America motivated other Europeans to look north for profit and global power. For much of the sixteenth century, the French, English, and Dutch presence in North America was informal. The crucial process was trade, and the crucial commodities were fish and fur on one side, and European manufactured goods, including ironware and guns, on the other. Women were active in this process as both producers and consumers. As in Spanish America, sexual contact and disease accompanied and complicated trading relations. Permanent settlements of European men and women developed later, in the first years of the seventeenth century (see Chapter 2).

Hundreds of European ships yearly fished the waters from Newfoundland to Massachusetts, drawn by what seemed like an inexhaustible supply of cod, the source of protein at the base of the Western European diet. By the middle of the sixteenth century, more than half the cod consumed in Europe came from North American waters. Men cast the nets, but in European coastal cultures, women sold their catch on the streets. Fishwives, as these market women were called, impinged on the disreputable, male culture of the wharves and the ships, and the term outlived the occupation, becoming synonymous for any foul-mouthed, working-class, quarrelsome female.

By the 1580s, fur had overtaken fish as the primary source of European wealth gained in North America. Beaver fur in particular was a luxury commodity, the North American equivalent of Mexican gold. It was warm and, when properly tanned, waterproof, and thus highly prized. Men were still the fashionable gender in Europe in the sixteenth century and sported most of the large, jaunty beaver hats of the age. Famed Indigenous princess Pocahontas was one of the few women to be pictured in such a hat. (See Primary Sources: "European Images of Indigenous Women," Figure 1.10.) Most women wore lesser furs as collars and cuffs on their gowns. The French dominated that trade. Indigenous males were the hunters, while females were responsible for scraping, tanning, and preparing the skins. The European commodities that Indigenous peoples received in exchange fell along gendered lines, as women received beads, iron kettles, and metal needles to use in fur preparation, while men received guns and knives, as well as alcohol. Both males and females got and valued cloth and clothing.

The fur trade with the French affected Indigenous family and gender relationships. Instead of hunting communally for larger animals such as moose and caribou, men trapped in small groups for beaver. Hunting and trapping for the market also left men with less time and energy for subsistence activities. Thus, Indigenous societies required more and more European trade goods, including clothing and food. As the hunt for fur intensified, Indigenous men had to travel farther and farther away from home to satisfy the demands of the market, intensifying intertribal warfare. Looking over this process from the perspective of the late nineteenth century, ethnologist Lewis Henry Morgan, writing about the Iroquois, hypothesized that the rise of capitalist economies was responsible for the subordination of women.

Indigenous women played another role in the fur trade, especially in the Great Lakes region, through their marriages with European men. Although some fur traders formalized their marriages to Indigenous women, most of these relationships were what the French called *mariage à la façon du pays* (marriage in the custom of the country, that is, without formal church recognition). Begun in the late sixteenth century, this practice flourished over the next two centuries until significant numbers of European women arrived. These so-called country marriages were somewhat different from the interracial liaisons in Spanish America, because they tended to accept European men into Indigenous culture rather than Indigenous women or their children into European culture. Indigenous wives gave their French husbands, in the words of one historian, "an entrée into the cultures and communities of their own people. In this way, Indian women were the first important mediators of meaning between the cultures of two worlds."[13] The children of these liaisons formed a mixed, or *métis*, society along the trade routes of rivers and lakes deep into the North American heartland.

Early British Settlements

The British were slow to follow the Spanish and Portuguese in settling in the Americas. During the first half of the sixteenth century, the British ignored America in favor of subduing and occupying Ireland, a promising colony much closer to home. In 1558, the half-century reign of Elizabeth I began, and England's interest in the other side of the Atlantic grew. Elizabeth wanted to challenge the legacy of Isabella of Spain, who had established her country's control of the seas and access to the New World's wealth.

In contrast to the highly religious Spanish queen, Elizabeth was a thoroughly worldly monarch. She, like her father Henry VIII, abjured the Catholic Church in favor of heading the Church of England. She did so more as a source of political than spiritual identity and authority. Elizabeth brilliantly maneuvered through the difficulties of being a female monarch by refusing to marry, having no children, and maintaining a public reputation for chastity. She did, however, have numerous male "favorites." To one of these favorites, Sir Walter Raleigh, she granted dominion over the large, undefined American territory north of the Spanish lands that Raleigh named Virginia to honor the Virgin Queen Elizabeth.

◆ **Queen Elizabeth I**

In 1588, the Spanish navy, or Armada, attempted to invade England. This epochal event was commemorated in this extraordinary portrait by George Gower. Elizabeth is encased in symbols of royal and imperial power, including pearls from the New World. The channel storm that helped the English defeat the much larger and better-armed Spanish is depicted on the upper right as a sign of England's divine destiny as ruler of the seas. The globe in the lower left is turned to show the Americas, and Elizabeth's hand rests on the continent's northern lands, above New Spain, which were to become British North America. The defeat of the Spanish Armada helped to clear the way for England's growth as a transatlantic power. *Woburn Abbey, Bedfordshire, UK/Bridgeman Images.*

Unlike the Catholic colonists, the Protestant English had few structures for and little interest in converting Indigenous peoples to Christianity. While the Spanish and French created "frontiers of inclusion" by liaisons between European men and Indigenous women, the English created "frontiers of exclusion," bringing in white women very early. Instead of integrating themselves into Native American society, they pushed out Indigenous peoples to make room for their own exclusively English settlements.

The initial effort at British colonization of the North American mainland was a famous failure. In 1587, more than a hundred British emigrants (including seventeen women and nine children) sailed across the Atlantic to the island of Roanoke, on the North Carolina coast. They were following an earlier expedition composed entirely of men, during which the English had launched a surprise attack on the Indigenous inhabitants and had murdered women and children as well as warriors. The inclusion of English women this time may have been an attempt to signal a less confrontational approach.

The head of this effort at settlement was John White, who had accompanied the first expedition as official painter. Many of his extraordinary drawings from that trip focused on Indigenous women (see Primary Sources: "European Images of Indigenous Women," Figures 1.4 and 1.6). In addition to providing a kind of ethnographic record of these women's labors, his images suggest the English men's fascination with the physical appearance and "nature" of Indigenous women: their beauty, strength, labor, and of course partial nudity.

On the 1587 expedition, however, White was traveling not as an observer, but as Raleigh's replacement. The symbol of British hopes for establishing a colonial settler society on American soil as part of an expanding empire and the centrality of families to that effort was the birth, barely a month after landing, of White's granddaughter, Virginia Dare. Imagining this series of events through women's eyes leads us to wonder about the experience of Virginia's mother, nineteen-year-old Eleanor White Dare, pregnant during the grueling two- to three-month transatlantic journey.

As food and other necessities dwindled, John White sailed back to England to replenish the community, leaving most of the other colonists behind. White did not return to Roanoke until 1590, only to discover that the entire community — including his own daughter and granddaughter — had disappeared. Current hypotheses are that most of the surviving settlers moved north and lived among Indigenous peoples. Rumors circulated for many years of local children with blond hair and blue eyes, presumably the product of Indigenous intermarriage with English men and women. Groups of North Carolina Native Americans continue to regard themselves as descendants of the Roanoke community.

Twenty years later, in 1607, the British attempted another settlement along the more sheltered banks of the Chesapeake Bay, naming the community after the new British monarch, James. This time, British investors provided greater support and Jamestown survived, though just barely. As in Roanoke, the first shipments of colonists were heavily biased toward adventurous gentlemen, and singularly unprepared to provide the labor to survive. Recognizing that settlers had to be committed to permanent lives in the new land, subsequent groups of emigrants included more unmarried English women meant to become settlers' wives. For women who were servants back in England, Virginia, for all its trials, may have promised a step up in the world. However, British women never constituted more than about 20 percent of the population in the early years. By the winter of 1609, the inability of the settlers to feed themselves became lethal, and more than three-quarters died. Recent archaeological research suggests that they may have resorted to cannibalism to survive.

It was the agricultural productivity of the women of the surrounding peoples, the Algonquian-speaking Powhatans, that made the difference between life and death for the surviving few. As in so many Indigenous communities, women planted, harvested, and controlled the crops that were the core of their diet. English observers recorded with considerable astonishment and unconcealed disdain that, unlike in their home cultures, women were the primary agriculturists in this "New World." To them, women's labor in the fields made them unfeminine drudges and their husbands lazy, uncivilized examples of manhood. Yet Indigenous female labor kept the colonists from total starvation.

Certainly, the most well-known female in the first years of permanent British settlement on the Virginia coast was Amounte, also known as Pocahontas (see Primary Sources: "European Images of Indigenous Women," Figures 1.9 and 1.10). She was the "favorite" daughter of one of the many wives of the powerful chief Powhatan, who was paramount over more than thirty tribes. The British appreciated Native American structures of power and chieftainship. From a very young age, Pocahontas had the authority to serve as an intermediary between her people and the English colonists. Had she never become involved with the English settlers of Jamestown, she might have become a powerful female leader in her own right.

The legend of Pocahontas as it has come down through history follows suspiciously close to the lines of a typical European romance, with the young 11- or 12-year-old girl saving Jamestown leader John Smith from death at the hands of her father out of personal passion for the dashing Englishman. This version comes from Smith, who published it upon returning to England several years later. A more likely explanation is that Pocahontas was participating in a Powhatan ritual by which Smith was being absorbed into the community by some sort of adoption process, as was often the case with valuable captives of war.

Several years later, male colonists kidnapped Pocahontas, and she remained as part of their community for the rest of her short life. She was treated as a woman of noble birth, converted to Christianity, renamed Rebecca, and married in a church ceremony to planter John Rolfe. It is possible that she took on the role of cultural intermediary out of her sense of service to her people and her father's need to know more about the newcomers. Several portraits of her survive because in 1616 Pocahontas, along with her husband, her son, and a considerable Native entourage, sailed to England, where they were presented to the royal court as evidence of the promising future of the colonial experiment in Virginia. Interestingly, Pocahontas's role as Indigenous female aide for British America brought her historical praise from her adopted people, rather than the reputation of traitor, as in the case of Malintzin a century before in Spanish America. Pocahontas never returned to Virginia, dying at the age of twenty-one of an unknown respiratory illness.

One final detail of Pocahontas's life bears emphasis: with her help, John Rolfe became Virginia's first successful European cultivator of tobacco, the next in a long line of valuable commodities, beginning with sugar, produced in America and traded around the world. Tobacco cultivation allowed for the development of market-based plantation agriculture in Virginia, which was critical to the wealth and power of the British Empire. Tobacco cultivation also encouraged the development of African slavery in North America, and to this we now turn.

◆ AFRICAN WOMEN AND THE ATLANTIC SLAVE TRADE

The first Africans to be recorded in Virginia arrived in 1619, forty-three years before the Virginia legislature passed the initial laws establishing African chattel slavery. Ndongo women, from Kongo, like those baptized and renamed Isabella and Angela by their captors, were among them. The origins of this institution, with its incalculable significance for American history, lie in the Atlantic slave trade developed long before British settlement of North America. In what simplistically has been called the "triangular trade," Europeans brought goods to Africa to trade for gold, ivory, spices, and enslaved people, whom they shipped to the New World to trade for agricultural commodities such as sugar, rice, indigo, and tobacco. These commodities, grown by Black labor, were then shipped to Europe for consumption. The roots of North American slavery can be found in the European trade of African peoples during the fifteenth and sixteenth centuries, in the understanding that Europeans used to classify Africans as inferior, and in the development of a commercial plantation economy in the eastern Atlantic and Brazil. In each of these constructs, the ideologies of gender roles were important dimensions.

Women in Western Sub-Saharan Africa

West African women were productive, sometimes truly powerful members of their societies. They were agriculturalists, with responsibilities for cultivating major foodstuffs, such as yams and rice, and innovating new agricultural methods. They helped to produce textiles by spinning, weaving, and dyeing cloth. In towns and along trading routes, women were often the local traders, an economic practice that West African women have maintained to this day. Though productive and family roles were divided by gender, women could cross over into male roles under exceptional circumstances. In the internal slave trade, discussed in the following section, some African women aimed to augment their families' wealth by buying enslaved people.

Just as this was a period of female monarchs in Europe, so too in Africa. In the middle of the sixteenth century, Queen Amina, a renowned warrior, ruled the Hausa Zazzau peoples in what is now northern Nigeria. More is known about

Tom. 4 . pag. 37.

Audiance du Vice Roy d'angole à la Reine Anne Zingha.

◆ **Queen Nzinga**

Nzinga was undoubtedly one of the most politically and diplomatically skilled monarchs of the early modern period. She expertly used her father's royal lineage and manipulated gender roles to move with authority among powerful African and European men. She led armies against the Portuguese, required her soldiers to view her as a man, and dressed her husband and male concubines in women's clothing. This late seventeenth-century image portrays Nzinga's 1622 negotiations with the Portuguese governor of Luanda. Faced with the governor's humiliating suggestion that she sit on the floor, Nzinga ordered one of her female attendants to serve as her human chair. Behind her is a large, imposing view of the Angolan landscape. How does the image convey Nzinga's authority in relation to both the Portuguese and her own subjects? *Widener Library, Harvard University.*

a Cabocero's wife   *a Country Girl*   *a Merchant's Wife*   *a Woman of the good sort Suckling her Infant*

◆ Female Clothing Styles, Gold Coast, Late Seventeenth Century

John Barbot, an agent of the Royal African Company, provided detailed descriptions of Gold Coast men and women that accompanied his sketches. Note the varying forms of dress for different ranks of women, such as "A Country Girl" and "A Merchant's Wife." Why might Barbot, a slave trader for the English Crown, be interested in the social hierarchies of West African societies? What messages about African women did these illustrations convey to European readers? *David M. Rubenstein Rare Book & Manuscript Library, Duke University.*

Queen Nzinga. Born to the Ndongo king and his favored concubine in what is now Angola, Nzinga rose to power just as the Portuguese attempted to expand their colonial rule and slave trading. In her later years, Nzinga's strategies for consolidating power shifted from fighting the Portuguese and sheltering runaways to converting to Catholicism and conducting peace negotiations. An astute ruler and military strategist, Nzinga interacted with both African and European officials. In 1660, she even corresponded directly with Pope Alexander VII, who addressed her as "our Daughter Anna Queen Nzinga."[14]

In contrast to Queen Nzinga's exceptional story, most women in sub-Saharan West Africa of the sixteenth and seventeenth centuries lived ordinary lives grounded in the collective identities of their lineage groups. Girls were likely to come of age learning skills of cultivation, harvesting, and pottery from their mothers and other older women. As they entered puberty, many underwent specific initiation rituals with other females of similar age. In the Upper Guinea region of West Africa, for example, older women initiated younger generations into the secret female society *Sande*. During their training, girls received ancestral knowledge about healing, sexuality, maternity, and other responsibilities of adult womanhood. In these societies, motherhood served as a central institution that could elevate a woman's social status and even lead to political authority.[15]

However, European records of sixteenth-century encounters with sub-Saharan Africans record little of this. Early European slave traders dealt primarily with African men. When they did come across women, they mainly commented on their nakedness and the way they carried, fed, and cared for their children. Their likening African females and mothers to animals laid the groundwork for racial distinctions between African and European women that provided an ideological defense of New World slavery and rampant sexual abuse.

The Early Trade in African Peoples

Trading in African peoples predates the involvement of Europeans. Long-standing slaving practices in Africa allowed victors to keep captives taken in war or, more likely, sell them to trans-Saharan caravans trading them elsewhere on the continent. Within Africa, women were more desirable than men because they could provide both agricultural labor and offspring. They could be absorbed by marriage and motherhood as inferior members of the kin structures of the peoples who acquired them.

Beginning in the mid-fifteenth century, European enslavers on the west coast of Africa developed working relationships with African traders from inland Africa. The European trade drew primarily from the West African coast south of the Sahara, initially from the Upper Guinea area and shifting to the region south of the mouth of the Congo River. The growing demand among Europeans for African labor drove the internal African trade to new heights. Africans traded in order to get the latest weaponry needed to protect their societies and to garner individual and communal wealth. For all the European nations involved, the trade in Black captives became the source of immense wealth, both because of the profit involved in buying and selling human beings and because of the fruits of unfree labor in the commercial enterprises of the New World.

The Spanish and Portuguese of the Iberian Peninsula were the first Europeans to trade in African people. At first, the Iberians brought their Black captives to their own countries, where they served as domestic and personal servants. By the turn of the sixteenth century, there were as many as ten thousand Africans in Lisbon and almost that number in Seville.

Within two decades, captured Black Africans were being shipped off the mainland to Spanish and Portuguese colonists on a small group of Atlantic islands midway between the Iberian Peninsula and the Guinea coast. On Madeira, São Tomé, and the Canary and Cape Verde Islands, displaced Africans formed the labor force of a new large-scale, commercially oriented agriculture. This was the beginning of the plantation system, which, along with Black chattel slavery, eventually flourished in the Caribbean and Americas, including the British North American colonies. On these sixteenth-century plantations, mostly male and some female enslaved Africans cultivated and processed crops meant for sale around the known world. Sugar set the pattern later taken up by tobacco: both were luxury products, not meant for local consumption but of interest instead to people far away with disposable wealth and a desire for different and exotic tastes.

In the late sixteenth century, sugar cultivation crossed the Atlantic, arriving in the massive Portuguese colony of Brazil and the Spanish island colonies of Hispaniola (now Haiti and the Dominican Republic) and Cuba. There, the gradual shift to an African labor force in the late sixteenth century was the ironic consequence of the protests by Bartolomé de Las Casas and others against the mistreatment and high death rates of American Indigenous peoples. Thus one tragedy, the near eradication of the Indigenous peoples of the Americas, was compounded by a second one, the development of a brutal traffic in human beings, brought from Africa to work in developing colonial economies. By one estimate, at the end of the sixteenth century, there were 150,000 African peoples enslaved in the Spanish West Indies and 50,000 more in Portuguese Brazil (see Map 1.2).[16]

The transatlantic trade in enslaved peoples was much larger and more violent than the intra-African trade that preceded it. Captive Africans were employed in a modern, commercial, globally oriented form of production. Far from home, surrounded by strangers, they had little means of escape. Unlike the intra-African trade, which was mostly young females, the majority of Africans taken across the Atlantic to be enslaved were adolescent boys and men. And in the Americas, enslaved people were distinguished from their enslavers by the highly visible physical differences in skin color, phenotype, and hair texture.

Racializing Slavery

Long before European colonists to the Americas solidified the legal status of Black Africans and their offspring as lifelong captives, skin color differentiated Black Africans from other unfree persons, such as white indentured servants. The long history of prior bondage systems rested on various sorts of difference, such as kinship, religion, military allegiances, or geography. The Spanish and Portuguese were particularly experienced with distinctions of religion, as they were busy "cleansing" their society of Jews and Moors at the same time as they were initiating a transatlantic trade in enslaved peoples. But these other systems of differentiating and relegating people to slavery allowed for some individuals to cross over to freedom, by conversion for instance, or by adoption and marriage.

A new, far more inescapable form of human categorization was emerging in connection with the enslavement of Africans in Europe and the Americas, that of "race." Nothing but generations of racial mixture could make a Black person

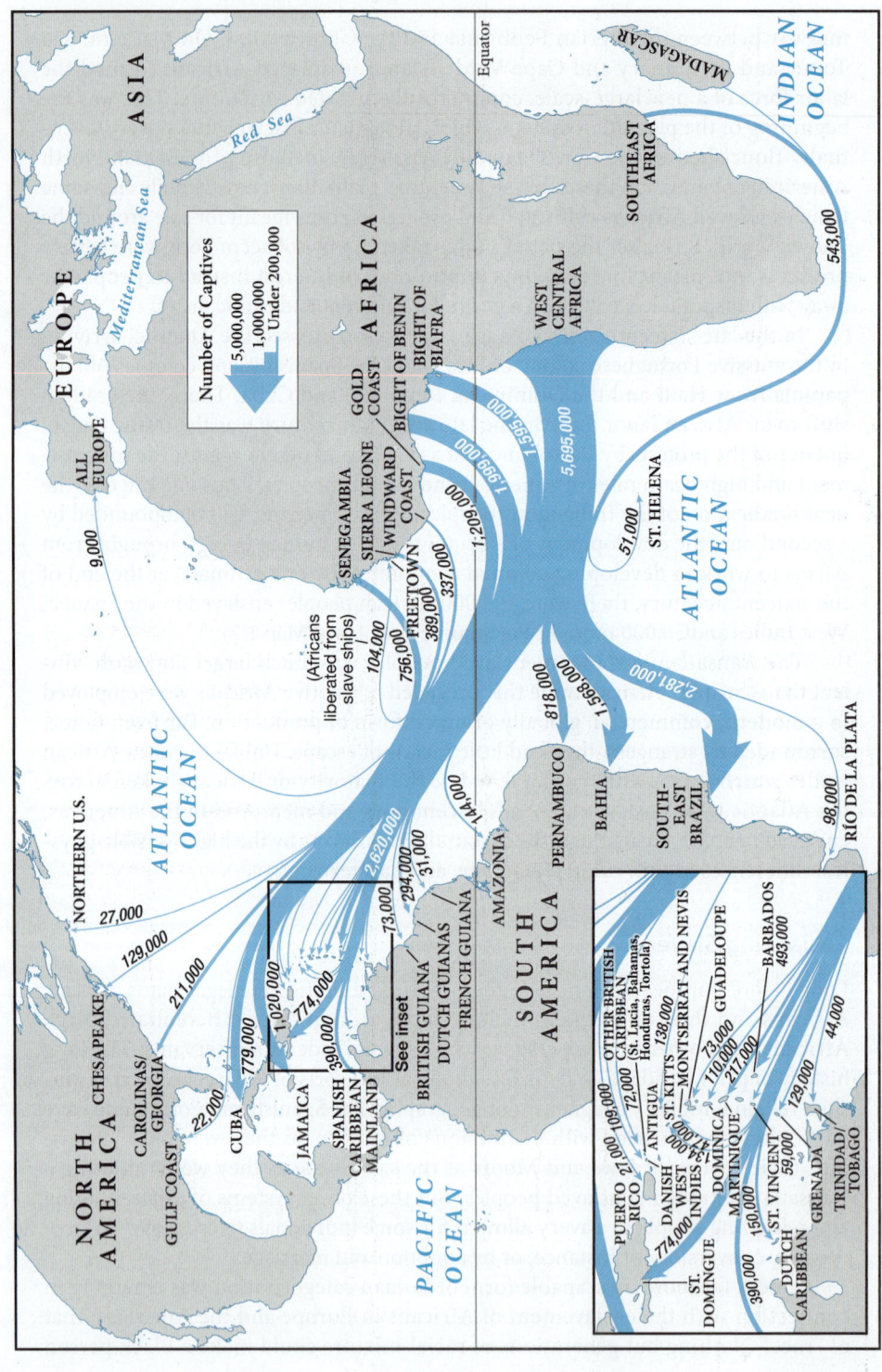

Number of Captives

- 5,000,000
- 1,000,000
- Under 200,000

ASIA

EUROPE

Mediterranean Sea

Red Sea

Equator

AFRICA

INDIAN OCEAN

MADAGASCAR

SOUTHEAST AFRICA

543,000

WEST CENTRAL AFRICA

BIGHT OF BIAFRA

BIGHT OF BENIN

GOLD COAST

1,595,000

1,999,000

5,695,000

ST. HELENA

51,000

SENEGAMBIA

SIERRA LEONE

WINDWARD COAST

2,000

1,209,000

ALL EUROPE

9,000

ATLANTIC OCEAN

FREETOWN

(Africans liberated from slave ships)

104,000

756,000

389,000

337,000

818,000

1,568,000

1,999,000

2,281,000

NORTHERN U.S.

27,000

CHESAPEAKE

129,000

CAROLINAS/ GEORGIA

211,000

GULF COAST

22,000

CUBA

779,000

JAMAICA

390,000

SPANISH CARIBBEAN MAINLAND

1,020,000

774,000

2,620,000

73,000

See inset

BRITISH GUIANA

DUTCH GUIANAS

FRENCH GUIANA

294,000

31,000

144,000

AMAZONIA

SOUTH AMERICA

PERNAMBUCO

BAHIA

SOUTH-EAST BRAZIL

RIO DE LA PLATA

98,000

PACIFIC OCEAN

Inset (Caribbean):

PUERTO RICO 21,000

DANISH WEST INDIES 109,000

ST. KITTS 72,000

ANTIGUA 138,000

MONTSERRAT AND NEVIS

GUADELOUPE 73,000

BARBADOS 493,000

OTHER BRITISH CARIBBEAN (St. Lucia, Bahamas, Honduras, Tortola)

DOMINICA 110,000

MARTINIQUE 217,000

ST. VINCENT 59,000

GRENADA 129,000

TRINIDAD/ TOBAGO 44,000

DUTCH CARIBBEAN 150,000

ST. DOMINGUE 390,000

774,000

non-Black. The "science" of racial classification and hierarchy was not fully formed until the nineteenth century. But the idea of an ineradicable and unbridgeable difference inscribed on the face and the body of a person from Africa was already beginning to appear in the sixteenth century. The profitable prospect of enslavement encouraged debasing, dehumanizing images of Africans. Europeans' contempt for Black Africans as closer to animals than themselves encouraged enslavement. The two worked hand in hand.

African women were fundamental to this development. Although sexually intrigued by the nakedness and exoticness of African women, Europeans were rarely interested in "elevating" them through marriage — unlike their attitude toward some Native Americans. On the contrary, once the idea of the inherited differentiation called "race" hardened, African women became crucial to the development of permanent and inherited enslavement. At the point that transatlantic slavery shifted away from working Africans to death in the Caribbean and Brazil toward a system of slavery in North America that could reproduce its own labor force, the reproductive capacity of African women's bodies and their nurture as mothers were the key.

African Slavery in the Americas

By the middle of the sixteenth century, 25 percent of the people who came across the Atlantic to the New World were African. By the first half of the eighteenth century, that percentage had risen dramatically to 75 percent. The sparse evidence for gender ratios on known slave ship voyages indicates an average of 41.5 percent female captives in the period between 1525 and 1700 compared to 34.7 percent female captives after 1700.[17] Although the great majority of Africans shipped to the pre-nineteenth-century Americas were men, African women constituted a significant majority of non-Indigenous women there. Put another way, although men outnumbered women among enslaved peoples, African women outnumbered European women in early migration to the New World. Unlike most other female immigrants in this period, African women were not sent to America as wives or daughters within male-headed family systems.

◄ **Map 1.2 Major Trends in the Atlantic Slave Trade**
A global team of scholars led by historian David Eltis have compiled records of specific enslavers' ship voyages in a ground-breaking project on the history of the Atlantic slave trade. According to *Voyages: The Trans-Atlantic Slave Trade Database* estimates, enslavers forcibly carried a minimum of 12.5 million captive Africans into the Americas. Millions died, but at least 10.7 million survived the brutal Middle Passage. Two hundred thousand of these survivors were intercepted at sea by naval patrols during the nineteenth-century era of abolition. The Spanish and Portuguese dominated the transatlantic trade in the sixteenth century. The entry of first Dutch and then British and French traders in the mid to late 1600s, however, caused a sharp increase in the numbers of trafficked Africans. By 1837, all slaving nations had abolished the transatlantic slave trade, but a vigorous illegal trade nonetheless transported another 1.2 million captive Africans into slavery, primarily to Brazil and Cuba.
David Eltis and David Richardson, Atlas of the Transatlantic Slave Trade *(New Haven, 2010), reproduced with the permission of Yale University Press.*

The daily work of African women on the plantations of the sugar islands also differed from European patterns of gendered labor. Plantation society was unusual in that it did not distinguish African workers by gender in the agricultural labor they performed. In a perverse version of their farming roles in their own lands, African women were incorporated alongside men into gangs of workers on the sugar plantations of the Caribbean and South America. Enslaved women seem to have had special responsibility for the dangerous work of guiding the freshly cut cane between millstones. According to one historian, the pace at which sugarcane was brought into the mills and ground down was so furious that "in northeastern Brazil slave women with a missing arm were a common sight."[18] These grim conditions repeated themselves as the plantation economy spread to the British Caribbean by the 1640s, which came to rival Brazil in the global sugar market.

As a result of brutal working conditions, violence, skewed gender ratios, and poor health, African women in early New World slave societies had very low fertility rates. In fact, both African men and women in Brazil and the Caribbean (British and French) were generally worked to death, because it was less costly to replace them than to sustain them. There is also some evidence that enslaved women turned to contraceptives and abortifacients to keep from giving birth to children whom they would then lose to slavery. Yet, even in the early seventeenth century, before all the laws of inheritance and bondage had been written, English enslavers began to use a language of "breeding" and "increase" in wills and other legal documents that indicated their awareness of the potential of enslaved women's childbearing. In the British and other European colonies, racialized ideas about Black women's reproductive capacity proved foundational to a system of chattel slavery where children would inherit their status as enslaved from African-descended mothers.

Not until the turn of the eighteenth century did the use of enslaved African labor for plantation production take off substantially in the British North American colonies. By this time, the Dutch and the British had overtaken the Portuguese and Spanish as the major powers in the transatlantic trade. By the mid-eighteenth century, more people were born into slavery in British North America than were imported into the institution from abroad. The consequences of this shift became clearer over the next century: even though fewer than 4 percent of Africans traded into the New World ended up in British North American colonies, the population of African Americans emancipated after the U.S. Civil War constituted the largest population of freed Black people anywhere in the western hemisphere.[19]

The climate in most parts of mainland North America did not favor sugar, so other crops became the focus. In Maryland and Virginia, tobacco was the first "cash crop." In lowcountry South Carolina, rice was a challenge to grow and difficult to mill, yet cheap to ship. In the Senegambian region of West Africa, cultivating and milling rice were women's tasks, and numerous legends on either side of the Atlantic suggest that the first rice crops in America came from seeds that enslaved women hid in their hair, perhaps to remind themselves of their homeland, or in the hair of the children sold away from them, to make sure that they would be properly fed.

◆ CONCLUSION: MANY BEGINNINGS

The beginnings of all nations are difficult to identify, even a nation as relatively young as the United States. Our cherished national narratives tell us that our roots were in the wilderness. By contrast, in this account, the beginnings of America are set in the wide world: in the diverse cultures of the Americas of course, but also in those of western sub-Saharan Africa and of Western Europe. The distinctions between the two American continents had not yet hardened, except that the southern one offered mineral riches that the northern one did not. Perhaps most surprisingly, the history of our nation reaches back at least a full century before the first permanent European settlements, not only in the British Atlantic colonies, but also in Spanish incursions into Florida, the Southwest, and the lower Mississippi River valley.

Of all these conflicting and intersecting cultures in North America, only Indigenous societies involved men and women from the same society in approximately equal numbers, living together in family and kin groupings, engaged in complementary productive tasks and varying political roles as determined by their communities. The others, the Europeans who came freely and the Africans who did not, were mostly men. Women would not arrive in significant numbers for another hundred years. Thus, many of the interactions between men and women in sixteenth-century America were also between peoples largely unknown to each other, and many of the cross-cultural contacts that characterized the New World of the 1500s were accomplished via relations between men and women, the inequalities of culture intersecting with those of gender.

CHAPTER 1 REVIEW

KEY TERMS

Pueblo peoples (p. 7)
matrilineal system (p. 7)
matrilocal (p. 8)
Iroquois Confederacy (p. 9)

berdache (p. 12)
Columbian exchange (p. 13)
encomienda (p. 14)

Nuestra Señora de la
    Concepción (p. 18)
Zuñis (p. 19)

REVIEW QUESTIONS

1. Compare the economic roles of Iroquois and Pueblo women. In general, across North America, how did Indigenous women's economic contributions shape their political and social roles within their communities?

2. How did the fact that early European invaders of the Americas were mostly male influence the way they interacted socially, militarily, culturally, and economically with Indigenous societies and Indigenous women in particular?

3. How did the sex ratio of captives in the African slave trade and the conditions of early plantation societies affect African women's experiences of work and motherhood?

4. **Making Connections** How did European, African, and Native American women meet at the "crossroads of gender" in early colonial America? Compare and contrast experiences of family and sexuality, gendered divisions of labor, and opportunities for female authority among these three large groups of women.

SUGGESTED READING

America in the World, to 1650: Overview

James Axtell, *Beyond 1492: Encounters in Colonial North America* (1992).

Thomas Bender, *America's Place in World History* (2006).

J. H. Elliott, *Empires of the Atlantic World: Britain and Spain in America, 1492–1830* (2007).

Peter C. Mancall and James H. Merrell, eds., *American Encounters: Natives and Newcomers from European Contact to Indian Removal, 1500–1850*, 2nd ed. (2006).

Philip Morgan and Molly A. Walsh, *Early North America in Global Perspective* (2013).

Mary P. Ryan, *Mysteries of Sex: Tracing Women and Men through American History* (2006).

Indigenous Peoples' Lives and Encounters

James Axtell, *The Indian Peoples of Eastern America: A Documentary History of the Sexes* (1981).

Karen Olsen Bruhns and Karen E. Stothert, *Women in Ancient America*, 2nd ed. (2014).

Carl J. Ekberg, *Stealing Indian Women: Native Slavery in Illinois Country* (2013).

Matthew Jennings, *New Worlds of Violence: Cultures and Conquests in the Early American Southeast* (2011).

Andrew Lipman, *The Saltwater Frontier: Indians and the Contest for the American Coast* (2015).

Karen Vieria Powers, *Women in the Crucible of Conquest: The Gendered Genesis of Spanish American Society, 1500–1600* (2005).

Daniel K. Richter, *The Ordeal of the Longhouse: The Peoples of the Iroquois League in the Era of European Colonization* (1992).

Spanish America

Mary Giles, *Women in the Inquisition: Spain and the New World* (1998).

Ramón Gutiérrez, *When Jesus Came, the Corn Mothers Went Away: Marriage, Sexuality, and Power in New Mexico, 1500–1846* (1991).

Susan Migden Socolow, *The Women of Colonial Latin America*, 2nd ed. (2014).

Lisa Sousa, *The Woman Who Turned into a Jaguar, and Other Narratives of Native Women in Archives of Colonial Mexico* (2017).

Roanoke and Jamestown

James Horn, *Jamestown and the Forging of American Democracy* (2018).

James Horn, *A Kingdom Strange: The Brief and Tragic History of the Lost Colony of Roanoke* (2010).

Camilla Townsend, *Pocahontas and the Powhatan Dilemma* (2005).

African Women and the Atlantic Slave Trade

Judith Carney, *Black Rice: The Origins of Rice Cultivation in the Americas* (2009).

David Eltis and David Richardson, *Atlas of the Transatlantic Slave Trade* (2010).

Linda M. Heywood, *Njinga of Angola: Africa's Warrior Queen* (2017).

Herbert Klein, *The Atlantic Slave Trade* (2010).

Jennifer Lyle Morgan, *Laboring Women: Reproduction and Gender in New World Slavery* (2004).

Sowande' M. Mustakeem, *Slavery at Sea: Terror, Sex, and Sickness in the Middle Passage* (2016).

Claire C. Robertson and Martin A. Klein, eds., *Women and Slavery in Africa* (1997).

PRIMARY SOURCES

European Images of Indigenous Women

IN EXPLORING THE LIVES OF early Indigenous women, historians rely on the images and narratives produced by Europeans eager to describe the peoples they encountered in what they viewed as the New World. How does this essay on European images of Indigenous women reveal the advantages and limitations of such sources in conveying women's lives accurately and clearly?

Europeans' representations of Indigenous women tell us about European perceptions of their conquest of the Americas. However, depending on the artist, and with careful critical tools, we can also learn about the women depicted. Figure 1.1 uses allegory, a device common in Western European art — employing the female form to symbolize a country or abstract qualities such as virtue or liberty. Images of America represented by an idealized Indigenous woman were highly popular

◆ Figure 1.1 **Theodor Galle,** *America* **(c. 1580)**
The Stapleton Collection/Bridgeman Images.

◆ **Figure 1.2 Indians Planting Corn, from Theodor de Bry,** *Great Voyages* **(1590)**
Beinecke Rare Book and Manuscript Library, Yale University.

in Europe. The illustration here, titled *America*, is an engraving created around 1580 by Flemish engraver Theodor Galle, based on a drawing from around 1574 by Jan van der Straet. The striking image represents Amerigo Vespucci, the Italian explorer whose name was eventually given to the landmass he first explored in 1499,* as he "awakens" America. The animal at bottom right is a sloth, and in the background naked people are roasting a human leg on a spit, indicating the widespread belief that Indigenous peoples in America were uncivilized, barbaric, and cannibalistic. The engraving projects America as a bountiful land, but with savage peoples. The phrase in Latin may be translated in two ways: "Amerigo rediscovers America; he called her once and thenceforth she was always awake" or "Amerigo laid bare America; once he called her and thenceforth she was always aroused." How might these translations elicit different interpretations of the engraving? What is the significance of Vespucci being clothed and standing while the woman representing America is largely naked and reclining? Why would western Europeans choose to depict America as a woman? What does the engraving reveal about Western European society and values?

More helpful to us in understanding the reality of Indigenous women's lives are the illustrations and descriptions made by Europeans who encountered them in the sixteenth and seventeenth centuries. Often these accounts aimed to promote enthusiasm and funding for exploration, colonization, or missionary activity, so

---

* Historians dispute the exact year of Vespucci's arrival in the Americas.

◆ Figure 1.3 **Canadian Iroquois Women Making Maple Sugar, from Joseph-François Lafitau, *Moeurs des Sauvages Amériquains* (1724)**
Beinecke Rare Book and Manuscript Library, Yale University.

they presented Indigenous peoples in ways that would appeal to their readers. But they also reflect their artists' ethnographic intentions to record, with more or less accuracy, the appearance and ways of strange new peoples. Publications such as Theodor de Bry's multivolume *Great Voyages* (1590) provided texts with illustrations detailing geography, information about flora and fauna, and accounts of Indigenous peoples. A native of Flanders, de Bry had a fervent interest in promoting the colonization schemes of Protestant nations on a continent where the Catholic French and Spanish had already established a foothold. His depiction in Figure 1.2 must be analyzed with his point of view and purpose in mind. The image is based on the work of artist Jacques Le Moyne de Morgues, who had spent time in Florida when the French had an outpost there. The drawing purports to describe the

◆ **Figure 1.4** **John White, *Theire Sitting at Meate* (c. 1585–1586)**
GRANGER — Historical Picture Archive.

Timucuas, a Muskogean-speaking people. The Timucuas were a matrilineal, agricultural people who raised corn, beans, and squash. Scholars believe that details in this image such as the dress, the baskets, and the sticks used to punch holes in the ground for planting may be accurate, but the straight rows are apparently modeled after the plowed fields of Western Europe, and the hoes depicted are Flemish tools. The bodies of the women reflect European ideas of classical beauty (female nudes were common in European painting). What does this image suggest about the Timucuas' sexual division of labor?

A much later depiction of women's work (Figure 1.3) appeared in *Moeurs des Sauvages Amériquains* (1724) by Joseph-François Lafitau, a Jesuit missionary in the region of Montreal, Canada. It is included here because there are no such depictions of Iroquois women's traditional work in the Great Lakes area from the sixteenth century. Accompanying his illustration of Canadian Iroquois women making maple sugar, Lafitau wrote,

> The women are busy going to get the vessels which are already full of the sap which drips from the trees, taking this sap and pouring it into the kettles which are on the fire. One woman is watching over the kettles while

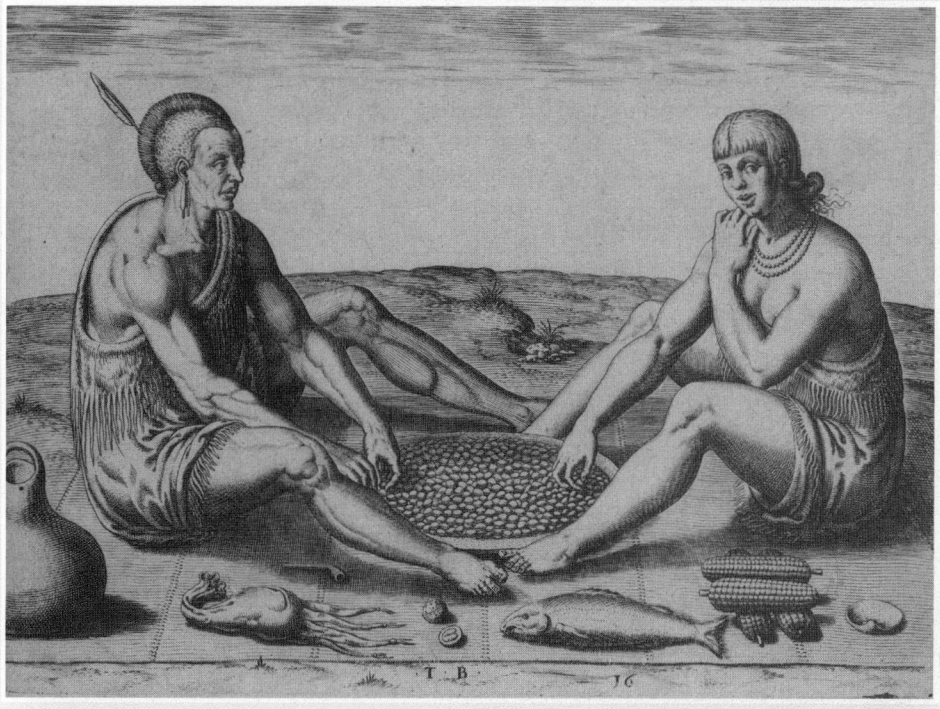

◆ Figure 1.5 **Theodor de Bry, *Their Sitting at Meate* (1590), based on a drawing by John White**
Courtesy of the John Carter Brown Library at Brown University.

another one, seated, is kneading with her hands this sap which is thickening and in condition to be put in the shape of sugar loaves. Beyond the camp and the woods appear the fields as they look at the end of winter. We can see the women busy putting the fields into shape for the first time and sowing their corn.[20]

What does this drawing and description suggest about the work patterns of these Iroquois women? What are the similarities and differences with Figure 1.2?

Undoubtedly the most comprehensive set of sixteenth-century North American illustrations are those of John White, who was not only the most prolific and accomplished European artist of the New World but also governor of Roanoke, the first English attempt at settlement on the North American continent (see "Early British Settlements"). Sir Walter Raleigh commissioned White to illustrate plant and animal life and the Indigenous peoples encountered in the three Roanoke voyages of 1584–1590. White's extraordinary watercolors, such as

Figure 1.4, appear to have been accurately painted from his careful observations of the coastal Algonquians, who lived on the Outer Banks of today's North Carolina. Among most Algonquian peoples, men and women ate separately, although those White encountered seem to have had different practices. Who may have made the mat on which the couple sits? "They are very sober in their eatinge, and drinkinge, and consequentlye verye longe lived because they doe not oppress nature," Thomas Harriot wrote in the accompanying text.[21] How is White's admiration for these people portrayed visually?

Theodor de Bry modified White's drawings when he published them in 1590. In White's version (Figure 1.4), the only dish the couple is eating is boiled maize. De Bry's version (Figure 1.5) adds nuts, a fish, and corn; there is also a gourd, a pipe, and a shell. What are the other differences between the two versions of the image *Their Sitting at Meate*? Why might de Bry have changed White's original drawing?

White's detailed depiction of clothing and ornamentation is particularly valuable. Why might the English have been so interested in such details? Figure 1.6, *A Chief Lady of Pomeiooc and Her Daughter*, features the wife of the chief in an Algonquian town in what is now North Carolina. Although not clear from the drawing, the accompanying text indicates that the marks on the woman's arms and face are "pounced," or tattooed.[22] In what other ways has the woman decorated herself? Her fringed skirt is made of skins and covers her front only, not her back. She is wearing a three-strand necklace, probably made of pearls and/or copper, hanging to her waist. Her daughter also wears a beaded necklace and, though it is hard to see, a skin covering her genitals. She carries a doll — a European one, dressed in Elizabethan clothing. A similar illustration that appeared in a de Bry engraving in 1590 adds a background landscape and shows the girl holding both the doll and an armillary sphere — a globelike ornament commonly used to depict the earth and its heavens. What is the significance of the inclusion of these European items?

More than a century later, when British colonization had been well established, the Virginian Robert Beverley reproduced an altered version of *A Chief Lady of Pomeiooc and Her Daughter*. In this image, *A Woman and a Boy Running after Her* (Figure 1.7), the doll and armillary sphere have been replaced with an "Indian rattle" and an ear of corn, and the daughter has become a boy. Historian Joyce Chaplin observes, "It is as if the English had initially been eager to place European objects in native hands, but later they were just as eager to take these things away."[23] What shifts in European views of Indigenous peoples might these newly substituted items represent? What is the significance of the text labels added to the later image? Why might the eighteenth-century version have changed the gender of the child?

While most of White's paintings focus on the Atlantic Coast Algonquians with whom he met and lived, a small part of his work focused on Aleutian Islanders. The British explorer Martin Frobisher sailed in search of a Northwest Passage to Asia in the 1570s and landed in what is now Baffin Island, northern Canada,

◆ Figure 1.6 **John White, *A Chief Lady of Pomeiooc and Her Daughter***
© The Trustees of the British Museum/Art Resource, NY

between Greenland and Quebec Province. He brought back two captives with him, one man and one woman. White either sailed with Frobisher or met these Indigenous people in London in 1577. In either case, White's attention to detail is once again evident. Figure 1.8 is that of a woman in a sealskin dress and distinctive high boots. Her face is tattooed, but what is most striking about the image is the baby's face visible inside her hood. Why did White paint yet another image of Indigenous

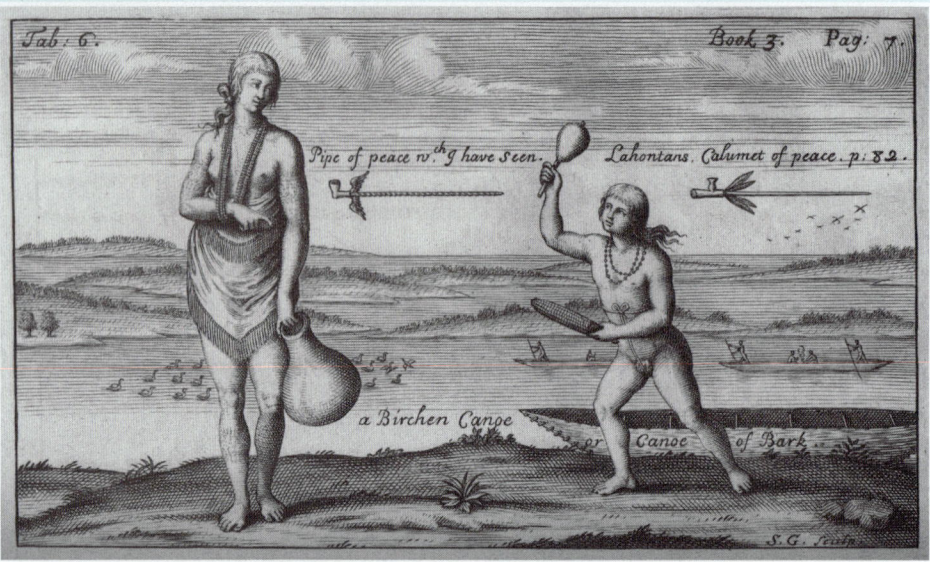

◆ Figure 1.7 Robert Beverley, *A Woman and a Boy Running after Her* (1705)
Documenting the American South, University Library, The University of North Carolina at Chapel Hill.

motherhood? What other similarities, if any, does this woman bear to the women near Roanoke that White painted a decade later?

Pocahontas of the Algonquian-speaking Powhatan people in Virginia is perhaps the most famous Indigenous woman. Figure 1.9 represents the well-known story of how she convinced her father, the powerful chief Powhatan, to spare the life of Captain John Smith. An unidentified illustrator prepared this image for Smith's account of his adventures, published in London in 1612. As Smith recounted it (writing about himself in the third person),

> At last they brought him to Meronocomo, where was Powhatan their Emperor. Here more than two hundred of those grim Courtiers stood wondering at him, as he had beene a monster; . . . having feasted him after their best barbarous manner they could, a long consultation was held, but the conclusion was, two great stones were brought before Powhatan; then as many as could laid hands on him, dragged him to them, and thereon laid his head, and being ready with their clubs, to beate out his braines, Pocahontas the Kings dearest daughter, when no intreaty could prevaile, got his head in her armes, and laid her owne upon his to save him from death.[24]

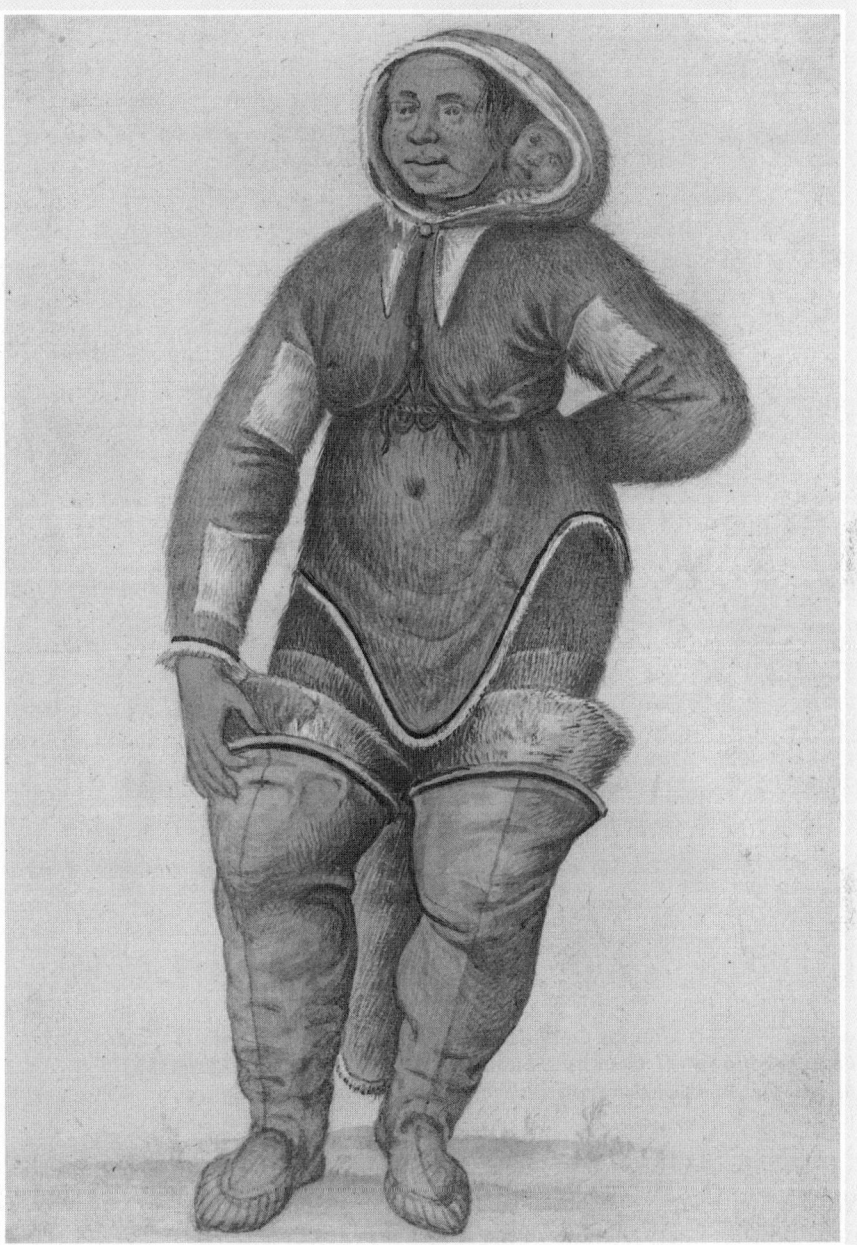

◆ Figure 1.8 **John White, *Eskimo Woman* (1577)**
© *The Trustees of the British Museum/Art Resource, NY.*

King Powhatan comands C.Smith to be slayne his
daughter Pokahontas beggs his life his thankfullness
and how he Subiected 39 of their kings reade $ histor

◆ **Figure 1.9** *Pocahontas Convinces Her Father, Chief Powhatan, to Spare the Life of Captain John Smith,* **from John Smith,** *Generall Historie of Virginia* **(1612)**
Beinecke Rare Book and Manuscript Library, Yale University.

What is Smith suggesting about Pocahontas and about himself by this story? What other possible interpretations of the events depicted here can you suggest?

Other images of Pocahontas come from her brief, celebrated trip to England, where she was presented as Native American royalty and as proof of the promise and success of the Jamestown settlement and of the eventual transplantation of English culture in the New World. Figure 1.10, a 1616 portrait engraved shortly before her death, represents her as John Smith later described her: "a gracious lady" with a "very formall and civill . . . English manner."[25] The Virginia Company, which

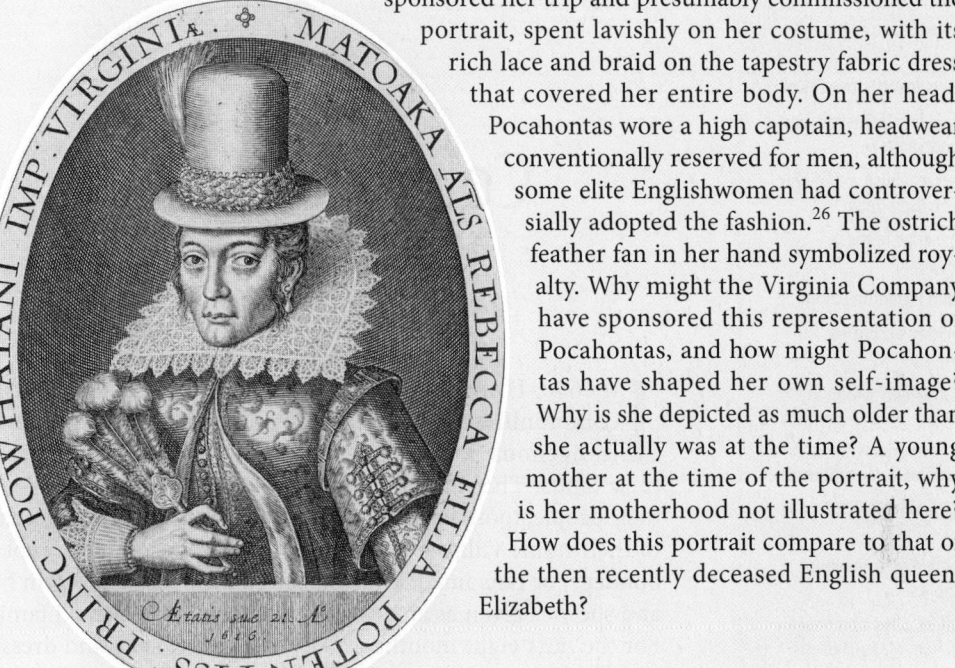

sponsored her trip and presumably commissioned the portrait, spent lavishly on her costume, with its rich lace and braid on the tapestry fabric dress that covered her entire body. On her head, Pocahontas wore a high capotain, headwear conventionally reserved for men, although some elite Englishwomen had controversially adopted the fashion.[26] The ostrich feather fan in her hand symbolized royalty. Why might the Virginia Company have sponsored this representation of Pocahontas, and how might Pocahontas have shaped her own self-image? Why is she depicted as much older than she actually was at the time? A young mother at the time of the portrait, why is her motherhood not illustrated here? How does this portrait compare to that of the then recently deceased English queen, Elizabeth?

◆ **Figure 1.10 Simon Van de Passe, *Pocahontas* (1616)**
Beinecke Rare Book and Manuscript Library, Yale University.

ANALYZING PRIMARY SOURCES

1. This visual essay features European images of early Indigenous women and cautions that we must "read" these images carefully in using them to understand Indigenous women's lives. What limitations do these images have as historical sources?

2. What commonalities do you find among the different representations here of Indigenous women? What differences?

3. One important characteristic of Indigenous societies was the sexual division of labor. In what ways do these images depict women's economic participation in their communities?

2

Colonial Worlds

1607–1750

In 1690, Hannah Swarton's village, like many other communities on the New England frontier, was raided by Indigenous peoples angered by European incursions on their lands. The Abenaki warriors, following the practices of their people, took the surviving men, women, and children back to their home villages as captives, there to be adopted, kept in bondage, or ransomed. Swarton's children were taken from her, and she was given as an enslaved woman to an Abenaki family. For the next eight months, she lived, traveled, ate, and dressed as an Indigenous woman. She was hungry, cold, exhausted, and terrified of being killed. Upon arriving in French Canada, her Indigenous enslaver sold Swarton to local Catholics, who dressed her in European clothes, gave her a bed to sleep in, and fed her relatively well. But now that Swarton's outer self was saved, she felt that her inner self was endangered. As a Protestant, Swarton had been taught to view Catholics as papists, or people who mindlessly followed the pope, and to view Catholic practices and beliefs such as the veneration of Mary and the saints as idolatry. Swarton felt pressured to convert to Catholicism: "The Lady, my mistress, the nuns, the priests, the friars, and the rest set upon me with all the strength of argument they could." Still, she held on to Protestanism for four long years, until intercolonial negotiations permitted her to return to New England.[1]

Hannah Swarton's story, which we know because the renowned Puritan cleric Cotton Mather published it to teach the power of faith, shows modern readers that colonial North America was home to a wide range of cultures and societies, close geographically yet sometimes far apart in lifestyles and expectations for women. These different peoples, not just "Europeans," "Africans," and "Indigenous peoples" but also French, English, and Spanish peoples, Mbundus, Igbos, Pueblos, Powhatans, Iroquois, Hurons, and Ojibwas, just to name a few, knew one another as neighbors, trading partners, allies, and enemies. Women rarely fought, but they were caught up in these conflicts. Hannah Swarton was unusual in crossing not just one boundary, but three, the first between English and Indigenous, the second between Indigenous and French, and the third between Catholic and Protestant. Her experience, first as a free woman and then as a captive and enslaved person, reminds us that slavery in North America took many forms before it became synonymous with African origins. Swarton's religious devotion and her family attachments link her to other women whose stories reveal the history of seventeenth- and early eighteenth-century North America through women's eyes.

◆ A CHANGED WORLD FOR INDIGENOUS PEOPLES

After the first century of contact, Indigenous peoples of North America entered a long period of trade, exchange, and conflict with European invaders. For some, their changed world meant merging shattered communities and rebuilding new identities. Many Indigenous peoples survived by migrating as a group and reestablishing new territory. Along the Eastern Seaboard, the growing population of English families, like Hannah Swarton's, caused the most harmful Indigenous dispossession and displacement during the seventeenth and early eighteenth centuries. Elsewhere, in the Great Lakes, Great Basin, interior Plains, and Southwest, Indigenous societies continued to exert and, in some cases even expand, their sovereignty effectively.

Although the political economies of Indigenous peoples varied widely, one historian tells us that "all of them governed and defended bounded, sovereign domains."[2] They established their borders in various ways, including through strategic assignment of place names, tree markings, and passport systems. Rather than imagining the expansion of European colonists across a blank North American map, we must understand that European newcomers continually bumped up against Indigenous geospatial boundaries (see Map 2.1). In the resulting interactions, many Indigenous women gradually lost political and economic power relative to men in their groups. Where war erupted with Europeans or other Indigenous groups, Indigenous women (and

1. Klallam	19. Chinook	37. Yuki	55. Halchidhoma	73. Houma
2. Cowichan	20. Tlatskanai	38. Pomo	56. Mohave	74. Chitimacha
3. Quileute	21. Tillamook	39. Wappo	57. Walapai	75. Acolapissa
4. Quinault	22. Alsea	40. Coast Miwok	58. Havasupai	76. Biloxi
5. Twana	23. Siuslaw	41. Costano	59. Hopi	77. Mobile
6. Sanpoil	24. Coos Bay	42. Salina	60. Zuni	78. Alabama
7. Kalispel	25. Chastacosta	43. Chumash	61. Hidatsa	79. Apalachee
8. Klikitat	26. Takelma	44. Wintun	62. Mandan	80. Hitchiti
9. Spokan	27. Klamath	45. Washoe	63. Arikara	81. Yuchi
10. Coeur D'Alene	28. Karok	46. Miwok	64. Menominee	82. Cusabo
11. Walla Walla	29. Shasta	47. Tubatulabal	65. Winnebago	83. Tuscarora
12. Wishram	30. Tolowa	48. Kawaiisu	66. Omaha	84. Pamlico
13. Tenino	31. Hepa	49. Gabrielino	67. Missouri	85. Powhatan
14. Umatilla	32. Yurok	50. Luiseno	68. Kiowa-Apache	86. Nanticoke
15. Cayuse	33. Wiyot	51. Cahuilla	69. Karankawa	87. Metoac
16. Molala	34. Wailaki	52. Kamia	70. Chakchiuma	88. Mohegan
17. Chehalis	35. Achomawi	53. Yuma (Quachan)	71. Tunica	89. Massachuset
18. Kwalhioqua	36. Yana	54. Maricopa	72. Natchez	90. Pennacook

◆ **Map 2.1** **Indigenous Claims to Sovereignty in North America, c. 1600**
While most early maps of the North American colonial era depict Indigenous names
floating above a blank continent, this map attempts to outline the bounded domains of
Indigenous nations. Although it is dated about 1600, the Indigenous peoples depicted here
in the continent's interior and west retained their claims and sovereignty well into the 1700s.
Imagine this map overlaid on Map 2.2 and consider the zones where conflict arose between
these Indigenous claims of sovereignty and the territorial claims of European nations.

children) bore the brunt as captive, hostaged, and enslaved people. Yet women also played a crucial part in rebuilding their societies and mediating culture exchange and evolution. The dilemmas of negotiation and survival faced by singular women like Malinztin and Pocahontas (see Chapter 1) spread to Indigenous women across North America as they encountered colonists with their own gendered ways. Nowhere was this more urgently the case than in the regions of British colonialism.

◆ SOUTHERN BRITISH COLONIES

Although colonists came from many European nations, the English dominated the Eastern Seaboard region, which eventually formed the political foundation of the United States as the thirteen English colonies. English cultural values were particularly influential in shaping early American assumptions concerning women's proper place. The male-headed, "heteronormative" family was the primary unit of society. Women's work was expected to be confined to household production, even though prevailing notions concerning the sexual division of labor were not always met, particularly among the poor and very wealthy. Both Protestant religious values and English law, especially as it related to property, reinforced women's subordination to men.

Ideas about women's roles framed the experiences of the Englishwomen who came as settlers to Britain's southern colonies as well as the African women who came enslaved. But the special circumstances of the New World also powerfully shaped migrant women's lives. The chronic shortage of marriageable (read English) women put them under irresistible pressure to marry quickly but also gave them some leverage in choosing a husband. The economic goals that dominated the plantation societies of the South not only created potential class conflict among whites but also led to the institution of a new form of chattel slavery and the evolution of distinct African American cultures.

British Women in the Southern Colonies

As noted in Chapter 1, the English finally succeeded in establishing a permanent beachhead in North America at Jamestown in 1607. Economic hopes for Virginia came to center on colonists raising tobacco in mass quantities for the European market. Plantation-grown export crops became crucial to the economies of the other southern British colonies as well: tobacco in Maryland, settled by the British in 1634; rice, indigo, and certain varieties of cotton in the Carolinas (colonized in 1663) and Georgia (settled in 1732). (See Map 2.2.)

With these marketable crops, merchants who sought to exploit the potential wealth of North America needed a steady supply of laborers to make their ventures successful. A population explosion in England and rising levels of poverty facilitated the recruitment of thousands willing (and some forced) to make the hazardous journey across the Atlantic. The first colonists were overwhelmingly male. To redress this imbalance, in 1620 and 1621 the Virginia Company imported

◆ Map 2.2 European Claims in North America, c. 1750
Of the four European nations that had permanent colonies along the Eastern Seaboard of North America in 1650, only England had substantial numbers of colonists. Approximately twenty-five thousand British subjects lived in New England, and another fifteen thousand lived in the Chesapeake region. Europeans in the interior, particularly Dutch and French fur traders, established diplomatic relationships with Indigenous peoples, bringing with them European trade goods, diseases, and gendered cultural disruptions.

approximately 150 **"tobacco brides"** — "respectable" young women whose passages (and whose persons) were paid for with 120 pounds of tobacco by men eager to acquire wives who could serve not only as sexual partners and mothers but also as another pair of domestic and agricultural hands. The disappearance of most of these women from historical records suggests that many died, some from disease and starvation in the hardship years of 1622–1623, others in the 1622 military attack of Powhatan's brother Opechancanough. Thus the imported brides made hardly a dent in improving the balance between the sexes. Women continued to immigrate in small numbers compared to men (in 1635, only 14 percent of the 2,010 colonists arriving from London were women), and the lack of marriageable women (it was illegal for Englishmen to marry the African or Indigenous women whom they pursued sexually) was a constant complaint among Englishmen. Maryland, founded in 1634 to provide refuge for Catholics, had an even greater disproportion of men to women: in the colony's first decade, men outnumbered women by 6 to 1. In Maryland and Virginia, it was not until after 1700, when the numbers of European women migrants increased and subsequent American-born generations began to reproduce, that the English sex ratio came into balance.

Even so, mortality rates remained exceptionally high in the Chesapeake region throughout the seventeenth century as a result of harsh conditions and diseases such as malaria and dysentery. Men's average life span was forty-eight years; women's was thirty-nine. (The hazards of childbirth caused the disparity; women who survived their childbearing years lived much longer than men.) The death of a spouse, usually an older husband, often cut marriages short; in Maryland, for example, only one in three couples could expect their marriage to last ten years. Widows, especially with inherited wealth from first husbands, remarried quickly, creating complicated households of stepsisters and stepbrothers.

The circumstances of the Chesapeake colonies made it difficult to reestablish as strong a patriarchal system as the one that flourished in England, but patriarchy was a coveted ideal especially among the landed elite and those who hoped to imitate them. While colonial political and religious leaders insisted upon formal marriages, their authority was limited, especially in the backcountry. Some couples cohabited without legal sanction and separated and created new relationships that ignored the law and the church. The many children who came to adulthood with just one living parent, particularly if that parent was the mother, had more freedom from parental oversight in their marriage choices. In the scattered homesteads of the southern colonies, premarital sex was not rare. The availability of land and the uncertainty of life induced some elite Chesapeake fathers to leave land to their daughters, once they had assured their sons' inheritances.

Married women, however, generally were just as subordinate to their husbands as in England. Under the English common law of coverture, which the Chesapeake colonies followed, a married woman became a *feme covert* (meaning her legal identity was absorbed into that of her husband). Naming practices by which a married woman took her husband's family name embodied this system. Without any separate legal identity, married women could not sue or be sued, hold public office, or vote. If they did not have a legally defined "separate estate" established before marriage, their husbands had legal control over their property, their children, and even their bodies. When a married woman was brought before the court for an offense, her husband was held responsible. Further, given that a wife's sexual services were the property of her husband, he could be found guilty if she committed the crime of adultery.

Upon her husband's death a widow did receive a portion — a dower right, which was at least one-third of the estate — for the duration of her lifetime. Those few women who remained single or who remained widowed had the status of *feme sole*, which gave them some individual rights before the law. Chesapeake widows also had decent opportunities to improve their circumstances by remarrying well. Husbands often left their wives more than the accustomed one-third dower rights — perhaps because they were so uncertain that their children would live to adulthood — and even made wives executors of their estates. Thus astute elite women could amass wealth and achieve a degree of economic autonomy. Elizabeth Digges, the widow of the former governor of Virginia, had an estate valued at 1,100 pounds, which was the largest in York County.

The most famous Chesapeake woman who acted independently was not a widow, but someone who never married. Margaret Brent, a well-connected English Catholic, came to Maryland in 1638. Both she and her sister Mary acquired substantial landholdings that they managed independently. Margaret Brent actively exercised her *feme sole* rights, making contracts, appearing in court to reclaim debts, and conducting her business freely. Her business acumen, her status as a large landholder and English gentlewoman, and the fact that she was not burdened by a husband with political entanglements led the governor of Maryland, Lord Calvert, to name her as his executor. When Calvert died in 1647, Maryland had recently experienced a local rebellion, and the troops that had put it down had yet to be paid. The responsibility of bringing order to the colony fell to Brent. The Maryland Assembly resolved that "the colony was safer in her hands than any man's in the Province and she rather deserves favor and thanks from your Honour for her so much concerning for the public safety."[3] Despite this show of trust and respect, the Assembly refused in 1647 to honor Brent's novel demand that she be given two votes in the Assembly, one based on her role as landowner and another on her role as representative of her male clients. Although Brent's story illustrates the fluid circumstances in the seventeenth-century Chesapeake colonies that allowed some women to have unusual economic power — and in very rare cases even limited political power — it is clearly an exceptional one.

In contrast to Brent, the vast majority of the early white immigrants to the Chesapeake — male and female — came as indentured servants. In Virginia and Maryland, and later in the Carolinas and Georgia, a system of "bound" labor predominated. Impoverished young people, seeking opportunities unavailable in Europe, and some who had to leave or face punishment for criminal activity, bound themselves via a legal document (an indenture) to "masters" for fixed periods of time — usually between four and seven years — exchanging their labor for their passage to the colonies. Recognizing the importance of women in creating a stable colony, the Virginia Company eagerly recruited young women by using propaganda that assured them that they would be treated well and would find it easy to marry at the conclusion of their service. Although the Company also promised that indentured women would not be "put into the ground to worke, but occupie such domestique imployments and housewifery as in England," this was often not the case.[4]

As many as three-quarters of the women who migrated to the Chesapeake colonies in the seventeenth century were indentured. Despite the promises of the colonies' promoters, indentured women servants found life harsh (see Primary Sources: "By and About Colonial Women"). They carried out their responsibilities for food preparation and housekeeping in meager circumstances in small dwellings. In the early years, the zeal to produce a cash crop overrode the English sensibilities about proper gender roles. Instead of concentrating on domestic production, women servants often were sent into the tobacco fields — planting seedlings, hoeing, weeding, and, at harvest, stripping and processing the leaves for market.

Other conditions of their servitude added to the hardships of indentured women. Prohibited from marrying while servants, they were subject to sexual exploitation. When they became pregnant — and an estimated 20 percent of indentured women did — they were punished with a public whipping and a fine. Those unable to pay the fine had their time of servitude extended, usually by one to two years, but their children were bound to adulthood. A servant who claimed that her master was the father of her child was not released from service, for fear that if a "woman got with child by her master should be freed from that service it might probably induce such loose persons to lay all their bastards to their masters."[5] Rather, a pregnant servant's indenture was transferred to a new master, who paid the county for her services.

Because of the indenture system, most young white women who came to the Chesapeake colonies married relatively late, at age twenty-four or twenty-five. Marriage helped to mark a woman's freedom from bound labor, but it did not necessarily lighten her load. Some women married "up" — and found themselves the "mistress" of servants — but others married men less well off than their former masters. Until the legal codification of perpetual slavery for Africans in the later 1600s, some of them married enslaved African men. In addition to the responsibilities of childbirth and child care, in poorer families wives worked in the fields. In middling families, women conducted business and trade in their husbands' absences. Wives' contributions to the household economy were valued, but as elsewhere in the English world, married women lived highly circumscribed lives.

Discontent among indentured servants, female as well as male, played a major role in **Bacon's Rebellion**. In 1676, a rebel faction of the Virginia colony's British elite, led by Nathaniel Bacon, recruited white indentured servants and enslaved Africans to protest the high-handed rule of his uncle, royal governor Sir William Berkeley. These men protested the governor's control over land and trade. They also argued that his policies shielding the lands of Indigenous peoples from seizure and sale interfered with colonial men's ability to establish their own economic independence. They especially resented the shortage of Englishwomen to marry. Women also joined the ranks of protesters. Sarah Drummond, the wife of one of Bacon's closest advisors, famously defied royal authority by declaring, "I fear the power of England no more than a broken straw."[6] Sarah Drummond's husband was hanged as a punishment for his part in the rebellion and the couple's property seized. Governor Berkeley was recalled to England, leaving his spouse to deal with the destruction of their home and his diminished political status. He died soon after arriving back in England. This "rebellion" concerning men's right to Indigenous property and greater power had, not surprisingly, enormous impact on the lives of their spouses.

Although the rebels had forced an unprecedented crisis in Virginia affairs, the resolution of the rebellion taught the ruling powers of the colony how to quell cross-class conflicts among Englishmen and thus stabilize their own leadership.

The colony's rulers went to great lengths to forestall any future alliance between white servants, free Blacks, and enslaved Africans, and they made it easier for land-hungry whites to seize treaty-protected territory from Indigenous peoples. Colonial legislators also lifted restrictions on the enslavement of Indigenous peoples. In the next half century, English captors sold between thirty thousand and fifty thousand Indigenous peoples into slavery either in British North America or to the British Caribbean colonies.[7]

At the same time, economic and political power remained consolidated in the hands of large plantation owners, who continued to acquire not only the best land but also more and more enslaved people. Some began to build large, elegant mansions for themselves, conspicuously displaying their wealth and social prominence as a class of landed gentry. Girls and single women of the planter class, aided by a large retinue of bound workers and supervised by the married woman of the home for household tasks, were able to devote time to such leisurely pursuits as studying French, playing music, writing letters, and doing needlework. Married wealthy women participated in a growing consumer economy, importing from English merchants gowns, china, silver, and furniture with income that their husbands, nonetheless, tightly controlled. Privileged white women's attention to hospitality and fashion, as well as to domestic and maternal labor, eventually became essential elements in the ideal of the "genteel lady" that reinforced southern patriarchal culture in European American households.

African Women

Whether plantation wives, wives of yeomen, or indentured servants, white women in the southern colonies were inextricably tied up with slavery. Until the mid-seventeenth century, relatively few Africans had been imported into North America, and the historical records on them are spotty. One of the first African women was "Mary," who arrived in Virginia in 1622 and ended up at the same plantation as "Antonio a Negro." Eventually the two won their freedom, married, had children, adopted the surname Johnson, and became modest landowners, even owning enslaved Blacks. The couple's experience points to an important fact about early African servitude: initially the system was a fluid one that allowed some Africans opportunities for freedom and created a small nucleus of free Blacks in the region. By the end of the seventeenth century, however, chattel slavery had become a nearly inescapable status for those of African descent.

The harshness of African women's American existence began when they were kidnapped or sold into the Atlantic slave trade (see Reading into the Past: "Florence Hall's Account of the Slave Trade"). Of all people captured in Africa, 10 to 20 percent died in transit. The numbers of women, men, and children being bought, shipped, and sold increased significantly as the scale of the transatlantic trade grew. Of the estimated 1 million Africans forcibly shipped to the British American colonies between 1650 and 1750, some 39 percent were female, including girls as well as adult women.[8] The two- to three-month voyage across the Atlantic is known as the Middle Passage. Female captives made the Middle Passage in gender-segregated quarters, stripped naked and terrorized by crew members who routinely sexually abused them. Olaudah Equiano struggled for words to describe his Atlantic passage after being abducted from his Nigerian home: "The shrieks of the women, and the groans of the dying, rendered the whole a scene of horror almost inconceivable."[9] When African women arrived in the mainland colonies in the late 1600s, they found a new system of Black chattel slavery emerging that relied on both their physical labor and their childbearing.

Diverse systems of bondage were operative on the seventeenth-century British colonial frontier, and some Africans initially had experiences similar to the indentured servitude of poor white immigrants. Their "unfree" condition, however, began a decided shift toward a lifelong and inherited status starting in the middle of the seventeenth century. Scholars have pointed out that African bound women were particularly crucial to this shift. Virginia's laws reveal some of the steps by which perpetual Black slavery became customary and was institutionalized. A 1643 law placed a tax on the labor of African women, putting them in the same category as adult male (European and African) laborers. White women were exempt from this tax. By making a sharp distinction between Black women's and white women's labor, the law contributed to the view of African females as fundamentally distinct from European females. Eventually, the increased use of African men and women in the fields allowed the reinstitution of traditional English gender roles for white women. By 1722, Virginian William Beverly could write that "slaves of both sexes are employed together in tilling and manuring the ground" while "a white woman is rarely or never put to work in the ground."[10]

This first law that distinguished the roles of Black and white women was followed by others. Particularly important was the 1662 law known as **partus sequitur ventrem** that made bondage an inherited condition, derived only from the mother. Enslavement now extended beyond an individual's lifetime and was passed to offspring through the female parent, a major break with traditional English patrilineage. The principle of *partus sequitur ventrem* increased enslaved women's vulnerability to rape, even though the 1662 law imposed stiff penalties on whites who had sexual intercourse with Blacks. Sexual relations between white female servants and enslaved Black males, which had once been common, were now deemed illegal. By contrast, sexual relations between white men and Black women were largely ignored by the law. Indeed, should a slaveholder impregnate an enslaved woman, the child's birth only added to his wealth. Laws that centered on women and their bodies illustrate the intersection of gender, sexuality, bondage, and reproduction in differentiating among free, indentured, and enslaved, and among white, Black, and Indigenous.

Most Africans were initially sent to the Chesapeake Bay colonies of Maryland and especially Virginia. In 1650 there were only 300 enslaved Africans in all of Virginia; by 1700 there were 13,000, and by 1750 there were 150,000. The majority of these captives cultivated and processed tobacco. Tobacco could be raised on small farms as well as on large plantations; thus, slaveholding was widespread in the Chesapeake region. On small farms, African women performed both field work and domestic tasks, including spinning and weaving. On the great plantations, by contrast, all the labor of most enslaved people, Black women and men

READING INTO THE PAST

Florence Hall's Account of the Slave Trade

Florence Hall, born Akeiso and an Igbo girl when she was kidnapped and sold into the Atlantic slave trade, managed to leave behind one of the very few firsthand accounts by a female of her life before enslavement, her capture, the Middle Passage, and the transition from freedom in Africa to enslavement in the Americas. The source is especially precious because of her revelation of the various emotions she experienced and the sense of extreme loss and alienation as a result of her enslavement in a foreign land and culture.

Africa is my Country — In the Country of the Eboe [Igbo], on the banks of the great [missing word] river, my people lived. The manner of my life before I was taken, and sold to the white people, I can scarcely remember beyond that I was still unclothed, sometimes employed in attending our people, while engaged in fishing, at other times guarding the fowls and chickens from hawks, or more frequently at play with other children. In one of those evening plays, while at a distance from our houses a party of the enemy came around and drove us, into an enclosed place, and immediately secured us — our hands were tied — while in vain our cries and screams were raised, but raised unheard, if heard, unattended, and by force we were hurried along and rested not until the sun arose, and marked our [illegible word] and distance from our homes. The day we lay concealed, and in the night our journey was performed. Day and night succeeded each other, in hunger, weariness, and grief at the end of

alike, went to cultivating tobacco. The records of Robert Parnafee indicate that the enslaved females on his tobacco plantation produced a crop worth 1,140 pounds, a figure nearly equal to that produced by the enslaved males.

Because of the initially skewed sex ratio favoring males and the low fertility rates of African immigrant women, Africans living in the Chesapeake region did not have enough children to offset their deaths until the 1720s. The change was the result of declining disease rates and a lower sex ratio, as females came closer in number to males. Even so, the hard labor, poor living conditions, and separations of partners meant that African women's fertility rates remained lower than those of English-women. The gradual creation of family units among enslaved people changed not only the history of the slave institution but also the lives of African Americans.

the 15th night, our travelling was at an end and the dawn of day shewed us the Great Sea, and the ship, [on? in?] which we were soon embarked, and at once left our Country, and our freedom, and consigned to foreigners and Slavery. The enemies of our Country seized and sold us to the White people, for the love of drink, and from the quarrels of their Chiefs — The white people received, and stripped us of all our beads, and shells, and while the naked children were permitted to walk about the ship, the men and women were chained and kept in darkness below. Our food was sparing, and ever bad. Our punishment was frequent and severe, and death became so frequent an occurrence, that at last it [illegible word] on, without fear on the dying, or grief on those left behind, as we believed that those who died, were restored to their people and Country. A long voyage at length brought the ship to Jamaica. My Eboe name was Akeiso, the loss of which soon put an end to all recollections of my people — another name — a strange language, & a new master, confused my mind, and while ignorance of each, made my labour more troublesome, yet the dread of punishment compelled me to work, [end of existing manuscript]

SOURCE: Florence Hall (Akeiso), *Memoir of the Life of Florence Hall,* The Powel Family Papers (Historical Society of Pennsylvania, 1808–1820?).

ANALYZING PRIMARY SOURCES

1. Why might the traumas that Florence experienced hinder her memory of her people and culture?

For women, the birth and survival of their children were powerfully mixed blessings, as surviving children could be and often were sold away from their mothers.

By the early eighteenth century, second- and third-generation enslaved people were forming African American cultures, adapted from multiple African origins but also including European elements. Enslaved people whose parents and grandparents spoke different languages began to evolve a common language, a mixture of European and African words. While many African religious practices, including Islam, continued, African Americans also incorporated parts of Christianity as it began to spread among them in the 1740s, with the beginning of the First Great Awakening (see "Social Change in the Eighteenth Century" in Chapter 3). Women seem to have been especially responsible for transferring and adapting medicines, foods, and some cultural practices such as making quilts following distinct sub-Saharan West African patterns of decoration.

◆ **John Rose, *The Old Plantation***

The Old Plantation depicts the evolution of the enslaved community in eighteenth-century North America. By the time that John Rose painted this scene about the lives of Black people enslaved on a South Carolina plantation, the numbers of adult men and women had become roughly equal, allowing for families and communities to develop. Community life is demonstrated here in dance, ritual, musical contributions, and courtship. On their one workday off per week, women donned their best clothes and head wraps to fully participate in communal recreation and representation. *HIP/Art Resource, NY.*

In addition to the development of African American cultures, communities of free Blacks began to develop throughout the mainland colonies as small numbers were freed by slaveholders or bought their own freedom. By one estimate, in some Virginia counties in the 1660s, free Blacks made up as much as one-third of the Black population.[11] Overall, a disproportionate number of free Black colonial households were headed by women, reflecting African traditions of matrilocality as well as the legal restrictions that made it difficult for their marriages to be recognized as legitimate. The intensification and growth of slavery affected free Blacks for the worse. They were, in the words of one historian, "an anomaly in a society committed to racial slavery," and their very presence was taken as incitement to slave rebellion.[12] Denied the rights of free persons, Black men could not vote or carry guns. Despite the efforts of legislatures, however, some white servant women continued to bear children by Black fathers. These interracial relationships were a major factor in the increase of an indentured and/or free African American population well into the eighteenth century.[13]

Many of the first Africans in North America were sent from the British colonies of the Caribbean, in particular from the wealthy sugar island of Barbados

◆ **Hulling Rice in West Africa**
Southern white slaveholders drew on the tools of West and West Central African women's traditional work as agriculturists. African women's contributions to the technology of southern rice cultivation were particularly notable. They were responsible for introducing methods for sowing and processing harvested rice. They usually did the backbreaking work of hulling and polishing the rice, pounding open the outer shell, and then scouring out the inner germ. Their tools were fashioned according to those they remembered from West Africa, particularly those from the "Grain Coast," today known as Sierra Leone and Liberia. Using a hollowed-out log and a pine branch, they pounded away in a method that required prolonged movement and tremendous strength. This engraving is an eighteenth-century depiction of women's work in West Africa. *Library of Congress.*

to the British colony in the Carolinas. One of the earliest enslaved women in the Carolinas — we know her only as "Sara" — came in 1678, with no family of her own, accompanying her captor for reasons about which we can only speculate. In South Carolina, slave importation was so dramatic after 1700 that Africans formed a majority of the population. "A fruitful woman . . . is very much valued by planters, and a numberous Issue esteemed the greatest Riches in this country," an observer wrote in 1737.[14]

African women were particularly involved in the Carolinas' two major export crops, one of which was the indigo plant, the source of a valuable blue-black textile dye. The other, rice, was South Carolina's most important and valuable product, in large part because African women had useful knowledge about its cultivation. They used African techniques for processing the rice, but with a critical difference. Women in Africa had spent a small part of their day pounding rice for their families; African women in America spent whole long days shelling rice for distant markets.

After two centuries of English colonization, tobacco, indigo, and rice planta-tions that were sustained by Black labor had created a distinctive economy and cul-tures in the Chesapeake and Carolinas. Enslaved peoples of course could be found elsewhere in North America, too — an active African slave trade helped define port cities such as New York, Boston, and Newport, while shipbuilding companies, insurance and banking firms, lawyers, dockworkers, molasses and rum factories, tax collectors, newspaper editors, scriveners, ironworkers, caulkers, coopermen, and farmers who provided food for voyages all benefited from the trade in Black bodies and the labor they were forced to perform.

◆ NORTHERN BRITISH COLONIES

Despite their common English origins, the colonies of New England differed dra-matically from the Chesapeake and Carolina settlements. Although climate and geography accounted for some of the differences — the land there did not typically offer possibilities for commercially oriented agriculture — at the center of the dis-tinctive quality of New England was religious fervor.

The people who founded the colonies of Plymouth (1620), Massachusetts Bay (1630), Connecticut (1635), and New Hampshire (1638) were **Puritans**, dissenters from the established Church of England. Puritans believed that the Anglican Church, despite the English Reformation, retained too many vestiges of Catholicism. Calling for a more thorough "purification" of Christian worship and ecclesiastical, hierarchical organization, they emphasized religious conversion as a deeply personal experience. Each church stood as an autonomous congregation of baptized saints who could testify to their conversion, as well as children and others who still awaited the conversion experience. While not the moralistic prudes of popular stereotype, the Puritans did strive to reverse what they saw as England's moral, including sexual, degeneracy and closely monitored the behavior not only of other Puritans, but also of the larger community. Given all these characteris-tics, Puritans placed great emphasis on the family as a "little commonwealth," the essential foundation of reformed churches and a virtuous and orderly community.

Puritanism acknowledged women's spiritual equality before God. Nonetheless, both the little commonwealth of the family and the greater one of the community were male-headed, and women's role in Puritan society was definitely subordinate. The contradiction between Puritanism's religious radicalism and its social conser-vatism helps to account for some of the contradictions in women's experience in the northern British colonies. While the majority accepted the Puritan "goodwife" ideal, a minority followed the word of God into unconventional behaviors or were accused — as witches — of female behavior gone horribly awry.

Subject to religious persecution in England and inspired by the idea of cre-ating a harmonious Christian commonwealth in the New World — what Puritan leader John Winthrop described as "a city on a hill" that would be a model for all peoples — nearly fifty thousand Puritans arrived in North America between 1620 and 1640. Dedicating themselves to a righteous and disciplined life based on a covenant with God, they established a society in which church and state, while officially separate, were in reality intertwined, giving the religious and moral values of Puritanism the force of law. Whereas in the South commercial agriculture and slavery were the defining factors shaping women's lives, in New England religion served as the major force constructing gender roles and framing women's experiences. In a different way, the Quaker religion shaped the lives of women in the settlement of the Pennsylvania colony.

The Puritan Search for Order: The Family and the Law

In contrast to virtually all other groups of Europeans who settled on the North American continent, the Puritans did not send men alone: nearly three-quarters of Puritan migrants to New England came in family groups that included wives and daughters. Puritan notions of marriage, like those of other Protestants, Catholics, and other faiths, combined mutuality and hierarchy. Husband and wife had reciprocal responsibilities, were enjoined to recognize their mutual dependence, and were charged with creating social order and community virtue together through their gendered domestic order and conduct. As one historian puts it, they were "sturdy mates and fellow travelers on the road to salvation."[15] At the same time, patriarchal authority characterized their families, and wives were clearly secondary to their husbands in almost all matters. Indeed, female deference to male authority was the Puritans' model for humanity's relation to God. (See Primary Sources: "Depictions of 'Family' in Colonial America.")

New England women married early and had an astonishingly high childbirth rate, considerably more than women in England or the Chesapeake colonies. First-generation Plymouth women bore an average of 7.8 children, the majority of whom lived to adulthood. The family and the church stood as lynchpins of social order, a value magnified by frontier conditions. Although Puritans encouraged love and respect within the family, each person's role was clearly delineated by gender and age, as indicated in their biblical teachings. So crucial was the family unit and the church to social order that all were expected to attend regular religious services, and single adults were required to live with a family.

Religion deeply shaped New England laws governing marriage and women's status. The Massachusetts colonies, like other British colonies, followed the English principle of *feme covert*. However, Puritans, in keeping with Protestant Reformation theology, viewed marriage as a civil contract rather than as a religious sacrament; thus they permitted divorce, offering women more legal options than they had in England. Nonetheless, remarriage after divorce was rarely allowed, and women were still legally subordinate. A northern woman, like a southern one, might be released from marriage to a husband who abandoned his family completely, but while married, she had to obey her husband's decisions, even if those decisions included abusive, destructive, or promiscuous behavior.

The Puritan moral code, at least in the early years of settlement, punished both men and women — though not equally — for sexual crimes such as intercourse outside of marriage. Despite popular notions of Puritans as sexually repressed, they valued sexual pleasure for men and women within marriage, though they viewed extramarital sexuality as damaging to social order and Christian piety. Puritan religious leaders in both Europe and New England sought to reform the indulgent sexual culture of their times, but with mixed success. In New England, premarital pregnancy was fairly common: records for the 1690s in New Haven County, Connecticut, for example, reveal that 19 percent of women were already pregnant at the time of their marriage.[16] For the most part, neither men nor women were harshly condemned as long as the couple married, but an unmarried woman giving birth was pressured to name the father so that he could care for her and the child, preventing them from becoming burdens on the community. A liaison between a married man and an unmarried woman was a less serious offense than that between a married woman and an unmarried man. The former crime was deemed "fornication," while the latter was given the much more serious label of "adultery." As Puritan William Gouge put it, a woman's crime created "greater infamy before men, worse disturbance of the family, more mistaking of legitimate, or illegitimate children."[17] Similarly, the rape of a married white woman was regarded, in the words of one historian, as "not the offense against the woman but the offense against her husband."[18]

Women's subordination to men was evident in disparities in education, too. Although the New England colonies mandated that all children be taught to read so that they could study the Scriptures (and women did have a high literacy rate), few girls attended school. Not surprisingly, few women wrote diaries or books. (See Primary Sources: "By and About Colonial Women.") Only four women authors were represented in the 911 books produced in seventeenth-century New England. Of these, the most famous was Anne Bradstreet, whose works included *The Tenth Muse, Lately Sprung Up in America* (1650) and the posthumously published *Several Poems Compiled with Great Variety of Wit and Learning* (1678). Bradstreet's brother, the pastor Thomas Parker, wrote to Bradstreet, "Your printing of a Book, beyond the custom of your sex, doth rankly smell."[19]

Mary Rowlandson's *A True History of the Captivity and Restoration of Mrs. Mary Rowlandson* (1677) was also one of the most important books authored by a North American woman. Rowlandson, who had emigrated from England in 1639, wrote powerfully about her captivity and enslavement during the brutal colonist/Indigenous conflict known as King Philip's War (1675–1676; King Philip was the colonists' name for the Wampanoag leader Metacom). During this conflict, which came at the same time as Bacon's Rebellion in Virginia and reflected the Indigenous peoples' growing desperation at the hands of whites, one thousand white colonists and three thousand Nipmucs, Wampanoags, and Narragansetts were killed. Half the towns of Massachusetts were attacked, including Lancaster, where Rowlandson and her minister husband lived. Rowlandson's tale of her captivity includes her interactions with her mistress, Weetamoo, Metacom's sister-in-law and a powerful woman in her own right. Among other things, Rowlandson survived by sewing shirts and stockings for her Indian captors, who appreciated her skill with a needle. Eventually she was ransomed by Massachusetts authorities. When the conflict ended, both Metacom and Weetamoo were killed, and their

◆ **Esther Wheelwright**
Esther Wheelwright (1696–1780), who was born into a Puritan family in Maine, became an Ursuline nun after being captured and adopted by a Catholic Wabanaki family. When New England soldiers retaliated, the Wabanaki band who raised Esther took shelter in mission towns near Quebec. Esther lived as a Wabanaki girl from ages seven to twelve and then enrolled as a student at a nearby Ursuline convent school in 1709. In later life, she became mother superior of the convent. This oil painting was most likely painted by a sister artist, as the Ursulines were known for their fine brushwork. Her biographer notes that "across every political, religious, and linguistic border, Esther was surrounded by communities of women."[20] How do her experiences of religion in the northeastern colonial borderlands compare with those of Mary Rowlandson and Kateri Tekakwitha, also discussed in this chapter? *Massachusetts Historical Society/Bridgeman Images.*

families sold into slavery in the Caribbean. King Philip's War was a watershed in the history of New England. In the aftermath of the war, some Indigenous survivors looked for safety by adopting English customs, while others joined distant relatives in Canada or west of the Hudson River. Rowlandson viewed her own survival and rescue as a sign of God's blessing on the Puritan community.

While Puritan leaders valued Rowlandson for her pious example, they drew clear rules to discipline women who presumed to offer their own doctrinal interpretations. Even though Puritan women shared with men the right to be members of the church once they satisfactorily testified to their salvation, the male clergy and male community leaders periodically punished or banished heretical women who challenged male religious authority.

Disorderly Women

In the 1630s, Massachusetts' patriarchal leaders faced a major controversy regarding both religious orthodoxy and gender assumptions: the case of Anne Hutchinson. Hutchinson, a midwife, arrived in the colony with her merchant husband William in 1634 and began proselytizing among women only. She believed that people were "saved" by a direct infusion of God's spirit and contended that the Puritan ministers were wrong in preaching that salvation came from earthly obedience to Puritan laws. Her provocation went even deeper than her theological notions; she also contested the status of women in the Puritan religious world, if only by her assertion of religious authority. Hutchinson began holding informal

READING INTO THE PAST

Trial of Anne Hutchinson

This excerpt from the published transcript of the 1637 trial of Anne Hutchinson (1591–1643) before a panel of Massachusetts Bay colony judges headed by Governor John Winthrop can only begin to suggest the theological intricacies of the interrogation. Hutchinson was accused of several religious crimes. Not only did she act in the male role of a religious teacher, but she compounded this crime by ministering to men as well as women. She was further accused of preaching various doctrines contrary to Puritan teaching. Not reflected in this excerpt is an intricate debate between Hutchinson and Winthrop about whether she diverged from the Protestant belief in salvation by God's grace to advocate the doctrine of salvation by "works," that is, human effort.

GOV.: Why do you keep such a meeting at your house as you do every week upon a set day? . . .

MRS. H.: I conceive there lyes a clear rule in Titus [Titus 11:3–5], that the elder women should instruct the young and then I must have a time wherein I must do it. . . . If any come to my house to be instructed in the ways of God what rule have I to put them away? . . .

GOV.: But suppose that a hundred men come unto you to be instructed will you forbear to instruct them? . . .

MRS. H.: No Sir for my ground is they are men. . . .

GOV.: You must shew your rule to receive them.

MRS. H.: I have done it.

GOV.: I deny it because I have brought more arguments than you have.

MRS. H.: I say, to me it is a rule. . . .

GOV.: . . . [W]e must therefore . . . restrain you from maintaining this course. . . . We are your judges, and not you ours and we must compel you to it. . . .

religious meetings in her home that included both men and women. Although male leaders worried that her radical religious views were heretical and posed a threat to the colony, their court proceedings focused on her behavior as a woman: in their view, Hutchinson had "rather been a Husband than a Wife and a preacher than a Hearer; and a Magistrate than a Subject."[21] (See Reading into the Past: "Trial of Anne Hutchinson.") Trial records indicate that Hutchinson ably defended both her religious ideas and her right as a woman to expound upon them. However, after days of unrelenting interrogation, she began to openly claim to have received

MRS. H.: It is one thing for me to come before a public magistracy and there to speak what they would have me to speak and another when a man comes to me in a way of friendship privately there is difference in that. . . . [I]f you do condemn me for speaking what in my conscience I know to be truth I must commit myself unto the Lord.

MR. NOWEL [ASSISTANT TO THE COURT]: How do you know that that was the spirit?

MRS. H.: How did Abraham know that it was God that bid him offer his son . . . ? . . . So to me by an immediate revelation. . . .

DEP. GOV.: How! an immediate revelation. . . .

MRS. H.: By the voice of his own spirit to my soul. . . .

GOV.: . . . [T]he ground work of her revelations is the immediate revelation of the spirit and not by the ministry of the word, and that is the means by which she has very much abused the country that they shall look for revelations and are not bound to the ministry of the Word, but God will teach them by immediate revelations and this hath been the ground of all these tumult and troubles. . . . [T]he sentence of the court you hear is that you are banished from out of our jurisdiction as being a woman not fit for our society.

SOURCE: Mr. [Thomas] Hutchinson, *The History of the Province of Massachusets-Bay, From the Charter of King William and Queen Mary in 1691, Until the Year 1750*, vol. 2, 2nd ed. (London: Printed by J. Smith, 1828), 484–87, 489, 508, 513, 520.

ANALYZING PRIMARY SOURCES

1. How does Hutchinson threaten ministerial authority when she claims to receive a direct revelation from God?

2. What does Winthrop's last comment here reveal about his central criticism of Hutchinson and her spiritual errors?

direct revelation from God. The Puritan magistrates used this statement as evidence that she was "delusional." Excommunicated and banished, she moved first to Rhode Island, established in 1636 as a haven for the growing number of refugees from Massachusetts Puritan orthodoxy, before finally settling in New Netherland, where she died during an Indigenous attack on the Dutch settlement.

The Hutchinson controversy represented not just a theological position that impacted men and women, but also an undercurrent of female rebelliousness that community leaders felt compelled to repress. In the aftermath of Hutchinson's trial, churches began to drop the requirement that women make their conversion statements publicly. Instead, they could relay their experience to their ministers, who, in turn, would convey their words to the congregation. Moreover, one historian has found that during this crisis the percentage of female defendants brought before the courts rose significantly. Either women were becoming more assertive, or the magistrates were becoming more determined to extinguish their public voice.

The most dramatic kind of disorderly act associated with women was witchcraft. Of the 344 people accused of being witches in the colonial period, 80 percent were female; of the men accused, half were relatives of accused women. Two major witch hunts occurred in New England: one during the period 1647–1663, in which 79 people were accused and 15 hanged, and an even larger episode in 1692 in Salem, Massachusetts, in which over 200 were accused and 19 were hanged. Witch trials occurred elsewhere as well. Some have been documented for New York, Maryland, and South Carolina; several took place in North Carolina; and over 20 occurred in Virginia between the 1620s and 1730.

Witchcraft was a complex crime. Sometimes women associated with heresy were charged with being Satan's servants. Many of Anne Hutchinson's critics, for example, hinted that she was a witch. For others, it was less their religious positions than their *maleficia*, or malicious actions against their neighbors, that brought such women to trial. Did milk sour, an animal die, a child take sick? Did a midwife assist at — or perhaps cause — a deformed birth? Did young girls have fits and see an unpopular village woman in spirit form? Did men believe themselves sexually ravaged by a neighbor woman with supernatural powers? (See Primary Sources: "By and About Colonial Women.")

The finger often pointed at an older, poor, and powerless woman, although the first implicated in the **Salem witch trials**, Tituba, was an enslaved Indigenous woman whose cultural difference and slave status no doubt contributed to suspicions about her. Of the white women accused, some had reputations for being argumentative, discontented, or prideful. Some were suspected of causing abortion, committing infanticide, or, if they were midwives, using their healing power for ill instead of good. Another major category of witches — more evident in the Salem cases — were those with some measure of authority or prestige. For example, a widow engaged in a dispute with her husband's heirs over property rights was a likely candidate for suspicion. Indeed, as the frenzy escalated in Salem, some elite men and women were accused by young women who claimed the witches had "possessed" them. The young women's accusations gave them an unprecedented opportunity to influence community affairs and to exercise a degree of power, thus complicating the gendered dimensions of the incidents. Indeed, the clergy and the magistrates quickly lost control of the situation and ceased to support the prosecutions. Eventually, the governor of Massachusetts interceded and brought the trials to a halt in 1692, but at least twenty of those accused were already dead.

What accounts for these tumultuous outbursts of witchcraft accusations? Most historians believe that societal tensions laid the groundwork. Many Salem residents were refugees from Indigenous wars on the southern Maine frontier.

The Salem cases suggest a link between the community's susceptibility to believing in the malevolent power of witches among them (and those witches' ability, for example, to aid the "heathen" in massacring the Christian colonists) and the insecurities of living near the frontier at a time of heightened Indigenous resistance to colonial encroachment. In addition, by the 1690s the stability of New England's Puritan order was being eroded by the growth of trade, an influx of immigrants, and the inroads of secularism and materialism. These tensions were compounded by a rise in population that put pressure on land acquisition, which in turn created intergenerational tensions as young people chafed at the older generation's control of family property. While these anxieties help to explain the dynamics of witchcraft accusations, they do not fully explain why the witch hunts had such a strong gendered component. Whatever the source of the frenzy, the accused women had seemingly violated their prescribed gender roles and certainly were easier targets of societal surveillance, control, and punishment than men.

Women's Work and Consumption Patterns

Only a small minority of women were involved in the dramatic events connected to mid- to late seventeenth-century witch hunts or religious dissent. Most led ordinary, work-filled lives. Wealthier women's labor was less physically demanding than poorer or rural women's, but all women's work was valued for its contribution to the family economy. The division of labor followed English patterns: men's duties concentrated outside the home in family security, farming, hunting, fishing, or trade; women's duties centered within the home around food preparation, cleaning, childbearing, and childrearing. Goodwives, as hard-working married women were called, raised, butchered, and preserved domestic animals, produced dairy products, tended orchards and vegetable gardens, and fashioned meals with the few cooking utensils available. They produced their own candles, soap, thread, cloth, and clothing and exchanged their excess home-produced goods for their families' additional needs.

Women without servants created networks of female friends and relatives to help with their tasks. Since few women excelled at all necessary household trades, they usually bartered, especially in more remote areas where women's lives were harder and their time more constrained. Women were expected to train their own daughters in wifely responsibilities and often took in daughters of neighbors to apprentice them in exchange for their household labor. And for another form of distinctly female labor — childbirth — women came together in close communion, often spending days at a prospective mother's home, giving practical assistance and emotional comfort during a time when almost one in ten New England women died during childbirth or of related complications.

As elsewhere in the colonies, midwives were central figures in the New England world of women; their existence demonstrates that women could and did engage in work beyond their own homes. They generally were highly respected and often tended to other "female" ailments with herbal remedies. Their assistance was rewarded with payment in kind — chickens, eggs, cloth, sugar, and so on — or with coin from more prosperous citizens. Occasionally other women, too, moved outside the sexual division of labor. If her husband was away hunting, serving in the militia, or trading, a wife could conduct family business or represent her husband in legal matters. Widows, who as *femes sole* could act on their own, ran taverns, inns, shops, or printing establishments. Many took pride in their abilities to manage their estates. Bostonian Ann Pollard reported that "[by my] own proper gettings by my Labour and Industry [the estate of my husband] is Considerably Advanced and bettered."[22]

As commerce in the colonies increased, mercantile cities such as New York, Philadelphia, Boston, and Charleston grew in size and importance. At the same time, King William's War (1689–1697) and Queen Anne's War (1702–1713), European conflicts that also played out in the American colonial empires, created a dramatic rise in widows. These women often moved with their children to urban centers like Boston, for example, where widows represented 16 percent of the population by 1725. Poorer town women, encouraged to work by community leaders eager to keep them off the charity rolls, found employment as spinners, weavers, seamstresses, domestics, and in other trades that drew on their wifely skills. Shopkeeping was another avenue for urban women, and historians estimate that between 1740 and 1775, more than ninety Boston white women operated commercial enterprises.

In addition to urban/rural distinctions in colonial women's lives, other divisions were growing in New England. Approximately 3 percent of working women in the eighteenth century were bound Africans. Northern slaveholders tended to have small numbers of enslaved people (one or two) and to buy and sell them frequently in response to labor demands, making it difficult for enslaved people to live with family members. Most northern female captives lived in the cities, where they worked as domestics and contributed to the leisure of their white female enslavers, usually the wives of merchants, professionals, and craftsmen. These prosperous women and their daughters enjoyed increased free time, often taking up activities like fancy needlework that demonstrated their genteel feminine skills. Well-to-do urban women increasingly bought what they needed instead of making it themselves, and imported goods were especially popular. Boston milliner and merchant Elizabeth Murray offered satin gloves, ebony fans, and ermine muffs. Although this kind of opulence was unusual, it pointed to the emergence of an urban consumer culture.

This consumer culture was part of a broad pattern of economic change evident in New England life, especially after 1700. High white childbirth rates and immigration meant that the population of the four New England colonies (Massachusetts, Connecticut, Rhode Island, and New Hampshire) doubled every twenty-five years — in 1775 it was 345,000. As urban areas and commerce grew and class distinctions hardened, men increasingly focused on economic success and moved away from religion. They left women to predominate in most churches, thus underscoring a distinctive association of white married women with moral and spiritual matters that deepened over time. Puritans' political control slipped as well, as the British Crown revoked the Massachusetts charter in 1684. In a new charter of 1692, the influence of the Puritan church was greatly reduced when property holding, not church membership, became the basis for freeman — and voting — status.

Some scholars argue that the breakdown of the Puritan commonwealth also eroded the power of the patriarchal family, giving women a greater degree of freedom. Certainly new prosperity and urban growth stimulated female education and opened increased economic opportunities for some women. Changes in church membership patterns gave women more voice (though never open leadership) in the religious sphere of life, but only at a time when church influence was declining. Perhaps the most significant change toward the end of the colonial period in New England was the increased group diversification in women's experiences — the continued hard labor of farmwomen, the variety of work available for women to take up in the cities, the increased presence of enslaved Black females, and new goods for consumption for prosperous urban women. These patterns pointed to a coalescing segmentation of women's communities that would persist throughout the course of American history, in New England and beyond.

Dissenters from Dissenters: Women in Pennsylvania

Although the Puritans had come to North America to be able to practice their religion free from persecution in England, they did not tolerate dissent in their own midst. Another group of dissenting English Protestants, the **Quakers**, who did not rely on an institutionalized clergy (and thus allowed for a much greater religious role for women), were banned in Massachusetts. Mary Dyer, a follower of Anne Hutchinson, was hanged in Boston in 1660 when she returned from exile as a Quaker. In 1681, Quaker William Penn received a charter from the British king giving him authority to establish a colony in the lands west of the Delaware River that had once been part of New Netherland. Pennsylvania was thus founded as a haven for the beleaguered Quakers.

Quaker women had no distinctive economic privileges, yet religious values made their society relatively egalitarian. The Quakers believed that "the Inner Light of Christ" was available equally to all. This experience stressed the individual's direct relationship with God and deemphasized ceremony and sermonizing. Among American Quakers, a number of women, such as Elizabeth Norris of Philadelphia, were noted for articulating the idea that women should not be subordinate to men. In contrast to the Puritan effort to suppress women's religious speech, Quaker women were often respected religious teachers, in part because religious ministry was not ordained or institutionalized among them.

Quaker institutions reflected women's elevated status. In Pennsylvania, white women's local monthly groups sent representatives to quarterly meetings, which in turn sent representatives to the annual convocation in Philadelphia. Created "for the better management of the discipline and other affairs of the church more proper to be inspected by their sex," the meetings monitored marital and family life in the community.[23] In particular, they forwarded petitions that determined whether a betrothed couple embraced appropriate Quaker values. By formalizing the responsibility of some Quaker matrons to monitor the behavior of other women, Quaker practice offered an additional degree of religious authority to older women.

Pennsylvania Quakers' relation to African slavery was complex. On the one hand, British Quakers were among the first to develop a full-fledged critique of slavery as a violation of God's law. On the other hand, the leadership of the Quaker community in Pennsylvania was made up of wealthy merchants, for whom traffic in African captives was an important element of their trade. Quakers also owned enslaved people. As a result, about 20 to 30 percent of Pennsylvania's labor force before 1750 consisted of enslaved people, and at least 10 percent of Philadelphia Quakers were enslavers. Their slaveholding numbers were even greater in Virginia, Maryland, and North Carolina, where they also settled. A combination of religious objections and the migration of Germans and other immigrants to work as indentured servants in Pennsylvania's fertile farmlands led to a gradual decline in dependence on African slavery. Sometime after 1760, an enslaved woman named Margaret, already married to a free Black man, secured her freedom. She began to have children in her forties, knowing that they would be free. Her son, James Forten, became leader of one of the most activist and elite free Black communities in British America.

◆ BEYOND THE BRITISH SETTLER COLONIES

Despite the growing size and strength of the British colonies, the North American continent continued to be the site of other European nations' expansionist hopes, as well as Native American persistence. As with North America's Indigenous peoples, European groups too had their differences. Cultural variation went hand in hand with different economic purposes and gender patterns in colonial endeavors. For example, the Dutch competed fiercely with England in matters of trade. In addition, both the Spanish and the French kept their agricultural and settlement projects to a minimum, concentrating, especially in the French case, on trade. Thus their need for female labor and family formation was considerably less and their toleration for marriages with Native Americans much greater. Meanwhile, Indigenous peoples incorporated new European goods into their economies and, where possible, developed new strategies of defending their borders and cultures.

New Netherland

The Dutch sojourn in North America was one of the briefest of colonizing Europeans, lasting only from 1614 to 1664. The center of New Netherland was the port town of New Amsterdam (later New York City). In 1647, the stern reformer Peter Stuyvesant was brought in to administer the colony; he relinquished his post when the British laid claim to it in 1664.

Women's lives in New Netherland differed from those in the British colonies. Although both societies paid a great deal of attention to proper domestic arrangements, Dutch women had more legal rights and economic authority. In contrast to the British concept of *feme covert*, Dutch women could choose a form of marriage in which women were considered their husband's partners and maintained their independent legal identities. Husband and wife viewed their possessions as community property and usually constructed a mutual will in which each left the estate to the other, postponing the children's inheritance until both died. Married women could and did own property, including enslaved people, and managed their own businesses.

Margaret Hardenbroeck perfectly exemplified a New Netherland businesswoman. She immigrated to North America in 1659 and established herself as a successful trader and debt collector who also represented other merchants. When she married her first husband, Peter de Vries, she maintained her business and at his death became even wealthier by acquiring his property. In her second marriage, she and Frederick Philipse drew up a marriage contract that delineated her control over her own property and ensured that she would be able to continue her commercial activities. Husband and wife were highly successful traders and partners in their own shipping enterprise, often acting as each other's agent in business matters and in court.

In part because of the prominent role that the Dutch played in the slave trade, New Amsterdam was home to many enslaved Africans, and substantial numbers of captives were shipped through the port. African men worked on the wharves, and African women were domestic servants to wealthy families. (Stuyvesant himself enslaved forty African people.) Concentrated in one city, enslaved people could develop explosive discontent, and there were at least two such uprisings in New Amsterdam in the seventeenth century. In 1991, an excavation of an African burial ground in lower Manhattan unearthed the remains of a twenty-two-year-old woman with a musket ball lodged near her ribs, a likely casualty of one of these upheavals.[24]

The great growth in the New York enslaved population occurred under the British, and most of it was urban. By the middle of the eighteenth century, 20 percent of New York City's population was Black, and half of the households in the cities owned enslaved people. Unlike Black men, who frequently learned skilled crafts from slaveholders, enslaved women did a variety of household tasks. A 1734 ad for the sale of a twenty-year-old captive woman emphasized that "she does all sorts of housework, she can brew, bake, boil soft soap, wash, iron and starch and is a good dairy woman, she can card and spin at the great wheel."

New Amsterdam was also the home to some of the first Jews to arrive in North America. Many European Jews, expelled from Spain and Portugal in the 1490s, had migrated to the Netherlands. Some went on to Dutch colonies in the New World, where tolerance was considerably less. Among the first Jews to arrive in North America were twenty-three people, including six women and thirteen children, who had been driven out of another Dutch colony, Recife, Brazil, in 1654. Jews suffered under the anti-Semitism of Peter Stuyvesant but were determined to remain and re-create their community. Miriam Israel Levy, the widow of one of the men in the original group, followed the Dutch practice of serving as executor of her husband's estate.[25] Even after the Dutch lost control of the colony to the British, Dutch Jews continued to migrate to New York, sometimes intermarrying with British colonists.

When the English conquered New Netherland, they decreed that Dutch inheritance laws could be sustained and Dutch contracts honored. However, as more

NEGROES, TO BE SOLD

A Parcel of young able bodied Negro Men, one of whom is a Cooper by Trade, two Negroes Wenches, and likewise two Girls, one of 12 Years old, and the other 16, the latter a good Seemſtreſs, and can be well recommended.

◆ **The Sale of Enslaved People in the North** This slave auction notice, so typical in the British colonies, demonstrates the importance of the institution of slavery, not only in the southern colonies, but also in the northern ones. This advertisement also indicates the growing importance of females in the slave trade, particularly those of childbearing age and with skills. Women, like men, brought skills from Africa and were also trained by owners, thus becoming more "valuable" than most who were agricultural workers. The notice also underscores the anonymity of those enslaved, reduced in these descriptions to age, gender, and skill level. There is, for example, no mention of name, family ties, culture, or personality as is often found in fugitive-slave advertisements in the same colonial newspapers. *GRANGER — Historical Picture Archive.*

English people settled in New York, they implemented English common law practices that circumscribed married women's property rights. Dutch women gradually became less visible in the public sphere. In Albany, for example, forty-six women were listed as traders before the British conquest, but by the turn of the eighteenth century, there were none. Women's names also became less prevalent in the rosters of skilled artisans and proprietors — brewers, bakers, and the like — and women were less likely to appear in court representing themselves or others. Margaret Hardenbroeck continued her business ventures, but when she bought land in New Jersey, her husband had to make the purchase for her. In 1710, the New York assembly passed a law that placed married women in the same legal category as minors and people of unsound mind. All these people presumably were not capable of acting on their own. Perhaps the reversal of women's property rights contributed to making New York the birth place of American women's fight for equal economic rights in the nineteenth century.

New France

New France was a large territory, covering almost as much of North America as the lands claimed by the British. Beginning in 1608 with the small settlement of Quebec, traders and missionaries spread south and west through the Great Lakes region and down the Mississippi, ultimately founding the city of New Orleans in 1718. Lightly populated and barely supported by the French Crown, New France was organized as a series of small communities closely linked to Indigenous villages. Although some farming took place, the major focus was trade, not agricultural settlement. Emigration from France was almost entirely made up of single men until between 1663 and 1673, when almost eight hundred marriageable women, known as *filles du roi* ("the king's daughters"), were shipped to Quebec; the families they formed with French men grew rapidly. Still, by 1700, the population amounted to less than 20 percent of British America's and included a substantial portion descended from the liaisons of French men and Indigenous women.[26] Native wives of French traders, along with the French religious women who worked to convert these *métis*, or "mixed-race," families to Catholicism, were important historical actors in the growth of New France.

The fur traders who moved into the upper Great Lakes and Illinois territories learned quickly that connection to an Indigenous woman through the practice of country marriage (see "Fish and Furs in the North" in Chapter 1) was the most important resource a French man could have on the frontier. Ojibwa, Huron, Illini, Missouri, and Osage women had excellent fur-preparation skills, could act as translators, and, most importantly, connected European traders to the Native American societies that provided them their wares. Indigenous women retained their relatively easy rights of divorce and the ability to retreat into their birth families. At the same time, country marriages gave Indigenous women more direct access to trading goods, such as the prized European cloth most frequently exchanged for furs. Indigenous wives gave their European husbands, in the words of one historian, "an entrée into the cultures and communities of their own people. In this way, Indigenous women were the first important mediators of meaning between the cultures of two worlds."[27]

By the eighteenth century, however, increasing numbers of these French-Indigenous alliances were undertaken with the blessings of the church. Indigenous women seem to have been more attracted to Catholicism than Indigenous men. Some historians see conversion as providing these women with external resources as they became major conduits for the expansion of Catholicism into Indigenous lands. Others argue that Catholic conversion, with its encouragement of female submission, destroyed these women's traditional sources of strength and independence. Either interpretation can be sustained by the experience of the Kaskaskia woman Aramapinchue, renamed Marie Rouensa. When her father urged her to marry a dissolute French trader in 1694, she was reluctant; already a convert, she turned to her priest, who supported her, telling her parents that "she alone was mistress" of her own life and decisions. In the end, Aramapinchue agreed to the marriage on the condition that her parents convert to Catholicism. Was this her assertion or her concession to the church's priorities?[28]

French Catholic women exerted influence in France's efforts to convert Indigenous peoples. Particularly important in this regard were the Ursulines, a religious order with a special commitment to the education of women. Marie de l'Incarnation, a woman with great energy and organizational gifts, came from Rouen, France, in 1639 to establish the first Ursuline community in New France.

◆ **Kateri Tekakwitha**
Kateri Tekakwitha exemplified the attraction Catholicism
held for some Indigenous women whose lives were
upended by violence and Old World diseases. Daughter
of an Algonquian mother and Mohawk father (both of
whom died of smallpox), Kateri arrived at a Jesuit mission
near Montreal in 1677, already a convert. She developed a
following of Indigenous women who physically tortured
themselves to demonstrate their faith. After her death in
1680, she became associated with miracles and healing,
heightening the veneration she is still accorded today
(she was canonized by the Catholic Church in 2012). This
1690 painting of Kateri, by Father Chauchetière, hangs
in the St. Francis-Xavier Church in Kahnawake, Quebec,
Canada. *Alessandra Tarantino/AP Photo.*

Although she was successful in establishing a community of **Ursuline sisters**
in Quebec, she did not convert as
many young Huron women as she had
hoped would spread the faith among
the Native population. The second
Ursuline convent in North America
was more successful in its educational
mission. It opened in New Orleans in
1727, charged by French authorities
with helping to clean up the chronically
disorderly and raucous port city. The
girls who boarded at the convent school
included elite European and multiracial
girls, although other free and enslaved
women of color and some Indigenous
females also received rudimentary education for religious purposes. Marie
Charlotte, a biracial girl, was sent to the
sisters by the terms of her dead father's
will. An unnamed Osage young woman
was also entrusted to the convent by
her enslaver upon his death. Although
distinctions of race and hierarchies of
class certainly existed in the New Orleans Ursuline community, the sisters
succeeded comparatively well.

New Spain

In 1608, the same year in which the
French established Quebec City, the
Spanish established Santa Fe in the heart
of Pueblo territory (see "Pueblo Peoples" in Chapter 1) as a center for their
soldiers, administrators, and merchants.
Throughout the seventeenth century,
tensions built both among and between
Indigenous peoples and colonists. Euro-
pean priests and soldier/settlers had very different ideas about how to absorb the
Indigenous peoples — as a tributary labor force or as converted Christians. The Pueblos' resentment over their economic and physical exploitation and the failure of the
Spanish God to protect them from Spanish disease and abuse led to what became
known as the **Pueblo Revolt**. In 1680, only a few years after both King Philip's War
in New England and Bacon's Rebellion in Virginia, Pueblo peoples drove the Spanish

out of New Mexico. In the aftermath, the revolt's leaders did all they could to rid the Pueblos of Christianity and return to the traditional religions exemplified by the Corn Mothers who had given birth to the world as they once knew it.

One of the most important areas of Indigenous restoration was with respect to women, marriage, and gender roles. Spanish priests had sought to impose monogamous marriages on the Pueblos, angering Pueblo men and helping to spark the revolt. It is not clear to what extent Indigenous women welcomed back their indigenous spiritual and sexual powers, nor is it known if they had any appreciation for the kinds of female roles that Catholicism introduced. After twelve years, Spanish colonial forces retook Santa Fe and killed or enslaved the Indigenous resisters, including four hundred women and children. From this point on, Spanish control over the colony went largely uncontested militarily.

Indigenous Grounds of the North American Interior

In the continent's heartland, neither French nor Spanish colonists succeeded in controlling terms of engagement with Indigenous groups. In the Arkansas River valley (present-day Arkansas, Oklahoma, and Kansas), for example, Quapaws who had newly migrated to the valley in the mid-seventeenth century used alliances with French traders to establish their own sovereignty. Rather than being conquered or mounting a war of resistance, the Quapaws incorporated French traders into their political networks. Quapaw women, however, contributed essential agricultural goods used in gift-exchange rituals that forged interdependent relations with Europeans and other Indigenous groups. The ability of Quapaw society to retain relative control over its "native ground" may have been rooted in its patrilineal rules of descent.[29] In contrast to Algonquian matrilineal practices, the Quapaw patrilineal system meant that mothers and children of interracial unions would no longer belong to Quapaw society. French priests may have encouraged intermarriages for purposes of cultural assimilation and conversion, but Quapaws rejected these suggestions and guarded their political strength and autonomy well into the eighteenth century.

To the west and south of Quapaw native ground, Comanches used the upheaval of the early colonial period to create a new equestrian empire on the grassy plains between 1700 and 1750. Indigenous groups living in the New Mexico mountains appropriated horses, guns, and metal goods left behind when the Spanish retreated after the Pueblo Revolt. From a small, relatively egalitarian group of hunter-gatherers, the Comanches grew in population, centered their culture around equestrian prowess and bison hunting, and intensified their trading relations with markets in New Mexico. Their military strength proved highly significant in preventing French and Spanish colonists from setting up permanent posts in a wide swath of land stretching from present-day eastern New Mexico to northern Texas.

Female labor — free and enslaved — proved central to Comanche expansion and the power of the **Comanche empire**. The increased emphasis on warfare heightened the cultural value of the male lineage head, whose prestige came from raiding and hunting exploits. Masculine respect and honor rested on a Comanche

◆ *Comanche Village, Women Dressing Robes and Drying Meat*
George Catlin, riding with the U.S. dragoons, painted this image in 1835 when his unit
encountered a Comanche encampment near the Wichita Mountains. Although he portrayed
the Comanche empire at a later phase of its history, the work of processing bison meat and
hides belonged to women, even in the eighteenth century. *Smithsonian American Art Museum,
Gift of Mrs. Joseph Harrison, Jr.*

man's "ability to protect and expand his kinship network."[30] Women and child
captives of raided Apache, Pawnee, and Navajo towns could be incorporated into
Comanche lineages or sold as enslaved people to the Spanish. At the same time,
Comanche women and girls also grew skilled in horse riding, as entire families
traveled on horseback. To traditional female skills of food gathering, clothing
making, and child care, women now added care of horses, leather skills for
making harnesses and halters, and curing of bison hides, all critical to Comanche
trade relations. Without women's skills and the exchange of female captives, the
Comanche people could not have taken and held their sovereign ground.

◆ CONCLUSION: THE DIVERSITY OF AMERICAN WOMEN

As diverse as the lives of North American women were in the seventeenth and
eighteenth centuries, there were some commonalities. All women operated
within a fairly rigid sexual division of labor, although the actual tasks assigned to
them varied from culture to culture. Most women's roles included childbearing,
childrearing, and food preparation. Within their communities, women tended
to form strong bonds with other women in similar circumstances — whether

grinding corn in the Pueblo communities, planting it in Iroquoia, bartering in female networks, or forming supportive communities of enslaved women. With some exceptions, women shared an exclusion from direct political participation. They also shared the burdens — which varied widely — of adjusting to the new societies created by both contact and conflict in North America.

Despite these commonalities, the differences among women of this period also were striking. With the emergence of transgenerational chattel slavery, the legal significance of African women's childbearing veered sharply away from that of European and many Native American women. Moreover, there were significant variations not only among Native American, African, and European women, but also within each group. Indigenous women encompassed perhaps the richest cultural variety. But Africans as well represented various linguistic, religious, social, and political backgrounds. Among European women, too, distinctions emerged. Between first- and second-generation settlers, there were major differences in quality of life, especially in the southern colonies. Beyond that, ethnic, religious, and regional differences proved powerful determinants of women's legal and economic circumstances. And by the mid-eighteenth century, class — both in growing cities and in the plantation regions of the South — had become as important as any other factor that shaped women's experiences.

Earlier generations of historians tended to see the colonial period as a monolithic one in which women's lives were static. Reading back from nineteenth-century middle-class gender roles, which relegated women firmly to the private world of the home, white colonial women's participation in a preindustrial household economy can be seen as empowering. A similar tendency to romanticize the hard life of Indigenous women contrasted their freedom and influence with the patriarchal structure within which European women lived. Although comparisons are perhaps inevitable, they can obscure the complexities of women's lives — both the diversity that characterized them and the points of common ground they shared. Such comparisons also deflect attention from the historical changes that shaped females' lives: the challenge to Native American sovereignty, the importation and enslavement of Africans, the massive immigration of Europeans, and the economic and political maturation of the European colonies.

CHAPTER 2 REVIEW

KEY TERMS

"tobacco brides" (p. 50)	Puritans (p. 60)	Ursuline sisters (p. 74)
feme covert/feme sole (p. 51)	Salem witch trials (p. 66)	Pueblo Revolt (p. 74)
Bacon's Rebellion (p. 53)	Quakers (p. 69)	Comanche empire (p. 75)
partus sequitur ventrem (p. 55)	*filles du roi* (p. 73)	

REVIEW QUESTIONS

1. Compare the information offered by Maps 2.1 and 2.2. How did the expansion of European colonization in the Americas create a "new world" for Indigenous peoples and, in particular, Native American women? How would the answer to this question vary depending on the perspective of Powhatan, Iroquois, Comanche, and Pueblo peoples?

2. How did laws passed in seventeenth-century Virginia that related specifically to African women serve to institutionalize a system of chattel slavery?

3. How did the lives of planter-class women differ from those of indentured European and enslaved African women?

4. How did Christianity shape northern free women's identity and family relations? How did both church and state respond to women who were considered "disorderly"?

5. **Making Connections** Given the wide diversity of women in colonial North America, can you name any similarities in women's experiences across cultures and empires? What major historical developments most changed women's lives between 1607 and 1750? How does geographic location matter in your answer to these questions?

SUGGESTED READING

General Works

James Axtell, ed., *The Indian Peoples of Eastern America: A Documentary History of the Sexes* (1981).

Beryl Lieff Benderly and Hasia R. Diner, *Her Works Praise Her: A History of Jewish Women in America from Colonial Times to the Present* (2003).

Ira Berlin, *Many Thousands Gone: The First Two Centuries of Slavery in North America* (1998).

Sharon Block, *Rape and Sexual Power in Early America* (2006).

Elaine Forman Crane, *Witches, Wife Beaters, and Whores: Common Law and Common Folk in Early America* (2011).

Richard Godbeer, *Sexual Revolution in Early America* (2002).

Darlene Clark Hine, ed., *Black Women in American History: From Colonial Times through the Nineteenth Century* (1990).

Peter C. Mancall and James H. Merrell, eds., *American Encounters: Natives and Newcomers from European Contact to Indian Removal, 1500–1850*, 2nd ed. (2006).

Mary Beth Norton, *Founding Mothers and Fathers: Gendered Power and the Forming of American Society* (1996).

Marylynn Salmon, *Women and the Law of Property in Early America* (1986).

Nancy Shoemaker, *A Strange Likeness: Becoming Red and White in Eighteenth-Century North America* (2004).

Alan Taylor, *American Colonies* (2001).

Women in the Southern Colonies

Kathleen M. Brown, *Good Wives, Nasty Wenches, and Anxious Patriarchs* (1996).

Patricia Cleary, *Elizabeth Murray: A Woman's Pursuit of Independence in Eighteenth-Century America* (2000).

Kirsten Fischer, *Suspect Relations: Sex, Race, and Resistance in Colonial North Carolina* (2002).

Gunlog Für, *Nations of Women: Gender and Colonial Encounters among the Delaware Indians* (2011).

David Barry Gaspar and Darlene Clark Hine, eds., *More than Chattel: Black Women and Slavery in the Americas* (1996).

Jessica Marie Johnson, *Wicked Flesh: Black Women, Intimacy and Freedom in the Atlantic World* (2020).

Catherine Kerrison, *Claiming the Pen: Women and Intellectual Life in the Early American South* (2006).

Cynthia A. Kierner, *Beyond the Household: Women's Place in the Early South, 1700–1835* (1998).

Allan Kulikoff, "The Beginnings of the Afro-American Family in Maryland," in Aubrey Land, Lois Green Carr, and Edward C. Papenfuse, eds., *Law, Society, and Politics in Early Maryland* (1977).

Gloria L. Main, *Tobacco Colony: Life in Early Maryland, 1650–1720* (1982).

Ben Marsh, *Georgia's Frontier Women: Female Fortunes in a Southern Colony* (2007).

Jessica Millward, *Finding Charity's Folk: Enslaved and Free Black Women in Maryland* (2015).

Jennifer L. Morgan, *Laboring Women: Reproduction and Gender in New World Slavery* (2004).

Philip D. Morgan, *Slave Counterpoint: Black Culture in the Eighteenth-Century Chesapeake and Lowcountry* (1998).

Mary Beth Norton, "Gender and Defamation in Seventeenth-Century Maryland," *William and Mary Quarterly* 44 (January 1987).

John Ruston Pagan, *Anne Orthwood's Bastard: Sex and Law in Early Virginia* (2002).

Theda Perdue, *Cherokee Women: Gender and Cultural Change, 1700–1835* (1998).

Darret B. Rutman and Anita H. Rutman, *A Place in Time: Middlesex County, Virginia, 1650–1750* (1984).

Carole Shammas, "Black Women's Work and the Evolution of Plantation Society in Virginia," *Labor History* 26 (1985).

Terri L. Snyder, *Babbling Women: Disorderly Speech and the Law in Early Virginia* (2003).

Brenda E. Stevenson, *Life in Black and White: Family and Community in the Slave South* (1997).

Lorena S. Walsh, " 'Till Death Us Do Part': Marriage and Family in Seventeenth-Century Maryland," in Thad W. Tate and David L. Ammerman, eds., *The Chesapeake in the Seventeenth Century: Essays on Anglo-American Society* (1979).

Monica C. Witkowski, *Women at Law in Early Colonial Maryland* (2012).

Peter H. Wood, *Black Majority: Negroes in Colonial South Carolina: From 1670 through the Stono Rebellion* (1974).

Women in the Northern Colonies

Linda Briggs Biemer, *Women and Property in Colonial New York: The Transition from Dutch to English Law, 1643–1727* (1983).

Ava Chamberlain, *The Notorious Elizabeth Tuttle: Marriage, Murder, and Madness in the Family of Jonathan Edwards* (2012).

Michelle Coughlin, *One Colonial Woman's World: The Life and Writings of Mehetabel Chandler Coit* (2012).

Cornelia Hughes Dayton, *Women before the Bar: Gender, Law, and Society in Connecticut, 1639–1789* (1995).

John Demos, *A Little Commonwealth: Family Life in Plymouth Colony* (1970).

Lorri Glover, *Eliza Lucas Pickney: An Independent Woman in the Age of Revolution* (2020).

Leslie Harris, *In the Shadow of Slavery: African Americans in New York City, 1626–1863* (2003).

Carol F. Karlsen, *The Devil in the Shape of a Woman: Witchcraft in Colonial New England* (1987).

Lyle Koehler, *A Search for Power: The "Weaker Sex" in Seventeenth-Century New England* (1980).

Ann M. Little, *Abraham in Arms: War and Gender in Colonial New England* (2006).

M. Michelle Morris, *Under Household Government: Sex and Family in Puritan Massachusetts* (2012).

David E. Narrett, "Men's Wills and Women's Property Rights in Colonial New York," in Ronald Hoffman and Peter J. Albert, eds., *Women in the Age of the American Revolution* (1989).

Deborah A. Rosen, "Women and Property across Colonial America: A Comparison of Legal Systems in New Mexico and New York," *William and Mary Quarterly* 60 (April 2003).

Mary Beth Norton, *In the Devil's Snare: The Salem Witchcraft Crisis of 1692* (2002).

Rebecca Tannenbaum, *A Healer's Calling: Women and Medicine in Early New England* (2002).

Teresa A. Toulouse, *The Captive's Position: Female Narrative, Male Identity, and Royal Authority in Colonial New England* (2006).

Laurel Thatcher Ulrich, *Good Wives: Image and Reality in the Lives of Women in Northern New England* (1991).

Wendy Warren, *New England Bound: Slavery and Colonization in Early America* (2016).

New Spain, New France, and Native America beyond British Colonies

Karen Anderson, *Chain Her by One Foot: The Subjugation of Native Women in Seventeenth-Century New France* (1993).

Stephen Aron, *American Confluence: The Missouri Frontier from Borderland to Border State* (2005).

Julianna Barr, *Peace Came in the Form of a Woman: Indians and Spaniards in the Texas Borderlands* (2007).

James Brooks, *Captives and Cousins: Slavery, Kinship, and Community in the Southwest Borderlands* (2002).

Emily Clark, *Masterless Mistresses: The New Orleans Ursulines and the Development of a New World Society* (2007).

Natalie Zemon Davis, *Women on the Margins: Three Seventeenth-Century Lives* (1995).

Kathleen DuVal, *The Native Ground: Indians and Colonists in the Heart of the Continent* (2006).

Allan Greer, "Colonial Saints: Gender, Race, and Hagiography in New France," *William and Mary Quarterly* 57 (April 2000).

Ramón A. Gutiérrez, *When Jesus Came, the Corn Mothers Went Away: Marriage, Sexuality, and Power in New Mexico, 1500–1846* (1991).

Pekka Hämäläinen, *The Comanche Empire* (2008).

Susan Sleeper-Smith, *Indian Women and French Men: Rethinking Cultural Encounter in the Western Great Lakes* (2001).

Jennifer Spear, *Race, Sex, and Social Order in Early New Orleans* (2009).

Richard White, *The Middle Ground: Indians, Empires, and Republics in the Great Lakes Region, 1650–1815* (1991).

Michael Witgen, *An Infinity of Nations: How the Native New World Shaped North America* (2012).

PRIMARY SOURCES

By and About Colonial Women

LITTLE MATERIAL WRITTEN BY AMERICAN WOMEN in the seventeenth century is available to historians. Even in New England, where literacy was prized and most women were taught to read, relatively few women could write, as historians who have examined the signatures on deeds and other legal documents have discovered. In seventeenth-century New England, women produced only two of the fifty-seven surviving diaries from that period. More records exist from the mid-eighteenth century, when educational opportunities for women expanded slightly. But for most of the period from 1600 to 1750, men wrote much of the material we rely on to learn about women's experiences. Even our knowledge of a famous and knowledgeable woman such as Anne Hutchinson comes from accounts written by men, such as ministers like John Cotton and John Winthrop. Yet historians have managed to mine the historical record imaginatively to capture the voices of at least some women of the era.

LAWS ON WOMEN AND SLAVERY

ALTHOUGH ENSLAVED WOMEN OF THIS PERIOD left behind no written documents, references to them appear in newspapers, in court cases, and in their owners' letters, wills, and diaries; property inventories and business records also provide clues that historians use to determine something of enslaved women's environment. More impersonal, but vital to understanding their experiences, are the laws that, taken together, created the system of perpetual slavery.

In the southern colonies, the laws that created boundaries between enslaved and free and among Black, Indigenous, and white were added in a piecemeal fashion. One of the first legal distinctions between Blacks and whites concerned the labor of women. Instead of taxing land, Virginia taxed planters according to the numbers of the laborers who worked in their tobacco fields.

In this first sentence of a 1643 statute designed to support the colony's ministers, the Assembly refers specifically to taxing ("tithing") the labor of "negro women." Although white women worked in the tobacco fields, they are not mentioned here. What does the presence of Black women and the absence of white women in this law suggest about the distinctions being made between the two?

Laws of Virginia (1643)

Be it further enacted and confirmed That there be tenn pounds of tob'o. per poll & a bushell of corne per poll paid to the ministers within the severall parishes of the collony for all tithable persons, that is to say, as well for all youths of sixteen years of age as upwards, as also for all negro women at the age of sixteen years.

SOURCE: William Waller Hening, ed., *The Statutes at Large, Being a Collection of All the Laws of Virginia* (Charlottesville: University Press of Virginia, 1969), 1:242, 2:170.

AN EVEN MORE DRAMATIC INDICATION of the hardening of lines between Black and white is the short 1662 law that assigned the child of a Black woman to the status of the mother, regardless of the race or status of the child's father. The statute also assigned penalties for interracial sex. The use of the term "Christian" was common, to distinguish English people from Africans and Native Americans, both of whom were considered heathens. What are the implications of this act for the institutionalization of slavery?

Laws of Virginia (1662)

WHEREAS some doubts have arrisen whether children got by any Englishman upon a negro woman should be slave or free, Be it therefore enacted and declared by this present grand assembly, that all children borne in this country shalbe held bond or free only according to the condition of the mother. And that if any christian shall committ fornication with a negro man or woman, hee or shee soe offending shall pay double the fines imposed by the former act.

SOURCE: William Waller Hening, ed., *The Statutes at Large, Being a Collection of All the Laws of Virginia* (Charlottesville: University Press of Virginia, 1969), 1:242.

LEGAL PROCEEDINGS

ALTHOUGH IN ENGLISH AND BRITISH COLONIAL LAW, married women as *femes covert* had no legal identity, women appear frequently in legal documents. Unmarried women and widows could act for themselves, and even some married women successfully petitioned the courts for *feme sole* rights in order to conduct a business — usually in the absence of their husbands. They sued and were sued, sold and bought property. Women appeared as beneficiaries or as servants and enslaved people in men's wills. Women were also brought to court as defendants, on trial for sexual offenses, slander, theft, infanticide, and witchcraft. The documents offered here are from courts in the Chesapeake and New England regions, but they have many similarities to those from other European colonies.

SLANDER AND THE COURTS

Slander cases were common throughout the colonies, revealing the way in which individuals in small communities placed great store on their reputations and how, collectively, they could control gendered social behaviors. When their neighbors engaged in gossip accusing them of inappropriate actions, many victims turned to the court for satisfaction. In analyzing defamation cases from seventeenth-century Maryland, historian Mary Beth Norton has discovered that while white women participated in only 19 percent of the colonies' civil cases, they appeared in over 50 percent of the slander cases.[31] Cases that men brought against their defamers tended to concern questions of business and honesty, while those by women focused on sexual irregularities, although witchcraft was another common accusation. While some women came to court to protect their reputations, others were summoned for having spread rumors.

The following case featuring Michael Baisey's wife revolves around issues of sexuality and paternity. What does women's gossiping indicate about their role in the community? What does this suggest about privacy in colonial towns?

Michael Baisey's Wife (1654)

Richard Manship Sworne Saith that the wife of Peter Godson related . . . that Michael Baiseys wifes Eldest Son was not the Son of Anthony Rawlins her former husband, but She knew one at Maryland that was the father of him, but Named not the man, and that the Said Michael Baisey's wife was a whore and a Strumpett up and Down the Countrey, and Said that Thomas Ward of Kent tould her Soe.

Elizabeth Manship Sworne Saith the Same.

Margaret Herring Sworne Saith that the wife of Peter Godson affirmed that Anthony Rawlins Son was not his Son but the Son of another man at Maryland. . . .

Whereas Peter Godsons wife hath Slandered the wife of Michael Baisey & Saying She was a whore & a Strumpet up and Down the Countrey, It is ordered that the Said Godson's wife Shall be Committed into the Sheriffs hand untill She Shall find Security for the behaviour which the plf^t [plaintiff] is Satisfied with as he hath declared in Court. . . .

Whereas Mrs Godson was bound in a bond of Good behaviour from the 21st of October till the 5th of December towards the wife of Michael Baisey, and none appearing to renew the Said Bond, It is ordered that she be remitted from her Bond of Good behaviour.

SOURCE: *Archives of Maryland Judicial and Testamentary Business of the Provincial Court*, 1649/50–1675, ed. William Hand Browne (Baltimore, 1887), 10:399.

WOMEN "JURORS"

Other court cases reveal the ways in which women could expand their limited public power. When women were accused of witchcraft, the court might ask a group of women, which usually included a midwife, to examine the defendant's body for telltale signs of witchcraft. They might also be called to duty in cases in which it was crucial to determine whether a woman had given birth or had naturally shaped female reproductive organs.

In the following complex murder accusation, the court officially termed the group of women a "jury." What does the case suggest about women's access to authority in their communities?

Judith Catchpole (1656)

At a Generall Provinciall Court Held at

Putuxent September 22th

Present Capt William ffuller, m^r John Pott Present

m^r Richard Preston: m^r Michael Brooke

m^r Edward Lloyd

Whereas Judith Catchpole being brought before the Court upon Suspicion of Murdering a Child which She is accused to have brought forth, and denying the fact or that She ever had Child the Court hath ordered that a jury of able women be Impannelled and to give in their Verdict to the best of their judgment whether She the Said Judith hath ever had a Child

Or not . . .

The Names of the Jury of women Impannelled to Search the body of Judith Catchpole . . .

Rose Smith	m^rs Bussey
m^rs Belcher	m^rs Brooke
m^rs Chaplin	Elizabeth Claxton
m^rs Brooke	Elizabeth Potter
m^rs Battin	Dorothy Day
m^rs Cannady	

We the Jury of Women before named having according to our Charge and oath Searched the body of Judith Catchpole doe give in our Verdict that according to our best judgment that the Said

Judith Catchpole hath not had any Child within the time Charged.

Whereas Judith Catchpole Servant to William Dorrington of this Province of Maryland Was apprehended and brought before this Court upon Suspicion of Murthering a Child in her Voyage at Sea bound for this Province in the Ship Mary and ffrancis who Set forth of England upon her intended Voyage in or about october Last 1655 and arrived in this Province in or about January following, and her accuser being deceased and no murther appearing upon her Examination denying the fact; was Ordered that her body Should be Searcht by a Jury of able women, which being done the Said Jury returning their Verdict to this Court that they found that the Said Judith had not had any Child within the time Chargd[.] And also it appearing to this Court by Severall Testimonies that the party accusing was not in Sound Mind, whereby it is Conceived the Said Judith Catchpole is not Inditable, The Court doth therefore order that upon the reasons aforesaid, that She the Said Judith Catchpole be acquitted of that Charge unless further Evidence appeare.

SOURCE: *Archives of Maryland Judicial and Testamentary Business of the Provincial Court*, 1649/50–1675, ed. William Hand Browne (Baltimore, 1887), 10:456–58.

A PRENUPTIAL AGREEMENT

Court records are a vital source of information about property holding. Through wills and property settlement documents, we can determine the range of goods that people owned and make distinctions between rich and poor; we can discover patterns of slaveholdership and servant holding; and we can acquire some information about women's economic circumstances.

The following is a prenuptial settlement by Ralph Wormeley, a wealthy man, on a widow, Mrs. Agatha Stubbings, whose first husband had been a successful merchant. How does it shed light on the economic advantages widows in early Virginia might have experienced? What clues does the reference to Black "servaunts" give us about African Americans' circumstances in early Virginia?

Mrs. Agatha Stubbings (1645)

To All to whom these presents shall come I Ralph Warmley [sic] of the Parrish and County of Yorke in Virginia gentleman send Greeting etc. Knowe Yee, That I the sayde Ralph Wormley For and in consideration of the unfayned love and affection That I beare unto Mrs. Agatha Stubbings late the wife of Luke Stubbings of the County of Northampton gentleman deceased, And especially in Consideration of Matrimony intended presently (by gods grace) to bee solemnized betweene the sayde Ralph and the sayde Agatha doe by these presents give graunt confirme and endow, And by these presents have given graunted and in nature of a Free Joynture endowed unto Nathaniell Littleton Esquire and Phillip Taylor gentlemen . . . in trust For and on the behalfe of the sayde Agatha six Negro servaunts . . . Fower Negro men, and Two women, To say Sanio, and Susan his wife, and greate Tony, and his wife Dorothis, Tony the younger, and Will, Tenn Cowes, six Draught Oxen, two young Mares, two Feather Bedds and Furniture, sixe paire of sheetes of Holland, two Dyaper table cloathes, two dozen of Napkins and Cubboard Cloath to it, two dozen of Napkins, Twelve pewter dishes, one dammaske table cloath, one Dozen of Napkins and cubboard Cloath to it, To have and to hold, the said Recited promisses and every parte thereof, unto her the sayde Agatha, and the heyres [heirs] Lawfully ingendered between mee the said Ralph Wormley and shee the sayde Agatha whether Male or Female or both to bee equally devided after his decease Provided always that the same and every parte thereof graunted as aforesaid shalbe and

Remayne to the only use benifitt and behoofe of mee the said Ralph Wormley during my naturall Life, And in case I the said Ralph shall happen to depart this lyfe without issue begotten betweene mee the said Ralph and shee the said Agatha as aforesayde, Then the said demised promisses and every parte thereof with the proceeds and increase thereof shalbe and Remayne to the only use benifitt and behoofe of the sayde Agatha her heyres Executors or Administrators And For the true and reall performance of this deede and every parte and parcel thereof in manner and Forme aforesaid I the said Ralph Wormley doe bynde over unto the said Nathaniell Littleton Esquire and Phillip Taylor gentlemen the said Six Negroes and Six other Negroes, the sayde Tenn Cowes and other tenn Cowes, the sixe Oxen and other sixe Oxen, one plantation and houses whereon I now live scituate at Yorke aforesaid Conteyning Five hundred Acres more or lesse according to the purchase lately made by mee of Jefery Power to bee all Lyable and Responsable For the full Assurance of makeing good the abovesaid Joynture for the use of the said Agatha her heyres Executors or Administrators as aforesaid In Witnes whereof I the sayde Ralph Wormley have hereunto sett my hand and Scale the second day of this instant July Annoque Domini 1645.

Ralph Wormeley
The Seale

SOURCE: Susie M. Ames, ed., *County Court Records of Accomack-Northampton, Virginia 1640–1645* (Charlottesville: University Press of Virginia, 1973), 433–34.

WITCHCRAFT TESTIMONY

The Salem witch trials of 1692 brought women into the courtroom not only as defendants, but also as plaintiffs and witnesses. The following first three witnesses accused Sarah Bibber (known also as Vibber) of malevolent behavior. Notably, Bibber also swore testimony against Sarah Good (who was executed for witchcraft less than one month later). The accusations against Bibber are followed by testimony from the accused "Goody" Mary Bradbury and her husband, Thomas Bradbury. The seventeenth-century spellings can be difficult to decode, but if you read the passages out loud, their meaning will be clearer. According to her accusers, how did Sarah Bibber appear to have violated the norms of Puritan motherhood? How does Thomas's testimony compare with Mary's defense of herself? What ideals of Puritan womanhood can you see in these statements? Bradbury, whose husband was well connected, received a guilty verdict and a death sentence but managed to evade execution. Little is known about Bibber's life beyond her testimony.

Testimony of John Porter and Lydia Porter v. Sarah Bibber (June 29, 1692)

The Testimony of John Porter: And Lidia Porter These The Testimony of John Porter, who Testifieth & sayth that Goodwife Biber Somtime living amongst us I did observe her to be a woman of An unruly turbulent Spirit; And shee would often fall into strange fitts; when shee was crost of her humor: Likewise Lidia Porter Testifieth, that Goodwife Bibber And her Husband would often quarrel & in their quarrels shee would call him, very bad names, And would have strange fitts when she was crost, And a woman of an unruly turbulent spirit, And double tongued[.]

Testimony of Joseph Fowler v. Sarah Bibber (June 29, 1692)

The Testimony of Joseph fowler, who Testifieth that Goodman Bibber & his wife, Lived at my house, and I did observe and take notice, that Goodwife Bibber was a woman, who was very idle in her calling And very much given to tatling & tale Bareing makeing mischeif amongst her neighbo'rs, & very much given to speak bad words and would call her husband bad names & was a woman of a very turbulent unruly spirit[.]

Testimony of Thomas Jacobs and Mary Jacobs v. Sarah Bibber (June 29, 1692)

The testymony of Thomas Jacob and mery his wife doth testify and say that Good Bibbor #[and] now that is now counted aflicketed parson she did for a time surgin in our hous and Good Bibber wood be very often spekeking against won and nother very obsanely and thos things that were very falls. and wichshing very bad wichchis and very often and she wichs that wen hor chill fell into the rever that she had never pull #[out] hor childd out and Good Bibbor yous to wich ill wichches to horselfe and hor chilldren and allso to others: the nayborhud werr she liveued amonkes aftor she bered: hor fust housbon hes told us that this John Bibbor wife coud fall into fitts as often as she pleased[.]

Answer of Mary Bradbury (September 9, 1692)

The Answer of Mary Bradbury in the charge of Witchcraft or familliarity with the Divell I doe plead not guilty.

I am wholly inocent of any such wickedness through the goodness of god that have kept mee hitherto. I am the servant of Jesus Christ & Have given my self up to him as my only lord & saviour: and to the dilligent attendance upon him in all his holy ordinances, in utter contempt & defiance of the divell, and all his works as horid & detestible; and accordingly have endevo'red to frame my life; & conversation according to the rules of his holy word, & in that faith & practise resolve by the help and assistance of god to contineu to my lifes end:

for the truth of what I say as to matter of practiss I humbly refer my self, #[my selfe,] to my brethren & neighbors that know mee and unto the searcher of all hearts for the truth & uprightness of my heart therein: (human frailties, & unavoydable infirmities excepted) of which i bitterly complayne every day:

Mary Bradbury

Testimony of Thomas Bradbury for Mary Bradbury (July 28, 1692)

Concerning my beloved wife Mary Bradbury this is that I have to say: wee have been maried fifty five yeare: and shee hath bin a loveing & faithfull wife to mee, unto this day shee hath been wonderfull laborious dilligent & Industryous in her place and imployment, about the bringing up o'r family (w'ch have bin eleven children of o'r owne, & fower grand-children): shee was both prudent, & provident : of a cheerful Spiritt liberall Charitable: Shee being now very aged & weake, & greived under her affliction may not bee able to speake much for herselfe, not being so free of Speach as some others may bee: I hope her life and conversation hath been such amongst her neighbours, as gives a better & more reall Testimoney of her, then can bee exprest by words.

own'd by mee
Tho: Bradbury

SOURCE: Essex County Court Archives, Salem, Massachusetts.

NEWSPAPER ADVERTISEMENTS

ANOTHER SOURCE THAT ALLOWS US to recapture women's voices is newspaper ads that appeared in colonial publications. While men predominate among those offering services and goods for sale, as the eighteenth century wore on, women's names appeared with greater frequency. What does this ad suggest about the expansion of women's economic roles in urban colonial America?

South Carolina Gazette, Charleston (October 22, 1744)

This is to give Notice, to all Persons inclinable to put their Children to board, under the Care of the Subscriber [illegible], that she has noow Vacancies; where there is taught, as usual, Writing, and all sorts of fine Needle work. Masters likewise attend to teach Writing, Arithmetick, Dancing, and Musick, if required. Mary Hext.

OTHER ADVERTISEMENTS OFFERED ENSLAVED PEOPLE for sale or for hire; indentured servants were also hired out. What clues do the following ads give about these women's experiences?

South Carolina Gazette, Charleston (December 23, 1745)

To be hired out a home born Negro girl about thirteen or fourteen years of age who has been for some years past kept employed at her needle and is a handy waiting maid. Enquire at the Printer [illegible].

Boston Gazette (April 28, 1755)

A likely Negro woman, about 25 years of age, has had the smallpox, and been in the country ten or twelve years, understands all household work, and will do either for town or country.

Boston Gazette (June 20, 1735)

A white Servant Maids Time to be disposed of for about four years and a half; she is a Scotch woman that can do all sorts of Household Business and Knit, and thoroughly honest. Enquire of The Publisher.

LETTERS

LETTERS, THOUGH RELATIVELY RARE, are a major source for exploring early colonial women's experiences. The following examples offer insight into very diverse southern women's lives, those of the prosperous Eliza Lucas Pinckney and a desperate indentured servant, Elizabeth Sprigs.

Eliza Lucas Pinckney (1722–1793), a South Carolinian woman, left numerous records detailing her life among her colony's elite. Daughter of a wealthy planter and invalid mother, Eliza Lucas ran the large household, supervised her father's estates in his lengthy absences, experimented with new crops, and was instrumental in introducing indigo to the region. She made good use of her father's legal library and represented not only her family in court but neighbors as well. Lucas married a much older man, the recently widowed Charles Pinckney, and became a devoted wife and energetic mother. At her husband's death, she again employed her business skills to run the complex estate of her family. Pinckney's letters and diaries reflect on the privileged life of an elite woman in the mid-eighteenth-century South, with enslaved people and servants at her disposal. As you read these letters, consider the factors in early South Carolinian life that shaped her opportunities and limits.

In the following passage from a letter to a Miss Bartlett, Pinckney is unusual in her concern for teaching reading to the people her family has enslaved, but typical of wealthy plantation women in how she spends her time.

ELIZA LUCAS PINCKNEY
To Miss Bartlett

In general then I rise at five o'Clock in the morning, read till Seven, then take a walk in the garden or field, see that the Servants are at their respective business, then to breakfast. The first hour after breakfast is spent at my musick, the next is constantly employed in recolecting something I have learned least for want of practise it should be quite lost, such as French and short hand. After that I devote the rest of the time till I dress for dinner to our little Polly and two black girls who I teach to read, and if I have my paps's approbation (my Mams I have got) I intend [them] for school mistres's for the rest of the Negroe children — another scheme you see. But to proceed, the first hour after dinner as the first after breakfast at musick, the rest of the afternoon in Needle work till candle light, and from that time to bed time read or write. 'Tis the fashion here to carry our work abroad with us so that having company, without they are great strangers, is no interruption to that affair; but I have particular matters for particular days, which is an interruption to mine. Mondays my musick Master is here. Tuesdays my friend Mrs. Chardon (about 3 mile distant) and I are constantly engaged to each other, she at our house one Tuesday — I at hers the next and this is one of the happiest days I spend at Woppoe. Thursday the whole day except what the necessary affairs of the family take up is spent in writing, either on the business of the plantations, or letters to my friends. Every other Fryday, if no company, we go a vizeting so that I go abroad once a week and no oftener.

SOURCE: *The Letterbook of Eliza Lucas Pinckney 1739–1762*, ed. Elise Pinckney (Columbia: University of South Carolina Press, 1997), 34, 35, 38.

OTHER LETTERS FROM PINCKNEY show the energetic businesswoman at work. In the following excerpt from a 1740 letter to a friend, she explains her plans for one of her father's plantations, which she clearly considers her property.

Wont you laugh at me if I tell you I am so busey in providing for Posterity I hardly allow my self time to Eat or sleep and can but just snatch a minnet to write to you and a friend or two now. I am making a large plantation of Oaks which I look upon as my own property, whether my father gives me the land or not; and therefore I design many years hence when oaks are more valueable than they are now — which you know they will be when we come to build fleets. I intend, I say, 2 thirds of the produce of my oaks for a charity (I'll let you know my scheme another time) and other 3rd for those that shall have the trouble of putting my design in Execution. I sopose according to custom you will show this to your Uncle and Aunt. "She is [a] good girl," says Mrs. Pinckney. "She is never Idle and always means well." "Tell the little Visionary," says your uncle, "come to town and partake of some of the amusements suitable to her time of life." Pray tell him I think these so, and what he may not think whims and projects may turn out well by and by. Out of many surely one may hitt.

I N STARK CONTRAST to the lives of elite southern women like Pinckney were the lives of those bound to them, for life or for years. Details about the thousands of European women who came to the colonies as indentured servants in the seventeenth century are largely lost to historians because such women left few written records.

The following is a rare document, a letter written by a distressed servant in Maryland to her father. We cannot know what she had done to so displease her parent, but what does her letter indicate about the hardships facing indentured servants in America?

ELIZABETH SPRIGS

To Mr. John Sprigs White Smith in White Cross Street near Cripple Gate London

Maryland Sept'r 22'd 1756.

Honred Father

My being for ever banished from your sight, will I hope pardon the Boldness I now take of troubling you with these, my long silence has been purely owing to my undutifullness to you, and well knowing I had offended in the highest Degree, put a tie to my tongue and pen, for fear I should be extinct from your good Graces and add a further Trouble to you, but too well knowing your care and tenderness for me so long as I retain my Duty to you, induced me once again to endeavour if possible, to kindle up that flame again. O Dear Father, belive what I am going to relate the words of truth and sincerity, and Ballance my former bad Conduct [to] my sufferings here, and then I am sure you'll pitty your Destress[ed] Daughter, What we unfortunat English People suffer here is beyond the probibility of you in England to Conceive, let it suffice that I one of the unhappy Number, am toiling almost Day and Night, and very often in the Horses druggery, with only this comfort that you Bitch you do not halfe enough, and then tied up and whipp'd to that Degree that you'd not serve an Annimal, scarce any thing but Indian Corn and Salt to eat and that even begrudged nay many Negroes are better used, almost naked no shoes nor stockings to wear, and the comfort after slaving dureing Masters pleasure, what rest we can get is to rap ourselves up in a Blanket and ly upon the Ground, this is the deplorable Condition your poor Betty endures, and now I beg you have any Bowels of Compassion left show it by sending me some Relief, C[l]othing is the principal thing wanting, which if you should condiscend to, may easely send them to me by any of the ships bound to Baltimore Town Patapsco River Maryland, and

give me leave to conclude in Duty to you and Uncles and Aunts, and Respect to all Friends

Honred Father

Your undutifull and Disobedient Child

SOURCE: Nancy Cott, ed., *Root of Bitterness: Documents of the Social History of American Women* (New York: E. P. Dutton, 1972), 89–90. Original source: Isabel Calder, ed., *Colonial Captivities, Marches, and Journeys* (New York: Macmillan, 1935), 151–52.

ANALYZING PRIMARY SOURCES

1. What evidence do these documents offer about the diversity of women's experiences in colonial America? What are some of the hardships or challenges that women encountered? In what ways did women of this period seek control over their lives?

2. What do these documents suggest about societal expectations for white elite women's roles? About the roles of white servants and enslaved women?

3. How do legal documents allow us to understand the experiences of women who left no personal writings behind? What insights can descriptions of property give about the social circumstances of colonial women? How do the court cases concerning slander and witchcraft portray women and expectations about their behavior?

PRIMARY SOURCES

Depictions of "Family" in Colonial America

I N THE VARIED CULTURES OF seventeenth- and eighteenth-century North America, "family" meant different things — different groupings of people, different relations of affection, different hierarchies, and different implications for the larger society. One of the only characteristics that all these different meanings of "family" had in common was male dominance. Visual sources can convey relationships of power within the family in ways that written sources sometimes cannot.

The period explored in this chapter predates the sentimental ideal of the nuclear family that characterized nineteenth-century white middle-class American society. Nonetheless, family relations were especially crucial to daily life in the seventeenth and eighteenth centuries because family was a system not only of emotions and kinship, but also of protection, economics, and production. While some of the family bonds illustrated here may seem unusual to modern Americans, they were nonetheless deeply felt and fundamental to the people who lived them.

Although family paintings were a luxury of the wealthy, American painters were struggling artisans more than they were purveyors of high culture. In these earlier years, we do not even know the names of the artists; scholars identify them by the families who patronized them rather than by their own reputations. Traveling from place to place and looking for commissions, American painters, unlike their British counterparts, were usually not formally trained.

One of the earliest family group paintings from colonial British America was the 1674 portrait of Elizabeth Clarke Freake (b. 1641) and child shown in Figure 2.1. By 1674, Freake had already borne six children, and although tradition identifies this baby as a girl, in fact infant boys and girls were dressed exactly alike, so it is difficult to distinguish them. This portrait is part of a series that includes a separate painting of the husband and father, Boston merchant John Freake. Painted as standing and facing toward his left, John Freake's portrait was probably meant to hang alongside that of his wife and child. John Freake died just a year after the painting was completed, and his widow — like so many other New England women — went on to remarry.

Art historians have discovered that this version of Elizabeth Freake and child was painted over a previous portrait created three years earlier. The major difference is that, in the later version, the mother's right arm is around her child, whereas in the earlier version, it was crossed in front of her chest. Why do you think, after three years, the painter was asked to make this change? What aspects of the painting convey Elizabeth Freake's piety? What details suggest her wealth

◆ Figure 2.1 **Elizabeth Freake and Child**
GRANGER — Historical Picture Archive.

and social standing? How do these two dimensions come together in the overall portrait of mother and child?

Joint portraits of husband and wife from this period are very rare. Family portraits were meant to illustrate intergenerational family descent, not conjugal affection. Art historians are not sure who painted the example in Figure 2.2, but it is generally attributed to John Watson, a Scots immigrant who arrived in the colonies in 1714. A traveling artist in New Jersey, Pennsylvania, and New York, Watson is one of the first generation of painters working in America whose name is known to us. His style is much more refined than that of the anonymous painter of Elizabeth Freake and child in Figure 2.1.

Figure 2.2 records the alliance through marriage of two of the wealthiest Dutch American families in New York State, the Schuylers and the Wendells. Both were located in Albany and began to accumulate their wealth in the late seventeenth

◆ Figure 2.2 **Johannes and Elsie Schuyler**
New-York Historical Society/Bridgeman Images.

century through trade with the Mohawks and through extensive agricultural hold-ings. The husband, Johannes Schuyler, was an Albany merchant and later became the city mayor. The wife, Elsie Staats Wendell, also a member of a founding Dutch American family, was a decade older than her husband and already quite wealthy from her father and her first husband. A widow, she had given birth to nine chil-dren before she married Schuyler. Their first child was born eight months after their marriage, and together they had three more. How do the details of this mar-riage help to explain the Schuylers' decision to commission a joint portrait? Notice that she chose to be pictured with a book in her hands; what might she be trying to indicate about her tastes and activities? What other aspects of this portrait signal the Schuylers' social status?

While there are paintings of enslaved people at work and at leisure, we have no paintings in which Black families from the early eighteenth century, enslaved

◆ **Figure 2.3 The Potter Family**
The Newport Historical Society (53.3).

or free, are clearly depicted. Indeed, by the mid-eighteenth century most Africans in the American colonies were just beginning to live long enough to establish multigenerational kinship ties. Some portraits of white families, however, included a Black servant among the family grouping.

The group portrait of the Potter family of southern Rhode Island in Figure 2.3 was painted around 1740 by an unknown artist. The Newport Historical Society identifies the white male head of household as John Potter, a wealthy landowner who later became a Quaker and released the enslaved people he had kept in bondage. The Potters lived near Narragansett Bay, on one of several large plantations in the area whose land had been seized from Indigenous peoples. Included in the picture are three unidentified women, no doubt Potter's wife, their daughter, and probably a collateral relative or friend of his wife. But what draws our modern attention is the young Black boy holding a tea tray. Newport, Rhode Island, was the center of New England slave trading, and Potter was both a slave trader and slaveholder. Unlike most of Potter's captives, who worked in the fields, this child was likely a full-time domestic. How does the picture itself signal this information? Curiously, this enslaved child and Mr. Potter are portrayed as looking directly at the viewer, while the three women look slightly away. Why might the painter have chosen to do this?

Why do you think that the Potters made the deliberate decision to include this child in the painting of their family grouping? The painting was permanently installed over the family's mantelpiece. How might it have affected master, mistress, and captive to see themselves together in the portrait day after day? Remember that the enslaved boy, in addition to being a worker, was also a marker of white wealth: the Potters owned many enslaved people. What else about the portrait suggests their wealth?

Figures 2.1, 2.2, and 2.3 are portraits of particular families, each with its own intentions, relationships, and personalities. All are products of Protestant New England and New Netherland societies, which revered domestic life and parent-child and husband-wife relations. Spanish America grew out of a very different religious and artistic tradition. Like the artists of Catholic Europe, most of its painters concentrated on religious themes. Undoubtedly the family they painted most frequently was Mary, Joseph, and the baby Jesus.

Casta paintings were a genre unique to New Spain and represent a distinct pictorial approach to family relationships. The collective term *castas* — in English, "castes" — refers to the intricate system, part racial and part economic, that constituted the social and political hierarchies of New Spain. Among English colonists, racial inequality was enforced by legal prohibitions against interracial marriage and a system in which only three racial identities were available: white, Black, and Indigenous. By contrast, in New Spain, where white women never were equal in number to white men, interracial marriage was deemed something of a necessity as well as sometimes a means to "civilize" nonwhite populations. The resulting racial system still was hierarchical and white-dominated.

The *casta* system was a kind of taxonomy, or system of racial classification, and the paintings themselves contained indicators of that system. Most *casta* paintings consisted of sixteen different categories, painted on either a single canvas or separate canvases. The paintings depicted highly stylized categories rather than real people, and each family's racial composition was painted in the color of the skin of family members and specifically inscribed on the canvas. Both as idealizations of interracial families and as depictions of New World well-being, the *casta* paintings were a kind of advertisement for the exoticism and resources of New Spain. Scholars note the emphasis on hierarchical categorization as indicators of anxiety about the potential disorder of racial mixing, a reminder "to the Spanish Crown that Mexico was still a rigidly structured society."[32]

The actual lives of interracial families, and their experience of racial inequality and hierarchy, bore little relationship to the depictions of the *casta* paintings. *Castas* were usually painted in the urban centers of Mexico City and Lima, but we can be confident that the images they purveyed and the system they represented would have been familiar on the northern borders of Mexico, among the colonists who came to Santa Fe and El Paso, for whom interracial liaisons and difficult living conditions were major factors of life.

The elaborate depiction of interracial combinations and offspring in Figures 2.4, 2.5, and 2.6, dated about 1715 and attributed to Juan Rodríguez Juárez, conveys the abstract and idealized quality of the *casta* genre. The two family combinations in Figures 2.4 and 2.5 are labeled along the top of the images: "D ESPAÑOL Y D INDIA PRODUCE MESTISO" and "D ESPAÑOL Y NEGRA PRODUCE MULATO." In both these paintings, the man is white and the woman is not. Significantly, according to the *casta* system, Indigenous blood ("India"), in contrast to African heritage ("Negra"), could be redeemed (Christianized and

◆ **Figure 2.4**
"D Español y D India Produce Mestiso"
Breamore House, Hampshire, UK/ Bridgeman Images.

◆ **Figure 2.5**
"D Español y D Negra Produce Mulato"
Breamore House, Hampshire, UK/ Bridgeman Images.

◆ Figure 2.6
"Indios Barbaros"
*Breamore House,
Hampshire, UK/
Bridgeman Images.*

civilized) by a mixture with Spanish blood ("Español"). The child of a white man and a Black woman was labeled a "mulatto," a derogatory term widely used in the eighteenth century. Figure 2.6 portrays an *India Barbara*, an Indigenous family unredeemed by any Spanish blood. What are the differences between the three images that suggest the hierarchical *casta* system? Why does each family unit consist only of mother, father, and child, rather than the much more diverse and numerous family units depicted in the Protestant portrait tradition?

ANALYZING PRIMARY SOURCES

1. In what different ways is male headship of family life depicted in these paintings?
2. What do these images tell us about women's roles in family relations?
3. What similarities and differences do you see among the women portrayed in these images?
4. Why are no elderly women depicted?

3

Mothers and Daughters of the Revolution

1750–1810

Y EARS AFTER THE AMERICAN REVOLUTION ENDED British colonial rule in 1783, Sarah Osborn applied for a widow's pension from the U.S. government. In her 1837 deposition, she described not only her husband's service as a soldier but also her contributions to the war effort. During one battle she took "her stand just back of the American tents, say about a mile from the town, and busied herself washing, mending, and cooking for the soldiers, in which she was assisted by the other females. . . . She heard the roar of the artillery for a number of days."[1] Osborn's account of life close to the fighting suggests a significant break from notions of women's traditional place at the hearth. But that she performed domestic work for her husband and his fellow soldiers also reveals that, even in the disruptive context of war, women's customary domestic roles prevailed. Osborn's experiences were hardly universal, yet her deposition underscores a crucial point. Even though the dramatic events of the second half of the eighteenth century centered on political and international concerns — which were customarily viewed as exclusively male terrain — women of all status actively participated, albeit usually in distinctly gendered ways, in the American Revolution and the founding of the United States of America.

Historians vigorously debate the long-term impact of the American Revolution on women's lives. Some scholars argue that while white men enjoyed expanded legal and political rights in the postrevolutionary period, women's relative status declined. Others contend that women developed a new consciousness that led to improved education and increased opportunities to influence public life. These historians also point out that the religious revival that preceded the Revolution, the First Great Awakening, similarly offered women a greater voice in the world beyond their homes. Neither scenario, however, neatly fits the experience of all women. Free Black women strove to make a living and build communities as full citizenship became increasingly tied not only to being male, but also to being white and well-to-do. Immigrant women, often urbanized or living on contested western territories, faced poverty, danger, and few gendered "protections." Women of many Indigenous nations faced a newly empowered, expanding U.S. republic and a transforming continent that violently reduced Indigenous claims to ownership, influence, and independence. This chapter emphasizes the ways in which women participated in the Revolution and traces the complex changes the revolutionary era brought to their lives. Although traditional expectations about women's roles were challenged, they were rarely overturned.

◆ BACKGROUND TO REVOLUTION, 1754–1775

For two centuries North America was the site of contesting colonial powers, with France, Spain, and Britain struggling with Indigenous peoples and each other to dominate the continent's land and resources. The transformation by which the region came to be controlled largely by Britain, and later the United States, was rooted in the French and Indian War of 1754–1763 and further consolidated by the American Revolution of 1776–1783. A number of factors led to the outbreak of the Revolution. Social changes from the First Great Awakening and new ideas introduced during the Enlightenment loosened the strict hierarchy that had defined social relations up to the eighteenth century. Further, British attempts to recoup the economic losses incurred by colonial wars led to a tightening of economic and political controls on their settler colonists in North America, leading to colonial resistance that brought about the American Revolutionary War.

Social Change in the Eighteenth Century

Two important social factors paved the way for rebellion against imperial power in the eighteenth century. The first was the evangelical revival known as the **First Great Awakening** (1730–1770).

Waves of Protestant revivalism began as early as the 1730s and 1740s, inspired in part by English minister George Whitefield's preaching tours throughout the British colonies. Outpourings of evangelical fervor reached their greatest intensity between the 1750s and the 1770s, especially in the South, where revivalism touched both Blacks and whites. Evangelical worshippers gathered outside at camp meetings, in fields and pastures, where their religious joy could have physical expression. The First Great Awakening split established churches and created increasing numbers of converts to new denominations, such as the Baptists and the Methodists, whose evangelicalism emphasized an emotional spiritual rebirth and validated the religious experience and participation of ordinary people.

In challenging established religious authority and church hierarchy, the First Great Awakening promoted a leveling of some of the social hierarchies that cut across gender, class, and race. Evangelicals within the Methodist and Baptist churches, especially the Southern Baptists, reached out to the poor and uneducated, generally welcoming Black converts. A few churches like the Quakers and some Methodists condemned the institution of slavery, and while most slaveholders refused to accept that condemnation, some were moved to encourage the people they enslaved to become Christians. This set of evangelical revivals, in which women were prominent participants, promoted a rough spiritual egalitarianism that many scholars think fostered political unrest as well.

In addition to the religious awakening, the onrushing crisis with Britain led some colonists to examine closely not only their relationship to the Crown but also their conceptions of the existing social order and government itself. Among educated elites, the ideas of the Enlightenment had a powerful impact. This European intellectual movement emphasized the rights of individuals, the role of reason, the promise of social progress, and the importance of the scientific method. In America, it contributed to the questioning of the British Crown's authority and to an appreciation for the rights of the individual. Particularly influential was the seventeenth-century political philosopher John Locke, whose *Two Treatises of Government* was widely circulated in the colonies.

These public debates, which were occasioned by the British efforts to control the colonies more tightly in the latter half of the eighteenth century, were conducted almost exclusively by men. Although many addressed the questions of hierarchical structures within the British Empire and within the colonial governments, few questioned the hierarchy embedded in their gender or race systems. Despite societal assumptions that the weighty considerations of government, diplomacy, and the economy were outside the realm of women's concerns, many women from diverse groups actively participated in the events surrounding the revolutionary conflict. But while many women found themselves acting in novel ways, for the most part their activities followed the traditional lines of household production and family obligation.

The Growing Confrontation

In the British colonies, settlers on the frontier experienced the events leading up to the Revolution as part of an ongoing struggle over colonial freedom from British intervention. During the early years, colonists had enjoyed a high degree of freedom from British intrusion in their domestic affairs. But the French and Indian War, in which British and colonial troops conquered New France, brought dramatic changes. It was a costly war, and Britain insisted that the colonials pay a large share through increased taxation, a burden that women, as consumers, often experienced firsthand. Moreover, the victory had opened up more land for British settlement: by the terms of the Treaty of Paris that ended the war, the French yielded their vast lands in North America to the British, who now claimed all the territory east of the Mississippi River (see Map 3.1). The war also drew in various Indigenous peoples, who sided and fought with whichever European power they thought most likely to honor individual tribal claims to territory. Usually this was the French, who, unlike the British, had learned to live with the Indigenous people rather than drive them off their lands. The British victory imperiled Native Americans in part because they could no longer play European powers against one another, and in part because of British colonists' desire for the newly acquired territories.

◆ **Map 3.1 British Colonies in North America, 1763**
Following the French and Indian War, the Treaty of Paris gave Britain control over all of New France east of the Mississippi and all of Spanish Florida. At the same time, Britain imposed the Proclamation Line of 1763, which prohibited white settlement west of the Appalachian Mountains. Subsequent legislation designated most of the western lands reserved for Indigenous peoples. This western policy angered settlers hungry for land and land speculators eager to make a profit, and it contributed to the crisis in the British colonies that eventually led to the American Revolution.

The promise of land won during the war accelerated European emigration. Irish, Scots, Ulster Scots, German, and English peoples expanded the population of the British colonies, which counted almost 2 million settlers by 1765. Cities grew, but so did the population of the backcountry. Pressured for years by a scarcity of good, affordable land, settlers as well as land speculators coveted Indigenous lands along the colonial frontier. The British, hoping to put an end to the recurring wars with Indigenous peoples, issued the Proclamation of 1763, which temporarily closed the land west of the Appalachians to settlement. Expansion-minded colonists resented (and often ignored) the Proclamation Line, thus fomenting conflict with Native Americans and creating tension between the colonies and the mother country.

Other British efforts to exert more control over the American colonies included a series of fiscal and administrative reforms. The Revenue Act of 1764 (known as the Sugar Act) lowered duties on sugar but firmly established the means of enforcing their collection. Designed to defray the cost of keeping British troops in North America, the Sugar Act was followed by the 1765 Stamp Act, which required the use of embossed paper for legal documents and other printed matter. Forced to rescind the Stamp Act because of colonial protests, the British Parliament in 1767 passed the Townshend Act. By placing new duties on tea, coffee, and other items of household consumption, the Townshend Act directly affected free women's domestic responsibilities and consequently heightened their political consciousness. At the same time, the British increased their bureaucratic presence in the colonies — the number of Crown officials doubled during this period — and sought to limit the autonomy of the colonies' governing assemblies.

As tensions between Britain and the colonists took center stage in the years after the French and Indian War, waves of social and economic problems roiled the colonies. Seaport towns and cities suffered an economic downturn after the war boom, and the colonists, especially those indebted to English creditors, became all the more resentful of British taxation. Tax-related unrest prompted the British occupation of Boston, where a 1770 clash between colonists and British soldiers resulted in the death of five colonists, including the fugitive enslaved man Crispus Attucks. This "Boston Massacre" set off a wave of anti-British sentiment and propaganda. Hard times widened the gap between rich and poor in the colonies, deepening dissatisfaction. Extraordinary unrest in the backcountry regions of the southern and middle colonies — where poor farmers went on rampages against Indigenous peoples and resisted the authority of colonial elites on the seaboard — also promoted the desire for change. While perhaps resenting the wealthy colonial merchants and landed gentry who controlled so much of the economic and political life of the colonies, poor people in the mid-Atlantic colonies in particular diverted much of their anger toward British authority and its efforts to bring the American colonies more tightly into the imperial fold.

Liberty's Daughters: Women and the Emerging Crisis

Women made critical contributions to colonists' resistance to the new British policies. When the colonists resisted the new taxes by boycotting British goods, women, and their domestics, were necessarily involved. Where colonists had formerly relied on imported cloth, they now proposed to make their own cloth. Even though most textile production was the work of free and enslaved women, initial reports of the substitution of homespun cloth for imported fabric often ignored women's contributions. In 1768, the *Providence Gazette* commended one man for the large quantities of cloth and yarn "spun in his own house," without reference to the women who were doing the work. But male patriots (as colonials who protested British domination were called) quickly realized their dependence on women's efforts — even as they continued to ignore those of enslaved people — and northern newspaper reports of patriotic women's production of homespun cloth escalated.[2] In New England, spinning bees for manufacturing the yarn for homemade cloth were particularly popular.

Southern white women also produced homespun, but because they lived on farms and plantations often widely separated from one another, they rarely did so in the large groups typical in the North. Nor was there much publicity for their work, and indeed the southern press tended to criticize elite women for their extravagant taste in clothes and to suggest that men would have to persuade their wives to provide the necessary assistance.[3] Although free white women did provide assistance, owners of large plantations also bought equipment and set groups of enslaved women to spinning. Robert Carter of Virginia had his overseer "sett a part, Ten black Females the most Expert spinners . . . — they to be Employed in Spinning, solely."[4] This method of using enslaved women to produce cloth continued through the Revolutionary War, allowing some of these women to rely on old skills and acquire new ones.

While enslaved Black women had little choice in the matter of assisting their captors in their boycotts against the British, free white women could and did see themselves as acting in a patriotic cause, and many called themselves **"Liberty's Daughters."** Their spinning bees may not have produced a large amount of cloth, but their efforts took on symbolic importance and reinforced their importance as consumers — or nonconsumers — in the boycott. The spinning bees were, says one historian, "ideological showcases" that demonstrated women's contribution to the colonial struggle.[5]

Beyond producing homespun, women practiced all sorts of economies as they spurned a wide variety of British goods. Tea became the focus of boycotts in the early 1770s, especially after 1773, when the British instituted new regulations designed to undercut the colonials' illegal importation of non-British tea. Some women substituted herbal teas and coffee and engaged in collective efforts to encourage other women to do the same. In Edenton, North Carolina, Penelope Barker declared, "We women have taken too long to let our voices be heard." She organized fifty-one women who signed a proclamation acknowledging their "duty" to support the nonimportation resolutions passed by the First Continental Congress in 1774.[6] (See Primary Sources: "Gendering Images of the Revolution," Figure 3.1.) Women boycotters were roundly applauded in the press for their sacrifice. Presbyterian leader William Tennent III told women that "you have it in your power more than all your committees and Congresses, to strike the Stroke, and make the Hills and Plains of America clap their hands."[7]

Articles attributed to women appeared in both northern and southern newspapers. Whether these were actually written by women or by men using female pseudonyms, they helped to legitimize the idea of women as authors with valuable insights to impart. Phillis Wheatley, an enslaved woman in Boston, published poems in support of patriot efforts and liberty for all. (See Primary Sources: "Phillis Wheatley, Enslaved Poet.") Others produced thoughtful essays, such as one that appeared in 1774 in the *Virginia Gazette*, which was edited and published by Clementina Rind. The essay explained that American women "will be so far instrumental in bringing about a redress of the evils complained of, that history may be hereafter filled with their praises, and teach posterity to venerate their virtues."[8]

Despite the widespread sense that politics was not a woman's affair, women did participate in political action through boycotts and the production of homespun, and these acts of resistance encouraged them to see themselves as part of a larger American whole. Even someone as young as thirteen-year-old Anna Green Winslow wrote in her diary in 1771, "As I Am (as we say) a daughter of liberty, I chuse to wear as much of our own manufactory as possible."[9] Another young girl, Betsy Foote, recorded her daily labor at spinning and carding, and reported that she "felt Nationly into the bargain."[10] Women wrote of duty, of civic virtues, of freedom, and of sacrifice. However, despite the centrality of women's contributions to the success of the Americans' resistance, their efforts were extensions of their roles within the home — as goodwives, mothers, skilled laborers, and consumers — and, as such, the potential challenge to the gender order was minimized.

◆ WOMEN AND THE FACE OF WAR, 1775–1783

Colonial resistance escalated from boycotts and protests to armed conflict in April 1775, when British troops marched on Lexington and Concord, Massachusetts, in an effort to put down the growing rebellion. Although colonial leaders did not issue the Declaration of Independence until July 1776, the Revolution had begun. A struggle between imperial Great Britain and thirteen of its colonies, the American Revolution was also a civil war in which British subjects fought one another and former friends and neighbors became enemies. While many colonists tried to avoid taking sides, historians estimate that about one-fifth of the white population were loyalists (that is, loyal to Britain and opposed to the Revolution), also called Tories by their enemies. Probably two-fifths were patriots, supporters of the Revolution. Indigenous peoples and Blacks, too, became embroiled in the conflict on both sides of the fence. A wide spectrum of Americans, both male and female, thus faced profound disruptions and complex decisions.

Choosing Sides: Indigenous, Enslaved, and Free Black Women

Indigenous communities confronted particularly weighty choices. In part because their experiences with land-grabbing colonists had been so negative, many Indigenous nations opted to side with the British — who had made some efforts to control the colonists' encroachment into Indigenous territory — and they waged war against the patriots and their Indigenous allies throughout the backcountry. In many of the Indigenous nations, including the Iroquois and the Cherokees, women traditionally exerted significant influence over the decision to go to war; the causes were often linked to the desire to avenge deaths of loved ones killed by enemies. As Indigenous peoples became enmeshed in European and American conflicts, the rationale for warfare shifted from kinship issues, and women's role may have diminished. Nonetheless, when some of the Iroquois peoples (the Mohawks, Cayugas, Senecas, and Onondagas, but not the Oneidas and Tuscaroras) decided to ally with the British, they announced that the "mothers also consented to it," and some well-known Indigenous women were highly visible in the war effort. Molly Brant, the Mohawk wife of Sir William Johnson, a British official on the frontier, followed the path of many Native American women who had married white men and then mediated between the two cultures (see "Fish and Furs in the North" in Chapter 1). After Johnson died, Brant returned to her people and enjoyed unusual wealth and status. She so actively engaged in revolutionary era diplomacy on the side of the British that one officer claimed that her influence among her people was "far superior to that of all their Chiefs put together."[11]

Black women's choices in the Revolution were of a completely different nature. Although small communities of free Blacks existed throughout the colonies, the Revolution affected enslaved people far more profoundly. For example, slaveholders gave the needs of those they enslaved a low priority when allocating scarce foodstuffs and clothing. However, wartime labor shortages and political circumstances gave enslaved persons more room for maneuvering in their relations with their enslavers. Southern whites repeatedly complained that their demands were being met with insolence and resistance. Slaveholders were particularly worried about the prospects of insurrection and flight, especially after November 1775, when Virginia's royal governor Lord Dunmore offered freedom to rebels' enslaved men and indentured servants who agreed to fight for the British. His goal was twofold: to acquire troops and laborers, and to pressure white slaveholders to stay within the loyalist fold. His offer led to a massive flight of enslaved people from plantations, including men expecting to serve as soldiers and also women and children often linked by family ties to these men.

Throughout the war, enslaved men and women pondered their choice: Could they make it safely to the British lines? Would the British be true protectors? Would the British or the rebels win? Would the patriot leadership ever offer them freedom for fighting as had the British? General George Washington and many of the other slaveholding founding fathers were opposed to recruiting enslaved men until state legislators, desperate to fill their troop quotas, convinced Washington to allow it. Approximately 10,000 fought for the British, but half that number for the patriots. Is there any wonder why? Many more than those who joined military forces took advantage of the chaos and threat of the war to flee.

An estimated 55,000 enslaved Blacks escaped during the Revolution. Some made their way to the British; others had the British come to them. When the British left after occupying the plantation home of Mary Willing Byrd, for example, forty-nine enslaved people went with them. Many others simply escaped, looking for freedom independent of the British. Some, particularly those in South Carolina and Georgia, tried to reach the Spanish in Florida, where they more easily found freedom. Those who went over to the British often did so in groups, frequently with family members. Historians estimate that one-third of those who fled were women, a much higher proportion of runaways than before the Revolution. With nearby British troops offering some sanctuary to males who could fight, related women were willing to take the risk, some with their children in tow.

Escape from an owner, however, did not mean escape from danger and hardship. The British forced Black women to do laundry, cook, clean, and tend to the wounded. Some worked as spies. They often had to perform some of the most disagreeable and dirty tasks. When the British occupied Philadelphia, for example, they formed a "Company of Black Pioneers." This group of seventy-two men, fifteen women, and eight children were to "assist in Cleaning the Streets and Removing all Newsiances being thrown into the Streets."[12] Living conditions were harsh. In the British camps, many succumbed to smallpox and other diseases. In 1781, the British general Alexander Leslie reported that "about 700 Negroes are come down the River in the Small Pox." In an eighteenth-century version of germ warfare, he decided to "distribute them about the Rebell Plantations."[13] This callous attitude toward these Black men and women underlines the fact that most British officers viewed the enslaved people seeking freedom only as pawns in the imperial struggle. Despite the unsettled conditions of wartime, Black men and women fought an uphill battle to escape to freedom and survive.

White Women: Pacifists, Tories, and Patriots

White women also had to make decisions about the war, but of a very different sort than those of enslaved Black women. The war created a painful situation for Quaker women, whose pacifism was a tenet of their religion. Patriots were often suspicious of Quakers, and Quakers themselves clearly struggled with their political identity. Margaret Morris, a Quaker from New Jersey, proudly recounted her success in hiding a loyalist friend from a group of armed patriots who appeared at her door. At the same time, she described General George Washington's troops as "our side."

American or British, patriot or Tory: Did a woman's political identity follow her husband's, her brother's, her father's? To whom would the wife of a Tory man show allegiance? Women whose loyalist husbands had been exiled or who had gone to fight with the British were subject to ostracism. They sometimes found their land and personal goods, including their enslaved property, claimed by patriots. State laws permitting the confiscation of land of known Tories differed slightly regarding the rights of the wife or widow of an "absentee." Massachusetts, for example, acknowledged the female spouse's dower rights in the estate only if she had remained in the state and not followed her husband. Most generally, states presumed that a woman's allegiance followed her husband's, in accordance with the assumptions of *feme covert*. Significantly, most states did not require the loyalty oaths of women that they required of men, an indication that women were not viewed as political actors.

Not all women followed the allegiance of their husbands. A few took up the patriot cause despite their husbands' loyalty to the British Crown. Florence Cook of Charleston, South Carolina, attempted to regain her family's dispossessed property after the war. In her petition, she described herself as a "Sincere friend to her Country," who taught her daughter "the love of Liberty and this her Native Country." Jane Moffit of Albany, New York, was protected from expulsion despite her husband's political sentiments because, said city leaders, she "has always been esteemed a Friend to the American Cause."[14]

In case after case, decisions about the fate of wives were based on the assumption that they could not act independently of their husbands, but they also reflected the reality that some women directly aided the loyalist cause. Many women did serve as couriers and spies or in other ways assisted the British after their loyalist husbands had left for war. In Albany, thirty-two women were brought to the attention of the New York State commissioners for "detecting and defeating conspiracies" in 1780. Some, like Lidia Currey and Rachael Ferguson, were jailed for hiding loyalists in their homes. Others smuggled messages to British troops. In Philadelphia, Margaret Hutchinson carried "Verbal Intelligence, of what she had seen of their [the rebels'] different Movements" to British spies. While in absolute numbers such daring women were not many, they were considered so serious a threat that patriot committees of safety sought the help of "discreet Women, of Known attachment to the American Cause" to search for contraband and hidden letters on the persons of suspected female Tory couriers.[15]

Maintaining the Troops: The Women Who Served

Service to one's country during wartime often becomes a defining moment of citizenship. Sacrifices become emblems of civic virtue and worthiness. Since the ultimate signs of service are bearing arms and risking death, women's contributions, outside of their sons who served, are frequently less valued than men's. During the Revolution, few women actually fought in combat. But the exceptions are notable. In South Carolina, one woman joined her son-in-law to resist 150 British soldiers who were trying to destroy a cache of ammunition. Pennsylvanian Mary Hays McCauley, perhaps the inspiration for the legendary Molly Pitcher, routinely carried water to troops in battle. When her husband fell at the Battle of Monmouth, New Jersey, in 1778, she took his place, keeping a cannon loaded in the face of enemy fire, for which she later received a pension from the state of Pennsylvania "for services rendered in the revolutionary war." Deborah Sampson, later Gannett, was one of a handful of women who disguised themselves as men in order to join the troops. Donning men's clothing and enlisting as Robert Shurtleff in the Fourth Massachusetts Regiment, Sampson served eighteen months from 1782 to 1783 and was wounded twice before her sex was discovered and she was discharged. Another woman attempted to enlist in 1778 at Elizabethtown,

DEBORAH SAMPSON.
Published by H. Mann, 1797.

◆ **Joseph Stone, *Deborah Sampson* (1797)**

In 1797, Herman Mann commissioned Joseph Stone to paint this image for the frontispiece of his book on Deborah Sampson's life, titled *The Female Review: or Memoirs of an American Lady.* Sampson had come of age as an indentured servant in Middleborough, Massachusetts. When her period of indenture concluded at age eighteen, she became a "masterless" woman, an unusual status in the colonial era, having neither husband, father, nor an indenture holder to whom she was bound. This gave her rare freedom for a woman, and she moved from town to town, working sometimes as a teacher, sometimes as a weaver. After her service and honorable discharge from the Fourth Massachusetts Regiment, she married and had three children. With the help of her friend Paul Revere, she obtained a small military pension from the U.S. Congress. Although in later statements she appeared at times apologetic for her "uncouth actions," she also pronounced, "I burst the tyrant bonds which held my sex in awe and clandestinely or by stealth, grasped an opportunity which custom and the world seemed to deny, as a natural privilege."[16] *GRANGER — Historical Picture Archive.*

New Jersey. A suspicious officer required that she submit to a physical exam, and the following day he "ordered the Drums to beat her . . . Threw the Town with the whores march."[17]

More generally, women's role in the military was one they had historically taken in warfare: the so-called camp follower. Most who attached themselves to the patriots' Continental Army under George Washington's command were soldiers' wives, but some were sex workers. While officers' wives did make protracted visits to encourage their husbands and to participate in entertainments, most women who followed the army were poor men's spouses. Their presence may have signaled a patriotic fervor to aid the cause, but more probably it indicated their desire to attend to their husbands' welfare as well as their inability to function on their own financially. Camp followers, often with their children, faced extraordinary challenges, risking disease, injury, kidnapping, and death. Living under primitive conditions with scanty provisions, some even gave birth in army camps.

But camp followers did provide valuable services. Some were "sutlers," merchants who sold provisions to the troops. More commonly, women such as Sarah Osborn, whose story opens this chapter, did laundry or worked as cooks. Women served as nurses, both in the fields and at the general hospitals for the sick and wounded where conditions were primitive. While male doctors and their assistants performed the skilled work, female nurses were assigned "to see that the close-stools or pots are emptied as soon as possible after they are used . . . they are to see that every patient, upon his admission into the Hospital is immediately washed with warm water, and that his face and hands are washed and head combed every morning."[18] The sexual division of labor relegated women to menial tasks, and no matter how important this work was, free women's compensation was small.

Thus female camp followers lived and worked in the very midst of war, drawing on a physical fortitude associated with male activities, but did not break down traditional expectations about women's proper role. Their presence with the army was for the most part a reflection of their dependence. Women continued to be controlled not only by their husbands, but also by what one historian terms "that most male of institutions, the military."[19] Their activities were extensions of white women's traditional household work. Although many undoubtedly took pride in their patriotic contributions, most did not exhibit a new sense of independence.

Some women did not follow the armies but did observe the fighting as it came to them. Occupying armies commandeered homes for quartering soldiers, and women, along with their servants and bondspersons, frequently bore the brunt of their demands for food, firewood, and domestic labor. In September 1777, Elizabeth Drinker, alone with her children in Philadelphia, found herself the unwilling hostess to a British officer: "Our officer mov'd his lodging from the bleu Chamber to the little front parlor, so that he has the two front parlors, a chamber up two pair of stairs for his bagge, and the Stable wholly to himself, besides the use of the kitchen."[20] Catherine Van Cortlandt, a Tory woman, wrote disparagingly to her husband about the patriot troops who commandeered her house in New Jersey and complained that "the farmers are forbid to sell me provisions, and the millers to grind our grain. Our woods are cut down for the use of their army, and that which you bought and left corded near the river my servants are forbid to touch, though we are in the greatest distress for the want of it."[21]

Women caught in the crossfire worried about their personal safety and that of their children. While reported rapes were infrequent, British soldiers were brutal on occasion. More commonly, women had to adjust to being the only white adult in their households and handling the day-to-day affairs of running a farm or managing a business in a husband's prolonged absence. Their independent management of labor and business enterprises proved to be one of their most significant roles in the revolutionary era.

A small group of elite patriot women, reminiscent of the Daughters of Liberty who had organized spinning bees in the early stages of the Revolution, carved out more public ways of participating in the war effort by raising funds for the beleaguered Continental Army. Following a discouraging defeat at Charleston in 1780, Esther DeBerdt Reed, the wife of the governor of Pennsylvania, and Sarah Franklin Bache, the daughter of Benjamin Franklin, organized the **Ladies Association of Philadelphia** to raise the considerable sum of $300,000 for the troops. In a powerfully worded broadside, Reed announced that "the Women of America manifested a firm resolution to contribute as much as could depend on them, to the deliverance of their country." The broadside urged prosperous women to go without luxuries to aid the cause and asked poorer women to offer what they could. After outlining the rationale for the fund-raising, Reed challenged anyone who would doubt the group's patriotic purpose: "He cannot be a good citizen who will not applaud our efforts for the relief of the armies which defend our lives, our possessions, our liberty."[22]

The Pennsylvania women publicized their efforts and sent letters to women in other states, urging them to raise funds as well. In Virginia, the scattered nature of settlement made an exact duplication of Pennsylvania's door-to-door effort impossible, but Martha Wayles Jefferson, wife of Governor Thomas Jefferson, did encourage other elite Virginia women to raise funds (Martha herself was not in good health), describing it as an "opportunity of proving that they also participate on those virtuous feelings."[23] In most cases, the sums raised were modest. In New Jersey, women collected $15,488 in paper dollars, but because of high inflation, the money purchased only 380 pairs of stockings for the state's soldiers.

The distribution of donations that the Philadelphia women collected offers a revealing insight into perceptions of women's supporting role. Writing to General Washington, Esther Reed explained that the women did not want the money to go into a general fund that would provide soldiers "an article to which they are entitled from the public." Rather, the women hoped that their money — approximately $2 per soldier in hard currency — might be given directly to the soldiers. Washington demurred: the men might waste it on liquor, and having hard currency, when they were generally paid in paper money, might create discontent and exacerbate inflation. He declared that their "benevolent donation" should be used to provide men with shirts and requested further that the women make the shirts themselves. In the midst of the exchange, Reed died of dysentery, but Sarah Bache followed through with the project, eventually sending Washington 2,200 shirts. A French visitor to Bache's home reported that "on each shirt was the name of the married or unmarried lady who made it."[24]

Thus, however novel the Philadelphia women's plan may have been, General Washington's response placed their efforts firmly in the realm of woman's more traditional sphere — of sewing for her family. The Philadelphia women's efforts may have been more overtly political than the service of poor women following the army, but in both cases women's contributions were constrained by traditional notions of women's roles. The link between white women's patriotism and the domestic sphere was to be one of the principal ideological legacies of the Revolution.

◆ REVOLUTIONARY ERA LEGACIES

The patriots emerged victorious in 1781 when the British surrendered at Yorktown, Virginia. In that same year, the colonies, now states, ratified the Articles of Confederation, their first attempt at national governance. Weaknesses in that body led eventually to adoption of the U.S. Constitution in 1788 and the inauguration of George Washington as the new nation's first president in 1789. As a national government was being framed, the various states also wrote constitutions. The period was rich with debates about the nature of government and the rights of citizens, as Americans pondered the implications of their Revolution. What were the legacies of the Revolution for women? For many, war and revolution translated into hardship and poverty; for others, new opportunities emerged, but these were always constrained by prevailing assumptions about white women's marginal role in public life. For enslaved and Indigenous women, there was no assumption of a public role or improved status.

A Changing World for Indigenous Women

The American victory realigned European colonial claims on the continent and brought changes to many Indigenous women's lives as their people encountered a new republic intent on western expansion onto their lands. Indigenous groups that sided with Britain, in particular, suffered devastating losses in the war. American forces in New York invaded Iroquois territory in 1779, killing many, burning forty towns, and destroying crops. The Cherokees in the Appalachian region to the south suffered a similar destruction. Native American men's preoccupation with warfare and their role in diplomacy may have heightened their power within their own communities, but it also increased women's responsibilities in maintaining their communities in the men's prolonged absences, and in the face of destruction, disease, and starvation.

In the postwar period, as weakened Native American societies started to come under the power of a new, neighboring nation, challenges to traditional gender roles arose. Men acted as primary mediators between their nations and the U.S. government. As men's roles took on magnified political importance, women may have correspondingly lost influence in their own communities. The example of Cherokee leader Nancy Ward, however, diverges from this general trend. Since her participation in a battle against the Creeks in the 1750s, Ward had been recognized as a "War Woman," a position that garnered high esteem and broader authority over the fates of war captives. Along with Cherokee male leaders, Ward spoke to U.S. commissioners in treaty negotiations during and after the Revolutionary War. At the 1781 meeting at the Holston River in present-day Tennessee, Ward used a language of kinship and her symbolic maternal authority to call for peace between the United States and the Cherokees: "Let your women's sons be ours; our sons be yours. Let your women hear our words."[25] Almost forty years later, at the age of eighty, Ward would still be invoking her authority as an elder "Beloved Woman" to protect her people's land and sovereignty. (See Reading into the Past: "Beloved Children: Cherokee Women Petition the National Council" in Chapter 4.) By that time, however, Cherokee women's pathways to political authority had narrowed considerably.

◆ **Redefining Gender Roles among the Creeks**

This early nineteenth-century painting features Creek people as U.S. agent Benjamin Hawkins introduces them to plows as a first step in "Americanizing" them. Hawkins focuses his attention on the men, placing his back to a woman who stands amid the foodstuffs she has produced. This stance represents white officials' and missionaries' goal of redefining gender roles among the Creeks so that men would abandon hunting in exchange for farming, while women would give up their traditional role of raising crops to undertake domestic roles in the home. *GRANGER — Historical Picture Archive.*

The U.S. government's efforts to encourage Indigenous peoples to assimilate to white norms also disturbed traditional patterns of gender behavior and spheres of activity. American leaders insisted that men give up hunting to become farmers and that Native American women become farmers' wives. In a letter to the Cherokees in 1796, President Washington was explicit about his expectations. "You will easily add flax and cotton which you may dispose of to the White people; or have it made up by your own women into clothing for yourselves. Your wives and daughters can soon learn to spin and weave."[26] But if white Americans envisioned a family order in which women were subordinate, Cherokee women adapted to the new expectations in ways that maintained their traditional roles in the community. They continued their customary farming work, tended livestock, and took on the responsibilities of spinning and weaving. Elite Cherokee women among them did this work with the assistance of enslaved Black women and men — another detail of their assimilationist agenda. In contrast, men found it far more difficult to adjust to their changed circumstances. Loss of land and depletion of fur-bearing animals deprived males of hunting, an important masculine activity with both economic and spiritual significance. Native Americans' use of alcohol also contributed to their exploitation and to unhappy family situations that sometimes resulted in domestic abuse.

After the Revolution, Indigenous peoples with the most proximity to the expanding white population became the objects of Protestant missionary activity. Although white missionaries sought to convert Indigenous peoples, calls for change also came from within Native American nations. Handsome Lake, a Seneca religious prophet who had been influenced by the Quakers, called for major reforms for his people. He promoted a return to some of the old ways, especially in regard to religion. He condemned the abuse of alcohol and criticized men's physical mistreatment of their wives. At the same time, however, Handsome Lake also urged that the Iroquois follow the family patterns of whites: men should take up farming and women should limit themselves to spinning and weaving. Privileging the nuclear family and the husband-wife relationship, he downplayed the older emphasis on kinship relations and was especially critical of Iroquois matrons. In the long run, assimilative pressures and a changed economic and political order undermined women's position among many Native American peoples, especially where men took on economic roles of increased importance to the community and their families. But that process was neither immediate nor universal.

For Indigenous women farther to the west, however, the American Revolution paled in importance to other changes in economy, culture, and health. In 1776, for example, the Lakota Sioux expanded into the Black Hills and incorporated this mountainous region as a sacred site for their expanding horse- and bison-based society. California Native Americans attacked a San Diego mission in 1775, responding in part to the abuse of Indigenous women by Spanish soldiers. Northwest Coast Indigenous peoples found their economy and gendered labor transformed by the late eighteenth-century international rush for sea otter pelts. Similar to the earlier fur trade of the Northeast, the otter skin trade introduced new textiles and metal goods into Indigenous culture. In some cases, Northwest Coast groups offered Indigenous female captives as sex workers to European, American, and Russian traders who appeared on their coast. Finally, between 1779 and 1784, a terrible smallpox pandemic decimated Indigenous western communities — hitting pregnant women and children especially hard — as it spread along continental trade routes. Some Plains Indigenous bands lost up to 80 percent of their members, causing further migration and regrouping for survival.[27]

These were some of the transformed Indigenous societies that the young Shoshone woman Sacagawea observed as part of the Meriwether Lewis and William Clark transcontinental journey to the Pacific Ocean in 1804–1806. Sacagawea first met Lewis and Clark in the Mandan-Hidatsu village in what is now North Dakota. As a young girl, she had been taken from her homeland in the Rocky Mountains and eventually sold to the man who would become her husband, a French Canadian trader named Toussaint Charbonneau. Sacagawea

◆ **Sacagawea Monument, Portland, Oregon**
The Shoshone woman known as Sacagawea left a powerful legacy, although differing versions of her biography, and even her name, continue to be debated. This statue of Sacagawea was commissioned in 1905 by the white women's clubs of Portland, Oregon, in recognition of the Shoshone guide and translator to the Lewis and Clark expedition a hundred years before. The statue, by Denver sculptor Alice Cooper, was one of the first monuments to depict an actual historical woman in the United States. From this point on, Sacagawea's role as national symbol, both of the contribution of Indigenous peoples to American history and of their tragic fate at the hands of white colonists, began to grow. She is almost always represented as she is here: with her baby on her back and her hand pointing the way west. *MPI/Getty Images.*

accompanied Charbonneau when he was hired by Lewis and Clark's exploratory expedition of the newly acquired (1803) Louisiana Purchase. Pregnant when she began this journey, Sacagawea gave birth to her son as the party traveled westward. Other Shoshone women also labored for Lewis and Clark as they crossed the Continental Divide, driving pack horses and carrying burdens, as women, especially captives, were expected to do in both Mandan and Shoshone society. Sacagawea proved invaluable to the expedition as someone who knew the Rocky Mountain terrain and Shoshone language. Although Lewis's diary entries on Shoshone people emphasized the "drudgery" of the women, he also inadvertently recorded female skills of child care and domestic work, as well as the horse care, transportation, and gathering of "wild fruits and roots" necessary to cross-country travel.[28] By focusing on Sacagawea, we can understand that Lewis and Clark's much-celebrated journey utilized the linguistic, geospatial, and cultural knowledge, labor, physical strength, and mobility of Native American women.

Black Women: Freedom and Slavery

For Black women, the Revolution also left a complex, but completely different, legacy. Most significantly, chattel slavery remained a federally recognized institution with a Constitution that equated enslaved Blacks as two-thirds of a person, allowed the African slave trade, and supported legislation that authorized local governments to capture and return people who had fled enslavement. The Constitution also was silent on citizenship for Blacks, even those who were free or hoped to gain their release from bondage. Some individual states and territories designed legislative means of ending both the international trade and the institution itself, resulting in a national political, economic, and cultural sectionalism centered on slavery that had long-lasting consequences.

At the end of the war, a fraction of enslaved people known as "Black Loyalists," who had fled to the British to achieve their freedom, were evacuated by ship from New York, Charleston, and Savannah. Of those who left from New York and whose sex is known, 42.3 percent were women, and apparently many had their children with them. Some were sold again into slavery in the West Indies; others were shipped to Nova Scotia, where they eked out an existence in harsh conditions; and some eventually ended up in another marginal environment, a new British-sponsored colony in Sierra Leone, West Africa. Mary Perth, born into slavery in Virginia, joined this migration along with her children and her husband, Caesar. The Perth family traveled in company with other devout Black Methodists who had established a new meetinghouse in Sierra Leone. Perth supported her family by running a boardinghouse and restaurant near the Freetown wharves, where she had to interact with sailors from the British slave ships working close to the small West African colony of free migrants.[29] For Mary Perth and other Black loyalist women, the revolutionary conflict resulted in global migration and great risks taken to establish new lives in another part of the British Empire.

For some Blacks who had not joined the British, the most important legacy of the Revolution was freedom. Crispus Attucks's death at the Boston Massacre publicly pronounced the enslaved man's investment in the fight for freedom, as did the many others who had attempted to escape prior to the Revolution. Even before the conflict, a small movement of white colonists had supported manumission (release from bondage), primarily the result of the Quakers' growing revulsion against slavery. The ideological issues at the center of the Revolution, especially those concerning natural rights and liberty, encouraged some white Americans to examine the institution of slavery. So too did the teachings of John Wesley during the First Great Awakening. Even for those with little humanitarian interest in enslaved people themselves, the moral and philosophical incongruity of building a nation based on notions of liberty while maintaining chattel slavery was troublesome. More mundane concerns also promoted antislavery sentiment — white immigrant workers who were increasingly available and who were easily hired and fired became more attractive in the urban commercial culture of the North. Anxieties about Black insurrections during the war raised further questions about the slave system.

Blacks were active participants in the emancipation process, especially in Massachusetts. Mum Bett, later known as Elizabeth Freeman, was enslaved by Colonel John Ashley in Sheffield, Massachusetts. In 1781, she petitioned a Massachusetts county court for her freedom. Freeman's suit, *Brom and Bett v.*

◆ **Susan Anne Livingston Ridley Sedgwick,** *Elizabeth Freeman ("Mum Bett")* **(1811)**
After her successful freedom suit that led to the end of slavery in Massachusetts, Mum Bett adopted the name Elizabeth Freeman. She lived the remainder of her life as a paid servant in the family of Theodor Sedgwick, who had served as her lawyer. Theodor's daughter Catherine Sedgwick later wrote an account of her freedom suit, and Catherine's sister-in-law Susan Sedgwick painted the watercolor shown here. In the portrait, Freeman's dress is vivid blue, and she wears a gold necklace around her neck. Why do you suppose the Sedgwick family members made the effort to document Freeman's life in words and portrait? What is the artist hoping to convey about Freeman in this image? *GRANGER — Historical Picture Archive.*

Ashley, combined with several others, led to the state court's 1783 decision that "there can be no such thing as perpetual servitude of a rational creature."[30] In other northern states, manumission came through legislation. Only Vermont, in 1777, provided for immediate emancipation. Elsewhere, the process was protracted. In Pennsylvania, children of enslaved females were apprenticed until they were twenty-eight years old. Although each year more enslaved people became free in the North, one-fourth of northern Blacks were still enslaved as late as 1810. This gradualism meant that enslaved women would continue to bear children who would not be fully free until they were adults, but they could take some comfort in their grandchildren's future freedom.

The emancipation laws, as well as individual manumissions in the North and the Upper South (usually at the death of their enslaver or as a reward for a "heroic" act) and the migration of southern free Blacks, created growing free Black populations in the last years of the eighteenth century, especially in cities such as Baltimore, Philadelphia, Boston, and New York. Although a small number were able to carve out a modest financial success, constrained education and pervasive discrimination limited their opportunities. Most women worked at jobs similar to those that had occupied them when they were enslaved — domestic work, washing, cooking, and child care. Some Black women were proprietors, especially of board-inghouses, where they would have been important resources for the freed Blacks migrating to the cities during this period. Others opened shops and restaurants that built upon their domestic skills. Some worked as seamstresses, weavers, hat makers, caterers, and, of course, midwives. In Portsmouth, New Hampshire, Dinah Gibson, locally well known for her baking, established "Dinah's Cottage."

A handful of Black women were prominent enough to make a mark in the historical record. Lydia York, for example, petitioned the Philadelphia Abolition Society to assist her in finding a position for her niece Hetty as an indentured servant. Jane Coggeshall, who gained her freedom during the war when she and two other enslaved people gave information about British troops to Rhode Island patriots, later petitioned the state to confirm her freedom, lest her former owners attempt to reenslave her. Catherine Ferguson, who had purchased her own freedom, established a school for poor Black and white children in New York in 1793. Another former enslaved woman, Eleanor Harris, became the first Black teacher in Philadelphia. Ona Judge gained notoriety as the fugitive from Martha Washington who escaped the Executive Mansion in Philadelphia for a free home in New Hampshire. (See Reading into the Past: "Ona Judge's Escape.") Many others could be read about in the copious fugitive-slave advertisements in every regularly published newspaper.

As they worked at their jobs and cared for their families, many urban free Black women participated in building a network of Black institutions, including churches and the literary and benevolent societies devoted to self-help efforts that had emerged by the turn of the century. These free Black institutions were a source of strength and pride for the community, but they also exemplified the segregated lives that African Americans lived in the North and a small, but significant class difference in the Black community. Emancipation brought freedom for some Black women and men, but within the constraints of a racial and economic hierarchy. The egalitarian promises implicit in revolutionary ideology were closed to African Americans, as they were to many poor whites and first-generation immigrants.

In the South, these promises were even less in evidence. In the Upper South, there was a spate of individual manumissions, especially through the wills of slaveholders, and the free Black population did expand significantly. But there was no widespread sentiment for dispensing with the institution altogether, and many states and locales legally forbade free Black residents from remaining. Most slaveholders were not troubled by the implications of a rhetoric of individual freedom and natural rights for their system of chattel labor. Indeed, slaveholders became more deeply entrenched in the institution after the war, especially in the Deep South, where access to more land for large-scale agriculture grew with the diminishment of Indigenous property rights and the acquisition of the Louisiana Purchase lands. The 1793 patent of the cotton gin, which mechanically removed the seed and hull from short-staple cotton, made it possible to process the crop more quickly, increasing profitability. Until 1808, when the Constitution outlawed the importation of enslaved Africans, enslavers brought increasing numbers of captives to southern markets, where demand for their labor was high.

READING INTO THE PAST

Ona Judge's Escape

Ona Maria Judge, listed as "Oney" in this runaway ad, was born in 1773 on the Mount Vernon estate of George and Martha Washington to her enslaved mother, Betty. She was the "property" of Martha Washington and a skilled seamstress. At the age of sixteen, Judge was sent north to serve as the First Lady's domestic in New York. When the U.S. capitol moved to Philadelphia in 1790, Judge was again moved with other enslaved men and women to work in the new Executive Mansion. But Philadelphia had passed a law that required all incoming slaveholders to free any enslaved adults who stayed in the state longer than six months. George Washington and his legal advisors worked out a plan to get around the manumission requirement by circulating the Washingtons' enslaved people back and forth between Philadelphia and Mount Vernon every six months. These periodic visits between 1791 and 1796 to Mount Vernon allowed Judge to stay connected to friends and family she had left behind, but they also kept her in bondage. When Judge learned that she was to be sent back to Virginia permanently as a wedding present for Martha's granddaughter, Elizabeth Parke Custis, the twenty-two-year-old Judge gathered her courage, took advantage of the aid offered by local free Blacks, and escaped from Philadelphia to Portsmouth, New Hampshire. Although the Washingtons tried repeatedly to recapture her and although her life in New England was often hard, Ona Judge lived the rest of her days as a free woman until her death at age fifty-two. She married and had two free children.

The document here is a copy of the ad placed in several newspapers by Frederick Kitt, Executive Mansion steward. Runaway ads like this appeared frequently in the newspapers of the early republic.

The regional differences in patterns of Black slavery grew after the Revolution, with slavery eventually disappearing in the Northeast and upper Midwest (via the **Northwest Ordinance** of 1787) and deepening in the actual number of those bound and depended on for the agrarian-based economies of the Lower South and frontier Southwest. In the Chesapeake region, tobacco declined in importance and the region's farming economy diversified to include grains. While some enslaved women had developed textile skills, for the most part it was men who were trained as wagon makers, blacksmiths, mill workers, or builders. The vast majority of both genders were field workers. Enslaved people also became extremely important to the growing urban areas of the region, and women

Ten Dollars Reward.

ABSCONDED from the household of the President of the United States, on Saturday afternoon, ONEY JUDGE, a light Mulatto girl, much freckled, with very black eyes, and bushy black hair — She is of middle stature, but slender and delicately made, about 20 years of age. She has many changes of very good clothes of all sorts, but they are not sufficiently recollected to describe.

As there was no suspicion of her going off, and it happened without the least provocation, it is not easy to conjecture whither she is gone — or fully, what her design is; but as she may attempt to escape by water, all masters of vessels and others are cautioned against receiving her on board, altho' she may, and probably will endeavour to pass for a free woman, and it is said has, wherewithal to pay her passage.

Ten dollars will be paid to any person, (white or black) who will bring her home, if taken in the city, or on board any vessel in the harbor; and a further reasonable sum if apprehended and brought home, from a greater distance, and in proportion to the distance.

May 24   FRED. KITT, Steward

SOURCE: *Claypoole's American Daily Advertiser*, May 25, 1796, in Erica Armstrong Dunbar, *Never Caught: The Washingtons' Relentless Pursuit of Their Runaway Slave, Ona Judge* (New York: 37Ink/Atria, 2017), 99.

ANALYZING PRIMARY SOURCES

1. What language does the ad use to speculate about Judge's motives for running away, and what assumptions does this wording reveal?
2. What evidence can such ads offer about the history of enslaved women during the postrevolutionary period? What silences do they contain?

in particular were used in the tobacco factories of Petersburg and Richmond, Virginia. Women and girls also served as domestic workers and participated in city markets, selling wares such as cakes, oysters, and garden produce, an occupation that gave them, as females, an unusual amount of liberty to move about urban spaces.

Most Black captives, however, enjoyed little personal freedom. This was particularly evident in the way in which slaveholders in the Upper South increasingly sought to reproduce the enslaved population, encouraging people to form families that they would later break up and sell for profit. Thomas Jefferson provided gifts for at least one couple on his Virginia plantation and explicitly commented on the

◆ **Enslaved Women in the Tobacco Fields**

In 1798, architect Benjamin Henry Latrobe produced this image labeled "An overseer doing his duty. Sketched from life near Fredericksburg." Latrobe apparently recognized the irony presented by the overseer, a white male in the employ of the plantation owner, standing idly on a tree stump, his duty merely to watch the two enslaved women hard at work hoeing in a tobacco field. *GRANGER — Historical Picture Archive.*

value of a fertile bondswoman: "I consider a woman who brings a child every two years as more profitable than the best man on the farm."[31]

Despite their appreciation of the females' fertility, male and female slaveholders expected pregnant captives to work well into their pregnancies and to return to their work almost immediately after delivery. The hardships of being a mother under these conditions were magnified by the constant threat of separation. A white observer in Wilmington, North Carolina, in 1778 described the trauma he witnessed: "A wench clung to a little daughter, and implored, with the most agonizing supplication, that they might not be separated."[32] Children could be sold from their parents, husbands from their wives, and vice-versa. Financial reversals or the death of the slaveholder, in particular, often led to sales that destroyed Black families.

White Women: An Ambiguous Legacy

Just as the Revolution had mixed results for some Black women, its meaning for white women eludes easy generalizations. Petitions from widows and soldiers' wives provide eloquent evidence for the personal tragedies that came with war. Sarah Welsh's husband had died in 1780, but "being a destress widow not knowing how to or whom aplication was to be made . . . untill it was too late," she waited until 1791 to ask the government for his back pay.[33] Many wives of Tory men, too, found themselves in dire straits. After the war, they waged lengthy, and only rarely successful, legal battles to regain property seized when their husbands left to fight with the British. Many impoverished women worked in the few avenues of employment offered to women, such as shopkeepers, teachers, innkeepers, servants, seamstresses, or milliners. By 1800, as the nation moved toward the first stages of industrialization and the "putting-out" industries (those industries focused on producing goods such as textiles, shoes, and straw bonnets) expanded, poor and immigrant women increasingly turned to doing piecework in their homes (see "From Market Revolution to Industrial Revolution" in Chapter 4). For more privileged educated women, war and revolution contributed to a changed conception of self, as many expanded their horizons beyond the narrow sphere of the hearth and marriage. Women whose husbands served in the army or in the new state or federal governments were left alone for extended periods but benefited from their spouses' secure income. As women had been doing since the early colonial period, they became **deputy husbands**, managing farms and businesses and often rising impressively to the new challenges, but receiving little lasting credit for their efforts.[34]

In the extant correspondence and diaries from this period, primarily from the wives of officers and politicians, a distinct pattern concerning women's roles as deputy husbands emerges. Men originally left detailed instructions, urging their wives to consult male kin or neighbors. Through time, many men began to trust their wives' judgment. New Yorker James Clinton, for example, commented to his wife, Mary, "I Can't give any Other Directions About Home more than what I have done but must Leave all to your good Management."[35] Women themselves often made pointed reference to their own competence, and some even asserted a new language of companionate marriage. When Lucy Flucker Knox in New York wrote to her husband, Henry Knox, she commented that she was "quite a woman of business," adding, "[I hope that in the future] you will not consider yourself as commander in chief of your own house — but be convinced that there is such a thing as equal command."[36]

Although few women challenged their subordinate position as overtly as Lucy Knox, the postwar years did see a significant questioning of white women's status in the home and, to some extent, in politics. Early in the revolutionary crisis, women speaking about politics often made apologies, almost ritualistically accepting their inferiority. In a June 1776 letter to a female friend, Elizabeth Feilde followed her comments on contemporary politics with the following self-deprecating remark: "No; I assure you it's a subject for which I have not either Talents or Inclination to enter upon."[37] But in the turmoil of rebellion and war, the apologies became less evident as astute women got caught up in the dramatic events unfolding before them. Eliza Wilkinson of South Carolina frankly resented men's claim that women had no business with politics, writing to a friend in 1782, "I won't have it thought that because we are the weaker sex as to bodily strength, my dear, we are capable of nothing more than minding the dairy, visiting the poultry-house, and all such domestic concerns. . . . They won't even allow us the liberty of thought, and that is all I want."[38]

READING INTO THE PAST

Thirteen Toasts

It was customary and socially obligatory for men at the time of the American Revolution to give thirteen toasts to celebrate the thirteen colonies that made up the new nation as a popular expression of national unity. The following list of toasts is significant because it was authored and performed by women as a unique example of gendered political expression.

1. Lady Washington
2. The Congress
3. A long continuance to our glorious peace.
4. The Thirteen United States.
5. Success to Independence.
6. May internal disturbance cease.
7. Trade and Commerce throughout the world.
8. Reformation to our husbands.
9. May the gentlemen and the ladies ever unite on joyful occasions.
10. Happiness and prosperity to our families.
11. Reformation to the men in general.
12. May the Protestant religion prevail and flourish throughout all nations.
13. May reformed husbands ever find obedient wives.

SOURCE: "Thirteen Toasts," *Massachusetts Gazette*, 1783, recorded in David Waldstreicher, *In the Midst of Perpetual Fetes* (Chapel Hill: University of North Carolina Press, 1997), 83.

ANALYZING PRIMARY SOURCES

1. What are the "female" issues embedded in these toasts? Would enslaved or Indigenous women have crafted similar toasts? If not, what might have been some of theirs?

As Wilkinson's term "liberty of thought" suggests, some women made overt connections between the ideology of the Revolution concerning natural rights, liberty, and equality and the position of women (see Reading into the Past: "Thirteen Toasts"). Abigail Adams's admonition to her husband, John Adams, that the men drawing up the new government and its code of laws should "remember the ladies" is probably the most famous expression of the handful of white women who hoped to see at least modest changes in their status. The issue attracted a significant amount of attention in the decade after the Revolution. Following publication in the United States in 1792 of *A Vindication of the Rights of Woman* by the English activist Mary Wollstonecraft, American ladies' magazines debated women's rights and roles. Some articles referred to marriage as a form of slavery. Others blamed women's limited education for women's vanity and superficiality.

Limited Citizenship: White Women's Legal Status and Education

Did the flurry of attention to women's rights in the postrevolutionary era lead to an improvement in white women's status? The states in the new nation were now free of British legal statutes and could theoretically construct laws in keeping with the new emphasis on protecting individual rights. Divorce law was one area in which women did benefit. British common law did not allow divorce, but now all states except South Carolina permitted it. Still, the procedure was difficult. In most states, divorce petitions required action by the state assembly. Courts in Pennsylvania and the four New England states could decree divorce. Causes offered for divorce changed over time, hinting at a slight shift in marital expectations. During most of the colonial period, women were far more likely than men to seek a divorce, usually doing so on the grounds of desertion. After the Revolution, the grounds women used expanded to include adultery, and more men began to seek divorce, usually for desertion. Still, husbands had the upper hand when it came to child custody, financial support for divorced wives, and retention of a spouse's property even if the couple were no longer together. The changes were subtle ones, as one historian concedes: "All one can say, and perhaps it is enough, is that after the war women were physically moving out of their unhappy households, an action that, judging from the divorce literature, had been relatively uncommon before the war."[39]

In other legal matters, white women gained little. In many states, widows' rights to their dower were, if anything, eroded in the years after the Revolution. In addition, states maintained the British system of coverture, a major impediment to married women's autonomy. Women continued to be excluded from juries and from legal training and thus were excluded from the male political culture that centered at the courthouse.

Most significantly, women in the new nation were denied the vote. Despite the revolutionary rhetoric of equality, the majority of the founding fathers believed that in a democratic republic only independent people should be permitted to vote, and independent people, by definition, owned property. Thus propertyless men and all women were excluded. In the case of women, however, exclusion was less a matter of property than of sex. Married or not, women were assumed to be dependent creatures by nature. The fleeting exception to this assumption was New Jersey, whose 1776 state constitution did not explicitly define the qualifications for voters, declaring only that "all inhabitants" who met certain property and residence requirements "shall be entitled to vote," thus technically permitting both white women and Blacks to vote. In the 1780s, some property-holding women seized the initiative and voted in local elections. A 1796 statute specifically excluded Black people of both sexes but reaffirmed white women's right to vote.

By 1800, however, criticism of women as voters in New Jersey had mounted. Some concern was voiced about occasional voting by wives and daughters who lived at home (and were thus not independent) and by men without property. When an 1807 referendum election revealed extensive fraud, the legislature moved to tighten suffrage requirements. All women were excluded on the grounds that they were easily manipulated by men. But at the same time, the state expanded suffrage to include propertyless white men and sons living at home, further emphasizing the different political stature of men and women.

The results in New Jersey lend credence to the conclusion that, while white men gained rights as a result of the Revolution, white women actually lost ground. After 1800, as states granted universal white male suffrage, women's exclusion from suffrage defined their political dependence and inequality more sharply than ever before. But to define women's experience solely in terms of their formal political and legal roles obscures other significant factors that shaped their lives. For many women, the revolutionary years sparked a political consciousness, one that encouraged women to move outside their preoccupations of home and family. At the same time, improvements in white women's education — the substantial number of revolutionary women's diaries and letters indicate that more women had become fully literate — helped to broaden women's vision and open some opportunities.

The move for improved education for both men and women accelerated after the war — for practical as well as ideological reasons. As the new nation began the long process of industrialization, its more complex economy required literacy and other skills. Formal education became more necessary as print replaced oral traditions. Americans also believed that the new republic required an educated, enlightened citizenry. For women, the interest in educational reform was linked to the civic good. Observers roundly criticized the type of education that elite white women most often received. Beyond basic literacy, women were taught domestic skills and refinements meant to enhance their position in the marriage market. But what sort of wife and mother could such a poorly educated woman become? The image of flighty women concerned primarily with fashion and sentimental novels seemed especially out of step with the expectations of the new nation.

Critics who addressed the issue of women's education at length included Mercy Otis Warren, Judith Sargent Murray, and Dr. Benjamin Rush. Although they challenged conventional assumptions that more fully educating women would make them less feminine and more discontented with their lot, these critics continued to recommend that women be educated primarily to remain within the domestic sphere. Most of the proponents of improved education for women articulated an ideology that historians have called **Republican Motherhood**, the idea that women had vital roles in educating their children for their duties as citizens. One notable advocate, Abigail Adams, wrote, "If we mean to have heroes, statesmen, and philosophers, we should have learned women. If much depends as is allowed upon the early education of youth and the first principles which are instilled take the deepest root, great benefit must arise from the literary accomplishments in women."[40] In addition to this emphasis on children, the ideology of the postrevolutionary years stressed that women's enlightened and virtuous influence on their husbands could contribute mightily to civic culture and order. (See Primary Sources: "Education and Republican Motherhood.")

The new thinking about women's education bore some fruit. Not only did some states, like Massachusetts in 1789, institute free elementary public schooling for all children, but academies and boarding schools specifically designed for middle-class and elite women proliferated in the North and eventually appeared in the South. Parents and educators expected that this enhanced education would, according to one historian, "allow women to instruct their sons in the principles of patriotism, to make their homes well-run havens of efficiency, to converse knowledgeably with their husbands on a variety of subjects, and to understand family

◆ **John Singleton Copley,** *Mercy Otis Warren* **(1763)**

The 1763 portrait by John Singleton Copley makes Mercy Otis Warren's high status quite clear. The picture also emphasizes her femininity. Contemporaries understood the nasturtiums entwined in her hands as symbols of fertility, and indeed she had given birth the year before she sat for this portrait and would have another child the following year. Through her prolific writing and elite social networks, Warren carried on an active political and intellectual life. She wrote plays and poetry and commented astutely on political questions of the day, such as the debate over ratification of the Constitution. Her 1805 *History of the Rise, Progress and Termination of the American Revolution*, a monumental three-volume work, reflected Warren's deep commitment to the cause of the Revolution and her hope for America's future as a repository of republican virtue. Consider Warren's bearing and pose in this portrait. What sort of personality is suggested? How does Copley reveal Warren as a woman of many accomplishments? *Photograph © 2022 Museum of Fine Arts, Boston. All rights reserved/ Bequest of Winslow Warren/Bridgeman Images.*

finance."[41] Rather than discouraging women from domestic pursuits, education was expected to improve their chances for a suitable and happy marriage. But many of the women educated at the new academies apparently were inspired to move beyond the household sphere. Some became writers, missionaries, or reformers, and a substantial number became teachers themselves, pursuing jobs that offered the earliest form of professional opportunity for American women. The ideology of Republican Motherhood and the educational reforms it inspired began a long process of expanded opportunities for white women. Eventually women would demand opportunities to learn as much as, and even alongside, men.

Women and Religion

In addition to the impact of new educational opportunities, religious communities and the continued influence of evangelical revivals offered important venues of expression for Black and white women living in the early republic. Two radical religious groups centered around charismatic women who broke dramatically with traditional female piety and gender conventions. After recovering from a serious illness in 1776, Jemima Wilkinson, a former Quaker, believed that she had been resurrected for the sole purpose of preaching repentance before the final days of judgment. Wilkinson traveled the Northeast, primarily in Rhode Island and Connecticut, attracting a host of devoted followers. Mother Ann Lee, a founder of the "Shaking Quakers," or **Shakers** (so named for the ecstatic dances that were part of their worship), styled herself as a preacher and prophet. In different ways, both of these remarkable women minimized their femaleness. Wilkinson dressed in male-style clothing and insisted on the gender-neutral title of Public Universal Friend. Followers consistently referred to the Friend with the pronouns "he" and "him." Mother Ann Lee required celibacy not only for herself but also for her followers. Lee's adamant denial of sexuality kept the issue of gender from undercutting her religious leadership.

In newer congregations, such as northern Baptist churches, white women, and some Black women as well, could vote to elect deacons and even "exhort," or act as a lay preacher. One of the more radical groups, the Separates, or Strict Congregationalists, explicitly affirmed women in their "just Right . . . to speak openly in the Church."[42] In the South, Quakers and the Separate Baptists permitted women official roles, appointing them as deaconesses and eldresses. A Baptist minister traveling in Virginia and the Carolinas in the early 1770s described the duties of the eldresses as "praying, and teaching at their [women's] separate assemblies; presiding there for maintenance of rules and government; consulting with sisters about matters of the church which concern them, and representing their sense thereof to the elders; attending at the unction of sick sisters; and at the baptism of women, that all may be done orderly."[43]

But none of the larger denominations accepted women as preachers equal to male ministers. In backcountry regions, some women may have been traveling preachers, but generally their roles, even in evangelical churches, were unofficial. Typically, they served as counselors. Women created informal religious groups, encouraging friends and families along the road to conversion. Sarah Osborn,

◆ *Jemima Wilkinson (The Public Universal Friend)* **(1844)**
This lithograph of the self-styled Public Universal Friend was based on a painting made by John L. D. Mathies in 1816 near the end of Wilkinson's life. The image conveys Wilkinson's lifelong adoption of men's clothing. After hearing the Friend preach in New Haven, Connecticut, one critical observer described Wilkinson in 1787 as wearing "a light cloth Cloke with a Cape like a Man's — Purple Gown, long sleeves to Wristbands — Mans shirt down to the Hands with neckband — purple handkerchief or Neckcloth tied around the neck like a man's — No Cap — Hair combed turned over & not long — wears a Watch — Man's Hat."[44] How does the artist present the preacher's gender in this portrait? Although Wilkinson's style of dress may have stemmed from the religious belief that it was possible to transcend sex, why else might Wilkinson have preferred male attire? *Library of Congress.*

a white woman of Newport, Rhode Island (not the same Sarah Osborn who participated in the Revolutionary War), organized a young women's religious society in 1737 that met more or less continuously for fifty years. In the 1760s, she expanded her focus and on Sunday evenings taught a group of Black people in her home. Although Osborn was criticized for usurping the role of male ministers, throughout her life she continued to exert considerable influence within her congregation, an experience shared by many women in evangelical churches throughout the country.

By 1800, white women's ability to be active in doctrinal disputes and matters of church discipline and procedures diminished. In northern Baptist churches, for example, women's public voices were increasingly silenced after the Revolution. As the Baptists matured as a religious denomination, a growing bureaucracy and a new emphasis on an educated ministry eroded women's position in favor of men. Establishing respectability for the church often meant controlling "disorderly" women. This shift in women's influence was accomplished despite the fact that women outnumbered men in the congregation almost two to one, yet another indication that the egalitarian spirit of the postrevolutionary era did not encompass white women.

This suppression of women's voices was not long-lived, however. Beginning around 1795, another series of revivals, loosely categorized as the **Second Great Awakening**, swept the nation in periodic waves, lasting through the 1830s. In the eighteenth century, women's role in evangelical religion paralleled their course in the public sphere, where the ideas formulated around Republican Motherhood articulated a civic role for patriotic women that was only partially realized. Yet both evangelical religion and Republican Motherhood formed an important rationale for women's expanding roles in a wide range of benevolent and reform associations, other areas of informal public space that white and free Black women claimed as their own in the nineteenth century.

The religious ferment that so powerfully affected white women also touched the lives of many enslaved Black women. A wide diversity of religious practices existed among the enslaved population of the early American republic. By the late eighteenth century, a minority of African-born elders lived alongside a younger American-born majority. In certain regions, such as the Lowcountry Sea Islands, some families continued to practice Islam, brought with them from West Africa. Although poorly documented, ritual practices of West African and Kongo-Angolan ancestors also persisted in areas with large enslaved populations. Women played significant roles in such religious expression, often serving as healers, mediums, or priestesses.

In addition, both free and enslaved Blacks continued to adopt Christianity by infusing their theology and worship practice with West African–influenced elements, creating a distinctive religious style. Some scholars suggest that the evangelical emphasis on spontaneous conversion harmonized with West African beliefs that "the deity entered the body of the devotee and displaced his or her personality."[45] In turn, African influences — especially dances and ring shouts typical of West African religious rituals — influenced the shape of white evangelicalism. Black women were highly visible in their communities of worship. They consistently made up the majority of congregants in Baptist and Methodist churches of Virginia in the 1790s, for example. Barred from being ordained formally as preachers, Black women made their voices heard in Black and interracial evangelical meetings through personal testimony and a form of spiritual encouragement known as "exhortation." In these ways, Black women were able to create a sphere of influence and spiritual power for themselves, roles that would assume even greater importance in the nineteenth century, as independent Black denominations emerged in the North and Black Christianity spread in the quarters of southern enslaved people.

◆ CONCLUSION: TO THE MARGINS OF POLITICAL ACTION

Whatever their social or racial group, women living on the eastern part of the continent in the late eighteenth century were affected by the imperial conflicts that eventually resulted in the founding of a new nation. Most women's activities were filtered through traditional expectations about their female roles: enslaved women tried to protect their children; Indigenous women maintained villages while men were at war; elite ladies sewed shirts for George Washington's army; poor women cooked for soldiers. Yet despite these traditional trajectories — and despite the fundamentally male character of eighteenth-century diplomacy, politics, economics, and warfare — women did exercise some choice in the revolutionary era. They acted politically when they decided to escape slavery by fleeing to the British, when they participated in their Indigenous councils' deliberations over alliances, or when they chose to be loyalists or patriots.

The revolutionary era's dramatic events affected women in widely varying ways. Enslaved women in the North benefited from gradual emancipation, while many in the South suffered from their owners' deepening commitment to the institution of slavery. Both free and enslaved Black women confronted a deepening racial ideology that defined citizenship as a white inheritance of the Revolution. Many Indigenous women saw their traditional roles erode under the pressures of assimilation, yet most scholars marvel at their resilience and adaptability. White women's positions became more limited in some respects, as white men's political rights expanded.

But if the Revolution did not prompt a deep-seated questioning of women's rights and roles, it did embody harbingers of change, especially for white women. The economic expansion of the new nation would lead to industrial development and an expanded presence of women in the paid workforce. The U.S. territorial expansion would not only promote western migration of white women and their families but also significantly affect Indigenous peoples and enslaved Blacks. In addition, revolutionary ideology, educational advancements, and the egalitarianism of the Great Awakening sowed the seeds for greater participation of middle-class and elite women in public life, not in politics per se, but in informal spheres of public spaces — churches, benevolent societies, and reform movements — which were to be such an important part of nineteenth-century American culture.

CHAPTER 3 REVIEW

KEY TERMS

First Great Awakening (p. 99)
"Liberty's Daughters" (p. 103)
Ladies Association of
  Philadelphia (p. 110)

Northwest Ordinance (p. 118)
deputy husbands (p. 121)
Republican Motherhood
  (p. 124)

Shakers (p. 126)
Second Great Awakening
  (p. 128)

REVIEW QUESTIONS

1. What were some of the factors leading to open conflict between Britain and its North American colonies? What forms of colonial resistance particularly depended on women's participation?

2. Discuss the various kinds of "profound disruptions and complex decisions" that the Revolutionary War brought to Anglo-American women colonists, enslaved and free Black women, and Indigenous women. What did "taking sides" mean for each of these groups of women?

3. What changes in free women's status during the late eighteenth century, if any, can be attributed to the legacy of the American Revolution? How was the shift from colony to nation significant for enslaved Black women? For Indigenous women? How did the impact of the Revolution on white, Black, and Indigenous women vary depending on geographic region?

4. **Making Connections** Between the 1750s and 1800s, how did women's gendered labor and relationship to the family change? Was the American Revolution a "revolution" for America's women? How did free versus enslaved status and colonist versus Indigenous identity matter in answering these questions?

SUGGESTED READING

General Works

Carol Berkin, *Revolutionary Mothers: Women in the Struggle for American Independence* (2005).

Edward Countryman, *Enjoy the Same Liberty: Black Americans and the Revolutionary Era* (2012).

Linda K. Kerber, *Women of the Republic: Intellect and Ideology in Revolutionary America* (1980).

Susan E. Klepp, *Revolutionary Conceptions: Women, Fertility, and Family Limitation in America, 1760–1820* (2010).

Mary Beth Norton, *Separated by Their Sex: Women in Public and Private in the Colonial Atlantic World* (2011).

Marylynn Salmon, *The Limits of Independence: American Women, 1760–1800* (1994).

Women and the American Revolution

Catherine Adams and Elizabeth H. Pleck, *Love of Freedom: Black Women in Colonial and Revolutionary New England* (2010).

Vincent Carretta, *Phillis Wheatley: Biography of a Genius in Bondage* (2014).

Patricia Cleary, *Elizabeth Murray: A Woman's Pursuit of Independence in Eighteenth-Century America* (2000).

Linda Grant De Pauw, *Four Traditions: Women of New York during the American Revolution* (1974).

Elizabeth Ellett, *Women of the American Revolution*, 3 vols. (2015–2018).

Joan R. Gunderson, *To Be Useful to the World: Women in Revolutionary America, 1740–1790*, revised edition (2006).

Kate Haulman, *The Politics of Fashion in Eighteenth-Century America* (2011).

Cynthia Kierner, *Beyond the Household: Women's Place in the Early South, 1700–1835* (1998).

Charlene M. Boyer Lewis, *Women in George Washington's World* (2022).

Mary Beth Norton, *Liberty's Daughters: The Revolutionary Experience of American Women, 1750–1800* (1980).

Barbara Oberg, ed., *Women in the American Revolution: Gender, Politics and the Domestic World* (2022).

Alfred F. Young, *Masquerade: The Life and Times of Deborah Sampson, Continental Soldier* (2004).

Revolutionary Legacies for Women

Norma Basch, *Framing American Divorce: From the Revolutionary Generation to the Victorians* (1999).

Catherine A. Brekus, *Strangers and Pilgrims: Female Preaching in America, 1740–1845* (1998).

Erica Armstrong Dunbar, *Never Caught: The Washingtons' Relentless Pursuit of Their Runaway Slave, Ona Judge* (2017).

Kathleen DuVal, *Independence Lost: Lives on the Edge of the American Revolution* (2016).

Sylvia R. Frey and Betty Wood, *Come Shouting to Zion: African-American Protestantism in the American South and British Caribbean to 1830* (1998).

Cassandra Good, *Founding Friendships: Friendships between Men and Women in the Early American Republic* (2017).

Susan Juster, *Disorderly Women: Sexual Politics and Evangelicalism in Revolutionary New England* (1994).

Linda K. Kerber, *No Constitutional Right to Be Ladies: Women and the Obligation of Citizenship* (1998).

Lester D. Langley, *The Long American Revolution and Its Legacy* (2019).

Lucia McMahon, *Mere Equals: The Paradox of Educated Women in the Early American Republic* (2012).

Jessica Millward, *Finding Charity's Folks: Enslaved and Free Black Women in Maryland* (2015).

Paul B. Moyer, *The Public Universal Friend: Jemima Wilkinson and Religious Enthusiasm in Revolutionary America* (2015).

Theda Perdue, *Cherokee Women: Gender and Culture Change, 1700–1835* (1998).

PRIMARY SOURCES

Gendering Images of the Revolution

IN ADDITION TO THE REPRESENTATIONS OF American women contained in the portraits of the late eighteenth century are a variety of other images specifically connected to the American Revolution. Many of these — whether paintings or cartoons — had propagandistic purposes. Few portray actual women and instead render females as abstractions, often as icons of "Liberty."

Englishmen on both sides of the Atlantic often ridiculed women's interest in fashion and represented them as weak-minded and frivolous. These negative stereotypes about women took on propagandistic value in Figure 3.1, "A Society

◆ **Figure 3.1** *A Society of Patriotic Ladies* (1774)
Library of Congress Prints and Photographs Division, Washington, D.C. (LC-USZ62-12711).

of Patriotic Ladies." This British cartoon was created as a response to the fifty-one women of Edenton, North Carolina, who signed a pledge in 1774 to uphold the boycotts against British goods. By depicting fashionable women neglecting their children (note the child on the floor being licked by a dog) and acting in unfeminine ways (note the grotesque woman with the gavel), the cartoon devalues the boycott and American women at the same time.

Consider the choices of the cartoonist. Why do you think he decided to include a Black servant in his drawing? Why did he depict the woman in the center being fondled by a man?

A number of images of women holding muskets circulated during the revolutionary era. Scholars think that the 1770 drawing in Figure 3.2 was modeled after a 1750 woodcut of Hannah Snell, an Englishwoman who had joined the British Navy in 1745. Though *Miss Fanny's Maid* predates the outbreak of fighting, it reflects the disruptive atmosphere of Boston in the 1770s. The American illustration was probably not intended to refer to a specific woman bearing arms; the story of Deborah Sampson was not made public until 1781, for example (see "Maintaining the Troops: The Women Who Served"). What do you think might have been the purpose of this image for revolutionary propagandists?

The tendency to depict women as abstractions was most evident in the widespread popularity of images of "Liberty." The convention of using a stylized woman to represent political virtues such as liberty or justice was a long-standing one in Western European art, though, as one historian explains, "the female form [of liberty] does not refer to particular women, does not describe women as a group, and often does not even presume to evoke their natures."[46] Instead, this idealized image was intended to embody the principles for which men were fighting.

During the 1770s, the American colonies were sometimes personified as an Indigenous woman, as in Figure 3.3, "The Female Combatants." This hand-colored engraving by an unknown artist appeared in January 1776, the same month in which Thomas Paine published *Common Sense*. Decoding the image, which portrayed the conflict between Britain and the North American colonies as a lively fistfight between women,

◆ Figure 3.2 *Miss Fanny's Maid* (1770)
Courtesy, American Antiquarian Society/Bridgeman Images.

◆ Figure 3.3 *The Female Combatants* (1776)
Courtesy of The Lewis Walpole Library, Yale University.

requires attention to both words and material objects. Begin with the speech bubbles. How does the artist use sexual insult and familial relations ("Rebellious Slut" and "Mother") to comment on political resistance to Britain? Next, move to the visual symbolism. What is the meaning of the white Mother Britain's aristocratic dress? Why is America portrayed as a bare-breasted Indigenous woman? Note the Phrygian liberty cap on America's tree (look for this ancient icon elsewhere in this document set). The combatants' shield and banner slogans also differ. The shield on the left holds a compass pointing north, while the one on the right depicts a Gallic rooster, symbol of France. The banners juxtapose British "Obedience" with American "Liberty." A historian who has analyzed the image asks, "Does the artist believe Britain holds the moral right; does the cartoon display America's winning ideology?"[47] How would you answer this question using specific evidence from the image?

An alternative rendering of a female version of Liberty appeared in the well-known painter Edward Savage's engraving *Liberty in the Form of the Goddess of Youth Giving Support to the Bald Eagle*, created in 1796. In Figure 3.4, the youthful Liberty, clad in white with a garland of flowers, nourishes an eagle, who symbolizes the Republic. In the background is the flag of the union with a liberty cap. At the bottom right, lightning surrounds the British fleet in the Boston harbor. Crushed under Liberty's feet are symbols of the British monarchy: a key, a broken scepter, and the garter of a royal order. This version of Liberty was so popular that it was reproduced in many forms — including needlework — well into the nineteenth century. Why do you think Savage depicts Liberty as a "goddess of youth"? Why was the image so popular with Americans?

A somewhat unusual depiction of a female Liberty had more radical political meaning than most versions. Figure 3.5 suggests the way in which revolutionary ideology ignited questions about women's and enslaved people's freedom. *Liberty Displaying the Arts and Sciences*, by Samuel Jennings (1792), was initially

◆ **Figure 3.4 Edward Savage,** *Liberty in the Form of the Goddess of Youth Giving Support to the Bald Eagle* **(1796)**
Library of Congress Prints and Photographs Division, Washington, D.C. (LC-USZ62-15369).

◆ **Figure 3.5** Samuel Jennings, *Liberty Displaying the Arts and Sciences* (1792)
GRANGER — Historical Picture Archive.

suggested by the artist himself to the Library Company of Philadelphia, an institution founded by Benjamin Franklin and others in 1731. The directors specifically asked Jennings to portray a tableau of "Liberty (with her Cap and proper Insignia) displaying the arts by some of the most striking Symbols of Painting, Architecture, Mechanics, Astronomy, &ca. whilst She appears in the attitude of placing on the top of a Pedestal, a pile of Books, lettered with, *Agriculture, Commerce,*

Philosophy & Catalogue of Philadelphia Library.[48] The directors, many of whom were active antislavery advocates, also requested the inclusion of Blacks and the symbolic broken chains. In the image, Liberty is offering a book to the grateful African Americans. Examine the images associated with Liberty. What do they suggest? What did the library directors hope to convey in combining a depiction of Liberty, books, and freed Blacks?

ANALYZING PRIMARY SOURCES

1. How do these diverse images of women contribute to our understanding of how gender shaped the experience of the American Revolution?

2. The images presented here have propagandistic purposes. What do these images suggest about the roles that gender and sexuality play in conceptualizing both war aims and patriotic service?

3. How can historians analyze these propagandistic images in the effort to reconstruct the actual experiences of women in the revolutionary era?

PRIMARY SOURCES

Phillis Wheatley, Enslaved Poet

Eighteenth-century American women left behind far more written material than those in the seventeenth century; we have diaries, letters, essays, wills, and books to help us flesh out the lives of many women, especially educated white women. The experiences of individual Black women are far more obscure in the historical record, with the important exception of poet Phillis Wheatley (c. 1753–1784). At age seven or eight, Wheatley made a terrifying passage from the Senegambia region of West Africa to Boston in the hold of her namesake, the slave ship *Phillis*; nearly a quarter of her fellow captives died along the way. In Boston she was purchased by John and Susannah Wheatley, who, informed by their own expectations of African intellectual inferiority, were immediately impressed with her precociousness. "Without any Assistance from School Education, and by only what she was taught in the Family, she, in sixteen Months Times from her Arrival, attained the English Language, to which she was an utter Stranger before, to such a Degree, as to read any, the most difficult Parts of the Sacred Writings, to the great Astonishment of all who heard her."[49] The Wheatleys, especially Susannah and her daughter Mary, took pride in Phillis's learning but also in her quick and deeply felt conversion to Protestantism. Their own evangelical beliefs, reflecting the First Great Awakening sweeping through the colonies, made them open to the notion of Blacks' spiritual equality and led them to encourage Wheatley's religious and intellectual gifts.

Phillis Wheatley began writing poetry as early as 1765 and apparently published her first poem in 1767 at age fourteen. By 1772, she had attempted, with the help of Susannah Wheatley and other sponsors, to publish a book of collected works in Boston. When that venture failed, she found a publisher in London and had the opportunity to accompany the son of her owner to London, where she was able to complete the arrangements for *Poems on Various Subjects, Religious and Moral* (1773).

Figure 3.6, a portrait of Phillis Wheatley, was commissioned as the frontispiece for her book. John and Susannah had sent Phillis's poems to the London bookseller Archibald Bell. He in turn had taken them to an antislavery noblewoman, the Countess of Huntington, to receive permission for Wheatley to dedicate the book to her, a common practice designed to enhance a book's prestige. Huntington, enthusiastic about the poems, apparently asked for reassurance that the author was "*real*, without a deception." Perhaps to offer proof to future readers that Wheatley was indeed of African descent, the countess requested a picture of Wheatley for the frontispiece. The painting was executed by an enslaved artist, Scipio Moorhead, owned by a Boston minister, and sent to England for engraving.

Wheatley appreciated Moorhead's talents and wrote the following poem to "SM. a young *African* painter":

> To show the lab'ring bosom's deep intent,
> and thought in living characters to paint,
> When first thy pencil did those beauties give,
> And breathing figures learnt from thee to live,
> How did those prospects give my soul delight,
> A new creation rushing on my sight?
> Still, wond'rous youth! each noble path pursue,
> On deathless glories fix thine ardent view:
> Still may the painter's and the poet's fire
> To aid thy pencil, and thy verse conspire![50]

Why do you think Wheatley was so pleased by the portrait? What details in the image convey Wheatley's literacy and authorship? Why do you suppose the painting includes the information that Wheatley was "servant to Mr. John Wheatley"?

Shortly after Wheatley became a published author, her owners granted her freedom. Wheatley continued to write, undeterred by such life-changing events as the deaths of her former owners, Susannah Wheatley in 1774 and John Wheatley in 1778, and her own marriage in 1778 to a free Black, John Peters. Her poems, such as one in honor of General George Washington, were published individually, but she failed to gain backing for her proposal, printed in the *Evening Post & General Advertiser* (1779), in which she described herself as a "female African" who sought subscriptions to print a second book of poems and letters to be dedicated to Benjamin Franklin. Other disappointments followed. Toward the end of her life, she worked as a scrubwoman in a boardinghouse. Two of her children died, and she and her third baby died of complications in childbirth on December 8, 1784.

Because of the profoundly religious content of much of her work, Wheatley's poetry was warmly received by evangelical Protestants, both in England and in America. Apparently some slaveholders read

◆ Figure 3.6 **Scipio Moorhead,** ***Phillis Wheatley*** **(1773)**
GRANGER — Historical Picture Archive.

Wheatley's poems to the people they enslaved to encourage their conversion. Opponents of slavery also welcomed the poet's work, viewing her as proof of the humanity and capabilities of Africans and therefore useful evidence in their campaigns against both slavery and the slave trade.

LETTERS

Twenty-two of Wheatley's letters have survived. The first one, printed below, is to a Black friend, Arbour Tanner, a servant to James Tanner in Newport, Rhode Island, who shared Wheatley's religious ardor. The letter refers to a frequent theme in the poet's work: the conversion of her fellow Africans. What is the purpose of Wheatley's letter to Tanner? How might her abduction from Africa as a child have informed her views of her land of birth as a place of "darkness"?

To Arbour Tanner

Boston May 19th 1772

Dear Sister

I rec'd your favour of February 6th for which I give you my sincere thanks, I greatly rejoice with you in that realizing view, and I hope experience, of the Saving change which you So emphatically describe. Happy were it for us if we could arrive to that evangelical Repentance, and the true holiness of heart which you mention. Inexpressibly happy Should we be could we have a due Sense of the Beauties and excellence of the Crucified Saviour. In his Crucifixion may be seen marvellous displays of Grace and Love, Sufficient to draw and invite us to the rich and endless treasures of his mercy, let us rejoice in and adore the wonders of God's infinite Love in bringing us from a land Semblant of darkness itself, and where the divine light of revelation (being obscur'd) is as darkness. Here, the knowledge of the true God and eternal life are made manifest; But there, profound ignorance overshadows the Land, Your observation is true, namely that there was nothing in us to recommend us to God. Many of our fellow creatures are pass'd by, when the bowels of divine love expanded towards us. May this goodness & long Suffering of God lead us to unfeign'd repentance.

It gives me very great pleasure to hear of so many of my Nation, Seeking with eagerness the way to true felicity, O may we all meet at length in that happy mansion. I hope the correspondence between us will continue, (my being much indispos'd this winter past was the reason of my not answering yours before now) which correspondence I hope may have the happy effect of improving our mutual friendship. Till we meet in the regions of consummate blessedness, let us endeavor by the assistance of divine grace, to live the life, and we Shall die the death of the Righteous. May this be our happy case and of those who are travelling to the region of Felicity is the earnest request of your affectionate

Friend & hum. Sert. Phillis Wheatley

SOURCE: Julian D. Mason Jr., ed., *The Poems of Phillis Wheatley* (Chapel Hill: University of North Carolina, 1989), 190.

THE FOLLOWING LETTER, to Rev. Samson Occom, a Mohegan and Presbyterian minister, was published in the *Connecticut Gazette; and the Universal Intelligencer* on March 11, 1774, and widely reprinted. Written after Wheatley had gained freedom, it is her most critical statement about slavery. What is the essence of her criticism? To whom is she referring in the phrase "our modern Egyptians"?

To Rev. Samson Occom

Rev'd and honor'd Sir,

I have this Day received your obliging kind Epistle, and am greatly satisfied with your Reasons respecting the Negroes, and think highly reasonable what you offer in Vindication of their natural Rights: Those that invade them cannot be insensible that the divine Light is chasing away the thick Darkness which broods over the Land of Africa; and the Chaos which has reign'd long, is converting into beautiful Order, and [r]eveals more and more clearly the glorious Dispensation of civil and religious Liberty, which are so insep[a]rably united, that there is little or no Enjoyment of one without the other. Otherwise, perhaps, the Israelites had been less solicitous for their Freedom from Egyptian slavery; I do not say they would have been contented without it, by no means, for in every human Breast, God has implanted a Principle which we call Love of Freedom; it is impatient of Oppression and pants for Deliverance; and by the Leave of our modern Egyptians I will assert, that the same Principle lives in us. God grant Deliverance in his own Way and Time and get him honour upon all those whose Avarice impels them to countenance and help forward the Calamities of their fellow Creatures. This desire not for their Hurt, but to convince them of the strange Absurdity of their Conduct whose Words and Actions are so diametrically opposite. How well the Cry for Liberty, and the reverse Disposition for the exercise of oppressive Power over others agree, — I humbly think it does not require the Penetration of a Philosopher to determine.

SOURCE: Mason, *Poems of Phillis Wheatley*, 203–4.

POEMS

OVER FIFTY OF WHEATLEY'S POEMS have survived. They encompass a wide range of topics, from elegies to thoughts "On Virtue," from religious commentaries to a patriotic ode to George Washington. With references to Africa, Africans, and slavery, her poetry insists on the humanity of Africans and makes criticisms — sometimes veiled — of slavery.

On the surface, this 1772 poem seems to adopt white Christians' condescension toward "pagan" Africans, but what does the final line suggest? Is it possible to read this troubling poem as Wheatley's challenge to biological theories of white superiority?

On Being Brought from Africa to America

'Twas mercy brought me from my *Pagan* land,
Taught my benighted soul to understand
That there's a God, that there's a *Saviour* too:
Once I redemption neither sought nor knew.
Some view our sable race with scornful eye,

"Their colour is a diabolic die."
Remember, *Christians*, Negroes, black as Cain,
May be refin'd, and join th' angelic train.

———————————

SOURCE: Mason, *Poems of Phillis Wheatley*, 53.

THE FOLLOWING POEM, addressed to the British secretary of state for North America, was written in a period when tensions had eased — temporarily — between the colonies and the mother country, hence Wheatley's statement in the second stanza about grievances being addressed. The poem reveals not only her sensitivity to the political turmoil of the period but also her understanding of the parallels between the colonists' desire to resist British "enslavement" and her own people's experience of slavery. What does she seem to be asking Lord Dartmouth for in the final stanza?

To the Right Honourable William, Earl of Dartmouth, His Majesty's Principal Secretary of State for North America

HAIL, happy day when, smiling like the morn,
Fair *Freedom* rose *New-England* to adorn:
The northern clime beneath her genial ray,
Dartmouth, congratulates thy blissful sway:
Elate with hope her race no longer mourns,
Each soul expands, each grateful bosom burns,
While in thine hand with pleasure we behold
The silken reins, and *Freedom's* charms unfold.
Long lost to realms beneath the northern skies
She shines supreme, while hated *faction* dies:
Soon as appear'd the *Goddess* long desir'd,
Sick at the view, she languish'd and expir'd;
Thus from the splendors of the morning light
The owl in sadness seeks the caves of night.
No more, *America*, in mournful strain
Of wrongs, and grievance unredress'd complain,
No longer shalt thou dread the iron chain,

Which wanton *Tyranny* with lawless hand
Had made, and with it meant t' enslave the land.
Should you, my lord, while you peruse my song,
Wonder from whence my love of Freedom sprung,
Whence flow these wishes for the common good,
By feeling hearts alone best understood,
I, young in life, by seeming cruel fate
Was snatch'd from *Afric's* fancy'd happy seat:
What pangs excruciating must molest,
What sorrows labour in my parent's breast?
Steel'd was that soul and by no misery mov'd
That from a father seiz'd his babe belov'd:
Such, such my case. And can I then but pray
Others may never feel tyrannic sway?
For favours past, great Sir, our thanks are due,
And thee we ask thy favours to renew,
Since in thy pow'r, as in thy will before,

To sooth the griefs, which thou did'st once deplore.
May heav'nly grace the sacred sanction give
To all thy works, and thou for ever live
Not only on the wings of fleeting *Fame*,
Though praise immortal crowns the patriot's name,
But to conduct to heav'ns refulgent fane,

May fiery coursers sweep th' ethereal plain,
And bear thee upwards to that blest abode,
Where, like the prophet, thou shalt find thy God.

———————

SOURCE: Mason, *Poems of Phillis Wheatley*, 82–83.

ANALYZING PRIMARY SOURCES

1. What do these selections of Wheatley's poems and letters reveal about the importance and role of religion in her life?

2. What are the grounds for her criticism of slavery?

3. How might opponents of slavery have used her poetry to criticize the institution?

4. How did Wheatley use both her image and her writing to challenge prevailing ideas about racial difference and African intellect?

Education and Republican Motherhood

FOR MUCH OF THE COLONIAL PERIOD, women's opportunities for education were quite limited. A small number of enslaved women received lessons from their owners, particularly by Quakers, and some Indigenous women had access to missionary schools, where the emphasis was on assimilation rather than education. Elite women sometimes had private tutors. Most other white women had little formal schooling, and their training usually emphasized domestic skills with a smattering of reading and sums. By the time of the Revolution in New England, 90 percent of white men could write, while fewer than half of white women could.

The Revolution and its aftermath ushered in significant changes. Outside the South, where public schools were rare, primary public education for white women and men became more common. Women's opportunities for higher education — while not universally endorsed — also expanded. While some of the most famous schools, like Philadelphia's Young Ladies Academy, were in urban areas, educational entrepreneurs also established them in small towns such as Litchfield, Connecticut, where Sarah Pierce's school attracted young women from throughout the region, as well as from other states. The Bethlehem, Pennsylvania, Moravian Seminary had special appeal for parents eager to give their daughters a rigorous education; in addition to academic subjects, the school encouraged its students' industry and moral development. While the new schools still offered ornamental skills such as needlework and dancing, they emphasized academic subjects such as history, grammar, math, geography, logic, and philosophy.

The post-Revolution improvement in northern white women's education was in part a product of the efforts of reformers, who eagerly promoted the idea that in a republic, all citizens needed education to contribute to the general public good. In keeping with the ideas associated with Republican Motherhood (see "White Women: Pacifists, Tories, and Patriots"), supporters of women's education argued that mothers needed to be well educated to prepare their children, especially their sons, for their duties as citizens. Advocates also emphasized the importance of women's moral influence on their husbands and other family members. While a number of people called for women's education, including Mercy Otis Warren and Sarah Pierce, two of the most significant were Dr. Benjamin Rush and Judith Sargent Murray.

BENJAMIN RUSH SIGNED the Declaration of Independence and was the pre-eminent physician and medical teacher of the revolutionary era. His essay *Thoughts upon Female Education* reflects both increased expectations as well as the limits to new ideas about women's education. The curriculum he promoted included geography, bookkeeping, reading, and arithmetic and omitted the traditional female accomplishment of needlework. But he did not recommend that women study advanced mathematics, natural philosophy, or Latin or Greek, subjects that remained hallmarks of educated men. Rush and most other reformers emphasized the utilitarian potential of an academic curriculum for women. Although Rush lectured to both men at the College of Philadelphia and women at the Young Ladies Academy on natural philosophy, his presentation for the latter — "Lectures, Containing the Application of the Principles of Natural Philosophy, and Chemistry to Domestic and Culinary Purposes" — was tailored to their perceived future roles. Still, Rush's views were progressive for his time, when many people felt that too much learning might "unsex" a woman and make her unfeminine.

The following selection is from an essay based on a speech Rush gave to the Board of Visitors of the Young Ladies Academy of Philadelphia in 1787. As you read, take note of Rush's major justifications for educating women.

BENJAMIN RUSH
Thoughts upon Female Education (1787)

There are several circumstances in the situation, employments and duties of women in America which require a peculiar mode of education.

I. The early marriages of our women, by contracting the time allowed for education, renders it necessary to contract its plan and to confine it chiefly to the more useful branches of literature.

II. The state of property in America renders it necessary for the greatest part of our citizens to employ themselves in different occupations for the advancement of their fortunes. This cannot be done without the assistance of the female members of the community. They must be the stewards and guardians of their husbands' property. That education, therefore, will be most proper for our women which teaches them to discharge the duties of those offices with the most success and reputation.

III. From the numerous avocations to which a professional life exposes gentlemen in America from their families, a principal share of the instruction of children naturally devolves upon the women. It becomes us therefore to prepare them, by a suitable education, for the discharge of this most important duty of mothers.

IV. The equal share that every citizen has in the liberty and the possible share he may have in the government of our country make it necessary that our ladies should be qualified to a certain degree, by a peculiar and suitable education, to concur in instructing their sons in the principles of liberty and government.

V. In Great Britain the business of servants is a regular occupation, but in America this humble station is the usual retreat of unexpected indigence; hence the servants in this country possess less knowledge and subordination than are required from them; and hence our ladies are obliged to attend more to the private affairs of their families than ladies generally do of the same rank in Great Britain. "They are good servants," said an American lady of distinguished merit . . .

in a letter to a favorite daughter, "who will do well with good looking after." This circumstance should have great influence upon the nature and extent of female education in America.

[Rush proceeds to discuss the most important "branches of literature most essential for a young lady in this country," in which he emphasizes "a knowledge of the English language," "the writing of a fair and legible hand," "some knowledge of figures and bookkeeping," so that she "may assist her husband with this knowledge," "an acquaintance with geography and some instruction in chronology [history]," vocal music and dancing, "the reading of history, travels, poetry, and moral essays," and the "regular instruction in the Christian religion."]

A philosopher once said, "let me make all the ballads of a country and I care not who makes its laws." He might with more propriety have said, let the ladies of a country be educated properly, and they will not only make and administer its laws, but form its manners and character. It would require a lively imagination to describe, or even

to comprehend the happiness of a country where knowledge and virtue were generally diffused among the female sex. . . .

The influence of female education would be still more extensive and useful in domestic life. The obligations of gentlemen to qualify themselves by knowledge and industry to discharge the duties of benevolence would be increased by marriage; and the patriot — the hero — and the legislator would find the sweetest reward of their toils in the approbation and applause of their wives. Children would discover the marks of maternal prudence and wisdom in every station of life, for it has been remarked that there have been few great or good men who have not been blessed with wife and prudent mothers.

SOURCE: Benjamin Rush, *Thoughts upon Female Education Accommodated to the Present State of Society, Manners, and Government, in the United States of America: Addressed to the Visitors of the Young Ladies' Academy in Philadelphia, 28 July, 1787, at the Close of the Quarterly Examination* (Philadelphia: Printed by Prichard & Hall, 1787).

ALTHOUGH JUDITH SARGENT MURRAY (1751–1820), the daughter of a distinguished and wealthy Gloucester, Massachusetts, family, also believed in the tenets of Republican Motherhood, she was far more radical than Rush in her approach to women's capabilities and needs. Murray's parents denied her the extensive education that they provided for her brother, but she was a voracious reader of both American and European writers. A contemporary of the English historian Catharine Macaulay and the English women's rights activist Mary Wollstonecraft, Murray was an early American proponent of women's rights and an accomplished writer. Intensely religious, she had left the Puritan fold for Universalism, a far more egalitarian faith that encouraged her to challenge traditional authority. Influenced by her religion as well as her frustration over her limited schooling, Murray was further energized by the ideas swirling around the American Revolution that led her to articulate her belief in men's and women's mental and spiritual equality. As she contemplated the themes of liberty, equality, and independence, she struggled with her own dependence.

After she was widowed in 1787, her second marriage in 1788, like her first, provided little financial security, and she was highly conscious of the legal and financial constraints on women. It is not surprising, then, that many of her essays call for an education that would help women to be self-reliant and even self-supporting. She pointed out that she would want her daughters to be taught "industry and order." They "should be enabled to procure for themselves the necessaries of life; independence should be placed within their grasp."[51] Unlike reformers such as Rush, who saw women's education primarily as a tool for promoting the family and the public good, Murray understood it as something contributing to women's independence, to a reverence of self. But she shared with more conventional reformers the assumption that most women would marry and have children and that women's improved education would make them better wives and virtuous Republican Mothers.

In 1782, Murray anonymously published her first work, a religious piece titled *Catechism*. By that time, however, she had already drafted a much more radical piece, "On the Equality of the Sexes," which appeared finally in the *Massachusetts Magazine* in 1790, under the pseudonym "Constantia." Although writing under pen names was a common eighteenth-century practice, Murray probably did so with a knowledge of how subversive it was for women to write publicly at all, let alone on political matters. In addition, her biographer suggests, she enjoyed the game of hiding her identity under multiple names and may have thought that the pseudonym helped readers to focus on the content of the piece rather than on the identity of the writer.[52] Murray began this essay with a poetic question for "the lordly sex." Why, she queried, do "they rob us of the power t' improve / And then declare we only trifles love"? She then went on to argue that if women's intellect was deficient, it was because of men's advantage in education, rather than birth. A good part of her essay, excerpted here, focuses on reason — a prominent theme in Enlightenment ideas about human intellectual abilities. What curriculum does Murray favor for girls' education? What consequences does she see for the inferior education women receive? In what sense is she arguing that women and men are equal? In what ways does this piece reflect Murray's upper-class identity?

Judith Sargent Murray
On the Equality of the Sexes (1790)

Is it upon mature consideration we adopt the idea, that nature is thus partial in her distributions? Is it indeed a fact, that she hath yielded to one half of the human species so unquestionable a mental superiority? I know that to both sexes elevated understandings, and the reverse, are common. But, suffer me to ask, in what the minds of females are so notoriously deficient, or unequal. . . .

Are we [women] deficient in reason? we can only reason from what we know, and if an opportunity of acquiring knowledge hath been denied us, the inferiority of our sex, cannot fairly be deduced from thence. . . . Yet it may be questioned, from what doth this superiority in this determining faculty of the soul, proceed. May we not trace its source in the difference of education, and continued advantages? Will it be said that the judgment of a male of two years old, is more sage than that of a female's of the same age? I believe the reverse is generally observed to be true. But from that period what partiality! how is the one exalted, and the other depressed, by the contrary modes of education which are adopted! the one is taught to aspire, and the other is early confined and limited. As their years increase, the sister must be wholly domesticated, while the brother is led by the hand through all the flowery paths of science. Grant that their minds are by nature equal, yet who shall wonder at the *apparent* superiority, if indeed custom becomes second nature; nay if it taketh place of nature, and that it doth the experience of each day will evince. At length arrived at womanhood, the uncultivated fair one feels a void, which the employments allotted her are by no means capable of filling. What can she do? to books she may not apply; or if she doth, *to those only of the novel kind*, lest she merit the appellation of a *learned* lady; and what ideas have been affixed to this term, the observation of many can testify. Fashion, scandal, and sometimes what is still more reprehensible, are then called in to her relief; and who can say to what lengths the liberties she takes may proceed. Meantime she herself is most unhappy; she feels the want of a cultivated mind. Is she single, she in vain seeks to fill up time from sexual employments or amusements. Is she united to a person whose soul nature made equal to her own, education hath set him so far above her, that in those entertainments which are productive of such rational felicity, she is not qualified to accompany him. She experiences a mortifying consciousness of inferiority, which embitters every enjoyment. Doth the person to whom her adverse fate hath consigned her, possess a mind incapable of improvement, she is equally wretched, in being so closely connected with an individual whom she cannot but despise. Now, was she permitted the same instructors as her brother, (with an eye however to their particular departments) for the employment of a rational mind an ample field would be opened. In astronomy she might catch a glimpse of the immensity of the Deity, and thence she would form amazing conceptions of the august and supreme Intelligence. In geography she would admire Jehovah in the midst of his benevolence; thus adapting this globe to the various wants and amusements of its inhabitants. In natural philosophy she would adore the infinite majesty of heaven, clothed in

condescension; and as she traversed the reptile world, she would hail the goodness of a creating God. A mind, thus filled, would have little room for the trifles with which our sex are, with too much justice, accused of amusing themselves, and they would thus be rendered fit companions for those, who should one day wear them as their crown. Fashions, in their variety, would then give place to conjectures, which might perhaps conduce to the improvement of the literary world; and there would be no leisure for slander or detraction. Reputation would not then be blasted, but serious speculations would occupy the lively imaginations of the sex. Unnecessary visits would be precluded, and that custom would only be indulged by way of relaxation, or to answer the demands of consanguinity and friendship. Females would become discreet, their judgments would be invigorated, and their partners for life being circumspectly chosen, an unhappy Hymen would then be as rare, as is now the reverse.*

Will it be urged that those acquirements would supersede our domestick duties. I answer that every requisite in female economy is easily attained; and, with truth I can add, that when once attained, they require no further *mental attention*. Nay, while we are pursuing the needle, or the superintendency of the family, I repeat, that our minds are at full liberty for reflection; that imagination may exert itself in full vigor; and that if a just foundation is early laid, our ideas will then be worthy of rational beings. If we were industrious we might easily find time to arrange them upon paper, or should avocations press too hard for such an indulgence, the hours allotted for conversation would at least become more refined and rational. Should it still be vociferated, "Your domestick employments are sufficient" — I would calmly ask, is it reasonable, that a candidate for immortality, for the joys of heaven, an intelligent being, who is to spend an eternity in contemplating the works of Deity, should at present be so degraded, as to be allowed no other ideas, than

---

* Hymen was the Greek god of marriage.

those which are suggested by the mechanism of a pudding, or the sewing the seams of a garment? Pity that all such censurers of female improvement do not go one step further, and deny their future existence; to be consistent they surely ought.

Yes, ye lordly, ye haughty sex, our souls are by nature *equal* to yours; the same breath of God animates, enlivens, and invigorates us; and that we are not fallen lower than yourselves, let those witness who have greatly towered above the various discouragements by which they have been so heavily oppressed; and though I am unacquainted with the list of celebrated characters on either side, yet from the observations I have made in the contracted circle in which I have moved, I dare confidently believe, that from the commencement of time to the present day, there hath been as many females, as males, who, by the *mere force of natural powers*, have merited the crown of applause; who, thus unassisted, have seized the wreath of fame. I know there are who assert, that as the animal powers of the one sex are superiour, of course their mental faculties also must be stronger; thus attributing strength of mind to the transient organization of this earth born tenement. But if this reasoning is just, man must be content to yield the palm to many of the brute creation, since by not a few of his brethren of the field, he is far surpassed in bodily strength. Moreover, was this argument admitted, it would prove too much, for occular demonstration evinceth, that there are many robust masculine ladies, and effeminate gentlemen. Yet I fancy that Mr. Pope,* though clogged with an enervated body, and distinguished by a diminutive stature, could nevertheless lay claim to greatness of soul; and perhaps there are many other instances which might be adduced to combat *so unphilosophical an opinion*. Do we not often see, that when the clay built tabernacle is well nigh dissolved, when it is just ready to mingle with the parent soil, the immortal inhabitant aspires to, and even attaineth heights the most sublime, and which were before wholly unexplored. Besides, were we to grant that animal strength proved any thing, taking into consideration the accustomed impartiality of nature, we should be induced to imagine, that she had invested the female mind with superiour strength as an equivalent for the bodily powers of man. But waving this however palpable advantage, for *equality only*, we wish to contend.

---

*"Mr. Pope" refers to Alexander Pope, an English poet and writer famous for such pieces as "An Essay on Man" (1733–1734) and "The Rape of the Lock" (1712).

SOURCE: Constantia [Judith Sargent Murray], "On the Equality of the Sexes," *Massachusetts Magazine; or Monthly Museum Containing the Literature, History, Politics, Arts, Manners and Amusements of the Age 2* (March 1790): 132–35 and (April 1790): 223–24.

ANALYZING PRIMARY SOURCES

1. What do Rush and Murray see as the benefits of female education? How does the proper education of females differ from that of males? Are there any differences between Rush's and Murray's arguments?

2. What do Rush and Murray assume about the abilities of females?

3. How do Rush's and Murray's ideas accord with the ideas associated with Republican Motherhood?

4

Pedestal, Loom, and Auction Block

1800–1860

LUCY LARCOM SPENT HER TEENAGE YEARS as a mill worker in the new factory town of Lowell, Massachusetts, on the Merrimack River. In 1835, at the age of eleven, she had moved to Lowell with her widowed mother, who had taken a job as manager of one of the company-owned board-inghouses to support herself and her children. For Lucy, working in the textile factory, a "rather select industrial school for young people," was the formative experience of her life, and she carried the memory into her future career as a poet and writer.[1] She loved doing work that was significant to the larger society and wrote of "the pleasure we found in making new acquaintances among our workmates." But in later years, she became uneasy with the condescension toward her humble past as a factory girl. "It is the first duty of every woman to recognize the mutual bond of universal womanhood," Larcom wrote in her memoirs. "Let her ask herself whether she would like to hear herself or her sister spoken of as a shopgirl or a factory-girl or a servant-girl, if necessity had compelled her for a time to be employed."[2]

Larcom's experiences embodied two of the three crucial elements shaping the lives of women in the United States during the first half of the nineteenth century. First, she subscribed to the influential ideology of womanhood, home life, and gender relations that treated women as fundamentally different from men; this ideology placed women on a pedestal, simultaneously elevated and isolated by their special domestic role. Second, Larcom was participating in the first wave of American industrialization, a process that dramatically redirected the young nation's economy and created new dimensions of wealth and poverty, new levels of production and consumption, and new ways of life. Historians tend to identify these two elements with two different and emerging classes — domestic ideology with the middle class, industrialization with the working class — but through the eyes of women like Lucy Larcom, it is possible to see that they were mutually influential.

The very cotton fibers that mill girls like Larcom spun and wove symbolize the third major element considered in this chapter: slavery. By the nineteenth century, slavery was a southern social, cultural, and economic system but one with profound national implications. Slavery was of incomparable importance to American women in the antebellum (pre–Civil War) years, not only to enslaved people and those who lived by or profited from unfree labor, but also to those who dedicated themselves to ending slavery and, ultimately, to all who would endure the devastating conflict fought over it.

◆ THE IDEOLOGY OF TRUE WOMANHOOD

Lucy Larcom's concern with the implications of her factory years for her character as a woman reflects a powerful ideology of gender roles that historians have variously labeled **"the cult of true womanhood,"** "the ideology of separate spheres," or simply "domesticity." This system of ideas, which took hold in the early years of the nineteenth century just as the United States was coming into its own as an independent nation, treated men and women as complete and absolute opposites, with almost no common human traits that transcended the differences of gender. The ideology of true womanhood also saw the larger society as carved into complementary but mutually exclusive "spheres" of public and private concerns, work and home life, politics and family. "In no country has such constant care been taken as in America to trace two clearly distinct lines of action for the two sexes," exaggerated Alexis de Tocqueville, the French observer of American culture in the 1830s. "American women never manage the outward concerns of the family, or conduct a business, or take a part in political life; nor are they, on the other hand, ever compelled to perform the rough labor of the fields, or to make any of those laborious exertions, which demand the exertion of physical strength. No families are so poor, as to form an exception to this rule."[3]

151

The experience of innumerable women in antebellum America — the enslaved women of the South, the mill girls of the North, the impoverished widows of the new cities, the rising number of female immigrants, even the hardworking farm wives — contradicted these assertions. Yet no aspect of this complex reality seemed to interfere with the widespread conviction that this gender ideology was "true." The challenge of understanding American women's history in the first half of the nineteenth century is to reconcile the extraordinary hegemony — that is, breadth and power — of the ideology of separate spheres with the wide variety of American women's lives in these years, many of which tell a very different story.

Christian Motherhood

An ideology as culturally widespread as that of true womanhood is difficult to reduce to a set of beliefs, but several basic concepts do stand out. First and foremost, proponents situated true women in an exclusively domestic realm of home, family, and childrearing. They considered housewifery and childrearing not as work but as an effortless expression of women's feminine natures. Action and leadership were reserved for man; inspiration and assistance were woman's province. The home over which women presided was not merely a residence or a collection of people but, to use a popular phrase, "a haven in a heartless world," where men could find solace from a grueling public existence. "The perfection of womanhood . . . is the wife and mother, the center of the family, that magnet that draws man to the domestic altar, that makes him a civilized being, a social Christian," proclaimed the popular women's magazine *Godey's Lady's Book* in 1860. "The wife is truly the light of the home."[4]

At the core of the idea of woman's sphere was motherhood. This basic contention was present in late eighteenth-century rhetoric about the importance of Republican Motherhood to the success of the American democratic experiment (see "Limited Citizenship: White Women's Legal Status and Education" in Chapter 3). In stark contrast to the self-serving individualism expected of men and rewarded by economic advancement in the larger world, proponents of true womanhood described motherhood as a wholly selfless activity built around service to others. Oddly enough, given the importance that American political culture placed on independence of character, maternal selflessness was seen as the very source of national well-being, training citizens of the new nation to be virtuous, concerned with the larger good, and yet industrious and self-disciplined. Even women without children could bestow their motherly instincts on society's unloved and ignored unfortunates. "Woman's great mission is to train immature, weak and ignorant creatures, to obey the laws of God," preached author and domestic ideologue Catharine Beecher in one of her many treatises on true womanhood, "first in the family, then in the school, then in the neighborhood, then in the nation, then in the world."[5] Beecher herself was unmarried and childless (see Reading into the Past: "The Peculiar Responsibilities of the American Woman").

Women's expansive maternity was thought to make them natural teachers and underlay the feminization of this profession in the early nineteenth century.

◆ **Teaching the Scriptures:**
The Religious Souvenir **(1839)**
Edited by Lydia H. Sigourney,
The Religious Souvenir collected
devotional poems and stories
for Christian readers. This
engraving of a mother and
daughter studying the Bible
vividly conveys the ideals of
domesticity and piety at the
heart of white women's true
womanhood. Fine furniture,
clothing, and decorative objects
also reflect the increased
consumer activity of the
middle-class home. A Romantic
landscape fills the background,
while abundant foliage inside
and out suggests the woman's
fertility and the child's growth
under her tutelage. *Harvard
University Libraries.*

Whereas in the eighteenth century teaching was seen as a fundamentally male vocation, by the nineteenth century women were increasingly regarded as best suited to instruct the young, and primary school teaching became an overwhelmingly female occupation. Especially in New England, public education was becoming widespread, and classrooms were staffed by young Yankee women, literate but less expensive to hire than men. By one estimate, one-quarter of all white women born in New England between 1825 and 1860 were schoolteachers at some point in their lives.[6]

Women's motherly vocation had a deeply religious dimension. True womanhood was a fervently Christian notion, which gave a redemptive power to female devotion and selfless sacrifice. The true woman functioned as Christ's representative in daily life, and the domestic environment over which she presided served as a sort of sacred territory, where evil and worldly influences could be cleansed away. Beecher insisted that "the preparation of young ministers for the duties of the church does not surpass in importance the training of the minister of the nursery and school-room."[7]

The special identification of women with Christian piety was firmly established by a new wave of religious revivals that swept through American society in the late eighteenth and early nineteenth centuries. Beginning in the frontier communities of Ohio, Kentucky, and Indiana, the **Second Great Awakening** moved

READING INTO THE PAST

CATHARINE BEECHER
The Peculiar Responsibilities of the American Woman

In the first chapter of A Treatise on Domestic Economy *(1841), a book devoted to the details of childrearing and homemaking, author and domestic ideologue Catharine Beecher (1800–1878) elaborates her theory of American democracy and women's place in it. She insists that women's inclusion in the American promise of equality is completely compatible with the subordination that she believed was divinely ordained in wives' relations to their husbands.*

In this Country, it is established, both by opinion and by practice, that woman has an equal interest in all social and civil concerns; and that no domestic, civil, or political, institution, is right, which sacrifices her interest to promote that of the other sex. But in order to secure her the more firmly in all these privileges, it is decided, that, in the domestic relation, she take a subordinate station, and that, in civil and political concerns, her interests be intrusted to the other sex, without her taking any part in voting, or in making and administering laws. . . . In matters pertaining to the education of their children, in the selection and support of a clergy-man, in all benevolent enterprises, and in all questions relating to morals or manners, [women] have a superior influence. In such concerns, it would be impossible to carry a point, contrary to their judgement and feelings; while an enterprise, sustained by them, will seldom fail of success.

If those who are bewailing themselves over the fancied wrongs and injuries of women in this Nation, could only see things as they are,

east by the 1810s and 1820s. Western New York was known as the "burned-over district" because of the zealous religiosity that swept through it in these years. Conveyed by preachers inspired by personal spiritual conviction rather than theological training, religious fervor especially thrived outside large cities. In the South, Blacks and whites were drawn together in similar extended revivals. A cultural phenomenon with many different sources, the Second Great Awakening was a reaction both to the political preoccupations of the revolutionary period and to swift changes in the American economic system. This religious revivalism also had a populist element, as it bypassed established clerical authority in favor of more direct spiritual experience among the broad mass of the American people.

they would know, that . . . there is nothing reasonable, which American women would unite in asking, that would not readily be bestowed. . . . To us [Americans] is committed the grand, the responsible privilege, of exhibiting to the world, the beneficent influences of Christianity. . . . But the part to be enacted by American women, in this great moral enterprise, is the point to which special attention should here be directed. . . . The proper education of a man decides the welfare of an individual; but educate a woman, and the interests of the whole family are secured. . . .

The woman, who is rearing a family of children; the woman, who labors in the schoolroom; the woman, who, in her retired chamber, earns, with her needle, the mite, which contributes to the intellectual and moral elevation of her Country; even the humble domestic, whose example and influence may be moulding and forming young minds, while her faithful services sustain a prosperous domestic state; — each and all may be animated by the consciousness, that they are agents in accomplishing the greatest work that ever was committed to human responsibility.

SOURCE: Catharine Beecher, *A Treatise on Domestic Economy* (New York: Marsh, Capen, Lyon, and Webb, 1841), chap. 1.

ANALYZING PRIMARY SOURCES

1. What does this passage, written more than a half century after the American Revolution, indicate about Beecher's vision of the grand political purposes served by women's "special" domestic role, for both the United States and the rest of the world?

2. How do Beecher's ideas compare to the Republican Motherhood concept of the earlier revolutionary years?

New evangelical forms of Protestant worship, especially in Baptist and Methodist congregations, stressed personal conversion and commitment to rooting out sin.

Religious enthusiasm and activism gave women, who were the majority of converts in these revivals, an arena for individual expression and social recognition that they were denied in secular politics. To establish their reputations as effective religious leaders, popular evangelical preachers relied on their female followers. Catharine Beecher's father, Lyman, and her brother, Henry Ward, were two such evangelical ministers. As for Catharine herself, she was never able to experience a full personal conversion and always doubted the depth of her religious conviction. Nonetheless, the career she was able to build for herself as an authority on proper Christian womanhood was much assisted by the association of the Beecher name with evangelical piety.

Women's reputation for deeper religious sentiment was closely related to the assumption that the true woman was inherently uninterested in sexual expression, that she was "pure." The notion of a white woman's natural sexual innocence was a relatively modern concept. In traditional European Christian culture, women had been considered more dangerously sexual than men. The belief in women's basic "passionlessness," as one historian has named it, was a new idea that, in the context of the time, served to raise white women's stature.[8] In the hierarchical nineteenth-century Protestant worldview, woman was less tied to humanity's animal nature than man was and was thus closer to the divine. Sexual appetite in the white, middle-class female was virtually unimaginable.[9] However, poor women, and especially women of African and Indigenous descent, continued to be viewed by white Americans as excessively sexual beings. These class- and race-based assumptions about female sexuality made the presence of sex workers profoundly disturbing to nineteenth-century moralists. If women were as lustful as men, there would be no one to control and contain sexual desire. As Dr. William Sanger wrote in his pathbreaking 1858 study of sex work in New York City, "Were it otherwise, and the passions in both sexes equal, illegitimacy and prostitution would be far more rife in our midst than at present."[10] (See Primary Sources: "Sex Work in New York City, 1858.")

THE GREAT SOCIAL EVIL.

TIME:—Midnight. A Sketch not a Hundred Miles from the Haymarket.

Bella. "AH! FANNY! HOW LONG HAVE YOU BEEN *GAY*?"

◆ **New York City Sex Worker** Whether the number of sex workers rose dramatically in the mid-nineteenth century, as many observers charged, in large cities they were certainly more visible and thus more disturbing to the middle-class public. Sex workers and their clients commonly frequented the "third tier" of theaters, which was informally reserved for them. As this contemporary cartoon indicates, they could even be found at the most elegant theaters. The joke in this cartoon refers to the difficulty of distinguishing between sex workers and reputable women of fashion. The term "gay" referred to sex work, not homosexuality, in the nineteenth century. *Look and Learn/Peter Jackson Collection/ Bridgeman Images.*

Starting in the 1820s, pious women expanded their religious expression beyond churchgoing to participation in a wide variety of voluntary organizations that promoted the spiritual and moral uplift of the poor and unsaved. They formed the first female moral reform society in 1834, during the decade when many participants also helped to organize widespread temperance campaigns. Female benevolent associations sponsored missionary efforts to bring Christianity to unbelievers at home and abroad. By the 1830s as well, an extensive network of Protestant women's organizations was sending money to church missions throughout Asia and Africa. A handful of adventuresome women went to preach the gospel abroad, mostly as wives of male missionaries. Ann Hasseltine Judson, who served with her husband in the 1820s in Rangoon, Burma, was the first American woman missionary in Asia. Closer to home, female missionaries brought Christian solace to the American urban poor. Pious middle-class women joined their ministers in "friendly visiting" to preach the word of Christ to society's downtrodden and outcast.

Many free Black women in the northern states embraced the culture of middle-class female Christian piety, yet entrenched racial and economic inequality created tensions between the ideals of true womanhood and the realities of free Black life. By 1840, almost 171,000 free Blacks resided in the northern states, especially in the cities of New York, Philadelphia, and Boston. Hundreds of mutual aid societies, churches, and schools sprang up in these Black communities. The first independent Black Protestant denomination, the **African Methodist Episcopal (AME) Church**, founded in Philadelphia in 1816, had a large membership of free Black women. Most free Black women worked as domestics or laundresses, and others became accomplished seamstresses and milliners. A few were teachers.

◆ **Peter S. Duval, *Mrs. Juliann Jane Tillman* (c. 1844)**
Juliann Jane Tillman's portrait demonstrates her command over holy text and her audience as she peers forward with quiet determination, one hand outstretched in an inclusive gesture and the other placed on an open Bible as her foundation. Her bonnet, tie, and dark coat provide a "female" version of a minister's dress and establish her gendered respectability at a time when women who lectured publicly, even those who identified with the clergy, were still considered out of place, even promiscuous. *Library of Congress, Prints and Photographs Division, Washington, D.C. (LC-USZ62-54596).*

Those solidly in the middle class drew their economic status, and the leisure it afforded them to invest in reform efforts, from well-to-do husbands and fathers. Even when economic reality did not match the domestic ideal, free Black women asserted their dignity and personhood through a culture of respectability based on moral conduct and self-improvement.

A Middle-Class Ideology

Despite the wide range of those who subscribed to its tenets, the ideology of true womanhood was a thoroughly middle-class social ethic. Certainly, the assumption that a woman should be insulated from economic demands to concentrate on creating a stable and peaceful home environment presumed that she was married to a man able to support her as a dependent wife. The middle-class wife in turn was responsible for what Beecher characterized as "the regular and correct apportionment of expenses that makes a family truly comfortable."[11] The idealized true woman, presiding over a virtuous family life, was a crucial staple of the way Americans contrasted themselves with European aristocratic society. Adherence to the ideology of true womanhood also helped people of the middle classes to distinguish themselves from those they regarded as their social and economic inferiors. In their charitable activities among the poor, true women preached the gospel of separate sexual spheres and female domesticity, convinced that the absence of these family values, rather than economic forces, was what made poor people poor.

These ideas reflected changing conditions in middle-class American women's lives. The birthrate for the average American-born white woman fell from 6 in 1800 to 4.9 in 1850, in part because economic modernization meant that children were less important as extra farm hands to help support the family and more likely to be a financial drain. Also, technological developments — for example, the new cast-iron stove, which was easier and safer than open-hearth cooking — were just beginning to ease women's household burdens. As the industrial production of cloth accelerated, women no longer had to spin and weave at home, although they still cut and sewed their family's clothes. Depending on their husbands' incomes, women might be able to hire servants to help with their labors. Even so, the middle-class housewife did plenty of work herself. Despite technological developments, leisure time was a privilege for only the very richest women. Laundry, the most burdensome of domestic obligations, remained a difficult weekly chore.

The doctrine of domesticity was elaborated by ministers in sermons and by physicians in popular health books. But middle-class women themselves did much of the work of spreading these ideas. The half century in which this rigid ideology of gender first flourished was also the period in which writing by women first found a mass audience among middle-class women. Lydia Sigourney, a beloved woman's poet; Mrs. E. D. E. N. Southworth, popular author of numerous sentimental novels; and Sarah Josepha Hale, editor of the influential women's magazine *Godey's Lady's Book* (with 150,000 subscribers in 1860), all built successful careers elaborating the ideology of true womanhood. (See Primary Sources: *"Godey's Lady's Book."*) In her influential and much-reprinted *Treatise on Domestic Economy* (1841), Catharine Beecher taught that woman's sphere was a noble "profession," equal in importance and challenge to any of the tasks assigned to men. Her younger half sister, Harriet Beecher Stowe, relied heavily on the ideas of woman's sphere in her book *Uncle Tom's Cabin* (1851), which became the most widely read American novel ever written.

In the judgment of such women, the tremendous respect paid to woman's lofty state was one of the distinguishing glories of nineteenth-century America. While proponents of true womanhood insisted that woman's sphere differed from man's, they regarded it as of equal importance to society and worthy of respect. Lucy Larcom put it this way: "God made no mistake in her [woman's] creation. He sent her into the world full of power and will to be a *helper*. . . . She is here to make this great house of humanity a habitable and a beautiful place, without and within, a true home for every one of his children."[12]

The many women of the nineteenth century who energetically subscribed to the ideas of true womanhood were not brainwashed victims of a male ideological conspiracy. Private writings of middle-class women from this period, letters and diaries notably, show women embracing these ideas and using them to give purpose to their lives. Not only could the true woman claim authority over the household and childrearing, but the widespread belief in her special moral vocation legitimated certain kinds of activity outside the domestic sphere such as teaching, church activities, and advocacy for social reform. Despite its middle-class character, the doctrine of true womanhood was strikingly widespread throughout antebellum American society. Almost the only white women during this period who openly challenged its tenets were the women's rights radicals (see "Entering New Territory: Women's Rights" in Chapter 5).

Domesticity in a Market Age

By fervently insisting that white women had to be insulated from the striving and bustle of the outside world, the advocates of true womanhood were implicitly responding to the impact of larger economic pressures on women's lives. The ideology of separate spheres and women's sheltered domesticity notwithstanding, much of women's history during this period can be understood only in the context of the burgeoning market economy. The development and growth of a cash-based market-oriented economy — as opposed to one in which people mostly produced goods for their own immediate use — reaches back to the very beginnings of American history when in the colonial South crops like tobacco, rice, and indigo were essential exports — and forward into the twentieth century. But early nineteenth-century America is rightly seen as the time in which the fundamental shift toward market-oriented production took place nationally instead of just regionally or in limited locations.

The spread of market relations had particular implications for women. In preindustrial society, men's work as well as women's was considered fundamentally domestic. Both sexes worked within and for the household, not for trade on the open market. By the eighteenth century, commercial transactions were growing in significance. Within urban areas, various household goods — soap and candles, for example, or processed foods like flour and spices — were available for purchase. By the early nineteenth century, white households needed to acquire more and more cash to buy consumer goods to fill the needs of daily life. Acquiring this money became men's obligation.

Much of men's work moved outside the home while the work of adult and elderly women, their daughters, servants, and the enslaved remained the domestic realm. Because work was increasingly regarded as what happened outside the home, done by men and compensated for by cash or credit, what females did in the home was becoming invisible as productive labor. From this perspective, the lavish attention the proponents of true womanhood paid to the moral significance of white woman's domestic sphere might be seen as ideological compensation for the decline in its economic value.

Industrial depressions, which affected the entire society and not just the lower rungs of wage earners, were becoming a regular, seemingly inescapable characteristic of the nation's developing industrial society — the busts that inevitably followed the booms. In 1837, the U.S. economy, which had been growing by leaps and bounds, violently contracted. Prices dropped precipitously, banks collapsed, and wages fell by as much as a third. The Panic of 1837, as it was called, was an early and formative experience in the lives of many women, among them the future women's rights leader Susan B. Anthony, whose father lost his grain mill business in that year.

Despite waning recognition of white women's role in economic production, popular nineteenth-century ideology assumed that in the household women could counteract some of the more disturbing aspects of economic expansion. A woman's household management skills, moral high ground, and emotional steadiness were supposed to be crucial in helping her family weather the shifting financial winds that were such an unnerving aspect of the new economy. "When we observe the frequent revolutions from poverty to affluence and then from extravagance to ruin, that are continually taking place around us," wrote Mrs. A. J. Graves in her popular handbook *Woman in America* (1841), "and their calamitous effects upon families brought up in luxury and idleness, have we not reason to fear that our 'homes of order and peace' are rapidly disappearing?"[13] Seen this way, the proper conduct of woman's sphere virtually became a matter of economic survival.

◆ WOMEN AND WAGE EARNING

As Mrs. Graves's admonition indicates, the depiction of woman's sphere as unconnected to the striving and bustle of the outside world is misleading. Indeed, women felt the pressures of a consumer-based (or cash-based) market economy in many ways. Some women found ways to make money from within their households — for instance, by selling extra butter or eggs. Barely visible to a society focused on its own capacity for productive prosperity, impoverished urban women and mothers, widowed or deserted by men, scrounged or begged for pennies to buy shelter, food, and warmth.

Of all women's intersections with the cash economy and the forces of the market revolution, none was more important for women's history than the employment of young, single New England women like Lucy Larcom as factory operatives at the power-driven spindles and looms of the newly established American textile industry. Though their numbers were small, these young women constituted the first emergence of the female wage labor force (see the Appendix, Table 1).

From Market Revolution to Industrial Revolution

To understand the experiences of early nineteenth-century women factory workers, we must place them in the setting of the era's industrial transformations. The growth of a market economy encouraged the centralization and acceleration of the production of goods. This industrializing process was gradual and uneven, a fact that becomes especially clear when we focus on the distinct contribution of women workers. For a long time after industrialization began, people continued to produce goods at home, even as their control over what they made and their share of its value were seriously eroded. In this transitional form of manufacture for sale, male entrepreneurs, or "factors," purchased the raw materials for production and distributed them to workers in their homes, then paid for the finished goods and sold them to customers. Workers no longer received the full cash value of what they had produced since the factor also made money from the process. In essence, the workers were receiving a wage for their labor instead of being paid for their products, which were no longer theirs to sell. Their labor was increasingly considered only a part, not the entirety, of the production process.

Shoemaking is a particularly interesting example, both because its transition to full industrialization was prolonged and because women and men underwent this transition at different rates. Making shoes for sale was already an established activity by the early nineteenth century, especially in cities north of Boston, notably Lynn, Massachusetts. At first, shoes were manufactured in home-based workshops in which the male head of the household was the master artisan and his wife, children, and apprentices worked under his direction. Starting in the 1820s and 1830s, a new class of shoemaking entrepreneurs brought male shoemakers, who specialized in cutting and sewing soles, to a centralized site, while women continued to sew the shoes' uppers and linings at home. By the 1840s and 1850s, women's piecework labor was being directed and paid for by the male entrepreneurs. It was not until later in the nineteenth century, after the Civil War, that women's part in shoe production moved into factories.

Clothing manufacture remained in a similar "outwork" phase for a long time. Women working at home produced most of the clothing manufactured for sale in the antebellum period. By 1860, there were sixteen thousand seamstresses in New York City alone.[14] Industrialization ravaged many of these mid-nineteenth-century poor women and their families. Other than for enslaved people, manufacture of clothing did not begin to shift into factories until after the Civil War — and well into the twentieth century the workshop form of production continued to thrive, in sweatshops. Other industries that relied on women outworkers included straw-hat making and bookbinding. Limited to their homes by childrearing and other domestic responsibilities, married women remained home-based industrial outworkers much longer than did men or unmarried women. The more exclusively female that outwork was, the more poorly it paid.

Manufacturing could be said to be fully industrialized only when it shifted to a separate, centralized location, the factory, at which point home and work were fully separated. In factories, entrepreneurs could introduce more expensive machinery and supervise labor more closely, both intended to maximize their profits. Factories and the machines within them were the manufacturers' contribution to the process, the "capital" that gave them control and ownership over the product of the workers.

Male artisans, no longer the masters of their family workshops, experienced the shift to the factory as absolute decline even if it meant a guaranteed income; for women the shift of manufacturing to outside the home offered a more mixed experience. Factory ownership was entirely in the hands of men, and women, whose secondary status had already been established in home manufacturing, earned a much lower wage than men for tasks that were inevitably considered less skilled. Yet white women's turn to factory labor also gave them the chance to earn wages as individuals, and at times to experience a taste of personal freedom. As Lucy Larcom explained, young women like herself "were clearing away a few weeds from the overgrown track of independent labor for other women."[15]

The Mill Girls of Lowell

By the 1820s, textile production, one of the most important of America's early industries — and certainly the most female dominated — was decisively shifting in the direction of factory labor. If the impoverished "tailoresses" working out of their dark urban garrets stood for the depredation of women by industrial capitalists, the factory girls of the textile industry came to represent the better possibilities that wage labor might offer white, immigrant women. And "girls" they were — unmarried, many in their teens. (See Primary Sources: "Early Photographs of Factory Operatives.") Though they were only a tiny percentage of women — as of 1840, only 2.25 percent[16] — these first female factory workers understood themselves, and were understood by others in their society, as opening up new vistas of personal independence and economic contribution for their sex.

The story of the first women factory workers began in the American textile industry during and immediately after the War of 1812. At the beginning of the nineteenth century, Americans who did not produce textiles in their rural homes bought wool, linen, and cotton cloth manufactured in the textile factories of Great Britain. The war with England interrupted the transatlantic trade in factory-made cloth, creating an irresistible opportunity for wealthy New England merchants, who had heretofore made their money by importing enslaved people and British textiles, to invest in American-based industry. In 1814 in Waltham, Massachusetts, a group of local merchants opened the first American factory to house all aspects of textile production under one roof. In an early and daring example of industrial espionage, they had spirited out of England designs for water-driven machinery for both spinning and weaving. The investors enjoyed quick and substantial profits, and in 1823 the same group of venture capitalists opened a much larger operation twenty-three miles away, on Merrimack River farmland north of Boston. The new factory town, named after the leading figure in the merchant capital group, Francis Cabot Lowell, soon became synonymous with the energetic American textile industry and with the young women who provided its labor force.

Previously, in England and in earlier, unsuccessful efforts at factory textile production in the United States, whole families who would otherwise be destitute were the workers: children worked the spinning machines and looms. This impoverished working population gave factory production a bad name, best captured by British poet William Blake's terrifying 1804 image of the "dark satanic mills" soiling "England's green and pleasant land."[17] Textile factories were regarded as poorhouses designed for keeping indigent people from disrupting society. Given the availability of land for farms in the United States, this type of labor force was not as obtainable for aspiring American textile industrialists. But an alternative had been identified as early as the 1790s by President George Washington's secretary of the treasury, Alexander Hamilton, an early promoter of American industrial production. Hamilton advocated hiring the unmarried daughters of farming families, who could move in and out of industrial production without becoming a permanent and impoverished wage labor force like that which haunted England. By laboring for wages in textile factories, these young women could for a time help provide their families with the cash that they increasingly required. The fact that the spinning of fiber for cloth had been the traditional work of women in the preindustrial household (especially unmarried women, hence the term "spinster," and elderly females) provided an additional argument for turning to a female labor force.

To the delight of New England textile capitalists, girls from Yankee farm families took to factory labor in the 1820s and early 1830s with great enthusiasm. Earning an individual wage offered them a degree of personal independence that was very attractive to these young women. Many were eager to work in the factories, despite thirteen-hour days, six-day workweeks, and wages of $1 to $2 per week.[18] "I regard it as one of the privileges of my youth that I was permitted to grow up among these active, interesting girls," Lucy Larcom wrote in her memoirs, "whose lives were not mere echoes of other lives, but had principles and purposes distinctly their own."[19] Even though they saved their wages and sent as much as possible to their families, the mill girls occasionally spent some of their earnings on themselves; for this they were regarded by contemporaries as spoiled and self-indulgent. And although their workdays were extraordinarily long and the labor much more unrelenting than that to which they were accustomed, they reveled in the small amounts of time they had for themselves in the evenings. Larcom's

◆ The *Lowell Offering*

The *Lowell Offering* was the mill owner–sponsored publication of original writings by women workers known as "factory girls." Conditions in the mills had already begun to deteriorate by 1845, the date of this publication. Nonetheless, the image's foreground shows a confident, literate, individual woman stepping out into the larger world. In the background are the mills and boardinghouses in which the working girls lived and worked. Note the idealized pastoral frame, so different from the actual reality of the industrial process and its impact on the city, factories, and workers of Lowell. *Everett Collection/Alamy.*

reminiscences detail the classes she and her sister attended, the writing they did, and the friendships they made. Factory girls at Lowell and elsewhere even formed female benevolent societies, as did their more middle-class counterparts.

One problem, however, stood in the way of the success of this solution to the problem of factory labor: Where were the young women workers to live? Given the scale of the labor force required by the large new factories and the decentralized character of the New England population, young women would have to be brought from their homes to distant factories. Parents were reluctant to allow their daughters to be so far from home and away from family supervision. Factory work for women, probably because it had been so dreadfully underpaid in England, was suspected of being an avenue to prostitution. The manufacturers' solution to both the housing and moral supervision dilemmas was to build boardinghouses for their young workers and to link work and living arrangements in a paternalistic approach to industrial production. Four to six young women shared each bedroom, and their behavior was closely supervised. The boardinghouses, and the camaraderie among young women that flourished there, added to the allure of factory labor. To the farm girls of New England, this was greater cosmopolitanism than they had ever known.

For about a decade, the city of Lowell and the Lowell system (as the employment of young farm girls as factory workers was called) were among the glories of the new American nation. Visitors came from Europe to see and sing the praises of the moral rectitude and industry of the women workers in this new type of factory production, free of the corruptions of the Old World. "They were healthy in appearance, many of them remarkably so," Charles Dickens wrote after a visit in 1842, "and had the manners and deportment of young women; not of degraded brutes of burden."[20] The dignity and probity of the Lowell girls were crucial elements in the optimism that temporarily thrived regarding the possibilities of a genuinely democratic American version of industrial factory production, in which all could profit from the new levels of wealth. "The experiment at Lowell had shown that independent and intelligent workers invariably give their own character to their occupation," Larcom proudly wrote.[21] Young women workers wrote stories, essays, and poems about their experience at the factories for their own literary journal, the *Lowell Offering*, to put their uprightness and their intelligence on display. Larcom began a long career as a writer this way. Factory owners, not insensitive to the propaganda value of such efforts, underwrote the magazine, paid the editor's salary, and distributed issues widely.

The End of the Lowell Idyll

Eventually, however, economic pressures combined with gender discrimination took their toll on Lowell's great promise, at least for the female workers. Declining prices for cotton and wool and investors' expectations of high returns led factory owners to slash wages. Within the first decade, wages were cut twice. The factory owners counted on the womanly demeanor of their employees to get them to accept the cuts. But they were wrong. In 1834 and 1836, in response to lower wages, Lowell girls "turned out" — conducted spontaneous strikes — and in the process began to question notions of womanhood that forbade such demonstrations of individual and group assertion. They repudiated the deference and subordination expected of them on the grounds of their sex and championed, instead, their dignity and independence as proud "daughters of freemen." One young striker, Harriet Hanson, who went on to become a leader in the woman suffrage movement, remembered that the strike "was the first time a woman had spoken in public in Lowell, and the event caused surprise and consternation among her audience."[22] But the Panic of 1837, which triggered contraction of the entire industrial economy, doomed the efforts of the women operatives to act collectively, defend their jobs, and preserve the level of their wages. Workers were laid off and mills shut down. Young girls went back to their farm families to wait out the economic downturn.

When the economy revived and the mills resumed full production, workers were expected to increase their pace, tend more machines, and produce more cloth. Production levels rose, but wages did not. Moral concerns were giving way to the bottom line. In 1845, Lowell's women workers formed the **Lowell Female Labor Reform Association** and joined with male workers in other Massachusetts factories in petitioning the state legislature to establish a ten-hour legal limit to their workdays as a way to resist work pressure and keep up levels of employment. This turn to the political system to redress group grievance was part of the larger effort to extend the rights of ordinary white citizens during the period. It is striking to find women engaged in these methods at a time when politics was regarded as thoroughly outside of woman's sphere. Indeed, the legislative petitions of the women textile workers of the 1840s are an important indicator that women were beginning to imagine themselves as part of the political process not only in trying to impact general free working conditions, but also as part of the growing abolitionist movement. Women still, however, lacked whatever voting power male workers could muster and were unable to secure any labor gains by their legislative petitions.

Conditions of factory labor were changing in other ways as well, most notably in the composition of the labor force. The Lowell system had been devised in the context of a shortage of workers willing to take factory jobs. By the 1840s, however, immigrants were providing an ever-growing labor pool for industrial employment. Coming to the United States in large numbers, they poured into the wage labor force. The Irish were both the largest and the most economically desperate of all the new arrivals. Starting in 1845, a terrible blight on the potato crop that was the staple of the Irish diet, exacerbated by the harsh policies of England toward its oldest colony, threw the population into starvation conditions and compelled well over a million Irish men and women to emigrate to the United States. The textile capitalists, no longer pressured by labor shortages to make factory employment seem morally uplifting, paid low wages to and enforced harsh working conditions on these new immigrant workers, who soon constituted the majority of mill laborers.

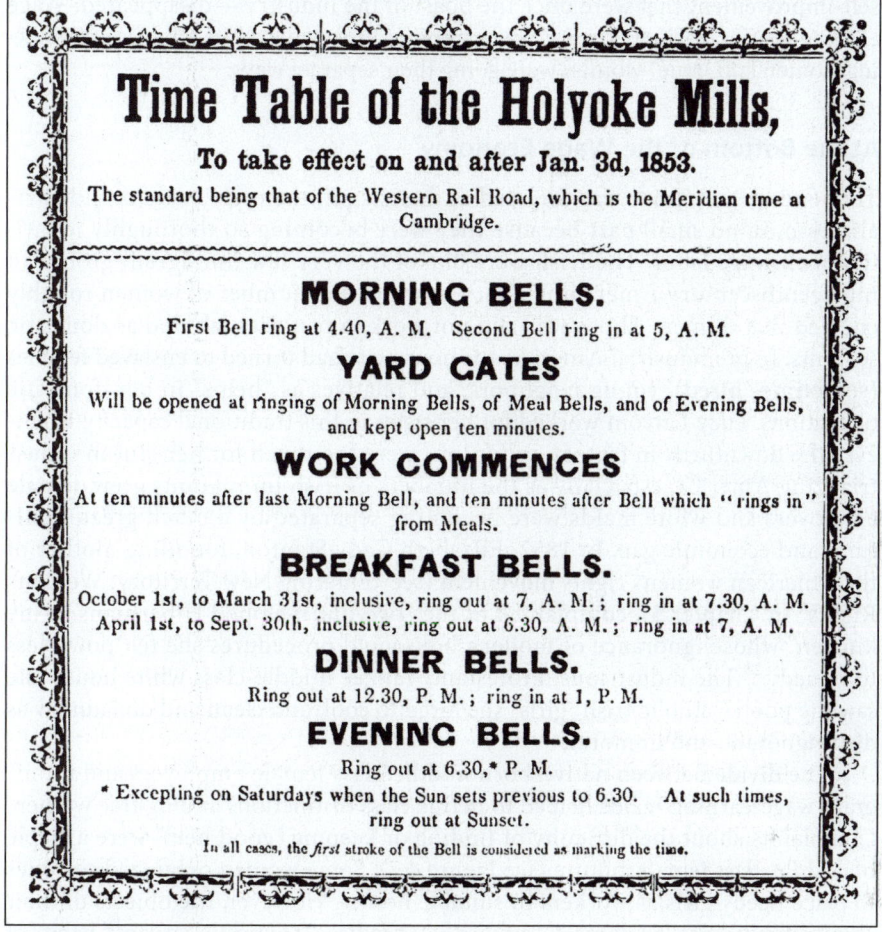

Time Table of the Holyoke Mills,

To take effect on and after Jan. 3d, 1853.

The standard being that of the Western Rail Road, which is the Meridian time at Cambridge.

MORNING BELLS.

First Bell ring at 4.40, A. M.   Second Bell ring in at 5, A. M.

YARD GATES

Will be opened at ringing of Morning Bells, of Meal Bells, and of Evening Bells, and kept open ten minutes.

WORK COMMENCES

At ten minutes after last Morning Bell, and ten minutes after Bell which "rings in" from Meals.

BREAKFAST BELLS.

October 1st, to March 31st, inclusive, ring out at 7, A. M. ; ring in at 7.30, A. M. April 1st, to Sept. 30th, inclusive, ring out at 6.30, A. M. ; ring in at 7, A. M.

DINNER BELLS.

Ring out at 12.30, P. M. ; ring in at 1, P. M.

EVENING BELLS.

Ring out at 6.30,* P. M.

* Excepting on Saturdays when the Sun sets previous to 6.30.   At such times, ring out at Sunset.

In all cases, the *first* stroke of the Bell is considered as marking the time.

◆ **Time Table of the Holyoke Mills (1853)**
The "Time Table of the Holyoke Mills" clearly indicates the temporal and other kinds of control pursued by male supervisors of mill workers, who were primarily female. Workers toiled from morning to evening and would be penalized if they did not adhere strictly to this schedule or to the other commands that bosses imposed. *GRANGER — Historical Picture Archive.*

Part of the initial attraction that native-born farm girls had for capitalists was the knowledge that they would eventually marry and return to their families and farms, and therefore their factory labor would be only a brief episode in their lives. The dreaded Old World fate of becoming a permanently degraded and dependent wage labor class went instead to the Irish Catholic immigrants, who by 1860 were well over half of the workers in the industry. Immigrant men now worked the looms and immigrant women the spindles. Public celebrations of the high moral character of the factory operatives — the womanly demeanor and hunger for self-improvement that were once the boast of the industry — disappeared. Wage earning was increasingly seen as undermining respectable white femininity. Working women and "true" women were going their separate ways.

At the Bottom of the Wage Economy

Tremendous prejudice was directed at the Irish in the early years of industrialization, in no small part because they were becoming so thoroughly identified with wage labor. The Irish were one of the very few immigrant groups in nineteenth-century American history in which the number of women roughly equaled that of men. Those who did not work in factories labored as domestic servants. In preindustrial America, the housewife had turned to enslaved females (sometimes hired), young neighbors, and relatives as "helps" in her domestic obligations. Lucy Larcom worked for her sister in this traditional capacity whenever the downturns in factory conditions were too much for her. But in industrializing America, especially as the numbers of Irish immigrants grew, female employers and white maids were becoming separated by a much greater cultural and economic gap. In 1852, Elizabeth Cady Stanton, founding mother of the American women's rights movement (see "Entering New Territory: Women's Rights" in Chapter 5), complained of the "two undeveloped Hibernians in my kitchen" whose ignorance of modern household procedures she felt powerless to remedy.[23] The industrious, Protestant, Yankee middle-class white housewife saw the poor, Catholic Irish "girls" she hired to cook and clean and do laundry as dirty, ignorant, and immoral.

The divide between native-born middle-class female employers and immigrant wage-earning maids helped to define class distinctions among free women. Complaints about the difficulty of finding or keeping "good help" were a staple of middle-class female culture (see Figure 4.7). Some women organized societies to place needy girls as workers in suitable homes. However, the objects of their charity rarely regarded domestic service as a privilege. Domestic servants' habits of working erratically, changing employers often, and presenting a sullen demeanor were means of protesting a form of employment they did not like and that was not respected in democratic America, where the deference expected in personal service already had given it a bad name. Their female employers could never understand why, even when wages were competitive, their domestic servants did their best to switch to factory employment. There, though the workday was long and the labor hard, a factory job ended with the dismissal bell, after which a young woman's time became her own.

At the very bottom of the economic ladder, beneath even the lower rungs of domestic service, were the urban poor. America had always had its poor people, but this destitute class was new, as it included able-bodied people willing to work but unable to find jobs that would support themselves and their families. The most desperate of the urban poor were the women, free Black and white, with children but without men (or, more precisely, without access to the higher wages a man could earn). These poor urban women were thought to be the antithesis of true

◆ **Irish Immigration**
Mary Anne Madden Sadlier, the author of the first American-written novel about an Irish immigrant woman, herself left Ireland in 1844. Living first in Montreal, she and her husband, James Sadlier, a book and magazine publisher, moved to New York City in 1860. Her novel *Bessy Conway, or The Irish Girl in America* (1861) modified the domestic focus of true womanhood ideology for a Catholic audience and blamed Protestant values and prejudices for the poverty and social ills that the Irish experienced in the United States. *The Irish Collection, John J. Burns Library, Boston College.*

womanhood. The rooms in which they lived often were not furnished or private. Their children played in the streets or worked for a pittance to help support their families. Housework was especially difficult for poor urban women, who had to carry water for their laundry or coal for warmth or small amounts of food for dinner up steps into tiny tenement apartments or down into cellar spaces (where twenty-nine thousand lived in New York City as of 1850).[24] After each downturn of the industrial economy, the numbers of urban poor swelled.

The Society for the Relief of Poor Widows, formed in New York City in 1799, was the first American charity organized by women for women.[25] The charitable ladies did not provide outright cash or employment, instead dispensing spiritual and moral ministrations along with occasional food, coal, and clothing. In such exchanges, just as in the relationship between female employers and maids, middle-class and poor women met each other across the class divide, probably struck more with what separated them than with what they allegedly shared by virtue of their common gender.

◆ **William Henry Burr, *The Intelligence Office***
This 1849 painting of an employment office dramatically portrays the harsh reality of poor working women in search of employment, as two young women are displayed before a potential employer by the male proprietor. The sign at the back reads "Agents for Domestics. Warranted Honest." *New-York Historical Society/Bridgeman Images.*

◆ WOMEN, SLAVERY, AND THE SOUTH

Perhaps the greatest irony embedded in the dynamic beginnings of industrial capitalism is the degree to which it rested on a very different social and economic system that also thrived in early nineteenth-century America: chattel slavery. As northern states gradually abolished slavery, the institution became identified exclusively with the South. At the same time, the North and the South were linked in important ways. Both regions added new states to the west that displaced Indigenous peoples through various wars and ineffectual treaties. In the South, the gigantic cotton crop grown by enslaved labor was the raw material of New England's textile industry. Among the greatest advocates of American democracy were numerous southern slaveholders, including four of this country's first five presidents. And at many levels, the North and South shared a national culture. Their citizens read the same books and magazines, worshipped in the same Protestant denominations, voted for the same political parties, and embraced a doctrine of Manifest Destiny. Southern white women followed many essentials of the cult of domesticity. But underlying these similarities were fundamental differences, signifying a conflict that eventually led to the Civil War.

The absence in the South of the wage relationship between producer and capitalist lay at the heart of these sectional differences. Property owners accumulated great profits in the South, and much of what was produced there was intended for sale. But the workers of the system were not paid any wages for their labor. They were *chattel* enslaved people, human property, the value of whose current and future labor, along with the land they worked, constituted the wealth of slaveholders. Like the factory buildings and machines that produced wealth in the Northeast, they were capital; but they were also human beings. While the cotton boom states expanded their system of human property and the numbers of enslaved people grew rapidly, white southern politicians also set their sights on the extensive territory of southeastern Indigenous peoples. Paired with aggressive state legislation, a new U.S. Indian removal law remade the map of Indigenous America and was part of the formula that eventually made the nation the largest Black slave society in the Americas.

Indigenous Peoples in the South and U.S. Removal Policy

While planters owned their growing captive labor force, Native American societies still claimed much of the land in the trans-Appalachian South. In the early nineteenth century, slavery and cotton began to expand into what was called the "new" or "lower" South (western Georgia, Florida, Alabama, Arkansas, Mississippi, Louisiana, and Texas). This move was greatly facilitated by the Louisiana Purchase and a sustained, concerted effort of land-hungry whites, aided by the state governments of Georgia and the Carolinas and legal manipulation by the U.S. government under President Andrew Jackson. Together, white settler violence backed by new state and federal laws as well as military force worked to push the Indigenous peoples of the Southeast — the Creeks, Chickasaws, Choctaws, and Cherokees — off their extensive lands. The Cherokees in particular had tried to adapt to American society and resist land sales (see Reading into the Past: "Beloved Children: Cherokee Women Petition the National Council"). The Cherokee leader Sequoyah had devised a written language, enabling the translation of the Christian Bible and the drafting of a political constitution. Some Cherokee families — as well as those in other southeastern Indigenous ethnic groups — grew wealthy as owners of large cotton plantations and enslaved African-descended workers. Although Native American societies already had long-standing practices of captivity and servitude, this new market-oriented form of chattel slavery supplanted the tradition of Indigenous women's agricultural labor and introduced racialized notions of Black inferiority.

All of these efforts to maintain sovereign Indigenous lands through assimilation proved ineffective, however, once Andrew Jackson was elected president.

READING INTO THE PAST

Beloved Children: Cherokee Women Petition the National Council

The United States assisted citizens who wanted to take over the lands of Indigenous peoples in order to expand plantation agriculture and, with it, chattel slavery. In the early nineteenth century, the federal government negotiated a number of land cessions in treaties with southern tribes, including the Cherokees. In 1817, thirteen Cherokee women sent this petition to their own National Council to warn against the transfer of any more lands to white ownership. Among the signers was eighty-year-old Nancy Ward, whose high standing among her people harked back to an earlier age in which women shared political and social authority with men (see "A Changing World for Indigenous Women" in Chapter 3). The signers spoke for those women who had given up their traditional agricultural responsibilities in favor of American domestic tasks, such as making clothing. Nonetheless, their words indicate a continuing identification through their gender with the land.

May 2, 1817: The Cherokee ladys now being present at the meeting of the chiefs and warriors in council have thought it their duty as mothers to address their beloved chiefs and warriors now assembled.

Our beloved children and head men of the Cherokee Nation, we address you warriors in council. We have raised all of you on the land which we now have, which God gave us to inhabit and raise provisions. We know that our country has once been extensive, but by repeated sales [it] has become circumscribed to a small track, and [we] never have thought it our duty to interfere in the disposition of it till now. If a father or mother was to sell all their lands which they had to depend on, which their children

Jackson pushed the **Indian Removal Act** of 1830 through Congress and then, ignoring Supreme Court decisions partially favoring Cherokee sovereignty, sent federal troops to Georgia to enforce a treaty that had been signed by only a small faction of the Cherokee Nation. In 1838, the Cherokees were forcibly driven into the newly established "Indian" Territory west of the Mississippi, across what the Cherokees called the "Trail of Tears." The lands taken from them were transformed into acres of cotton, tobacco, and other crops, owned by planters and grown by enslaved people. Meanwhile, in the older southern states of Virginia, Maryland, and the Carolinas, where soil had become exhausted and tobacco prices had slumped, enslaved people who were not used to grow grains and other marketable items themselves became a kind of commodity, a surplus for slaveholders to sell.

had to raise their living on, [it] would be indeed bad & [so would it to] be removed to another country. We do not wish to go to an unknown country to which we have understood some of our children wish to go over the Mississippi, but this act of our children would be like destroying your mothers.

Your mothers, your sisters ask and beg of you not to part with any more of our land. We say ours. You are our descendants; take pity on our request. But keep it for our growing children, for it was the good will of our creator to place us here, and you know our father, the great president, will not allow his white children to take our country away. Only keep your hands off of paper talks for it's our own country. For [if] it was not, they would not ask you to put your hands to paper, for it would be impossible to remove us all. For as soon as one child is raised, we have others in our arms, for such is our situation & [they] will consider our circumstance.

Therefore, children, don't part with any more of our lands but continue on it & enlarge your farms. Cultivate and raise corn & cotton and your mothers and sisters will make clothing for you which our father the president has recommended to us all. . . . Nancy Ward to her children: Warriors to take pity and listen to the talks of your sisters. Although I am very old yet [I] cannot but pity the situation in which you will here [sic] of their minds. I have great many grand children which [I] wish them to do well on our land.

SOURCE: Presidential Papers Microfilm: Andrew Jackson (Washington, D.C., 1961, series 1, reel 22).

ANALYZING PRIMARY SOURCES

1. How is Cherokee women's identification with the land reflected in their petition?
2. What sources of authority do Cherokee women invoke to validate their petition to "their beloved chiefs and warriors"?

Plantation Patriarchy

Over the first half of the nineteenth century, slaveholding became increasingly concentrated in the hands of fewer and fewer whites, even as slave territory expanded. By 1860 only an estimated 25 percent of southern white families were slaveholders; of these, only a small minority qualified for an elite status that often included significant political and economic power. These elite planters, owning anywhere from twenty to hundreds of enslaved people, controlled the large concentrations of land and labor that formed the power basis of southern slave society (see Map 4.1). On large market-oriented agricultural estates, enslaved people were organized into work gangs in which they raised the cotton, rice, sugar, and tobacco that made the

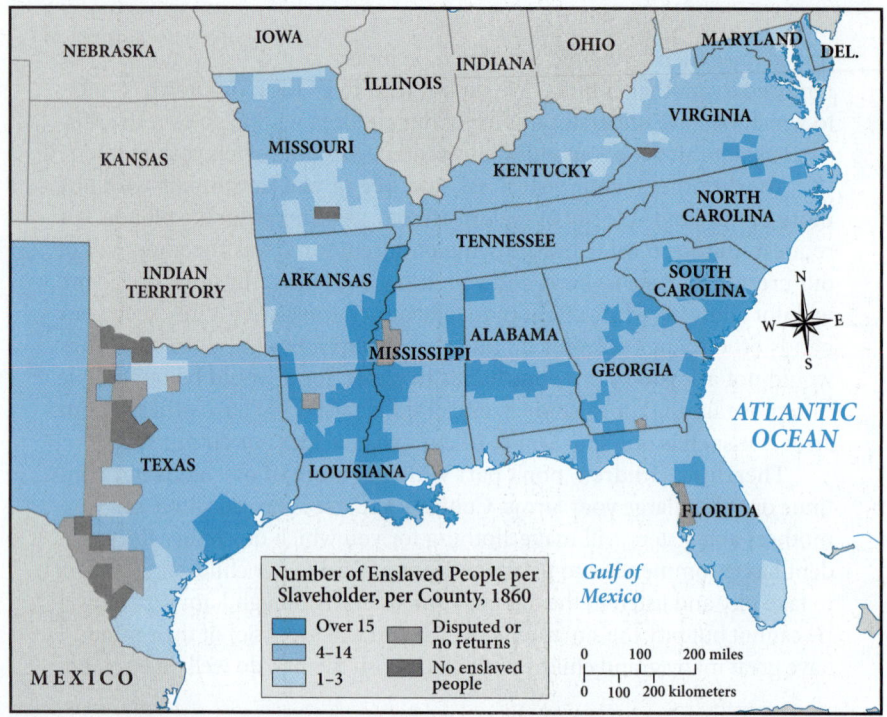

◆ **Map 4.1 Number of Enslaved People per Slaveholder, per County, 1860**
The cotton boom shifted enslaved African Americans to the lower and western South. In 1790, most lived and worked on the tobacco plantations of the Chesapeake and in the rice and indigo areas of South Carolina. By 1860, the centers of slavery lay along the Mississippi River and in an arc of fertile cotton land sweeping from Mississippi through Georgia west to Texas.

South wealthy and the nation wedded to items produced by enslaved people. These plantations were not only the economic core but also the social, political, and cultural centers of slave society. Laws centered on the control of Black bodies and labor, not on protecting the rights of all humankind. In general, the nineteenth-century slave South did not develop the dynamic civil society that flourished in the North. The growth of an industrial economy and of a wage labor class was limited in the South to a few urban centers, such as Richmond and Atlanta. With the sole exception of party politics, which wealthy men dominated, public life did not thrive. As a result, plantation women's lives varied significantly from those of northern women.

To begin with, family life was different. The ideological distinction between public and private, work and family — much touted in the North — was less visible on the great southern plantations. The plantation was residence and workplace simultaneously. Slave society was proudly, and publicly, patriarchal. Wealthy white southern men were fiercely protective of the honor of their women and their families. Female deference to white male authority was considered a virtue, and any moral superiority granted to women gave them power only over enslaved people and small children.

Owners, both male and female, regarded enslaved men and women as workers and dependents — lacking in judgment and authority. Proslavery advocates and benefactors constructed a self-serving, racist mythology that the plantation community was a single large family, with slaveholder parents and enslaved children, bound by devotion and reciprocal obligations of service and protection. One white woman, writing about her father's plantation, truly believed that "the family servants, inherited for generations, had come to be regarded with great affection. . . . The bond between master and servant was, in many cases, felt to be as sacred and close as the tie of blood."[26] Enslaved people certainly did not hold this view, mounting resistance efforts as an essential part of their personal and communal lives. When slavery was abolished, male and female slaveholders were often astounded to discover the degree of hostility these "family servants" felt toward them.

Plantation patriarchy was a gendered, class, and financial system, organized around racial difference, white privilege, and Black oppression. The structures and inequalities of race hierarchy, much like those of gender, were designated by whites as natural and God-given. In their imaginations and the culture that they imposed, "Black" equaled "enslaved" and was understood as the opposite not only of "white" but also of "free." In contrast to this belief, it is important to recognize that by 1830 there were a third of a million Black people in the United States who were not enslaved, half of them living in the South. The lives of these people and their claims to free status were deeply compromised by the power of the slaveocracy, racist citizens nationally, and the racial inequalities that white Americans insisted on in law and custom. In the South, free people of color were kept out of certain occupations, forbidden to carry firearms, denied the right to assembly, made to carry passes when traveling, and often legally required to register in court with a white guardian. In the Midwest and West, many were not allowed residence without posting woefully exorbitant bonds; had restricted housing and occupational access; could only send their children to segregated schools; were confined to segregated seating in public assemblies and public transportation; had harshly enforced curfews; and could not participate in electoral politics. Free Black women in slaveholding locales shared many of the same restrictions on occupations as their counterparts in the North and West. In Augusta County, Virginia, for example, the 1860 census revealed sixty-seven females of color, ranging from age fourteen to seventy-two, who listed their occupations. Domestic work was most common, followed by laundering, whereas only five of these women listed themselves as seamstresses.[27]

Despite slave society's insistence that the racial divide was absolute, the line that separated "Black" from "white" was constantly being breached. Slaveholders could — and certainly did — compel enslaved girls and women to have sexual relations with them. When a captive woman gave birth to her captor's child, how was the racial divide on which slave patriarchy was premised to be maintained? The legal answer was that the child followed the status of the mother: the child was permanently bound because her female parent was permanently bound. While slavery is usually considered a system for organizing labor and producing profit, it was also a way of controlling sexual and reproductive relations, of determining which sexual encounters produced legitimate and/or free children. In other words, gaining wealth by oppressing another race necessitated controlling gender expectations and roles as well as sexuality across the racial divide.

Female Slaveholders

The link between racial inequality and gender ideals is evident in the effusive literary and rhetorical praise devoted to the southern white feminine ideal. Elite white women in plantation society were elevated to a lofty pedestal that was the ideological inverse of the auction block on which enslaved women's fate was sealed. As in other part of the nation, white women were supposed to be selfless, pure, pious, and possessed of great, if subtle, influence over husbands and sons. But the difference in the South was that white women's purity was defined in contrast not only to the actions of white men but also to the condition of enslaved Black women.

As slavery came under more and more open criticism from northern opponents during the nineteenth century, rhetorical devotion to elite white women's leisure and culture, to the preservation of their beauty and their sexual innocence, and to their protection from all distress and labor intensified as part of the proslavery rhetoric. The message seemed to be that the purity of elite white womanhood, protected by a chivalrous, honor-driven manhood, and enabled by the dehumanization and enslavement of Black people, was one of the core values of southern society. "We behold," proclaimed southern writer Thomas Dew, "the marked efficiency of slavery on the conditions of woman—we find her at once elevated, clothed with all her charms, mingling with and directing the society to which she belongs, no longer the slave, but the equal and the idol of man."[28] Some women among the most elite of the slaveholding class also held to the opinion that a lady's life on a southern plantation was a great privilege. Any greater political and economic rights for white women were "but a piece of negro emancipation," declared Louisa McCord, daughter of an important South Carolina slaveholder and politician, in 1852.[29] She was sure that women like herself wanted no part of such a movement. Others, like the diarist Mary Chesnut who was married to a South Carolinian slaveholder and politician, complained bitterly of the difficulties some southern patriarchs stirred in their households. Chesnut wrote about the tyrannical control these men exercised over their daughters and the humiliations they caused their wives through sexual liaisons with enslaved girls and women.

Whereas in the North womanly virtues were meant to be universal, in the South they proudly excluded lower-class white women and all Black females, enslaved and free. Leisure was especially the privilege of the unmarried young woman of the slaveholding class, who was not only spared any household obligations, but also relieved of even the most intimate of responsibilities—dressing herself, for instance—by the presence of enslaved attendants. "Surrounded with them from infancy, they form a part of the landscape of a Southern woman's life," one woman romantically recalled of her captives long after slavery had ended. "They watch our cradles; they are the companions of our sports; it is they who aid our bridal decorations; and they wrap us in our shrouds."[30]

Once a wealthy woman married, however, she took on managerial responsibility for her household. Unlike some of their husbands who hired overseers and

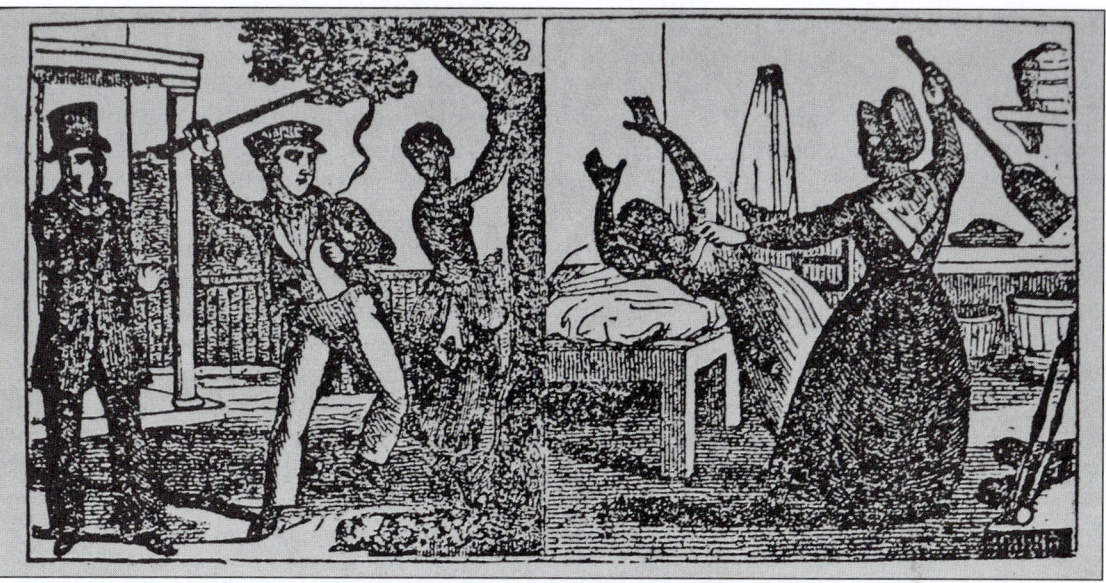

◆ **"How Slavery Improves the Condition of Women" (1838)**
This illustration was published in *The Anti-Slavery Almanac* in 1838, just as women in
abolitionism were becoming more assertive. The title ironically juxtaposes the evils of slavery
and the ideology of female purity and protection. Not only does it show enslaved women
being beaten, but it also suggests that the white slaveholder herself has become brutalized by
joining in the violence. *The Stapleton Collection/Bridgeman Images.*

drivers to manage field workers, female captors typically oversaw the labor and
punishment of domestics and the distribution of food, clothing, and medicine to
the Black labor force.

Because slavery was a labor system in which there were no positive incentives
for hard work, the management of workers relied almost entirely on threats and
punishments, including beatings and loss of one's family members. The association
of allegedly delicate womanhood with brutal violence was a disturbing aspect of the
system, even to its most passionate adherents. Opponents of slavery played endlessly
on this theme to indicate that the fundamental corruption of the system reached
even to the women of slaveholding families. "There are *female tyrants* too, who are
prompt to lay their complaints of misconduct before their husbands, brothers, and
sons, and to urge them to commit acts of violence against their helpless slaves," wrote
Angelina Grimké, daughter of a powerful southern slaveholder, who left the South
in 1829 to fight against the system.[31] (See "Crossing Political Boundaries: Abolitionism" in Chapter 5.) Fannie Moore, who came of age on a North Carolina plantation,
agreed with Grimké. Speaking of her former slaveholder, Moore said, "She shore was
a rip-jack." This particular woman viewed enslaved people as animals, who were
"not like other folks." Moore recalled, "She whip me, many time wif a cow hide, til I
was black and blue."[32] (See Primary Sources: "Mothering under Slavery.")

In the South, as in other parts of the young nation, marriage for free women legally prohibited them from the privileges of property ownership except when they, like Martha Washington, entered their marriage with a legally created "separate estate." Changing this practice of loss of property after marriage was one of the initial goals of the American women's rights movement, within which southern white women were notoriously absent. Thus it is ironic that the first states to liberalize property laws for married women were southern — Mississippi (in 1839) and Arkansas (in 1840). They did so to protect the inheritance of slaveholding. Far more than middle-class women in the country, elite southern women were expected to bring dowries — wealth packages — into their marriages, and it was not uncommon for a young woman to bring into her new home enslaved people from her parents' plantation. This was one of the many ways in which Black captives were separated from their own families. To protect their daughters — and the family property that had been transferred with them — against spendthrift husbands, southern patriarchs modified married women's property laws to allow wives to retain title to inherited property. By contrast, the first married women's property law to be reformed in the North in response to pressure from women's rights activists was not until 1848 in New York State.

In all other ways, however, the slave system made for more severe constraints on free women than in the North. The rhetorical weight that rested on the ideals of elite white women's purity meant that women's public activities were extremely limited. Unlike women in other parts of the nation, respectable southern white women had no means of earning money except as owners of the enslaved and sometimes as governesses, seamstresses, or midwives. Women who remained unmarried faced futures as marginal members in the households of their married kin. Whatever education existed for young women was oriented to the ornamental graces rather than more serious subjects. Fewer charitable societies of the sort that northern middle-class women formed to care for the indigent and poor existed in the South, although plantation female slaveholders, defensive about whether they were sufficiently benevolent, frequently claimed that caring for and feeding the people they enslaved constituted an equivalent moral responsibility.

Slaveholding women and men did not regard themselves as heading up a brutal and inhumane system. On the contrary, they were convinced that the society over which they presided, which elevated them to lives of enviable grace and culture, was the best of all possible worlds, certainly better than the lives led by money-grubbing capitalists and degraded wage workers. They regarded enslaved people as well treated compared to wage earners, whom they believed were ignored and eventually abandoned, their welfare of no concern to bosses who wanted only to exploit their labor and then dispose of them. "How enviable were our solidarity as a people, our prosperity and the moral qualities that are characteristic of the South," one southern matron mourned many years after the Civil War. In nostalgic retrospect, she believed that white southerners' "love of home, their chivalrous respect for women, their courage, their delicate sense of honour, their constancy . . . [all] are things by which the more mercurial people of the North may take a lesson."[33]

Non-elite White Women

While the power of southern society lay in the hands of the plantation elite, the majority of whites were not large slaveholders. Indeed, close to three-quarters of all white families could claim no captives at all and relied on their own labor, occasionally hiring an enslaved person or two from a neighbor. Even the great majority of those who did own enslaved people were working farmers themselves, living and laboring alongside the few people they enslaved. These small farmers are often called yeomen, a British term signifying the non-noble agricultural classes. The slave system would not have worked without the active support of the many white people who were not slaveholders. Non-elite white men patrolled the roads for enslaved people who had escaped, voted in favor of aggressively proslavery state governments, and served as overseers and skilled craftsmen on others' plantations.

Women on the small farms and modest households of the South had much less interaction with planter culture than did their husbands. The southern white women's common culture centered on practicing religion and setting the family's moral standard, bearing and rearing children, and attending to domestic upkeep; the difference in their lives was that poorer female yeoman performed the labor that enslaved workers performed for plantation women. Yeoman women produced goods for their own family's consumption, for instance, spinning and weaving homespun, even long after northern farmwomen were purchasing factory-made cloth.

Although men of the yeomen class had few or no captives over whom to establish their patriarchal authority, they did have wives. The ethic of male household headship, therefore, bonded white men across class boundaries. "As masters of dependents, even if only, or perhaps if especially, of wives and children," one historian observes, "every freeman was bound to defend his household, his property, against invasion."[34]

Enslaved Women

Far more than even the most impoverished, degraded wage worker in the North, enslaved people in the South were forbidden the basic elements of personal freedom — to live with their own families, to move about, to have control of their sexual behavior, to be educated, to work for their own benefit, to marry, and to raise their own children — not to mention the loftier rights of citizenship. The legal definition of enslaved people as property was recognized by the laws of all the southern states and protected by the careful wording of the U.S. Constitution. Indeed, the Constitution, in permitting legislation ending the transatlantic slave trade after 1808 and relegating control over the institution of slavery entirely to the states, laid the foundation for an enormous commerce in enslaved people within the United States that depended on enslaved women's childbearing. The profitable, vigorous internal market in enslaved people touched the lives of virtually all Blacks, for each man, woman, and child experienced either the horror of being sold, the fear of the possibility of being sold, or the heartrending knowledge of a loved one being sold. The auction block loomed over all, repeatedly.

When we recall Tocqueville's confident assertion in 1830 that American women were so privileged and honored that they "never labor in the fields," we begin to see the degree to which the enslaved women of the South were not only ignored in all the sweeping generalizations of true womanhood, but also excluded from the category of "woman" except in the ability to bear children. Ninety percent of enslaved women labored in the cotton, sugar, tobacco, and rice fields that generated the expanding region's wealth. A small minority worked as personal and domestic servants in planter households, despite the genteel image of slavery that plantation patriarchs extolled. It was the giant mass of captive agricultural workers on whom the power and wealth of the planter class rested.

Nowhere in early nineteenth-century America was labor less divided by gender than in the antebellum fields of the plantation South. Some farming tasks, such as enslaved women's sowing of rice fields, still relied on gendered divisions of labor. On many plantations, enslaved women spent some of their days in all-female work gangs. However, a great deal of agricultural labor was assigned according to skill, strength, and presence rather than gender. Enslaved women and men hoed and planted and reaped alongside each other in gangs that worked from sunup to sundown under constant surveillance and the threat of the overseer's whip. In lowcounty Georgia and South Carolina, in fact, enslaved women frequently made up the majority of field workers. African American oral histories are full of stories of individual women famous for their strength and ability to work as hard as any man. Cornelia, enslaved on a small Tennessee farm, proudly remembered her mother's speed and strength: "She cooked, washed, ironed, spun, nursed, and labored in the field. She made as good a field hand as she did a cook . . . I tell you, she was a captain."[35] Both men and women worked as domestics, estimated at about 10 percent of the Black labor force of the South, with men serving as personal valets, as butlers, and occasionally even as nurses for slaveholders' young sons.

In addition to their skilled agricultural work, enslaved women supplied knowledge and labor that sustained enslaved communities and supported the privileges of the slaveholding class. On the larger plantations, where some specialization of labor was possible, enslaved men had more access to trades such as blacksmithing and carpentering while individual women might gain reputations as expert midwives, seamstresses, and cooks. Large slaveholding estates often relied on enslaved women's knowledge of medicine and long hours of caregiving in plantation "hospitals" as well as white households. One Georgia planter in 1832 directed his overseer never to call a white doctor unless Elsey, "the Doctress of the Plantation" — also the neighborhood midwife — had first tried her hand at a cure.[36]

Although often made to "work like a man," enslaved women also became targets of gendered violence. The particular vulnerabilities of their sex were exploited when they were beaten. Numerous stories record that enslaved women's skirts were raised over their heads before whippings, to humiliate them and perhaps to make their physical sufferings greater. Only a woman in the late stages of pregnancy might be spared the worst whippings, and only then to protect her baby, who, when born, had the potential to be worth a great deal to the slaveholder. Similarly, after

ELLEN CRAFT,

The fugitive Slave.

◆ *Ellen Craft, The Fugitive Slave* **(1860)**
This engraving of Ellen Craft (1826–1891) serves as the frontispiece for her husband William Craft's slave narrative, *Running a Thousand Miles for Freedom*, published in London in 1860. As the daughter of an enslaved woman and her white captor, Ellen was able to use her light skin to masquerade as a young invalid white man traveling north with his enslaved valet (who was actually William). William stealthily procured an extra man's hat, shirt, and coat, while Ellen sewed a set of men's trousers for her escape. During their long journey, Ellen pretended to be deaf to avoid having to speak to fellow travelers. Her race- and gender-crossing ruse successfully fooled even a white acquaintance they encountered along the route from Georgia to Boston. William's dramatic narrative, self-authored after he learned to read and write, conveyed the perils braved by both Ellen and William Craft to reach a free community where their future children would not be born into slavery. *Mary Evans Picture Library.*

giving birth, women were suspended from field labor just briefly. Northern visitors commented frequently on the sight of an old enslaved woman bringing infants to the fields so that their young mothers could nurse them quickly and return to work. When beatings failed to discipline females who resisted their captors' control, sale was an even greater threat, especially if it meant separating a woman from her child. A runaway captive named Mrs. James Seward told the story of her sister in Maryland who was punished for resisting her captor in all these ways: after beating her, the slaveholder controlled her by "taking away her clothes and locking them up. . . . He kept her at work with only what she could pick up to tie on her for decency. He took away her child which had just begun to walk." Fearing the woman's physical strength, this slaveholder waited to whip her until she had just given birth. "Now I can handle you," he exclaimed, "now you are weak."[37]

As chattels rather than persons with rights, Black captives were not permitted legally binding marriage contracts, which might interfere with the slaveholder's right to buy and sell them away from their husbands or wives. Nonetheless, men and women under slavery went to great lengths to sustain conjugal and parental relationships. Frequently, such unions linked women and men of different slaveholders. In these "abroad marriages," it usually fell to the man to visit his wife and children. Often traveling at night to visit his family, without the slaveholder's knowledge or permission, the abroad husband risked being whipped or even sold away. To some extent, what enslaved husbands and wives expected of each other bore similarities to the gender roles of free couples. Yet, as one historian rightfully argues, "The daily realities of the slave system, bent on maximizing profits, meant that neither women nor men could strictly adhere to the gender assignments of the dominant society."[38] The daily aspirations of both enslaved wives and their husbands continually ran up against slaveholder attempts to control their time, labor, bodies, and mobility.

Coerced sexual relations between captors and enslaved women were an open secret in the South, heartily denied by slaveholders and yet virtually endemic to the society. The light complexions and western European features of numerous bondspeople were adequate testimony to this forced intimate connection between enslaved people and slaveholders. Mary Boykin Chesnut, a member of South Carolina's slaveholding aristocracy, knew this reality. Her diaries are much quoted by historians for what they reveal about slave society's contradictions (see Reading into the Past: "Slavery a Curse to Any Land").

While running afoul of Christian morality, slaveholders' sexual exploitation of enslaved women was encouraged by everything else about the slave system, from their control of bondwomen's bodies to their legal ownership of any resulting children. Slaveholders certainly did not limit their sexual abuse to females, but Black women and girls in the South bore the brunt of sexual coercion, ranging from gang rape to concubinage that extended over many decades. Southern rape laws specifically named only white women as capable of being raped, so free Black women also experienced considerable sexual violence. In one of the best-known accounts of a slaveholder's sexual aggression toward a female captive, Harriet Jacobs described how, when she was only fifteen, the slaveholder began to insist that she have sex with him. Some Black mothers attempted to prepare their daughters for the dangers ahead. Later in her life, Minnie Folkes recalled how her mother told her, "Don't let nobody bother yo' principle; cause dat wuz all yo' had."[39] Many who were unable to avoid abuse lived with deep trauma. Others erupted in rage. In 1856, nineteen-year-old Celia was executed by the state of Missouri for killing her captor Robert Newsome after five years of enduring his repeated sexual assaults. As Celia's case reminds us, the sexual exploitation of enslaved women cannot be understood solely in property terms, but must also be seen as reflecting dynamics of physical, social, and psychological domination under the racialized system of southern slavery.

The issue of deliberate breeding was an explosive one in the slave South. Opponents of slavery accused owners of encouraging and arranging pregnancies among their female captives to produce more people to sell on the lucrative internal slave market. Evidence suggests that they were right. "Marsa used to sometimes pick our wives fo' us," formerly enslaved person Charles Grandy recalled. "Marsa would . . . buy you a woman. . . . All he wanted was a young healthy one who looked like she could have children, whether she was purty or ugly as sin."[40]

READING INTO THE PAST

MARY BOYKIN CHESNUT
Slavery a Curse to Any Land

The diary kept by the South Carolina slaveholder Mary Boykin Chesnut (1823–1886) has long been regarded as a major source for insights into the minds of southern slaveholders. More recently, historians have explored Chesnut's views on the position of the women of this class.

March 14, 1861: I wonder if it be a sin to think slavery a curse to any land. . . . [W]e live surrounded by prostitutes. An abandoned woman is sent out of any decent house elsewhere. Who thinks any worse of a Negro or Mulatto woman for being a thing we can't name. God forgive us, but ours is a monstrous system & wrong & iniquity. Perhaps the rest of the world is as bad. This is only what I see: like the patriarchs of old, our men live all in one house with their wives & their concubines, & the Mulattos one sees in every family exactly resemble the white children — & every lady tells you who is the father of all the Mulatto children in everybody's household, but those in her own, she seems to think drop from the clouds or pretends so to think — . . . . My disgust sometimes is boiling over — . . . . Thank God for my countrywomen — alas for the men! No worse than men everywhere, but the lower their mistresses, the more degraded they must be.

SOURCE: Mary Boykin Chesnut, *A Diary from Dixie* (1905; repr., Boston: Houghton Mifflin, 1949), 21.

ANALYZING PRIMARY SOURCES

1. In her writings about the hidden but extensive sexual relations between slaveholding men and the women they enslaved, why does Chesnut seem so resentful of, rather than sympathetic to, these women?

2. What privileged assumptions is Chesnut making when she calls enslaved women who have had sexual relations with white slaveholding men "prostitutes"?

Women of childbearing age who were described as "good breeders" brought a higher price on the auction block. The painful imprint of these practices stayed with Black women for decades. Faced with the threat of being sold away from her family, for example, the sixteen-year-old Rose Williams "yielded" to forced breeding. Yet, as she told Federal Writers' Project (FWP) interviewers in the 1930s, the scarring experience left her unable or unwilling to have anything more to do with men or childbearing.[41]

Any hope that the solidarities of gender might have crossed the boundaries of race and class was crushed by a female slaveholder's financial and cultural attachments to her privilege vis-à-vis enslaved women and the tensions of the unacknowledged sexual exploitation of enslaved women. Jealous or suspicious women vented on their bonded females the anger and rage they dared not express to their husbands. Harriet Jacobs feared her female captor every bit as much as she did her male. Females who worked in the plantation house were at greatest risk, exposed day in and day out to slaveholders' sexual demands and their wives' grievances.

Bondwomen's narratives frequently describe an impatient or intolerant female slaveholder striking out at a cook or a nursemaid or even an enslaved child who was unable to handle an assigned task. In their diaries and letters, slaveholding white women recorded their secret fears of violent retribution. As the Civil War was breaking out, Mary Boykin Chesnut wrote anxiously about the death of a cousin who, it was suspected, had been "murdered by her own people."[42] Although both Black and white women suffered in the slave system, white women also benefited from it. Black women knew they could expect no sympathy from female captors. The luxury and culture of the white southern woman were premised on the forced labor and sexual oppression of captives. Violence against and violations of enslaved girls and women mocked southern deference to womanhood and female sexual purity. With only the rarest of exceptions, slavery turned Black and white women against each other and set their interests and their perspectives in direct opposition.

◆ CONCLUSION: TRUE WOMANHOOD AND THE REALITY OF WOMEN'S LIVES

Perhaps at no other time in American history were the prescriptions for a proper domestic role for white women more precise and widely agreed on than in antebellum America. Much of the young country's hope for stability and prosperity among its white citizens rested on the belief in a universally achievable middle-class family order for them, with the devoted, selfless wife and mother at the center.

As we shall see in the next chapter, some women were able to use the ideology of "true womanhood" to expand their sphere in subtle ways, but even so, this ideology was exceedingly rigid and limiting, ignoring the reality of women who led very different sorts of lives. Factory operatives were outside the boundaries of acceptable womanhood because they lived and worked in what *Godey's Lady's Book* editor Sarah Josepha Hale called "the accursed bank note world" that only men were supposed to occupy.[43] And enslaved and Indigenous women were deprived — absolutely — of the protection and privileges that were meant to compensate true women for their limited sphere. While the rhetoric of true womanhood seemed to place domestic women at the heart of American society, in reality the giant processes in which these other women were caught up — industrialization, marginalization, extermination, and slavery — were the dynamic forces shaping the young American nation and foreshadowing the trends and crises of its future.

CHAPTER 4 REVIEW

KEY TERMS

"the cult of true womanhood" (p. 151)

Godey's Lady's Book (p. 152)

Second Great Awakening (p. 153)

African Methodist Episcopal (AME) Church (p. 157)

Lowell Offering (p. 165)

Lowell Female Labor Reform Association (p. 166)

Indian Removal Act (p. 172)

REVIEW QUESTIONS

1. How did the "hegemonic" ideology of true womanhood shape northern women's lives, even when their economic and social realities didn't match the ideal? How does the answer to this question change when discussing enslaved women, working-class women, and middle-class women?

2. What made Lowell millwork so liberating for young white women from New England? When and why did millwork become more exploitive of its laborers?

3. The text notes that "slavery turned Black and white women against each other and set their interests and their perspectives in direct opposition." Explain this statement by explaining how the system of slavery both connected and divided slaveholding and enslaved females. Be sure to include nonslaveholding white women and slaveholding Indigenous and white women in this discussion.

4. **Making Connections** One of the most important developments of the first half of the nineteenth century was the emergence of commercial capitalism and a market economy. How was women's labor (Black and white, enslaved and free, northern and southern) central to this development? Consider both domestic and public labor in your answer.

SUGGESTED READING

True Womanhood

Nancy Cott, *The Bonds of Womanhood: "Woman's Sphere" in New England, 1780–1835*, 2nd ed. (1997).

Barbara Cutter, *Domestic Devils, Battlefield Angels: The Radicalism of American Womanhood, 1830–1865* (2003).

Cathy N. Davidson and Jessamyn Hatcher, eds., *No More Separate Spheres! A Next Wave American Studies Reader* (2002).

Amy S. Greenberg, *Manifest Manhood and the Antebellum American Empire* (2005).

Shawn Johansen, *Family Men: Middle-Class Fatherhood in Industrializing America* (2001).

Mary Ryan, *Cradle of the Middle Class: The Family in Oneida County, 1780–1835* (1983).

Kathryn Kish Sklar, *Catharine Beecher: A Study in American Domesticity* (1976).

Barbara Welter, *Dimity Convictions: The American Woman in the Nineteenth Century* (1976).

Early Industrial Women Workers

Mary Blewett, *Men, Women, and Work: Class, Gender, and Protest in the New England Shoe Industry, 1780–1910* (1988).

———, *We Will Rise in Our Might: Workingwomen's Voices from Nineteenth-Century New England* (1991).

Jeanne Boydston, *Home and Work: Housework, Wages, and the Ideology of Labor in the Early Republic* (1990).

Susanna Delfino and Michele Gillespie, eds., *Neither Lady nor Slave: Working Women of the Old South* (2002).

Thomas Dublin, ed., *Farm to Factory: Women's Letters, 1830–1860*, 2nd ed. (1993).

———, *Women at Work: The Transformation of Work and Community in Lowell, Massachusetts, 1826–1860* (1981).

Martha Hodes, *The Sea Captain's Wife: A True Story of Love, Race and War in the Nineteenth Century* (2006).

Bernice Selden, *The Mill Girls: Lucy Larcom, Harriet Hansen Robinson, Sarah G. Bagley* (1983).

Christine Stansell, *City of Women: Sex and Class in New York, 1789–1860* (1986).

Carole Turbin, *Working Women of Collar City: Gender, Class, and Community in Troy, New York, 1864–1886* (1992).

Sex Work

Patricia Cline Cohen, Timothy J. Gilfoyle, and Helen Lefkowitz Horowitz, eds., *The Flash Press: Sporting Male Weeklies in 1840s New York* (2008).

Barbara Meil Hobson, *Uneasy Virtue: The Politics of Prostitution and the American Reform Tradition* (1987).

Women in Slave Society

Daina Ramey Berry, *The Price for Their Pound of Flesh: The Value of the Enslaved from Womb to Grave in the Building of a Nation* (2017).

———, *"Swing the Sickle for the Harvest Is Ripe": Gender and Slavery in Antebellum Georgia* (2007).

Stephanie M. H. Camp, *Closer to Freedom: Enslaved Women and Everyday Resistance in the Plantation South* (2004).

Christie Anne Farnham, ed., *Women of the American South: A Multicultural Reader* (1997).

Sharla M. Fett, *Working Cures: Healing, Health, and Power on Southern Slave Plantations* (2002).

Elizabeth Fox-Genovese, *Within the Plantation Household: Black and White Women of the Old South* (1998).

Thavolia Glymph, *Out of the House of Bondage: The Transformation of the Plantation Household* (2008).

Tera W. Hunter, *Bound in Wedlock: Slave and Free Black Marriage in the Nineteenth Century* (2017).

Jacqueline Jones, *Labor of Love, Labor of Sorrow: Black Women, Work, and the Family from Slavery to the Present* (1985).

Barbara Krauthamer, *Black Slaves, Indian Masters: Slavery, Emancipation, and Citizenship in the Native American South* (2013).

Suzanne Lebsock, *The Free Women of Petersburg: Status and Culture in a Southern Town, 1784–1860* (1984).

Stephanie McCurry, *Masters of Small Worlds: Yeoman Households, Gender Relations, and the Political Culture of the Antebellum South Carolina Low Country* (1995).

Melton A. McLaurin, *Celia, A Slave: A True Story* (1999).

Tiya Miles, *The House on Diamond Hill: A Cherokee Plantation Story* (2010).

Deirdre Cooper Owens, *Medical Bondage: Race, Gender, and the Origins of American Gynecology* (2017).

Marie Jenkins Schwartz, *Birthing a Slave: Motherhood and Medicine in the Antebellum South* (2006).

Brenda E. Stevenson, *Life in Black and White: Family and Community in the Slave South* (1996).

Deborah Gray White, *Ar'n't I a Woman? Female Slaves in the Plantation South*, rev. ed. (1999).

PRIMARY SOURCES

Sex Work in New York City, 1858

As chief physician in the 1850s for the New York City "lock hospital" (where sex workers suspected of venereal diseases were both incarcerated and treated), Dr. William Sanger had both knowledge of and compassion for the women he attended. Although Sanger was hopeful that more accurate information would help to eradicate sex work, he originally relied only on the surveys conducted by other scholars regarding how various populations believed men and women should behave, including acceptable and forbidden sexual behaviors. His "global" study unfortunately adhered to biased, racialized, and classist notions of the day. He did, however, eventually try to bring the facts of late nineteenth-century New York sex work to light and to convey the sex workers' experiences and thoughts realistically by conducting his own inteviews. The originals of Sanger's interviews were destroyed in a fire the year after he gathered them, so his published report to the trustees of the New York Alms House brings us as close as we can get to the sex workers themselves. Interestingly, Sanger did no research into the men who were their clientele.

Sanger's sample, although not randomly selected, was large enough to allow for useful generalizations about white sex workers: most were from fifteen to twenty years old; three-fifths were native-born; among the immigrants, 60 percent were Irish; one-fifth were married; half had children; half were or had been domestic servants; half were afflicted with syphilis; and the average length of life after entering sex work was four years.

Sanger estimated that six thousand women were engaged in commercial sex in New York City, a number based on his careful survey of police records, lock hospitals, and known brothels. Others estimated much higher numbers. Even so, Sanger's estimates were distressing. As Sanger repeatedly insisted, they reflected not the inherent lack of virtue of the sex workers, but rather the relentless financial pressure on poor urban women. The effects of a sharp economic depression in 1857 are detected everywhere in the women's descriptions of their situations.

Sanger believed that women were too often blamed for prostitution. He wanted to show that they were the victims, both of men's callousness and their own lack of economic opportunity. Despite these reformist sentiments, however, Sanger held conventional notions of white femininity. Indeed, he championed sex workers because he was certain that most women would never of their own accord undertake a life of casual sex. Rather, he believed, they must have been deserted, seduced, driven by destitution, or forced into sex work by some other extraordinary event over which they had no control. Underlying his compassion for those who were remorseful, the traces of a harsher set of judgments can be found. Thus

Sanger's report can be read as evidence of middle-class attitudes toward white female sexuality, as well as of sex workers' own experience.

What follows is Sanger's summary and analysis of the two thousand answers given to one of his most revealing questions: "What are the causes of your becoming a prostitute?" As you read, think about how the personal stories that Sanger relates allow us to imagine a more complicated set of explanations for individual women's entry into sex work than the categories he uses.

WILLIAM W. SANGER
The History of Prostitution: Its Extent, Causes, and Effects throughout the World (1858)

[Question:] *What are the causes of your becoming a prostitute?* . . .

Causes	Numbers
Inclination	513
Destitution	525
Seduced and abandoned	258
Drink, and the desire to drink	181
Ill-treatment of parents, relatives, or husbands	164
As an easy life	124
Bad company	84
Persuaded by prostitutes	71
Too idle to work	29
Violated	27
Seduced on board emigrant ships	16
Seduced in emigrant boarding houses	8
Total	2000

This question is probably the most important of the series, as the replies lay open to a considerable extent those hidden springs of evil which have hitherto been known only from their results. First in order stands the reply [which 513 respondents chose], "Inclination," which can only be understood as meaning a voluntary resort to prostitution in order to gratify the sexual passions. . . .

The force of desire can neither be denied nor disputed, but still in the bosoms of most females that force exists in a slumbering state until aroused by some outside influences. . . . In the male sex nature has provided a more susceptible organization than in females, apparently with the beneficent design of repressing those evils which must result from mutual appetite equally felt by both. In other words, man is the *aggressive* animal, so far as sexual desire is involved. Were it otherwise, and the passions in both sexes equal, illegitimacy and prostitution would be far more rife in our midst than at present.

Some few of the cases in which the reply "Inclination" was given are herewith submitted, with the explanation which accompanied each return. C. M.: while virtuous, this girl had visited dancehouses, where she became acquainted with prostitutes, who persuaded her that they led an easy, merry life; her inclination was the result of female persuasion. E. C. left her husband, and became a prostitute willingly, in order to obtain intoxicating liquors which had been refused her at home. E. R. was deserted by her husband because she drank to excess and became a prostitute in order to obtain liquor. . . . Enough has been quoted to prove that, in many of the cases, what is called willing prostitution is the sequel of some communication or circumstances which undermine the principles of virtue and arouse the latent passions.

Destitution is assigned as a reason in five hundred and twenty-five cases. In many of these it is unquestionably true that positive, actual want, the apparent and dreaded approach of starvation, was the real cause of degradation. . . .

During the progress of this investigation in one of the lower wards of the city, attention was drawn to a pale but interesting-looking girl, about seventeen years of age, from whose replies the following narrative is condensed, retaining her own words as nearly as possible.

"I have been leading this life from about the middle of last January (1856). It was absolute want that drove me to it. My sister, who was about three years older than I am, lived with me. She was deformed and crippled from a fall she had while a child, and could not do any hard work. . . . One very cold morning, just after I had been to the store, the landlord's agent called for some rent we owed, and told us that, if we could not pay it, we should have to move. The agent was a kind man, and gave us a little money to buy some coals. We did not know what we were to do, and were both crying about it, when the woman who keeps this house (where she was then living) came in and brought some sewing for us to do that day. She said that she had been recommended to us by a woman who lived in the same house, but I found out since that she had watched me, and only said this for an excuse. When the work was done I brought it home here. I had heard of such places before, but had never been inside one. I was very cold, and she made me sit down by the fire, and began to talk to me, saying how much better off I should be if I would come and live with her. . . . When I got home and saw my sister so sick as she was and wanting many little things that we had no money to buy, and no friends to help us to, my heart almost broke. However, I said nothing to her then. I laid awake all night thinking, and in the morning I made up my mind to come here. . . . I thought that, if I had been alone, I would sooner have starved, but I could not bear to see her suffering. She only lived a few weeks after I came here. I broke her heart. I do not like the life. I would do almost any thing to get out of it; but, now that I have *once done wrong*, I can not get any one to give me work, and I must stop here unless I wish to be starved to death."

These details give some insight into the under-current of city life. The most prominent fact is that a large number of females, both operatives and domestics, earn so small wages that a temporary cessation of their business, or being a short time out of a situation, is sufficient to reduce them to absolute distress. Provident habits are useless in their cases; for, much as they may feel the necessity, *they have nothing to save*, and the very day that they encounter a reverse sees them penniless. The struggle a virtuous girl will wage against fate in such circumstances may be conceived: it is a literal battle for life, and in the result life is too often preserved only by the sacrifice of virtue. . . .

Moralists say that all human passions should be held in check by reason and virtue, and none can deny the truthfulness of the assertion. But while they apply the sentiment to the weaker party, who is the sufferer, would it not be advisable to recommend the same restraining influences to him who is the inflictor? No woman possessed of the smallest share of decency or the slightest appreciation of virtue would voluntarily surrender herself without some powerful motive, not pre-existent in herself, but imparted by her destroyer. Well aware of the world's opinion, she would not recklessly defy it, and precipitate herself into an abyss of degradation and shame unless some overruling influence had urged her forward. This motive and this influence, it is believed, may be uniformly traced to her weak but truly feminine dependence upon another's vows. . . . Thus there can be little doubt that, in most cases of seduction, female virtue is trustingly surrendered to the specious arguments and false promises of dishonorable men.

Men who, in the ordinary relations of life, would scruple to defraud their neighbors of a dollar, do not hesitate to rob a confiding woman of her chastity. They who, in a business point of view, would regard obtaining goods under false pretenses as an act to be visited with all the severity of the law, hesitate not to obtain by even viler fraud the surrender of woman's virtue to their fiendish lust. Is there no inconsistency in the social laws which condemn a swindler to the state prison *for his offenses*, and condemn a woman to perpetual infamy *for her wrongs*? Undoubtedly there are cases where the woman is the seducer, but these are so rare as to be hardly worth mentioning.

Seduction is a social wrong. Its entire consequences are not comprised in the injury inflicted on the woman, or the sense of perfidy oppressing the conscience of the man. Beyond the fact that she is, in the ordinary language of the day, ruined, the victim has endured an attack upon her principles which must materially affect her future life. The world may not know of her transgression, and, in consequence, public obloquy may not be added to her burden; but she is too painfully conscious of her fall, and every thought of her lacerated and bleeding heart is embittered with a sense of man's wrong and outrage. . . . It can not be a matter of surprise that, with this feeling of injustice and insult burning at her heart, her career should be one in which she becomes the aggressor, and man the victim; for it is certain that in this desire of revenge upon the sex for the falsehood of one will be found a cause of the increase of prostitution. . . .

In one of the most aristocratic houses of prostitution in New York was found the daughter of a merchant, a man of large property, residing in one of the Southern states. She was a beautiful girl, had received a superior education, spoke several languages fluently, and seemed keenly sensible of her degradation. Two years before this time she had been on a visit to some relations in Europe, and on her return voyage in one of her father's vessels, she was seduced by the captain, and became pregnant. He solemnly asserted that he would marry her as soon as they reached their port, but the ship had no sooner arrived than he left her. The poor girl's parents would not receive her back into their family, and she came to New York and prostituted herself for support. . . .

"Ill-treatment of parents, husbands, or relatives" is a prolific cause of prostitution, one hundred and sixty-four women assigning it as a reason for their fall. . . .

J. C.: "My father accused me of being a Prostitute when I was innocent. He would give me no clothes to wear. My mother was a confirmed drunkard and used to be away from home most of the time." Here we have a combination of horrors scarcely equaled in the field of romance. The unjust accusations of the father, and his conduct in not supplying his child with the actual necessaries of life, joined with the drunkenness of the mother, present such an accumulation of cruelty and vice that it would have been a miracle had the girl remained virtuous. It is to be presumed that no one will claim for this couple the performance of any one of the duties enjoined by their position. . . .

Great as are the duties and responsibilities of a father, they are equaled by those devolving upon a husband. He has to provide for the welfare of his wife besides caring for the interests of his children. . . . All married prostitutes can not be exonerated from the charge of guilt, yet the facts which will be hereafter quoted prove that many were driven to a life of shame by those who had solemnly sworn to protect and cherish them. . . .

C. H.: "I was married when I was seventeen years old, and have had three children. The two boys are living now; the girl is dead. My oldest boy is nearly five years old, and the other one is eighteen months. My husband is a sailor. We lived very comfortably till my last child was born, and then he began to drink very hard, and did not support me and I have not seen him or heard any thing about him for six months. After he left me I tried to keep my children by washing or going out to day's work, but I could not earn enough. I never could earn more than two or three dollars a week when I had work, which was not always. My father and mother died when I was a child. I had nobody to help me, and could not support my children, so I came to this place. My boys are now living in the city, and I support them with what I earn by prostitution. It was only to keep them that I came here." . . . In order to feed her helpless offspring she was forced to yield her honor; to prevent them suffering from the pains of hunger, she voluntarily chose to endure the pangs of a guilty conscience; to prolong their lives she periled her own. And at the time when this alternative was forced upon her, the husband was lavishing his money for intoxicating liquor. If she sinned — and this fact can not be denied, however charity may view it — it was the non-performance of his duty that urged, nay, positively forced her to sin. She must endure the punishment of her offenses, but, after reading her simple, heart-rending statement, let casuists* decide what amount of condemnation will rest upon the man whose desertion compelled her to violate the law of chastity in order to support his children. . . .

Seventy-one women were persuaded by prostitutes to embrace a life of depravity. One of the most common modes by which this end is accomplished is to inveigle a girl into some house of prostitution as a servant, and this is frequently done through the medium of an intelligence office. . . . [At such establishments] servants who wish to obtain situations register their wants and pay a fee. . . .

Keepers of houses sometimes visit these offices themselves, but generally some unknown agent is employed, or, at times, one of the prostitutes is plainly dressed, and sent to register her name as wishing a situation, so as to be able to obtain admission into the waiting-room. There she enters into conversation with the other women, whom she uses all the art she possesses to induce to visit her employer. . . .

Some of the sources of prostitution have been thus examined. To expose them all would require a volume; but it is hoped that sufficient has been developed to induce observation and inquiry, and prompt action in the premises.

SOURCE: William W. Sanger, *The History of Prostitution: Its Extent, Causes, and Effects throughout the World* (New York: Harper & Brothers 1858, 1921), 488–522.

ANALYZING PRIMARY SOURCES

1. Why does Sanger think it highly unlikely that women ever are responsible for their entry into sex work? Do you agree with him on this point?

2. How does Sanger distinguish his approach to and opinions about sex work from the views of those he calls "moralists"?

3. Where do economic conditions show up in Sanger's account of what causes women to become sex workers?

4. Do you think that Sanger is writing about Black and other women of color when he draws his conclusions? If so, how specifically does he engage these women's experiences? What more might he have done to include them in his study?

---

* Those who are logical yet unfeeling.

PRIMARY SOURCES

Mothering under Slavery

Motherhood was simultaneously the source of an enslaved woman's greatest personal satisfaction and her greatest misery, because her children ultimately belonged to her enslavers. Mothers had the immensely difficult task of teaching their children to survive their captors' power and at the same time to know their own worth as human beings. The woman Cornelia remembered her spirited mother's lessons in self-defense: "I'll kill you, gal, if you don't stand up for yourself. . . . Fight, and if you can't fight, kick; if you can't kick, then bite."[44] Not all enslaved women chose the dangerous route of open resistance. Many worked collectively with other enslaved women to impart lessons of survival and care for one another's children in the face of sale and high mortality.

Motherhood, therefore, so elevated in the ideology of true womanhood, presented enslaved women with dilemmas that free women simply did not have to face. Nineteenth-century slave states still followed the principle of *partus sequitur ventrem*, instituted during the colonial period, which imposed a property claim on each and every bonded woman's child (see "African Women" in Chapter 2). Once the United States outlawed the transatlantic slave trade in 1808, slaveholders and their physicians placed greater emphasis on enslaved women's fertility to ensure the future of the plantation economy. Southern doctors like the well-known J. Marion Sims even targeted some enslaved women and Irish immigrant females for experimental surgeries that contributed to the emergence of obstetrics and gynecology as a medical specialty. The public and derogatory way in which whites, male and female, discussed Black women's sexuality and childbearing led an older woman in the 1930s to describe slavery as a time when "women wasn't nothing but cattle."[45] Added to their reproductive labor of childbearing and child care — not only of their own children, but also of white women's children — enslaved women also shouldered the burden of agricultural labor in the fields and skilled work in spinning and sewing rooms. Motherhood thus pulled enslaved women in conflicting directions while the wider society denied them any of the respect or status accorded to free white middle-class mothers.

One way to think about the multiple meanings of motherhood for enslaved women is through the history of Black women's bodies. In theory, suggests one historian, enslaved women "possessed at least three bodies."[46] The first body was the body dominated by slaveholders and subjected to commodification, coerced labor, and sexual violence. Motherhood from this perspective was strictly an exploitive institution, reinforced by both the law and the customs of white society. The second body was the site of sorrow and pain that resulted from this process of domination. Viewed through the second body, enslaved motherhood primarily entailed suffering, as women mourned the sale, mistreatment, and neglect that led to the deaths of their sons and daughters. Yet enslaved people were never defined solely by slaveholders' domination or by their own suffering. For this reason, an exploration of enslaved motherhood would not be complete without the inclusion of a third body: "a thing to be claimed and enjoyed, a site of pleasure and resistance." For these Black mothers, the third body could be expressed in moments of stolen enjoyment, acts of fierce protection and resistance, and even in the rejection of motherhood under the slaveholder's terms.

The many facets of mothering under slavery can best be grasped by reading several different types of sources. Because of the emphasis on oral culture within enslaved communities and white society's devaluation of enslaved people's history, much first-person testimony from enslaved women has been dismissed. Yet the historical record is still plentiful. Antebellum narratives, retrospective oral histories, plantation records, newspaper ads, and photographs such as Figures 4.2 and 4.3, just to name a few of the extant sources, all carry important evidence of enslaved women's mothering histories. As you examine these sources, carefully consider the perspective, audience, assumptions, and insights of each document or image.

DURING A PERIOD WHEN MOST MEDICAL CARE still occurred at home, antebellum domestic medicine manuals dispensed advice about treating common ailments. Physician J. Hume Simons's guide, aimed at the households of southern planters, included a section titled "General Directions for Raising Negroes." At the time of this manual's publication, deepening racial ideology painted Black mothers as inept and uncaring. Georgia lawyer Thomas R. R. Cobb, for example, wrote that the Black person's "natural affections are not strong, and consequently he is cruel to his offspring, and suffers little by separation from them."[47] Where do you see racialized ideas about Black mothering and inept child care reflected in the following passage? What consequences for enslaved mothers might have resulted from the author's assumption that white planters should be the providers and protectors of the health of enslaved people?

The Planter's Guide and Family Book of Medicine (1848)

On every plantation . . . there should be a capable and trusty nurse, to attend the sick and to report all new cases. A faithful and trusty woman (not as is commonly the case, a decrepit old woman), but a strong, able, and healthy woman to attend the negro children; for mothers who have infants at the breast will frequently obtain leave of absence from the field to nurse their infants and employ the time given them in sleeping [instead].

The person selected for the little negroes should also be made to cook for them, and to see that they are fed regularly with victuals well cooked. For it is a common practice among negroes to eat victuals half raw, and of course to give the same to their children. Some do it from laziness, others from ignorance of cooking, and some leave the feeding of their children entirely to their little nurses. I have several times been called to attend little children on plantations, who were poor and emaciated, and as the planter or overseer termed it, not thriving, but who were evidently suffering actually from starvation and want of water, owing to the negligence of their parents and little nurses.

SOURCE: J. Hume Simons, M.D., *The Planter's Guide and Family Book of Medicine* (Charleston, SC, 1848), 208.

IN THE 1930s, AS PART OF THE NEW DEAL Works Progress Administration, federally funded interviewers from the Federal Writers' Project (FWP) were sent throughout the South to record the memories of the last generations of Black people to have lived under slavery, all of whom had been children or young adults at the time and were now almost eighty or older. Preserved only as typescripts (and in a few cases, as primitive tape recordings), the FWP oral histories were finally made available in published form in the 1960s. Despite their valuable content, these twentieth-century sources, like most other sources of historical comment, also have limitations. Most of the interviewers were white, and some of the interviewees were deferential to or intimidated by them. Some interviewers were expected to render the testimony in dialect.

Nevertheless, Fannie Moore (Figure 4.1) provided an unvarnished portrait of her girlhood in bondage on a South Carolina plantation. What does Moore remember most about her mother and grandmother? Many FWP interviewees spoke of their mothers' and grandmothers' knowledge of herbal medicines. A Texas woman named Harriet Collins, for example, began her lengthy account of plant-based remedies with this assertion: "My mammy larned me a lots of doctorin', what she larnt from old folkses from Africy, and some de Indians larnt her."[48] In Fannie Moore's account below, who was responsible for the care of sick children? How might memory and the conditions of the FWP interviews have shaped the way that Moore told her life story?

Fannie Moore Remembers Her Mother and Grandmother (1937)

My granny she cook for us chillens while our mammy away in de fiel. Dey wasn't much cookin to do. Jes make co'n pone and bring in de milk. She hab a big wooden bowl wif enough wooden spoons to go 'roun'. She put de milk in de bowl and break it up. Den she put de bowl in de middle of de flo' an' all de chillum grab a spoon.

My mammy she work in de fiel' all day and piece and quilt all night. Den she hab to spin enough thread to make four cuts for de white folks ebber night. Why sometime I nebber go to bed. Hab to hold de light for her to see by. She hab to piece quilts for de white folks too. . . .

I never see how my mammy stan' sech ha'd work. She stand' up fo' her chillum tho'. De ol' overseeah he hate my mammy, case she fight him for beatin' her chillun. Why she git more whuppins for dat den anythin' else. She hab twelve chillun. . . .

◆ **Figure 4.1 Fannie Moore, Age 88 (c. 1937)**
Library of Congress.

My mammy she trouble in her heart 'bout de way they treated. Ever night she pray for de Lawd to git her an' her chillum out ob de place. . . .

My mammy grieve lots over brothah George, who die wif de fever. Granny she doctah him as bes' she could, evah time she git way from de white folks kitchen. My mammy nevah git chance to see him, 'cept when she git home in de evenin'. George he jes lie. One day I look at him an' he had sech a peaceful look on his face, I think he sleep and jes let him lone. Long in de evenin I think I try to wake him. I touch him on de face, but he was dead. Mammy nebber know til she come at night. Pore mammy she kneel by de bed an' cry her heart out'. Ol' uncle Allen, he make pine box for him an' carry him to de graveyard over on de hill. My mammy jes plow and cry as she watch em' put George in de groun'. . . .

Folks back den never heah tell of all de ailments de folks hab now. Dey war no doctahs. Jes use roots and bark for teas of all kinds. My ole granny uster make tea out o' dogwood bark an' give it to us chillum when we have a cold, else she make a tea outen wild cherry bark, pennyroil, or hoarhound. My goodness but dey was bitter. We do mos' enythin' to git out a takin' de tea, but twarnt no use granny jes git you by de collar hol' yo' nose and you jes swallow it or get strangled. When de baby hab de colic she git rats vein [a local medicinal plant] and make a syrup an' put a little sugar in it an' boil it. Den soon as it cold she give it to de baby. For stomach ache she give us snake root. Sometime she make tea, other time she jes cut it up in little pieces an' make you eat one or two ob dem. When you hab fever she wrap you up in cabbage leaves or ginseng leaves, dis made de fever go.

SOURCE: *Federal Writers' Project: Slave Narrative Project, Vol. 11, North Carolina, Part 2, Jackson-Yellerday*, 1936. 128–35. Manuscript/Mixed Material.

ONE OF THE CURIOUS, AND HAUNTING, aspects of material culture items created during the long era of Black enslavement is the inclusion of captives in the drawings, paintings, and photographs of their captors. These images of enslaved people, both individually and in spatial relationship to slaveholders, signify much about the power relationships between these subjects. Figures 4.2 and 4.3 capture the ambiguity of mothering in slave societies. Enslaved women often were taken away from their own children and made to turn their attention and labor to the children of slaveholders, as denoted in Figure 4.2. Captive mothers also had to withstand the physical "loss" of their own children when slaveholders employed young girls (and boys) to work as companions to their children or to themselves, as is indicated in Figure 4.3. Both images suggest the better, comparatively speaking, material conditions such as dress that these Black females reaped while in domestic service. It was, however, a high price to pay for their familial isolation while in service to slaveholders and their kin. No complaint was more repeated in the memoirs or accounts of enslaved females than, as mothers, their separation from their children or, as children, their loss of their mothers as a result of forced labor regimes or sale.

◆ Figure 4.2 **Lucy Cottrell and Child**
Kentucky Gateway Museum Center.

◆ Figure 4.3 **Female Slaveholder and Enslaved Child**
The History Collection/Alamy.

ADVERTISEMENTS FOR WET NURSES

Even intimate moments of nurture could be given a price in the market economy of chattel slavery. Evidence from newspaper ads and white women's diaries and letters suggests an "informal market in enslaved wet nurses, in which white women were the primary arbiters and beneficiaries."[49] Enslaved mothers were both hired and sold in the colonial and early nineteenth-century American South, in part, for the purpose of breastfeeding white infants. What words do advertisers use to promote enslaved wet nurses? What is the significance of the first advertisement's use of the phrase "without a child" as an attractive feature of this particular wet nurse? What other kinds of labor might wet nurses also be expected to do? How do these ads hint at white expectations for Black women's relationships to their own children?

City Gazette and Daily Advertiser, Charleston, South Carolina (October 28, 1795)

> To Be Hired,
> A Healthy Black Wet Nurse, without a child, with a good breast of milk. Enquire of Mrs. Dawson, at Mr. Patrick Hind's, in Beausain-Street. October 24

The Southern Patriot, Charleston, South Carolina (May 10, 1842)

> Wet Nurse, Seamstress, Washer, Ironer, and House Servant to Hire — A young healthy Woman with her child about 6 weeks old, and a Boy to attend to it. She will be hired either as a Wet Nurse, or either of the above capacities. She is a complete Seamstress, Washer and Ironer, and House Servant; to be seen at my house until hired. Apply to

> Theodore A. Whiteney,
> Broke and Auctioneer,
> 24 Holrlbeck's Alley, next to King St., May 10

The Charleston Mercury (June 7, 1856)

> Private Sales.
> *Healthy Young Wet Nurse.*
> *Capers & Heyward*
> Offer at private sale, a young and healthy Wet Nurse. For further particulars, apply at our office, South Side Adgers' Wharf, June 7

Source: Stephanie Jones-Rogers, " '[S]he Could . . . Spare One Ample Breast for the Profit of Her Owner': White Mothers and Enslaved Wet Nurses' Invisible Labor in American Slave Markets," *Slavery and Abolition* 38, no. 2 (2017): 337–55.

Narratives published by enslaved women who managed to escape to the North in the antebellum period provide valuable first-person accounts. Harriet Jacobs's (1813–1897) narrative, *Incidents in the Life of a Slave Girl*, is the most well known of the female-authored accounts. Jacobs was born into bondage in Edenton, North Carolina. From the age of fifteen, she was sexually harassed and abused by a slaveholder, the white physician James Norcom (whose young daughter was Jacobs's legal slaveholder). To escape the constant predation of Norcom, Jacobs sought the protection of another white man by whom she had two children.

In the midst of fear and sexual abuse, Jacobs described each of her beloved children as a "tie to life" that motivated her survival. After a decade, she escaped from Norcom, but because of her attachment to her children, she stayed nearby, hidden in the cramped attic room of her free grandmother. There she remained for seven years until she and her two children finally escaped the South.

In the following excerpt, Jacobs describes the atmosphere of violence and tension surrounding the birth of her second child, a daughter. Note that Jacobs uses pseudonyms in her narrative — Linda Brent for herself and Dr. Flint for Norcom. With a northern audience in mind, Jacobs was well aware of her readers' assumptions about Christian women's piety and sexual purity. What does she mean when she says that there was "no chance for me to be respectable"? How does Jacobs's grandmother attempt to provide maternal protection, and what are the limits to her efforts? How did Jacobs's grandmother respond to her granddaughter's sexual liaison with Dr. Flint/Norcom? What are Jacobs's feelings about giving birth to a daughter?

HARRIET JACOBS
Incidents in the Life of a Slave Girl (1861)

Chapter 14: Another Link to Life

I had not returned to my master's house since the birth of my child. The old man raved to have me thus removed from his immediate power; but his wife vowed, by all that was good and great, she would kill me if I came back; and he did not doubt her word. Sometimes he would stay away for a season. Then he would come and renew the old threadbare discourse about his forbearance and my ingratitude. He labored, most unnecessarily, to convince me that I had lowered myself. The venomous old reprobate had no need of descanting on that theme. I felt humiliated enough. My unconscious babe was the ever-present witness of my shame. I listened with silent contempt when he talked about my having forfeited his good opinion; but I shed bitter tears that I was no longer worthy of being respected by the good and pure. Alas! slavery still held me in its poisonous grasp. There was no chance for me to be respectable. There was no prospect of being able to lead a better life.

Sometimes, when my master found that I still refused to accept what he called his kind offers, he would threaten to sell my child. "Perhaps that will humble you," said he.

Humble me! Was I not already in the dust? But his threat lacerated my heart. I knew the law gave him power to fulfil it; for slaveholders have been cunning enough to enact that "the child shall follow the condition of the mother," not of the father; thus taking care that licentiousness shall not interfere with avarice. This reflection made me clasp my innocent babe all the more firmly to my heart. Horrid visions passed through my mind when I thought of his liability to fall into the slave trader's hands. I wept over him, and said, "O my child! perhaps they will leave you in some cold cabin to die, and then throw you into a hole, as if you were a dog."

When Dr. Flint learned that I was again to be a mother, he was exasperated beyond measure. He rushed from the house, and returned with a pair of shears. I had a fine head of hair; and he often railed about my pride of arranging it nicely. He cut every hair close to my head, storming and swearing all the time. I replied to some of his abuse, and he struck me. Some months before, he had pitched me down stairs in a fit of passion; and the injury I received was so serious that I was unable to turn myself in bed for many days. He then said, "Linda, I swear by God I will never raise my hand against you again"; but I knew that he would forget his promise.

After he discovered my situation, he was like a restless spirit from the pit. He came every day; and I was subjected to such insults as no pen can describe. I would not describe them if I could; they were too low, too revolting. I tried to keep them from my grandmother's knowledge as much as I could. I knew she had enough to sadden her life, without having my troubles to bear. When she saw the doctor treat me with violence, and heard him utter oaths terrible enough to palsy a man's tongue, she could not always hold her peace. It was natural and motherlike that she should try to defend me; but it only made matters worse.

When they told me my new-born babe was a girl, my heart was heavier than it had ever been before. Slavery is terrible for men; but it is far more terrible for women. Superadded to the burden common to all, they have wrongs, and sufferings, and mortifications peculiarly their own.

ANALYZING PRIMARY SOURCES

1. What claims about mothering for the enslaved does each primary source make, and what contradictions can you see between various sources?

2. What ideals of motherhood did enslaved women develop out of their daily experiences? How did these ideals compare to those of various groups of free women?

3. Interpret the sources here using the model of the three different "bodies" discussed in the introduction. Which sources best reveal the agency of enslaved mothers' "third body"?

PRIMARY SOURCES

Godey's Lady's Book

———————

BY 1850 *GODEY'S LADY'S BOOK*, with forty thousand subscribers, was the most widely circulated "ladies' magazine" in the United States. For $3 a year, readers from all over the country enjoyed a rich monthly collection of fiction, history (specializing in heroes and heroines of the American Revolution), poetry, and illustrations. Contributors to the magazine included well-known writers such as Nathaniel Hawthorne, who elsewhere bitterly castigated women writers as "that damned mob of scribbling women."[50] Lavish pictorial "embellishments," printed from full-page, specially commissioned steel engravings and hand-colored by the magazine's special staff of 150 female colorists (wage laborers, unlike most of the magazine's readers), lifted *Godey's* above the run-of-the-mill periodicals published for the literate female public. Subscribers treasured their issues, circulated them among friends, and preserved them in leather bindings. The magazine's large readership was testimony to the degree to which *Godey's* both reflected and affected the sympathies and values of its subscribers.

Godey's Lady's Book was edited by a woman and published by a man. Sarah Josepha Hale, a schoolteacher, mother, and widow from Boston, had turned to magazine editing to support herself and her children after the death of her husband in 1828. Like Catharine Beecher, she had pronounced views on the dignity and power of white woman's distinct domestic sphere. In the aftermath of the Panic of 1837, she joined forces with a commercially minded publisher, Louis Godey, to become the editor of *Godey's Lady's Book*, which he had founded in 1830. Her concerns for feminine values were now combined with his eye for women's possibilities as consumers. The magazine's illustrations thus combined advertisements for the latest fashions (which readers took to their seamstresses to duplicate) with illustrations promoting the feminine ideal of selflessness, purity, and subtle maternal influence. Although as the editor Hale was consistent in preaching this notion of women's redemptive, domestic influence throughout her career, her position became more defensive in the 1840s in reaction to the rising tide of the women's rights movement, which she thought dangerous both to women and to the nation: "The elevation of the [female] sex will not consist in becoming like man, in doing man's work, or striving for the dominion of the world. The true woman . . . has a higher and holier vocation. She works in the elements of human nature."[51]

Through stories and images, *Godey's Lady's Book* preached a compelling if conservative doctrine of women's importance to the nation. In a society rapidly being transformed by economic growth and political upheaval, domestic women were expected to provide emotional and spiritual stability. They were to function, as Figure 4.4 advocates, as "the constant" to middle-class American family life.

◆ Figure 4.4 ***The Constant, or the Anniversary Present*** **(1851)**
P 201.2 (v.42, Jan. 1851), Houghton Library, Harvard University.

This drawing illustrated a story of a young white wife whose quiet, steady love wordlessly convinced her wandering husband to join with her in embracing the healing "close communion of home life."[52] Note the woman's pose, at once submissive to her husband and protective of her child. This image was juxtaposed against another illustration warning women against being a flirtatious "coquette."

The ideology of true womanhood imbued motherhood with both secular and spiritual roles. *Godey's Lady's Book* considered white mothers as crucial to preserving the memory of the American Revolution and to securing its legacy within a stable, peaceful, and permanent American nation. Mothers accomplished this task by raising the next generation of citizens. The citizen-child was usually figured as male. "How Can an American Woman Serve Her Country?" *Godey's* asked. The answer: "By early teaching her sons to consider a republic as the best form of government in the world."[53]

While preaching the virtues of motherhood and domesticity, female ideologues of middle-class femininity portrayed teaching as a natural profession for

◆ **Figure 4.5 *The Teacher* (1844)**
GRANGER — Historical Picture Archive.

white women, drawing as it did on maternal virtues and emotions. Hale wrote that "the reports of common school education show that women are the *best* teachers," in response to which she sponsored a petition to Congress urging public support for women's teacher training.[54] Teaching had previously been the province of men and began changing into a woman's occupation only during the 1820s and 1830s. Outside the South, public education, considered essential to a virtuous citizenry, was expanding at a rapid rate. Inasmuch as female teachers were usually paid a third or less of what men were paid, the reasons for the shift were economic as well as ideological. How does the image in Figure 4.5 reconcile a woman working for wages with the ideology of true womanhood?

◆ **Figure 4.6** *Purity* **(1850)**
The New York Public Library/Art Resource, NY.

Barbara Welter, the first modern historian to examine the ideology of true womanhood, identified its four basic elements as domesticity, piety, submission, and purity.[55] Purity, of course, referred to sexuality (not just experience but also desire), of which the true woman was expected to be innocent. In Figure 4.6, the feminine virtue of purity is illustrated at the same time as it is used to advertise designs for fashionable wedding dresses. How do ideological and economic concerns come together in this image?

The middle-class character of the doctrine of domesticity was revealed in the frequent illustrations of the difficulties that the true woman had in hiring and supervising household servants. Although — or because — the relation between

◆ **Figure 4.7** *Cooks* **(1852)**
The New York Public Library/Art Resource, NY.

female employer and maid was one of the more distressing of the middle-class housewife's domestic obligations, the stories and drawings about this dilemma were invariably humorous, with the "incompetent" and "stupid " housemaid or cook as the butt of the joke. The very face and figure of the cook in Figure 4.7 indicate a female quite different from her employer. How is the employer designated as a true woman while the cook is not? What does the illustration suggest about the relationship of husband and wife, as well as that of female employer and maid?

Although *Godey's Lady's Book* insisted on the distinction between white woman's domestic sphere and man's worldly obligations, it hinted at the ways that

◆ Figure 4.8 *Shoe Shopping* (1848)
The New York Public Library/Art Resource, NY.

economic realities and the larger society impinged on middle-class women's efforts to practice their home-based ideals. Hale preached women's special virtues as an antidote to the distressingly materialistic world outside the home, but *Godey's* itself purveyed those same worldly values. The true woman was a frequent shopper, and in 1852 the magazine instituted a shopping service to assist its readers in the purchase of accessories and jewelry. Figure 4.8 portrays middle-class female consumers who have left their cloistered homes for the pleasures and luxury of an elegant shoe emporium, presided over by a male clerk. Looking at this mid-nineteenth-century illustration, keep in mind the women workers who manufactured these shoes. Note also how shopping is portrayed as a recreational activity already at this early stage in market society.

ANALYZING PRIMARY SOURCES

1. Examine the expressions, demeanor, and dress of the women from the *Godey's* illustrations shown here. What do they have in common? Why do they show so little variety? How might women readers have regarded these images and tried to imitate them?

2. Look at the profiles of the true women from *Godey's*. Notice their tiny waists, the composure of their hands, the elegance of their bearing. How do these and other details reinforce the message that white women are unfit for the public sphere?

3. Consider *Godey's* in light of fashion magazines you are familiar with today. What is the appeal of fashion magazines for women? How seriously do you take the lifestyle and the profiles modeled in the magazines you read? How can such sources be read critically to reveal something about contemporary times?

PRIMARY SOURCES

Early Photographs of Factory Operatives

PHOTOGRAPHY, INVENTED IN FRANCE in the 1830s, came to the United States in the 1840s. By 1850, commercial photographers were working in all the major cities. Compared to portrait painting, photography was quick and relatively inexpensive, exactly the modern form of artistic representation appropriate to a young nation. Perhaps also because so many Americans were on the move, they wanted these small, portable pictures of themselves to send to loved ones. In Massachusetts alone, there were four hundred photographic studios by 1855.[56] Nationwide, the estimate is three thousand by 1860.[57] Pocket-size portraits could be had for a few dollars, and common folks, even free Blacks, were eager to purchase their likenesses. In 1853, the *New York Tribune* estimated that 3 million photographs were being made annually. Unfortunately, only a relative few have survived.[58]

The earliest of these photographs are known as daguerreotypes, named for Louis Jacques Daguerre, the Frenchman who invented the technology in 1837. The daguerreotypist created a positive image on a metal plate treated with mercury and exposed to light. The finished product was enclosed in a case to protect it from light over time. In the United States, the technology gave way in the mid-1850s to simpler and less expensive processes: the tintype (which shortened the sitting time and reduced the cost) and the ambrotype (which used glass instead of metal for the photographic plate and produced a negative rather than a positive image).[59] By the early 1860s, photographers were learning how to make multiple positive prints on paper from negative glass plates. In the early studio photographs, sitters had to remain still for minutes, sometimes with their heads in braces to keep them still; not surprisingly, few smiled. The images that resulted were extremely fragile but also often stunning in their intimacy and delicacy. The sitters seem to look out at us across time, inviting us to study them and detect their sentiments.

For modern students of history, who rely on images for a great deal of information, photographs are particularly satisfying as a source of historical documentation. In our eagerness to see precise, seemingly objective images of the past, however, it is important to realize that the objects of these early historical photographs are selective: some things — and people — were photographed relatively frequently and others not at all. To put it another way, we cannot see photos of everything about which we are curious, only of what previous generations wanted to be seen. Thus, in addition to the obvious visible information that these early photographs convey about the American past, they also document what versions and aspects of themselves nineteenth-century Americans wanted to preserve.

The images of female factory workers that follow represent women living and working outside the dominant, middle-class ethic of mid-nineteenth-century true womanhood. Their existence prompts us to ask: who took care to purchase and preserve these images and why?

Female textile factory operatives arranged to have their own photographs taken. They posed in their work clothes and held shuttles as symbols of their work as spinners and weavers of cloth. The tools signified that the sitter was a skilled worker, with valuable knowledge, experience, and ability. As these images indicate, the women were proud of their presence in and contribution to the burgeoning industrial economy of those years.

Workers often posed for these portraits in groups, which suggests that they thought of their labor as collective and of their coworkers as friends. For women, coworkers were often relatives as well; sisters and cousins followed their kin into the mills, took jobs that had been secured for them, and worked in the same room at the same task. Factory work was a new experience for most of these young women, and the presence of familiar faces may have eased their transition into a strange environment. Family relations were still crucial elements of their lives, even in the impersonal environment of the textile factory.

By 1860, textile factories and the women who worked in them were found throughout much of New England. The four young women shown in Figure 4.9

◆ Figure 4.9 **Four Women Mill Workers (1860)**
Cornell University Library, ATHM Textile Photographs Collection.

were photographed near Winthrop, Maine. The two Lowell weavers pictured in Figure 4.10 look enough alike to have been sisters. By 1860, when both of these tintypes were taken, Irish newcomers were beginning to take over from Yankee workers in the textile industry, and these women may have been Irish-born. As you study the photographs presented in Figures 4.9 and 4.10, examine the poses, settings, and props. What do they suggest about these women's identities and perhaps even their thoughts? What do the photographs capture about these women's relationships? How do Figures 4.9 and 4.10 represent the pride that early factory workers took in their position?

ANALYZING PRIMARY SOURCES

1. These two early photographs show women defined by their labor. How are the women in these photographs different from those in in *Godey's Lady's Book* (Figures 4.4 to 4.8) of middle-class "true women"? What do you think of the fact that the former were more likely to come down to us in photographs, while the images of the latter were preserved in illustrations and paintings?

2. Consider what photographs add to historical documentation. What can photographs, even at this early stage, tell us about women's history that other sorts of images cannot? Conversely, how should we analyze photographs to avoid the temptation of regarding them simply as mirrors of a lost historical reality?

◆ **Figure 4.10 Two Women Mill Workers (1860)**
Cornell University Library, ATHM Textile Photographs Collection.

5

Shifting Boundaries

EXPANSION, REFORM, AND CIVIL WAR, 1840–1865

THE YEAR 1848 WAS A DECISIVE ONE IN THE HISTORY of the nation and its women. Mexico, on the losing side of a grueling war with the United States, had just signed the Treaty of Guadalupe Hidalgo and transferred 1.5 million square miles of land and thousands of human beings to U.S. sovereignty. The term "Manifest Destiny," coined a few years before, described the young nation's ambition to wrest much of the continent from Indigenous peoples, who, U.S. expansionists claimed, could not be trusted to exploit its potential riches. Responding to this violent crusade, tens of thousands of land-hungry American women and men crossed the central Plains to settle on the Pacific Coast. Less than a year after the end of the Mexican War, the discovery of gold in California dramatically accelerated this migration.

The beginning of the organized American women's rights movement also dates from 1848. Female reformers, white and Black, had been engaged for several decades in efforts to reshape and perfect American society. As proponents of temperance and opponents of slavery, women had pushed at the boundaries of the so-called woman's sphere and moved into more public roles in these years. With the inauguration of the women's rights movement at the Seneca Falls Convention of 1848, they openly breached these boundaries, directing their utopian hopes and activist energies toward the freedom of women themselves.

Finally in 1848, the issue of slavery began to move more directly into American party politics. Although Congress had been evading the issue of slavery for decades, in that year the first political party to oppose the expansion of slavery, the Free-Soil Party, was established, followed by the formation of the

Republican Party six years later. On the basis of its antislavery platform, the Republican Party captured the presidency in 1860, prompting eleven southern slave states to secede and fracturing the nation. The resulting Civil War threw the lives of all women, Union and Confederate, white, Black, and Native American, into upheaval for four deadly years and beyond.

In different ways, each of these historical processes was a kind of "movement." In this dynamic period in American history, when traditional social and economic arrangements were being challenged and reformulated, when national politics were confronting fundamental questions about the nature of American democracy and the future of the American nation, when the physical nation itself was breaking and remaking its borders, and when these vital sources of growth gave way to war and destruction and death, American women were on the move as well. Despite cultural conventions about white women's rootedness at home, American women of all backgrounds struck out in all sorts of directions, playing a distinctive part in the nation's history and transforming themselves in the process.

◆ AN EXPANDING NATION, 1843–1861

For a century before and a half century after 1848, continental expansion was a defining aspect of the American experience. Starting in the 1840s, however, the westward movement of American settlers entered a distinctive phase. The Oregon Trail was mapped in 1843 — the first of the overland routes across the Rocky Mountains — and over the next two decades approximately 350,000 Americans crossed the continent, moving through the Indigenous lands of mid-America and the West to reach the Pacific Coast. The migrants were mostly young American families: men charged with economic obligation and women with housekeeping, childbearing, and childrearing responsibilities. Except for enslaved people brought by southerners, they were for the most part white and, given the costs of the trek, from the middle ranks of society. When gold was discovered in California in 1848, the character and purposes of American migration changed. Hordes of eager, ambitious men (white, Black, and immigrant) — and a few intrepid women — rushed to California to realize their dreams of quick wealth rather than permanent settlement. The outbreak of the Civil War effectively curtailed the overland migration, and when expansion resumed

1848	Oneida, New York, utopian community formed
1848	Treaty of Guadalupe Hidalgo transfers much of northern Mexico to the United States
1848	First New York State Married Women's Property Act passed
1848	Seneca Falls Convention initiates women's rights movement
1848	Free-Soil Party founded
1850	Compromise of 1850, including Fugitive Slave Law, passed
1850	California becomes a state
1850	First National Women's Rights Convention held in Worcester, Massachusetts
1851	Susan B. Anthony and Elizabeth Cady Stanton's partnership begins
1852	New York women's temperance society formed
1852	Harriet Beecher Stowe's *Uncle Tom's Cabin* published
1854	Republican Party formed
1854	Elizabeth Cady Stanton addresses New York legislature on women's rights
1856	Margaret Garner tried in Cincinnati
1857	Supreme Court decides *Dred Scott v. Sandford*, rejecting possibility of Black citizenship
1860	Second New York State Married Women's Property Act passed
1860	Republican candidate Abraham Lincoln elected president
1860–1861	Southern states secede
1861	Civil War begins
1863	Emancipation Proclamation declares enslaved people in rebel territory free
1863	Women's National Loyal League established
1863	Battle of Gettysburg proves turning point in war
1863	Food riots in Richmond, Virginia, and draft riots in New York City erupt
1865	Robert E. Lee surrenders
1865	Lincoln assassinated
1865	Thirteenth Amendment ratified

211

during the last decades of the century, it took a different form, following the nation's new railroad system to concentrate on the great expanse of the trans-Mississippi Plains (see "Colonial Settler Families in the West" in Chapter 7).

Throughout the period of migration along the overland trails, women from the diverse cultures that converged in the West came into conflict. Mexican women who lived in the Southwest were pushed aside as white American women moved onto their lands. Self-identified "respectable" women shunned sex workers and female adventurers. Black women found some spaces to live more freely, but most still were forced to live and work on the margins of society and as inferior to other women. Through it all, Indigenous women and girls were used by newcomers for domestic and sexual labor. By the outbreak of the Civil War, many Mexican women were beginning to be confined in the labor market as domestics for white women. The conflicts between different groups of women were sometimes overt, sometimes implicit, but always more significant than the commonalities that the ideology of true womanhood could ever deliver.

Overland by Trail

Historians and American popular culture have long celebrated migrant women as "selfless wives" and "pioneer mothers" for their roles on the overland crossing, and it is undoubtedly true that men alone could not have made the new claims of continental nationhood a reality. But what of the actual experience of the individual women who pulled up stakes, cooked and laundered out of their primitive wagons for half a year or longer, and gave birth and tended children across more than two thousand miles? Husbands and fathers usually made the decision to move with little or no requested input from wives, children, or those kin who inevitably would be left behind because of old age, infirmity, or reluctance. In 1852, Martha Read wrote to her sister of her reluctance to leave New York with her husband: "It looks like a great undertaking to me but Clifton was bound to go and I thought I would go rather than stay here alone with the children."[1] Other women undertook the crossing with the same eagerness as did men. Looking west from the banks of the Missouri River that same year, Lydia Rudd wrote in her diary, "With good courage and not one sign of regret . . . [I] mounted my pony."[2] Individual families joined together in long lines ("trains") of thirty to two hundred covered wagons to share the cost, effort, and danger of the trip. Many single men made the overland crossing, but few unmarried women did. Enslaved women had no choice in the matter when southern slaveholders decided to take their households westward.

Occasionally, documents left by the migrants provide glimpses into the domestic tension that accompanied the difficult decision to uproot and migrate. A month into her 1848 trip to Oregon Territory, Keturah Belknap recorded a quarrel she overheard in a nearby wagon between a husband and wife: "She wants to turn back and he won't, so she says she will go and leave him . . . with that crying baby." Then Belknap heard a "muffled cry and a heavy thud as if something was thrown against the wagon box." She heard the wife say, "Oh you've killed it," to which the husband responded that "he would give her more of the same."[3] In another of these rarely recorded incidents of desperate female resistance, one woman on the trail was so determined to turn back that she set the family's wagon on fire.[4]

Throughout the crossing, men and women had distinctive responsibilities. Men drove the wagons and tended the animals. Women fed their families, cared for their children, and did their best to "keep house" in a cramped wagon bumping its way across the country. As the months wore on and the horses and oxen weakened, women walked more often than they rode. Men's tasks were concentrated during the day; after the wagons stopped and the animals were tended, they could snatch a bit of time to relax while they took turns keeping a security watch. If decisions about direction or pace had to be made, the men met alone and made them. The women's workdays were effectively the reverse. Wives and older girls woke up

◆ **Daniel Jenks,** *Camp 100* **(July 1859)**
Camp 100 — Humbolt River is a somewhat romanticized view of life for women (and men) on the overland trails to the West. The clothing, cooperative labor, and pleasant landscape belie the difficulty of the trip, particularly for the women. Females (and enslaved people) performed much of the domestic labor, including washing, cooking, nursing, and child care. Unlike many images of the West during this era, there is little hint of the dangers of criminals, illness, or the owners of this land on which these people camped — the Indigenous inhabitants. *Library of Congress, Prints and Photographs Division, Reproduction number LC-DIG-ppmsc-04819 (digital image from original).*

earlier to prepare breakfast, feed, clean, clothe, teach, and care for children as the train moved forward, and they worked for many hours after the wagons stopped to prepare for the next day. On an overland trail, everyone worked to the full limit of her or his capacities. Even so, the average woman's workday was several hours longer than that of a man.

Overlanders took care to bring with them some of the few household improvements American women had gained in settled areas by the mid-nineteenth century, such as industrially spun cloth, rudimentary schoolbooks, machine-sewn shoes, prepared flour, and soap. Other modern inventions — iron stoves, for example — could not be carried easily, returning women to the domestic conditions of their mothers' and grandmothers' generations. On the rare days when the wagon train stopped, many women did laundry, pounding the dirt out of clothes in cold running streams where they bathed themselves and their children and collected water for cooking. Often women convinced men to stop the train to observe the Sabbath, but instead of resting, women caught up on their work.

In certain situations, women also had to help the men drive the wagons or tend the stock. Rather than seize the chance to show that they could do a man's job, white women were frequently reluctant to undertake new and difficult obligations on top of their regular work, clinging to the ideas of true womanhood as a way to preserve feminine dignity on the trail. As Catherine Haun's party crossed the Rockies, she described how she joined in to keep the wagons from plunging uncontrollably back and forth. She complained bitterly, not so much that the work was difficult as that it was "unladylike."[5] Enslaved women were even more exposed than free women to hard and never-ending labor in these westward caravans. Bridget "Biddy" Mason, for example, made the overland journey in 1848 with her Mormon owners. Although a nursing mother with three daughters, Mason was charged with the dirty jobs of tending the cattle trailing the wagon trains and collecting waste to burn for fuel, as well as assisting in all of the domestic work her female enslavers undertook and lending medical assistance when someone fell ill.

Women had exclusive responsibility for children on the trip. Since the average period between births for white women in 1850 was twenty-nine months, it is reasonable to assume that many, perhaps most, women of childbearing age were either pregnant or nursing and caring for infants in the wagons. Pregnancy was not discussed publicly, although "confinement" was not possible on a wagon train. Often the only way that a historian reading a woman's letters or diary can detect a pregnancy is through the woman's references to "getting sick," followed soon afterward by mention of a new child. "Still in camp, washing and overhauling the wagons," Amelia Stewart Knight wrote in her 1853 trail diary. "Got my washing and cooking done and started on again . . . (here I was sick all night, caused by my washing and working too hard)." Within two weeks, just as their trip ended, she gave birth to her eighth child. She had been pregnant but had not referred directly to it for the entire six-month trip west.[6]

In contrast to the infrequent references to birth, deaths — especially of children but also adults — were amply described. On her way to Oregon, Jane Gould Tortillott wrote about overtaking a particularly ill-fated wagon train. "There was a woman died in this train yesterday," she wrote. "She left six children, one of them only two day's [*sic*] old."[7] As the number of overlanders rose, more and more graves marked the trail. Lydia Rudd, who had begun her trip west so optimistically, within weeks was counting the graves she passed. Many migrants died of cholera, a swift-moving infectious disease that killed by severe dehydration. The disease had come with European immigrants in the mid-nineteenth century, and the overland migrants brought it with them as they traveled west. Sarah Royce wrote in her diary about the death of a man in her group: "Soon terrible spasms convulsed him. . . . Medicine was administered which afforded some relief . . . but nothing availed and in two or three hours the man expired." After the body was buried and the wagons were cleansed, Royce could only wait. "Who would go next?"[8]

Women's relief at having arrived at their destination in Oregon or Washington or California was quickly replaced by the realization that they still had to build homes and establish communities. Long after they had moved west, many continued to miss the lives and families they had left behind. Yet, while individual women suffered during the crossing, their ways of life and standards for womanhood eventually triumphed, and for most, their willingness to move west was vindicated. In contrast, Indigenous women and the resident Mexican citizens experienced the United States's growing continental reach as violence, conquest, and displacement. The process of American expansion set women against one another on the grounds of culture, race, class, and ethnicity.

The Underside of Expansion: Indigenous Women and Californianas

In the Far West, three groups — white migrants, Indigenous peoples, and Californios (Mexican citizens who lived in California prior to American statehood) — came upon one another with various combinations of curiosity, hospitality, alliance, exploitation, and violence. In the late eighteenth century, Californios — many of whom had Indigenous and African ancestry — inhabited the thinly populated Pacific Coast up to the San Francisco Bay. Significant numbers of coastal Indigenous peoples became their laborers and servants. Inland and to the north, larger numbers of Indigenous peoples retained their cultures and traditional lifestyles. The arrival of non-Indigenous migrants beginning in the mid-1840s brought rapid change. Within a few years, the Californios had lost control of the coastal lands; the lives of the Indigenous peoples had been profoundly disrupted by epidemics, warfare, and genocide; and California had become the thirty-first state of the United States.

As migrating overlanders crossed through Indigenous lands in large numbers, they imagined that they were constantly at risk from the "red man." Over and over, trail accounts speak of Indigenous "attacks" that turn out to be something quite different. Hunger and epidemics were spreading among the Plains peoples, a consequence of encroaching American settlement. To alleviate their poverty, some requested food and money from the migrants as they passed through their lands. In 1849, Sarah Royce's wagon train was stopped outside of Council Bluffs, Iowa, by Sioux who wanted payment of a toll. A tense encounter ensued, but the Americans refused to pay and declared that "the country we were traveling over belonged to the United States and that these red men had no right to stop us." Royce recorded that the Sioux had the "the expression of sullen disappointment, mingled with a half-defiant scowl" as the wagon train moved on.[9]

In and around the U.S. Army forts and trading posts in the West were Indigenous women who had been forced or had gone to live with white men in informal sexual and domestic unions, but who had been abandoned when the men married white women. In some cases, their Indigenous communities did not allow them to return. These women ended up on the edges of white society, laboring as domestic servants or sex workers. Many were met with scorn and labeled as "black dirty squaws."[10] "Squaw" had originally been used by white people simply to mean "Indian woman," but the word came to hold exclusively negative connotations of gendered sexual degradation, cultural inferiority, and unrelenting, unrewarded, and unskilled female labor.

Compared to the numerous accounts from white women who feared Indigenous people, few Native women left records of how they felt about the white encroachers. In her autobiography, Sarah Winnemucca, a Paiute from the eastern side of the Sierra Nevada, related her encounter with American emigrants who crossed into her people's lands when she was a small child: "They came like a lion, yes, like a roaring lion, and have continued so ever since, and I have never forgotten their first coming." The Paiutes had their own rumors of American emigrants' unrelenting violence and destruction: that the white people "were killing everybody and eating them." The men of her father's band were away from camp and the women and children were gathering seeds when they realized that whites were approaching. The terrified but resilient women buried their children up to their necks in mud and then hid their faces with bushes. "Can any one imagine my feelings buried alive?" Winnemucca recalled. "With my heart throbbing and not daring to breathe, we lay there all day." Her parents rescued her later that night. Soon after, the band's winter supplies were destroyed by a party of white raiders, and their impoverishment began.[11]

Indigenous peoples on the Pacific Coast suffered severe losses as Americans poured into their lands. Indigenous peoples in California were particularly devastated. Their traditional sources of food were destroyed by American mining and agriculture. Sarah Winnemucca's mother feared that her "young and very good-looking" sister was unsafe among white men, even those whom her family considered friends. These assaults, along with the sexually transmitted diseases that American men brought with them, dramatically reduced Indigenous women's fertility. The Indigenous population of California, which had already been cut in half by disease and poverty in the years of Mexican rule, declined even more precipitously — from 150,000 to 30,000 — during the first ten years of the gold rush.

The descendants of the original Mexican colonists also experienced loss of land as well as status under American rule. Mexican and American legend romanticized the women of the small class of grand Mexican landholders. Starting in the 1830s, American men who went to California made their way into Mexican society by marrying the women, including multiracial ones, of these elite families.

AN INDIAN WOMAN GATHERING ACORNS.

◆ An Indian Woman Gathering Acorns (1859)

Collecting acorns was part of California Indigenous women's traditional gathering work. Women dried and ground the acorns as a staple of their diets. However, by the time the *Hutchings' California Magazine* published this image, California's Indigenous peoples had already undergone a horrific decade of intentional decimation and forced removal to reservations carried out by American colonists. The accompanying article stated that Indigenous peoples were "the lowest in morality and intellectual ability on this continent." Like European colonists of earlier eras, the unnamed author pointed to the subsistence labor of Indigenous women as a sign of Indigenous backwardness. The scene of acorn gathering therefore both romanticized and racialized the work of Indigenous women.

In 1841, Abel Stearns, an ambitious merchant from Massachusetts, married Arcadia Bandini, daughter of one of the largest landholders in California. Arcadia, who was fourteen when she married the forty-year-old Abel, outlived her husband; when she died in 1912, she was the richest woman in southern California.

Arcadia Bandini Stearns was unusual. While Mexican law gave married women more control over their property than did U.S. law, this did not protect them from the loss of wealth and standing that they, along with their men, suffered once California was absorbed into the United States. (See Reading into the Past: "Narrative of Mrs. Rosalía Vallejo de Leese.") This was the experience of Maria Amparo Ruiz de Burton, a Californiana who married an American army officer when she was seventeen and he was thirty. She became the first person to chronicle her people's experience for an English-speaking audience. In her 1885 historical romance, *The Squatter and the Don*, she gave a powerful fictional account of the long legal process by which the U.S. government's guarantees to the citizens of Mexican California were abrogated and their lands gradually taken from them. Despite Ruiz de Burton's high literary and political standing, she died landless and impoverished in 1895. Instead of Ruiz de Burton's work, which was based on personal experience, the more enduring fictional account of the Californio experience has become the 1880 novel *Ramona: A Romance of the Old Southwest*, written by the Massachusetts writer Helen Hunt Jackson.

READING INTO THE PAST

Narrative of Mrs. Rosalía Vallejo de Leese, Who Witnessed the Hoisting of the Bear Flag in Sonoma on the 14th of June, 1846

Rosalía Vallejo was born in Monterey in 1811 to a prominent military family who helped to colonize Alta California for Spain. In the late 1830s, after Mexican independence, she married a naturalized citizen named Jacob Leese. After residing several years in Yerba Buena (now San Francisco), Rosalía and Jacob built a family ranch on a land grant in Sonoma that had been secured by Rosalía's brother Mariano Vallejo. In Sonoma, Rosalía Vallejo de Leese encountered the small group of American settlers who had invaded Sonoma and declared an independent "republic" in June of 1846. Almost thirty years later, she shared her testimonio in Spanish with Henry Cerruti, one of the interviewers hired by Hubert Howe Bancroft to gather materials for a comprehensive history of California. The interview focused on the event known in American history as the "Bear Flag Revolt," but which Vallejo de Leese described as the "all-out robbery of California." Cerruti, a European immigrant whose first language was neither Spanish nor English, wrote down Vallejo de Leese's words in English. In this version of her testimonio, bilingual scholars have revised Cerruti's awkward translation for clearer expression.

As soon as the Bear Flag was raised, I was told by the thieves' interpreter that I was now a prisoner. This interpreter's name was Solís. He was a former servant of my husband's. Solís pointed to four ragged desperados who were standing close to me with their pistols drawn. I surrendered because it would have been useless to resist. They demanded the key to my husband's storehouse and I gave it to them. No sooner had I given them the key than they called their friends over and began ransacking the storehouse. There were enough provisions and liquor there to feed two hundred men for two years. A few days after my husband was taken away, John C. Frémont arrived in Sonoma. He said that his sole purpose for coming was to arrange matters to everyone's satisfaction and protect everyone from extortion or oppression. Many paid writers have characterized Frémont with a great number of endearing epithets, but he was a tremendous coward. Listen to me! I have good reason to say this. On June 20, we received news that Captain Padilla was on his way to Sonoma with a squad of one hundred men to rescue us. As soon as Frémont heard about this, he sent for me. He ordered me to write

Padilla a letter and tell him to return to San José and not come near Sonoma. I flatly refused to do that, but Frémont was bent on having his own way. He told me that if I refused to tell Padilla exactly what he told me to say, and if Padilla approached Sonoma, he would order his men to burn down our houses with us inside. I agreed to his demands, not because I wanted to save my own life, but because I was pregnant and did not have the right to endanger the life of my unborn child. Moreover, I judged that a man who had already gone this far would stop at nothing to attain his goals. I also wanted to spare the Californio women from more trouble, so I wrote that ominous letter which forced Captain Padilla to retrace his steps. While on alert for Padilla's possible attack, Frémont changed out of his fancy uniform into a blue shirt. He put away his hat and wrapped an ordinary handkerchief around his head. He decided to dress like this so he would not be recognized. Is this the way a brave man behaves?

During the whole time that Frémont and his ring of thieves were in Sonoma, robberies were very common. The women did not dare go out for a walk unless they were escorted by their husband or their brothers. One of my servants was a young Indian girl who was about seventeen years old. I swear that John C. Frémont ordered me to send that girl to the officers' barracks many times. However, by resorting to tricks, I was able to save that poor girl from falling into the hands of that lawless band of thugs who had imprisoned my husband. . . .

I could tell you about the many crimes committed by the Bear Flag mob, but since I do not wish to detain you any longer, I will end this conversation with this: those hateful men instilled so much hate in me for the people of their race that, even though twenty-eight years have gone by since then, I still cannot forget the insults they heaped upon me. Since I have not wanted to have anything to do with them, I have refused to learn their language.

SOURCE: Rose Marie Beebe and Robert M. Senkewicz, trans. and eds., *Testimonios: Early California through the Eyes of Women, 1815–1848* (Berkeley: Heyday Books, Bancroft Library, University of California, Berkeley), 28–29.

ANALYZING PRIMARY SOURCES

1. What parts of Vallejo de Leese's testimonio emphasize her experiences as a woman and a mother?

2. How did Vallejo de Leese draw on ideals of manhood to challenge the prevailing heroic narratives about Frémont and the Bear Flag "revolt"?

◆ **Rosalía Vallejo de Leese, with Spouse and Children (c. 1850)**
Rosalía Vallejo came from an extended family of colonial Mexican military officers. Against the wishes of her brother, she married Jacob Leese, who converted to Catholicism and became a Mexican citizen. Through dress and posture, this landowning Californio family conveyed their dignity and privilege, which at the time of the photograph had been upset by American occupation. By the end of the Civil War, Jacob Leese had returned to New York, leaving Rosalía and her children in California. *SAN FRANCISCO HISTORY CENTER, SAN FRANCISCO PUBLIC LIBRARY.*

Once California became a state in 1850, legislators sought to preserve some of the advantages that Mexican law provided married women, but gradually state courts and legislatures began to rewrite and reinterpret the laws of marital property to conform to the American standard, which favored husbands over wives. These legal shifts may have helped to accelerate the transfer of California lands from Mexican to American ownership in the 1850s and 1860s. As this happened, many Californianas followed the path of Indigenous women into landlessness, domestic service, and even poverty.

The Gold Rush

The combination of the discovery of gold in 1848 with the end of the Mexican War and the achievement of statehood in 1850 greatly accelerated the "Americanization" of California. The year before the discovery of gold, there were four thousand overland migrants; the year after, there were thirty thousand. Overlanders were joined by other gold-seekers who sailed around the southern tip of South America or crossed the Panamanian isthmus. International migrants flocked to the goldfields from Chile, Sonora Province in Mexico, and even China. At the end of the war with Mexico, California had been populated by one hundred thousand Indians, perhaps a tenth as many Mexicans, and only a few thousand white Americans. After the discovery of gold, it became one of the most cosmopolitan places on earth. Based on almost unlimited hopes for the quick achievement of fortune, California society was thoroughly cash-dependent; anything could be bought, and everything cost dearly.

Most of the gold-seekers were men. For every one hundred men who came to gold country, there were only three females.[12] Some of these women came with their husbands, either to share in the adventure or to fulfill a sense of conjugal duty. But some longed to go west to pursue their own adventurous dreams. In a letter to her mother soon after news broke of the discovery of gold, Susan B. Anthony, one of the founders of the women's rights movement, wrote, "I wish I had about $100,000 of the precious dust. I would no longer be [a] School marm."[13] Anthony did not go, but there were women who did join the rush, some to work close to the mines and others to set up businesses in San Francisco or Sacramento and make their fortunes at a distance. (See Primary Sources: "Female Labor in the Gold-Rush Economy.") One of the few African American women in gold-rush San Francisco was Mary Ellen Pleasant, who ran a boardinghouse and a restaurant from 1849 through 1855 and became very rich. "A smart woman can do very well in this country," one woman wrote to a friend back east. "It is the only country that I ever was in where a woman recev'd anything like a just compensation for work."[14]

Despite the economic unpredictability of gold-rush California, women continued to maintain class differences among themselves. Only rarely did middle-class women live at the goldfields. Most white women at the diggings lived more hardscrabble lives. While their husbands sought their fortunes at the mines, they supported their families by feeding, housing, sewing, and laundering for the hordes of unmarried men who were willing to pay well for such services. Mary Ballou, who ran a supper table for miners, was astounded at the money she could make in California compared to how little women's labor was worth in the East. Even so, she concluded, "I would not advise any Lady to come out here and suffer the toil and fatigue that I have suffered for the sake of a little gold."[15]

Of all the women in gold-rush California, sex workers have drawn the most attention from historians, much of it either romantic or salacious. "The first females to come were the vicious and unchaste," wrote Hubert Howe Bancroft, the state's first historian. "Flaunting in their gay attire, they were civilly treated by the men, few of whom, even of the most respectable and sedate, disdained to visit their houses."[16] This image of the gold-rush sex worker who was accorded the respectability in California denied to her elsewhere in American society is inaccurate. So, too, is the claim that sexual labor provided these women with wealth and independence. The glamorous whores of California legend were few and limited to San Francisco. Closer to the goldfields, the majority worked in seedy "crib hotels,"

FIG. 95. — Croquis californien par Cham.
Allusion aux Agences matrimoniales.

◆ **"Entreprise de Mariages" (1849)**

This French satirical cartoon demonstrates the immense international interest in the California gold rush and the notable scarcity of women in the goldfields. In the wake of the 1848 French revolution, which encouraged republican freedom of the press, Parisian humor magazines poked fun at the absurdities of gold-rush life. Here, a magazine called *Le Charivari* lampoons writer and reformer Eliza Farnham's plan to send brides to California miners. The sign behind the merchant indicates a wedding business that promises an "assortment of widows" to repair California bachelor households, and the caption indicates that this commercial item is in "high demand." *The New York Public Library/Art Resource, NY.*

where they had sex with many men for $1 or $2 per customer. All were at great risk for venereal disease, violence, unwanted pregnancy, and early death.

The hierarchy of sex service in midcentury California reflected sharp racial and national distinctions, with white American and French women in the top strata, and Mexicans, South Americans, and Blacks much lower. At the very bottom were the Chinese. By the late 1850s, approximately thirty-five thousand Chinese men had come as miners but had been forced by discriminatory laws into low-paid, unskilled labor. The much smaller numbers of immigrant Chinese women were registered as working almost exclusively in sex work, a skewed record due in part to the bias of census takers. By 1860, approximately two thousand women had been kidnapped or purchased in China and sent to the United States, where they were resold for tremendous profits, some as picture brides — females whose only representation to their potential spouses was a photograph of them.

Those who were indentured were forced into sex work and held in virtual slave conditions. Their terms of indenture were repeatedly extended for all sorts of spurious reasons, and many did not outlive their terms. Should they somehow elude their captors and the Chinese syndicates that organized the trade, they had no place to turn. U.S. courts ruled that sex workers who had run away were guilty of the crime of property theft (of themselves) and brought them back to their slaveholders. Some were able to marry Chinese laborers, but American law prohibited marriage between Chinese women and white men and between white women and Asian, Black, Mexican, or Indigenous peoples.

◆ ANTEBELLUM REFORM

The physical expansion of the United States, along with the economic transformation of early industrialization, generated a thriving spirit of moral and social activism from 1830 to the Civil War. Antebellum reformers pushed beyond established social and cultural norms in their attempts to improve, even perfect, both the individual and the society. The centers of this reform ferment were in New York, Philadelphia, and New England. Initially rooted in deeply religious conviction, the antebellum reform movement eventually followed the lodestar of moral virtue to arrive at the deeply political and social issues of abolition, women's rights, temperance, and public education. Reform activism centered on abolition was virtually nonexistent in the slave South.

White and free Black women played a notable role in antebellum reform. By one estimate, at any given time as many as 10 percent of adult women in the Northeast were active in benevolent and reforming societies in these years.[17] The influential ideology of true womanhood credited women with the selflessness necessary to counterbalance male individualism. Women's modest efforts on behalf of the community's welfare were thus compatible with domesticity and female respectability. But over time, women's dedication to moral and social causes led them beyond their homebound roles and to the edges of woman's allotted sphere. In the case of women's rights, some women crossed over into new gender territory altogether.

Expanding Woman's Sphere: Maternal, Moral, and Temperance Reform

Following the intense wave of revivals in the late 1820s known as the Second Great Awakening (see "Christian Motherhood" in Chapter 4), women from an ever-wider swath of American society became involved in efforts to deepen and broaden the Protestant faith. Initially their role was to support male missionaries in bringing Christianity to the unconverted at home and abroad. For the most part, they deferred to male clergy and kept to their place, but the fervor of their faith inspired some to venture into new territory, figuratively and literally. In 1836, for instance, Narcissa Whitman and Eliza Spaulding traveled with their minister husbands to Oregon Territory by wagon, probably the first white American women to do so, to convert the Nez Perce and Cayuse people.

Even in these supportive roles, however, pious women began to form their own organizations dedicated to aspects of their religious duty. They formed mothers' societies to protect the virtue of their children from the rampant immorality they perceived in a society constantly on the move and in social and economic flux. These organizations published magazines to advise mothers and established and administered orphanages and Sunday religious schools. By emphasizing the Christian exercise of maternal responsibility, their members wielded their maternal role to expand social authority for their sex. Pious women also formed **moral reform societies** to combat the upsurge of drink, sex work, and other forms of what they called "vice." By the early 1840s, there were four hundred female moral reform societies in New England and New York. Moral reform enthusiasm was expansive enough to cross boundaries of race and class. Black middle-class women formed their own societies, and integrated men's and white women's organizations, to encourage standards of sexual decorum and family respectability in the free Black community. One such Black female organization in Lynn, Massachusetts, brought together artisans' wives and unmarried seamstresses to guard against the sex work that they feared would take root in factory towns.

Moral reform societies were particularly concerned with the increase in casual sexuality among young women caught up in the forces of rapid urbanization and industrialization. Female moral reformers raised money to send ministers to save the souls of those women who had already "fallen" and campaigned to exclude from upstanding society "persons of either sex known to be licentious."[18] Eventually they became bolder and reached out directly to sex workers, despite the threat that such actions posed to their own womanly respectability. Because they considered sexual excess as fundamentally male and regarded all women, even sex workers, as its victims, they felt that sexual immorality represented sin in its most distinctly male form. To be sure, if sex workers were not sufficiently penitent, they lost their claim to Christian women's sympathy. Nonetheless, women's moral reform activism deepened middle-class women's gender consciousness and expanded their sense of common womanhood, thus helping to lay the foundations for the women's rights movement.

Women's religiously motivated social activism in the mid-nineteenth century reached its height in the temperance movement. The temperance fervor focused on more than alcohol abuse. In an era of rapid and disorienting economic growth, the lack of self-restraint expressed through drunkenness provided a convenient explanation for why so many people suffered dramatic downward social mobility. The gospel of temperance promised that if a man could just control his impulses, subdue his appetites, and redirect his energies, his family might survive and even prosper through physical moves and economic shifts. No reform movement was more widely supported in the 1840s and 1850s.

Although alcoholism was considered exclusively male and a vice, images of its female victims — the suffering wives and children of irresponsible drunkards — figured prominently in anti-alcohol propaganda. Not content to remain mere symbols for the tragedies that "King Alcohol" wreaked, women became active proponents of temperate living. They began to form their own **Daughters of Temperance**

◆ *The Drunkard's Home* (1850)
Temperance was thought to be a vicious enemy to a peaceful, productive, and happy home. This image depicts what was believed to be the gendered violence and distress that women and children endured when under the control of a drunken patriarch. *The Library Company of Philadelphia.*

societies to challenge both the morality and the legality of commerce in alcohol. When New York women activists created a women's temperance society in 1852, five hundred women attended the convention.

Like moral reform associations, women's temperance organizations incubated the expression of female discontent with middle-class family life and marital practices. Temperance activism allowed women to criticize men for their failure to live up to the marital bargain, by which wives would subordinate themselves to their husbands so long as the men were reliable breadwinners and evenhanded patriarchs. Numerous female activists began their reform careers within the temperance movement, among them Susan B. Anthony, the women's rights pioneer, and Frances Ellen Watkins Harper, a prominent Black woman writer and speaker. After the Civil War, women's temperance activism continued to grow until it led to the most important women's organization of the Gilded Age, the Woman's Christian Temperance Union (see "The Woman's Christian Temperance Union" in Chapter 6).

Exploring New Territory: Radical Reform in Family and Sexual Life

As women's enthusiasm for moral reform and temperance suggests, family and sexual life were important concerns of antebellum female reformers. The private nuclear family that was so central to the middle-class cult of domesticity was also a locale for domestic violence, sexual abuse, and female disempowerment. Some antebellum reformers called for more radical changes in women's sexual and reproductive lives and for the establishment of alternative social systems not based on the private family.

Women's menstrual, reproductive, and sexual complaints made them eager advocates and consumers of health reform. Unwilling to rely on the questionable diagnoses of regular physicians, health activists developed alternative therapeutic regimes to increase physical vitality. They made use of natural, non-invasive methods and urged against too much sensual stimulation, believing it unhealthy. The "water cure," a system that emphasized cold-water baths and loose clothing, offered comfort to women worn out from too many and too frequent pregnancies. A program developed by reformer Sylvester Graham stressed the benefits of cold, unspiced foods (from which we inherited the Graham cracker) and promised to remedy sexual as well as digestive complaints.

Mary Gove Nichols, an outspoken critic of the sexual abuses hidden within marital life, advocated both the Graham and water-cure systems. Through the 1840s, she spoke forcefully and wrote explicitly about women's physical frustrations and sufferings in marriage. Insistent that "a healthy and loving woman is impelled to material union" — that is, sexual intercourse — "as surely, often as strongly as man," she declared that "the apathy of the sexual instinct in woman is caused by the enslaved and unhealthy condition in which she lives."[19] The **Ladies Physiological Society of Boston**, active between 1837 and 1841, enthusiastically sponsored Nichols's direct speech about female sexuality. In addition to hosting lectures on physiology and anatomy, Society members gathered in one another's homes, cultivating an "intimate, confessional peer education model" where white women activists could support one another in achieving sexual virtue.[20] Black abolitionist Sarah Mapps Douglass also embraced the cause of women's health education in the 1850s, giving public lectures in Philadelphia on female physiology with the aid of a "French manikin."

Radical reformers of sexuality and the family could be found as residents of the many communitarian experiments that sprang up in the 1830s and 1840s. These intentional communities posed a range of challenges to conventional notions of marriage and the family. The Shakers occupied one end of the continuum, prohibiting all sexual relations, even within marriage. Men and women lived and worshipped in separate but conjoined communities, coming together to dance and sing their religious ecstasies. Obviously unable to enlarge their numbers by biological reproduction, Shakers took in orphans, apprentices, and individuals in flight from unhappy families, including destitute widows. In the 1830s, an estimated six thousand Shakers lived in nineteen communities throughout the country. Their celibate way of life and the alternative they offered to the private, patriarchal family strongly appealed to women, particularly inasmuch as their founder and chief saint was a woman. Mother Ann Lee had emigrated in the 1770s from England, where she had suffered marital rape and domestic abuse. She taught that God was both male and female and that marriage was based on the subjugation of women and thus violated divine law.

On the other end of the continuum, the Oneida community sanctified extra-marital sexuality. Moved by deep dissatisfaction with his own marriage, John Humphrey Noyes founded a community in 1848 in Oneida, near Syracuse, New York. Its members owned property collectively and raised children communally, but the collectivization of sexual relations was the source of the community's greatest notoriety. Both men and women were sexually active but foreswore monogamy, lest they substitute attachment to an individual for the exclusive love of God. They also practiced a strict contraceptive regime that required men to withhold ejaculation through prolonged sexual intercourse. Despite the Oneidans' sexual radicalism, they were deeply Christian and justified all their practices in biblical terms. The collectivization of housework, the availability of different sexual partners, male responsibility for contraception, and what might fairly be called the institutionalization of foreplay offered women at Oneida alternatives available nowhere else. Yet Noyes's insistence on retaining authority over all community life (including assigning sexual partners) also gave Oneida a deeply patriarchal air. Nonetheless, the Oneida community survived into the 1880s.

The Church of Jesus Christ of Latter-day Saints, commonly known as the Mormons, was the most historically significant of these intentional antebellum communities. It is also difficult to assess through the eyes of women, because the estimations of insiders and outsiders were so different with respect to women's status in it. Founded in 1830 in Palmyra, New York, the Mormons numbered fifteen thousand nine years later. The group migrated several times, eventually forming a cooperative community in Nauvoo, Illinois. Responding to rumors that Mormon leaders had multiple wives, non-Mormons drove them out, and starting in 1847, the community trekked farther west to Utah. There, polygamy became an open practice, a sign of special divinity. In 1870, in response to federal pressure against polygamy, the Utah Territory enfranchised its women to indicate their power and stature. When Elizabeth Cady Stanton, the great philosopher of nineteenth-century women's rights, brought her own critique of marriage to Salt Lake City in 1871, she reported that "the Mormon women, like all others, stoutly defended their religion, yet they are no more satisfied [with their marriage practices] than any other sect."[21] The Mormons held to the practice of polygamy until 1896, when they formally rejected it in order for Utah to be admitted as a state.

While the Shakers, the Oneidans, and the Mormons were inspired by radical Christian notions of human perfectibility, other communal experiments were based on more secular, indeed socialist, ideas. The most famous was Brook Farm, founded in Roxbury, Massachusetts, in 1841 by members of the Boston-based intellectual circle known as the Transcendentalists. For its brief existence, Brook Farm combined high culture and cooperative labor. Although young Georgiana Bruce, recently arrived from England, was not one of the luminaries of the experiment, she enthused, "The very air seemed to hold more exhilarating qualities than any I had breathed before."[22] Margaret Fuller was the most prominent woman associated with Brook Farm, which she visited frequently as she was writing the first full-length feminist treatise in American history, *Woman in the Nineteenth Century*. "What woman needs is not as a woman to act or rule," she wrote, "but as nature to grow, as an intellect to discern, as a soul to live freely and unimpeded."[23]

Crossing Political Boundaries: Abolitionism

Of all the forms of antebellum social activism, the movement to abolish chattel slavery had the most profound impact on American history, contributing significantly to the social, economic, and political tensions leading to the Civil War. Like temperance and moral reform, abolitionism arose out of a deep religious conviction that truly God-fearing Christians had the obligation to eliminate sin — in this case slaveholding. "Let but each woman in the land do a Christian woman's duty," implored the Boston Female Anti-Slavery Society in 1836, "and the result cannot fail to be [the enslaved person's] instant, peaceful, unconditional deliverance."[24] But unlike other reform movements, abolitionism brought its proponents, women along with men, into open conflict with America's basic political, economic, and religious institutions.

The call for immediate, uncompensated abolition of slavery and full civil rights for Black people first came from the free Black community, which by 1820 numbered over a quarter of a million. Many free Blacks were kin to enslaved people, whom they struggled to purchase or smuggle into freedom through the Underground Railroad, the elaborate system of escape routes developed to aid those fleeing slavery. Black women sustained their abolitionist work through fund-raising, writing, and public speaking.

In 1831, Maria Stewart became the first American woman known to have spoken publicly before mixed audiences of women and men. A Black domestic servant, Stewart had migrated from Connecticut to Boston, where she furthered her rudimentary education, married, was widowed, and befriended leading abolitionists David Walker and William Lloyd Garrison. Her strength and purpose derived from

◆ **Am I Not a Woman and a Sister?**
This image, widely used in antislavery literature, expresses the complex sentiments that underlay women's abolitionist activism. The rhetorical question "Am I Not a Woman and a Sister?" challenges the fundamental premise of chattel slavery that the enslaved woman was mere property. This version appeared in the special pages for women in William Lloyd Garrison's abolitionist newspaper, the *Liberator*. GRANGER — *Historical Picture Archive.*

her deep, abiding Christian faith. Maria believed that God had chosen her specifically to take on the power of the institution of slavery and all who would deny universal equality. Stewart gave four public lectures between 1831 and 1833 and published a pamphlet describing her personal philosophy and belief system. She championed the intellectual and morally exemplary contributions of Black women to the cause of racial equality. In one of her speeches, published by Garrison's abolitionist newspaper the *Liberator*, Stewart demanded: "How long shall the fair daughters of Africa be compelled to bury their minds and talents beneath a load of iron pots and kettles?"[25]

Black men and women who had experienced slavery directly also publicly challenged the institution. Frederick Douglass escaped slavery in Maryland in 1838 to become an internationally renowned advocate of freedom for his people. Sojourner Truth was born into slavery in New York in 1797 and remained enslaved until the institution was abolished in that state in 1827. After her emancipation, she spent several years in a religious community in New York City, dropped her "slave" name of Isabella Baumfree, and rechristened herself Sojourner Truth to signify her self-chosen vocation as an itinerant preacher and prophet. Starting in 1846, she also became an abolitionist lecturer, traveling as far west as Kansas. Unlike most other Black abolitionists, Truth did not present a respectable, middle-class face to the world. She spoke and acted like the woman she was — unlettered, emotionally intense, opinionated, and forthright. In her Dutch-inflected English dialect and style, she made a tremendous impact, especially on white audiences. Author Harriet Beecher Stowe praised "her wonderful physical vigor, her great heaving sea of emotion, her power of spiritual conception, her quick penetration, and her boundless energy."[26]

Knowing that their numbers and influence were insufficient to uproot slavery, Black abolitionists sought, and supported, sympathetic white allies, beginning with Quakers and others like William Lloyd Garrison. From 1831 until 1865, Garrison edited the *Liberator*. Women were always a substantial proportion of Garrison's followers. His radical principles, universalist notions of human dignity, and personal appreciation for women's discontent with their sphere made him a trusted leader. Elizabeth Cady Stanton — not one to bestow praise on men lightly — wrote of him: "I have always regarded Garrison as the great missionary of the gospel of Jesus to this guilty nation, for he has waged uncompromising warfare with the deadly sins of both Church and State. My own experience is, no doubt, that of many others. . . . [A] few bold strokes from the hammer of his truth and I was free!"[27]

In 1833, Garrison founded the American Anti-Slavery Society, which was committed to the immediate, uncompensated abolition of slavery. Its membership was racially integrated, although the majority of its members were white. At first, men led the organization and women took supporting roles. Lucretia Mott, an influential Quaker who went on to become a leader among female abolitionists, attended the founding meeting of the American Anti-Slavery Society, but neither she nor any other women were listed as members. "I do not think it occurred to any one of us at the time, that there should be propriety in our signing the [founding] document," she later wrote.[28]

Accordingly, women abolitionists, white and Black, organized separate auxiliary female societies. Black women were 10 percent of the members of the **Philadelphia Female Anti-Slavery Society**, formed also in 1833, and they were an even higher proportion of its officers.[29] Among the most prominent were Charlotte Forten (grandmother of the better-known Charlotte Forten Grimké); Forten's daughters, Margaretta, Sarah Louise, and Harriet as well as her daughter-in-law Mary Virginia Woods; and Grace Bustill and Sarah Mapps Douglass (not related to Frederick). Despite having greater wealth and education than the overwhelming majority of Blacks, these women were no strangers to racial prejudice. In 1838, when a nationwide meeting of women abolitionists was held in Philadelphia, a mob, infuriated by witnessing Black and white women meeting together, attacked them and burned down Pennsylvania Hall, the building they had just dedicated to the abolitionist movement.

Female abolitionists' willingness to go beyond the limits of female propriety to defeat slavery, combined with their increasing realization that free women, white as well as Black, experienced barriers to full personhood like those faced by enslaved people, pushed many of them in the direction of women's rights. Sarah and Angelina Grimké were prominent among these activists. Born into a wealthy and politically prominent slaveholding family in South Carolina, in 1829 the sisters left for Philadelphia, where they became Quakers and abolitionists. Driven by their deep conviction of slavery's profound sinfulness, they followed Maria Stewart's lead and in 1836 preached against slavery to "promiscuous" (mixed) audiences of men and women, providing shockingly detailed descriptions of the sexual corruptions of slavery. The Massachusetts General Association of Congregationalist Clergy publicly reprimanded them: "We appreciate the unostentatious prayers and efforts of woman in advancing the cause of religion at home and abroad . . . but when she assumes the place and tone of man as a public reformer, . . . her character becomes unnatural. . . . We especially deplore the intimate acquaintance and promiscuous conversation of females with regard to things 'which ought not to be named.' "[30] The sisters neither admitted error nor retreated. Instead, they insisted, again like Maria Stewart, that it was not man's place but God's to assign woman's sphere. Combining religious conviction and American democratic ideals, Sarah wrote: "Men and women were CREATED EQUAL; they are both moral and accountable beings; and whatever is *right* for man to do, is *right* for woman."[31]

The Grimkés' courageous defense of their equal rights as moral beings and social activists produced a split in the abolitionist movement over the role of women. One wing, led by Garrison, moved to include women as full and equal participants in the work of converting white Americans to realize the moral necessity of abolishing slavery. After 1840, women served as officers and paid organizers of the American Anti-Slavery Society. A second wing, which included among its leaders Frederick Douglass, insisted that the issue of women's equality needed to be kept separate from that of abolition. The non-Garrisonians moved in the direction of more pragmatic, political methods, including the formation of political parties against slavery. These two issues — separating abolition from women's rights and moving beyond moral to political methods — were connected, and remained so in the decades to come. Women, who were identified with moral purity and who lacked political rights, had little to offer a more political approach to abolitionism, at least until they began to make claims for suffrage.

The surfacing of political methods within abolitionism reflected the dramatic effort to democratize electoral politics for white males in this period. By 1840, virtually all adult white men, regardless of wealth, had the right to vote. White men of all ranks followed elections closely, boasted proudly of their partisan inclinations, and contended openly for the candidates of their choice. Historians have labeled this expansion of political involvement "Jacksonianism" because the Democratic Party, formed in 1828 to nominate Andrew Jackson for the presidency, was its first institutional embodiment, followed in 1834 by the formation of the Whig Party. While in 1824 only 30 percent of adult white men went to the polls, 80 percent did so in 1840. However, many free Black men lost political rights in these years, and by 1860 they were enfranchised in only four states — Maine, Massachusetts, New Hampshire, and Vermont.

Nor were women included in the Jacksonian expansion of the franchise. On the contrary, the right to vote was becoming the distinguishing characteristic of white American manhood. Yet, as the reformist spirit of the age began to spill over into politics, women were drawn into the excitement of electoral contests. They participated in political discussions and championed candidates and parties. When they felt compelled to formally register their political opinion on an issue, they turned to the only mechanism allowed to them: petitioning their legislators. As early as 1830, non-Indigenous women petitioned the U.S. government to halt the violent removal of the Cherokees from their own lands. Women also petitioned their state legislatures to ban the sale of alcohol and to make men's seduction of women punishable by law.

Women abolitionists conducted the most controversial of these petition campaigns. Starting in the 1830s, they began to gather thousands of signatures on petitions to Congress to ban slavery in the territories and in the capitol of Washington, D.C., and to end the domestic slave trade. "Let us know no rest til we have done our utmost to . . . obtain the testimony of every woman . . . against the horrible Slave-traffic," they declared.[32] In 1836, Congress passed a "gag rule" to table all petitions on slavery without discussion, but abolitionist women only intensified their efforts. Their congressional champion, John Quincy Adams (who had become a Massachusetts congressman after a single term as president), defended the movement of women beyond the boundaries of woman's sphere into the male world of politics. "Every thing which relates to peace and relates to war, or to any other of the great interests of society, is a political subject," he declared. "Are women to have no opinions or actions on subjects relating to the general welfare?"[33]

Entering New Territory: Women's Rights

Starting in the 1840s, all of these developments — moral reform and temperance, circulating petitions against slavery, hitting the lecture circuit, the Grimkés' and others' defense of their equal right to champion enslaved people — led many women reformers into women's rights. But unlike other activists, advocates of women's rights openly challenged the basic premise of true womanhood — that women were fundamentally selfless — and insisted that women had the same claim on individual rights to life, liberty, property, and happiness as men.

First articulated in 1792 by the English radical Mary Wollstonecraft, the doctrine of women's rights was first popularized in the United States in the 1820s by Frances Wright, a Scottish immigrant who gained great notoriety by her radical

BLOOMERISM—AN AMERICAN CUSTOM.

◆ **Bloomer Costumes**

The heavy skirts worn by middle-class women in the mid-nineteenth century were awkward and confining. In 1851, women's rights advocates began to adopt a "reform dress" that featured loose trousers under a shortened skirt. The fashion was named after Amelia Bloomer, a Seneca Falls neighbor of Elizabeth Cady Stanton. Bloomer championed the outfit in her reform magazine, the *Lily*, and "bloomerism" traveled widely. This image was published in 1851 in the British satirical magazine *Punch*. That year, London hosted the first World's Fair, where bloomer-outfitted women were frequently sighted. The cartoonist, John Leech, published over two dozen such cartoons, linking "bloomerism" with women engaged in unpleasant male activities such as smoking and drinking in pubs. The cartoonist visually exaggerates the bloomered women and their outfits and contrasts them with the respectable, modest women who shy away from them. In the image, street urchins also publicly ridicule them. Elizabeth Cady Stanton later observed that this ridicule is what eventually convinced her to abandon the outfit, much as she liked it. *Mary Evans Picture Library.*

pronouncements on democracy, education, marriage, and labor. The threat that Wright's ideas represented to notions of respectable Christian womanhood can be appreciated by Catharine Beecher's horrified description of her: "There she stands, with brazen front and brawny arms, attacking the safeguards of all that is venerable and sacred in religion, all that is safe and wise in law, all that is pure and lovely in domestic virtue."[34] For several years, any woman who publicly advocated radical ideas was derisively called a "Fanny Wright woman."

For women's rights to grow from a set of ideas associated with one publicly maligned individual into a reform movement took several decades. Changing state laws that deprived married women of all independent property rights was an early goal. These laws treated "free" wives as nonpersons before the law, on the grounds that they were dependent on and subordinate to their husbands' intelligence and authority. This pervasive Anglo-American legal principle was called "coverture," a term signifying the notion that marriage buried (or "covered") the wife's selfhood in that of the husband. A law to undo coverture by granting married women the same rights to earnings and property as single women and all free men was introduced into the New York State legislature in 1836 by Elisha Hertell. Hertell was assisted by Ernestine Rose, a Jewish immigrant who had fled from an arranged marriage in Poland to England. There she married a man of her own choosing and later settled with him in New York City, where she became a leader in the "free-thinking" (atheistic) community. Despite great effort, however, Rose was able to gather only a handful of women's names on a petition supporting Hertell's bill.

By the 1840s, two other women joined Rose to work on behalf of married women's economic rights. One was Paulina Wright (later Davis), an activist who had started her career as a women's health educator. The other was Elizabeth Cady Stanton, destined to become *the* iconic women's rights thinker of the nineteenth century. (See Primary Sources: "Women's Rights Partnership: Elizabeth Cady Stanton and Susan B. Anthony.") Born into a wealthy and politically conservative New York family, Elizabeth Cady possessed great intelligence and high spirits that consistently led her afoul of the boundaries of woman's sphere. Her father, Daniel Cady, was a prominent lawyer and a judge, and although she could never hope to follow in his footsteps, she studied law informally in his office. As a young woman, she was deeply influenced by her cousin, the abolitionist Gerrit Smith. In his home, a stop on the Underground Railroad, she met fugitive captives. She also met her future husband, the charismatic abolitionist orator Henry Stanton. In 1840, despite her father's opposition, Elizabeth and Henry married. When Henry introduced his new bride to Sarah and Angelina Grimké, they noted that they "were very much pleased" with Elizabeth but wished "that Henry was better calculated to help mould such a mind."[35]

Elizabeth Cady Stanton soon found her mentor in Quaker and abolitionist leader Lucretia Mott. On her honeymoon in London in 1840, she met Mott at an international antislavery convention at which female delegates were confined behind an opaque curtain and barred from participating in formal discussions. Both women were incensed, but the thrill of meeting each other outweighed the insult. "The acquaintance of Mrs. Mott, who was a broad, liberal thinker on politics, religion, and all questions of reform, opened to me a new world of thought," Cady Stanton later recalled.[36] For the next several years, Mott instructed her young protégée in the principles of women's rights. Cady Stanton lobbied in the New York legislature for reform of married women's economic rights. In April 1848, the legislature passed the first **New York State Married Women's Property Act**, which gave wives control over inherited (but not earned) wealth.

By this time, Cady Stanton was the mother of four boys and living in the small industrial town of Seneca Falls, New York. Her husband was often away working for the abolitionist cause. With Lucretia Mott as her teacher and Henry Stanton as her husband, Elizabeth Cady Stanton was perfectly situated to bridge the gap between the moral activist tradition of female reformers and the increasingly political focus within abolitionism. She was also eager for a dramatic change in her own life. "The general discontent I felt with woman's portion as wife, mother, housekeeper, physician, and spiritual guide," she wrote, "the wearied, anxious look of the majority of women impressed me with a strong feeling that some active measures should be taken to right the wrongs of society in general, and of women in particular."[37] In July 1848, Cady Stanton, Lucretia Mott, Mott's sister Martha Coffin Wright, and two other local female abolitionists called a public meeting in a local church to discuss "the social, civil and religious condition of Woman." Of the approximately three hundred women and men who attended the **Seneca Falls Convention**, one-third, including a large contingent of Quakers, endorsed a manifesto titled "Declaration of Sentiments and Resolutions," which, in part, rewrote the Declaration of Independence to declare that "all men *and women* are created equal" (emphasis added).[38]

The Seneca Falls manifesto went on to list eighteen instances of "repeated injuries and usurpations on the part of man toward woman." (See the Appendix Documents for the complete text.) Women were unjustly denied access to professions, trades, and education; their rights in marriage and motherhood; their self-confidence; and their moral equality before God. The most controversial resolution asserted women's equal right to vote. To abolitionist purists, however, resort to the ballot represented participation in a fundamentally corrupt system. Yet more and more issues about which women cared — including temperance and abolition — were being debated and resolved within the electoral arena. And, as Cady Stanton repeatedly insisted, all the other changes needed in women's condition would ultimately require women's ability to affect the law. Frederick Douglass, living nearby in Rochester, was the only man in the room who could not vote, and he supported the suffrage resolution eloquently. After debate, the delegates passed it, thirty-two men of the many there voting affirmatively.

In the years after the Seneca Falls Convention, the women's rights movement grew energetically but haphazardly. Lucy Stone, the first U.S. woman college graduate and a traveling lecturer on abolition and women's rights, inspired many women to join the ranks. Women learned about the new movement from friends and relatives. In 1851, Susan B. Anthony, living in nearby Rochester, heard about it from her mother and sister, traveled the short distance to Seneca Falls, and there met Cady Stanton. The two women immediately formed a working friendship that lasted sixty years. Women brought women's rights ideas with them as they migrated west. In 1850, California emigrants Eliza Farnham and Georgiana Bruce (later Kirby) debated women's rights as side by side they plowed their Santa Cruz farm. Beginning with a national women's rights meeting in Worcester, Massachusetts, in 1850, women's rights advocates met in conventions to share ideas, recruit new adherents, and fortify themselves for future efforts. At one such meeting, in 1851 in Akron, Ohio, abolitionist and former enslaved woman Sojourner Truth delivered a women's rights speech that has come down through the years as a forceful case for a new standard of womanhood expansive enough to include women like herself (see Reading into the Past: "I Am as Strong as Any Man").

READING INTO THE PAST

SOJOURNER TRUTH
I Am as Strong as Any Man

The most oft-cited version of Sojourner Truth's eloquent 1851 women's rights speech was published by a white activist, Frances D. Gage, twelve years after it was delivered. Recently, historian Nell Painter has drawn attention to a version of the speech published in the Anti-Slavery Bugle *at the time Truth made her remarks. In this presumably more accurate version, Truth makes her important argument for women's rights on the basis of her own experience of Black womanhood but without the southern dialect, the "Ain't I a woman" refrain, or the lament for her children lost to slavery, all of which Gage attributed to her.*

I am a woman's rights [woman]. I have as much muscle as any man, and can do as much work as any man. I have plowed and reaped and husked and chopped and mowed, and can any man do more than that? I have heard much about the sexes being equal; I can carry as much as any man, and can eat as much too, if I can get it. I am as strong as any man that is now. . . .

I can't read, but I can hear. I have heard the Bible and have learned that Eve caused man to sin. Well, if woman upset the world, do give her a chance to set it right side up again. The Lady has spoken about Jesus, how he never spurned woman from him, and she was right. When Lazarus died, Mary and Martha came to him with faith and love and besought him to raise their brother. And Jesus wept and Lazarus came forth. And how came Jesus into the world? Through God who created him and the woman who bore him. Man, where was your part?

SOURCE: Marius Robinson, *The Anti-Slavery Bugle*, June 21, 1851, reprinted in Nell Irvin Painter, *Sojourner Truth: A Life, a Symbol* (New York: Norton, 1996).

ANALYZING PRIMARY SOURCES

1. How is Truth using her own experience to expand the definition of womanhood?
2. How does Truth interpret the Bible through a women's rights lens?

Gradually, these pioneering activists began to reform the laws that denied women, especially wives, their rights, particularly their economic rights. Cady Stanton and Anthony conducted the most successful of these early campaigns in New York State. Cady Stanton, confined by her growing brood of children, wrote the speeches and petitions from her Seneca Falls home. In these years, she spoke in public only once, in 1854, before the members of the New York legislature. Anthony, freer as an unmarried woman, traveled through the state to collect signed petitions on behalf of women's civil and political rights. Women's rights reformers also confronted cultural practices such as fashion that, along with laws, constrained women.

In 1860, the New York State legislature finally passed a more comprehensive Married Women's Property Act that gave wives the rights to own and sell their own property, to control their own wages, and to claim rights over their children upon separation or divorce. Cady Stanton was ready to move on to a campaign to liberalize divorce laws, but this was too much even for women's rights radicals. Moreover, by this point, political conflicts over slavery between North and South had reached such a level of intensity that, like other Americans, women's rights activists were thoroughly preoccupied with the fate of the Union.

◆ CIVIL WAR, 1861–1865

Beginning with the Constitution, national political leaders had tried to find ways to assuage citizens of varying attitudes about Black slavery in different regions of the country. With the gradual abolition of slavery in northern states in the early decades of the republic, the nation's divide into slave and free states had challenged lawmakers to maintain national unity. In 1820, Congress responded with the Missouri Compromise, which drew a line across the territories of the Louisiana Purchase at the southern border of the new slave state of Missouri and declared that no further slave states (with the exception of Missouri itself) could be established north of it. The goal was to keep the number of slave and free states equal so as to give neither side an advantage in the Senate. Despite the petitions of abolitionist women, the two major parties — the Democrats and the Whigs — cooperated in keeping debate over slavery out of national politics. But continuing western expansion, especially the 1848 acquisition of lands from Mexico that lay outside the Louisiana Territory, eroded this fragile political balance.

In 1850, congressional leaders crafted a second compromise centered largely on the future of slavery in the United States. Slave trading was banned in the nation's capital. California would enter the Union as a free state. The white male voters in other new territories would decide whether their territory would enter the Union as a free or slave state, according to a doctrine known as popular sovereignty.

In a concession to slaveholders, legislators authorized the appointment of federal commissioners with the power to return people charged with being runaways to those who claimed to own them. Although bounty hunters of fugitives already

◆ Margaret Garner

Six years after the Fugitive Slave Act was passed, Kentucky captive Margaret Garner and her family fled across the Ohio River to freedom. When bounty hunters caught up with them, Garner killed her daughter Priscilla rather than see her returned to slavery. The ensuing trial, the longest in American history, defended Margaret from return to Kentucky on the grounds that she must be tried for murder under Ohio law. The strategy failed and she was reenslaved, sold farther south, and died of typhoid two years later. Both abolitionists and proslavery forces made her trial a cause célèbre. Which position does this 1867 painting of the episode support? *Library of Congress, Prints and Photographs Division, Washington, D.C. (LC-USZ62-845450)*

were protected by the Constitution and existing federal legislation, the 1850 Fugitive Slave Act strengthened the law in favor of slaveholders and increased the threat of kidnapping for free people of color in the North. What southerners regarded as proper federal protection of their property rights, northerners regarded as evidence that an expansive slave power was taking over the country. From this point forward, the expansion of slavery became an increasingly explosive national political issue, culminating in the secession of South Carolina in December 1860 and the beginning of the Civil War in April 1861.

Just as the Civil War pitted brother against brother, women, too, were intensely divided in their loyalties, with the difference, of course, that women were barred from both the ballot box and the battlefield. But as in all civil wars, the home front was impossible to separate from the battlefront. Women on both sides actively supported their causes and their armies. A small but surprising number participated directly, either on the battlefield or in the politics that shaped the changing purposes for which the war was fought. All women were affected by the war — its passions, victories, devastations, and deaths.

Women and the Impending Crisis

As the political conflict over slavery intensified, Black and white women were drawn into the growing crisis. Most famously, Harriet Beecher Stowe wrote **Uncle Tom's Cabin** to dramatize the dangers facing those escaping bondage under the new federal law. By far the most popular American novel ever written, the story of Eliza fleeing bounty hunters to save her child was avidly read when it first appeared in installments in an antislavery newspaper in 1851 and 1852. Inspired by Stowe's book and the memoirs of other formerly enslaved men and women, Harriet Jacobs, who had actually escaped from slavery twelve years before, determined to write her own story. *Incidents in the Life of a Slave Girl: Written by Herself* was published in 1861, with the help of white abolitionist Lydia Maria Child. (See Primary Sources: "Mothering under Slavery"in Chapter 4 for an excerpt.)

Throughout the political events of the 1850s, women's involvement was everywhere. In 1854, the Republican Party was founded to oppose the expansion (though not the existence) of slavery, and it succeeded in bringing the issue squarely into the center of national politics. The party's 1856 presidential nominee was U.S. senator John Frémont of California, one of the men who had originally surveyed the Oregon Trail. Frémont ran on a platform that proclaimed slavery to be a "relic of barbarism." His wife, Jessie Benton Frémont, was the first wife of a presidential candidate to figure significantly in a national campaign. Daughter of U.S. senator Thomas Hart Benton of Missouri, the young, attractive, and vivacious woman was considered a liberal influence on her husband. Campaign paraphernalia advertised Jessie as much as her husband. Although John Frémont was defeated by the Democratic candidate, James Buchanan, the Republicans succeeded in displacing the Whigs to become one of the two major national parties.

Then, in 1857, the Supreme Court ruled in favor of slavery in the momentous case *Dred Scott v. Sandford*. The case might more appropriately be called the Dred and Harriet Scott case since it involved not only Missouri captive Dred Scott but also his wife, Harriet. Together they sued their owner for their freedom and that of their two daughters. By being brought in 1834 into federal territory where slavery was not lawful, the Scotts argued, they had become free persons. A majority (7–2) of the Supreme Court ruled against the Scotts. In addition, Chief Justice Roger B. Taney wrote an opinion that the entire legal framework dating back to the Missouri Compromise was unconstitutional because it violated slaveholders' property rights. The Court's decision also clarified the citizenship status of Blacks, male and female, enslaved and free: they were not citizens. The sons of Dred Scott's original owner eventually bought the Scotts their freedom, but the larger battle between

135,000 SETS, 270,000 VOLUMES SOLD.

UNCLE TOM'S CABIN

FOR SALE HERE.

AN EDITION FOR THE MILLION, COMPLETE IN 1 Vol., PRICE 37 1-2 CENTS.
"   "   IN GERMAN. IN 1 Vol., PRICE 50 CENTS.
"   "   IN 2 Vols. CLOTH, 6 PLATES, PRICE $1.50.
SUPERB ILLUSTRATED EDITION, IN 1 Vol. WITH 153 ENGRAVINGS,
PRICES FROM $2.50 TO $5.00.

The Greatest Book of the Age.

◆ **A Bookseller's Announcement for Harriet Beecher Stowe's** *Uncle Tom's Cabin*

Harriet Beecher Stowe's *Uncle Tom's Cabin; or Life among the Lowly* (1852) was, without a doubt, the most influential publication of the nineteenth century, selling more than three hundred thousand copies in its first year of publication. Underscoring the cruelty of Black chattel slavery, *Uncle Tom's Cabin* influenced abolition not only in the United States but also globally. It was translated into twenty languages even before the outbreak of the Civil War and was performed both as a stage play and as some of the very first commercial films in the United States. *GRANGER — Historical Picture Archive.*

pro- and antislavery forces for control of the federal government had been profoundly intensified by the decision.

The election of 1860 took place against the background of abolitionist John Brown's abortive guerrilla raid on the federal armory in Harpers Ferry, Virginia, which was intended (but failed) to start a general Black uprising. To white southerners, the handful of Black and white antislavery warriors under Brown's command constituted exactly the violent threat that they long had feared from abolitionists. Many northerners regarded Brown quite differently, rather as a martyr. "I thank you that you have been brave enough to reach out your hands to the crushed and blighted of my race," Frances Ellen Watkins Harper wrote to Brown as he awaited execution after his capture by federal forces. "I hope from your sad fate great good may arise to the cause of freedom."[39]

For president, the Republicans nominated former Illinois congressman Abraham Lincoln, a moderate critic of slavery, hardly an abolitionist. Nonetheless, his election was intolerable to the South because he was a Republican. But to many northerners, Lincoln's election was cause to celebrate. Twenty-one-year-old Frances Willard, who would go on to head the Woman's Christian Temperance Union in the 1870s, observed events from her Illinois home: "Under the present system I am not allowed to vote for [Lincoln], but I am as glad on account of this Republican triumph as any man who has exercised the elective franchise can be."[40]

By April 1861, eleven southern states had seceded from the Union to form the Confederate States of America, with a constitution that clearly articulated the legality of slaveholding. On April 13, South Carolina slaveholder Mary Chesnut watched as southern gunboats fired on U.S. ships that Lincoln had sent to provision federal Fort Sumter in Charleston harbor. She recorded her reaction upon learning that federal forces had surrendered to the Confederates: "[I] sprang out of bed and on my knees — prostrate — I prayed as I never prayed before."[41]

Chesnut understood that war had begun in earnest. North and South, men and boys rushed to enroll in their local regiments, and wives and mothers prepared to say good-bye. "Love for the old flag became a passion," wrote Mary Livermore from Illinois, "and women crocheted it prettily in silk, and wore it as a decoration on their bonnets and in their bosoms."[42] Both sides hoped for a brief war and a glorious victory but got instead a four-year conflict, the deadliest war in American history.

Women's Involvement in the War

Although formally excluded from enlistment and armed service, both Union and Confederate women were deeply involved in the war. Eager and patriotic, a minority found their way to the battlefields as nurses, spies, and strategists; a few, disguised as men, even served as soldiers. (See Primary Sources: "Women on the Civil War Battlefields.") Far more women participated at a distance. Because both armies were decentralized and almost entirely unprovisioned — except for munitions — by their respective governments, women volunteers were responsible for much of the clothing, feeding, and nursing of the soldiers. In the South, this was done at a local level. Within a few months after the conflict had begun, Mary Ann Cobb, wife of a Confederate officer in Georgia, found herself charged with rounding up provisions for a company of eighty men, largely by going door-to-door among her neighbors.

In the North, where women had greater experience in running their own voluntary associations, soldiers' relief was better organized. Local societies were drawn together in a national organization known as the United States Sanitary Commission. Mary Livermore spent the war directing the Chicago branch. Her duties were manifold: "I . . . delivered public addresses to stimulate supplies and donations of money; . . . wrote letters by the thousand . . . ; made trips to the front with sanitary stores . . . ; brought back large numbers of invalid soldiers . . . ; assisted to plan, organize, and conduct colossal [fund-raising] fairs . . . ; detailed women nurses . . . and accompanied them to their posts."[43] The experience turned Livermore and others like her into skilled, confident organization women, and after the war they used these experiences to build even more ambitious women's federations. On the basis of her experience organizing relief supplies for northern soldiers, Clara Barton went on to found the American division of the International Red Cross.

The labors of such women earned them elaborate praise. But for the average woman on either side of the conflict, these were not so much years of uplifting service or patriotic heroism as years of prolonged suffering. Women struggled to care for their families without the aid of husbands, sons, and brothers. Anna Howard Shaw, who later became one of America's leading suffragists, was a young woman living in rural Michigan in 1861: "I remember seeing a man ride up on horseback, shouting out Lincoln's demand for troops. . . . Before he had finished speaking the men on the [threshing] machine had leaped to the ground and rushed off to enlist, my brother Jack . . . among them. . . . The work in our community, if it was done at all, was done by despairing women whose hearts were with their men."[44]

Since the North lost much of its labor force to the fighting, the South, which relied on enlaved workers, initially had the advantage. Even so, most white southerners were small-scale subsistence farmers who relied almost entirely on their own labor rather than on that of captives. Numerous women from these families demanded that the Confederate government excuse their husbands from service or provide them with the wherewithal to support their families. For a group of women who had long served only as symbols of southern patriotism and objects of husbandly protection, this signaled the beginning of direct political engagement. With or without official leaves, numerous southern soldiers responded to the entreaties of their wives to leave their posts, come home, and bring in the harvest. "Since your connection with the Confederate army, I have been prouder of you than ever before . . . ," one such woman wrote to her husband, "but before God, Edward, unless you come home we must die."[45] By the middle of the war, such seasonal desertions, conservatively estimated at more than one hundred thousand, as much as 10 percent of the Confederate forces, were a major strain on the South's capacity to fight.

As the conflict wore on, patriotism and optimism gave way to discontent on both sides. In the South, the situation was exacerbated by a Union naval blockade that led to food shortages and triple-digit inflation. In the spring of 1863, the women of Richmond rampaged through the streets protesting the high cost of food and demanding that they be able to buy bread and meat at the same prices as the Confederate armies. Three months later, New York City was paralyzed by mobs protesting passage of a federal Conscription Act that allowed wealthy men to buy themselves out of the draft for $300. Elizabeth Cady Stanton, who had just moved to the city with her three youngest children, found herself in the middle of the upheaval. She watched with horror as one of her older sons was recognized by the rioters as "one of those three-hundred-dollar fellows." Alone with her children, Cady Stanton prepared a speech to deliver, if necessary, that aimed to "appeal to them as Americans and citizens of the Republic."[46] As the mob redirected their violence toward the city's free Black population, Adelaide Butler, the matron of the Colored Orphan Asylum, also sprang into action to shepherd over two hundred children to safety while the orphanage burned to the ground behind them.

Emancipation

While the South was fighting to preserve slavery and defend its sovereignty, the war aims of the North remained muddled. For more than a year, Lincoln insisted that his only goal was to end secession and restore the Union. The president was unwilling to declare opposition to slavery for fear that the border states of Kentucky, Missouri, Maryland, and Delaware, where slavery was still being practiced, would leave the Union and join the Confederacy. The abolition of slavery became the Union's goal only after the enslaved themselves took action through a massive, prolonged process of what has been characterized as "self-emancipation." Like the Black captives who for decades had run away, enslaved men and women in large numbers began to flee into the arms of the Union army, buoyed by news of Union victories and hoping that they would be freed. One woman described her escape onto a Union gunboat sailing down the Mississippi River. "We all give three times three cheers for the gunboat boys and three times three cheers for big Yankee sojers an three times three cheers for gov'ment," she recalled; "an I tell you every one of us, big and little, cheered loud and long and strong, an' made the old river just ring ag'in."[47]

Female teachers, missionaries, and doctors, supported by northern aid societies and churches, traveled in droves to help educate, clothe, nurse, and minister to the children, men, and women who escaped to Union camps in Virginia, South Carolina, Georgia, and beyond. Charlotte Forten, the brilliant granddaughter of

◆ **Timothy O'Sullivan, *Plantation in Beaufort, South Carolina* (1862)**
The photographer Timothy O'Sullivan was traveling with the Union army when he posed this picture of a multigenerational family just freed from enslavement. The army had seized and occupied the coastal Sea Islands of eastern Georgia and South Carolina early in the war. The plantation owners having fled, these Black people continued to work the land where they lived but now under the supervision of northern officers, in anticipation of the relationship later formalized within the U.S. Army's Freedmen's Bureau. *Library of Congress, Prints and Photographs Division, Washington, D.C. (LC-B8171-152-A).*

◆ Charlotte Forten Grimké
This photo of Charlotte Forten (who married Francis J. Grimké in 1878) captures her impressive beauty and poise. As a well-educated female of an upper-class family, Charlotte defied contemporary stereotypes of the Black woman and was thought by abolitionists to be a perfect example of what free Black womanhood could be if released from enslavement, poverty, and illiteracy. *From The New York Public Library.*

pioneering Black abolitionist James Forten, was among them, arriving in the South Carolina lowcountry in 1862 with a teaching commission from the Port Royal Relief Society. (See Reading into the Past: "Life on the Sea Islands.")

Union officers disagreed on how to respond to the masses of Black refugees. Those unsympathetic to the antislavery cause wanted to, and sometimes did, return them to their owners; but the army eventually decided on a policy of accepting refugees under the category of "confiscated" enemy property. Thousands of these human "contraband" provided crucial aid to the Union army as laborers, cooks, nurses, spies, and domestics. As many as forty thousand gathered in Washington, D.C., alone, where Sojourner Truth, Harriet Jacobs, and others organized a Freedmen's Village.

As their numbers increased, President Lincoln realized that the steady flight of the southern Black labor force offered an irresistible military advantage to the Union. Accordingly, he issued the Emancipation Proclamation, to take effect on January 1, 1863, which declared all enslaved people in Confederacy territory "forever free" and instructed the Union army and navy to "recognize and maintain the freedom of such persons." The status of Black captives living in the Union border states, however, was left untouched. Since the Union could not actually emancipate people in lands it did not control, the Proclamation was meant to encourage Blacks in the renegade regions to abandon their captors and free themselves. Despite its limits, the Emancipation Proclamation finally made the Civil War a war against Black slavery.

READING INTO THE PAST

Charlotte Forten Grimké
Life on the Sea Islands

Charlotte Forten Grimké, one of the most important Black female advocates of abolition and the expansion of free Black rights in the pre–Civil War era, traveled to the Sea Islands of South Carolina at the time of Union army occupation to help the newly freed people to gain literacy. Forten, a member of the wealthy, activist Forten family of Philadelphia, spent her youth and early adulthood not only participating in abolitionist efforts in the U.S. North, but also gaining an excellent education and training to be a teacher. She was determined to contribute to the education of freedpeople. An avid diarist, she meticulously recorded her reflections and experiences during her work in South Carolina in 1862 and 1863. She published some of her diary entries in a two-part article in the Atlantic. *Culturally distinct from the Black people she encountered given their Gullah (African-derived) cultures and her assimilationist upbringing, Forten was an intensely curious observer of southern Black life as it emerged out of the slave regime.*

It was on the afternoon of a warm, murky day late in October that our steamer, the United States, touched the landing at Hilton Head. A motley assemblage had collected on the wharf, — officers, soldiers, and "contrabands" of every size and hue: black was, however, the prevailing color. The first view of Hilton Head is desolate enough, — a long, low, sandy point, stretching out into the sea, with no visible dwellings up-on it, except the rows of small white-roofed houses which have lately been built for the freed people. . . .

Little colored children of every hue were playing about the streets, looking as merry and happy as children ought to look, — now that the evil shadow of Slavery no longer hangs over them. Some of the officers we met did not impress us favorably. They talked flippantly, and sneeringly of the negroes, whom they found we had come down to teach, using an epithet more offensive than gentlemanly. They assured us that there was great danger of Rebel attacks, that the yellow fever prevailed to an alarming extent, and that, indeed, the manufacture of coffins was the only business that was at all flourishing at present. Although by no means daunted by these alarming stories, we were glad when the announcement of our boat relieved us from their edifying conversation. We rowed across to Ladies Island, which adjoins St. Helena, through the splendors of a grand Southern sunset. The gorgeous clouds of crimson and gold were reflected as in a mirror in the smooth, clear waters below. As we glided along, the rich tones of the negro boat-men broke upon the evening stillness, — sweet, strange, and solemn — "Jesus make de blind to see, Jesus make de cripple walk, Jesus make de deaf to hear. Walk in, kind Jesus! No man can bender me." . . .

The first day at school was rather trying. Most of my children were very small, and consequently restless. Some were too young to learn the alphabet. These little ones were brought to school because the older children — in whose care their parents leave them while at work — could not come without them. We were therefore willing to have them come, although they seemed to have discovered the secret of perpetual motion, and tried one's patience sadly. But after some days of positive, though not severe treatment, order was brought out of chaos, and I found but little difficulty in managing and quieting the tiniest and most restless spirits. I never before saw children so eager to learn, although I had had several years' experience in New-England schools. Coming to school is a constant delight and recreation to them. They come here as other children go to play. The older ones, during the summer, work in the fields from early morning until eleven or twelve o'clock, and then come into school, after their hard toil in the hot sun, as bright and as anxious to learn as ever.

Of course there are some stupid ones, but these are the minority. The majority learn with wonderful rapidity. Many of the grown people are desirous of learning to read. It is wonderful how a people who have been so long crushed to the earth, so imbruted as these have been, — and they are said to be among the most degraded negroes of the South, — can have so great a desire for knowledge, and such a capability for attaining it. One cannot believe that the haughty Anglo-Saxon race, after centuries of such an experience as these people have had, would be very much superior to them. And one's indignation increases against those who, North as well as South, taunt the colored race with inferiority while they themselves use every means in their power to crush and degrade them, denying them every right and privilege, closing against them every avenue of elevation and improvement. Were they, under such circumstances, intellectual and refined, they would certainly be vastly superior to any other race that ever existed.

SOURCE: Charlotte Forten Grimké, "Life on the Sea Islands (Part 1)," *The Atlantic* (May, 1864) 587–91.

ANALYZING PRIMARY SOURCES

1. How are Charlotte Forten's class and cultural biases displayed in her writing?
2. What sexism and racism did Forten detect in the conversations of some of the Union officers?

Women's rights leaders Elizabeth Cady Stanton and Susan B. Anthony were among those determined to push Lincoln to enact a more comprehensive abolition policy. "If it be true that at this hour, the women of the South are more devoted to their cause than we to ours, the fact lies here," wrote Cady Stanton. "The women of the South know what their sons are fighting for. The women of the North do not."[48] (See Primary Sources: "Women's Rights Partnership: Elizabeth Cady Stanton and Susan B. Anthony.") Along with Lucy Stone and other women's rights activists, they formed the Women's National Loyal League to force Lincoln to adopt a broader emancipation policy. As white and Black abolitionist women had done thirty years before, they gathered signatures on petitions to Congress to "pass at the earliest practicable day an act emancipating all persons of African descent."[49] The League collected and submitted to Congress 260,000 signatures, two-thirds of them from women. The first popular campaign ever conducted on behalf of a constitutional amendment, these efforts contributed significantly to the 1865 passage and ratification of the Thirteenth Amendment, which permanently abolished Black slavery, with little exception, throughout the United States.

In 1863, after two years of grueling warfare, the military tide began to turn in the Union's favor. An important factor was the Union army's decision to permit Black men to fight. Close to two hundred thousand enlisted, among them Charlotte Forten's father Robert, providing a final burst of military energy as well as a manly model of Black freedom for the public. Black women such as Susie King Taylor and Harriet Tubman lived and traveled with these troops, serving as nurses, spies, and military laborers. (See Primary Sources: "Women on the Civil War Battlefields.") On July 4, 1863, the Union won a decisive battle at Vicksburg, Mississippi, just one day after its equally decisive victory at Gettysburg, Pennsylvania. Still, the war lasted two more years. In the autumn of 1864, General William Tecumseh Sherman marched the western division of the Union army across Georgia and South Carolina, determined to break the spirit of the rebellion by destroying everything of value (except enslaved Blacks) as he went. At her plantation, Mary Chesnut found that "every window was broken, every bell torn down, every piece of furniture destroyed, every door smashed in."[50]

Finally, on April 9, 1865, almost four years to the day after the attack on Fort Sumter, General Robert E. Lee, head of the Confederate army, surrendered at Appomattox Courthouse in Virginia. Fannie Berry, who had been enslaved close to the site of Lee's surrender, recalled that when they found out that they were free, many began to sing: "Mammy don't yo' cook no mo: Yo ar' free, yo' ar' free. Rooster don't yo' crow no mo', Yo ar' free, yo' ar' free."[51] An ex-captive woman from South Carolina remembered, "[On] de fust day of freedom we was all sittin' roun' restin' an' tryin' to think what freedom meant an ev'ybody was quiet an' peaceful."[52] "The people poured into the streets, frenzied with gladness," wrote Mary Livermore, "until there seemed to be no men and women in Chicago, — only crazy, grown-up boys and girls." Then, five days later, Lincoln was assassinated. "From the height of this exultation," Livermore wrote, "the nation was swiftly precipitated to the very depths of despair." She continued,

"Never was a month so crowded, with the conflicting emotions of exultation and despair, as was the month of April 1865."[53] Not all women saw it the same way. "Thank God, the wretch has gotten his just deserts," exulted a woman from the defeated Confederacy.[54]

◆ CONCLUSION: RESHAPING BOUNDARIES, REDEFINING WOMANHOOD

In the years from 1840 to 1865, the women of the United States had traveled a tremendous distance. They had taken a country across a continent. They had joined in a series of social movements to remake and reform American society. They had challenged Black slavery and undertaken systematic reform in their own status as women. They had begun to demand their inclusion in the democratization of American politics. And, along with men but in their own ways, they had joined in the fight over the character and existence of the Union, participating in the Civil War both on and off the battlefield.

Their experiences through these changes had by no means been the same. Some women had taken possession of new land, in the process displacing Indigenous and enslaved women from their homes of long standing. Some had challenged crucial elements of American society and culture and ended up challenging conventional notions of womanhood itself. And while some had defended and lost their right to own Blacks, those two million who had been enslaved became free women and could look forward to their daughters being free. Through all of this, however, American women, of all races and classes, had been deeply involved in these years of momentous national change and had been changed in the process. In the decades after the Civil War, in the victorious North, the defeated South, and the contested West, many began to enter more fully into public life, as workers and socially engaged citizens, in civic organizations, in public and private schools, and in colleges. Like 1848, 1865 was a decisive year in the history of the nation and of its women.

CHAPTER 5 REVIEW

KEY TERMS

moral reform societies (p. 224)
Daughters of Temperance
    (p. 224)
Ladies Physiological Society of
    Boston (p. 226)

Philadelphia Female Anti-
    Slavery Society (p. 229)
New York State Married
    Women's Property Act (p. 233)

Seneca Falls Convention
    (p. 234)
Uncle Tom's Cabin
    (p. 238)

REVIEW QUESTIONS

1. What was the significance of U.S. territorial expansion for American women? How did expansion bring different groups of women into conflict with one another across lines of race, ethnicity, region, and class?

2. How did women's reform movements either strengthen or challenge the tenets of true womanhood? Analyze the underlying connections *between* various women's reform movements — for instance, the relationship between abolition and health reforms.

3. Although war is often viewed through a male lens, how would you describe diverse American women's involvement in the Civil War, both on the home front and on the battlefield?

4. **Making Connections** How did America's diverse women engage with the overarching idea of Manifest Destiny and the increasingly controversial institution of Black slavery in these decades of national expansion? When considering various women's labor and family roles, what changes and continuities can you identify in the antebellum period?

SUGGESTED READING

Women and the Antebellum West

Gae Whitney Canfield, *Sarah Winnemucca of the Northern Paiutes* (1983).

María Raquél Casas, *Married to a Daughter of the Land: Spanish-Mexican Women and Interethnic Marriage in California, 1820–1880* (2009).

John Mack Faragher, *Women and Men on the Overland Trail* (1979).

Winifred Gallagher, *New Women in the Old West: From Settlers to Suffragists, An Untold Story* (2021).

Ramón A. Gutiérrez and Richard J. Orsi, eds., *Contested Eden: California before the Gold Rush* (1997).

Lisbeth Haas, *Saints and Citizens: Indigenous Histories of Colonial Missions and Mexican California* (2013).

Katie Hickman, *Brave Hearted: The Women of the American West* (2022).

Albert L. Hurtado, *Intimate Frontiers: Sex, Gender, and Culture in Old California* (1999).

Anne F. Hyde, *Empires, Nations, and Families: A New History of the North American West, 1800–1860* (2011).

Susan Lee Johnson, *Roaring Camp: The Social World of the California Gold Rush* (2000).

JoAnn Levy, *They Saw the Elephant: Women in the California Gold Rush* (1990).

Shirley Ann Wilson Moore, *Sweet Freedom's Plains: African Americans on the Overland Trail* (2016).

Women and Reform Movements

Bonnie S. Anderson, *Joyous Greetings: The First International Women's Movement, 1830–1860* (2000).

Erica L. Ball, *To Live an Antislavery Life: Personal Politics in the Antebellum Black Middle Class* (2012).

Charles Capper, *Margaret Fuller: An American Romantic Life*, vols. 1 and 2 (1994 and 2010).

Lee Chambers, *The Weston Sisters: An American Abolitionist Family* (2014).

Ellen Carol DuBois, *Feminism and Suffrage: The Emergence of an Independent Women's Movement in America, 1848–1869*, 2nd ed. (2003).

Carol Faulkner, *Lucretia Mott's Heresy: Abolition and Women's Rights in Nineteenth-Century America* (2011).

Lori D. Ginzberg, *Women in Antebellum Reform* (2000).

April R. Haynes, *Riotous Flesh: Women, Physiology, and the Solitary Vice in Nineteenth-Century America* (2015).

Nancy A. Hewitt, *Women's Activism and Social Change, Rochester, New York, 1822–1872* (1984).

Julie Roy Jeffrey, *The Great Silent Army of Abolitionism: Ordinary Women in the Antislavery Movement* (1998).

Andrea Moore Kerr, *Lucy Stone: Speaking Out for Equality* (1992).

Bonnie Laughlin-Schultz, *The Tie That Bound Us: The Women of John Brown's Family and the Legacy of Radical Abolitionism* (2013).

Carolyn Lawes, *Women and Reform in a New England Community, 1815–1860* (2021).

Gerda Lerner, *The Grimké Sisters from South Carolina* (1967).

Scott C. Martin, *Devil of the Domestic Sphere: Temperance, Gender, and Middle-Class Ideology, 1800–1860* (2008).

Jean L. Silver-Isenstadt, *Shameless: The Visionary Life of Mary Gove Nichols* (2002).

Kathryn Kish Sklar and James Brewer Stewart, *Women's Rights and Transatlantic Antislavery in the Era of Emancipation* (2007).

Lisa Tetrault, *The Myth of Seneca Falls: Memory and the Women's Suffrage Movement, 1848–1898* (2014).

Margaret Washington, *Sojourner Truth's America* (2009).

Shirley J. Yee, *Black Women Abolitionists: A Study in Activism, 1828–1860* (1992).

Women and the Civil War

Karen Abbott, *Liar, Temptress, Soldier, Spy: Four Women Undercover in the Civil War* (2014).

Jean H. Baker, *Mary Todd Lincoln: A Biography* (1987).

Sarah Hopkins Bradford, *Harriet: The Moses of Her People: A Biography of Harriet Tubman* (2020).

Mary Farmer-Kaiser, *Freedwomen and the Freedmen's Bureau: Race, Gender, and Public Policy in the Age of Emancipation* (2010).

Drew Gilpin Faust, *Mothers of Invention: Women of the Slaveholding South in the American Civil War* (1996).

——, *This Republic of Suffering: Death and the American Civil War* (2008).

Thavolia Glymph, *The Women's Fight: The Civil War Battles for Home, Freedom and Nation* (2022).

Libra R. Hilde, *Worth a Dozen Men: Women and Nursing in the Civil War South* (2012).

Shelby Harriet Hildebaugh, *Behind the Rifle: Women Soldiers in Civil War Mississippi* (2022).

Stephanie McCurry, *Confederate Reckoning: Power and Politics in the Civil War South* (2012).

——, *Women's War: Fighting and Surviving the American Civil War* (2019).

Victoria E. Ott, *Confederate Daughters: Coming of Age during the Civil War* (2008).

Barbara A. White, *The Beecher Sisters* (2003).

Female Labor in the Gold-Rush Economy

T HE GOLD RUSH PRESENTED CALIFORNIA'S working women with both unusual entrepreneurial opportunities and greater vulnerability to exploitation. The 1850 census showed that women and girls made up only 8 percent of California's nonnative population. By 1860, the proportion of females increased to 28 percent. Within communities of new migrants, the scarcity of females put a premium on the domestic and sexual labor traditionally demanded of women. With access to capital and a bit of luck, some women were able to take advantage of their circumstances and even accumulate family property. Many working-class women and women of color living near mining camps pursued the same promise of upward mobility but frequently encountered isolation, poverty, and violence. Indigenous women, who had long been hired as domestic workers on Californio ranches, now encountered new and lethal forms of racialized coercive labor under U.S. occupation. While individual stories offer examples of remarkable resourcefulness and initiative, the overall economic prospects of California's women in the gold-rush era divided along lines of race, class, and indigeneity.

The new technology of photography produced many images of diverse communities of men at work panning gold. Figure 5.1 offers a rare photograph of a woman at a mining site. Judging from her clothing and the basket in her hand, what economic contributions is she likely to be making to this group of miners?

FAMILY ECONOMIES AND WOMEN'S DOMESTIC WORK

A S THE FOLLOWING DOCUMENTS ON WHITE, BLACK, AND INDIGENOUS women and girls reveal, women's working lives during the gold rush varied as much as their ethnic and class backgrounds. Although some women spent time prospecting for gold, they were more likely to do cooking, laundering, boarding, and sewing for miners willing to pay high prices. In many migrant households, married women's domestic work brought much-needed cash to the family economy, especially when prospecting proved fruitless. The sources that follow reflect a range of women's experiences with economic success and failure in the goldfields northeast of Sacramento. Compare and contrast the documents by or about white "49er" Luzena Wilson, freedperson Nancy Gooch, and Cherokee migrant Barbara Longknife. How did the gender segregation of labor shape the earning abilities of gold-rush women? How might each of these women have viewed their work for money in relation to their unpaid labor for their families?

◆ **Figure 5.1 Panning for Gold in Auburn Ravine (c. 1852)**
GRANGER — Historical Picture Archive.

LUZENA STANLEY HUNT WAS BORN TO A QUAKER FAMILY in North Carolina, but she later moved to Missouri and married Mason Wilson. Luzena and Mason traveled overland to California in 1849 with their two small boys. In 1881 she recounted her days as a "Forty-niner" to her daughter Correnah Wilson Wright, who typed up her narrative. Mills College, Correnah's alma mater, published the memoir in 1937. After a grueling continental crossing and six months of residence in Sacramento, the Wilsons moved out to the mining camp of Nevada City, where Luzena looked for an opportunity to contribute to her family's income. From Wilson's vantage point, women's scarcity elevated their position and opened the door to economic opportunity. How does Wilson use her domestic skills to her family's advantage? In doing so, does she adhere to the conventions of true womanhood or transgress them? What do you make of Wilson's statement that "I shortly after took my husband into partnership"? Who might she have hired for her cook and waiters? How might this account have been different if Wilson had been keeping a diary instead of retelling the family history to her daughter thirty years later?

Luzena Stanley Wilson
Memories Recalled Years Later for Her Daughter (1937)

Chapter Six

From the brow of a steep mountain we caught the first glimpse of a mining camp. Nevada City, a row of canvas tents lining each of the two ravines, which, joining, emptied into Deer Creek, lay at our feet, flooded with the glory of the spring sunshine. The gulches seemed alive with moving men. Great, brawny miners wielded the pick, and shovel, while others stood knee deep in the icy water, and washed the soil from the gold. Every one seemed impelled by the frenzy of fever as men hurried here and there, so intent upon their work they had scarcely time to breathe. Our entrance into the busy camp could not be called a triumphal one, and had there been a "back way" we should certainly have selected it. Our wagon wheels looked like solid blocks; the color of the oxen was indistinguishable, and we were mud from head to foot. I remember filling my washbasin three times with fresh water before I had made the slightest change apparent in the color of my face; and I am sure I scrubbed till my arms ached, before I got the children back to their natural hue. We were not rich enough to indulge in the luxury of a canvas home; so a few pine boughs and branches of the undergrowth were cut and thrown into a rude shelter for the present, and my husband hurried away up the mountain to begin to split out "shakes" for a house. Since our experience of rain in Sacramento, we were inclined to think that rain was one of the daily or at least weekly occurrences of a California spring, and the first precaution was to secure a water-tight shelter. Our bedding was placed inside the little brush house, my cook stove set up near it under the shade of a great pine tree, and I was established, without further preparation, in my new home. When I was left alone in the afternoon — it was noon when we arrived — I cast my thoughts about me for some plan to assist in the recuperation of the family finances. As always occurs to the mind of a woman, I thought of taking boarders. There was already a thriving establishment of the kind just down the road, under the shelter of a canvas roof, as was set forth by its sign in lamp-black on a piece of cloth: "Wamac's Hotel. Meals $1.00."

I determined to set up a rival hotel. So I bought two boards from a precious pile belonging to a man who was building the second wooden house in town. With my own hands I chopped stakes, drove them into the ground, and set up my table. I bought provisions at a neighboring store, and when my husband came back at night he found, mid the weird light of the pine torches, twenty miners eating at my table. Each man as he rose put a dollar in my hand and said I might count him as a permanent customer. I called my hotel "El Dorado."

From the first day it was well patronized, and I shortly after took my husband into partnership. The miners were glad to get something to eat, and were always willing to pay for it. As in Sacramento, goods of all kinds sold at enormous figures, but, as no one ever hesitated to buy on that account, dealers made huge profits. The most rare and costly articles of luxury were fruits and vegetables. One day that summer an enterprising pioneer of agricultural tastes brought in a wagon load of watermelons and sold them all for an ounce (sixteen dollars) each. I bought one for the children and thought no more of the price than one does now of buying a dish of ice-cream. Peaches sold at from one to two dollars each and were miserable apologies for fruit at that. Potatoes were a dollar a pound and for a time even higher. As the days progressed we prospered. In six weeks we had saved money enough to pay the man who brought us up from Sacramento the seven hundred dollars we owed him. In a little time, the frame of a house grew up around me, and presently my cook stove and brush house were enclosed under a roof. This house was gradually enlarged room by room, to afford accommodation for our increasing business. . . . We had then from seventy-five to two hundred boarders at twenty-five dollars a week. I became luxurious and hired a cook and waiters. Maintaining only my position as managing housekeeper, I retired from active business in the kitchen.

SOURCE: *Luzena Stanley Wilson, '49er: Memories Recalled Years Later for Her Daughter Correnah Wilson Wright* (Oakland, CA: The Eucalyptus Press, 1937).

Like Luzena Wilson, Nancy Gooch traveled from Missouri to California, but her overland journey was a forced one. Slaveholder William Gooch took Nancy and Peter with him when he struck out for the goldfields, leaving behind the enslaved couple's three-year-old son Andrew. In 1850, when California passed a constitution outlawing chattel slavery, Nancy and Peter began to work for themselves. Nancy Gooch did domestic work and took in laundry. The Gooches bought farmland in Coloma by 1858 and eventually even acquired the original gold discovery site of Sutter's Mill. They did so in a hostile legal environment in which state laws prevented Blacks from voting or testifying against whites in court. The state even passed its own Fugitive Slave Law in 1852 to allow former slaveholders to claim enslaved people who arrived with them in California before the 1850 state constitution was ratified. After Peter passed away in 1861, Nancy Gooch continued her domestic work, carefully accumulating the $700 needed to send for her son Andrew and his family.[55] Postwar emancipation opened the door Gooch had been waiting for, and by 1870 she had used her savings to bring her son to California. She lived until 1901 in Coloma, surrounded by her extended family.

Domestic portraiture for both white and Black Americans in the mid-nineteenth century served as a sign of respectability and middle-class aspiration. The photo shown in Figure 5.2 was taken in 1857, when Nancy and Peter Gooch were still struggling to acquire land and save enough money to reunite their family. At this point, their son remained enslaved and beyond their reach. Figure 5.3 portrays the Gooch/Monroe family around 1870, when Nancy had finally managed to bring together her son, Andrew (seated with a child on his lap), along with his wife and other sons. Considered together, what do these photographs convey to you about the importance of marriage and extended family for Black Californians? What is the possible significance of the book Nancy Gooch is holding in Figure 5.3? What comparisons can you make between Nancy Gooch's status as a domestic worker and laundrywoman and her self-presentation in these family portraits? Note the photographers' backgrounds and the clothing, facial expressions, and postures of the people.

◆ Figure 5.2 **Peter and Nancy Gooch Portrait, San Francisco (1858)**
Courtesy of California State Parks, 2023.

◆ Figure 5.3 **Nancy Gooch and the Monroe Family (c. 1870)**
El Dorado County Historical Museum.

Living in Coloma during the 1850s, the Cherokee woman Barbara Longknife could easily have known Nancy Gooch. The migration to California wasn't her first overland journey, for as a ten-year-old girl, Barbara had been forcibly removed with her family from Cherokee traditional lands in the East to Indian Territory (see "Indigenous Peoples in the South and U.S. Removal Policy" in Chapter 4). In 1850, pregnant with her first child, Barbara and her husband, William Longknife, journeyed with a larger group of Cherokees to California. Barbara's letters to Stand Watie, head of a prominent family in the Cherokee Nation, offer a "counter narrative of the gold rush" that speaks mainly of a working woman's economic struggle and homesickness.[56] Responsibilities for her family — in particular for her sick daughter — compounded the burden of Longknife's domestic work. The letters preserve Longknife's original spelling. What insight do these letters give you into Longknife's contributions to her family's survival? What are the main sources of her dissatisfaction? How did Longknife use her letters to maintain her ties with family in the Cherokee Nation?

Barbara Longknife to Stand Watie, Coloma (June 8, 1854)

Dear Sir,

I gladly embrace the present opertunity of addressing you by the way of this letter. we are in moderate health at the present time and hope these lines may find you and your family emjoying the same blessing. we have made nothing in this country as yet more than barely supported the family. William has been trying his luck in the mines, did not make it pay over board, we have had a great deal of sickness in our family since we came to this Country and our doctor bills has cost us a great many dollars together with other expenses connected with Dr. Bills. we are still living in Coloma and I think it is very probable we will remain here as long as we stay in this Country. I would like very much to see all my old friends in the nation. California is not what it was represented to be, if I was back again I would let California be the last place that I would go to. I am engage in washing at present and have been for a considerable length of time it pays better than anything else that I can do. give my best respects to Mr. Huss and all enquiring friends & receive for your self and family the same. You will please write when this comes to hand and give me all the news of importance. William & myself are the only ones of the mess that I know anything about. R. Tuff died on the plains. Welch died after we got here, the last I heard of your Brother Charles he was going north in 52, have'nt heard from him since. John Candy is in this country somewhere, was in this place a few days since, he has not made his pile yet. when you write you will direct your letter to Coloma Eldorado Co California

Very respectfully your friend
Barbary Longknife

Barbara Longknife to Stand Watie, Coloma (October 11, 1857)

Dear Cir

I take this oppertunity of wrighting you a few lines to let you no we are yet in the land of the living. Charles E. Watie was hear to day, he is working at 3 dolars per day, that is good wages for this time. we are all well except my little girl, she has had the bilious fevor and it has left her all most blind of boarth eays. I live in hopes that her site will come back a gain. if I had money I would take her to some other Doctor but as it is I have the best Doctor thir is in this place. we have made a living in this Country and that is all. to rase money enough to take us home we could not if it was to save us all. we could not do that mush and we have not had that mush at one time cince we have bin in the country and Charles says he dont know wether he ever will make that mush or not; that he feels old now that he has worked so hard. not only him that has worked I have worked hard as the next one in the Country and all I have is a living. if I did not work as I do we would be so mush behind that we never would get strate again and if I had never come to this Country I would have now what I have not and that is good health. We have dun the best we could cince hire we have been. Every thing has been hy and is yet. baken is 28c per pound pork 25c per pound and beef 25c per pound . . . no the times is gon when Labor was from 5 to 8 a day for some people. It was good for some but not all. . . . now I say to Mr. Longknife if we doe not have moeny enought in two years to take us home I will then Baige min and my childs way home. to stay hear and work as I do any longer than that time I will not put up with it if I can help it. I am willing to help all I can but I an tyeard of this Country. . . .

Mrs. Barbra Longknife

SOURCE: Edward Everett Dale and Gaston Litton, eds., *Cherokee Cavaliers* (Norman: University of Oklahoma Press, 1939).

ENSLAVEMENT AND APPRENTICESHIP OF INDIGENOUS WOMEN AND GIRLS IN CALIFORNIA

THE RAPID GROWTH OF CALIFORNIA'S POPULATION that brought economic opportunity to some migrant women proved disastrous for Indigenous females. Tens of thousands of Indigenous women and girls living in California on the eve of the gold rush suffered extreme violence and terror, including wars of extermination, rape, and de facto slavery in the ensuing years of white expansion.

Figure 5.4 is a hand-colored engraving of a young Indigenous woman created in the 1850s during peak years of anti-Indigenous violence. The sobering French caption reads, "Sixteen-year-old Southern California Indian female at the price of a pound of gunpowder and a bottle of brandy."[57] Everything else, from the girl's own story to the artist's name and the purpose of the image, is unknown. What details do you notice in the portrait of the young woman? What further questions would you want to ask about her image and its context?

APART FROM DE FACTO TRAFFICKING, California Indigenous children also became subject to an institutionalized system of child labor. The ironically named 1850 Act for the Government and Protection of Indians regulated relations between whites and Indigenous peoples in matters dealing with labor, land, and court procedures. It established an Indigenous convict leasing system, institutionalized whipping as a legal penalty for Indigenous peoples convicted of stealing, and denied Indigenous testimony in court against a white person. Section 3, excerpted

◆ **Figure 5.4 "Indienne Californienne du Sud" (c. 1850s)**
Robert B. Honeyman, Jr., collection of early Californian and Western American pictorial material [graphic], BANC PIC 1963.002:1305:F — ALB. Courtesy of The Bancroft Library, University of California, Berkeley.

here, claimed to guard against the "compulsory" detention of Indigenous minors, but in reality it opened the door to dissolving Indigenous families, numerous child kidnappings, and other abuses and even the murder of Indigenous parents. One historian argues that these laws made Indigenous children's bonded labor "culturally invisible" because they placed Indigenous children alongside other family dependents under the patriarchal oversight of white male household heads.[58]

California Statutes, Chapter 133: "An Act for the Government and Protection of Indians," Section 3 (1850)

Any person having or hereafter obtaining a minor Indian, male or female, from the parents or relations of such Indian minor, and wishing to keep it . . . shall go before Justice of the Peace in his Township, with the parents or friends of the child, and if the Justice of the Peace becomes satisfied that no compulsory means have been used to obtain the child from its parents or friends, shall enter on record, in a book kept for that purpose, the sex and probable age of the child, and shall give to such person a certificate, authorizing him or her to have the care, custody, control and earnings of such minor, until he or she obtain the age of majority. Every male Indian shall be deemed to have attained his majority at eighteen, and the female at fifteen years.

SOURCE: Kimberly Johnson-Dodds, *Early California Laws and Policies Related to California Indians* (Sacramento: California Research Bureau, September 2002), 28.

THE CASE OF THE YUKI GIRL "Shasta" (so named for her Shasta mountain origins) demonstrates how guardianship laws worked to give white families legal control over Indigenous minors. In 1857, San Francisco courts heard white physician Oliver Wozencraft's plea for the return of a young Indigenous girl he claimed as his ward. Wozencraft charged that a "negro woman" named Charlotte Sophie Gomez had abducted the child from him three years earlier. The details of the case are not fully clear, but some additional background is known. Wozencraft had served as a delegate to the California state constitutional convention, where he unsuccessfully proposed a ban on admitting free Blacks into the state. Around the time Wozencraft first took Shasta into his household, he had served as a federal Indian commissioner who attempted to negotiate treaties with northern California Indigenous tribes. Charlotte Gomez lived in a small community of Black San Franciscans who were involved in aiding free Blacks whose former owners attempted to have them sent illegally back into southern states. Thus, it is possible that Gomez had attempted to shelter Shasta because she believed Wozencraft was holding her captive. Yet, under California law, Gomez could not have testified against Wozencraft in court, and she found herself facing perjury charges for denying any role in Shasta's removal from Wozencraft's household. In July 1857, a San Francisco probate court, following the law allowing apprenticeship of Indigenous minors, determined that Wozencraft was a "suitable person to be appointed guardian." Shasta returned to the Wozencraft household, where she resided until at least the 1880s.

Nineteenth-century newspapers can be read for both surface facts and underlying biases. For example, the following *Sacramento Daily Union* article related Wozencraft's version of Shasta's story from her "adoption" to her "abduction." Under what circumstances did Shasta first come into Wozencraft's family? Was she actually an orphan? How does the newspaper describe the actions of Charlotte Gomez and other free Blacks involved in the case? How do they discuss Shasta's Yuki family of birth? It isn't clear whether Shasta, like so many other Indigenous minors, was being held as a domestic laborer or sex captive. Is it possible that Wozencraft truly considered Shasta to be a member of his family?

Story of "Shasta," an Indian Orphan Child (1856)

An application was made, yesterday, to the Judge of the 4th District Court, for a *habeas corpus* to bring up the person of a little Indian girl, aged about 8 years, and named "Shasta." The application was made by Dr. Oliver M. Wozencraft, and it is from him that we learn the following romantic story:

In the year 1851, Dr. Wozencraft was Indian Commissioner and Agent, and was engaged in making treaties with the various aboriginal tribes living in the remoter portions of the State. In the month of August, of that year, he made arrangements to go among the Uka [Yuki] tribe, who inhabited the Shasta mountains. . . . His object was to chastise the Ukas, for having a short time before surprised a train of packers, whom they murdered and despoiled of all their pack animals and merchandise. They had also endeavored to burn the town of Shasta. . . . Accordingly, the Commissioner, with twenty mounted dragoons and thirty Ylackas [a different group of California Indians] proceeded against the Ukas, and chased them for several days along the stream on which they were located, but the Indians continually escaped up the mountains. . . .

[*After more than a day's pursuit, the soldiers managed to chase the Yuki men into the remote mountains, but captured a group of "squaws and children secreted in the bushes." The following morning, Wozencraft learned that the "captives" had silently escaped from the area under cover of night.*]

[They] left a little orphan girl about three years old, whom they had during the march treated with great neglect. Dr. Wozencraft took charge of the little unfortunate, and sent her to Mrs. Wozencraft, in San Francisco. That lady adopted, as it were, the orphan, and raised her; becoming more and more attached to her, until some time in September, 1853, "Shasta," for that was the appropriate name bestowed upon the girl, disappeared. Nothing more was heard of her until only a few days ago, when the Doctor and his lady as they were returning from church, met their former ward in the streets. On investigation it was discovered that she was living with certain colored persons, name Collyer and Charlotte Sophie Gomez. The Doctor immediately took measures to regain the custody and care of "Shasta," and procured the issuance of the writ of *habeas corpus*, to which we have referred above.

It may not be uninteresting to state, in connection with the story of Shasta, that the stream upon which the Commissioner encamped has since been named "Squaw Creek," in commemoration of the capture of the Uka women, which took place there. Many miners are located in its region, and the town of Natches is built upon its banks. We also learn that the Uka Indians afterwards accepted the alternative of peace, and became friendly.

SOURCE: "Story of 'Shasta,' an Indian Orphan Child," *Sacramento Daily Union*, December 15, 1856.

ANALYZING PRIMARY SOURCES

1. What role did class, race, and family networks of support play in shaping the kind of gendered labor done by each of the women represented here?

2. How might discriminatory legislation like the testimony laws or the Indigenous apprenticeship law have curtailed the ability of some groups of women to make a living and acquire property?

3. What opportunities and vulnerabilities to exploitation did girls and women encounter during the California gold rush? How were some women's opportunities related to other women's vulnerabilities? Were there any possibilities for female bonding across race and class lines?

PRIMARY SOURCES

Women's Rights Partnership:
Elizabeth Cady Stanton and Susan B. Anthony

Tracing the early nineteenth-century women's rights movement through the half-century-long relationship between Elizabeth Cady Stanton and Susan B. Anthony reminds us that many aspects of that history are best understood in terms of the types of bonds, or absence of connection, between women. This particular relationship, though always oriented toward important political events, also illustrates the degree to which domestic demands constrained and informed female reformers, not just wives and mothers like Cady Stanton but also single, self-supporting women like Anthony.

The documents excerpted here allow us to follow the first decade of their relationship through their rich correspondence, augmented by autobiographical and biographical reminiscences, excerpts from the speeches they worked together to produce, and occasional newspaper reports of their activities. A photograph from 1891 speaks to their enduring collaboration.

The following account from Cady Stanton's autobiographical reminiscences recalls the friends' first meeting in Seneca Falls, sometime in 1850 or 1851, in connection with an antislavery meeting. The two lived in booming industrial towns only a few hours from each other in upstate New York. Cady Stanton wrote her account thirty years after the fact. How might the intervening years have affected her memories of the event?

Elizabeth Cady Stanton Recalls Meeting
Susan B. Anthony (1881)

It was in the month of May, of 1851, that I first met Miss Anthony. . . . There she stood with her good earnest face and genial smile, dressed in gray silk, hat and all the same color, relieved with pale blue ribbons, the perfection of neatness and sobriety.

It is often said by those who know Miss Anthony best, that she has been my good angel, always pushing and guiding me to work. . . . Perhaps all this is in a measure true. With the cares of a large family, I might in time, like too many women, have become wholly absorbed in a narrow family selfishness, had not my friend been continually exploring new fields for missionary labors. Her description of a body of men on any platform, complacently deciding questions in which women had an equal interest, without an equal voice, readily roused me to a determination to throw a firebrand in the midst of their assembly. . . .

[From 1848 through 1860], Susan B. Anthony circulated petitions both for the civil and political rights of woman throughout the State [New York], traveling in stage coaches and open wagons and sleighs in all seasons, and on foot from door to door through towns and cities, doing her uttermost to rouse women to some sense of their natural rights as human beings, to their civil and political rights as citizens of a republic; . . . they would gruffly tell her they had all the rights they wanted, or rudely shut the door in her face, leaving her to stand outside, petition in hand, with as much contempt as if she were asking alms for herself. None but those who did that petition work in the early days for the slaves and the women, can ever know the hardships and humiliations that were endured.

SOURCE: Elizabeth Cady Stanton, Susan B. Anthony, and Matilda J. Gage, eds., *History of Woman Suffrage* (Rochester, NY: Susan B. Anthony, 1881), 1:56–62.

A PARTICULARLY RICH EXCHANGE OF LETTERS between the two coworkers in 1856 concerns Anthony's involvement in the educational reform movement of the time. Two-thirds of the teachers in the state of New York were women — including, for a while, Anthony herself. Yet only men were allowed to speak at the annual state teachers' conventions. Since 1853, Anthony had challenged that exclusion, and now that she had succeeded, she was getting ready to address the meeting on behalf of an issue of great meaning to her: coeducation. While she was struggling to prepare for one of her first public speeches, her friend was herself preparing for the birth of her sixth child. (This daughter would grow up to be the feminist reformer Harriot Stanton Blatch.) What do these letters tell us about the psychological challenges that women like these faced in undertaking careers as public reformers? How do the personal obstacles that the two women faced differ?

Anthony to Cady Stanton, Rochester
(May 26, 1856)

I hear the [women's rights] movement much talked of & earnest hopes for its spread expressed. But these women dare not speak out their sympathy. . . . Don't you think it would be a good plan to first state what we mean by educating the sexes together, then go on to show how the few institutions that profess to give equal education fail . . . and lastly that it is folly to talk of giving to the sexes equal advantages, while you withhold from them equal motive to improve those advantages. . . . When will you come to Rochester to spend those days, I shall be most happy to see whenever it shall be . . . [you may bring your servant] Amelia and the two babies of course and as many more as convenient. With love.[59]

SOURCE: Ellen Carol DuBois, ed., *The Elizabeth Cady Stanton–Susan B. Anthony Reader: Correspondence, Writings, Speeches* (Boston: Northeastern University Press, 1992), 60–61.

Anthony to Cady Stanton, Home-Getting, along towards 12 O'Clock (June 5, 1856)

And Mrs. Stanton, *not a word written* on that Address for *Teachers Convention. This* week was to be *leisure* to me and lo, our [servant] *girl, a wife,* had a *miscarriage* . . . and the Mercy only knows when I can get a moment; and what is *worse,* as the *Lord knows full well,* is, that if I *get all the time* the *world has,* I *can't get up a decent document.* So for the love of me, and for the saving of the *reputation* of *womanhood,* I beg you, with one baby on your knee and another at your feet, and four boys whistling, buzzing, hallooing *Ma, Ma,* set your self about the work. . . .

. . . [N]o man can write from *my stand point,* nor no woman but *you,* for all, all would base their *strongest* argument on the *un*likeness of the *sexes.* . . . Those of you who have the *talent* to do honor to poor — oh! how poor — womanhood, have all given yourselves over to baby-making; and left poor brainless me to battle alone.[60]

SOURCE: DuBois, *Cady Stanton–Anthony Reader,* 61–62.

Cady Stanton to Anthony, Seneca Falls (June 10, 1856)

Dear Susan, Your servant is not dead, but liveth. Imagine me, day in and day out, watching, bathing, nursing, and promenading the precious contents of a little crib in the corner of my room. I pace up and down these two chambers of mine like a caged lioness, longing to bring nursing and house keeping cares to a close. Is your speech to be exclusively on the point of educating the sexes together, or as to the best manner of educating women? . . . Come here and I will do what I can to help you with your address, if you will hold the baby and make the puddings. . . . It is not well

to be in the excitement of public life all the time. . . . You, too, need rest Susan; let the world alone awhile. We cannot bring about a moral revolution in a day or two. Now that I have two daughters, I feel fresh strength to work for women. . . . It is not in vain that in myself I feel all the wearisome cares to which woman even in her best estate is subject. Good night.

SOURCE: Ann D. Gordon, ed., *The Selected Papers of Elizabeth Cady Stanton and Susan B. Anthony,* vol. 1, *In the School of Anti-Slavery, 1840–1866* (New Brunswick, NJ: Rutgers University Press, 1997), 325.

THE FOLLOWING ARE THE FRAGMENTARY NOTES that Anthony left on the speech on coeducation she was struggling to compose in the winter of 1856–1857. Her notes are supplemented [in brackets] by quotations of her speech from a contemporary newspaper report. From the bullet point–like notes, can you imagine Anthony delivering her ideas to an audience of not particularly sympathetic men? How does Anthony's approach focus on education as a route to equality for the sexes? What connections does she make between equal education and economic independence for women, an issue to which she was especially attuned?

SUSAN B. ANTHONY
Why the Sexes Should Be Educated Together (1856)

Because their life work is so nearly identical . . . [To earn their bread and live is the work of both sexes. Every woman is born into the world alone and goes out of the world alone. . . . All women do not have husbands, and, besides, fathers and husbands die sometimes, and their wives and daughters may be obliged to earn a livelihood. Every father should educate his sons and daughters alike for upon each may devolve the task of earning their own bread.] The grand thing that is needed is to give the sexes like motives for acquirement — very rarely a person studies closely without hope of making that knowledge useful — as means of support or house or something to them.

That man may learn from his boyhood that woman is his intellectual equal and thus no longer look upon her as his inferior — Oh, dear dear there is so much to say & I am so without constructive power to put in symmetrical order —

Because separation and restraint stimulates the desires and passions . . . [Is it possible that boys and girls who have always associated together cannot go to college together? . . . The sexes behave better and learn better together.]

SOURCE: Enclosure in June 5, 1856, letter, in Gordon, *Selected Papers*, 323–24; and "Address by SBA on Educating the Sexes Together," *Rochester Daily Democrat*, February 4, 1857, in Gordon, *Selected Papers*, 334–38.

BY THE END OF THE 1850s, the two friends were immersed in the national crisis over slavery. Not only were North and South at odds, but so were radical and moderate opponents of slavery. Both Cady Stanton and Anthony, who were strong partisans of the abolitionist movement to end slavery immediately, absolutely, and without compensation to slaveholders, were among the former.

The following are two abolitionist speeches, one given by Anthony in 1859 and the other by Cady Stanton in 1860. While the nation was poised on the brink of civil war, neither the newly arisen Republican Party nor the Lincoln administration it had elected was ready to commit to the abolition of slavery. How do you think Anthony and Cady Stanton sought to increase popular support in the North for the more radical policy of making emancipation of the enslaved the purpose of the impending war? How do you think each connects her own condition as a free woman to the suffering of enslaved males and female?

SUSAN B. ANTHONY
Make the Slave's Case Our Own (1859)

Let us, my friends, for the passing hour, make the slave's case our own. . . . Let us feel that it is our own children, that are ruthlessly torn from our yearning mother hearts, and driven into the "coffle gang," . . . That it is our own loved sister and daughter, who are shamelessly exposed to the public market, and whose beauty of face, delicacy of complexion, symmetry of form, and grace of motion, do but enhance their monied value, and the more surely victimize them to the unbridled passions and lusts of their proud purchasers.

. . . If, by some magic power, the color of our skins could be instantly changed and the slave's fate made really our own, then would there be no farther need of argument or persuasion, or rhetoric or eloquence. But we . . . look upon the slave, as a being all unlike ourselves. . . . [T]he fact that

he has for so many generations been the victim of the white man, seem conclusive evidence to the masses, that a condition that would be torture worse than death to us, is quite endurable, nay, congenial to him. Again, it is argued that we of the North are not responsible for the crime of slave holding, that the guilty ones dwell in the South. . . . Thus, do we put the slave's case far away from us.

Source: Susan B. Anthony, "Make the Slave's Case Our Own," c. 1859, original in Susan B. Anthony Papers, Library of Congress, Washington, DC.

ELIZABETH CADY STANTON
To the American Anti-Slavery Society (May 8, 1860)

Eloquently and earnestly as noble men have denounced slavery on this platform, they have been able to take only an objective view. . . . [B]ut a privileged class can never conceive the feelings of those who are born to contempt, to inferiority, to degradation. Herein is woman more fully identified with the slave than man can possibly be, for she can take the subjective view. She early learns the misfortune of being born an heir to the crown of thorns, to martyrdom, to womanhood. For while the man is born to do whatever he can, for the woman and the negro there is no such privilege. . . . [A]ll mankind stand on the alert to restrain their impulses, check their

aspirations, fetter their limbs, lest, in their freedom and strength, in their full development, they should take an even platform with proud man himself. To you, white man, the world throws wide her gates; the way is clear to wealth, to fame, to glory, to renown, the high places of independence and honor and trust are yours; all your efforts are praised and encouraged; . . . all your successes are welcomed with loud hurrahs and cheers; but the black man and the woman are born to shame. The badge of degradation is the skin and sex.

Source: DuBois, *Cady Stanton–Anthony Reader*, 82–83. The original transcript appeared in the *Liberator*, May 18, 1860, p. 78.

TAKEN IN 1891, FIGURE 5.5 is a photographic portrait of a political and personal partnership lasting over four decades. Together Anthony (left), the organizer, and Cady Stanton (right), the writer, speaker, and orator, continued to provide leadership to the U.S. woman suffrage movement as it grew from a radical offshoot of antislavery into a mature, mass-based women's movement (see "Consolidating the Gilded Age Women's Movement" in Chapter 6). By the 1890s, Anthony was widely admired as the personification of dedication to the cause of women while Cady Stanton continued to push at the edges of acceptable opinion. How are their leadership roles reflected in the image?

◆ Figure 5.5 **Susan B. Anthony and Elizabeth Cady Stanton (1891)**

Universal History Archive/Getty Images.

ANALYZING PRIMARY SOURCES

1. What tensions did Cady Stanton and Anthony each experience as they moved into public life?

2. How were Cady Stanton and Anthony able to support each other in their reform work?

3. How did the reforms and political developments of the 1850s affect Cady Stanton's and Anthony's beliefs and arguments relating to women's rights?

PRIMARY SOURCES

Women on the Civil War Battlefields

THE BATTLEFIELD has not always been an exclusively male space. During the Civil War, wives and mothers of common soldiers came to cook, launder, and nurse the men of their families, while officers' wives were permitted social visits with their husbands. But women went to the scene of fighting for other reasons too. Political passions are no respecter of gender, and patriotism, dedication to cause, eagerness to be a part of historic events, and the simple desire for adventure brought women to the bloody heart of the Civil War.

The most common battlefield role of women was nurse — the "angel" of the battlefield who comforted wounded and dying soldiers, representing feminine care and domestic tranquility in the midst of armed conflict. Despite the desperate need for medical personnel to care for the enormous number of casualties, female nurses had to fight their own kinds of battles with male medical officers for the opportunity to serve. A much smaller number of women also served the Union and Confederate armies in less conventionally womanly ways, as spies, strategists, and even soldiers.

While the Civil War had a tremendous impact on women overall, generating aspirations for greater public responsibilities and more rights, those who had had direct battlefield experience found it difficult to have their particular contributions fully appreciated. Northern male veterans could count on an old-age army pension in recognition of their services. Finally, in 1890, the U.S. government granted pensions to twenty thousand women who served as paid nurses. Approximately one-tenth of these were Black women. Southern white women, of course, had no government to whom they could turn.

Many of the images in this essay are taken from memoirs written by women who served on and around battlefields, who wrote to make sure that the historical record included their stories. They succeeded in permitting us to see the Civil War through women's eyes.

THE NURSES

An estimated ten thousand women served as nurses during the Civil War.[61] Nursing was not yet a profession requiring special training and would not become so until the turn of the twentieth century. At first, both military hospitals and battlefield infirmaries were run by male surgeons, who had little to offer the wounded beyond the removal of a limb and whiskey to blunt the pain. Their assistants were also men, themselves often recuperating from battlefield injuries. Nursing under wartime conditions seemed too brutal for white women, an unacceptable offense against their modesty.

Nonetheless, care of the sick and injured was traditionally a female skill, and women began to offer their services as soon as the first call for troops was issued. In the North, Dorothea Dix, already well known for her work to improve the treatment of the insane, persuaded Edwin Stanton, U.S. secretary of war, to appoint her as superintendent of nursing for the Union army. "All nurses are required to be plain looking women," Dix declared. "Their dresses must be brown or black with no bows, no curls, no jewelry and no hoop skirts."[62] Clothing had to be not only respectable but also functional in the gory environment of the military hospitals. Louisa May Alcott, unmarried and struggling to become a writer, was one of those Dix recruited. "I love nursing and *must* let out my pent-up energy in some new way," she wrote in the journal that became her first published book, *Hospital Sketches*. "I want new experiences and am sure to get 'em if I go."[63] In 1861 Congress authorized pay of $12 a month for the female nurses under Dix's supervision, about a third of what male nurses received.

In the regimental hospitals away from Washington, D.C., women whose relatives had been wounded or who felt moved to care for the troops convinced local medical staff to allow them to serve without army commission or pay. Mary Ann Bickerdyke of Illinois became a legend for her battlefield stamina and disregard for military hierarchy. Bickerdyke was a mother and widow in her mid-forties. She was a dedicated caregiver, moving from battlefield to battlefield, cooking and laundering as well as tending to the Union army wounded. Eventually, she was appointed field agent for the United States Sanitary Commission, which, despite its name, was not part of the government but rather a massive, largely female, volunteer organization that provided clothing and medical supplies to the Union army.

Like other nineteenth-century women with commanding personalities, Bickerdyke assumed the powerful female appellation of "Mother." In an environment that reserved official control for men, the title of "Mother" could be translated into informal public authority. Bickerdyke insisted that she had the right to be near the action and to tend to the troops as she saw fit, on the basis of selfless concern for "her" boys. Indeed, Mother Bickerdyke seems to have treated most of the military men with whom she came into contact, including surgeons and generals, as overgrown boys for whom she knew best. Like other such female figures with unusual public standing who called themselves Mother — such as the late nineteenth-century labor organizer Mother Jones — Bickerdyke used this reworked maternal ideal as a framework for venturing beyond the genteel middle-class role of true womanhood.

Bickerdyke saw much military action. She arrived in Vicksburg, Mississippi, in time for the city's surrender to General Ulysses S. Grant and escorted home Union soldiers released from the notoriously brutal Confederate prison at Andersonville, Georgia. In 1864, she joined General William Tecumseh Sherman, with whom she claimed a special bond, for his devastating march across the heart of the South. At the end of the war, when Sherman and his troops paraded through Washington, D.C., to

◆ **Figure 5.6 F. O. C. Darley,** *Midnight on the Battlefield* **(1890)**
The New York Public Library/Art Resource, NY.

celebrate victory, Mother Bickerdyke rode in a place of honor. Then she slipped back into private life. In 1886, the army awarded her a pension of $25 a month.

Figure 5.6 depicts the initial episode of the Bickerdyke story, her role at the battle of Fort Donelson, Tennessee, site of an early Union victory. Bickerdyke achieved renown for her courage in remaining at the killing fields late at night, until she was absolutely sure that she had found all survivors. The illustration, a steel engraving, was commissioned for *My Story of the War*, an account of the wartime contribution of the women of the Sanitary Commission, written in 1889 by Mary Livermore. It pictures Bickerdyke as a female savior, alone in her attempt to sustain life in a field of death. How did the artist choose to idealize her? How does the use of light (and dark) suggest women's role on the battlefield?

Although the gender conventions of southern society were more restrictive and less encouraging of the kind of public presence and demonstration of organizational talent that characterized women's nursing involvement with the Union cause, southern white women, and their enslaved women and girls, provided hospital care for Confederate soldiers as well. They could be found in the mammoth military hospitals in the capital of Richmond and at temporary medical facilities close to the battlefields and near their own homes and communities. Because records of the Confederacy, including lists and numbers of women who served as nurses, were destroyed in the Union seizure and burning of Richmond, it is impossible even to estimate their numbers.

White women showed their patriotic dedication to the Confederate cause by attending wounded soldiers' bedsides, talking them through their suffering and dying, reading to them, and writing letters to their families. The dirtier jobs — bathing wounds, cleaning up the bloody sites of surgery, preparing corpses — were often done by enslaved women brought along by their female captors. Relatively early, in 1862, the Confederate Congress began paying women for their nursing services. Their wages ranged from $30 to $40 a month, figures that seem quite high until the wildly inflated currency of the Confederacy is taken into account. Wages were allotted even for enslaved women, although the money was no doubt paid to slaveholders who claimed them as property.

The painting depicted in Figure 5.7 is one of the few images we have of southern women acting as nurses for Confederate soldiers. The painting is not a portrait of a particular woman, but a generalized image of southern white womanhood devoted to the Confederate cause. The artist, William Ludwell Sheppard, served in the Army of Northern Virginia and began his career as an illustrator and watercolorist of the war from a romanticized, southern perspective. *In the Hospital* was painted in the first year of the war. What audience did Sheppard have in mind? If we could compare it with an image from 1863 or 1864, what might be different? What are the similarities and differences between this and the prior image, of Mother Bickerdyke ministering to a Union soldier? How did this image help to build what later became, as one historian puts it, "the legend of female sacrifice, . . . of Confederate women's unflinching loyalty"?[64]

Catholic religious women were the only group of women on the battlefield with any prior experience in caring for the wounded. Their selflessness and virtue were unassailable. For these reasons, they were more welcomed than other Civil War nurses by the male military establishment, an attitude that is particularly remarkable given the rampant anti-Catholic prejudice of the era. Civil War chronicler Mary Livermore, no admirer of "the monastic institutions of that [Catholic] church," nonetheless praised the Catholic nurses: "They gave themselves no airs of superiority or holiness, shirked no duty, sought no easy place, bred no mischief."[65] Livermore thought the sisters represented a model of organized public service that Protestant women would do well to follow. Dorothea Dix, on the other hand, resented the Catholic women, who were not under her supervision.

Dedicated to the service of God and humanity rather than the victory of North or South, the sisters attended both Confederate and Union wounded. During the

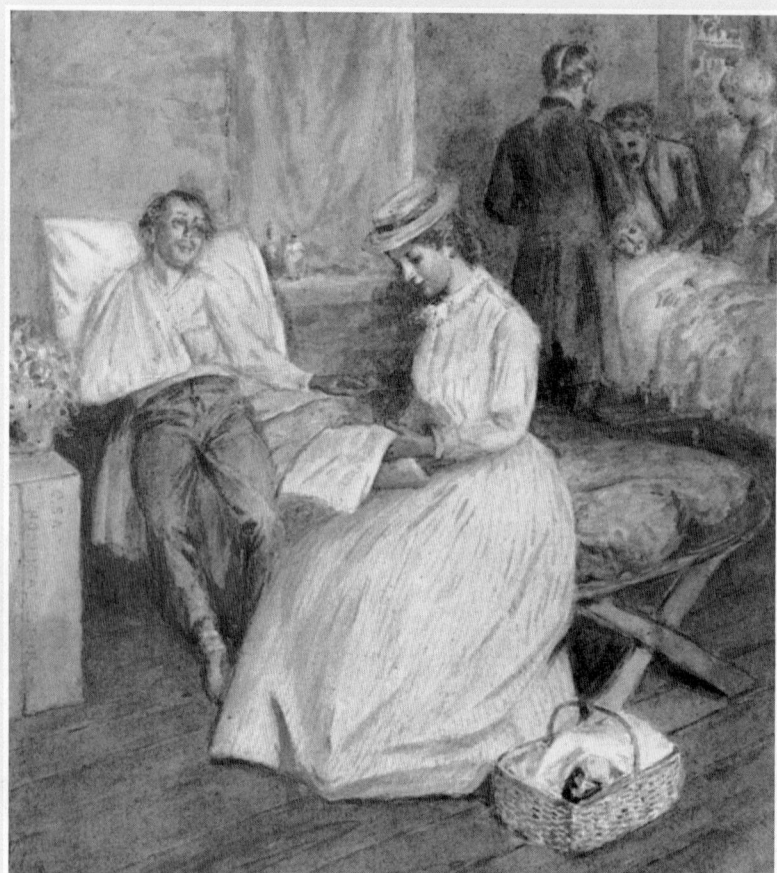

◆ Figure 5.7 **William Ludwell Sheppard, *In the Hospital* (1861)** *GRANGER — Historical Picture Archive.*

long Union siege of Vicksburg, the Daughters of Charity cared for Confederate soldiers and civilians alike. A similar community provided nurses for the giant Satterlee Hospital in Philadelphia, which received many of the Union wounded from the war's deadliest battle, Gettysburg. Figure 5.8 shows most of the forty sisters who served at Satterlee. How did the sisters' religious habits solve the problems of uniform and functional clothing for nurses? While other Civil War nurses were portrayed individually, why and with what effect did these women appear as a group?

THE SPIES

By far, the most well-known Black woman on the battlefield was Harriet Tubman (Figure 5.9), renowned for her role as conductor on the Underground Railroad. Born enslaved in Maryland about 1821, she ran away from the slaveholder in 1849 and returned numerous times, often disguised as a man, to rescue as many as

◆ **Figure 5.8 Daughters of Charity with Doctors and Soldiers, Satterlee Hospital, Philadelphia (c. 1863)**

Daughters of Charity, Province of St. Louise Archives, Emmitsburg, MD.

seventy enslaved relatives and friends. When the war began, she came back from Canada, where she had gone to evade the 1850 Fugitive Slave Law, and made her way to the Union-occupied South Carolina coastal islands to offer her services. In and around the fighting, she functioned in virtually every role available to women and more. She was a nurse, a liaison between the Union army and the many refugees from slavery, a spy, and a military strategist for Union coastal invasions into Georgia and South Carolina.

Tubman began her military service in the way that most women did, as a nurse, first to the formerly enslaved and then to Black troops along the Carolina coast. There is some indication that cures she learned as a bonded woman made her especially valuable in this role. But it soon became clear that, as a Black woman who could appear to be a common captive, she could move easily about the South, gathering information for the Union army. Union officers asked her to organize a corps from among the Black male refugees to serve with her as military spies and scouts.

◆ Figure 5.9 **Harriet Tubman**
Hulton Archive/Getty Images.

In 1863, on the basis of Tubman's reports, a regiment of 150 Black Union soldiers sailed up South Carolina's Combahee River to cut the enemy's supply lines, seize or destroy foodstuffs, and encourage the desertion of the Black labor force of the plantations along the banks. Eight hundred Black men and women — "thousands of dollars worth of property," according to a contemporary newspaper account — fled to the Union gunboats and were transferred to the freedmen's encampments on the Union-occupied Sea Islands.[66] The raid was commemorated more than a century later when a group of Black feminists from Massachusetts took as their name the Combahee River Collective.

Despite influential supporters, after the war Tubman was never able to secure the back pay or army pension that white women such as Mother Bickerdyke received. In 1867, her husband, John Tubman, was murdered by a white man, who was acquitted of the crime. She spent the rest of her life in Auburn, New York, struggling to raise money to support herself and an old-age home for ex-captives that she established. Proceeds from her memoir, *Scenes in the Life of Harriet Tubman*, were her major source of income. Tubman was not literate, and so her oral reminiscences were recorded in book form by a neighbor and friend, Sarah H. Bradford. Figure 5.9, the book's frontispiece, is described as a woodcut likeness of Tubman in her "costume as scout." Like other women on the battlefield (see Figure 5.11), Tubman wore a combination of men's and women's clothing. The jacket may have been military issue. What about this outfit reconciles her femaleness with the largely male nature of the battlefield? What might have been the impact on her readers of showing this former enslaved woman posed in front of a military camp, carrying an ammunition pouch and a gun?

If Tubman's race allowed her to spy for the North, white southerner Rose O'Neal Greenhow's sex allowed her to spy for the South. In the Union capital of Washington, D.C., nearby southern sympathizers were able to conduct a brisk trade in military information. Some of these spies were women who made use of their sexual attractiveness to serve their cause. Greenhow, one of the best known, was described by a contemporary as possessed of "almost irresistible seductive powers."[67]

When the war broke out, Greenhow was a widow and mother in her mid-thirties. She was prominent in Washington, D.C., social circles and had connections to important congressmen, including her nephew, Senator Stephen A. Douglas of Illinois. Committed to the Confederate cause and opposed to freedom for Black people, she gathered political and military information helpful to the South from her numerous admirers and lovers, allegedly including information that helped the Confederates win the first battle of Bull Run. Although constantly under suspicion, she avoided arrest by appealing to principles of gentlemanly chivalry shared by North and South alike.

Eventually, however, Greenhow was arrested and sent to a special Washington prison reserved for enemy agents, many of them women. She was subsequently released to Virginia. The circumstances of her death, soon after, were as extraordinary as those of her life. In 1864, she was a passenger on a British boat running the Union naval blockade off the Carolina coast. Northern gunships fired, and Greenhow's lifeboat capsized. She was close to shore and would have made it to land except that she held on to her purse, which was heavy with gold, and therefore drowned.

The photograph in Figure 5.10 was taken by a member of the studio of renowned Civil War photographer Mathew Brady, when Greenhow was imprisoned. One historian writes that her gender was her disguise.[68] What comment does the photographer's artful posing make on Greenhow's career as a Confederate spy? What do Greenhow's dress, pose, and the presence of her daughter suggest about her imprisonment at Union hands?

◆ **Figure 5.10 Rose O'Neal Greenhow in the Old Capitol Prison with Her Daughter (1862)**
Library of Congress Prints and Photographs Division, Washington, D.C. (LC-DIG-cwpbh-04849).

THE SOLDIERS

Although we will never know their numbers, hundreds of women, possibly more, fought on the battlefields of the Civil War. These women warriors fall into two categories: those who were known to be women at the time and those who passed themselves off as men. In the first category were the so-called daughters of the regiment. Often arriving in camp with their newly enlisted husbands, a few may have also been as motivated by the desire to see military action as by marital sentiment. After performing such womanly tasks as nursing, cooking, and laundering, occasionally these women took on the all-important job of carrying the regiment's flag (or standard) into battle. Soldiers, who were recruited at the local and state level, fought as much out of loyalty to their regiment as out of allegiance to the army or the nation, and the way their regimental colors were displayed represented their comradeship and military fervor. The standard bearer's job was to lead and encourage the troops, and women who undertook this role inspired tremendous devotion from their comrades.

Bridget Divers, known as "Michigan Bridget," was one of these regimental daughters. An Irish immigrant, she came to the First Michigan Cavalry with her husband. Early in the war, her regiment was the object of a surprise attack, and the troops panicked. One of Divers's comrades remembered how she leaped to her feet, grabbed the flag, and yelled, "Go in Boys and bate [beat] Hell out of them."[69] Divers found army life so much to her liking that, after the war, she continued to serve with her husband in the western Native American conflicts.

As with other such women, the legends that accrued around Michigan Bridget emphasized her combination of manly bravery and female sympathy. Figure 5.11, a steel engraving commissioned, like that of Mary Ann Bickerdyke (Figure 5.6), by Mary Livermore for *My Story of the War*, portrays Divers bearing the U.S. flag in the midst of battle. Divers knew how to shoot, and Livermore approvingly wrote of her, "When a soldier fell she took his place, fighting in his stead with unquailing courage."[70] How and with what purpose does the artist position Divers with respect to the battle? Why might she have been pictured with a flag instead of the gun that she allegedly knew how to use? And why might the artist have chosen to show her carrying not the regimental colors but the U.S. flag?

"Of the three hundred and twenty-eight thousand Union soldiers who lie buried in national cemeteries," the editors of the *History of Woman Suffrage* (1881) wrote, ". . . hundreds are . . . women obliged by army regulation to fight in disguise."[71] Women have assumed male identities to fight in many wars, but they seem to have been particularly numerous in the U.S. Civil War. The Union army discovered and dismissed many women among its recruits, and the sex of others was not discovered until they were wounded or killed. During the war, authorities' greatest fear was that women who had sneaked into the ranks would engage in immoral sexual activities with male soldiers. Stories of women who disguised themselves as men in order to fight continued to surface for many decades. In 1910, an Illinois Civil War pensioner who had gone by the name Albert Cashier was discovered to be biologically female, and as a result they were declared insane, sentenced to an asylum, and forced to dress as a woman.[72] For a long time after the war, some, like Cashier, lived as trans men. They worked in men's occupations and even married women, who invariably claimed to have believed their husbands to be men, which is hard to believe but impossible to dismiss.

With one exception, all of the well-known "trans men" of the Civil War era were Union soldiers. Loreta Velazquez, a Cuban immigrant, began their career in the Confederate army with their husband's support but continued to live as a man after the husband was killed. Using the name Harry T. Buford, Velazquez fought as an officer with several regiments and participated in the Confederate victory at the first battle of Bull Run. Although wounded, Velazquez escaped detection and continued to live a life of high adventure after the war.

◆ Figure 5.11 **F. O. C. Darley, *A Woman in Battle—"Michigan Bridget" Carrying the Flag* (1888)**

The New York Public Library/Art Resource, NY.

In 1876, Velazquez wrote a popular and controversial memoir, *The Woman in Battle*, in which they described their lifelong habit of wearing men's clothes and the attraction that being able to make money like a man held. The book included the illustrations shown in Figure 5.12 of Velazquez's female and male personae. How did Velazquez depict themselves as a woman, and what designated them visually as a man? Above all, what point might Velasquez have been seeking to make by demonstrating through illustrations that they could shift from role to role? How does Velasquez's story begin to suggest what today is called the social construction of gender?

◆ **Figure 5.12 Madam Velazquez in Female Attire (*left*) and Harry T. Buford, 1st Lieutenant, Independent Scouts, Confederate States Army (*right*)**
GRANGER — Historical Picture Archive.

ANALYZING PRIMARY SOURCES

1. What are the similarities in the images of women who served as Civil War nurses? What attitudes toward women help explain these similarities?

2. Male soldiers are issued official uniforms to designate their rank and military affiliation. What similarities do you notice in Divers's and Tubman's outfits? How might this clothing have constituted a kind of informal uniform for women on the battlefield?

3. The Civil War was fought between two cultures as much as between two economic and racial systems. Do you detect patterns in the images of northern versus southern women? What do these differences tell you about the gender dimensions of the North-South divide?

4. Taken as a group, do these images indicate that the women who participated directly in the war maintained or undermined standard gender roles?

5. What roles did females and nonbinary people take on in the war effort?

6

Reconstructing Women's Lives North and South

1865–1900

IDA B. WELLS and MARY KENNEY were both daughters of the Civil War era. Wells was born in 1862 to enslaved people in Mississippi and Kenney in 1864 to Irish immigrants in Hannibal, Missouri. Despite their great differences in background, the unfolding of both women's lives illustrates the forces that affected American women's history in the years after the Civil War and, in turn, women's capacity to be forces in the making of American history.

Wells (later Wells-Barnett) was shaped by the violent struggles between freedpeople seeking to realize their emancipation and equal rights, and white southerners seeking to retain their racial dominance. As a journalist, Wells exposed the continuing brutal methods of white supremacy, and her work sparked an organized women's movement among Blacks and some white allies. Kenney (later O'Sullivan) was a lifelong wage earner who recognized that workers needed to act collectively, rather than individually, to improve their lives. A pathbreaking female labor organizer, she helped form the Women's Trade Union League (WTUL) in 1903 (see "Organizing Women Workers" in Chapter 8). Both women, and so many more illustrated in this chapter, laid the basis for an era of extraordinary achievement by American women.

"Reconstruction" is the term used to describe the period of American history immediately following the Civil War, the revision of the U.S. Constitution to deal with the consequences of emancipation and racial inequalities, the rebuilding of the South after the losses of war, and the reconstitution of some sort of national unity after the trauma of sectional division. The formal period of Reconstruction lasted twelve years. It ended in 1877 when anti-Reconstruction politicians took full control of state governments in the South, leaving recently freed Black southerners without the power to defend their hard-won rights; the North to concentrate on industrial development and economic growth; and the West to continue to displace Indigenous societies.

The word "reconstruction" also can be used to cover a longer period, during which much of the U.S. economy was reconstituted around industrial capitalism. The free-labor ethic on which the Republican Party was founded evolved into a commitment to unbridled progress. For many, that meant rampant industrialization. The resulting wealth, optimism, and productivity were not shared equally. On the contrary, the gap between rich and poor grew enormously during the postbellum years, producing great tension and violence between owners and workers. With chattel slavery largely eliminated, industrial society could no longer ignore its internal class divisions. By the end of the century, conflict between labor and capital rivaled the inequalities of race as the most overt challenge to national unity.

Women also were reconstructing their lives in these years. In the defeated South, women emancipated from slavery grappled with the challenges of and dangers to their tentative freedom, while former female slaveholders sought to maintain the privileges of white supremacy under new conditions. In the North, a determined group of women sought equal political rights, and the woman suffrage movement came into its own. Industrial capitalism generated both a rapidly expanding female labor force and new leisure and wealth for middle- and upper-class white, native-born women. Between 1865 and 1900, women's wage labor, the terms of appropriate womanhood within which women lived, and their scope for public action all expanded. By the end of the nineteenth century, the basis had been laid for an epoch of female assertion and accomplishment unparalleled in American history.

◆ GENDER AND THE POSTWAR CONSTITUTIONAL AMENDMENTS

American history's first presidential assassination (Abraham Lincoln), followed quickly by its first presidential impeachment (Andrew Johnson), left the executive branch in shambles and the legislative branch in charge of national Reconstruction. Republicans controlled Congress, and former abolitionists, known as Radicals, controlled the Republican Party. To protect the North's victory and their party's control over Congress, the Radicals were determined to enfranchise the only population on whom the Republicans could depend in the defeated Confederacy—free Black men. In 1866, Radicals proposed an amendment to the U.S. Constitution to establish the citizenship of freedpeople. The **Fourteenth Amendment** began with a simple, inclusive sentence: "All persons born or naturalized in the United States, and subject to the jurisdiction thereof, are citizens of the United States and of the State wherein they reside."

Leaders of the women's rights movement hoped to further revise the Constitution and reconstruct democracy without distinction of either race *or* gender. Despite their best efforts, however, the ratification of the Fourteenth Amendment in 1868, followed by that of the Fifteenth Amendment in 1870, established Black suffrage without reference to white or Black female suffrage. Thwarted in Congress, these women turned to the U.S. Supreme Court to argue that women's political right to the franchise was included within the new constitutional definitions of national citizenship and political rights.

Their efforts failed. The only actual enfranchisement of women in the Reconstruction era occurred in the territories of Wyoming (1869) and Utah (1870), where a handful of legislators accorded women the vote in territorial and local elections. Even so, the movement for women's enfranchisement changed and expanded, drawing new adherents from the Midwest and the Pacific Coast. Some old alliances with male abolitionists were shattered, and most white women's efforts for women's equality were no longer linked to those for racial equality. The advocates of woman suffrage undertook a campaign that would require an additional half century and another constitutional amendment—the Nineteenth, ratified in 1920—to complete (see "Winning Woman Suffrage" in Chapter 8).

Constitutionalizing Women's Rights

In 1865 and 1866, as Congress was considering how to word the Fourteenth Amendment, women's rights activists called for woman suffrage to be joined with Black male suffrage in a single constitutional act. Many northern women, white and Black, had fought for the end of slavery, so, in the memorable words of Elizabeth Cady Stanton, "Would it not be advisable, when the constitutional door is open, for [women] to avail ourselves of the strong arm and blue uniform of the black soldier to walk in by his side?"[1] To pursue this goal, Cady Stanton, Anthony, and others formed the American Equal Rights Association, dedicated to both racial and gender equality in suffrage. "We resolved to make common cause with the colored class—the only other disfranchised class," observed Lucy Stone, "and strike for equal rights for all."[2]

But Radicals in Congress contended that pursuing woman suffrage and Black male suffrage simultaneously would doom the latter, which was their priority. Accordingly, they wrote the second section of the Fourteenth Amendment, meant to encourage states to grant voting rights to those formerly enslaved, to apply only to "male inhabitants . . . twenty-one years of age and citizens of the United States." This was the first reference to gender in the U.S. Constitution. Woman suffragists petitioned Congress to get the wording changed, but abolitionist Wendell Phillips told them, "This hour belongs to the Negro," leaving Cady Stanton to wonder impatiently if "the African race is composed entirely of males."[3]

Two years after the 1868 ratification of the Fourteenth Amendment, congressional Radicals wrote the **Fifteenth Amendment** to advance Black male suffrage more forcefully, explicitly forbidding states from enacting disfranchisements on the grounds of "race, color or previous condition of servitude." Again gender was not included, leading Cady Stanton to charge that "all mankind will vote not because of intelligence, patriotism, property or white skin but because it is male, not female."[4]

The American Equal Rights Association collapsed, and in its wake, woman suffragists divided over whether to endorse the Fifteenth Amendment. Elizabeth Cady Stanton and Susan B. Anthony broke with their former Radical allies and formed the rival National Woman Suffrage Association (NWSA). To reconcile woman suffrage advocacy with the Radical Republican agenda, Lucy Stone and her husband, Henry Ward Blackwell, took a different route. In 1869, they organized the American Woman Suffrage Association. They focused on campaigns for suffrage at the state level and in 1870 inaugurated the *Woman's Journal*, a weekly newspaper that was published for the next fifty years.

Of the two societies, NWSA pursued the more aggressive, independent path. The organization's newspaper, defiantly named the *Revolution*, lasted only two years. It proclaimed on its masthead: "Women their rights and nothing less; men their rights and nothing more." NWSA gained political autonomy for the suffrage movement but at the cost of an important part of the women's rights legacy: attention to the interrelation of the hierarchies of race and gender. As the larger society left behind the concerns of freedpeople and of Radical Reconstruction, much of the white woman suffrage movement did, too, envisioning women's emancipation largely in terms of themselves.

A New Departure for Woman Suffrage

Once the new constitutional amendments had been ratified, NWSA proposed an inventive, bold interpretation of them. The argument was both simple and profound: first, women were "persons" whose rights as national citizens were established by the first sentence of the Fourteenth Amendment; second, the right to vote was central to and inherent in national citizenship. Third, and most important, women's right to vote was thus already established and did not require any additional constitutional change.

This argument, which was called the New Departure, brought to prominence one of the most unusual advocates in the history of woman suffrage, Victoria Claflin Woodhull. Born into poverty, Woodhull made her way into the highest ranks of New York society, first as a "healer," and then as a newspaper owner, Wall Street trader, and associate of powerful men like Cornelius Vanderbilt. Aided by a congressman friend and without the knowledge of other suffragists, in 1871 she presented the case for the New Departure before the Judiciary Committee of the U.S. House of Representatives. Within a year, however, Woodhull, who had boldly criticized sexual hypocrisy within middle-class marriages, had become involved in the most notorious sexual scandal of the age. In her newspaper, she went public with her knowledge that Henry Ward Beecher, powerful Brooklyn minister and brother of Catharine Beecher and Harriet Beecher Stowe, had had an adulterous affair with one of his parishioners. Under a new federal anti-obscenity law, the **Comstock Act** (named for Anthony Comstock, the "social purity" crusader who drafted the legislation), Woodhull was jailed for using the federal mail system to distribute her newspaper, which included accounts of the scandal. Cady Stanton, one of the few suffragists who steadfastly defended Woodhull, insisted, "We have already women enough sacrificed to this sentimental, hypocritical prating about purity. If this present woman be crucified, let men drive the spikes."[5] Woodhull avoided jail, but dropped out of public life. She eventually moved to England, where she married a wealthy man, remade her reputation, became prominent among eugenicists (championing a fringe set of flawed ideas for creating "perfect children"), supported women's rights to an abortion, and lived until 1927.

Independent of Woodhull, suffragists around the country pursued their voting rights on the basis of the New Departure theory that they needed only to take hold of the right to vote, which was already theirs. During the elections of 1871 and 1872, groups of women went to their local polling places, put forth their constitutional understanding to stunned election officials, and stepped forward to submit their votes. In Washington, D.C., the Black journalist Mary Ann Shadd Cary was able to register but not to vote. Susan B. Anthony convinced polling officials in her home-town of Rochester, New York, to let her vote. "Well I have been & gone & done it!!" she wrote exuberantly. "Positively voted the Republican ticket."[6] Two weeks later, she was arrested for the crime of illegal voting, based on a federal law meant to disfranchise former Confederates. Her trial was a spectacle from start to finish. The judge ordered the jury to find Anthony guilty, which it did, and the judge's final insult was to refuse to jail Anthony so as to keep her from appealing her verdict.

The U.S. Supreme Court finally considered the suffragists' argument in 1875, in the case of Virginia Minor of St. Louis, Missouri, who sued the official who had not allowed her to vote. In ***Minor v. Happersett***, one of the most important rulings in the history of women's rights (see the Appendix: Documents), the Supreme Court ruled unanimously that, while Minor was indeed a citizen, voting was not a right but a privilege bestowed by the federal government as it saw fit. Not only did this decision strike the New Departure theory legally dead, but it also indicated that the Court was bent on narrowing the meaning of the Fourteenth and Fifteenth Amendments in general. Subsequently, the Court also permitted more and more ways to deprive Black men of their franchise and constitutional civil rights.

After the *Minor* decision, NWSA began to advocate a separate constitutional amendment, modeled on the Fifteenth, to bar states from disfranchising "on the grounds of sex." This was the wording that would eventually go into the Nineteenth Amendment (1920), but for the time being, the proposed amendment made little headway. In 1876, NWSA leaders, uninvited, forced their way into the national celebration in Philadelphia of the hundredth anniversary of the Declaration of Independence. "Our faith is firm and unwavering in the broad principles of human rights proclaimed in 1776, not only as abstract truths, but as the corner stones of a republic," they declared. "Yet we cannot forget, even in this glad hour, that while all men of every race, and clime, and condition, have been invested with the full rights of citizenship under our hospitable flag, all women still suffer the degradation of disfranchisement."[7]

◆ WOMEN'S LIVES IN SOUTHERN RECONSTRUCTION AND REDEMPTION

Meanwhile, life in the defeated South was being reconstructed as well. No element of freedom came easily or automatically for freedpeople, and southern whites changed their lives and expectations very reluctantly. Black women fought for their dignity and for control over their labor, their children, and their bodies. Elite white women sought new capacities and strengths to accommodate the loss of the labor and wealth that slaveholding had given them. White women from the middle and lower ranks remained poised between loyalties of race and the resentments of class that always relegated them to the margins of their society.

By 1870, all the southern states had met the lenient terms Congress mandated for readmission to the Union. After the final removal of federal troops in 1877, white southerners, in a process known as Redemption, moved to reclaim political control and to reassert white supremacy. As they did so, new laws institutionalized racial apartheid in every aspect of life and a race-based system of convict labor that resembled slavery. The region's economy, still largely agricultural, slowly began to industrialize. Black men and women were forced to remain mostly at the bottom of the economy as sharecroppers and tenant farmers. The complex result of these post-Reconstruction social, political, and economic changes was known as the New South.

Black Women in the New South

After the defeat of the Confederacy, some freedwomen and freedmen stayed on with former slaveholders for months — some because they did not know they had been freed, some because they had nowhere to go, and even more so because white vigilantes terrorized them into staying. Others took to the road to find long-lost spouses and other family members, reunite with them, and start afresh in a place that promised a more fully formed freedom. Those who could not travel to find their stolen kin posted advertisements, such as this one in the *Anglo-African Magazine*: "Martha Ward Wishes information concerning her sister, Rosetta McQuillan, who was sold from Norfolk, Va. About thirty years ago to a Frenchman in Mobile, Ala."[8]

Some hard-won family reunions of freedpeople did not end happily. Some spouses had formed new unions. Laura Spicer, sold away from a Virginia plantation, was contacted by her husband three years after the war ended. He had since become attached to another woman and was deeply conflicted. "I do not know which I love best, you or Anna," he wrote to Spicer. "Try and marry some good, smart man . . . and do it because you love me, and not because I think more of the wife I have got than I do of you."[9] Nor were parents always recognized by the children they had been forced to leave behind. "At firs' I was scared of her, 'cause I didn't know who she was," one

◆ **The Right to Marry**

As abolitionists considered disregard of enslaved people's marriages one of the fundamental immoralities of slavery, immediately after the Civil War the Freedmen's Bureau rushed to legalize marriages among freedpeople, who were eager to have their unions recognized. To indicate that enslaved people had been married in fact, if not in law, Bureau officials "solemnized" rather than authorized these marriages. In "The Ebony Bridal: Some salient scenes of life in the Sunny South," the artist captures the absolute importance that the freed Black community placed on marriage. The formality of the event, the bride's clothing and that of her groom and attendants, the large, diverse Black audience, some whites present, and the Black minister presiding celebrated marriage as a visual and cultural mark of freedom and social progress. *Library of Congress, Prints & Photographs Division, Reproduction number LC-USZ62-55057.*

child remembered of her mother. "She put me in her lap an' she most' nigh cried when she seen de back o' my head . . . where de lice had been an' I had scratched em."[10]

In 1865, the U.S. Army, charged with occupying and governing the defeated territories, organized a special division to deal with freedpeople. The Freedmen's Bureau provided temporary aid, oversaw freedpeople's labor, promoted legal marriages, and adjudicated disputes with former slaveholders. One of its tasks was to ensure that freedpeople had rights to their own children. On returning to the Union, southern states had passed laws, known as Black Codes, to limit the freedoms of newly emancipated people. Apprenticeship laws provided for the indenture of children into servitude regardless of the wishes of their parents. Black mothers and grandmothers fought especially hard against this abusive legislation. "We were delighted when we heard that the Constitution set us free," Lucy Lee of Baltimore explained, "but God help us, our condition is bettered but little; free ourselves, [but] deprived of our children. . . . Give us our children and don't let them be raised in the ignorance we have [been]."[11]

The deepest financial ambition of most freedpeople was to have their own family farms. However, Congress was unwilling to reapportion the southern lands that might have established genuine Black self-sufficiency. Some freedpeople became homesteaders on public lands in Florida, Kansas, Arkansas, Texas, and Alabama, and a handful were able to buy their own property. But the overwhelming majority found that they had to continue to work for others, rather than independently. A fundamental dilemma of Reconstruction for most centered on their returning to work for white people: On what terms? With what degree of personal freedom? And for what compensation?

One of the most subtle and complex aspects of this dilemma concerned the disposition of Black women's labor. During slavery, women worked alongside men in the fields. Black women began to leave field work immediately after emancipation, much to the horror of white landowners, who knew women's importance to the agricultural labor force. Some observers reported that Black men, eager to assert the rights of manhood over their families, were especially determined that their wives not work for whites. Black women, who discovered that any assertion of autonomy toward white employers might be violently punished as unacceptable "uppityness," had their own reasons for withdrawing their labor.

To achieve even a small degree of independence from direct white oversight, three out of four Black families ended up accepting an arrangement known as sharecropping. Working on small farms carved out of the holdings of white landowners, sharecropping families kept only a portion of the crops they grew. And, in bad times, which were frequent, the value of their yield did not equal the high interest credit that white landowners extended, and most ended up in permanent indebtedness.

Freedpeople were more successful in realizing their desire for education. Even before the war ended, Black and white women from the North had gone south to areas occupied by the Union army to begin teaching the Black population. Throughout Reconstruction, freedpeople built their own schools, funded by the Freedmen's Bureau and northern missionary societies, to gain the basics of literacy. Charlotte Forten (later Forten Grimké), for one, brought her idealism and hopes of

◆ **Women Exodusters (late 1800s)**
This late nineteenth-century photograph shows LeAnna Samuels and her daughters (from left to right) Harriet, Margaret, and Mary in the yard of their Nicodemus, Kansas, home. Nicodemus was founded by "Exodusters," a group of about six thousand African Americans who set out in 1879 to escape white violence and economic oppression in Mississippi and Louisiana. As the image shows, Black women and men were able to acquire homesteads in Kansas and live in relative safety compared to the Deep South. *Nicodemus Historical Society Collection, Kenneth Spencer Research Library, University of Kansas Libraries.*

racial uplift to her post in coastal South Carolina. "I shall gather my scholars about me, and see smiles of greeting break over their dusky faces," she wrote. "My heart sings a song of thanksgiving, at the thought that even I am permitted to do something for a long-abused race, and aid in promoting a higher, holier, and happier life on the Sea Islands."[12]

Many of the colleges and universities that are now referred to as "historically Black" began during the era of Reconstruction. Unlike long-standing prestigious white institutions, many of these institutions — for instance, Howard University, established in 1867 in Washington, D.C. — were open to women as well as to men. In 1881, famously wealthy John D. Rockefeller founded the Atlanta Baptist Female Seminary, an all-female school that later became Spelman College. These institutions provided both high school and college-level courses, and they played a major role in educating Black leaders. They educated women who went on to become teachers throughout the South and beyond. This educational infrastructure helped, in part, to create a small southern Black middle class in the urban South.

The right to vote awarded to formerly enslaved men by the Fourteenth and Fifteenth Amendments lay at the very core of their hopes for the future. During Reconstruction, freedmen's exercise of the ballot, protected by federal troops, helped to elect approximately two thousand Black men to local, state, and national political office. Despite their own disfranchisement, Black women understood the political franchise as a communal rather than an individual right. They regularly attended political meetings and advised men, who had the vote, how to use it. Southern white women, by contrast, regarded the enfranchisement of Black men as yet another insult to their sex and their race.

White Women in the New South

At the end of the war, white women in the South faced loss and defeat. Food shortages were compounded by the collapse of the economy. More than a quarter million southern white men died on Civil War battlefields, leaving one generation of widows and another that would never marry. Occupation by federal troops after the war deepened white southerners' seething anger and humiliation. One historian argues, perhaps exaggeratedly, that southern white women, who did not share some of men's sheer relief at getting off the battlefield, harbored greater resentment than southern white men toward the North.[13]

Elite white women felt the loss of their human "property" acutely. If they wanted Black men in their fields and Black women in their kitchens, they had to concede to some of the freedpeople's new expectations for wages, personal autonomy, and respect. Elite white women began for the first time to cook and launder for themselves and their families. "We have most of the housework to do all the time," complained Amanda Worthington of Mississippi, "and . . . it does not make me like the Yankees any better."[14]

Non-elite white southerners were less affected by the withdrawal of enslaved Black labor, but because they lived much closer to the edge of subsistence, they suffered far more from the collapse of the economy and the physical devastation of the South. Economic pressures drove many into the same sharecropping arrangement and permanent indebtedness as Blacks. Poor southern white women and their children, however, did find jobs in the textile mills that northerners and a new class of southern industrialists began building in the 1880s. Inasmuch as Black people were not allowed to work in the mills, white women experienced textile work as a kind of racial privilege. Many poor white women believed as fervently as those who had been slaveholders in the inviolability of racial hierarchies.

Even so, the collapse of the institution of Black slavery provided new opportunities for public life for those white women who chose to take them. Well-off women became involved in the memorialization of the Confederacy. They raised funds, built monuments, and lionized the men who had fought for southern independence, all the while creating an expanded civic role for their sex. Poor farm women found some of their opportunities in the Grange, a social and educational movement that later fed into the rise of Populism (see "Rural Protest, the People's Party, and the Battle for Woman Suffrage" in Chapter 7). With few exceptions, however, southern white women kept their distance from woman suffrage efforts, which reminded them all too much of the northern abolitionist and federal intervention to free and enfranchise Black people who had been enslaved.

Racial Conflict in Slavery's Aftermath

Changes in gender and race relations together generated considerable violence in the postwar South. Whites experienced African American autonomy as a profound threat. The Ku Klux Klan, founded in 1866 in Pulaski, Tennessee, terrorized freedpeople for asserting their new freedoms. Klan members sexually humiliated, raped, and murdered many freedwomen. In Henry County, Georgia, two Klansmen pinned down Rhoda Ann Childs; she told a congressional investigation in 1871, "[They] stretched my limbs as far apart as they could . . . [and] applied the Strap to my Private parts until fatigued into stopping, and I was more dead than alive." She was then raped with the barrel of a gun.[15] Through such actions, white men meant both to punish Black men and to reassert their slavery-era control over Black women's bodies.

Having had no legal recourse under slavery, however, Black women determined to use their newly won rights to defend themselves. According to one historian, "black women articulated a radical vision of sexual citizenship" that sought to include bodily sovereignty as part of their equal protection under the law.[16] After the deadly 1866 Memphis race riots, for example, five Black women who had been raped by rampaging white men came forward to give testimony before a congressional committee. Among them, sixteen-year-old Lucy Smith told how a group of men assaulted her in her own home. The women's courageous stand led the Republican committee report to acknowledge and condemn sexual violence against Black women.

Eventually, the region's hidden history of cross-racial sex took an even more deadly form. Whites charged that Black men were sexual predators seeking access to white women. The irony, of course, was that under slavery, it was white men who had unrestricted sexual access to Black women. Southern white women of all classes supported these charges against Black men, and most white northerners assumed that they were true. At the slightest suspicion of the merest disrespect to a white woman, Black men could be accused of sexual aggression and lynched — killed (usually hanged) by mobs who ignored legal process to execute their own form of crude justice. Lynchings, often involving gruesome mutilation, murder, and burning, were "popular" events in the post-Reconstruction South, with white women and children attending amid a carnival-like atmosphere. In 1892, the high point of this practice, 160 Black people, some women included, were lynched.[17]

Ida B. Wells, a Black journalist from Memphis, Tennessee, inaugurated a campaign, eventually international in scope, to investigate and expose the false charges behind the epidemic of lynchings and to get leading white figures to condemn it. In her publication *Southern Horrors: Lynch Law in All Its Phases*, Wells recognized that false allegations of Black men's lewd behavior toward white women were closely related to assumptions of Black women's sexual disreputability and that Black women had a major role to play in challenging the system that led to lynchings. Her efforts helped to catalyze the organization of a Black women's reform movement. (See Primary Sources: "Ida B. Wells, 'Race Woman.'")

Southern Blacks' efforts to claim their rights suffered many major setbacks in the late nineteenth century. One by one, all-white Democratic parties "redeemed" state governments from Republicanism and ended what they called "Black rule," instituting legal devices to disfranchise Black men, such as requiring voters to demonstrate literacy, to pay exorbitant poll taxes, or to prove that their grandfathers had been voters. By the beginning of the twentieth century, Black voting had been virtually obliterated throughout the South.

In addition to repudiating civil rights legislation, southern states also instituted new penal codes that shunted Black women and men into involuntary labor as leased convicts and prison farmworkers. In Georgia, for instance, the state rented out the labor of Black women, alongside Black and white men, to railroad, mining, and brickmaking companies as well as plantations. By the 1890s, reform efforts resulted in a sex-segregated system that assigned Black women to hard labor on all-female prison plantations where deprivation and sexualized violence were the norm. Moreover, Georgia's penal system reinforced elevated notions of white southern

♦ Mary Tape and Her Family (c. 1884–1885)

Pictured from left to right are Joseph, Emily, Mamie, Frank, and Mary Tape, Chinese American residents of San Francisco in the 1880s. Mary Tape emigrated from China in the 1860s and married Chinese immigrant Joseph Tape in 1875. The family became well known for a legal challenge to school segregation that culminated in a landmark 1885 California Supreme Court decision, *Tape v. Hurley*. (See Reading into the Past: "What Right Have You?") Mary Tape took her Anglicized maiden name from Mary McGladery, the matron of the San Francisco Ladies Protection and Relief Society, where Mary lived when she first arrived from China as a young orphan. *Archive Photos/Smith Collection/Gado/Getty Images.*

READING INTO THE PAST

MARY TAPE
"What Right Have You?"

De jure (stated by law) racial segregation was not limited only to the South or to Black people. Chinese immigrants Mary and Joseph Tape established their home in San Francisco in the expectation that their children could attend public schools. When the principal of their local primary school refused to enroll their daughter Mamie, Mary Tape sued the school. In the 1885 Tape v. Hurley *case, the California Superior Court decided that Mamie Tape had a right to attend the school on the basis of both California law and the U.S. Constitution. Although the state Supreme Court upheld the decision, the school board lobbied the state legislature to quickly pass a provision that legalized the segregation of students of "Mongolian or Chinese descent." In response, Mary Tape wrote a fiery letter of protest to the San Francisco School Board, excerpted here with original spelling and punctuation. Though visionary, Tape's objections proved unsuccessful and her children ultimately attended the segregated Chinese primary school.*

Mary Tape, 8 April 1885

To the Board of Education — Dear Sirs: I see that you are going to make all sorts of excuses to keep my child out off the Public schools. Dear sirs, Will you please to tell me! Is it a disgrace to be Born a Chinese?

womanhood by granting clemency and medical care to white female convicts while denying Black women all forms of gendered concessions. Many Black clubwomen used their organizational clout to protest convict leasing, and Ida B. Wells decried convict leasing and lynching as the "twin infamies" of southern society.

Meanwhile, a new legal system of rigid racial separation in social relations was being put in place. Called Jim Crow, after a foolish minstrel character played by whites in blackface, these laws and practices were a way to humiliate, intimidate, and diminish Black people. Under slavery, when Black people had no rights, racial segregation operated as a customary practice, but now its codification became a way to reassert white domination. Recalling what enforced segregation felt like, a southern Black woman wrote, "I never get used to it; it is new each time and stings and hurts more and more. It does not matter how good or wise my children may be; they are colored. . . . Everything is forgiven in the South but color."[18]

Didn't God make us all!!! What right! have you to bar my children out of the school because she is a chinese Decend. . . . It seems no matter how a Chinese may live and dress so long as you know they Chinese. Then they are hated as one. There is not any right or justice for them. . . . It seems to me Mr. Moulder [school superintendent] has a grudge against this Eight-year-old Mamie Tape. I know they is no other child I mean Chinese child! care to go to your public Chinese school. May you Mr. Moulder, never be persecuted like the way you have persecuted little Mamie Tape. Mamie Tape will never attend any of the Chinese schools of your making! Never!!! I will let the world see sir What justice there is When it is govern by the Race prejudice men! just because she is of the Chinese decend, not because she don't dress like you because she does. Just because she is decended of Chinese parents I guess she is more of a American then a good many of you that is going to prewent her being Educated. Mrs. M. Tape.

SOURCE: "Chinese Mother's Letter," *Daily Alta California*, April 16, 1885.

ANALYZING PRIMARY SOURCES

1. What appeals to equality and American identity does Mary Tape use to make her case?

2. Why does Tape focus on the question of her daughter's dress versus her ethnicity in the letter?

Segregation affected many things, including education, public services, housing, medical attention, and public accommodations, but Black women particularly resented Jim Crow regulations in public transportation. Wells began her career as a defender of her race in 1884 by suing the Tennessee railroad company that ejected her from a special "ladies" car and sent her instead to the "colored" car. Twelve years later, the Supreme Court considered a similar suit by Homer Plessy against a Louisiana railroad for its segregation policy. In *Plessy v. Ferguson* (1896), the Court characterized the entire Jim Crow regime as "separate but equal" and thus compatible with the Fourteenth Amendment's requirement of equality before the law. This constitutional defense of segregation was practiced everywhere in the nation and survived legally for nearly sixty years. (See the Appendix: Documents.) (For a case of legal segregation outside the South, see Reading into the Past: "What Right Have You?")

◆ FEMALE WAGE LABOR AND THE TRIUMPH OF INDUSTRIAL CAPITALISM

Industrial growth accelerated tremendously after the defeat of the slave system and the northern victory in the Civil War. Intense competition between industrialists and financial magnates gradually gave way to economic consolidation. By 1890, industries such as steel, railroads, coal mining, and meat production were dominated by a handful of large, powerful corporate entities. The mirror reflection of the growth of capital, the American working class, also came into its own and organized to find ways to offset the power of its employers.

The growth of the female labor force was an important part of this development, although it flew in the face of the still-strong presumption that white women belonged exclusively in their homes. Domestic service was the largest sector, but manufacturing labor by women, especially the industrial production of garments, with its distinctive and highly exploitative form of production — the sweatshop — was growing faster.

The dynamic growth of industrial society produced a level of class conflict in the last quarter of the nineteenth century as intense as any in American history. Starting in 1877, as the federal army retreated from the South and postwar depression receded, waves of protests by disgruntled workers shook the economy and drew a powerful and violent response from big business and government. Coming so soon after the Civil War, escalating class antagonism seemed to threaten national unity again, this time along economic rather than sectional lines. Women played a major role in these upheavals and, in doing so, laid the groundwork for a female labor movement in the early twentieth century.

Women's Occupations after the Civil War

Between 1860 and 1890, the percentage of the nonagricultural wage labor force that was female increased from 10.2 to 17 percent (see Chart 6.1). Since the population in these years increased enormously, the change in absolute numbers was even more dramatic: by 1890, 3.6 million women were working for pay in nonagricultural labor, more than twice the number in 1870. The average pay for women remained a third to a half of the pay for men. The great majority of white working women were young and unmarried. The outlines of Black women's labor were somewhat different, remaining largely agricultural until well into the twentieth century. Black women also were much more likely to work outside the home after marriage.

Much of what historians have written about working women of the nineteenth century, especially the numbers and statistics, is guesswork. Although significant numbers of white women had been working for wages since the 1830s, it was not until 1890 that the U.S. census began to identify or count working women with any precision. After the Civil War, some states investigated female wage labor, framing their inquiries in moralistic terms. State labor bureaus paid a great deal of attention, for instance, to disproving the assertion that working women were inclined to prostitution. These statistical portraits were fleshed out by investigative reporting, usually by middle- or upper-class women who went among the

◆ Chart 6.1 **Women and the Labor Force, 1800–1900**

Year	Percentage of All Women in the Labor Force	Percentage of the Labor Force That Is Female
1800	4.6	4.6
1810	7.9	9.4
1820	6.2	7.3
1830	6.4	7.4
1840	8.4	9.6
1850	10.1	10.8
1860	9.7	10.2
1870	13.7	14.8
1880	14.7	15.2
1890	18.2	17.0
1900	21.2	18.1

SOURCE: W. Elliot Brownlee and Mary M. Brownlee, *Women in the American Economy: A Documentary History* (New Haven: Yale University Press, 1976); *Historical Statistics of the United States: Colonial Times to 1970*, part 1, Bicentennial Edition, Bureau of the Census, U.S. Department of Commerce, 1975; "Marital and Family Characteristics of Workers," March 1983, U.S. Department of Labor. *Statistical Abstract of the United States*, Bureau of the Census, U.S. Department of Commerce, 1983 and 1992; Daphne Spain and Suzanne Bianchi, *Balancing Act* (New York: Russell Sage, 1996).

working classes to report on their conditions. (See Primary Sources: "The Woman Who Toils.")

Nonetheless, it is clear that for white women, paid domestic work was on the decline. Domestic servants, who before the war were the majority of the white female labor force, constituted less than 30 percent by the end of the century. Working women had long been impatient with domestic service and left it whenever they could, usually for factory labor. After the Civil War, the end of slavery tainted personal service even more. Investigator Helen Campbell took testimony in the mid-1880s in New York City from women who had abandoned domestic service. "I hate the very words 'service' and 'servant,' " an Irish immigrant renegade from domestic labor explained. "We came to this country to better ourselves, and it's not bettering to have anybody ordering you around."[19]

As white women workers shifted out of domestic service, their percentage in manufacturing increased to 25 percent as of 1900. Women continued to work in the textile industry, and in the shoe industry women organized their own trade union, the Daughters of St. Crispin (named after the patron saint of their trade), but it survived only a few years. The biggest change in women's manufacturing labor was the rise of the garment industry, as the antebellum outwork system began to give way to more fully industrialized processes.

The industrial manufacture of clothing depended on the invention of the sewing machine at the turn of the nineteenth century, one of the most consequential technological developments in U.S. women's history. The introduction of the sewing machine accelerated the subdivision of clothing production into discrete tasks. Thus, a single worker no longer made an entire piece of clothing, but instead spent her long days sewing sleeves or seams, incurring the physical and spiritual toll of endless, repetitive motion. Unlike the power looms and spindles of the textile mills, sewing machines did not need to be housed in massive factories but could be placed in numerous small shops. As sewing machines were also comparatively inexpensive, the cost of buying and maintaining them could be shifted to the workers themselves, who were charged rent or made to pay in installments for them.

Profits in the garment industry came primarily from pushing the women workers to produce more for less pay. This system became designated as the "sweating" system, meaning that it required women workers to drive (or sweat) themselves to work ever harder. Women workers were usually paid for each piece completed, whereas men tended to be paid for time worked. Employers set a low piece rate, lowering it even further as women produced more. Often workers were charged for thread and fined for sewing errors. The work was highly seasonal, and intense periods of twelve-hour workdays alternated with bouts of unemployment. At the beginning of the Civil War, the average earnings of white sewing women were $10 per week; by 1865, they were $5 per week.

Regardless of their ability or speed, women in the garment, textile, and shoe industries were generally considered unskilled workers, in part because they worked in female-dominated industries, in part because they were easily replaced by other women, and in part because they learned their work on the job rather than through a formal apprenticeship or trade school. The higher pay associated with so-called skilled labor was reserved for trades that men dominated. A few women gained entrance to male-dominated trades, such as typesetting, where they earned up to $15 per week. Initially, women made their way into print shops by replacing male workers who were out on strike or engaged in the military, but they were let go when the men came back to work. Eventually, the printers' union voted to admit women as equal members, only the second national male trade union to do so.

In the 1870s, a new field became available for female wage earners: office work. Before 1860, the office environment had been majority male, filled by young men aspiring to careers in business or law. During the Civil War, young women began to replace men as government copyists and stenographers. The shift to female labor was accelerated by another crucial technological development, the typewriter. Women, with their smaller hands, were thought to be especially suited to typing. Office work required more than primary school education and a command of the English language, adding to its prestige as an occupation for native-born white women. It also paid more than textile mills or garment sweatshops. Yet from the employers' perspective, hiring women rather than men to meet the

♦ **Advertising Women and Typewriters**

A practical machine for mechanical writing was devised just after the Civil War. It was first manufactured for the mass market by the Remington Arms Company, which adapted the production process it had developed for rifles. The machine retained the name Remington even after production shifted to the Wyckoff, Seamans, and Benedict Company. This 1897 advertisement explicitly links the modernity of its product to its skilled women operators. The elegantly dressed, self-composed typist suggests a quite different image from that of the overworked, underpaid woman factory worker, a contrast that is made explicit by the claim that technology means "less labor" for her and yet more output for her boss. *Jay Paull/Getty Images.*

growing demand for clerical labor constituted a considerable savings since women always were paid less than men doing the same work, regardless of the occupation. By 1900, office work was still only 9 percent of the female labor force, but it was the fastest-growing sector, a harbinger of things to come in the twentieth-century female labor force (see the Appendix, Table 1).

Who Were the Women Wage Earners?

Age and marital status were crucial elements in the structure of the female labor force. In 1890, three-quarters of white working women were unmarried. Most married Black women, in stark contrast, worked. As a leading historian of working women puts it, "In the history of women's labor market experience in the United States the half century from about 1870 to 1920 was the era of single women."[20] Unlike working men, whose wages were supposed to provide for an entire family, these young women allegedly had only themselves to support. "Working girls" were expected to work for pay for only a few years, then marry and become dependent on

◆ **Stripping Tobacco Leaves in a Tobacco Factory (c. 1890)**
The filthy and exhausting work of processing tobacco leaves was one of the few industrial jobs open to Black women. In this Richmond, Virginia, factory during the 1890s, both women and children worked in close quarters to strip the leaves from tobacco plants. White southern photographer Huestis Cook made the photograph as part of a series on tobacco production from field to factory. What does the image tell you about the physical conditions of Black women and children's industrial labor?
© Cook Collection/The Valentine Richmond History Center. Courtesy of the Virginia Commonwealth University Libraries. https://thevalentine.org.

the earnings of their husbands. This was the principle of the so-called family wage, which justified men's greater wages as much as it did women's lesser. Wage labor for white women was meant to be an interlude between childhood and domestic dependence, while men expected to work throughout their adult lives.

The reality of working women's lives was considerably more complex. Approximately 10 to 15 percent of urban families were headed by single mothers and were acutely disadvantaged by the family wage system.[21] A working woman who was a wife and/or mother was considered at best an anomaly and at worst an indicator of family and social crisis. Black female wage earners were three times as likely as white women to be married, partly because their husbands' pay was so low and partly because many chose to work themselves rather than send their daughters into work situations where they would be vulnerable to sexual harassment from white men. In historical hindsight, Black women were pioneering the modern working women's pattern of combining wage labor and domestic responsibilities, but at the time, the high number of Black working mothers was the object of much disparagement.

Most unmarried wage-earning women lived in their parents' homes, where, contrary to the ideal of the single male breadwinner, their earnings were crucial supplements to family support. However, perhaps as many as a third of single women wage earners lived outside of families. Carroll Wright, a pioneering labor statistician, reported in *The Working Girls of Boston* (1889), a Massachusetts Bureau of Statistics of Labor report, that in Massachusetts many young women workers were "obliged to leave their homes on account of bad treatment or conduct of [a] dissipated father or because they felt the need of work and not finding it at home, have come to [a large city]."[22] Philanthropists established charity boardinghouses to protect these "women adrift," who seemed vulnerable without parents or husbands to protect them. One of the major purposes of the Young Women's Christian Association (YWCA), formed soon after the Civil War, was to provide supervised housing for white, single, urban working women.

Responses to Working Women

Contemporaries' attempts to grapple with the growing female labor force contained a revealing contradiction. On the one hand, social observers contended that only women driven by sheer desperation should work outside the home. Less desperate working women were taking work away from truly needy women and — even more disturbing — from male breadwinners. If young working women used any part of their pay to buy attractive clothing or go out with men, they were castigated for frivolity. "[Working girls] who want pin-money do work at a price impossible for the self-supporting worker, many married women coming under this head," observed journalist Helen Campbell.[23]

On the other hand, those women who were driven into wage labor by absolute necessity were so ill-paid, so unrelentingly exploited, as to constitute a major social tragedy. "All alike are starved, half clothed, overworked to a frightful degree," wrote the same Helen Campbell, "with neither time to learn some better method of earning a living, nor hope enough to spur them in any new path."[24] Sympathetic observers concluded that the only humane response was to remove young women from the labor force altogether. White wage-earning women were therefore criticized if they worked out of choice or pitied if they worked out of need. In either case, they seemed to be trespassing where they did not belong: in the wage labor force.

Set against middle-class social observers' steady chorus of criticism or lament, the lives and choices of working women hint at a different picture. Working girls objected to the constant supervision at philanthropic working girls' homes, stubbornly spent their wages as they pleased, engaged in recreational activities that were considered vulgar, occasionally continued to work even after they got married, and preferred their morally questionable factory jobs to the presumed safety of domestic service. Though they were criticized for taking jobs away from the truly needy, many regarded themselves simply as women who liked to earn money, preferred the sociability of sharing work with others, chose the experience of manufacturing over endless domestic routine, and enjoyed their occasional moments of hard-earned personal freedom.

Class Conflict and Labor Organization

Women participated in all the dramatic strikes and labor conflicts of the late nineteenth century. During the nationwide rail strikes in 1877, in which male workers protested layoffs and wage cuts, women joined the mobs that burned railroad roundhouses and destroyed railroad cars. Women's involvement in such violent acts underlined the full fury of working-class resentment at the inequalities of monopolistic wealth in postbellum America. "Women who are the wives and mothers of the [railroad] firemen," reported a Baltimore newspaper, "look famished and wild and declare for starvation rather than have their people work for the reduced wages."[25] President Rutherford B. Hayes sent federal forces, recently withdrawn from occupying the South, to suppress the riots. More than a hundred strikers were killed nationwide.

In the late 1870s, many angry male workers joined the **Knights of Labor**, originally a secret society that became the largest labor organization of the nineteenth century. The Knights aimed to unite and elevate working men and to protect the country's democratic heritage from unrestrained capitalist growth. In 1881, the Knights, unlike most unions, admitted white women (housewives as well as wage earners). At its peak, the Knights of Labor had 750,000 members, of whom some 10 percent were women. Its goal was to unite "the producing classes," regardless of industry or occupation or gender. Race was more complicated. In the South, the Knights admitted Black workers in segregated local chapters, but in the West, the organization excluded Chinese men, whom it regarded as unfair economic competitors rather than as fellow workers.

The Knights played a major role in the nationwide campaign to shorten the workday for wage earners to eight hours, a movement of obvious interest to women who had to leave paid work at the end of a long day and then go home to cook, clean, and care for husbands and children. On May 1, 1886, hundreds of thousands of workers from all over the country struck on behalf of the eight-hour day. At a related rally a few days later in Chicago's Haymarket Square, a bomb exploded, killing seven policemen. Although the bomb thrower was never identified, eight male labor leaders were charged with conspiracy to murder. Lucy Parsons, the wife of one of the accused, helped conduct their defense. A multiracial woman, Lucy had met her husband in Texas, where he had gone after the war to organize Black voters for the Republican Party. Defense efforts eventually won gubernatorial pardons for three of the accused men, although not in time to save Albert Parsons. The violence and repression unleashed by the Haymarket incident devastated the Knights of Labor. By 1890, it had ceased to play a significant role in American labor relations. The eight-hour workday would not be won for many decades.

After the collapse of the Knights, the future of organized labor was left to male-dominated trade unions and their umbrella organization, the American Federation of Labor (AFL), founded in 1886 by Samuel Gompers, a cigar maker from New York City. While the goal of the Knights was inclusive and aimed to unify the producing classes, the purpose of AFL unions was exclusive. These unions vowed to protect the jobs of skilled and relatively well-paid labor from

READING INTO THE PAST

LEONORA BARRY
Women in the Knights of Labor

Leonora Barry (1849–1930) was one of the first female labor organizers. Her first report after being appointed head of the Women's Department of the Knights of Labor revealed a wide variety of industries with often unhealthy, low-paid, and dangerous labor performed by women. Barry, a widow when she began her assignment, resigned in 1890 when she remarried. She frequently expressed her frustration with the difficulties of organizing female labor. This report began by calling for more education of working women by the Knights of Labor. Barry decried the "selfishness of their brothers in toil" who had "sworn to demand equal pay for equal work" but failed to invest energy in female laborers. She then went on to review her many factory inspections and meetings with women wage earners.

December 6th I went to Trenton, N.J., in compliance with the request of L.A. 4925 [the L.A., or local assembly, was the basic organizing unit of the Knights of Labor]. While there made an investigation in three woolen mills, and found the condition of the female operatives to be in every respect above the average. Also visited the potteries, where many women are employed. Those people stand greatly in need of having their condition bettered, as they receive poor wages for laborious and unhealthy employment. Also visited the State Prison, and noticed, with regret, the vast amount of work of various kinds the inmates were turning out to be put on the market in competition with honest labor. While in the city, I addressed five local assemblies and held one public meeting of working women. . . .

On January 6, 1887, took up the work again in Trenton, N.J., per instruction. Held several meetings, both public and private, of working-women for the purpose of getting them into the order, as the women of this city are not well organized. Went to Bordentown to a shirt factory there, but the unjust prejudice which they have always held towards organized labor cropped out on this occasion and they refused me admission.

SOURCE: Leonora Barry, Report to the Knights of Labor, October 1886–1887, reprinted in *Tenth Annual Report of the Bureau of Statistics of Labor and Industries of New Jersey* (Somerville: Unionist-Gazette Printing House, 1888), 202–3.

ANALYZING PRIMARY SOURCES

1. How did Leonora Barry use her position to attempt to both improve women's working conditions and heighten the political consciousness of working-class women?

◆ **Lucy Parsons**

Lucy Gonzalez Parsons was born in Texas of Black, Mexican, and Native heritage. She crossed the color line to marry and moved with her husband to Chicago, where they were both labor activists. Albert Parsons was one of the eight men arrested for the alleged conspiracy behind the Haymarket riot of 1886. Lucy fought and failed to prevent his conviction and execution. An avowed anarchist, she continued to lead protests and give speeches against social, racial, and gender inequality for another thirty years. *Atlas Archive/TopFoto.*

less-skilled, lower-paid workers. Most members of AFL unions regarded women and people of color as exactly this sort of threat: unskilled, underpaid workers who took men's jobs during strikes. Adapting the domestic ideal of true womanhood from the middle class, the AFL subscribed to the notion that white women belonged in the home and that a male worker deserved a wage sufficient to keep his wife out of the labor force.

Nonetheless, the late nineteenth-century labor movement did provide a few exceptional chances for some women to begin speaking and acting on behalf of female wage earners. Leonora Barry and Mary Kenney were among the first women appointed by unions to organize other women workers. In 1886, the Knights of Labor designated Barry, a widowed Irish-born garment worker, to head its Woman's Department (see Reading into the Past: "Women in the Knights of Labor"). Although meeting with her might mean being fired, women workers around the country shared with Barry their complaints about wages and working conditions. Barry was their devoted advocate, but after two years, frustrated with the timidity of many working women and perhaps also with the limits of her support from the male leadership of the organization, she resigned her position.

Mary Kenney's trade was bookbinding. She joined an AFL union in Chicago and in 1891 was appointed the federation's first paid organizer for working women. She believed that working women should organize themselves but that they also needed the moral and financial support of middle- and upper-class women. The AFL was less committed to working women than the Knights, and Kenney was dismissed from her post after only six months. In the decades to come, many more female labor activists followed Barry and Kenney to play important roles in shaping women's history.

◆ WOMEN OF THE LEISURED CLASSES

Paralleling the expansion of the American working class was the dramatic growth, both in numbers and wealth, of the white middle and upper classes. For this reason, one of several terms used for the post-Reconstruction years is the Gilded Age. The phrase, first used by Mark Twain in a novel about economic and political corruption after the Civil War, captured both the riches and superficiality of the wealthier classes in the late nineteenth century. In the United States, with its proud middle-class ethic, the distinction between upper and middle class has always been hard to draw with precision, but in these years what was more important was the enormous and growing gap between those who lived comfortable, leisured lives and those who struggled with poverty. While the poor labored unceasingly, the upper class enjoyed unprecedented new wealth and influence, and the middle class imitated their values of material accumulation and display. For women of the middle and upper classes, the Gilded Age meant both new affluence but also growing discontent with an exclusively domestic sphere.

New Sources of Wealth and Leisure

The tremendous economic growth of the post–Civil War era emanated from the railroads that wove together the nation and carried raw materials to factories and finished goods to customers. The great fortunes of the age were made especially in oil production, iron mining, steel manufacturing, and railroad building — and in financing these endeavors. New technologies, government subsidies, cutthroat competition, and the pressure on workers to work faster and more productively contributed to this development. Dominated by a few corporate giants, this wealth was distributed very unevenly; in 1890 an estimated 1 percent of the population controlled fully 25 percent of the country's wealth.[26] In New York City alone, the number of millionaires went from a few dozen in 1860 to several hundred in 1865. Indeed, many of the great American family fortunes were begun in the Gilded Age: John D. Rockefeller in oil, Cornelius Vanderbilt in railroads, J. P. Morgan in finance, and Andrew Carnegie in steel. One of the very few women to amass spectacular wealth on her own was Hetty Robinson Green. She began her financial career with a $10 million inheritance, which she multiplied tenfold through shrewd investment. Because she operated in the man's world of high finance, her womanliness was suspect. The popular press played up her eccentricities, dubbing her "the witch of Wall Street" rather than one of the brilliant financiers of the epoch.

Wives of wealthy men faced no such criticism. On the contrary, they were regarded as the ultimate in feminine beauty and grace. In the world of the extremely wealthy, men's obligation was to amass money while women's was to display and spend it. Wealthy women were also responsible for the conduct of "society," a word that came to mean the comings and goings of the tiny upper class, as if the rest of the population faded into insignificance by contrast. In *The Theory of the Leisure Class* (1899), sociologist Thorstein Veblen astutely observed that upper-class women not only purchased expensive commodities, but were themselves their husbands' most lavish and enviable possessions.

Shopping was a new and important role for leisure-class women in the capitalist-driven postbellum years. Middle-class women, who no longer had responsibility for a great deal of productive household labor, became active consumers. With the dramatic increase in the country's manufacturing capacity, their obligation was now to purchase rather than to produce, to spend rather than to

◆ **Rike-Kumler Co. Department Store, Dayton, Ohio**
Department store counters were one place where working- and leisure-class women met.
Neat dress, good English, and middle-class manners were job requirements, even though pay
was no better than for factory work. Customers like the woman being fitted for gloves in this
1893 photograph sat, but clerks stood all day, one of the conditions of their work to which
they most objected. *Bettmann/Getty Images.*

economize. They flocked to the many department stores established in this period,
grand palaces of commodities such as Marshall Field's in Chicago (founded
in 1865), Macy's in New York (1866), Strawbridge and Clothier in Philadelphia
(1868), Hudson's in Detroit (1887), and May's in Denver (1888). They filled the
elaborate interiors of their homes with furniture and decorative items. Even at
a distance from the proliferating retail possibilities of the cities, rural women had
mail order catalogs to look at, long for, and occasionally purchase the many commodities of the age.

Rising incomes lifted the burden of housekeeping off urban middle- and
upper-class women in other ways. Cities laid water and sewer lines, but only in

wealthy neighborhoods in which households could afford the fees; indoor plumbing and running water made housework easier for prosperous women. But the most important factor in easing the load of housekeeping for leisure-class women was undoubtedly the cheap labor of domestic servants. Despite constant complaints about the shortage of domestic help, middle-class families regarded having at least one or two paid domestic servants as a virtual necessity. The wealthy had small armies of them. Laundry, which required enormous energy and much time when done in an individual household, was sent out to commercial establishments, where poor white, Black, and immigrant women pressed and folded sheets and linens in overheated steam rooms.

Another important factor in freeing middle- and upper-class women from domestic demands was the declining birthrate (see the Appendix, Chart 1). Between 1850 and 1890, the average number of live births for white, native-born women fell from 5.42 to 3.87. Black birthrates were not recorded in the federal census until several decades later. Ironically, birthrates declined in inverse proportion to class status: the wealthiest, with money to spare, had proportionately fewer children than the very poor, whose earnings were stretched to the limit but who relied on their children for income in both rural and urban economies.

In understanding the many individual decisions that went into the declining birthrate among leisure-class women, the explanation is not obvious. There were no dramatic improvements in contraceptive technology or knowledge in these years. On the contrary, traditional means of controlling pregnancy — early versions of condoms and diaphragms — were banned by new laws that defined them as obscene devices; even discussions aimed at limiting reproduction were forbidden. Following the Comstock Act of 1873, which outlawed the use of the U.S. mails for distributing information on controlling reproduction, twenty-four states criminalized the dissemination of contraceptive devices.

Rather, declining birthrates seem to have been both a cause and an effect of the expanding sphere of leisure-class women. Women's decisions to limit their pregnancies reflected a growing desire for personal satisfaction and social contribution beyond motherhood. Even though maternity remained the assumed destiny of womanhood, many women were coming to believe that they could choose when and how often to become pregnant. In advocating **"voluntary motherhood,"** Harriot Stanton Blatch, Elizabeth Cady Stanton's daughter, encouraged women to choose for themselves when to have sexual intercourse. Her speeches brilliantly exploited the nineteenth-century belief that motherhood was woman's highest vocation, in order to argue for women's rights to control whether and when they had children. Reformers like Blatch did not yet envision the separation of women's sexual activity from the possibility of pregnancy, but they did believe that women should have control over both. The very term "birth control" and the movement to advance it came later in the twentieth century, but basic changes in female reproductive behavior were already under way.

As women's reproductive lives changed, so did their understanding of their sexuality. To be sure, many restrictive sexual assumptions remained in place. Some physicians still regarded strong sexual desire in women as a disease, which

◆ **Alice Austen and Friends Dress Up as Men (1891)**
This photograph is by and of Alice Austen, a brilliant amateur photographer who left a visual
record of Gilded Age leisure-class female lives. Here, Austen (on the left) posed in drag with
two of her female friends. "Maybe we were better looking men than women," she quipped
when, as an old woman, she looked once again at the photo. In the context of Austen's decision
not to marry but to live her life with another woman, this photo made her a historical icon for
modern lesbians. *Alice Austen Collection, Staten Island Historical Society.*

they treated by methods ranging from a diet of bland foods to surgical removal
of the clitoris. But the heterosexual double standard — that men's sexual desire
was uncontrollable and that women's was nonexistent — was beginning to come
under fire. By the end of the century, even the conservative physician Elizabeth
Blackwell was writing in carefully chosen language that "in healthy, loving
women, uninjured by the too frequent lesions which result from childbirth,
increasing physical satisfaction attaches to the ultimate physical expression of
love."[27]

Lesbianism, in the modern sense of women openly and consistently
expressing sexual desire for other women, had not yet been named, but there
is a long history of females forming intense attachments with each other. These

"homosocial" relationships, as modern historians have designated them, ranged from intense, lifelong friendships to relationships that were as emotionally charged, as beset by jealousy and possessiveness, and sometimes as physically intimate, as any heterosexual love affair. Mary (Molly) Hallock and Helena De Kay were two such friends. They met in 1868 as art students in New York and wrote frequently and passionately to each other. When Helena announced that she was marrying New York publisher Richard Gilder, Molly angrily wrote to him: "Until you came along, sir, I believe she loved me almost as girls love their lovers."[28]

Most of what we know about such homosocial relations comes from leisure-class women, perhaps because they wrote more letters that were preserved and handed down to families and archivists than working-class women did. But surely some working-class women experienced similar passions. A set of letters between two Black women living in Connecticut during the 1860s offers the rare example of a cross-class homosocial/lesbian relationship, moreover one that was strongly suggestive of physical intimacy. Rebecca Primus, a schoolteacher, and Addie Brown, a seamstress, domestic worker, and laundress, conducted what the historian of their bond calls "a self-consciously sexual relationship" focused on fondling breasts.[29]

By the late nineteenth century, such intense bonds were coming under scrutiny from physicians. Recognizing the obvious erotic qualities of these intense same-sex relationships, neurologists sought to give them the dignity of scientific recognition, even as they characterized them as "unnatural" or "abnormal." Women-loving women who, in an earlier time, would have believed unquestioningly in the asexual purity and innocence of their attachments, were beginning to read scientific writings about homosexuality and to wonder about the meaning and nature of their own feelings.

The "Woman's Era"

Before the Civil War, Black and white women had formed charitable and religious societies and had worked together on behalf of temperance, abolition, and women's rights. After the war, associational fervor among women was more diverse, secular, and independent of male oversight. Participation in Gilded Age women's societies provided numerous women with new opportunities for collective activity, intellectual growth, and public life. By the end of the nineteenth century, women had almost totally commandeered nongovernmental civic life from men. Thus, another apt label for the post-Reconstruction years is the **Woman's Era**.

The women's club movement began in the Northeast among middle-class women. Among Black middle-class women, this movement had its start before the Civil War, in literary and other societies that began to flourish in the 1830s. That decade saw them create the Ladies Literary Society and the Female Literary Society in New York; the Minerva Literary Society in Philadelphia; and the Ladies Literary and Dorcas Society in Rochester. Clubs for white middle-class women started later, just after the Civil War. In 1868, New York City women writers formed a group they named Sorosis (a botanical term that suggested sisterhood) to protest their exclusion from an event held by male writers. Simultaneously, a group of Boston reformers led by Julia Ward Howe (author of "The Battle Hymn of the Republic") organized the New England Women's Club, dedicated to the cultivation of intellectual discussion and public authority for leisure-class women. Despite their impeccable reputations, both groups were publicly lambasted for their unladylike behavior. "Woman is straying from her sphere," warned the *Boston Transcript*.[30]

Despite such criticisms, women's clubs thrived among those middle-aged married women whose childrearing years were behind them. The concerns of the women's club movement evolved from literary and cultural matters, to local social service projects, to regional and national federations for political influence. Many public institutions established in the Gilded Age — hospitals and orphanages as well as libraries and museums — were originally established by women's clubs. From the Northeast, the club movement went on to impact the South and the West.

Clubs by their nature are exclusive institutions, and the sororal bonds of women's clubs reflected their tendency to draw together women of like background. In the larger cities, class differences distinguished elite women's clubs from those formed by wives of clerks and shopkeepers. Working women's clubs were rarely initiated by wage-earning women themselves but were likely to be uplift projects of middle- and upper-class clubwomen. Race and religion were especially important principles of association. German Jewish women and Black women organized separately from the mainstream women's club movement, which was largely white and Protestant. Generally, middle-class Jewish or Black women formed their own clubs both to assist poorer women and to cultivate their own skills and intellectual refinement.

The ethic of women's clubs was particularly compelling to Black women. They formed organizations not just to enlarge their horizons as women but to play their part in the enormous project of racial progress both before and after the Civil War. "If we compare the present condition of the colored people of the South with their condition twenty-eight years ago," explained Sarah J. Early in 1893, "we shall see how the organized efforts of their women have contributed to the elevation of the race and their marvelous achievement in so short a time."[31] By her estimate, there were five thousand "colored women's societies" with half a million members by the end of the nineteenth century. Black women organized separately from white women because they were serving a different population with distinctive needs, but also because they were usually refused admission into white women's clubs and those of men of either race. Racism was as alive and well in the women's club movement as sexism was in the men's club establishment.

The relation of the Gilded Age women's club phenomenon to woman suffrage is complex. At first, white women who formed and joined clubs took care to distinguish themselves from the radicalism and notoriety associated with woman suffragists. Yet women's rights and woman suffrage were standard subjects for club discussion, and over time members came to accept the idea that women should have political tools to accomplish their public goals. Black clubwomen were less hesitant to embrace woman suffrage. Over time, women's clubs incubated support for woman suffrage within a wide swath of the female middle class and prepared the way for the tremendous growth in the suffrage movement in the early twentieth century.

The Woman's Christian Temperance Union

The largest women's organization of the Woman's Era was the **Woman's Christian Temperance Union** (WCTU). Following on women's temperance activities in the 1850s, the WCTU was formed in 1874 after a series of women's "crusades" in Ohio and New York that convinced local saloon owners to abandon the liquor trade. Initially focused on changing drinking behavior at the individual level, the organization soon challenged the liquor industry politically and undertook a wide range of public welfare projects such as prison reform, recreation and vocational training for young people, establishment of kindergartens, labor reform, and international peace. These projects and the ability of the WCTU to cultivate both organizational loyalty and individual growth among its members were characteristics it shared with other women's clubs, but the WCTU was different in crucial ways. On the one hand, it defined itself explicitly as Christian; on the other, it was racially more inclusive than the club movement. The writer Frances Ellen Watkins Harper was one of several Black WCTU spokeswomen, and Black women were welcomed into the organization, though in segregated divisions. Black women's religiosity and own legacy of religious-based organizations complemented the Christian nature of the organization. The WCTU's centers of strength were less urban and more western and midwestern than those of women's clubs.

Finally, unlike the women's club movement, the WCTU was to a large degree the product of a single and highly effective leader, Frances Willard. Willard was born in 1839 and raised on a farm in Ohio. She never married. Determined to serve "the class that I have always loved and that has loved me always — the girls of my native land and my times,"[32] she became the first dean of women at Northwestern University at age thirty-four. In 1879, she was elected president of the WCTU; she rapidly increased its membership, diversified its purposes, and made it the most powerful women's organization in the country. Disciplined and diplomatic, she was able to take the WCTU to levels of political action and reform that the unwieldy mass of clubwomen never attained. Notably, this included active advocacy of woman suffrage, which the WCTU formally and enthusiastically endorsed in 1884. "If we are ever to save the State," Willard declared, "we must enfranchise the sex . . . which is much more acclimatized to self-sacrifice for others. . . . Give us the vote, in order that we may help in purifying politics."[33]

Consolidating the Gilded Age Women's Movement

The endorsement of woman suffrage by the Woman's Christian Temperance Union convinced Susan B. Anthony to encourage and draw together the pro-suffrage leanings developing within so many women's organizations. "Those active in great philanthropic enterprises," she insisted, "[will] sooner or later realize that

◆ **Frances Willard Learns to Ride a Bicycle**
Frances Willard, president of the WCTU, combined sympathy with conventional Protestant
middle-class women and an advanced understanding of women's untapped capacities.
In 1895, "sighing for new worlds to conquer," she learned to ride a bicycle, one of the
signature New Woman activities of the period. "Reducing the problem to actual figures," she
methodically reported, "it took me about three months, with an average of fifteen minutes'
practice daily, to learn, first, to pedal; second, to turn; third, to dismount; and fourth, to
mount."[34] Willard, not yet sixty, died in 1898, after which the WCTU never regained its
prominence or progressive vision. *Courtesy of the Frances E. Willard Memorial Library and Archives.*

so long as women are not acknowledged to be the political equals of men, their
judgment on public questions will have but little weight."[35] Accordingly, in 1888,
in honor of the fortieth anniversary of the Seneca Falls Convention, the National
Woman Suffrage Association sponsored an International Congress of Women,
attended by representatives of several European countries and many U.S. women's
organizations. Out of this congress came an International Council of Women and
a U.S. National Council of Women, both formed in 1893. Both organizations were
so broadly inclusive of women's public and civic activities as to admit anti-suffrage
groups, and much to Anthony's disappointment, neither served as the vehicle for
advancing the prospects of woman suffrage.

Other overarching organizational structures were formed. In 1890, NWSA
and the American Woman Suffrage Association reconciled, forming the

National American Woman Suffrage Association (NAWSA), which led the suffrage movement for the next thirty years. On the international level, U.S. suffragists joined with European colleagues to initiate the formation of an International Woman Suffrage Association in 1902. The associative impulse was constantly tending to greater and greater combination, amalgamating women in clubs, clubs in state federations, and state federations in national organizations. The vision shared by these federative efforts was of a unity of women so broad and ecumenical as to obliterate all differences between women. But the vision of all-inclusivity was a fantasy. For as women's social activism and public involvement grew, so did their ambitions and rivalries. Even as the National Council of Women was formed, the leaders of the venerable Sorosis club, who felt they should have been chosen to head this endeavor, set up a rival in the **General Federation of Women's Clubs**. Nor were federations any more racially inclusive than individual clubs. The General Federation of Women's Clubs refused to admit Black women's clubs. In 1895, Black women's clubs federated separately as the **National Association of Colored Women**, and the next year the **National Council of Jewish Women** was formed.

The ambitious scope and unresolved divisions of "organized womanhood" were equally on display in Chicago in 1893 at the World's Columbian Exposition, America's first world's fair. The Board of Lady Managers received public funds to build and furnish a special Woman's Building. Eighty sessions held at the Congress of Representative Women addressed "all lines of thought connected with the

◆ **The American Jewess**

In the 1890s, many Jewish American women became active in promoting social reform and Americanization programs through the National Council of Jewish Women (founded in 1896), which was part of the broader movement toward women's clubs. Printed from 1895 to 1896, *The American Jewess* was the first English-language magazine for Jewish women. It was published by Rosa Sonneschein, a progressive who challenged the discrimination women experienced within the synagogue and sought to promote an Americanized Jewish identity for women. As she put it, *The American Jewess* was intended "to connect the sisters dwelling throughout . . . this blessed country, concentrate the work of scattered charitable institutions, and bring them to the notice of the various communities as an imposing and powerful unit." *Klau Library, Cincinnati, Hebrew Union College–Jewish Institute of Religion.*

progress of women." But Black women were excluded from the planning and management, and women from Indigenous cultures, including the Inuit and Yuit, were again relegated to the absolute margins of American womanhood — "on display" on the fair's midway only as "exotics."

Looking to the Future

By 1890, a new, more modern culture was slowly gathering force under the complacent surface of late nineteenth-century America. The Gilded Age was organized around grand and opposing categories: home and work, Black and white, capital and labor, virtue and vice, masculine and feminine. While nineteenth-century society subscribed to a rigid hierarchy of values and a firm belief in absolute truth, modernist convictions allowed for greater contingency and relativism in assessing people and ideas. The concept of morality, so crucial to nineteenth-century cultural judgment, was losing some of its coercive force, giving way to a greater emphasis on individuality, inner life, the free development of personality, and psychological variety.

An important sign of this cultural shift was the growing displacement of the ideal of the "true woman" by the image of the **New Woman,** both in women's rights circles and in popular representations of femininity. For modern women of the late nineteenth century, true womanhood no longer seemed virtuous and industrious but idle and purposeless. New Women pushed against the boundaries of woman's sphere to participate in public life. (See Primary Sources: "The New Woman.") Their ethic emphasized "woman's work," a term that sometimes meant paid labor, sometimes public service, but always an alternative to exclusive domesticity.

Clubwoman and author Charlotte Perkins Gilman was the first great spokeswoman for the New Woman. Gilman went so far as to criticize the single-family household and the exclusive dedication of women to motherhood. "With the larger socialization of the woman of today, the fitness for and accompanying desire for wider combination, more general interest, . . . more organized methods of work for larger ends," she wrote in her widely read *Women and Economics* (1898), "she feels more and more heavily the intensely personal limits of the more primitive home duties, interests, methods."[36] Gilman's writings emphasized a second element of the New Woman ethic, the importance of female individuation, of each woman realizing her distinctive talents, capacities, and personality. Individualism was a long-standing American value, but it had been traditionally reserved for men. Men were individuals with different abilities; women were members of a category with common characteristics. New Womanhood challenged this vision of contrasting masculinity and femininity and claimed the legacy of individualism for women.

At age seventy-seven, Elizabeth Cady Stanton stressed this individualist dimension in her 1892 speech "The Solitude of Self," presented to a committee of the U.S. Congress and then to the National American Woman Suffrage Association. "The point I wish plainly to bring before you on this occasion," she began, "is the individuality of each human soul. . . . In discussing the rights of woman, we are to consider, first, what belongs to her as an individual, in a world of her own, the arbiter of her own destiny."[37] The speech was Cady Stanton's swan song from suffrage leadership. Her inclination to challenge relentlessly women's conventional values contrasted with Anthony's vision of a moderate, broad-based suffrage movement. The greatest expression of her lifelong passion for individual women's freedom, "The Solitude of Self" speech looked forward to a future of women's efforts for emancipation so modern in its emphasis on the self and on psychological change, as to require a new name: **feminism**.

◆ CONCLUSION: TOWARD A NEW WOMANHOOD

The end of the Civil War ushered in a period of great conflict. Reconstruction sought to restore the Union and to replace sectionalism with a unified sense of nationhood, but at its end in 1877 unity remained elusive for all Americans. Various terms for the post-Reconstruction era indicate its different aspects. In the New South during Redemption, Black and white women regarded each other over an embattled racial, cultural, and economic gulf, altered and intensified by emancipation. Meanwhile, in the America of the Gilded Age, a new divide had opened up between labor and capital, between the very wealthy and the expanding classes of the impoverished. As the American economy became increasingly industrialized, the numbers and visibility of women wage earners grew, along with their determination to join in efforts to bring democracy to American class and gender relations. For their part, middle- and upper-class white and Black women created what is called the Woman's Era as they pursued new opportunities in education, civic organization, and public authority. (See Primary Sources: "The Higher Education of Women in the Postbellum Years.")

Two other aspects of the changing face of America in the late nineteenth century are considered in the next chapter: the massive immigration that underlay the growth, and much of the assertiveness, of the American working class; and the physical expansion and consolidation of the nation through the further incorporation of western lands. Women were important actors in the multifaceted political crisis in the 1890s, which brought together all of these phenomena — racial and class conflict, woman's expanding sphere, massive ethnic change, and the nation's physical expansion up to and beyond its borders. By 1900, women were poised on the brink of one of the most active and important eras in American history through women's eyes, the Progressive years.

CHAPTER 6 REVIEW

KEY TERMS

Fourteenth Amendment
  (p. 280)
Fifteenth Amendment (p. 281)
Comstock Act (p. 282)
Minor v. Happersett (p. 282)
Knights of Labor (p. 298)
"voluntary motherhood"
  (p. 303)

Woman's Era (p. 305)
Woman's Christian Temperance
  Union (p. 307)
National American Woman
  Suffrage Association (p. 309)
General Federation of Women's
  Clubs (p. 309)

National Association of
  Colored Women (p. 309)
National Council of Jewish
  Women (p. 309)
New Woman (p. 310)
feminism (p. 311)

REVIEW QUESTIONS

1. What was the impact of the Fourteenth and Fifteenth Amendments on the women's rights movement, and what new strategies did suffragists develop after their ratification?

2. Analyze the different meanings of emancipation for Black and white women of the South. How did race, class, and gender politics in the "New South" compare to those in the Old South?

3. What were the most significant changes in women's labor between 1865 and 1900? How, if at all, did labor organizations in this period attempt to address women worker's issues?

4. What new organizations did American middle-class and leisure-class women create to address the conditions resulting from industrialization?

5. **Making Connections** How did women shape American society in the post–Civil War decades as workers, social and political reformers, and intellectuals?

SUGGESTED READING

Woman Suffrage

Adele Logan Alexander, *Princess of the Hither Isles: A Black Suffragist Story from the Jim Crow South* (2022).

Bernadette Cahill, *No Vote for Women: The Denial of Suffrage in Reconstruction America* (2019).

Ellen DuBois, *Suffrage: Women's Long Battle for the Vote* (2020).

Faye Dudden, *Fighting Chance: The Fight over Woman Suffrage and Black Suffrage in Reconstruction America* (2011).

Eleanor Flexner and Ellen Fitzpatrick, *Century of Struggle: The Woman's Rights Movement in the United States*, enlarged ed. (1996).

Laura E. Free, *Suffrage Reconstructed: Gender, Race, and Voting Rights in the Civil War Era* (2015).

Christine L. Ridarsky and Mary M. Huth, eds., *Susan B. Anthony and the Struggle for Equal Rights* (2012).

Allison L. Sneider, *Suffragists in an Imperial Age: U.S. Expansionism and the Woman Question, 1870–1929* (2008).

Rosalyn Terborg-Penn, *African American Women and the Struggle for the Vote, 1850–1920* (1998).

Marjorie Spruill Wheeler, *New Women of the New South: The Leaders of the Woman Suffrage Movement in the Southern States* (1993).

Black and White Women in the New South

Mia Bay, *To Tell the Truth Freely: The Life of Ida B. Wells* (2010).

Laura F. Edwards, *Gendered Strife and Confusion: The Political Culture of Reconstruction* (1997).

Crystal N. Feimster, *Southern Horrors: Women and the Politics of Rape and Lynching* (2009).

Paula Giddings, *When and Where I Enter: The Impact of Black Women on Race and Sex in America* (1996).

Glenda Elizabeth Gilmore, *Gender and Jim Crow: Women and the Politics of White Supremacy in North Carolina, 1896–1920* (1996).

Sarah Haley, *No Mercy Here: Gender, Punishment, and the Making of Jim Crow Modernity* (2016).

Evelyn Brooks Higginbotham, *Righteous Discontent: The Women's Movement in the Black Baptist Church, 1880–1920* (1994).

Tera W. Hunter, *To 'Joy My Freedom: Southern Black Women's Lives and Labors after the Civil War* (1997).

Dolores Janiewski, *Sisterhood Denied: Race, Gender, and Class in a New South Community* (1986).

Talitha L. LeFlouria, *Chained in Silence: Black Women and Convict Labor in the New South* (2015).

Anne Firor Scott, *The Southern Lady: From Pedestal to Politics, 1830–1930* (1970).

Working Women in the North

Marjorie W. Davies, *Woman's Place Is at the Typewriter: Office Work and Office Workers, 1870–1930* (1982).

Alice Kessler-Harris, *Out to Work: A History of Wage-Earning Women in the United States* (1982).

Joanne J. Meyerowitz, *Women Adrift: Independent Wage Earners in Chicago, 1880–1930* (1988).

Kathy Peiss, *Cheap Amusements: Working Women and Leisure in Turn-of-the-Century New York* (1986).

Harriet Robinson, *Loom and Spindle: Or Life among the Early Mill Girls; with a Sketch of the "Lowell Offering" and Some of Its Contributors* (2011).

Lara Vapnek, *Breadwinners: Working Women and Economic Independence, 1865–1920* (2009).

Leisure-Class Women in the North

Elaine S. Abelson, *When Ladies Go A-Thieving: Middle-Class Shoplifters in the Victorian Department Store* (1989).

Deborah Davis, *Gilded: How Newport Became America's Richest Resort* (2009).

Anne de Courcy, *The Husband Hunters: Social Climbing in New York and London* (2017).

Maureen A. Flanagan, *Seeing with Their Hearts: Chicago Women and the Vision of the Good City, 1871–1933* (2002).

Helen Lefkowitz Horowitz, *Alma Mater: Design and Experience in the Women's Colleges from Their Nineteenth-Century Beginnings to the 1930s* (1984).

Anne Firor Scott, *Natural Allies: Women's Associations in American History* (1991).

Ian Tyrrell, *Woman's World/Woman's Empire: The Woman's Christian Temperance Union in International Perspective, 1880–1930* (1991).

Martha Vicinus, *Intimate Friends: Women Who Loved Women, 1778–1928* (2004).

Janet Wallach, *The Richest Woman in America: Hetty Green in the Gilded Age* (2012).

PRIMARY SOURCES

Ida B. Wells, "Race Woman"

IN THE YEARS AFTER 1877, when the federal protections of Reconstruction ended and the freed Black population of the South was left on its own to resist resurgent white supremacy, a generation of exceptional female Black leaders emerged. Of these, none was more extraordinary than Ida B. Wells. Born in 1862 in Mississippi, she was orphaned at the age of sixteen by a yellow fever epidemic. Determined to assume responsibility for her siblings and to keep her family together, she found work first as a teacher and then as a journalist. In 1889 in Memphis, she purchased part ownership of a Black newspaper, *Free Speech and Headlight*. Her goal was to expose and publicize the mistreatment of her people. In an age notable for its florid and euphemistic writing, Wells's style was straightforward and explicit. She was not afraid to use the word "rape" to describe the accusations against Black men and the experiences of Black women.

Wells was catapulted into the role that changed her life when her friend Thomas Moss, a prosperous grocer and mail carrier, was lynched by a Memphis mob in 1892. Taken in the months following the lynching, Figure 6.1 shows Ida B. Wells posing with widow Betty Moss and the Moss children. Wells spent time with the Moss family as they mourned the loss of a father, husband, and community leader. She recalled how "the baby daughter of Tom Moss, too young to express how she misses her father, toddles to the wardrobe, seizes the legs of his letter-carrier uniform, hugs and kisses them with evident delight and stretches her little hands to be taken up into arms that will never more clasp his daughter's form."[38] What details in the photograph provide clues to the close emotional bond between Ida Wells and Betty Moss?

◆ **Figure 6.1 Ida B. Wells (left) with the Family of Thomas Moss (1893)**
Special Collections Research Center, University of Chicago Library.

Although the country had a history of vigilantes lynching people they decided were criminals, whether Black or white, Black people were typically the targets of white accusers in the South during this period. Wells concluded that Moss's "crime" had been the competition that his successful grocery business posed to whites. Over a hundred years later, we take for granted the connections that she was the first to make: between the postwar political and economic gains made by freedpeople and the brutal violence unleashed on them by resentful whites; and between the long history of sexual exploitation of Black women that began during slavery and the inflammatory charges made after emancipation to justify lynching — that Black men were sexual predators.

Perhaps the most remarkable element of Wells's analysis was her insistence that Black and white people sometimes voluntarily chose to be each other's sexual partners. She was not particularly in favor of the practice. She was what was called in this period a "race woman," meaning that her concerns were less for integration than for the happiness and progress of Black people. "A proper self-respect is expected of races as individuals," she later wrote. "We need more race love; the tie of racehood should bind us [through] . . . a more hearty appreciation of each other."[39] Nonetheless, she appreciated the difference between willing and coerced sex and defended the former while criticizing the latter. She understood that so long as interracial sex was concealed as a fact of southern life, Black people would pay the deadly price.

Her investigations into the practice of lynching got her driven out of Memphis in 1892. This autobiographical account details the impact that her harrowing experience had on Black women in the North, who went on to form the National Association of Colored Women and to join in the work of exposing the true nature, extent, and causes of southern lynchings. Exiled from the South, she moved to Chicago, where in 1895 she married Frederick Barnett, also a journalist and activist, and continued to battle for justice for her race by working for greater political power for Black people. She played an early role in organizing Black women to secure and use the right to vote. Her autobiography remained unfinished and unpublished until brought into print by her youngest child, Alfreda Duster, more than a century after her mother's birth.

As you read, consider what led Wells to undertake an exposé of lynching and how doing so challenged the expectations of race and gender that she faced. What does Wells's analysis of the causes of and attitudes toward the lynching of African Americans reveal about the dynamics between whites and Blacks several decades after the end of slavery?

IDA B. WELLS

Crusade for Justice: The Autobiography of Ida B. Wells (1970)

While I was thus carrying on the work of my newspaper, . . . there came the lynching in Memphis which changed the whole course of my life. . . .

Thomas Moss, Calvin McDowell, and Henry Stewart owned and operated a grocery store in a thickly populated suburb. . . . There was already a grocery owned and operated by a white man who hitherto had had a monopoly on the trade of this thickly populated colored suburb. Thomas's grocery changed all that, and he and his associates were made to feel that they were not welcome by the white grocer. . . .

One day some colored and white boys quarreled over a game of marbles and the colored boys got the better of the fight which followed. . . . Then the challenge was issued that the vanquished whites were coming on Saturday night to clean out [Thomas's] Colored People's Grocery Company. . . . Accordingly the grocery company armed several men and stationed them in the rear of the store on that fatal Saturday night, not to attack but to repel a threatened attack. . . . The men stationed there had seen several white men stealing through the rear door and fired on them without a moment's pause. Three of these men were wounded, and others fled and gave the alarm. . . . Over a hundred colored men were dragged from their homes and put in jail on suspicion.

All day long on that fateful Sunday white men were permitted in the jail to look over the imprisoned black men. . . . The mob took out of their cells Thomas Moss, Calvin McDowell, and Henry Stewart, the three officials of the People's Grocery Company. They were loaded on a switch engine of the railroad which ran back of the jail, carried a mile north of the city limits, and horribly shot to death. One of the morning papers held back its edition in order to supply its readers with the details of that lynching. . . . The mob took possession of the People's Grocery Company, helping themselves to food and drink, and destroyed what

they could not eat or steal. The creditors had the place closed and a few days later what remained of the stock was sold at auction. Thus, with the aid of city and county authorities and the daily papers, that white grocer had indeed put an end to his rival Negro grocer as well as to his business. . . .

Like many another person who had read of lynchings in the South, I had accepted the idea meant to be conveyed — that although lynching was irregular and contrary to law and order, unreasoning anger over the terrible crime of rape led to the lynching; that perhaps the brute deserved death anyhow and the mob was justified in taking his life.

But Thomas Moss, Calvin McDowell and Henry Stewart had been lynched in Memphis, one of the leading cities of the South, in which no lynching had taken place before, with just as much brutality as other victims of the mob; and they had committed no crime against white women. This is what opened my eyes to what lynching really was. An excuse to get rid of Negroes who were acquiring wealth and property and thus keep the race terrorized and "keep the n-----* down."

I then began an investigation of every lynching I read about. I stumbled on the amazing record that every case of rape reported . . . became such only when it became public.

Many cases were like that of the lynching which happened in Tunica County, Mississippi. The Associated Press reporter said, "The big burly brute was lynched because he had raped the seven-year-old daughter of the sheriff." I visited the place afterward and saw the girl, who was a grown woman more than seventeen years old. She had been found in the lynched Negro's cabin by her father, who had led the mob against him in order to save his daughter's reputation. That Negro was a helper on the farm. . . .

---

*This textbook does not reproduce racial slurs in full. We have replaced some letters in the original source with dashes.

It was with these and other stories in mind in that last week in May 1892 that I wrote the following editorial:

Eight Negroes lynched since last issue of the *Free Speech*. They were charged with killing white men and five with raping white women. Nobody in this section believes the old thread-bare lie that Negro men assault white women. If Southern white men are not careful they will over-reach themselves and a conclusion will be drawn which will be very damaging to the moral reputation of their women.

This editorial furnished at last the excuse for doing what the white leaders of Memphis had long been wanting to do: put an end to the *Free Speech*. . . .

Having lost my paper, had a price put on my life, and been made an exile from home for hinting at the truth, I felt that I owed it to myself and to my race to tell the whole truth now that I was where I could do so freely. Accordingly, the fourth week in June, the *New York Age* had a seven-column article on the front page giving names, dates and places of many lynchings for alleged rape. This article showed conclusively that my editorial in the *Free Speech* was based on facts of illicit association between black men and white women.

Such relationships between white men and colored women were notorious, and had been as long as the two races had lived together in the South. . . . Many stories of the antebellum South were based upon such relationships. It has been frequently charged in narratives of slave times that these white fathers often sold their mulatto children into slavery. It was also well known that many other such white fathers and masters brought their mulatto and quadroon children to the North and gave them freedom and established homes for them, thus making them independent.

All my life I had known that such conditions were accepted as a matter of course. I found that this rape of helpless Negro girls and women, which began in slavery days, still continued

without . . . hindrance, check or reproof from church, state, or press until there had been created this race within a race — and all designated by the inclusive term of "colored."

I also found that what the white man of the South practiced as all right for himself, he assumed to be unthinkable in white women. They could and did fall in love with the pretty mulatto and quadroon girls as well as black ones, but they professed an inability to imagine white women doing the same thing with Negro and mulatto men. Whenever they did so and were found out, the cry of rape was raised, and the lowest element of the white South was turned loose to wreak its fiendish cruelty on those too weak to help themselves. . . .

The more I studied the situation, the more I was convinced that the Southerner had never gotten over his resentment that the Negro was no longer his plaything, his servant, and his source of income. The federal laws for Negro protection passed during Reconstruction had been made a mockery by the white South where it had not secured their repeal. This same white South had secured political control of its several states, and as soon as white southerners came into power they began to make playthings of Negro lives and property. This still seemed not enough "to keep the n----- down."

Here came lynch law to stifle Negro manhood which defended itself, and the burning alive of Negroes who were weak enough to accept favors from white women. The many unspeakable and unprintable tortures to which Negro rapists (?) [here Wells inserted a parenthetical question mark to indicate her skepticism of these charges] of white women were subjected were for the purpose of striking terror into the hearts of other Negroes who might be thinking of consorting with willing white women.

I found that in order to justify these horrible atrocities to the world, the Negro was branded as a race of rapists, who were especially after white women. I found that white men who had created a race of mulattoes by raping and consorting with Negro women were still doing so wherever they could; these same white men lynched, burned and tortured Negro men for doing the same thing with white women; even when the white women were willing victims.

That the entire race should be branded as moral monsters and despoilers of white womanhood and childhood was bound to rob us of all the friends we had and silence any protests that they might make for us. For all these reasons it seemed a stern duty to give the facts I had collected to the world. . . .

About two months after my appearance in the columns in the *New York Age*, two colored women remarked on my revelations during a visit with each other and said they thought that the women of New York and Brooklyn should do something to show appreciation of my work and to protest the treatment which I had received. . . . A committee of two hundred and fifty women was appointed, and they stirred up sentiment throughout the two cities which culminated in a testimonial at Lyric Hall on 5 October 1892.

This testimonial was conceded by the oldest inhabitants to be the greatest demonstration ever attempted by race women for one of their number. . . . The leading colored women of Boston and Philadelphia had been invited to join in this demonstration, and they came, a brilliant array . . . behind a lonely, homesick girl who was an exile because she had tried to defend the manhood of her race. . . .

So many things came out of that wonderful testimonial.

First it was the beginning of the club movement among the colored women in this country. The women of New York and Brooklyn decided to continue that organization, which they called the Women's Loyal Union. These were the first strictly women's clubs organized in those cities. Mrs. Ruffin of Boston, who came over to that testimonial . . . called a meeting of the women at her home to meet me, and they organized themselves into the Woman's Era Club of that city. Mrs. Ruffin had been a member of the foremost clubs among white women in Boston for years, but this was her first effort to form one among colored women. . . .

Second, that testimonial was the beginning of public speaking for me. I have already said that I had not before made speeches, but invitations came from Philadelphia, Wilmington, Delaware, Chester, Pennsylvania, and Washington, D.C. . . .

In Philadelphia . . . Miss Catherine Impey of Street Somerset, England, was visiting Quaker relatives of hers in the city and at the same time was trying to learn what she could about the color question in this country. She was the editor of *Anti-Caste*, a magazine published in England in behalf of the natives of India, and she was therefore interested in the treatment of darker races everywhere. . . . [Thus happened] the third great result of that wonderful testimonial in New York the previous month. Although we did not know it at the time, the interview between Miss Impey and myself resulted in an invitation to England and the beginning of the worldwide campaign against lynching.

Source: Alfreda M. Duster, ed., *Crusade for Justice: The Autobiography of Ida B. Wells* (Chicago: University of Chicago Press, 1970), 47–82.

ANALYZING PRIMARY SOURCES

1. What were the underlying tensions and larger conflicts that led to the lynching of Thomas Moss?

2. What was the prevailing opinion about lynching that Wells was determined to challenge?

3. What did Wells see as the relationship between the long history of white men raping Black women and the charges raised against Black men of raping white women?

4. How did Wells's campaign contribute to the consolidation of the organized Black women's movement?

PRIMARY SOURCES

The Woman Who Toils

T HE LIVES AND LABORS of white wage-earning women and leisure-class women intersected in numerous ways in the late nineteenth century. Maids, cooks, nannies, and laundresses provided the labor that made possible the elaborate homes and active social lives of leisure-class women. Working women and their children were the objects of the charitable and philanthropic projects that middle- and upper-class women, aiming for a larger role in community affairs, organized in these years. Above all, working women provided the labor to manufacture the food, clothing, and luxuries that distinguished the rich from the poor. As the authors of *The Woman Who Toils* explained to wealthy women, working women provided "the labour that must be done to satisfy your material demands."[40]

By the end of the century, working-class women were also the subject of professional women's journalistic and sociological investigations, of which *The Woman Who Toils: Being the Experiences of Two Ladies as Factory Girls* (1903) is a notable example. The authors, Bessie and Marie Van Vorst, were upper-class women. Marie was born a Van Vorst, and Bessie married into the family. Neither went to college. Both were educated instead in the manner preferred by the upper classes for their daughters, by private tutors and at female academies. After Bessie's husband (Marie's brother) died, the two women, both still in their thirties, decided together to establish greater economic independence for themselves. They moved to Paris and cowrote a novel about an upper-class American woman abroad. Their next collaborative effort was *The Woman Who Toils*, a journalistic account of the lives of wage-earning women. As upper-class New Women aspiring to independence, they were motivated by both their growing awareness of the lives of working-class women and their own authorial ambitions.

To research the book, they returned to the United States, assumed fictional identities, and took a series of working-class jobs. Marie worked in a New England shoe factory and a southern textile mill. Bessie became the Irishwoman "Esther Kelly" and took a job in a pickling factory in Pittsburgh, where she went from eagerness to exhaustion in a few short days. Moving from job to job in the factory, Bessie explored how different it felt to work for a preset daily wage and to work for payment by the piece — an arrangement that led workers to drive themselves to work faster. A day in the male workers' dining room allowed her to compare manufacturing to domestic service labor.

Throughout Bessie's account, the distance she maintained from the women she wrote about is evident. She and her sister-in-law chose a subtitle to clarify that they were still "ladies" despite their brief stint as factory girls. The young men with whom their coworkers associated, the recreation they sought, and the clothes they wore seemed to them "vulgar." Like most reformers, they did not endorse wage labor for women with children, a point emphasized by President Theodore Roosevelt in his introduction to their book. Nonetheless, Bessie came to appreciate the generosity of her coworkers, the pleasures of collective work, and the "practical, progressive" democracy of working-class life. Above all, it was the sheer physical demands of doing the job, descriptions of which are among the best parts of the Pittsburgh pickling section of *The Woman Who Toils*, that seem to have broken through her shield of gentility and brought her a measure of closeness to the women workers about whom she wrote.

As you read this account of working in the pickle factory, identify what Bessie Van Vorst finds attractive about the jobs she does and the women who do them, and what she finds repellent. Consider the points at which her class prejudices emerge and the points at which she gets beyond them.

Mrs. John (Bessie) Van Vorst and Marie Van Vorst
The Woman Who Toils: Being the Experiences of Two Ladies as Factory Girls (1903)

"What will you do about your name?" "What will you do with your hair and your hands?" "How can you deceive people?" These are some of the questions I had been asked by my friends.

Before any one had cared or needed to know my name it was morning of the second day, and my assumed name seemed by that time the only one I had ever had. As to hair and hands, a half-day's work suffices for their undoing. And my disguise is so successful I have deceived not only others but myself. I have become with desperate reality a factory girl, alone, inexperienced, friendless. I am making $4.20 a week and spending $3 of this for board alone, and I dread not being strong enough to keep my job. I climb endless stairs, am given a white cap and an apron, and my life as a factory girl begins. I become part of the ceaseless, unrelenting mechanism kept in motion by the poor. . . .

My first task is an easy one; anybody could do it. On the stroke of seven my fingers fly. I place a lid of paper in a tin jar-top, over it a cork; this I press down with both hands, tossing the cover, when done, into a pan. In spite of myself I hurry; I cannot work fast enough—I outdo my companions. How can they be so slow? Every nerve, every muscle is offering some of its energy. Over in one corner the machinery for sealing the jars groans and roars; the mingled sounds of filling, washing, wiping, packing, comes to my eager ears as an accompaniment for the simple work assigned to me. One hour passes, two, three hours; I fit ten, twenty, fifty dozen caps, and still my energy keeps up. . . .

When I have fitted 110 dozen tin caps the forewoman comes and changes my job. She tells me to haul and load up some heavy crates with pickle jars. I am wheeling these back and forth when the twelve o'clock whistle blows. Up to that time the room has been one big dynamo, each girl a part of it. With the first moan of the noon signal the dynamo comes to life. It is hungry; it has friends and favourites—news to tell. We herd down to a big dining room and take our places, five hundred of us in all. The newspaper bundles are unfolded. The menu varies little: bread and jam, cake and pickles, occasionally a sausage, a bit of cheese or a piece of stringy cold meat. In ten minutes the repast is over. The dynamo has been fed; there are twenty minutes of leisure spent in dancing, singing, resting, and conversing chiefly about young men and "sociables."

At 12:30 sharp the whistle draws back the life it has given. I return to my job. My shoulders are beginning to ache. My hands are stiff, my thumbs almost blistered. The enthusiasm I had felt is giving way to numbing weariness. I look at my companions now in amazement. How can they keep on so steadily, so swiftly? . . . New girls like myself who had worked briskly in the morning are beginning to loiter. Out of the washing-tins hands come up red and swollen, only to be plunged again into hot dirty water. Would the whistle never blow? . . . At last the whistle blows! In a swarm we report: we put on our things and get away into the cool night air. I have stood ten hours; I have fitted 1,300 corks; I have hauled and loaded 4,000 jars of pickles. My pay is seventy cents. . . .

For the two days following my first experience I am unable to resume work. Fatigue has swept through my body like a fever. Every bone and joint has a clamouring ache. . . .

The next day is Saturday. I feel a fresh excitement at going back to my job; the factory draws me toward it magnetically. I long to be in the hum and whir of the busy workroom. Two days of leisure without resources or amusement make clear to me how the sociability of factory life, the freedom from personal demands, the escape from self can prove a distraction to those who have no mental occupation, no money to spend on diversion. It is easier to submit to factory government which commands five hundred girls with one law valid for all, than to undergo the arbitrary discipline of parental authority. I speed across the snow covered courtyard. In a moment my cap and apron are on and I am sent to report to the head forewoman. . . .

She wears her cap close against her head. Her front hair is rolled up in crimping-pins. She has false teeth and is a widow. Her pale, parched face shows what a great share of life has been taken by daily over-effort repeated during years. As she talks she touches my arm in a kindly fashion and

looks at me with blue eyes that float about under weary lids. "You are only at the beginning," they seem to say. "Your youth and vigour are at full tide, but drop by drop they will be sapped from you, to swell the great flood of human effort that supplies the world's material needs. You will gain in experience," the weary lids flutter at me, "but you will pay *with your life* the living you make."

There is no variety in my morning's work. Next to me is a bright, pretty girl jamming chopped pickles into bottles.

"How long have you been here?" I ask, attracted by her capable appearance. She does her work easily and well.

"About five months."

"How much do you make?"

"From 90 cents to $1.05. I'm doing piecework," she explains. "I get seven-eighths of a cent for every dozen bottles I fill. I have to fill eight dozen to make seven cents. . . ."

"Do you live at home?" I ask.

"Yes; I don't have to work. I don't pay no board. My father and my brothers supports me and my mother. But," and her eyes twinkle, "I couldn't have the clothes I do if I didn't work."

"Do you spend your money all on yourself?"

"Yes."

I am amazed at the cheerfulness of my companions. They complain of fatigue, of cold, but never at any time is there a suggestion of ill-humour. The suppressed animal spirits reassert themselves when the forewoman's back is turned. Companionship is the great stimulus. I am confident that without the . . . encouragement of example, it would be impossible to obtain as much from each individual girl as is obtained from them in groups of tens, fifties, hundreds working together.

When lunch is over we are set to scrubbing. Every table and stand, every inch of the factory floor must be scrubbed in the next four hours. . . .

The grumbling is general. There is but one opinion among the girls: it is not right that they should be made to do this work. They all echo the same resentment, but their complaints are made in whispers; not one has the courage to openly rebel. What, I wonder to myself, do the men do on scrubbing day. I try to picture one of them on his hands and knees in a sea of brown mud. It is impossible. The next time I go for a supply of soft soap in a department where the men are working I take a look at the masculine interpretation of house cleaning. One man is playing a hose on the floor and the rest are scrubbing the boards down with long-handled brooms and rubber mops.

"You take it easy," I say to the boss.

"I won't have no scrubbing in my place," he answers emphatically. "The first scrubbing day they says to me 'Get down on your hands and knees,' and I says — 'Just pay me my money, will you; I'm goin' home. What scrubbing can't be done with mops ain't going to be done by me.' The women wouldn't have to scrub, either, if they had enough spirit all of 'em to say so."

I determined to find out if possible, during my stay in the factory, what it is that clogs this mainspring of "spirit" in the women. . . .

After a Sunday of rest I arrive somewhat ahead of time on Monday morning, which leaves me a few moments for conversation with a piece-worker who is pasting labels on mustard jars. . . .

"I bet you can't guess how old I am."

I look at her. Her face and throat are wrinkled, her hands broad and scrawny; she is tall and has short skirts. What shall be my clue? If I judge by pleasure, "unborn" would be my answer; if by effort, then "a thousand years."

"Twenty," I hazard as a safe medium.

"Fourteen," she laughs. "I don't like it at home, the kids bother me so. Mamma's people are well-to-do. I'm working for my own pleasure."

"Indeed, I wish I was," says a new girl with a red waist. "We three girls supports mamma and runs the house. We have $13 rent to pay and a load of coal every month and groceries. It's no joke, I can tell you." . . .

Monday is a hard day. There is more complaining, more shirking, more gossip than in the middle of the week. Most of the girls have been to dances on Saturday night, to church on Sunday evening with some young man. Their conversation is vulgar and prosaic; there is nothing in the language they use that suggests an ideal or any conception of the abstract. . . . Here in the land of freedom, where no class line is rigid, the precious chance is not to serve but to live for oneself; not to watch a superior, but to find out by experience. The ideal plays no part, stern realities alone count, and thus we have a progressive, practical, independent people, the expression of whose personality is interesting not through their words but by their deeds.

When the Monday noon whistle blows I follow the hundreds down into the dining-room. . . . I am beginning to understand why the meager lunches of preserve-sandwiches and pickles more than satisfy the girls whom I was prepared to accuse of spending their money on gewgaws rather than on nourishment. It is fatigue that steals the appetite. I can hardly taste what I put in my mouth; the food sticks in my throat. . . . I did not want wholesome food, exhausted as I was. I craved sours and sweets, pickles, cakes, anything to excite my numbed taste. . . .

Accumulated weariness forces me to take a day off. When I return I am sent for in the corking-room. The forewoman lends me a blue gingham dress and tells me I am to do "piece"-work. There are three who work together at every corking-table. My two companions are a woman with goggles and a one-eyed boy. We are not a brilliant trio. The job consists in evening the vinegar in the bottles, driving the cork in, first with a machine, then with a hammer, letting out the air with a knife stuck under the cork, capping the corks, sealing the caps, counting and distributing the bottles. These operations are paid for at the rate of one-half a cent for the dozen bottles, which sum is divided among us. My two companions are earning a living, so I must work in dead earnest or take bread out of their mouths. . . .

There is a stimulus unsuspected in working to get a job done. Before this I had worked to make the time pass. Then no one took account of how much I did; the factory clock had a weighted pendulum; now ambition outdoes physical strength.

The hours and my purpose are running a race together. But, hurry as I may, as we do, when twelve blows its signal we have corked only 210 dozen bottles! This is no more than day-work at seventy cents. With an ache in every muscle, I redouble my energy after lunch. The girl with the goggles looks at me blindly and says: "Ain't it just awful hard work? You can make good money, but you've got to hustle."

She is a forlorn specimen of humanity, ugly, old, dirty, condemned to the slow death of the over-worked. I am a green hand. I make mistakes; I have no experience in the fierce sustained effort of the bread-winners. Over and over I turn to her, over and over she is obliged to correct me. During the ten hours we work side by side not one murmur of impatience escapes her. When she sees that I am getting discouraged she calls out across the deafening din, "That's all right; you can't expect to learn in a day; just keep on steady." . . .

The oppressive monotony is one day varied by a summons to the men's dining-room. I go eagerly, glad of any change. . . . The dinner under preparation is for the men of the factory. There are two hundred of them. They are paid from $1.35 to $3 a day. Their wages begin upon the highest limit given to women. The dinner costs each man ten cents. The $20 paid in daily cover the expenses of the cook, two kitchen maids, and the dinner, which consists of meat, bread and butter, vegetables and coffee, sometimes soup, sometimes dessert. If this can pay for two hundred there is no reason why for five cents a hot meal of some kind could not be given to the women. They don't demand it, so they are left to make themselves ill on pickles and preserves. . . .

[In the dining room] I had ample opportunity to compare domestic service with factory work. We set the table for two hundred, and do a thousand miserable slavish tasks that must be begun again the following day. At twelve the two hundred troop in, toil-worn and begrimed. They pass like locusts, leaving us sixteen hundred dirty dishes to wash up and wipe. This takes us four hours, and when we have finished the work stands ready to be done over the next morning with peculiar monotony. In the factory there is stimulus in feeling that the material which passes through one's hands will never be seen or heard of again. . . .

My first experience is drawing to a close. I have surmounted the discomforts of insufficient food, of dirt, a bed without sheets, the strain of hard manual labor. . . . In the factory where I worked men and women were employed for ten-hour days. The women's highest wages were lower than the men's lowest. Both were working as hard as they possibly could. The women were doing menial work, such as scrubbing, which the men refused to do. The men were properly fed at noon; the women satisfied themselves with cake and pickles. Why was this? It is of course impossible to generalize on a single factory. I can only relate the conclusions I drew from what I saw myself. The wages paid by employers, economists tell us, are fixed at the level of bare subsistence. This level and its accompanying conditions are determined by competition, by the nature and number of labourers taking part in the competition. In the masculine category I met but one class of competitor: the bread-winner. In the feminine category I found a variety of classes: the bread-winner, the semi-bread-winner, the woman who works for luxuries. This inevitably drags the wage level. The self-supporting girl is in competition with the child, with the girl who lives at home and makes a small contribution to the household expenses, and with the girl who is supported and who spends all her money on her clothes. It is this division of purpose which takes the "spirit" out of them as a class. There will be no strikes among them so long as the question of wages is not equally vital to them all. . . .

On the evening when I left the factory for the last time, I heard in the streets the usual cry of murders, accidents and suicides; the mental food of the overworked. It is Saturday night. I mingle with a crowd of labourers homeward bound, and with women and girls returning from a Saturday sale in the big shops. They hurry along delighted at the cheapness of a bargain, little dreaming of the human effort that has produced it, the cost of life and energy it represents. As they pass, they draw their skirts aside from us, the cooperators who enable them to have the luxuries they do; from us, the multitude who stand between them and the monster Toil that must be fed with human lives. Think of us, as we herd in the winter dawn; think of us as we bend over our task all the day-light without rest; think of us at the end of the day as we resume suffering and anxiety in homes of squalour and ugliness; think of us as we make our wretched try for merriment; think of us as we stand protectors between you and the labour that must be done to satisfy your material demands; think of us — be merciful.

Source: Mrs. John Van Vorst and Marie Van Vorst, *The Woman Who Toils: Being the Experiences of Two Ladies as Factory Girls* (New York: Doubleday, Page & Co, 1903), 21–58.

ANALYZING PRIMARY SOURCES

1. What different sorts of women does Bessie Van Vorst meet in the factory, and how and why do their responses to their work vary?

2. Why does Van Vorst conclude that working women are passive in accepting their working conditions and unwilling to stand up for themselves in the way of working men? Do you think she is right?

3. How might the working women described in *The Woman Who Toils* have responded on reading the book?

4. In light of Van Vorst's final comments, how do you think her life and attitudes were changed by her experience as a factory girl?

PRIMARY SOURCES

The Higher Education of Women in the Postbellum Years

WHEREVER WOMEN HAVE BEGUN to improve their lives, almost invariably they have started by aspiring to better education. "The neglected education of my fellow-creatures is the grand source of the misery I deplore," wrote British feminist Mary Wollstonecraft in 1792.[41] In the era of the American Revolution, grateful political leaders praised educated women for their role in mothering an enlightened (male) citizenry. Within fifty years, women were teachers in America's burgeoning system of public education. Even so, women continued to have far less access to education than men. Before the Civil War, women could rise no further than the high school level at all-female seminaries. Only Ohio's Oberlin College, an evangelical Protestant institution founded in 1833, admitted a few women to its regular baccalaureate course, most famously women's rights advocate Lucy Stone, who graduated in 1847. Even at Oberlin, however, most women students were educated in a special "ladies' program," with different language and mathematics requirements than those for men.

Two developments in the 1860s made higher education much more available to women. In 1862, the Morrill Land Grant Act provided federal lands to states and territories for the support of public institutions of higher education. While the act did not explicitly mention women, as one historian has explained, "taxpayers demanded that their daughters, as well as their sons, be admitted."[42] As coeducation spread, long-standing concerns that such easy association between the sexes would coarsen women students and distract men began to give way. Not only were many new land-grant institutions of higher education established throughout the West and Midwest in the 1860s and early 1870s, but public universities founded earlier changed their policies to admit women. Private institutions such as Northwestern and the University of Chicago in Illinois, Stanford in California, Tulane in Louisiana, and Grinnell in Iowa also followed the trend. By the end of the century, coeducational institutions granted college degrees to approximately four thousand women each year.

The University of California was one of the first of the newly established public universities to enroll women. Founded in 1868, "Cal" graduated its first woman, Rosa L. Scrivener, in 1874. By 1878, women's rights to equal education, including in the university's law school, were enshrined in the state constitution. By 1882, women constituted over 30 percent of the student body. Being a college student meant access not only to the serious matter of higher education, but also to a tradition of high-spirited and sometimes transgressive carousing. This part of the

◆ Figure 6.2 **Women Students Modeling Senior Plugs, University of California (c. 1900)**
University of California at Berkeley, Oliver Family Photograph Collections, BANC PIC 1960.010 ser. 1:0556—NEG (4 × 5), The Bancroft Library, University of California, Berkeley.

college experience was more difficult for women, with their obligations to maintain a ladylike demeanor, but by the end of the century at Cal they had broken through this barrier as well. In Figure 6.2, Berkeley women students are happily sporting the headgear that college juniors and seniors of the era prized — "plug" hats that had been battered and generally made to look as disgusting as possible. What do you imagine joining in these carefree practices meant to these young women?

After the Civil War, the establishment of all-women's colleges was the other source of increased women's opportunities for higher education. The first of these, Vassar College, opened in 1865, funded by a wealthy brewer from Poughkeepsie, New York, who wanted to create an educational institution "for young women which shall be to them, what Yale and Harvard are to young men."[43] Philanthropists endowed other all-female institutions, and by 1891 Smith and Wellesley Colleges in Massachusetts, Bryn Mawr College outside Philadelphia, and Goucher College near Baltimore were graduating women with bachelor's degrees. (Mount Holyoke in Massachusetts, begun many years before as a female seminary, upgraded to college level in 1890.) These all-women institutions produced about sixteen hundred white college graduates each year. According to statistics combining all-female and coeducational institutions, both public and private, by 1890 women were approximately 40 percent of the total of college graduates — an extraordinary development in less than four decades.

There was much debate about whether women students received a better education and had a better collegiate experience at an all-women's college or at a coeducational institution. To strengthen their claims to intellectual superiority, the top women's colleges were dedicated to providing a first-class education in the sciences, which were becoming increasingly important in modern higher education. The Wellesley College class pictured in Figure 6.3 is studying zoology. The students are examining a fish skeleton and a piece of coral to learn about animal physiology. This photograph, like so many photos of late nineteenth-century college women, is carefully posed. How does the deliberate positioning of the students convey the intellectual seriousness, intensity, and engagement of the scientific learning going

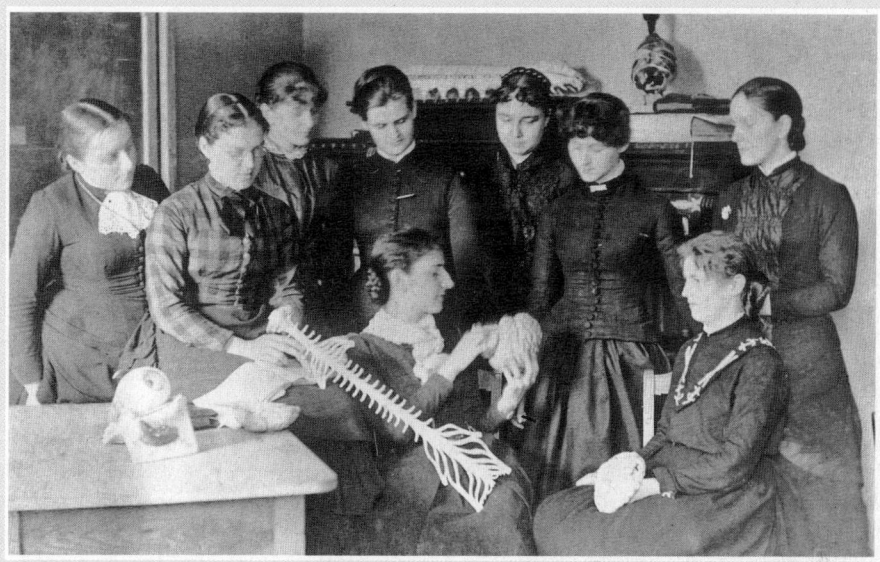

◆ Figure 6.3 **Class in Zoology, Wellesley College (1883–1884)**
Courtesy of Wellesley College Archives, photo by Seaver.

on in this all-female classroom? Consider the simple and functional character of the students' clothes, especially compared to the elaborate and costly appearance of elite women engaged in less serious pursuits.

Figure 6.3 also underscores the opportunities that all-female colleges in this period provided for the employment of educated women. Here, unlike in most coeducational schools, women could be professors and administrators. The zoology professor, the young woman seated at the center, is Mary Alice Wilcox, a graduate of Newnham College, the women's college of Britain's Cambridge University. Standing behind her and slightly to the right is Alice Freeman, the twenty-eight-year-old Wellesley College president. Freeman, an early graduate of the University of Michigan, was one of the first woman to head an institution of higher education in the United States. In 1886, she married Harvard professor George Herbert Palmer and resigned her position as college president. Why might women professors have been employed only at all-women's colleges? What difference do you think they made to women's experience of higher education? How might the youth of professors such as Wilcox and administrators such as Freeman have influenced the learning of these women students?

Concerns went beyond the intellectual. Did coeducation provide too many opportunities for undue familiarity between young unmarried men and women? Were women's colleges hotbeds for passionate female friendships? Anxiety that higher education would have a negative impact on women's health, in particular on their reproductive capacities, haunted the early years of women's higher education. In 1873, Dr. Edward Clarke published a controversial book, *Sex in Education*, in which he argued that higher education for women drained vital physical energy — literally blood — from the reproductive organs to the brain. Defenders of women's education rushed to challenge Clarke's argument that higher education endangered women's reproductive and maternal capacities. They undertook scientific studies of women college students to demonstrate that physical health and intellectual growth were not incompatible. Proponents of women's education were particularly anxious to prove that the menstruation of college girls was not disrupted by too much study.

Black women faced extraordinary educational challenges. In the first years of emancipation, the overwhelming goal for the formerly enslaved was basic literacy. During Reconstruction, Black educational institutions were founded, virtually all of them opened to women as well as men, but these schools provided secondary and vocational rather than baccalaureate education. Even the nation's premiere all-Black college, Howard University, founded in Washington, D.C., in 1867, did not open its collegiate program until 1897 and did not graduate its first woman BA until 1901. In the same year, Atlanta's all-female Spelman College also granted its first BA degree. The photo of the graduating class of 1909 (Figure 6.4) offers a window into the pride and commitment of those women who actively helped to lay the foundation for the upward mobility of Blacks regionally and nationally at the beginning of the new century.

By 1900, an estimated 252 African American women held bachelor's degrees, but almost all had been granted by predominantly white institutions, one-quarter from Oberlin College alone. Committed to equal education by both race and gender, Oberlin had produced the very first Black woman college graduate — Mary Jane Patterson — in 1862. Many of its Black female graduates, including Mary Church Terrell and Anna Julia Cooper, went on to become leading spokeswomen for their race and their sex.

In southern Black educational institutions, the dramatic downturn in race relations in the 1880s and 1890s had a discouraging impact on higher education for Black people. Many colleges concentrated on preparing their students to teach, preach, or take up skilled trades and manual vocations. This approach to higher education was promoted by Booker T. Washington, the era's premiere Black spokesperson. A school for freedpeople founded in 1868, Hampton Institute was a model for many similar institutions throughout the South. In a controversial experiment in interracial, but physically segregated, education, Hampton also began enrolling Indigenous students in 1878.

Freedpeople regarded the educational opportunities that the Hampton Institute and other such schools provided them as immense privileges. Speaking at the 1873 graduation, Alice P. Davis, born enslaved in North Carolina in 1852, praised Hampton as her alma mater: "A mother indeed she has been to us, for she has given us more instruction in these three years than our dear but illiterate mothers ever could."[44] Nonetheless, such institutions, which were often overseen by white benefactors and administrators, maintained strict controls over their Black students and trained them in the virtues of industriousness and self-discipline. The young women were prepared for jobs as teachers, but also as industrial workers.

◆ Figure 6.4 **Spelman College Graduating Class of 1909**
Spelman College.

In 1899, Hampton's white trustees hired America's first important female documentary photographer, Frances Benjamin Johnston, who was white, to portray the students' educational progress. Her photographs were displayed at the Paris Exposition of 1900, where they were much praised for both their artistic achievement and their depiction of racial harmony. Figure 6.5, titled "Class in American History," is an exceptionally rich image for the diversity of its subjects and the complexity of its content. A white female teacher stands among her female and male, Black and Indigenous, students. All are contemplating an Indigenous man in ceremonial dress. He can be likened in some way to the "scientific specimens" in Figure 6.3. Consider what the man himself might have been thinking as he was exhibited to the gaze of both the photographer and the history class.

◆ **Figure 6.5 Class in American History, Hampton Institute (1899–1900)**
Library of Congress Prints and Photographs Division, Washington D.C. [LC-USZ62-38149].

Historian Laura Wexler has unearthed the name of one of the students, the young Indigenous woman standing at the far right: she is Adele Quinney, a member of the Stockbridge tribe.[45] What lessons were she and the other students being taught about American history by the living exhibit of "traditional" Indigenous ways placed before them? What do their precise posing and uniform dress suggest about the discipline expected of Hampton students?

During the post–Civil War years, many "normal colleges" were established to concentrate exclusively on the training of teachers. Such schools provided a briefer, less demanding program of study than baccalaureate courses. With less competitive standards for admission and lower costs, they educated a much larger number of female students. The first teacher training institution supported with public funds was founded in 1839 in Framingham, Massachusetts.

◆ Figure 6.6 **Science Class, Washington, D.C., Normal College (1899)**
Library of Congress Prints and Photographs Division Washington, D.C. [LC-USZ62-14684].

Normal colleges also benefited from the 1862 Morrill Act and were an important avenue of upward mobility for the working class, immigrants, Blacks, and other people of color.

Many of these institutions survived into the twentieth century and became full-fledged colleges and universities. Figure 6.6 is a photo of a class at Washington, D.C.'s Normal College, established twenty-six years before in 1873. Because Washington was a southern city, public education there was racially segregated, and the Normal College enrolled only white students. Washington's Myrtilla Miner Normal School, founded in 1851 and named after a white woman educator of Black girls, enrolled only Black students. The two schools remained separate and segregated until 1955, one year after the Supreme Court found segregated education unconstitutional in the case of *Brown v. Board of Education*. Then they were merged into the District of Columbia Teachers College, now named the University of the District of Columbia.

As in Figure 6.3, the students in Figure 6.6 are studying science, once again illustrating the importance of this subject in meeting the ambitions of the leaders of women's higher education to offer young women a modern and intellectually challenging education. And yet the kinds of teaching and learning that went on in an elite college such as Wellesley and a teacher training institution such as the Normal College were very different. The former had a far more educated faculty and resources of equipment and specimens that the latter lacked. Consider what other differences can be detected by comparing this photograph with Figure 6.3. Figure 6.6 also invites comparison with Figure 6.5 because both photographs were taken by Frances Johnston. How has Johnston positioned her subjects in this picture, compared to those at Hampton Institute? What educational message is this different staging meant to communicate?

Like teachers, doctors were trained in specialized medical colleges. For most of the nineteenth century, a bachelor's degree was not a prerequisite to study medicine in the United States. Instead, students studied medicine at special medical schools and in undergraduate medical departments of large universities. The first major obstacle that women faced was gaining admission into these all-male programs of medical education. Anxieties about coeducation were particularly intense over the prospect of women sitting beside men at lectures about the human body. But women's desire for medical education was strong. Medicine, unlike other professions such as law or the ministry, fit comfortably with women's traditional role as healers. In 1849, after being rejected by a dozen major medical schools on the basis of her sex, Elizabeth Blackwell broke this educational barrier by graduating from Geneva Medical College in upstate New York.

One remedy was the establishment of all-female medical colleges. The Boston Female Medical College was established in 1849 by Dr. Samuel Gregory, who wanted to train women to attend their own sex in childbirth. Dr. Elizabeth Blackwell founded the Women's Medical College of New York in 1868 to help other women follow her into the profession. Figure 6.7 is a photograph of an anatomy class at the Woman's Hospital of Philadelphia, which was founded in 1861. Training female doctors as well as nurses, this teaching hospital focused on the treatment of women and children. What do you find most surprising about this image? What does this photo indicate about the opportunities available to women of color at this institution?

By 1890, women represented between 15 and 20 percent of all medical students. After 1890, the number of medical colleges shrank, even as their standards rose. Educationally, the crucial change came in 1893 when the Johns Hopkins University in Baltimore established the first postgraduate medical course in the United States. A group of women, led by Mary Garrett, donated $500,000 to the new postgraduate medical college on the condition that women be admitted along with men. Overall, however, women began to lose access to medical education after 1890, and the percentage of women in most medical schools dropped by half or more by the turn of the century.

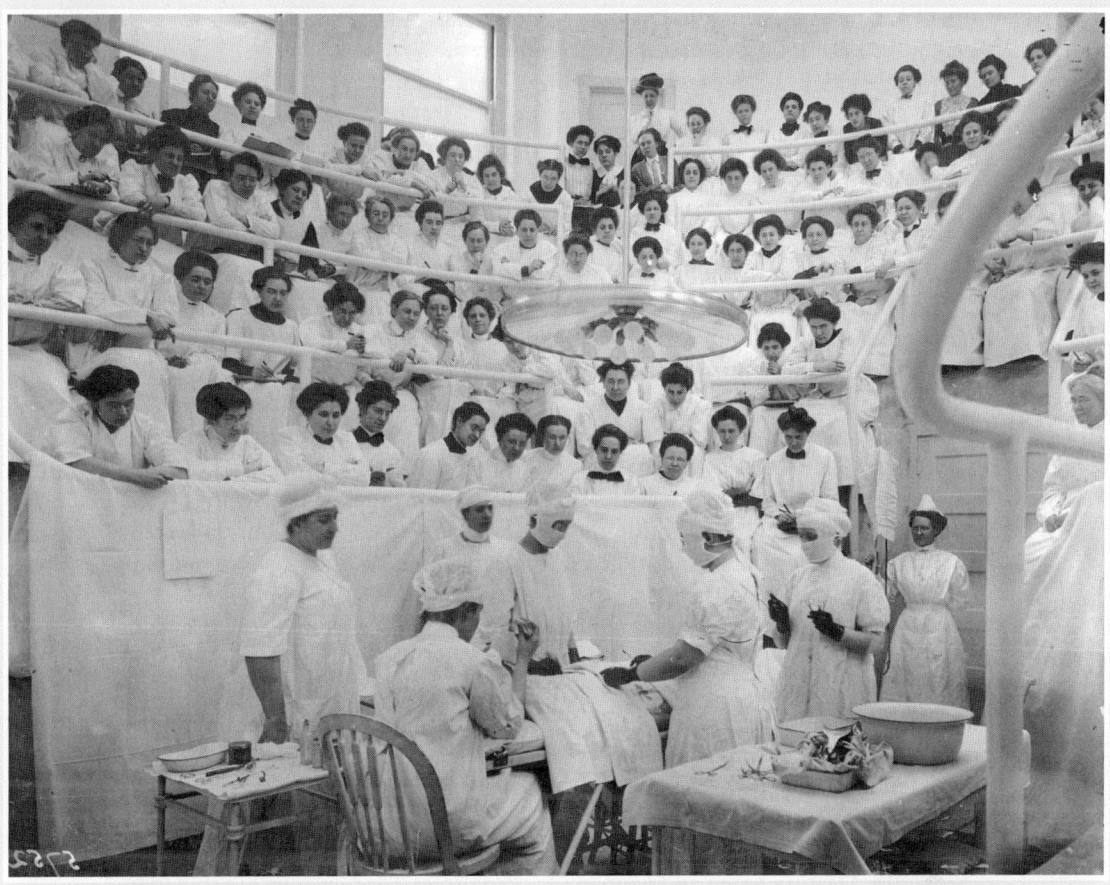

◆ **Figure 6.7 Medical Students Watching a Body Dissection at the Woman's College Hospital, Philadelphia**
Topical Press Agency/Getty Images.

ANALYZING PRIMARY SOURCES

1. Nineteenth-century women's higher education proceeded along two parallel lines: the struggle for coeducation and the establishment of all-women's institutions. What were the advantages and disadvantages of each approach?

2. In what way did the motivations for and rewards of higher education differ for white and Black women?

3. How did the growth of higher education for women relate to other major postbellum developments in women's history discussed in this chapter?

The New Woman

BEGINNING IN THE 1880S AND CONTINUING INTO THE 1920s, a new form of femininity evoked the ways in which women were beginning to break down barriers in both the public and private realms. Americans watched as the "New Woman" agitated for suffrage and reform, pursued higher education, and made modest gains in the professional world. She also demonstrated new patterns of private life, from shopping in the new urban department stores to riding bicycles and playing golf, hinting at changes in what was considered appropriate behavior. Black women, especially those associated with reform organizations, envisioned a New Black Woman, much in the mode of Ida B. Wells, Mary Church Terrell, and Anna Julia Cooper. But in the larger public imagination, the New Woman was white and of the leisure class.

The concept of the New Woman set off an immense controversy in the late nineteenth century. Critics insisted that voting, higher education, and athletic endeavors would damage women's health and undermine their femininity and that professional women's work and increased personal freedoms would harm the middle-class family ideal. Defenders praised the New Woman as an icon of progress and modernity. The many versions of this new phenomenon emerged particularly clearly in visual representations.

Critics of the New Woman in the 1890s often satirized her in cartoons and drawings that featured men and women swapping roles. Usually, men are shown in emasculating situations, doing housework or tending a baby, while women appear in mannish clothing and are depicted variously as attorneys, suffragists, and businesswomen. Figure 6.8, from the humor magazine *Puck*, is typical of this representation. How does the image convey the sense that "What We Are Coming To" is an alarming state of affairs? How are both man and woman made to appear ludicrous?

Contrast Figure 6.8 with Figure 6.9, an 1895 *Life* illustration titled "In a Twentieth Century Club," which features women at leisure, enjoying an atmosphere that replicated a men's drinking and eating club. Here, although role reversal still provides the humor, the women waitresses and patrons are physically attractive. While the women's unladylike posture and clothing would have been viewed as shocking, equally significant is the cross-dressing entertainer: a man dressed in an abbreviated female costume typical of the burlesque shows designed for male audiences. What is the artist suggesting about the New Woman's sexuality by the inclusion of the male dancer? What other features in the drawing hint at the possibility of new sexual patterns in the twentieth century?

In contrast to these negative or ambiguous portrayals of women's demands for political and economic advancement, the New Woman's physical vitality was

WHAT WE ARE COMING TO.

THE TYPEWRITER.— Beg pardon! Did you say " My learned *sister* is mistaken —? "
THE LAWYER.— Yes ; Miss Bigfee is the opposing counsel in this case.

◆ **Figure 6.8 "What We Are Coming To" (1898)**
© *New-York Historical Society/Bridgeman Images.*

attractive to some illustrators, most famously Charles Dana Gibson. Starting in the mid-1890s, his creation of the beautiful and statuesque "Gibson Girl" became a pervasive icon of American femininity. She appeared not only in print media, but also on jewelry and calendars, and her clothing and hairstyle were imitated across class and race lines. The Gibson Girl was independent, athletic, educated, and confident. Yet this self-assurance was oriented not toward careers, social reform, or politics, but toward attracting, and generally manipulating, men through her beauty. As one historian has noted, in many ways Gibson appropriated the New Woman and adjusted her attributes to more conservative ends.[46] Although the Gibson Girl often appeared engaged in genteel athleticism, such as bicycling or golfing, the beauties in Figure 6.10 sit somewhat languorously on the beach. As in Figure 6.9, the contours of women's legs are shown. How do these two depictions of the modern New Woman compare? Note that these hourglass figures are accomplished through corsets. What does that suggest about the extent of the New Woman's physical freedom?

Conservative critics argued that bicycling for women might damage their reproductive health and certainly undermined their femininity. Authors in medical journals even worried that a bicycle saddle might stimulate the rider sexually. Women's rights activists like Frances Willard, however, viewed the bicycle as a means of female independence. As Susan B. Anthony put it in 1896, the bicycle "has done more to

IN A TWENTIETH CENTURY CLUB.

"WHY DON'T YOU FETCH YOUR BROTHER HERE SOME NIGHT?"
"OH, I THINK IT'S A BAD ATMOSPHERE FOR A YOUNG MAN WHO HAS BEEN CAREFULLY BROUGHT UP."

◆ Figure 6.9 **"In a Twentieth Century Club" (1895)**
Beinecke Rare Book and Manuscript Library, Yale University.

emancipate women than anything else in this world. It gives her a feeling of self-reliance and independence the moment she takes her seat; and away she goes, the picture of untrammeled womanhood."[47] Although working-class women apparently used the bicycle to travel to and from work, its most common use was recreational. By 1895, the sight of women astride bicycles, dressed in a variety of costumes, including bloomers, had become commonplace. Certainly, the images of women bicyclists were everywhere in print media and advertising. Figure 6.11 is a coversheet for a dance tune, "The Scorcher." The title referred to a fast, speeding bicyclist. Why might the illustrator have chosen to feature the young woman in the foreground? What aspects of her demeanor and dress convey the qualities of the New Woman?

◆ **Figure 6.10 "Picturesque America" (1900)**
GRANGER — Historical Picture Archive.

An actual embodiment of the career-driven New Woman was Elizabeth Jane Cochran, a journalist who went by the pen name of Nellie Bly. Bly was one of the most famous of the many women "stunt" reporters who blended "hard" news, usually associated with male writers, with "soft" news, or emotional, personal interest stories. These reporters often engaged in gimmicks such as impersonation to get their stories, which moved them from the society page to the front page. Bly worked for the *New York World* and first came to fame when she pretended to be a madwoman in order to gain entrance to New York's Women's Lunatic Asylum. The serialized report established her as a crack investigative reporter whose sensational stories sold newspapers.

Bly's most famous exploit was a replication of the fictional journey of Phineas Fogg, Jules Verne's hero of *Around the World in 80 Days*. She set forth on November 24, 1889, alone and carrying only a small traveling bag and $250. As she sent back reports, the *World*'s circulation climbed. Close to a million readers sent in coupons for a contest to guess the exact length of time her journey would take. On her triumphant return to New York seventy-two days later, Bly commented, "It's not so

◆ **Figure 6.11** "The Scorcher" (1897)
Courtesy, Lilly Library, Indiana University, Bloomington, Indiana.

NELLIE BLY, ON THE FLY.

When Nellie Bly went on the fly,
To show what courage dared to try,
She made the startled world confess:
Men don't monopolize success.

USE
DR. MORSE'S Indian Root Pills,
for Biliousness, Headache, and Constipation.

◆ **Figure 6.12 "Nellie Bly, on the Fly" (1890)**
Old Paper Studios/Alamy Stock Photo.

very much for a woman to do who has the pluck, energy and independence which characterize many women in this day of push and get-there."[48] Bly's celebrity led to a successful board game and a thriving advertising, or "trade" card, market for a wide range of products. Figure 6.12 depicts "Nellie Bly, on the Fly." She wears her trademark plaid traveling coat and neat hat and carries her single bag. How does her clothing and bearing suggest Bly's New Womanhood? How does the surrounding imagery convey her adventurous spirit?

A Roof-top Study.

◆ Figure 6.13 **Women Bachelors in New York (1896)**
Yale Collection of American Literature, Beinecke Rare Book and Manuscript Library.

As a successful working woman, Bly represented the independent New Woman of the city. Single women professionals, such as doctors and lawyers, were part of this phenomenon, but so too were artists, illustrators, writers, teachers, and actresses. New Woman Mary Heaton Vorse, in reflecting on her own move to New York City, wrote of "the strange army of all the girls who in my mother's time would have stayed at home and I wonder what necessity sent us all out . . . more and more of us coming all the time, . . . and as we change the world, the world is going to change us."[49]

Mary Guy Humphreys's 1896 article, "Women Bachelors in New York," described the army Vorse identified. Although Humphreys argued that these women worked primarily to finance consumer goods and pleasures, she also stressed their pleasure in independence, in earning one's own income, and in living alone or with female flatmates. The article's illustrations show women reporters at work at night, commenting that "Mr. Edison's" electric lights offered women more freedom of the streets. Other images depict the women's small but cozy quarters. In commenting on the attention given to comfortable surroundings, Humphreys noted, "In the measure that women are determining their own lives, they want their own homes. . . . The woman who is occupied with daily work needs greater freedom of movement, more isolation, more personal comforts, and the exemption, moreover, from being agreeable at all times and places."[50] Figure 6.13 features the woman "bachelor" reading in her "roof-top study." In what ways does the artist convey a different kind of home life for women as part of their newfound freedom? What is the significance of the city skyline in the distance?

ANALYZING PRIMARY SOURCES

1. What qualities of the New Woman do these popular culture images convey?

2. How does the Gibson Girl (Figure 6.10) compare with other positive renditions of the New Woman (Figures 6.11, 6.12, and 6.13)?

3. Why do you suppose the New Woman, portrayed in either a positive or a negative light, was such a pervasive image in the popular culture of the era?

7

Women in an Expanding Nation

CONSOLIDATION OF THE WEST,

MASS IMMIGRATION, AND

THE CRISIS OF THE 1890s

Twenty-three-year-old Shige Kushida arrived in San Francisco in 1892. American influences had already reached her in her native Japan. She was Protestant, Western-oriented, and one of the few women who dared to speak in Japan before a mixed audience of men and women. She intended to get an education in the United States and return to her home country, but her experience, like that of so many other immigrants, did not go according to plan. Instead of studying, she married another Japanese Christian and settled in Oakland. There she raised her children and became a leader of the Issei (first-generation Japanese American) community. She saw to it that her daughters got the education she did not.[1]

The life of Shige Kushida Togasaki illustrates two grand historical processes that were reshaping American society at the end of the nineteenth century. First, the United States was beginning an unprecedented wave of immigration, which brought with it tremendous social challenges and national transformations. Second, the western part of the continent was being consolidated into the American nation. The frontier — in the sense of a westward-moving line of white settlers — was entering its final stages and, according to the 1890 census, coming to a close. White settlement, which seems like a quintessentially American phenomenon, and mass immigration, which brought the nation into greater interaction with the rest of the world, shared important links. Both involved enormous movements of people across oceans and continents, bringing different cultures into contact and sometimes into conflict. Both involved efforts to "Americanize," sometimes violently, different cultures into the national mainstream. Both developments were motivated at the individual level by hopes for better lives, greater prosperity, and more personal freedom. And yet both processes dashed hopes as much as they realized them, among the immigrant poor and especially among the Native Americans pushed aside by continuing westward expansion.

Mass immigration and the consolidation of the West together helped to set the stage for a major economic and political crisis in the 1890s, as discontented immigrants, farmers, and wage workers found ways to challenge what they saw as a failure of America's democratic promise, notably the unequal distribution of America's new wealth and the unwillingness of the two established political parties to offer any vision of a better social and political path. The resolution of the crisis in favor of corporate power and the established political parties prepared the way for America's first forays abroad as an imperial power.

In all these developments — western consolidation, mass immigration, the political and economic crises of the 1890s, and the beginnings of American imperialism — women were involved, active, influential, and, as a result, changed. In these two great movements of people into and through American society in the late nineteenth century, men initially predominated, but women soon followed. When they did, families were formed and temporary population shifts became permanent new communities. By the early twentieth century, American women's participation in the radical challenges of the 1890s, along with their support for or criticism of their country's ventures abroad, had made them a significant new force in U.S. political life.

◆ CONSOLIDATING THE WEST

American settlement reached the Pacific Coast before the Civil War, but the continent's broad heartland remained largely Indian territory. This situation changed in the last decades of the nineteenth century as white settlement and expansion overtook the Great Plains. The tremendous postbellum growth in industrial capitalism traced in Chapter 6 had as one of its major consequences the steady integration of the entire continent into the national economy. The growth of the transcontinental railroad system constituted the infrastructure for a booming national market that could provide eager consumers throughout the country with the beef, wheat, and lumber produced in abundance in the broad expanse of the trans-Mississippi West.

These western lands were consolidated as part of the American nation through two main processes that were distinguished as much by their gender practices as by anything else.

Large numbers of single men and a few women went west to realize quick profits or find jobs in the region's mines and on its cattle ranges. This form of American expansion has long been celebrated as the Wild West in national legend and popular culture. But there was also a Settler West in which primarily white migrants colonized the prairies of America's heartland. Women and women's labor were as fundamental to this Settler West as men and men's labor were to the other.

Indigenous Women in the West

Despite their differences, both kinds of westerners shared a basic premise: Indians would have to be removed to make way for the new settlers, for their economic ambitions, and for what they regarded as their superior civilization. Here, the U.S. Army, fresh from its victory over the Confederacy, was crucial. After 1865, federal forces moved with full strength against the Native nations to wrest control of the Great Plains and open these huge interior expanses to white settlement. Native American resistance to encroaching white settlers provoked military retaliation in an escalating series of wars that wore away at Native peoples' unity and resources. There were some victories for Indigenous peoples, most famously the 1876 Battle of the Little Big Horn in Montana, in which Lakota Sioux warriors annihilated the U.S. Seventh Cavalry commanded by George A. Custer. The army was able to keep Native peoples in a state of constant defense, however, wearing away at their ability to resist.

Bands of Native Americans who resisted pacification were regarded as "hostiles" who could be killed with impunity by Americans. Made up not only of male warriors but also of women and children, they moved constantly to elude pursuing troops. One of the last such groups was Geronimo's band of Warm Springs Apaches. His female lieutenant, Lozen, exemplified the Native American practice of allowing exceptional individuals to cross the gender divide. Lozen never married, was skilled in tracking the enemy, and performed the spiritual and military duties of a true warrior. Her brother called her "strong as a man, braver than most, and cunning in strategy."[2] For almost a decade, she helped her people evade and attack the U.S. Army, until the Apaches finally surrendered in southern New Mexico in 1886, and she along with others was incarcerated in Florida.

The **Wounded Knee massacre** in South Dakota in the winter of 1890 is often cited as the tragic end to the Indian wars. Following their defeat at the Little Big Horn, U.S. Army troops had relentlessly pursued the Lakota Sioux. Deeply dispirited, the Lakotas began a new religious practice, the Ghost Dance, that promised restoration of their traditional lands and lives. Male and female dancers alike wore special robes that they believed would protect them against bullets fired by white people. A white female observer reported that "the wife of a man called Return-from-scout had seen in a vision that her friends all wore a similar robe, and on reviving from her trance she called the women together and they made a great number of the sacred garments."[3] Believing that the Ghost Dance signaled a new organized insurgency, skittish soldiers fired on a camp of mostly unarmed Lakota people, killing many hundred. "Women with little children on their backs" were gunned down, one white witness to the Wounded Knee massacre recalled, and in blizzard conditions it was many days before their frozen bodies could be retrieved and buried in a mass grave.[4]

Assaults against the Plains Indians took forms other than outright military conflict. By the 1880s, hunters and soldiers with new high-powered rifles had decimated the buffalo herds that were the material basis of Plains Indians' traditional way of life. Hunger made the Plains peoples vulnerable to forced relocations on government reservations of the sort that had been pioneered in the 1850s among Pacific Coast nations (see Map 7.1). Allegedly designed to protect Native Americans from

◆ **Map 7.1 The Indian Frontier, to 1890**

As settlers pushed westward after the Civil War, Native Americans put up bitter resistance, which ultimately failed. Over a period of decades, they ceded most of their lands to the federal government. By 1890, they were confined to reservations, where the most they could expect was an impoverished and alien way of life. *Map reproduced courtesy of Colin Calloway.*

aggressive white settlers, these reservations instead became what one historian calls "virtual prisons."[5] Unable to support themselves by either farming or hunting, reservation Indians were dependent on food and clothing doled out by federal agents, who often embezzled as much as they dispensed. Instead of fulfilling their traditional role in gathering and preparing food, Native American women were relegated to standing in long lines, waiting for rations that frequently did not come.

On the reservations, Native Americans were subjected to intense pressures to assimilate. White women became central to this effort when the federal United States Indian Service began hiring women as superintendents and teachers and in a wide range of other jobs. Believing that the route to "civilizing" the Indian was through the restructuring of the family, or what scholars call "intimate colonialism" of a conquered people, policy makers thought that white women of exemplary character could teach through moral example. As Helen Hunt Jackson, a noted advocate for reforming federal Indian policy and author of the influential 1881 exposé of government mistreatment of Native peoples, *A Century of Dishonor*, explained, "Women have more courage and self-denying missionary spirit, sufficient to undertake such a life, and have an invaluable influence outside their school rooms. They go familiarly into the homes, and are really educating the parents as well as the children in a way that is not within the power of any man."[6] In the late nineteenth century, thousands of women, mostly single, served in this growing federal bureaucracy. By 1898, they made up 42 percent of the agency's employees. Many came with a missionary impulse, undoubtedly influenced by the efforts of the religiously based **Woman's National Indian Association**, a white women's reform organization founded in 1879 to publicize the plight of Native Americans. Others sought better salaries or the freedom from the restrictive lives many middle-class white women led. Despite the emphasis on moral suasion, many felt that they needed to use coercion — such as a threat to send a father to the local jail or remove a child from the home — to receive much cooperation from their clients, who resisted the efforts to suppress their culture.

In conjunction with this assimilative process on the reservations, U.S. policy coerced Native children into government-run boarding schools to be forcibly reeducated in the values and ways of dominant American culture. By the 1890s, several thousand children per year were removed from their parents' control and sent to schools where they were made to stop dressing, speaking, thinking, and believing "like Indians." Half the students were girls, whose forcible reeducation was regarded as crucial to the cultural transformation of Indigenous peoples. Too frequently, Native girls' assimilation into American culture consisted of training in menial occupations and in American standards of domesticity, which they learned as servants in the homes of nearby white families.

The goal of such programs was to save the child by "destroying the Indian," but the transformations sought were elusive. Evidence of repeated and harsh punishments testifies to the refusal of girls as well as boys to give up their Indigenous ways. One elderly woman recalled later, "Two of our girls ran away . . . but they got caught. They tied their legs up, tied their hands behind their backs, put them in the middle of the hallway so that if they fell asleep or something, the matron would hear them and she'd get out there and whip them and make them stand up again."[7]

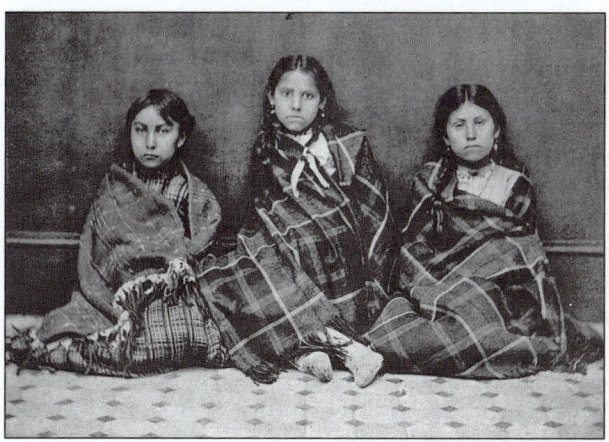

◆ **Before and after Americanization**
Native children were the primary targets of
Americanization at U.S. government-run boarding
schools. These "before-and-after" pictures were
common in the late nineteenth century and
were sometimes sent to philanthropic donors to
illustrate the schools' success in Americanizing
Indians. Within a little more than a year, these
three girls sat on chairs, not the floor, and had lost their blankets and braids, but they retained
their sad faces. The book on the lap of Sarah Walker, the girl on the right in the "after" photograph,
was meant to indicate her ability to read English. *Courtesy of the Peabody Museum of Archaeology
and Ethnology, Harvard University, 2004.24.26500B and 2004.24.26500C.*

Parents and tribal leaders protested the brutality of this coercive Americanization,
but they could not stop it.

Despite boarding schools' coercive practices, many Native American women were
able to acquire English literacy and other useful skills in the boarding school system.
Their training gave them access to jobs in the Indian Service. In 1899, Native Americans
made up 45 percent of those employed in the education division of the agency, mostly
in support services, but a significant number were teachers, clerks, or nurses. And while
some may have adopted the assumptions of their employer, others used their position
primarily to improve their charges' circumstances and even to oppose the government's
harsh assimilation policy. Because the Indian Service preferred not to place employees
with their own people, Native Americans who served outside their own communities
may have even encouraged a fledgling sense of intertribal identity.

A few graduates of boarding schools who also worked for the federal government in some capacity, such as Gertrude Simmons Bonnin (who wrote popular stories under her Yankton Sioux name, Zitkala-Ša) and the Omaha sisters Susan and
Susette La Flesche, became public advocates for their people. Sponsored by the white
women of the Woman's National Indian Association to attend the Women's Medical

College of Pennsylvania, Susan La Flesche graduated in 1889 to become the first white-trained Native American woman physician. She served her people for many years, both as a doctor and as a political leader. Susette La Flesche was a writer and speaker on behalf of Native American causes who made allies of several influential white women, including Helen Hunt Jackson. Bonnin became a well-known writer and activist for Native American causes. One renowned woman activist, Paiute Sarah Winnemucca, had little formal education and little use for the boarding school approach. In addition to serving as translator, negotiator, and lecturer, she created a short-lived bilingual school to offer Paiute children an education that would respect their own cultures. (See Primary Sources: "Representing Native American Women in the Late Nineteenth Century.")

Protests against corruption in the reservation system led in 1887 to congressional passage of the **Dawes Severalty Act**, which divided reservation lands into allotments for individual Native families, the remaining acreage to be sold to non-Indians. Allotment was meant as a reform alternative to demeaning reservation existence, a proposal encouraged by reformers like Jackson, but the way the system played out actually exacerbated Native peoples' misery. Where land was not very fertile, Native American families could not support themselves on their allotments, and whites managed to gain control of land that could be productively farmed. The allotment program also often deepened the dependency of Indigenous women on their men, following the pattern of white society. In contrast to communal landholding and farming practices, the allotment program meant that women who chose to divorce their husbands risked losing the economic resources that were under the control of male heads of household. A group of Hopi women vainly protested to the Bureau of Indian Affairs in 1894. "The family, the dwelling house and the field are inseparable," they insisted, "because the woman is the heart of these, and they rest with her."[8] In some areas, however, Native women found other means of contributing to the household economy. As tourism flourished in the West toward the end of the century, the baskets and blankets women produced became desirable commodities. In the Pacific Northwest's Puget Sound area, for example, Indigenous women from a number of Native nations, including the Snoqualmies, became migrant farm laborers, providing crucial labor as pickers on land that had once belonged to Indigenous peoples. These same women further supplemented their income by selling local crafts, including baskets, to white women consumers and tourists or by posing for photographs.

Colonial Settler Families in the West

As Native American control over the West weakened, American colonial settlement across the vast continent continued apace. The passage of the **Homestead Act** in 1862 granted 160 acres to individuals, including many immigrants and some women, who were willing to cultivate and "improve" the land. The railroads, themselves beneficiaries of federal largesse, also sold land to settlers to establish towns along their routes. Through this process, the broad central Plains — from Minnesota to Montana to Oklahoma — were settled and Americanized. By the early twentieth century, one-quarter of the U.S. population lived west of the Mississippi.

This population was diverse. After Reconstruction, a small but steady stream of African American families was drawn west by the hope of independent farming. In all-Black towns, such as Nicodemus, Kansas, and Langston, Oklahoma, African American women found ways to support their families that were less demeaning than working as domestic servants for white people. In Boley, Oklahoma, Lulu Smith started a dressmaking business; other women ran boardinghouses, catering services, and general stores.[9] European immigrants played a large role in western colonial settlement, especially in the northern territories. In the late nineteenth century, in the period of mass immigration, one out of every two western settlers was foreign-born. The Homestead Act allowed land grants to immigrants who intended to become citizens. They, too, formed their own communities where they could live and speak and farm as they had in their home countries.

For a while, in villages throughout New Mexico, Arizona, and southern California, Spanish-speaking women, descendants of original Mexican inhabitants, continued to live much as their mothers and grandmothers had. They maintained adobe homes and cultivated small plots, while the men in their families were increasingly drawn away to work in the mines, on the railroads, or on the commercial farms and ranches run by whites (known as Anglos). Ironically, while these Hispanic women were regarded by Anglo society as oppressed, they enjoyed considerable authority in their own communities. Local practices favored female property owning, and when widowed, women in these Hispanic enclaves preferred to head their own households rather than remarry. As the extension of the railroads brought national market pressures and a cash economy closer, however, the need for money became greater. Many of these women lost their distinctive advantages and followed their husbands into paid labor, as domestic servants in Anglo towns or agricultural wage laborers in Anglo fields.

Despite many differences, all these rural western communities relied on women's unpaid labor, in striking contrast to the emphasis on middle-class female leisure and working-class female wage labor in the more urbanized parts of American society. Western farm women did their homemaking in an environment where homes had to be built from scratch. On the Plains, after spending the first few months living in temporary shelters, settler families would move into huts made of sod, the top layer of soil so dense with the roots of prairie grass that it could be cut into bricks. Women sprinkled their dirt walls and floors with water to keep down the dust, and they decorated their unlikely homes as lavishly as they could, eager to banish the discomfort of being surrounded by dirt. Westering was an ongoing process; as families frequently moved and resettled on more promising land, it was left to the women to repeat the work of creating — both physically and emotionally — new home environments.

Western women cooked, did laundry, and made clothes without benefit of many of the technological improvements — such as running water — available in more industrialized areas. While their husbands cultivated specialized commercial crops, the wives cared for animals and grew food for the family table. One Arizona woman described her morning chores: "Get up, turn out my chickens, draw a pail of water, . . . make a fire, put potatoes to cook, then brush and sweep half inch of dust off floor, feed three litters of chickens, then mix biscuits, get breakfast, milk, besides work in the house, and this morning had to go half mile after calves." She also contributed to her family's unending need for cash by churning 24 pounds of butter in four days. "Quit with a headache," she wrote in her diary. "Done too much work."[10]

Some women were inspired to try homesteading on their own. Perhaps as many as 15 percent of late nineteenth-century American homesteads were at some point controlled by women. Unmarried women who controlled their own homesteads combined two resources irresistible to male settlers, land and female labor, and were besieged by marriage proposals. As one young Oklahoma woman wrote, as soon as she was awarded a claim, men started to court her: "The letters began pouring in — men wanting to marry me, men all the way from twenty-one to seventy-five."[11]

Of all the burdens for women settlers on the Great Plains, drudgery and loneliness seem to have been the worst, especially in the years when towns were still being established. Unlike their husbands, women rarely left the homestead — bound to the cookstove and the washtub. Ignored when she complained that she "never got to go nowhere, or see anybody . . . or [do] anything but work," one Oklahoma woman packed up the children and fled. Overtaken by a wind and ice storm, she almost froze to death and ended up back at the homestead, disabled for life.[12]

◆ **European Immigrants in the Great Plains**
As with the growth of American industry, the settling of the Great Plains required immigrant labor and determination. Scandinavians were particularly drawn to homesteading. This Norwegian immigrant to Minnesota, Beret Olesdater Hagebak, sits alone in front of a small house made of sod, the most common building material available on the treeless Plains. Her picture captures the experience of immigrant farmwomen, who suffered both the cultural disorientation of immigration and the isolation of Plains farm life. *Lac qui Parle County Historical Society/Museum.*

In 1867, the organization of an agricultural communities' group, the **National Grange** (the full title was the Order of the Patrons of Husbandry), helped overcome women's isolation on the prairies. By the mid-1870s, three-quarters of the farmers of Kansas had joined.[13] Based on the premise that farm families had to cooperate to succeed against the corporate power of railroads and other monopolies, the Grange established farmer-run stores and grain elevators and promoted laws against unfair railroad rates. It also sponsored social and cultural events that enriched local community life and were of special importance to women, who played a prominent role in the Grange. Local chapters were required to have nine female members for every thirteen male members, and women served as officers and delegates to the national meetings. The sense of community that the Grange created prepared the way for more overtly political expressions of agricultural discontent, including the farmers' alliances in the late 1880s and the Populist movement of the 1890s (see "Rural Protest, the People's Party, and the Battle for Woman Suffrage").

The Wild West

Alongside the families drawn by the promise of land and economic self-sufficiency were other westerners pursuing riskier schemes for getting rich. Both groups Americanized the West, but in different ways. While family settlement imported the American social and cultural values of industriousness and domesticity, these other westerners brought with them capitalism, wage labor, and subordination to growing corporate power. Despite their status as icons of individual freedom, the colorful cowboys of the cattle range and the grizzled miners of the gold and silver mines were wage laborers and suffered from wage dependence as much as industrial workers in New York and Chicago.

The contrasts between the Wild West and the Settler West are particularly clear in terms of the radically different gender practices on which they rested. In the mines and cattle ranges, women wage earners were rare. Annie Oakley's riding and roping skills made her a featured player in Buffalo Bill Cody's Wild West Show in the 1890s, but cowgirls were a staple only in the Wild West of popular culture. The rapidly expanding female labor force found elsewhere in America existed in the West only in the largest cities, such as Denver, San Francisco, and Seattle.

There were other sorts of women in the Wild West, however. At first, most were sex workers. Like the miners and cowboys who were their customers, they were Black and white, English- and Spanish-speaking, native- and foreign-born. Initially, many of these women worked for themselves, as what one historian calls "proprietor prostitutes."[14] A few were able to earn or marry their way into respectable society. Others bought or rented brothels, hired other women, and became successful, if disreputable, businesswomen. In 1890, in Helena, Montana, one of the most prosperous real estate entrepreneurs was an Irish-born former sex worker, "Chicago Joe." But for most, sex work was a thoroughly losing proposition. Two-thirds of sex workers died young of sexually transmitted diseases, botched abortions, alcohol or drug abuse, suicide, or homicide. As in other western businesses, the initial period of entrepreneurial exuberance was replaced by consolidated ownership. By the early twentieth century, men — pimps, landlords, and police — enjoyed most of the profits from western sex work.

More women — some rich, most poor — gradually began to move to western centers of industry. The wives of western mine owners lived in expensive, elegant homes, hired servants, and imported luxuries. The determination of a few to use their husbands' fortunes on behalf of their own social and philanthropic ambitions was legendary. Phoebe Appleton Hearst, whose husband got rich in the mines of California and Nevada, was a major benefactor of the University of California at Berkeley. Margaret (Molly) Tobin Brown, the daughter of Irish Catholic immigrants, married one of the rare individual prospectors to become wealthy off the mines. She bought and refurnished an elegant Denver mansion, hired tutors to teach her the ways of the upper class, and became a generous civic donor. In 1912, she survived the sinking of the ill-fated *Titanic*, earning herself the nickname of "Unsinkable Molly Brown." She used her wealth to support the Colorado suffrage movement (see "Rural Protest, the People's Party, and the Battle for Woman Suffrage").

At the other end of the class scale, wage-earning miners and cowboys also formed families. The immigrant copper miners of Anaconda, Montana, married the young Irish women who worked as domestic servants for their bosses or as waitresses in the local hotels. Mexican miners in Colorado brought their wives north to live with them and settle permanently in the United States. These working-class wives rarely took jobs outside the home, although they did earn money by feeding and housing single male miners, cowboys, and lumberjacks.

Western housewives lived with the constant fear of losing their husbands to violent death on the range or in the mines. Recognizing that unions would fight to raise wages and make working conditions safer, they were strong supporters of organized labor. They formed union auxiliaries that were very active during the militant strikes that rocked the region. In Cripple Creek, Colorado, miners' wives were involved in 1893 when the radical Western Federation of Miners won higher wages and in 1904 when the state militia drove union activists out of town. By far the most prominent female labor activist in the region was the legendary Irish-born Mary Harris ("Mother") Jones, who began her career as an organizer for miners' unions in the late 1890s. **Mother Jones** focused her attention on the miners — her "boys" — but she also understood the power of miners' wives and organized them into "mop and broom brigades" that effectively harassed strike-breakers. Referring to one of the family dynasties most identified with corporate greed, Jones declared: "God Almighty made women and the Rockefeller gang of thieves made the ladies."[15]

Jones's contempt for female gentility notwithstanding, western working-class wives were as careful as women of the leisure classes to maintain a distinction between their own status as respectable women and the status of the disreputable women who had preceded them. Family life was gradually displacing the world of the dance halls and brothels. Respectable women took care not to live in the same areas as "fast" women. "If the world of work was divided into laborers and employers," writes one historian of the western female experience, "the world of women was divided into good women and bad."[16]

◆ LATE NINETEENTH-CENTURY IMMIGRATION

While Americans were moving westward in the late nineteenth century, immigrants were pouring into the country, 27 million in the half century after 1880. These numbers dwarfed pre–Civil War immigration. Five million came from Italy and an equal number from Germany, as well as 2 million Eastern European Jews, 1 million Polish Catholics, and 1 million Scandinavians. A small but growing number of Asians and Mexicans also came to the United States in these years. By 1910, Asians constituted 2 percent of all arriving immigrants. Numbers of Mexican immigrants are harder to determine. Until 1924, when the U.S. Border Patrol was officially established, the Mexican-U.S. border was virtually unregulated, and those crossing back and forth melded into already existing Spanish-speaking American communities. This massive immigration turned the United States into a much more ethnically and religiously diverse people, no longer preponderantly English and Protestant but now broadly European, with a growing minority of resident Asians and Mexicans.

The gender patterns of these immigrations were complex. Among Slavic, Greek, and Italian immigrants, more men than women came to the United States. However, many men came as temporary workers and returned eventually to their homelands. As they did, and as more women came to marry those who remained, sex ratios tended to even out. Some groups, notably Eastern European Jews and new Irish immigrants, initially came in more gender-balanced numbers. Eventually, women constituted between 30 and 40 percent of all immigrants in these years (see the Appendix, Table 3: Immigration to the United States, 1900–2020).

The Decision to Immigrate

Women decided to leave their homelands and come to the United States for many reasons, some of which they shared with men. Faced with poverty, limited opportunity, and rigid class structures at home, families dispatched members to work in the United States and send money back to those who remained. The booming U.S. economy had an insatiable need for workers in its factories, mines, and kitchens, and it lured men and women alike with its promises of high wages and easy prosperity. "This was the time . . . when America was known to foreigners as the land where you'd get rich," remembered Pauline Newman, who arrived from Lithuania in 1901. "There's gold on the sidewalk! All you have to do is pick it up."[17] Political persecution also pushed people out of their homelands. Jews began emigrating in large numbers in the 1880s to escape growing anti-Semitism in Eastern Europe, especially the violent, deadly riots called pogroms. Similarly, the upheavals that culminated in the Mexican Revolution of 1910 drove men and women north.

Women also had their own distinctive reasons for emigrating. Many were drawn by the reputation that the United States was developing as a society that welcomed independence for women. A common story for young women of all groups involved fleeing from an overbearing, patriarchal father and from the threat of an arranged marriage. That was why Emma Goldman fled Russia in 1885. Upon arriving in America, she began a life of political activism that eventually made her the most notorious radical in the United States (see Reading into the Past: "Living My Life").

READING INTO THE PAST

EMMA GOLDMAN
Living My Life

Emma Goldman (1869–1940) was raised in Russia by an overbearing father and an uninterested stepmother. She was already interested in radical politics before she left in 1885 to follow her sister Helena and to become a garment worker in Rochester, New York. Within a few years, she had become deeply involved with the anarchist movement. Her autobiography, Living My Life *(1931), is one of the most widely read life stories in American women's history.*

Helena also hated to leave me behind. She knew of the bitter friction that existed between Father and me. She offered to pay my fare, but Father would not consent to my going. I pleaded, begged, wept. Finally I threatened to jump into the Neva [River], whereupon he yielded. Equipped with twenty-five roubles — all that the old man would give me — I left without regrets. Since my earliest recollection, home had been stifling, my father's presence terrifying. . . . [Father] had tried desperately to marry me off at the age of fifteen. I had protested, begging to be permitted to continue my studies. In his frenzy he threw my French grammar into the fire, shouting: "Girls do not have to learn much! All a Jewish daughter needs to know is how to prepare gefüllte fish, cut noodles fine, and give the man plenty of children." I would not listen to his schemes; I wanted to study, to know life, to travel. Besides, I never would marry for anything but love, I stoutly maintained. It was really to escape my father's plans for me that I had insisted on going to America.

SOURCE: Emma Goldman, *Living My Life* (1931; repr., New York: Courier Dover Publications, 1970), 1:11.

ANALYZING PRIMARY SOURCES

1. As an anarchist, Goldman was very critical of U.S. politics and economic organization, yet in this passage she suggests the positive qualities America could represent to a young immigrant woman. What were they?

Other women came to the United States as wives or to become wives, to join husbands who had migrated before them or to complete arranged marriages. Immigration from China was still largely banned by federal law. The Japanese government encouraged male immigrants to send back to Japan for women to marry. These women in turn sent letters and photographs to their potential husbands. This was a modern version of a traditional Japanese practice, but *shaskin kekkon* (literally, "photograph marriages") were regarded by Americans as akin to sex work and still another indication of the allegedly low morals of Asians. Similar arrangements were common among European immigrants. Rachel Kahn came from Ukraine to North Dakota in 1894 to marry a Russian immigrant farmer with whom she had only exchanged pictures.[18]

Some women undoubtedly migrated for reasons so personal and painful that they were hidden from public view. Unmarried women who had become pregnant might flee or be sent away so that the scandal could be more easily hidden. The father of Lucja Krajulis's child would not marry her but sent her instead to the United States, where she was shuttled about among fellow Lithuanians.[19] During the 1910 Mexican Revolution, women in the countryside were raped by armed marauders, and crossing the border provided them escape from their shame.

The Immigrant's Journey

Having decided to move to the United States, immigrant women had many obstacles to negotiate. Passage in the steerage class of a transoceanic steamship in 1900 cost the modern equivalent of $400. It took ten to twenty days to cross from Italy to New York and twice as long from Japan to San Francisco, during which time passengers slept in cramped, unhealthy conditions below deck. One can only imagine the experience of pregnant women or mothers of infants. Photos of arriving immigrants show dazed women, with babies held tightly in their arms and older children clinging to their skirts.

In 1892, the first federal receiving station for immigrants was established on **Ellis Island** in New York Harbor. The majority of immigrants were passed through quickly, although individuals judged "unfit" for admission could be isolated, confined, and eventually deported. Asian women were more likely to be kept for long periods at **Angel Island**, the equivalent site established in San Francisco Bay in 1910. Assumed to be sexually immoral, they were detained until they could establish their respectability by answering endless questions about themselves and the men they planned to marry. "Had I known it was like this," Mrs. Jew, a thirty-year-old wife of a Chinese merchant, recalled in 1922, "I never would have wanted to come."[20]

Young European women in transit were regarded as sexually vulnerable rather than sexually immoral. Stories circulated of unaccompanied and disoriented

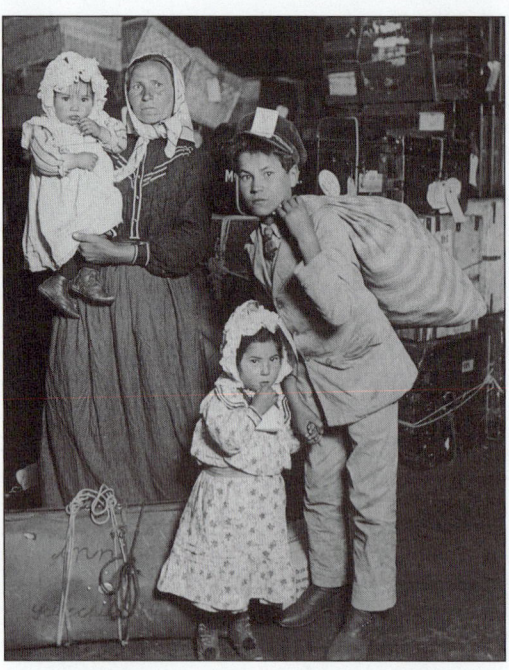

◆ **Italian Immigrant Family at Ellis Island (1905)**
Ellis Island became an official federal receiving station in 1894. This family's entire possessions were lost when they debarked the ship. There is no adult man with the mother and children, suggesting that he had arrived in the United States earlier and had then brought his family to be with him. The photographer, Lewis Hine, was an American-born sociologist who worked with the National Child Labor Society. *Gift of David Vestal/Art Institute of Chicago.*

immigrant girls tricked or forced into sex work. This phenomenon was known at the time as "white slavery," a term that invoked memories of Black chattel slavery. Feared as an international conspiracy to waylay and prostitute young women, this trafficking in women was a major focus for anxieties about women and immigration. The actual extent of the practice is difficult to determine.

Many immigrants kept on moving beyond their point of arrival in the United States, following friends or family or rumors of work. By the turn of the century, the populations of large midwestern cities such as Chicago and Milwaukee were preponderantly foreign-born. Numerous mining towns of the West were dense with immigrants as well. Many immigrants, wishing to retain something of their familiar homeland, preferred to live among people from their own village or region, but this practice could leave them ignorant of much about their new surroundings. Reformer Jane Addams told the poignant story of an Italian woman who had never seen roses in the few blocks of Chicago that she knew, thought they grew only in Italy, and feared that she would never enjoy their beauty again.[21]

Reception of the Immigrants

The United States's pride in its status as a nation of immigrants is embodied in New York Harbor's Statue of Liberty, a giant female figure presented to the United States by the people of France in 1885 to represent the two countries' common embrace of liberty. Suffragists, who were not allowed to participate in the unveiling, protested that a statue of liberty "embodied in a woman where no woman has political liberty" was totally inconsistent.[22] The poem inscribed on the statue's base was written by Emma Lazarus, a descendant of Sephardic Jews who had arrived in the mid-seventeenth century. The words she wrote welcome the world's oppressed, those "huddled masses yearning to breathe free, / The wretched refuse of your teeming shore." But Lazarus's sentiment was not the norm. In the late nineteenth century, many native-born Americans regarded the incoming masses as disturbingly different aliens who could never assimilate.

Anti-immigrant legislation initially targeted Asians. The **Page Law** of 1875, the very first federal legislation meant to discourage immigration, was directed at Chinese women, on the assumption that most were sex workers. In 1882, Congress passed a more comprehensive law, the **Chinese Exclusion Act**, that banned further immigration of Chinese laborers and their families. The few women who could prove that they were the wives or daughters of Chinese merchants already living in the United States were exempted. Chinese immigrants protested this new discrimination.

Once Chinese immigration had virtually ceased, Japanese workers began to come to the United States, but by the 1890s, anti-Asian sentiment on the West Coast had surfaced against them as well. In 1907, in the so-called Gentlemen's Agreement (a reference to the U.S. and Japanese governments), the United States and Japan agreed to restrict further immigration.

Laws against European immigrants were not passed until 1921 and 1924, when highly restrictive national quotas were established, remaining in place until 1965. Even before these laws, European immigrants were the targets of considerable prejudice and resentment. Degrading ethnic stereotypes were widely circulated as innocently amusing. Southern and Eastern European immigrants were seen as peoples whose strangeness and difference were fundamental, physical, and ineradicable. Religion was a major concern. The hundreds of thousands of Jews who arrived from Eastern Europe after 1880 were the first major group of non-Christians to settle in the United States. Even Catholics were regarded by American Protestants as so emotional and superstitious as barely to be fellow believers in Christ. Their devotion to a foreign pope was the source of much suspicion. Anti-Semitic and anti-Catholic attitudes abounded even among otherwise liberal-minded Americans. Susan B. Anthony could not understand by what logic "these Italians come over with the idea that they must be paid as much as intelligent white men."[23]

Americans were especially wary of immigrant gender relations, regarding their own attitudes as modern and those of the newcomers as backward and patriarchal. They were particularly uneasy with the reproductive behavior of immigrant women. While the birthrates of native-born women had been falling for some time (see the Appendix, Chart 1: U.S. Birthrate, 1820–2020), immigrant families were large. In 1903, President Theodore Roosevelt, concerned that immigrants' higher birthrates were overtaking those of native-born Americans, blamed middle-class women who were working or going to college instead of having babies for what he called "race suicide." "If the women do not recognize that the greatest thing

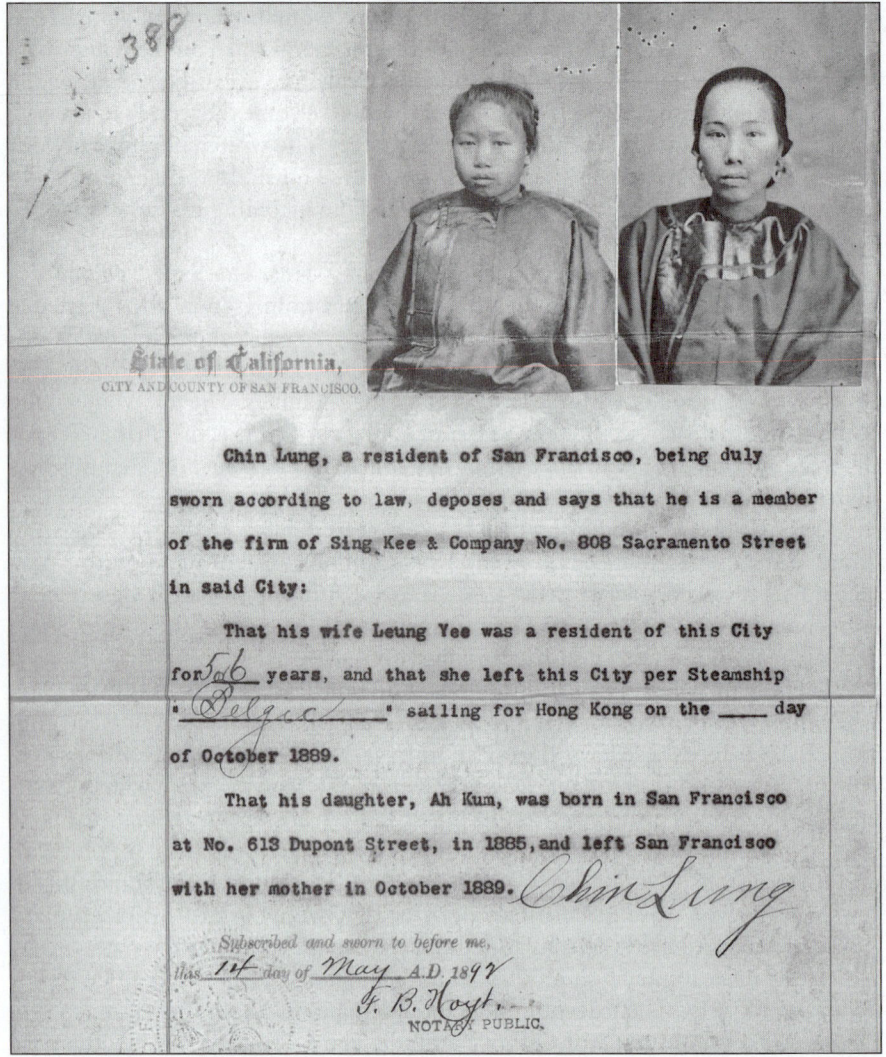

State of California,

CITY AND COUNTY OF SAN FRANCISCO.

Chin Lung, a resident of San Francisco, being duly sworn according to law, deposes and says that he is a member of the firm of Sing Kee & Company No. 808 Sacramento Street in said City:

That his wife Leung Yee was a resident of this City for 5 & 6 years, and that she left this City per Steamship "*Belgic*" sailing for Hong Kong on the _____ day of October 1889.

That his daughter, Ah Kum, was born in San Francisco at No. 613 Dupont Street, in 1885, and left San Francisco with her mother in October 1889. *Chin Lung*

Subscribed and sworn to before me, this *14* day of *May* A.D. 189*7*

F. B. Hoyt.

NOTARY PUBLIC.

◆ A Document of Chinese Immigration

Through diligent research, historian Judy Yung uncovered this sworn testimony given by her great-grandfather of her great-grandmother's immigration to the United States in 1892. She found that there were several strategic lies embedded within the document. First, his wife Leung Yee had not lived in the United States previously but was immigrating for the first time in 1892. Second, the daughter that she claimed on this document was in fact a young servant of the family. Such deceits were necessary — and common — to circumvent the prohibitions of the Chinese Exclusion Act of 1882. *File 12017/37232 for Leong Lee, Chinese Departure Application Case Files, 1912–1943, San Francisco District Office, Immigration and Naturalization Service, Record Group 85, National Archives and Records Administration — Pacific Region, San Bruno, CA.*

for any woman is to be a good wife and mother," he declared in the introduction to *The Woman Who Toils*, "why, that nation has cause to be alarmed about its future."[24] After some time in the United States, however, immigrant women started to want smaller families, too. Margaret Sanger, herself the daughter of Irish immigrants, founded the American birth control movement in the 1910s as a response to immigrant women's pleas for reliable ways to prevent unwanted pregnancy (see "The Birth Control Movement" in Chapter 8).

Immigrant Girls

Immigrant mothers and daughters confronted America very differently. Low wages made it difficult for immigrant men to meet the American standard of being the sole support of their families. Secondary wage earners were usually teenage children, not wives. Just as their families needed immigrant daughters' earnings, the expanding labor force needed their labor. Young girls were plunged immediately into the booming American economy, while their mothers remained largely homebound.

Young immigrant women predominated in the two largest categories of female wage labor, domestic labor and factory work. German, Irish, Polish, and Mexican girls met late nineteenth-century middle-class families' demand for servants. By contrast, Italian parents did not want their daughters to work as servants in strange households and preferred that they take jobs where other family members could oversee their activities, such as in seasonal fruit picking.

Young immigrant women were also drawn into factory work, making their greatest contribution to the garment industry. The mass production of clothes in the United States could not have occurred without their labor. By 1890, one out of three garment workers was a woman, and most of these women were immigrants. Some — Russian Jews, Japanese, Italians — had worked in clothing factories in their home countries. New York and Chicago were the centers of the ready-made clothing industry in the United States, but garment factories filled with immigrant women workers could be found throughout the country, from El Paso to San Francisco to Baltimore. Paid by the piece and pushed to work ever more quickly, young women earned low wages and risked occupational injuries. Sexual harassment was an additional problem for young immigrant women factory workers, as it was hard not to yield to the foremen who controlled their jobs.

Most of these teenage women workers lived with parents or other relatives, and intergenerational relations could be very tense. More than their brothers, girls were expected to turn over most of their wages to their parents. Mothers needed the money for household expenses, but daughters longed to spend some of their earnings on themselves. Disagreements did not end there. Daughters wanted to dress in the modern American style, while mothers wanted them to look and behave like respectable girls in the old country. Battles could be even more intense with fathers. No one resisted Old World patriarchy more intensely than its daughters. The Russian Jewish novelist Anzia Yezierska wrote often of this theme. "Should

I let him crush me as he crushed [my sisters]?" a character in her 1925 novel, *Bread Givers*, said of her father. "No. This is America. Where children are people. . . . It's a new life now. In America, women don't need men to boss them."[25]

Immigrant Wives and Mothers

While unmarried immigrant women were more likely to be wage earners than native-born women, the opposite was true of their mothers, very few of whom worked outside their homes. This behavior was not simply a carryover of Old World standards; Eastern European Jewish wives, for instance, had traditionally been shopkeepers or market vendors. Given the family wage system in the United States, in which it was assumed that adult men could and should support wives and dependent children, adult immigrant women had difficulty finding paid work. Immigrant wives were nonetheless expected to contribute to the family economy. Because of the numbers of single male immigrants and the preference of many groups for living among people from their own country, boarding was very common among immigrants. Middle-class observers, who regarded familial privacy as sacred, condemned the immigrant practice of boarders living within families. Immigrants recognized the tensions but regarded them more tolerantly, and stories of liaisons between amorous boarders and discontented housewives were a source of much amusement in immigrant culture.

Immigrant women's housekeeping and childrearing tasks were daunting, both because of poverty and the surrounding alien culture. In densely populated cities, apartments were crowded and residents still relied on backyard wells and outdoor privies, augmented by public baths. Children playing on busy city streets required additional supervision. Women hauled water up flights of stairs, as they did coal and wood purchased for fuel, and fought a constant battle against ash and soot. Photographer Jacob Riis did pioneering work documenting these conditions. (See Primary Sources: "Jacob Riis's Photographs of Immigrant Girls and Women.") Even so, American observers were frequently astonished at the levels of cleanliness immigrant women were able to maintain. While middle-class women dealt with their domestic obligations by hiring immigrant servants, immigrant women had no choice but to do their own scrubbing and ironing.

As Jane Addams observed, aging immigrant women were faced with particular dilemmas, especially if they did not have other generations to care for them. Unable to earn money, and with government old-age provisions many decades in the future, they were threatened with institutionalization in the American equivalent of workhouses.

Immigrant mothers had the added responsibility of preserving customary ways against the tremendous forces working to Americanize them and their families. They continued to cook traditional foods and observe religious obligations, while their husbands and children entered into the American economic mainstream to make the family's living. As practices that were ancient and reflexive became deliberate and problematic, it fell to women to defend and perpetuate the old ways, thus laying the basis for what would eventually become

American ethnic identity. Such practices constituted implicit resistance to the forces of Americanization and cultural homogenization. For the time being, however, such immigrant mothers were dismissed by their children as old-fashioned and quaint, their skills and knowledge irrelevant to the new world that their daughters mastered with such verve. Once again, Jane Addams subtly captured the emotional tenor of this role reversal in her description of the dilemma of immigrant women in search of runaway children in Chicago: "It is as if they did not know how to search for their children without the assistance of the children themselves."[26]

Despite these obstacles, adult immigrant women helped to construct lasting ethnic communities. In the mining town of Anaconda, Montana, Irish women, struggling to meet their family needs, nonetheless raised money to build St. Patrick's Catholic Church in 1888. This story was repeated in the immigrant neighborhoods within which the American Catholic Church developed. Occasionally, immigrant wives' community activism took a political turn, as in 1902, when New York City Jewish women demonstrated against the rising cost of meat in the city's kosher markets. Like native-born middle-class women, late nineteenth-century immigrant women formed and joined associations, but for different reasons. They had been drawn to the United States by the promise of greater freedom, if not for themselves, then for their children. But they were learning that to realize that promise, they had to find ways to work together.

◆ CENTURY'S END: CHALLENGES, CONFLICT, AND IMPERIAL VENTURES

For many of the women who immigrated to the United States or who migrated across the continent, the American dream remained elusive. Their frustrated hopes helped to fuel a dramatic crisis at century's end. The national economy, which had gone through a series of boom and bust cycles since the beginnings of industrialization in the 1830s, experienced its greatest economic crisis yet in 1893, as overextension of the railroad system, decline in gold reserves, and international collapse in agricultural prices set off a long, deep economic contraction that kept layoffs high, wages low, and economic growth stalled for four years. In the cities, the newest immigrants bore the brunt of massive unemployment and deep family disruption. In the agricultural heartland, crops could not be sold at a profit, and family farms failed. Factory workers and farmers were not natural allies; they were not even particularly sympathetic to each other. Nonetheless, the two groups moved together to confront the wealthy strata that ruled a complacent nation. The turmoil of the 1890s unleashed an unprecedented wave of industrial strikes and raised the prospects for a political movement, **Populism**, that mounted the first systematic challenge to entrenched political power since the rise of the Republican Party in the 1850s.

In the hotly contested presidential contest of 1896, the probusiness Republican candidate William McKinley defeated the Democratic-Populist nominee William Jennings Bryan, ending for the time being these challenges to entrenched power. In the wake of their victory, corporate leaders and Republican politicians brought the United States to join European nations in the race to acquire overseas colonies.

Women were active everywhere in the crises of the 1890s. They were the victims of desperate economic conditions, ardent supporters of strikes, spokeswomen for political challenges, and supporters and opponents of the new imperial ventures. During this decade, American women reached a new level of political prominence through two distinct achievements — winning the first victories for woman suffrage in the West and establishing settlement houses to assist urban immigrants.

Rural Protest, the People's Party, and the Battle for Woman Suffrage

The years after Reconstruction were difficult for American farmers. With the dream of economic independence and self-sufficiency receding, farming families were driven into debt by the pressures of falling prices and rising costs. Culturally, rural Americans also felt that they were losing ground — and often their children — to the magnet of city life. The powerful railroad corporations that set rates for transporting their crops were a particular target of farmers' anger. "It is an undeniable fact that the condition of the farmer and their poor drudging wives is every year becoming more intolerable," Minnesotan Mary Travis complained in 1880. "We are robbed and crowded to the wall on every side, our crop [is] taken for whatever the middlemen are of a mind to give us, and we are obligated to give them whatever they have the force to ask for their goods or go without, and all this means so . . . much toil, and less help for the farmer's wife."[27]

The Grange gave way in the 1880s to farmers' alliances. While continuing to encourage community life, the alliances encouraged farmers to form buying and selling cooperatives to circumvent the powers of the banks and railroads. The Southern Alliance, which began in Texas in 1877, was particularly strong. In it, non-elite southern white women began to take a visible, public role. Southern Black farmers organized a separate Colored Farmers' Alliance, approximately half of whose 750,000 members were women. African American sharecroppers, who were trapped in debt because they had to acquire their supplies from their landlords at exorbitant credit rates, were particularly attracted to cooperatives. The People's Grocery in Memphis, the lynching of whose owner in 1892 catapulted Ida B. Wells into her reform career (see Primary Sources: "Ida B. Wells, 'Race Woman,'" in Chapter 6), was probably one such cooperative enterprise.

By 1892, farmers' alliances in the Midwest and South came together to form a new political party, ambitiously named the **People's Party** and commonly known as the Populists. Women were active in its meteoric life. Frances Willard, an important figure at the founding convention in St. Louis, brought the large and powerful **Woman's Christian Temperance Union (WCTU)** with her into the new effort. Several of the People's Party's most successful organizers were also women. Kansan Mary Elizabeth Lease, daughter of Irish immigrants, was the fieriest of these radical female orators. "You wonder, perhaps, at the zeal and enthusiasm of the Western women in this reform movement," Lease proclaimed at the founding convention. "We endured hardships, dangers and privations, hours of loneliness, fear and sorrow; [w]e helped our loved ones to make the prairie blossom . . . yet after all our years of toil and privations, dangers and hardship upon the Western frontier, monopoly is taking our homes from us."[28]

The Populist insurgency lasted only four years, but it left an enduring mark on the history of women's rights. In the Reconstruction years, suffragists had fought for political rights via the U.S. Constitution. The very obstacles that the Supreme Court cited in its 1875 *Minor v. Happersett* case, that suffrage was not a right of national citizenship but a privilege controlled by the separate states, opened an alternate door to suffrage. During the 1890s, while national politics remained inhospitable to reform, the focus for woman suffrage, as for other democratic reforms, shifted to the state level. In several western states, the People's Party endorsed woman suffrage, giving it new life. Voter referenda were held to amend state constitutions to include votes for women.

The most important of these campaigns occurred in 1893, when the women of Colorado's suffrage societies, labor union auxiliaries, WCTU chapters, and Knights of Labor locals joined together to convince male voters to enfranchise them by amending the state constitution. In contrast to the violent, widespread class conflict in the western mining industry, the advocates of woman suffrage were proud of their ability to "work unitedly and well" for a common goal.[29] Middle- and upper-class women contributed money to hold giant rallies. Their respectability offset the charge that sex workers' votes would further corrupt the world of politics. Suffragists linked their cause to struggling farmers and wage earners and asked for the vote as a tool against the entrenched power of railroads and mining corporations. "The money question has power to reach into the most sheltered home and bring want and desolation," Lease proclaimed. "Women have not invaded politics; politics have invaded the home."[30] Although suffragists had appealed to all political parties, People's Party support was crucial to victory. "There is less prejudice against and a stronger belief in equal rights in the newer communities," wrote Denver journalist Ellis Meredith of this western victory. "The pressure of hard times, culminating in the panic of 1893, undoubtedly contributed to the success of the People's Party and to its influence the suffrage cause owes much."[31] Three years later, Idaho women won a similar victory by an even greater margin.

Campaigns to get male voters to support woman suffrage amendments to state constitutions were also waged in Kansas and California, but they failed because of partisan conflict. In Kansas in 1894, two out of three male voters voted against woman suffrage, and, according to Populist suffragist Annie Diggs, "the grief and the disappointment of the Kansas women were indescribable."[32] In 1896, the issue was put before the men of California. Seventy-six-year-old Susan B. Anthony went to the state to work for suffrage. At first, all three political parties endorsed the referendum, and labor, Socialist, Spanish-language, and immigrant newspapers also came out in its favor. But when national People's Party leaders decided to campaign in the presidential election that year solely on the issue of currency reform (establishing a more inflationary monetary standard based not just on the value of gold but also of silver and gold "bimetallism"), the political situation changed dramatically. The Democratic Party joined with the Populists in political unity, and the two parties "fused" behind the presidential candidacy of the charismatic Nebraskan orator

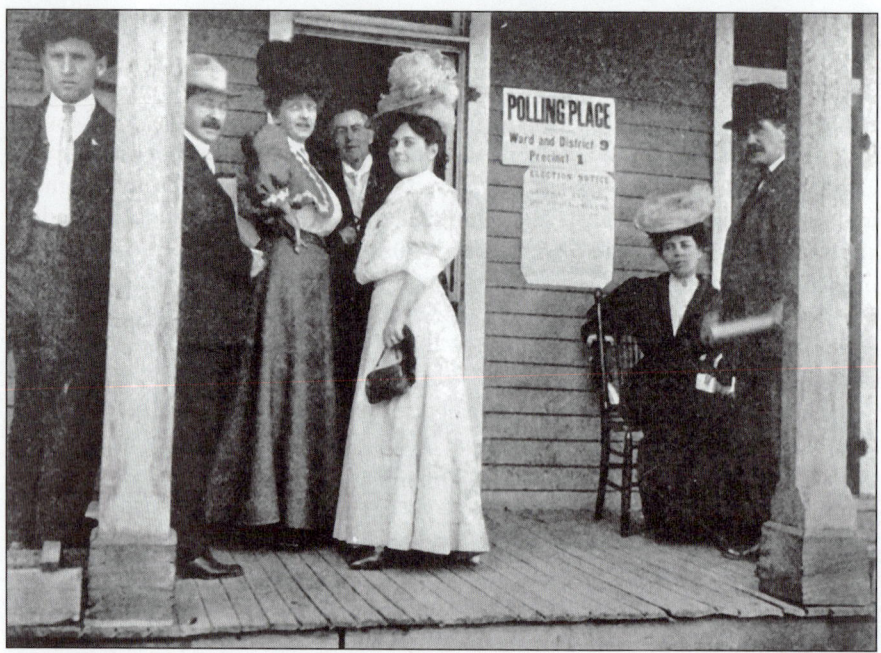

◆ **Early Women Voters in Colorado (1907)**
In 1893, the Populist-controlled legislature of Colorado called for a referendum to amend the state constitution to enfranchise women voters, the first time that the issue had been put before large numbers of male voters. Colorado was a booming state, the center of the mining industry, home both to the owners of great fortunes and a large, militant working class. The woman suffrage referendum won with a strong majority, passing in over three-quarters of the counties. Women followed up their victory by voting in substantial numbers for state and federal offices. The pride that they took in their new status as active, voting citizens is obvious in the faces and stances of these women, standing with male voters outside a Denver polling place. *Denver Public Library/Bridgeman Images.*

William Jennings Bryan. Woman suffrage became a liability, and the People's Party refused to agitate on its behalf. Republicans turned against it, and the California referendum was defeated 45 percent to 55 percent. "We feel defeated, and it doesn't feel good," Anthony told a newspaper reporter. "But we must save ourselves for other States. 'Truth crushed to earth will rise again.'"[33]

In the South, woman suffrage, which had been held back by its association with Black suffrage and with the determination to reverse the Reconstruction-era effort to subordinate states' rights to federal authority, also got its first sustained support in the Populist era. In 1888, Texan Ann Other defended woman suffrage against its critics in the pages of the *Southern Mercury*, a Populist newspaper. "Those men who could think less of a woman because she took a judicious interest in the laws of her country would not be worth the while to mourn over," she wrote.[34]

Eventually, however, southern Populism was felled by the racial divisions inherited from slavery and the deepening racial inequality at century's end. Established white political power countered the threat of electoral cooperation between angry Black and white farmers with the new system of segregation and disfranchisement known as Jim Crow (see "Racial Conflict in Slavery's Aftermath" in Chapter 6). When southern suffrage campaigns resurfaced again in the twentieth century, they were forced to do so in the context of this aggressive racism, often arguing for white women's votes as a means for countering Black men's votes.

Nationally, the election of Republican William McKinley in 1896 signaled the defeat of the People's Party. For women, however, the party's brief career had enormous consequences. The women of Colorado and Idaho now had full voting rights, in federal as well as state elections. Woman suffrage had become a live political issue, and its center had shifted from the Northeast, where the movement had begun, farther west, where male voters identified it with a more democratic political system. Having driven the People's Party from the electoral arena, the Republican Party absorbed some of its reform agenda. After 1896, the issue of woman suffrage passed into the hands of the reform-minded wing of the Republican Party, along with other Populist concerns, such as ameliorating the impact of economic growth on the poor and the need for government regulation of corporations. As with the People's Party, women activists and reformers would prove to be numerous and influential among these newly designated "Progressives" (see "The Female Dominion" in Chapter 8).

Class Conflict and the Pullman Strike of 1894

Just as Populism was reaching its high point in 1893, the national economy collapsed, thousands of businesses failed, and nearly a quarter of wage workers lost their jobs. The severe depression exposed critical problems and deep social rifts. Women suffered, both as out-of-work wage earners and as wives of unemployed men. Federal and state governments, following the laissez-faire principle of nonintervention in the marketplace, offered no help. Private charities provided a few paying jobs — street cleaning for men and sewing for women — but their efforts were inadequate to meet the massive need. Across much of the country, the winter of 1893–1894 was one of the coldest ever recorded. Rosa Cavalleri, a recent immigrant from Italy to Chicago, recalled waiting in a line for free food: "Us poor women were frozen to death."[35] The spread of disease under such conditions — smallpox and typhoid in Chicago, diphtheria in New York City — showed the middle and upper classes that, in a complex, modern society, misery and want could not be confined to one class. Poverty put entire communities at risk.

For a handful, the moment heralded a new American revolution. Amid rising working-class discontent, twenty-four-year-old Emma Goldman found her calling as a radical agitator and orator. She was already under suspicion for her role in the attempted assassination of the chairman of the Carnegie Steel Corporation during a violent strike at its Homestead, Pennsylvania, plant in 1892. The next year she led a phalanx of unemployed workers in New York City. An advocate of anarchism, the political philosophy that condemned all government as illegitimate authority, she challenged the crowd, "Do you not realize that the State is the worst enemy you have? . . . The State is the pillar of capitalism and it is ridiculous to expect any redress from it."[36] She was arrested, tried, and sentenced to a year in prison for "inciting to riot." In jail, Goldman learned the trade of midwifery and became an advocate of sexual and reproductive freedom for working-class women.

The most dramatic of the strikes against falling wages and massive layoffs began in May 1894 at the Pullman Railroad Car Company just south of Chicago. Company founder George Pullman was proud of his paternalistic policy of providing for all his workers' needs; but now, determined to maintain profits, Pullman refused to lower rents in the company-owned housing, where employees were expected to live despite their diminished pay packets. Pullman's policy drew workers' wives as well as women workers into the conflict. "Holding their babies close for shields," the antistrike *Chicago Tribune* reported of a workers' demonstration, "the women still break past the patrol lines and go where no man dares to step."[37] As railroad workers nationwide shut down the railroad system rather than transport Pullman cars, pressure grew on the federal government to intervene. President Grover Cleveland sent six thousand federal troops to quell riots and occupy the rail yards in Chicago. By early July, the strike was broken.

The Settlement House Movement

The Pullman strike also affected the future of middle- and upper-class women by putting a new development in female social reform, the **settlement house movement**, on the historical map. Settlement houses were pioneered in England in the 1880s by male college graduates who chose to live among and serve the urban poor. By 1890, settlement houses were beginning to appear in the United States, with the important difference that most of their participants were middle- and upper-class women. The most influential settlement house was Hull-House, established in Chicago in 1889 by Jane Addams. (See Primary Sources: "Jane Addams Remembers Hull-House.")

Soon Hull-House was serving several thousand people per week, helping immigrant mothers with child care and encouraging the spread of American values and culture. In contrast to later, more coercive forms of Americanization, however, Hull-House valued immigrants for their home cultures, struggling with the gulf between immigrant mothers and their Americanized children. Rooms were made available for union meetings and political discussion clubs. Immigrants in the neighborhood attended concerts and enjoyed the use of a gymnasium. Labor activist Mary Kenney established a cooperative residence, named the Jane Club in homage to Addams, as an alternative to commercial boardinghouses for young wage-earning women away from their families. "Hull-House is meant to be the centre for all the work needed around it," a sympathetic observer explained, "not committed to one line of work, but open to all that leads the way to a higher life for the people."[38]

The Pullman strike gave new prominence and impetus to the women of Hull-House, who suddenly found themselves in the midst of Chicago's violent class conflict. Jane Addams, who had a reputation as an effective conciliator, was appointed to a special citizens' arbitration committee, but its members were unable to find a way to resolve the strike. Meanwhile, Florence Kelley, another Hull-House member, was developing a more direct, long-term response to the frustration and demands of working-class immigrant families. The daughter of a Republican congressman and herself a Cornell University graduate, Kelley shared Addams's privileged background but had moved further beyond the expectations of women of her class. While living in Germany, she had become a socialist and corresponded with Karl Marx's collaborator, Friedrich Engels, about the condition of the Chicago poor. In 1892, she wrote him, "The most visible work is [being done] at the present moment by a lot of women who are organizing trade unions of men and women."[39] Kelley had come to Hull-House to escape her own abusive husband and so knew something of wives' dependency. She deserves much of the credit for moving Hull-House, and with it the entire settlement movement, decisively in the direction of modern social welfare reform.

Kelley crafted a body of labor laws designed to shield working-class families from the worst impact of the wage labor system. In 1893, she and others submitted a bill to the Illinois state legislature to prohibit the employment of children, constrain home-based manufacturing, establish an eight-hour workday for adult women workers, and enable state officials to visit and monitor work sites for safety and health conditions. Offered as a legislative response to the growing social and economic crisis of the poor, the Illinois Factory and Workshop Inspection Act was passed about a year before the Pullman strike. Kelley was appointed chief factory inspector for the state and empowered to search out and prosecute violations of the new laws. She and her deputy inspectors, including Jane Club founder Mary Kenney (see "Organizing Women Workers: The Women's Trade Union League" in Chapter 8), drew the attention of reformers, the state government, and labor unions to the extent and abuses of the "sweating" system of subcontracting clothing manufacture under unsafe and underpaid conditions in Illinois and helped to initiate a nationwide campaign to improve conditions in the industry. Many states began to pass similar factory and tenement inspection laws.

Other provisions of the law were not so successful. Illinois garment manufacturers united in opposition to the eight-hour workday for women workers. In the bitter aftermath of the Pullman strike, the Illinois Supreme Court ruled in 1895 that limitations on the working hours of women were a violation of their individual freedom of contract, enacted without "due process of law." Kelley's father had helped to write the Fourteenth Amendment, which had enshrined the principle of due process in the U.S. Constitution, and she railed against the 1895 decision as a perversion of this principle, making it into "an insuperable obstacle for the protection of women and children."[40] Ending child labor, a priority of both middle-class reformers and trade unionists, also proved extremely difficult, as immigrant parents resisted efforts to deprive their families of young wage earners. But Kelley had chosen her life's work — to find the political backing and constitutional basis for social welfare provisions that would aid working-class women and families.

Women-based settlement houses soon appeared in other immigrant-dense cities, among them the Henry Street Settlement in New York City, led by Lillian Wald; the Neighborhood House in Dallas; and the Telegraph Hill Neighborhood Association in San Francisco. While many white settlement leaders personally believed in greater racial justice, they yielded to the prejudices of the era and practiced racial segregation in the institutions they established. In the South, middle-class African American women organized their own settlements, most notably Atlanta's Neighborhood

◆ **Nurses and Babies in Front of "Neighborhood House," Atlanta**
Atlanta's Neighborhood Union was organized by Lugenia Burns Hope, African American social welfare activist and wife of John Hope (president of Morehouse College) and eight other African American women. Atlanta being a highly segregated city, the Neighborhood Union needed to provide the same kinds of services to African American neighborhoods as white-led settlements: day care and kindergarten, playgrounds, well baby clinics, and political pressure on the city government. *Atlanta University Center, Robert W. Woodruff Library.*

Union, organized in 1908 by clubwoman Lugenia Burns Hope. In the North, all-Black settlement houses were also organized. Ida B. Wells-Barnett (as she was known after marriage in 1895) set up the Negro Fellowship Association in a rented house on Chicago's south side. Hull-House, which had experimented with a few Black residents in the 1890s, switched in the twentieth century to encouraging and supporting a separate Black settlement house, the Wendell Phillips House. Similar Black-oriented settlement houses were the Robert Gould Shaw House in Boston, the Karamu House in Cleveland, the Sojourner Truth Industrial Club in Los Angeles, and the Lincoln House in New York City.

Epilogue to the Crisis: The Spanish-American War of 1898

In an atmosphere shaped by the crisis of the 1890s, the United States embarked on its first extracontinental imperialist efforts. Imperial advocates contended that the acquisition of overseas colonies could provide both new markets to revive the American economy and a military challenge to invigorate American manhood. In an influential paper titled "The Significance of the Frontier in American History," historian Frederick Jackson Turner considered the advantages of an imperial future for the United States. Mourning the end of an era in which the defining national purpose was to conquer the American continent, and concerned that immigrants

◆ **Art and Handicraft at the Woman's Building, World's Columbian Exposition, Chicago (1893)**
In the elegant Woman's Building, for which women were both architects and interior designers, exhibits showed women's long history of manufacture and industry, starting with the spinning wheel. Women were therefore part of the modern progress that the fair highlighted. This poster was designed by the noted French painter Madeline Lemaire. *(Maud Howe Elliott, editor,* Art and Handicraft in the Woman's Building of the World's Columbian Exposition *[Chicago and New York: Rand, McNally & Company, 1894]. Image retrieved from the Library of Congress, www.loc.gov /item/05028628/>)*

could not be fully Americanized in the absence of the frontier experience, Turner suggested that overseas expansion might be a way for the United States to continue to pursue its Manifest Destiny and maintain its frontier spirit.

Turner made his remarks in 1893 at the World's Columbian Exposition in Chicago. The fair was notable for its impressive "Woman's Building," which showcased women's accomplishments in the various industries, arts, and professions. Artist Mary Cassatt showcased a series of murals there. But the Woman's Building mostly celebrated white women, and like the rest of the fair its racial exclusivity reinforced the theme of the onward march of white American civilization. Along with the aged Frederick Douglass, Ida B. Wells protested the virtual exclusion from the exposition of African Americans, both their achievements in the few decades after slavery and the dangers they faced in freedom, especially the rising epidemic of lynchings. "Over a thousand black men, women and children have been thus sacrificed the past ten years," Wells wrote. "Masks have long since been thrown aside and the lynchings of the present day take place in broad daylight."[41]

In addition, the exposition displayed the nation's rising imperial aspirations. The spatial organization of the grounds reflected the country's new ambitions for world leadership. At the center was the Court of Honor, where the United States welcomed and joined the great nations of Europe. Meanwhile, on the riotous Midway Plaisance at the fair's periphery, belly-dancing Arabs, tribal Africans, and exotic Asians drew enormous crowds, fascinated and amused by the unprecedented spectacle of the world's strange variety of peoples. Much of the Midway traded on what scholars today term "Orientalism." Beginning in the late nineteenth century, white Americans and Europeans engaged in fantasies of the Middle East, North Africa, and East Asia as simultaneously primitive and exotic, which tell us more about those who fantasized than those of the East themselves. These fantasies reflected a longing for a sensuality and eroticism seemingly absent or repressed in more modern culture, embodied particularly by the women of these cultures. Significantly, industrial nations exoticized people of these countries just as industrial countries were also colonizing them in imperial ventures. The implication was clear: the people on the Midway, albeit fascinating, were inferior, uncivilized, and backward, and they needed the stewardship of the United States and other Christian nations to advance.

Some of the earliest manifestations of this crusading sense of American national superiority had come from Protestant missionaries, among whom women were prominent. Since the 1830s, women with a strong religious vocation had been bringing American values and culture along with the English language and Christian Bibles to the peoples of Asia and Africa. Women's overseas missionary efforts entered a new, more organized phase in 1883 when the WCTU created a division to undertake international work. Mary Clement Leavitt, a former schoolteacher from New Hampshire, became the first of the WCTU's "round the world missionaries," traveling around the Pacific, from Hawaii to New Zealand and Australia to Burma, Madagascar, China, and India, to spread the ideas of temperance.

Some Asian women were able to use the resources and perspective of the WCTU missionaries to address their own problems as they understood them. In Japan, for instance, the WCTU's combined message of female purity and activism became the basis for an anticoncubinage movement, while the antiliquor arguments were initially ignored by women. Nonetheless, the assumption of American superiority and world leadership constituted a kind of "soft" imperialism. Frances Willard made the link explicit when she said, "Mrs. Leavitt has been to the women of Japan what U.S. naval and economic power has been to its commerce: an opening into the civilized world."[42]

Willard wrote those words in 1898, the year that the United States entered into its first explicitly imperial overseas war and acquired its first formal colonial possessions. The Spanish-American War began in Cuba, which had long drawn American attention as a possible territorial acquisition. Cuban nationalists were showing signs of winning a prolonged insurgency against Spanish colonial control. In May, the United States joined the war on the side of the Cuban forces, ostensibly to avenge the destruction of the U.S.S. *Maine*, an American battleship blown up under suspicious circumstances in Havana harbor. (It was later determined that powder on the deck exploded, probably by accident.) Spain was quickly routed, but instead of supporting Cuban independence, the United States enforced a new type of foreign oversight on the island. While not making Cuba a formal colony, the U.S. Congress passed the Platt Amendment, giving the United States a supervisory role over Cuban affairs, which it retained until 1934.

As Spanish imperial power collapsed further, the United States claimed as colonies other Spanish possessions, including Puerto Rico and Guam. U.S. forces found it most difficult to consolidate control over the rich prize of the Spanish Philippines, the gateway to trade across the Pacific and throughout Asia. An indigenous Filipino independence movement fought back against the Americans, who had come in 1898 to liberate and stayed to control. The Filipinos turned what at first appeared to be a quick U.S. victory into a long and deadly conflict, which U.S. forces brought to an end only in 1902 through considerable expenditure of life (see Reading into the Past: "Women of the Philippines"). Unlike Cuba, the Philippines became a formal U.S. colony and remained so until 1946.

Alongside the economic justification for imperial expansion in search of new markets, a restless, insecure, and aggressive masculinity played a significant role in America's decision to go to war. Rising New York politician (eventually to be president) Theodore Roosevelt thoroughly embodied this phenomenon. With the memory of Civil War death tolls receding, men like Roosevelt were eager to demonstrate a middle-class American manliness they felt was being challenged by immigrant men and threatened by activist women. Newspapers encouraged popular support for intervention. In political cartoons, Americans were portrayed as the manly protectors of the Cuban people, who were regularly depicted as suffering women. These eager imperialists "regarded the war as an opportunity," says one historian, "to return the nation to a political order in which strong men governed and home-bound women proved their patriotism by raising heroic sons."[43]

Most American women joined the clamor and supported intervention on what they believed was the side of the Cubans. Remembering female service in the Civil War, they raised funds for military hospitals. But when it came to the unprecedented policy of taking overseas colonies, opinion was much more divided. By nature a pacifist, Jane Addams recognized the threat that rising militarism posed to a more general spirit of reform. On the streets around Hull-House, she observed, children were "playing war": "In the violence characteristic of the age, they were 'slaying Spaniards.' "[44] Susan B. Anthony also opposed the war, while her longtime friend and political partner, Elizabeth Cady Stanton, took the opposite position and believed that colonization would civilize the Filipino people.

The annexation of Hawaii during the war illustrates another aspect of the many roles women played in the U.S. move toward empire. In 1891, Queen Liliuokalani became the reigning monarch of the sovereign nation of Hawaii. She had been educated by American Protestant missionaries, was a devout Congregationalist, spoke English, and was married to a white American. Wealthy American planters already had enormous economic power in Hawaii, but U.S. tariff policies put them at a disadvantage in selling their fruit and sugar, and they pressed for a formal U.S. takeover of the islands. Now that its monarch was a woman, they redoubled their claims that only annexation could ensure Hawaii's stability and progress. The U.S. entry into the war against Spain created a political environment favorable to their aspirations, and in 1898 Congress voted to acquire Hawaii. Unlike Texas in 1845 and California in 1848, however, Hawaii was designated as a colonial territory, not to become a state for another six decades.

The response of U.S. suffragists was not to condemn acquiring Hawaii as a colony, even though the deposed head of state was a woman, or to object that Congress was imposing a government on the islands instead of allowing its residents to organize their own. Rather, they protested Congress's intention to write a territorial

READING INTO THE PAST

CLEMENCIA LOPEZ
Women of the Philippines

Clemencia Lopez and her brother, Sixto, were leading advocates to the American people of the cause of Philippine independence. She defended her people's dignity and sovereign rights in this 1902 address to the New England Woman Suffrage Association, many of whose members were active in the Boston-based Anti-Imperialist League. Subsequently she became a student at Wellesley College, one of the first Filipinas to attend a U.S. college.

You will no doubt be surprised and pleased to learn that the condition of women in the Philippines is very different from that of the women of any country in the East, and that it differs very little from the general condition of the women of this country. Mentally, socially, and in almost all the relations of life, our women are regarded as the equals of our men. . . .

. . . [I]t would seem to me an excellent idea that American women should take part in any investigation that may be made in the Philippine Islands, and I believe they would attain better results than the men. Would it not also seem to you an excellent idea, since representation by our leading men has been refused us, that a number of representative women should come to this country, so that you might become better acquainted with us?

. . . You can do much to bring about the cessation of these horrors and cruelties which are today taking place in the Philippines, and to insist upon a more humane course. I do not believe that you can understand or imagine the miserable condition of the women of my country, or how real is their suffering. . . . [Y]ou ought to understand that we are only contending for the liberty of our country, just as you once fought for the same liberty for yours.

SOURCE: Clemencia Lopez, "Women of the Philippines," address to the New England Woman Suffrage Association, published in *Woman's Journal*, June 7, 1902.

ANALYZING PRIMARY SOURCES

1. How does Lopez appeal to the ideals of the New England suffragists?

constitution for the Hawaiians that confined political rights to men only. As one historian writes, suffragists "substituted a critique of imperialism with a critique of patriarchy, and in the process lent their tacit approval to America's colonial project."[45] Even when they seemed to defend the rights of women in the colonies, late nineteenth-century suffragists did so within a framework that assumed the superiority of American culture and their right, as white Americans, to play a role in the nation's expansive "civilizing" mission.

◆ CONCLUSION: NATIONHOOD AND WOMANHOOD ON THE EVE OF A NEW CENTURY

While the end of the Civil War resolved, for the time being at least, the regional and racial divisions that had endangered the United States, the post-Reconstruction years brought new conflicts and dangers to American unity and national tranquility. Even as the American economy revived and geographic expansion reopened, new rifts in the American social fabric occurred over the distribution of these riches and resources. Immigrants were drawn into the booming economy and the growing cities, only to face ethnic discrimination, daunting poverty, and nativist legislation. Western families and ambitious entrepreneurs alike sought the removal of Native peoples to open up new lands for their own purposes.

Women were part and parcel of these two great movements of people — immigration and the removal of Native peoples — that did so much to transform the United States in the post–Civil War years. Their labor fueled dynamic new industries and contributed to growing corporate wealth, and their devotion relocated and rebuilt family lives. Native American women found ways to resist, record, or protest the relentless encroachment on their lands and the attacks on their cultures.

These conflicts culminated at century's end in a decade of political challenge and social turmoil. By the end of the century, the wealth produced by the U.S. economy more than equaled that of England, Germany, and France combined. The settlement of the western half of the continental United States gave a sturdy new physicality to American claims of nationhood. Strong and confident, the United States, once a colony itself, ended the century by acquiring its own colonies. The country was on its way to becoming a world power.

As this new era of national development and prominence dawned, women's prospects looked especially promising. Many, though not all, American women in 1900 were living more active, more public, more individualized, and more expansive lives than women of prior generations did. These women were prepared to make a major contribution to solving the problems that accompanied America's new prosperity and place in the world. In the coming era, important groups of women would achieve as much influence as in any period of U.S. history. Already the beneficiaries of American progress, they were about to become the mainstays of the Progressive era, in which America undertook the challenging task of both reforming and modernizing itself.

CHAPTER 7 REVIEW

KEY TERMS

Wounded Knee massacre (p. 344)

Woman's National Indian Association (p. 346)

Dawes Severalty Act (p. 348)

Homestead Act (p. 348)

National Grange (p. 351)

Mother Jones (p. 352)

Ellis Island (p. 355)

Angel Island (p. 355)

Page Law (p. 357)

Chinese Exclusion Act (p. 357)

Populism (p. 361)

People's Party (p. 362)

Woman's Christian Temperance Union (WCTU) (p. 362)

settlement house movement (p. 366)

REVIEW QUESTIONS

1. "Consolidating the West" had vastly different meanings for white women settlers and Native American women. What generalizations can you make about the two disparate groups' experiences?

2. How were women's experiences of immigration and settlement in the United States distinct from those of men? How were they similar?

3. How would you characterize the differences among women involved in industrial protest, the People's Party, and the settlement house movement? What similarities do you see in the methods or goals of these movements?

4. **Making Connections** The chapter's introduction states: "In all these developments — western consolidation, mass immigration, the political and economic crises of the 1890s, and the beginnings of American imperialism — women were involved, active, influential, and, as a result, changed." How might you characterize women's activity and influence, and how might they have been changed by their participation in these developments?

SUGGESTED READING

Women and Western Settlement and Conquest

Susan Armitage and Elizabeth Jameson, eds., *The Women's West* (1987).

Cathleen D. Cahill, *Federal Fathers and Mothers: A Social History of the United States Indian Service, 1869–1933* (2013).

Sarah Deutsch, *No Separate Refuge: Culture, Class, and Gender on an Anglo-Hispanic Frontier in the American Southwest, 1880–1940* (1987).

Lisbeth Haas, *Conquests and Historical Identities in California, 1769–1936* (1995).

Margaret D. Jacobs, *White Mother to a Dark Race: Settler Colonialism, Maternalism, and the Removal of Indigenous Children in the American West and Australia, 1880–1940* (2009).

Elizabeth Jameson and Susan Armitage, eds., *Writing the Range: Race, Class, and Culture in the Women's West* (1997).

Valerie Sherer Mathes, *Helen Hunt Jackson and Her Indian Reform Legacy* (1997).

Theda Perdue, ed., *Sifters: Native American Women's Lives* (2001).

Nancy Shoemaker, ed., *Negotiators of Change: Historical Perspectives on Native American Women* (1995).

Jane E. Simonsen, *Making Home Work: Domesticity and Native American Assimilation in the American West, 1860–1919* (2006).

Immigrant Women

Elizabeth Ewen, *Immigrant Women in the Land of Dollars: Life and Culture on the Lower East Side, 1890–1925* (1985).

Donna Gabaccia, *From the Other Side: Women, Gender, and Immigrant Life in the U.S., 1820–1990* (1994).

Katrina Irving, *Immigrant Mothers: Narratives of Race and Maternity, 1890–1925* (2000).

Mei Nakano, *Japanese American Women: Three Generations, 1890–1990* (1990).

Vicki L. Ruiz, *From Out of the Shadows: Mexican Women in Twentieth-Century America* (1998).

Rumi Yasutake, *Transnational Women's Activism: The United States, Japan, and Japanese Immigrant Communities in California, 1859–1920* (2004).

Judy Yung, *Unbound Feet: A Social History of Chinese Women in San Francisco* (1995).

Women Reformers

Mina Carson, *Settlement Folk: Social Thought and the American Settlement Movement, 1885–1930* (1990).

Rebecca Edwards, *Angels in the Machinery: Gender in American Party Politics from the Civil War to the Progressive Era* (1997).

Elisabeth Lasch-Quinn, *Black Neighbors: Race and the Limits of Reform in the American Settlement House Movement, 1890–1945* (1993).

Rebecca J. Mead, *How the Vote Was Won: Woman Suffrage in the Western United States, 1868–1914* (2004).

Kathryn Kish Sklar, *Florence Kelley and the Nation's Work* (1995).

Allison L. Sneider, *Suffragists in an Imperial Age: U.S. Expansion and the Woman Question, 1870–1929* (2008).

Ian Tyrrell, *Woman's World/Woman's Empire: The Woman's Christian Temperance Union in International Perspective, 1880–1930* (1991).

PRIMARY SOURCES

Representing Native American Women in the Late Nineteenth Century

POPULAR CULTURE IMAGES

IN POPULAR NINETEENTH-CENTURY MAGAZINES such as *Harper's Weekly*, one of the most pervasive images featured the Indigenous woman as "squaw," a hardworking drudge mistreated by her lazy husband. The stereotype had changed little since the eighteenth century (see "The Underside of Expansion: Indigenous Women and Californianas" in Chapter 5). The engraving in Figure 7.1 used technology that had revolutionized print media, making it cheaper to produce richly illustrated magazines in the post–Civil War era. The text that accompanied this 1875 drawing, "Indian Sledge Journey," explained the message of the image in clear terms:

> Among the noble red men, in the division of labor all the hard work falls upon the squaws; there is no question as to their mission in life. The frame-work of the sledge is generally made of some flexible, tough wood, over which dry hides are tightly stretched, forming a strong but very light vehicle, which slides easily over the surface of the snow.[46]

Note that the description of the sledge is far more precise than that of the family. Do you think this detail lent a sense of accurate reporting to the image? How do the image and caption reinforce the argument — popular since George Washington's administration and that would become so popular with white reformers — that the key to "civilizing" Native Americans was through restructuring gender relations?

Even as white observers were touting the modernization of Indigenous peoples, they also presented a romantic vision of a dying race. A subset of this nostalgia was the attention given to Native women's skill at traditional handicrafts such as basket making, rug weaving, and pottery. The interest in women's preindustrial work may have indicated anxiety about how modern industrial innovations had robbed modern women of traditional skills. The World's Columbian Exposition featured hundreds of displays of Native women's crafts and even showcased an actual Navaho woman at her loom. Dioramas (three-dimensional lifelike models) of Indigenous women at traditional tasks borrowed from the Smithsonian appeared in an ethnological exhibit titled "Woman's Work in Savagery," in which the figures were enclosed in glass cases like zoological exhibits.

◆ **Figure 7.1** **"Indian Sledge Journey,"** *Harper's Weekly* **(1875)**
Universal History Archive/UIG via Getty Images

Photographs were perhaps the most compelling demonstration of traditional crafts work, and there is a substantial archive of such images, part of an ambitious campaign of photographers to capture traditional cultures while they still existed. Figure 7.2 shows the Arizona Hopi Nampeyo, surrounded by her pottery in 1900. The photographer, A. C. Vroman, often arranged the pottery to suit his vision and in this case included some pots made by another woman. Most pictures of women

◆ Figure 7.2 **Hopi Potter Nampeyo**
National Archives, Identifier 520084.

with their crafts did not identify the women by name. Nampeyo is unusual in that she was well known in her lifetime as a superb artist, in particular for incorporating prehistoric designs into her ceramics, a technique that drew the attention of American museums and collectors. For her designs, Nampeyo borrowed from the artifacts archaeologists had recently uncovered of prehistoric Hopi people. Besides their artistic appeal, what other reasons might have prompted her to draw upon these ancient patterns?

One outlet for Nampeyo to sell her wares was a local trading post, and these emporia became an important part of the developing tourist industry of the West, where visitors could buy souvenirs to document their visit and adorn their homes. Postcards, many of them featuring "Indian princesses" or craftswomen like Nampeyo, helped to publicize the new tourist destinations. They suggest that not only had their blankets, pots, and baskets become commodities for white consumption, but so, too, had the women themselves.

Figure 7.3 is a particularly striking example of this phenomenon. Dating from 1902, the postcard shows Pueblo women at a railway station offering their

6848. PUEBLO INDIANS SELLING POTTERY.   COPYRIGHT, 1902, BY DETROIT PHOTOGRAPHIC CO.

◆ Figure 7.3 **Pueblo Women in a 1902 Postcard**
Library of Congress Prints and Photographs Division, Washington, D.C. (LC-DIG-ds-10121).

pottery to tourists while railroad staff look on. The postcard was part of a promotional campaign mounted by the Fred Harvey Company, which had a chain of hotels and restaurants. Why might this image have appealed to prospective tourists? Harvey initially hired Pueblo women to stand at train stations but eventually built permanent tourist shops that included "living" exhibitions of Native peoples.

Nampeyo worked at Harvey's Hopi House in 1905, and a promotional brochure included a photograph of the potter and her family, along with the caption "These quaintly-garbed Indians on the housetop hail from Tewa, the home of Nampeyo, the most noted pottery-maker in all Hopiland. Perhaps you [will be] so fortunate as to see Nampeyo herself." Inviting the tourist to step inside this re-creation of a Hopi dwelling and see the Hopi work at their crafts, it promised that "they are the most primitive Indians in America with ceremonies several centuries old."[47]

Although few images of Native American women identified them by name, notable exceptions were the photographs of a handful of women writers or activists such as the La Flesche sisters, Sarah Winnemucca, and Gertrude Simmons Bonnin, who wrote under the name Zitkala-Ša. Bonnin first gained fame as a writer of autobiographical stories, fiction, and poetry, based on her life among the Yankton Dakotas of South Dakota. Her autobiographical writings began to appear in such prestigious magazines as the *Atlantic Monthly* in 1900. By the 1910s she had become an outspoken activist for Native American rights. One of her most compelling stories detailed the trauma of the cultural shock she experienced when she first went to a Native American boarding school. That experience notwithstanding, she prized education and went on to study violin at the New England Conservatory of Music. Like many Native American intellectuals, Bonnin often struggled with the dilemma posed by valuing aspects of Euro-American culture, especially education, while hoping to sustain Native American cultures.[48]

Although Bonnin was often photographed wearing elaborate Indian clothing, other photos of the time offer a more subtle vision of her identity. Figure 7.4, an 1898 portrait by Joseph Keiley, shows Bonnin in a simple dress, probably made of buckskin, holding what seems to be a sheaf of papers. Her beads and the striped blanket signal her Native American identity. Keiley was part of a photography movement that promoted photographs as fine art. How does this image of Bonnin reflect his agenda?

◆ **Figure 7.4 Gertrude Simmons Bonnin, Photographed by Joseph T. Keiley (1898)**
National Portrait Gallery, Smithsonian Institution.

Like Bonnin, Angel De Cora, originally named Hinook-Mahiwi-Kilinaka, a Winnebago from Nevada, received her education at a boarding school. De Cora attended the African American Hampton Institute, where she studied for three years beginning in 1883. Eventually she trained as an artist at Philadelphia's Drexel Institute and the Museum of Fine Arts in Boston. She achieved substantial success as a commercial illustrator, contributing illustrations for many works by and about Native Americans in the early twentieth century. In 1901 she illustrated Zitkala-Ša's *Old Indian Legends.* Even before Zitkala-Ša published her works, De Cora's writing and illustrations appeared in *Harper's New Monthly Magazine.* In one of her two published stories, "Grey Wolf's Daughter," the main character reflected on the young women she knew, comparing "one who had been to school, to another who had staid at home and was a thorough Indian, comparing the life of the one with the life of the other."[49] She determined to go to boarding school to learn "the white man's ways." The night before her departure, she adorned herself with beads and jewelry and, with village girlfriends, underwent a purification ceremony. Then she removed all of her items, leaving herself with a simple dress and one ornament. Her father was sad to see her go but recognized that "she had always had her own way."

What is most striking about the story are the drawings that accompany it. Figure 7.5 is a stunning image that richly details the skilled beadwork on the title character's dress and belt. The painted hides behind her further illuminate a dazzling display of traditional Plains women's work. While the narrative might suggest a sense of loss as the young woman puts aside her Native adornments, historian Jane Simonsen maintains that the pensive expression and the celebration of the design work emphasize Grey Wolf's daughter's choice to establish a new identity in a new environment. "In the same way," Simonsen argues, "De Cora's identity as an artist began to take shape as she moved Native designs into the mainstream literary media. She removed her beads, as it were, only to place them in the pages of *Harper's*."[50] What do you make of this interpretation?

◆ Figure 7.5 **Grey Wolf's Daughter, by Angel De Cora (1899)**
Harvard Library.

THE WORDS OF SARAH WINNEMUCCA, PAIUTE ACTIVIST

SARAH WINNEMUCCA (1844?–1891), a member of the Nevada Paiutes* and daughter of one of the Paiutes' headmen, led an extraordinary life in which she served as U.S. Army messenger and translator, lectured extensively in western and eastern cities, visited Washington, D.C., at the request of President Rutherford B. Hayes in 1880, and wrote *Life among the Piutes: Their Wrongs and Claims* (1883), the first book written by a Native American woman. Winnemucca was a controversial figure. She provoked white hostility with her relentless condemnation of the reservation system and the numerous Indian Service agents she viewed as corrupt and incompetent. Some newspapers depicted her negatively, drawing on the squaw stereotype to question her morality. And, in keeping with many white assumptions about Native women's unrestrained sexuality, one Indian agent sought to undermine her credibility when she went to Washington by claiming that she was a prostitute. Even her own people were often suspicious, especially when she failed to secure improved conditions and also because she willingly worked with the U.S. Army as a translator. Yet the story that scholars have developed suggests that her most impressive legacy was her critique of white western expansion generally and U.S. Indian policy specifically. She did not look back to some romantic vision of her people returning to the old ways, but hoped that Native Americans would become educated, even "civilized," without surrendering their culture and their autonomy.

Winnemucca first began giving lectures to white audiences in San Francisco in 1879, primarily to draw attention to the government's removal of a group of Paiutes from their reservation in Nevada to one in Yakima, Washington, as punishment for their alleged attacks on whites, a claim they and Winnemucca roundly disputed. For her lectures Winnemucca appeared in Native American attire, which was described in detail by the *Daily Alta California*: "A head-dress of long feathers was fastened to her forehead by a bright red band, her long, jet-black hair falling below her waist. A bright buckskin shirt and cape were trimmed with beads and long buckskin string. A bead necklace shone around her throat and a blue bead bracelet was worn around the right wrist. Bright red hose showed below the short skirt, and it might have been the pair of gaily-embroidered moccasins worn on the feet that attracted the attention of the men in that way."[51] Figure 7.6 is a photograph that shows Winnemucca in

◆ **Figure 7.6 Sarah Winnemucca**
National Portrait Gallery, Smithsonian Institution.

---

* Winnemucca spelled it *PIUTE*, but the common modern spelling is *PAIUTE*.

similar clothing. Why might she have chosen traditional garb instead of the western dresses she was also accustomed to wearing?

In 1883, encouraged by the patronage of two Boston sisters, Elizabeth Palmer Peabody and Mary Mann, Winnemucca (who published under her married name, Sarah Winnemucca Hopkins) turned her lectures into a book that told her own story while also explaining Paiute cultural traditions and describing the devastating impact of white conquest of the West and its Native people. In the first of the following extracts from *Life among the Piutes*, Winnemucca explains women's duties and the nature of marriage in a discussion of tribal decision making. How might we read these passages as a response to white conventional representations of Indian families?

SARAH WINNEMUCCA
Life among the Piutes (1883)

We have a republic as well as you. The council-tent is our Congress, and anybody can speak who has anything to say, women and all. They are always interested in what their husbands are doing and thinking about. And they take some part even in the wars. They are always near at hand when fighting is going on, ready to snatch their husbands up and carry them off if wounded or killed. One splendid woman that my brother Lee married after his first wife died, went out into the battle-field after her uncle was killed, and went into the front ranks and cheered the men on. Her uncle's horse was dressed in a splendid robe made of eagles' feathers and she snatched it off and swung it in the face of the enemy, who always carry off everything they find, as much as to say, "You can't have that — I have it safe"; and she stayed and took her uncle's place, as brave as any of the men. It means something when the women promise their fathers to make their husbands *themselves*. They faithfully keep with them in all the dangers they can share. They not only take care of their children together, but they do everything together; and when they grow blind, which I am sorry to say is very common, for the smoke they live in destroys their eyes at last, they take sweet care of one another. Marriage is a sweet thing when people love each other. If women could go into your Congress I think justice would

soon be done to the Indians. I can't tell about all Indians; but I know my own people are kind to everybody that does not do them harm; but they will not be imposed upon, and when people are too bad they rise up and resist them. This seems to me all right. It is different from being revengeful. There is nothing cruel about our people. They never scalped a human being. . . .

[*In contrast to the respect Paiute men and women show each other, Winnemucca frequently comments on the sexual violence Indian women repeatedly experience at the hands of white men. In one passage she explains that a three-month war was started when white men raped and imprisoned two Paiute girls who had been out foraging for food. She also details her own experience with threatened assault, suggesting the ways in which Paiute women sought to protect themselves from the sexual violence that was a constant threat. She and a woman she describes as her sister, although she may have been a cousin or other kin, were traveling alone, heading to Yakima after Winnemucca had been in Washington, D.C. On the journey they were being chased by three men, and Winnemucca describes her plan to resist them.*]

Away we went, and they after us like wild men. We rode on till our horses seemed to drop from under us. At last we stopped, and I told sister what to do if the whole three of them undertook us. We could not do very much, but we must die fighting. If there were only two we were all right, — we would kill them; if only one we would see what he would do. If he lassoed me she was to jump off her horse and cut the rope, and if he lassoed her I was to do the same. If he got off his horse and came at me she was to cut him, and I would do the same for her. Now we were ready for our work. They were a long way back yet. We kept looking back to see how far off they were. Every time we would get out of sight, we would rest our horses, and at last, to our great joy, we only saw one coming. He would not dare to do us any harm. . . .

[*Winnemucca details yet another incident on the same trip when she was accosted at night in her bed by a white cowboy at the home of a white family. She rose up and "gave him a blow right in the face. I said, 'Go away, or I will cut you to pieces, you mean man!'" Here and elsewhere, Winnemucca makes it clear that she understood that white male sexual violence "was intertwined with racial and economic oppression."*[52]

Life among the Piutes also focuses on the grave injustice of federal Indian policy. In the following excerpts, how does she characterize the white conquest of the West? How does she attempt to appeal to white readers through a shared language of Christian ideals?]

Oh, for shame! You who are educated by a Christian government in the art of war; the practice of whose progression makes you natural enemies of the savages, so called by you. Yes, you, who call yourselves the great civilization; you who have knelt upon Plymouth Rock, covenanted with God to make this land the home of the free and brave. Ah, then you rise from your bended knees and seizing the welcoming hands of those who are the owners of this land, which you are not, your carbines rise upon the bleak shore, and your so-called civilization sweeps inland from the ocean wave; but, oh, my God! leaving its pathway marked by crimson lines of blood; and strewed by the bones of two races, the inheritor and the invader; and I am crying out to you for justice, — yes, pleading for the far-off plains of the West, for the dusky mourner, whose tears of love are pleading for her husband, or for their children, who are sent far away from them.

SOURCE: Sarah Winnemucca Hopkins, *Life among the Piutes: Their Wrongs and Claims* (New York: G. P. Putnam's Sons, 1883).

BEYOND CRITIQUING INDIAN POLICY, Winnemucca also challenged the assimilationist vision that shaped it, by establishing a short-lived bilingual school at Lovelock, Nevada, in 1885. Although she promoted learning English and other aspects of Western culture, in the words of her supporter Elizabeth Peabody, Winnemucca's school rejected the idea of "passive reception of civilizing influences proffered by white men who look down upon the Indian as a spiritual, moral, and intellectual inferior," and instead promoted "a spontaneous movement, made by the Indian himself, *from himself*, in full consciousness of free agency, for the education that is to civilize him."[53] The following document comes from a letter that Winnemucca sent to Paiute school trustees in Inyo, California; the letter was reprinted in a San Francisco newspaper. How does this passage convey Winnemucca's educational goals?

SARAH WINNEMUCCA
The Daily Alta California (July 24, 1886)

Brothers and Sisters: Hearing you are about to start a school to educate your children, I want to say a word about it. You all know me; many of you are my aunts or cousins. We are of one race — your blood is my blood, so I speak to you for your good. I can speak five tongues — three Indian tongues, English and Spanish. I can read and write, and am a school teacher. Now I do not say this to boast, but simply to show you what can be done. When I was a little girl there were no Indian schools; I learned under great difficulty. Your children can learn much more than I know, and much easier, and it is your duty to see that they go to school. . . . You are not asked to give money or horses — only to send your children to school. The teacher will do the rest. He or she will fit your little ones for the battle of life, so that they can attend to their own affairs instead of having to call in a white man.

A few years ago you owned this great country; today the white man owns it all, and you own nothing. Do you know what did it? Education. You see the miles and miles of railroad, the locomotive, the Mint in Carson, where they make money. Education has done it all. Now what it has done for one man it will do for another. You have brains same as the whites, your children have brains, and it will be your fault if they grow up as you have. I entreat you take hold of this school, and give your support by sending your children, old and young, to it, and when they grow up to manhood and womanhood they will bless you.

SOURCE: *The Newspaper Warrior; Sarah Winnemucca Hopkins's Campaign for American Indian Rights, 1864–1891*, ed. Cari M. Carpenter and Carolyn Sorisio (Lincoln: University of Nebraska Press, 2015), 261–62.

ANALYZING PRIMARY SOURCES

1. It is unlikely that Sarah Winnemucca saw the etching in Figure 7.1, but she was undoubtedly familiar with the squaw stereotype. How might she have responded to *Harper's Weekly*'s conception of a Native woman?

2. Taking into account the images and Winnemucca's writing, what conclusions can you draw about the variety of Native women's experiences in the West? What common themes, if any, do you see?

3. What were the greatest challenges for Native American women in their interactions with white Americans?

PRIMARY SOURCES

Jane Addams Remembers Hull-House

J ANE ADDAMS (1860–1935) was the leader of the American settlement house movement. After graduating in 1882 from Rockford Seminary (soon after to become Rockford College) in Illinois, she found herself trapped in what she called "the snare of preparation," the dilemma suffered by early college graduates who lacked a vocation in which to apply their education. She went to Europe in search of a larger purpose for her life. Like other daughters of wealthy families, she was looking for an alternative to the leisured, home-bound life for which her class and gender destined her. Addams and women like her did not require paid labor, but they did need work of large social purpose and a place and community in which to live.

Visiting London, Addams learned of a "settlement" project of male college graduates who lived among and served the urban poor. She returned to Chicago, determined to establish a similar community of female college graduates dedicated to social service. In 1889, Addams persuaded a wealthy member of the Hull family to donate a mansion, now in the center of a crowded immigrant district, to be the site of her project. Soon many similar "settlement houses" would dot the American urban landscape. Published by Addams in 1910, *Twenty Years at Hull-House* is a dual autobiography, focusing on Addams's path to social service and on Hull-House as an institution. Figure 7.7 is the author's photograph from her book.

The white, native-born, leisure-class women who joined Addams as "residents" of Hull-House combined a palpable sympathy with the urban poor and a determination to find a nonrevolutionary solution to the era's class and ethnic conflicts. Their neighbors were working-class and poorer immigrant families living around them (Figure 7.8). Both the leisure-class residents

◆ **Figure 7.7 Jane Addams**
GRANGER — Historical Picture Archive.

◆ Figure 7.8 **Alley Tenements near Hull-House; Illustration by Norah Hamilton, Hull-House Resident and Artist**

and the working-class neighbors showed considerable organizational ability and political savvy in addressing the difficult daily conditions of these immigrant neighborhoods. *Twenty Years at Hull-House* demonstrates that the public activism of the "Woman's Era" was not limited to native-born leisure-class women but characterized the immigrant working class as well.

There are many tensions at work in Addams's efforts to understand her neighbors and assist in their adjustment to American society. *Twenty Years at Hull-House* reveals both Addams's biases that she brought to her work and the compassion and understanding she developed while there. Her account of the development of the Labor Museum demonstrates her belief in steady economic progress alongside her realization that the loss of traditional culture — in this case the artisan skills of the older immigrant women — has gone unappreciated. She describes the ignorance that fuels ethnic clashes between different immigrant groups even as she recognizes that America's own "color problem" may be worse.

Addams's vignettes follow immigrant women through the many phases and challenges of their lives. She had a great deal to say about female immigrants at both the early and later years of their lives: Americanizing daughters, both wage earners and prostitutes (whom she euphemistically connects with "professional" or "disreputable" houses); and aged women left without means of support. To one degree or another, all suffer a common economic insecurity, based on both their class status and female dependence. Living among the immigrant poor, Addams recognized that financial security was probably the biggest difference between the classes in turn-of-the-century urban America.

JANE ADDAMS
Twenty Years at Hull-House (1910)

There was in the earliest undertakings at Hull-House a touch of the artist's enthusiasm when he translates his inner vision through his chosen material into outward form. Keenly conscious of the social confusion all about us and the hard economic struggle, we at times believed that the very struggle itself might become a source of strength. The devotion of the mothers to their children, the dread of the men lest they fail to provide for the family dependent upon their daily exertions, at moments seemed to us the secret stores of strength from which society is fed, the invisible array of passion and feeling which are the surest protectors of the world. We fatuously hoped that we might pluck from the human tragedy itself a consciousness of a common destiny which should bring its own healing, that we might extract from life's very misfortunes a power of cooperation which should be effective against them.

Of course there was always present the harrowing consciousness of the difference in economic condition between ourselves and our neighbors. Even if we had gone to live in the most wretched tenement, there would have always been an essential difference between them and ourselves, for we should have had a sense of security in regard to illness and old age and the lack of these two securities are the specters which most persistently haunt the poor. Could we, in spite of this, make their individual efforts more effective through organization and possibly complement them by small efforts of our own? . . .

At a meeting of working girls held at Hull-House during a strike in a large shoe factory, the discussions made it clear that the strikers who had been most easily frightened, and therefore first to capitulate, were naturally those girls who were paying board and were afraid of being put out if they fell too far behind. After a recital of a case of peculiar hardship one of them exclaimed: "Wouldn't it be fine if we had a boarding club of our own, and then we could stand by each other in a time like this?" After that events moved quickly. . . . [O]n the first of May, 1891, two comfortable apartments near Hull-House were rented and furnished. The Settlement was responsible for the furniture and paid the first month's rent, but beyond that the members managed the club themselves. . . . At the end of the third year the [Jane] club occupied all of the six apartments which the original building contained, and numbered fifty members. . . .

I recall our perplexity over the first girls who had "gone astray" — the poor, little, forlorn objects, fifteen and sixteen years old, with their moral natures apparently untouched and unawakened; one of them whom the police had found in a professional house and asked us to shelter for a few days until she could be used as a witness, was clutching a battered doll which she had kept with her during her six months of an "evil life." Two of these prematurely aged children came to us one day directly from the maternity ward of the Cook County hospital, each with a baby in her arms, asking for protection, because they did not want to go home for fear of "being licked." . . . I well remember our perplexity when we attempted to help two girls straight from a Virginia tobacco factory, who had been decoyed into a disreputable house when innocently seeking a lodging on the late evening of their arrival. Although they had been rescued promptly, the stigma remained, and we found it impossible to permit them to join any of the social clubs connected with Hull-House, not so much because there was danger of contamination, as because the parents of the club members would have resented their presence most hotly. . . .

. . .

That neglected and forlorn old age is daily brought to the attention of a Settlement which undertakes to bear its share of the neighborhood burden imposed by poverty, was pathetically clear to us during our first months of residence at Hull-House. . . .

Some frightened women had bidden me come quickly to the house of an old German woman, whom two men from the country agent's office were attempting to remove to the County Infirmary. The poor old creature had thrown herself bodily upon a small and battered chest of drawers and clung there, clutching it so firmly that it would have been impossible to remove her without also taking the piece of furniture. She did not weep nor moan nor indeed make any human sound, but between her broken gasps for breath she squealed shrilly like a frightened animal caught in a trap. The little group of women and children gathered at her door stood aghast at this realization of the black dread which always clouds the lives of the very poor when work is slack, but which constantly grows more imminent and threatening as old age approaches. . . . To take away from an old woman whose life has been spent in household cares all the foolish little belongings to which her affections cling and to which her very fingers have become accustomed, is to take away her last incentive to activity, almost to life itself. To give an old woman only a chair and a bed, to leave her no cupboard in which her treasures may be stowed, not only that she may take them out when she desires occupation, but that their mind may dwell upon them in moments of revery, is to reduce living almost beyond the limit of human endurance. . . .

We early learned to know the children of hard-driven mothers who went out to work all day, sometimes leaving the little things in the casual care of a neighbor, but often locking them into their tenement rooms. The first three crippled children we encountered in the neighborhood had all been injured while their mothers were at work: one had fallen out of a third-story window, another had been burned, and the third had a curved spine due to the fact that for three years he had been tied all day long to the leg of the kitchen table, only released at noon by his older brother who hastily ran in from a neighboring factory to share his lunch with him. . . . During our first summer an increasing number of these poor little mites would wander into the cool hallway of Hull-House. We kept them there and fed them at noon, in return for which we were sometimes offered a hot penny which had been held in a tight little fist "ever since mother left this morning, to buy something to eat with." Out of kindergarten hours our little guests noisily enjoyed the hospitality of our bedrooms under the so-called care of any resident who volunteered to keep an eye on them, but later they were moved into a neighboring apartment under more systematic supervision.

Hull-House was thus committed to a day nursery which we sustained for sixteen years first in a little cottage on a side street and then in a building designed for its use called the Children's House. . . .

While one was filled with admiration for these heroic women, something was also to be said for some of the husbands, for the sorry men who, for one reason or another, had failed in the struggle of life. . . . I could but wonder in which particular we are most stupid — to judge a man's worth so solely by his wage-earning capacity that a good wife feels justified in leaving him, or in holding fast to that wretched delusion that a woman can both support and nurture her children.

With all of the efforts made by modern society to nurture and educate the young, how stupid it is to permit the mothers of young children to spend themselves in the coarser work of the world! It is curiously inconsistent that with the emphasis which this generation has placed upon the mother and upon the prolongation of infancy, we constantly allow the waste of this most precious material. I cannot recall without indignation a recent experience. I was detained late one evening in an office building by a prolonged committee meeting of the Board of Education. As I came out at eleven o'clock, I met in the corridor of the fourteenth floor a woman whom I knew, on her knees scrubbing the marble tiling. As she straightened up to greet me, she seemed so wet from her feet up to her chin, that I hastily inquired the cause. Her reply was that she left home at five o'clock every night and had no opportunity for six hours to nurse her baby. Her mother's milk mingled with the very water with which she scrubbed the floors until she should return at midnight, heated and exhausted, to feed her screaming child with what remained within her breasts.

. . .

An overmastering desire to reveal the humbler immigrant parents to their own children lay at the base of what has come to be called the Hull-House Labor Museum. This was first suggested to my mind one early spring day when I saw an old Italian woman, her distaff against her homesick face, patiently spinning a thread by the simple stick spindle so reminiscent of all southern Europe. . . . It seemed to me that Hull-House ought to be able to devise some educational enterprise which should build a bridge between European and American experiences in such wise as to give them both more meaning and a sense of relation. . . . Could we not interest the young people working in the neighborhood factories in these older forms of industry, so that, through their own parents and grandparents, they would find a dramatic representation of the inherited resources of their daily occupation. If these young people could actually see that the complicated machinery of the factory had been evolved from simple tools, they might at least make a beginning toward that education which Dr. Dewey defines as "a continuing reconstruction of experience." . . .

We found in the immediate neighborhood at least four varieties of these most primitive methods of spinning and three distinct variations of the same spindle in connection with wheels. It was possible to put these seven into historic sequence and order and to connect the whole with the present method of factory spinning. The same thing was done for weaving, and on every Saturday evening a little exhibit was made of these various forms of labor in the textile industry. Within one room a Syrian woman, a Greek, an Italian, a

Russian, and an Irishwoman enabled even the most casual observer to see that there is no break in orderly evolution if we look at history from the industrial standpoint; that industry develops similarly and peacefully year by year among the workers of each nation, heedless of differences in language, religion, and political experiences. . . .

In some such ways as these have the Labor Museum and the shops pointed out the possibilities which Hull-House has scarcely begun to develop, of demonstrating that culture is an understanding of the long-established occupations and thoughts of men, of the arts with which they have solaced their toil. A yearning to recover for the household arts something of their early sanctity and meaning arose strongly within me one evening when I was attending a Passover Feast to which I had been invited by a Jewish family in the neighborhood, where the traditional and religious significance of the woman's daily activity was still retained. The kosher food the Jewish mother spread before her family had been prepared according to traditional knowledge and with constant care in the use of utensils; upon her had fallen the responsibility to make all ready according to Mosaic instructions. . . .

I recall a certain Italian girl who came every Saturday evening to a cooking class in the same building in which her mother spun in the Labor Museum exhibit; and yet Angelina always left her mother at the front door while she herself went around to a side door because she did not wish to be too closely identified in the eyes of the rest of the cooking class with an Italian woman who wore a kerchief over her head, uncouth boots, and short petticoats. . . . It was easy to see that the thought of her mother with any other background than that of the tenement was new to Angelina, and at least two things resulted; she allowed her mother to pull out of the big box under the bed the beautiful homespun garments which had been previously hidden away as uncouth; and she openly came into the Labor Museum by the same door as did her mother, proud at least of the mastery of the craft which had been so much admired. . . .

It is difficult to write of the relation of the older and most foreign-looking immigrants to the children of other people — the Italians whose fruit-carts are upset simply because they are "dagoes," or the Russian peddlers who are stoned and sometimes badly injured because it has become a code of honor in a gang of boys to thus express their derision. . . . Doubtless these difficulties would be much minimized in America, if we faced our own race problem with courage and intelligence, and these very Mediterranean immigrants might give us valuable help. Certainly they are less conscious than the Anglo-Saxon of color distinctions. . . .

. . .

It is easy for even the most conscientious citizen of Chicago to forget the foul smells of the stockyards and the garbage dumps, when he is living so far from them that he is only occasionally made conscious of their existence but the residents of a Settlement are perforce constantly surrounded by them. . . . The Hull-House Woman's Club had been organized the year before by the resident kindergartner who had first inaugurated a mother's meeting. The new members came together, however, in quite a new way that summer when we discussed with them the high death rate so persistent in our ward. After several club meetings devoted to the subject, despite the fact that the death rate rose highest in the congested foreign colonies and not in the streets in which most of the Irish American club women lived, twelve of their number undertook in connection with the residents, to carefully investigate the conditions of the alleys. During August and September the substantiated reports of violations of the law sent in from Hull-House to the health department were one thousand and thirty-seven. For the club woman who had finished a long day's work of washing or ironing followed by the cooking of a hot supper, it would have been much easier to sit on her doorstep during a summer evening than to go up and down ill-kept alleys and get into trouble with her neighbors over the condition of their garbage boxes. . . . Nevertheless, a certain number of women persisted, as did the residents, and three city inspectors in succession were transferred from the ward because of unsatisfactory services. . . .

Many of the foreign-born women of the ward were much shocked by this abrupt departure into the ways of men, and it took a great deal of explanation to convey the idea even remotely that if it were a womanly task to go about in tenement houses in order to nurse the sick, it might be quite as womanly to go through the same district in order to prevent the breeding of so-called "filth diseases."

SOURCE: Jane Addams, *Twenty Years at Hull-House* (New York: Macmillan, 1910), excerpts from chaps. 7, 8, 11, and 13.

ANALYZING PRIMARY SOURCES

1. What does Addams mean about her initial naïve attitude (she uses the word "fatuous") about the "common destiny" she hoped to experience by living in an immigrant neighborhood? What led her to shed this assumption?

2. In what ways was the assistance that Hull-House provided to poor immigrant women and children helpful, and in what ways was it not helpful?

3. To what degree can you rely on the personal stories Addams provides to understand the actual experiences of the immigrant poor?

PRIMARY SOURCES

Jacob Riis's Photographs of Immigrant Girls and Women

I N THE DECADE 1880–1890, more than 5 million immigrants came through the port of New York, and many remained in the city, swelling its population by 25 percent. By 1890, nearly half of the city's dwellings were classified as "tenements," overcrowded urban slums where vulnerable and desperately poor people were overcharged for filthy, cramped, and unsanitary lodgings.

This rise in immigration coincided with new forms of social documentation. Pioneering social scientists provided statistics on the growing industrial labor force, including the women who were entering the workplace in unprecedented numbers. Local and state health bureaus collected information on the epidemic diseases such as diphtheria, cholera, and tuberculosis that threatened family life in the burgeoning cities. And photographers captured searing images of the horrible living and working conditions of newly arrived immigrants.

One of the first and most enduring series of photographs of immigrant women and children in the United States was produced in the 1880s and 1890s by a man who was himself an immigrant. Jacob A. Riis arrived in New York City from Denmark in 1870. He began as a police reporter, writing in a male-oriented, journalistic genre that sensationalized the seamy side of "downtown" life. Riis's own impulses, however, were more humanitarian and allied him with urban reformers, many of whom were women. His particular focus was "the slum," by which he meant not only the dilapidated tenement homes of the poor but also the larger urban environment in which they lived and worked. He was especially concerned with children, and through them the mothers of immigrant families.

Convinced that only photographs could convey the shocking reality of urban poverty, Riis included them in *How the Other Half Lives: Studies among the Tenements of New York* (1890), a pioneering work of sociology that is still mined by historians and scholars for the insights it provides into urban immigrant life, nineteenth-century attitudes toward poverty and ethnicity, and the visual conventions of early documentary photography. Riis's pictures of women and girls give us glimpses of their lives. In its frequent resort to sensational and melodramatic conventions, *How the Other Half Lives* reflects its author's roots in mass commercial journalism, but it also skillfully adopts strategies from literary realism and the emerging field of social science to convey a probing portrait of poverty and its consequences.

Consistent with the late nineteenth century's preoccupation with ethnic and racial characteristics, *How the Other Half Lives* is organized like a guided tour for the middle-class reader through the ethnic geography of lower New York City. Not surprisingly, it invokes both positive and negative stereotypes in its descriptions and illustrations. Riis, as a northwestern European immigrant, had clear ethnic biases, but his prejudices were tempered by empathy and the recognition that "we are all creatures of the conditions that surround us."[54] His goal was to call attention to the plight of the poor, not to castigate them for their poverty.

Chapter 5 of Riis's book, "The Italian in New York," focuses on those who, as recent arrivals, were "at the bottom" of the economic and social hierarchy.[55] The photograph shown in Figure 7.9 depicts the wife and infant child of a "ragpicker" — one who barely made a living by picking through public rubbish cans and dumps for rags to sell — in their subterranean home. Riis developed the innovative technology used to make this photograph, a new chemical process that produced a "flash" bright enough to light up dark and windowless areas.

The pose of the Italian mother and her tightly swaddled child, as well as her mournful, upturned gaze, is reminiscent of religious paintings of the Madonna and Child in which the Virgin Mary's sad expression foreshadows the suffering that awaits her infant son. In the chapter that includes this photograph, Riis details the

◆ Figure 7.9 *In the Home of an Italian Ragpicker: Jersey Street*
Jacob A. Riis/Archive Photos/Getty Images.

high mortality rates of infants and children in this Italian neighborhood. What other explanations can be offered for her upward look?

In the text accompanying this photograph, Riis describes the Italian immigrant as "picturesque, if not very tidy."[56] Does his photograph support this characterization? What overall impression does it convey about Italian immigrant mothers? Also in the text relating to this image is Riis's description of Italian men as "hotheaded . . . and lighthearted" and of Italian women as "faithful wives and devoted mothers."[57] Note the man's straw hat hanging high on the wall. What are the possible explanations for the man's absence?

In Figure 7.10, Riis continues his progression through New York City's ethnic neighborhoods to "Jewtown," an area settled by large numbers of Eastern European Jews and marked by exceptional population density and industrial activity. As Riis notes, "Life here means the hardest kind of work almost from the cradle."[58] The "sweater" mentioned in the title of the photograph was a subcontractor who supplied garments to a larger manufacturer and hired other immigrants to do the work, often in his own tenement apartment. The ruthless competition to deliver finished goods at the lowest possible price pressured the boss to offer impossibly low wages and push (or "sweat")

◆ Figure 7.10 *Knee Pants at Forty-Five Cents a Dozen: A Ludlow Street Sweater's Shop*
Bettmann/Getty Images.

workers to their physical limits during a working day that "lengthened at both ends far into the night."[59] While Riis criticizes the "sweater's . . . merciless severity"[60] in exploiting his fellow Jews, he concedes that "he is no worse than the conditions that created him."[61]

Unlike the photograph shown in Figure 7.9, this photo was not posed and has no carefully arranged central figure. It catches its subjects off guard, and the blurring of some of their features suggests frantic activity and movement. The sweater is the moving figure with his back to the camera. The teenage girls in this picture are "greenhorns," newly arrived immigrant workers. One man looks up briefly from his work, but the other seems unwilling to lose a minute's time despite the photographer's presence. Piles of boys' short pants waiting to be finished are heaped on the floor and furniture. What visual clues tell us that this workshop is also a residence? What else goes on in this room? In what ways is it different from the living space of the Italian mother in Figure 7.9?

In contrast to the serious detachment of the adults, the young girl in Figure 7.10 turns to smile directly into the lens and casually touches to her lips the long-bladed scissors she is using to cut the garments. Maybe Riis regarded her direct gaze as somewhat immodest, a consequence of work conditions that placed unsupervised young girls amid grown men. Or did she simply find pleasure in having her picture taken? In his second book, *The Children of the Poor* (1892), Riis noted that in contrast to adults, who resisted and feared being photographed, children loved posing for the camera and had a "determination to be 'took' . . . in the most striking pose they could hastily devise."[62]

In *The Children of the Poor*, published originally as a series of articles in *Scribner's Magazine* in 1892, Riis turned his full attention to the group with whom he was most concerned, the children whose futures were being jeopardized by life in the tenements. Figure 7.11 is a rare individual portrait of an orphan, nine-year-old Katie, who attended the Fifty-Second Street Industrial School, a charitable institution for indigent children. Although Katie did not earn wages, she was not spared hard work, for she "scrubbed," cooked, and cleaned for her three older working siblings, for they all had been abandoned by their mother. "In her person and work, she answered the question . . . why we hear so much about the boys and so little about the girls," wrote Riis, "because the home claims their work earlier and to a much greater extent."[63] Consider Katie's clothing, posture, and expression. What do they suggest about her character and her prospects? In acknowledgment of Katie's contribution to her family's survival, Riis called Katie by the nickname often given to immigrant children who cared for siblings, "little mother." What does this tribute say about the economic role that mothers and other adult women played in the lives of poor families?

As an orphan, Katie attended an industrial school funded by a wealthy charity, the Children's Aid Society. The children learned trades, which for girls primarily meant housekeeping. In addition, the education of these mostly Catholic and

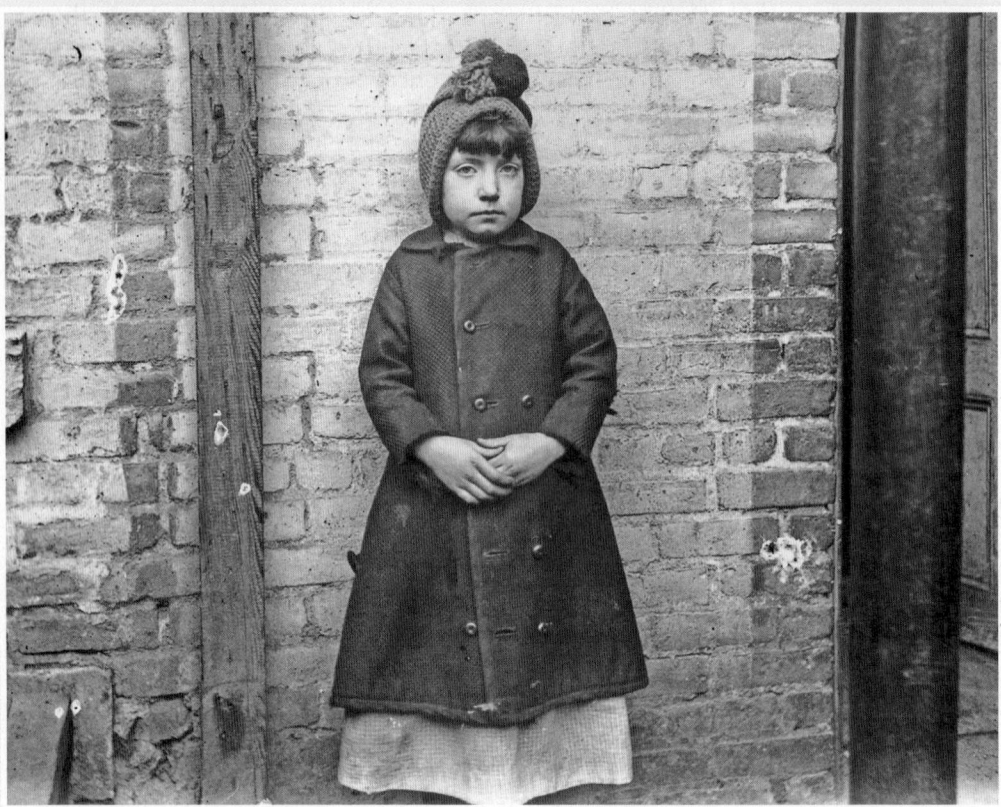

◆ Figure 7.11 *"I Scrubs": Katie Who Keeps House on West 49th Street*
GRANGER — Historical Picture Archive.

Jewish children was meant to assimilate them into Protestant-dominated American society.

A few of Riis's pictures focus on dependent and vulnerable women at the other end of life, the aged. Like very young Katie, the very old woman in Figure 7.12 "scrubs." Her "home," if it can be called that, was in the basement of a police station. These basements were the only public shelters available to homeless people. Riis probably had access to these sites because of his background as a police reporter. The plank behind her was her "bed" in the shelter, and the hand might have been Riis's. What do you read in the woman's closed eyes and downcast face?

◆ Figure 7.12 *An Ancient Woman Lodger in Eldridge Street Station—A "Scrub"*
The Museum of the City of New York/Art Resource, NY.

ANALYZING PRIMARY SOURCES

1. Riis clearly intended to shock comfortable Americans with his images of the slums. What might contemporaries have found most disturbing about his representations of immigrant women and girls?

2. Using Riis as an example, how would you evaluate the impact of documentary photography on middle-class America's reaction to poverty in the late nineteenth century?

3. How do we use these new methods of documentation, informed by a rising sense of public responsibility for improving social conditions and alleviating poverty, to look back through the perspectives of those who did the documenting, into the lives of late nineteenth-century immigrant girls and women?

4. In what ways did women's experiences of poverty and underpaid labor in this period differ from those of men?

APPENDIX

DOCUMENTS

Seneca Falls Declaration of Sentiments and Resolutions

I N 1848, ELIZABETH CADY STANTON, Lucretia Mott, and Martha Coffin Wright, among others, called a meeting in Stanton's hometown of Seneca Falls, New York, to discuss "the social, civil and religious condition of Woman." Over three hundred men and women attended, and one hundred signed a comprehensive document that detailed the discriminations women endured and demanded women's rights, most controversially the vote. The "Declaration of Sentiments" was forthrightly modeled on the Declaration of Independence, which is telling evidence of the Seneca Falls signers' understanding that the liberties and rights promised by the American Revolution had not been extended to the female half of the population.

DECLARATION OF SENTIMENTS

When, in the course of human events, it becomes necessary for one portion of the family of man to assume among the people of the earth a position different from that which they have hitherto occupied, but one to which the laws of nature and of nature's God entitle them, a decent respect to the opinions of mankind requires that they should declare the causes that impel them to such a course.

We hold these truths to be self-evident: that all men and women are created equal; that they are endowed by their Creator with certain inalienable rights; that among these are life, liberty, and the pursuit of happiness; that to secure these rights governments are instituted, deriving their just powers from the consent of the governed. Whenever any form of government becomes destructive of these ends, it is the right of those who suffer from it to refuse allegiance to it, and to insist upon the institution of a new government, laying its foundations on such principles, and organizing its powers in such form, as to them shall seem most likely to effect their safety and happiness. Prudence, indeed, will dictate that governments long established should not be changed for light and transient causes; and accordingly all experience hath shown that mankind are more disposed to suffer, while evils are sufferable, than to right themselves by abolishing the forms to which they were accustomed. But when a long train of abuses and usurpations, pursuing invariably the same object evinces a design to reduce them under absolute despotism, it is their duty to throw off such government, and to provide new guards for their future security. Such has been the patient sufferance of the women under this government, and such is now the necessity which constrains them to demand the equal station to which they are entitled.

The history of mankind is a history of repeated injuries and usurpations on the part of man toward woman, having in direct object the establishment of an absolute tyranny over her.

To prove this, let facts be submitted to a candid world.

He has never permitted her to exercise her inalienable right to the elective franchise. He has compelled her to submit to laws, in the formation of which she had no voice. He has withheld from her rights which are given to the most ignorant and degraded men — both natives and foreigners.

Having deprived her of this first right of a citizen, the elective franchise, thereby leaving her without representation in the halls of legislation, he has opposed her on all sides.

He has made her, if married, in the eye of the law, civilly dead.

He has taken from her all right in property, even to the wages she earns.

He has made her, morally, an irresponsible being, as she can commit many crimes with impunity, provided they be done in the presence of her husband. In the covenant of marriage, she is compelled to promise obedience to her husband, he becoming, to all intents and purposes, her master — the law giving him power to deprive her of her liberty, and to administer chastisement.

He has so framed the laws of divorce, as to what shall be the proper causes, and in case of separation, to whom the guardianship of the children shall be given, as to be wholly regardless of the happiness of women — the law, in all cases, going upon a false supposition of the supremacy of man, and giving all power into his hands.

After depriving her of all rights as a married woman, if single, and the owner of property, he has taxed her to support a government which recognizes her only when her property can be made profitable to it.

He has monopolized nearly all the profitable employments, and from those she is permitted to follow, she receives but a scanty remuneration. He closes against her all the avenues to wealth and distinction which he considers most honorable to himself. As a teacher of theology, medicine, or law, she is not known.

He has denied her the facilities for obtaining a thorough education, all colleges being closed against her.

He allows her in Church, as well as State, but in a subordinate position, claiming Apostolic authority for her exclusion from the ministry, and, with some exceptions, from any public participation in the affairs of the Church.

He has created a false public sentiment by giving to the world a different code of morals for men and women, by which moral delinquencies which exclude women from society, are not only tolerated, but deemed of little account in man.

He has usurped the prerogative of Jehovah himself, claiming it as his right to assign for her a sphere of action, when that belongs to her conscience and to her God.

He has endeavored, in every way that he could, to destroy her confidence in her own powers, to lessen her self-respect, and to make her willing to lead a dependent and abject life.

Now, in view of this entire disfranchisement of one-half the people of this country, their social and religious degradation — in view of the unjust laws above mentioned, and because women do feel themselves aggrieved, oppressed, and fraudulently deprived of their most sacred rights, we insist that they have immediate admission to all the rights and privileges which belong to them as citizens of the United States.

In entering upon the great work before us, we anticipate no small amount of misconception, misrepresentation, and ridicule; but we shall use every instrumentality within our power to effect our object. We shall employ agents, circulate tracts, petition the State and National legislatures, and endeavor to enlist the pulpit and the press in our behalf. We hope this Convention will be followed by a series of Conventions embracing every part of the country.

RESOLUTIONS

WHEREAS, The great precept of nature is conceded to be, that "man shall pursue his own true and substantial happiness." [William] Blackstone in his *Commentaries* remarks, that this law of Nature being coequal with mankind, and dictated by God himself, is of course superior in obligation to any other. It is binding over all the globe, in all countries and at all times; no human laws are of any validity if contrary to this, and such of them as are valid, derive all their force, and all their validity, and all their authority, mediately and immediately, from this original; therefore,

Resolved, That such laws as conflict, in any way, with the true and substantial happiness of woman, are contrary to the great precept of nature and of no validity, for this is "superior in obligation to any other."

Resolved, That all laws which prevent woman from occupying such a station in society as her conscience shall dictate, or which place her in a position inferior to that of man, are contrary to the great precept of nature, and therefore of no force or authority.

Resolved, That woman is man's equal — was intended to be so by the Creator, and the highest good of the race demands that she should be recognized as such.

Resolved, That the women of this country ought to be enlightened in regard to the laws under which they live, that they may no longer publish their degradation by declaring themselves satisfied with their present position, nor their ignorance, by asserting that they have all the rights they want.

Resolved, That inasmuch as man, while claiming for himself intellectual superiority, does accord to woman moral superiority, it is preeminently his duty to encourage her to speak and teach, as she has an opportunity, in all religious assemblies.

Resolved, That the same amount of virtue, delicacy, and refinement of behavior that is required of woman in the social state, should also be required of man, and the same transgressions should be visited with equal severity on both man and woman.

Resolved, That the objection of indelicacy and impropriety, which is so often brought against woman when she addresses a public audience, comes with a very ill-grace from those who encourage, by their attendance, her appearance on the stage, in the concert, or in feats of the circus.

Resolved, That woman has too long rested satisfied in the circumscribed limits which corrupt customs and a perverted application of the Scriptures have marked out for her, and that it is time she should move in the enlarged sphere which her great Creator has assigned her.

Resolved, That it is the duty of the women of this country to secure to themselves their sacred right to the elective franchise.

Resolved, That the equality of human rights results necessarily from the fact of the identity of the race in capabilities and responsibilities.

Resolved, therefore, That, being invested by the Creator with the same capabilities, and the same consciousness of responsibility for their exercise, it is demonstrably the right and duty of woman, equally with man, to promote every righteous cause by every righteous means; and especially in regard to the great subjects of morals and religion, it is self-evidently her right to participate with her brother in teaching them, both in private and in public, by writing and by speaking, by any instrumentalities proper to be used, and in any assemblies proper to be held; and this being a self-evident truth growing out of the divinely implanted principles of human nature, any custom or authority adverse to it, whether modern or wearing the hoary sanction of antiquity, is to be regarded as a self-evident falsehood, and at war with mankind.

[Signers, in alphabetical order]

Caroline Barker
Eunice Barker
William G. Barker
Rachel D. Bonnel
   (Mitchell)
Joel D. Bunker
William Burroughs
E. W. Capron
Jacob P. Chamberlain
Elizabeth Conklin
Mary Conklin
P. A. Culvert
Cynthia Davis
Thomas Dell
William S. Dell
Elias J. Doty
Susan R. Doty
Frederick Douglass
Julia Ann Drake
Harriet Cady Eaton
Elisha Foote
Eunice Newton Foote
Mary Ann Frink
Cynthia Fuller
Experience Gibbs
Mary Gilbert

Lydia Gild
Sarah Hallowell
Mary H. Hallowell
Henry Hatley
Sarah Hoffman
Charles L. Hoskins
Jane C. Hunt
Richard P. Hunt
Margaret Jenkins
John Jones
Lucy Jones
Phebe King
Hannah J. Latham
Lovina Latham
Elizabeth Leslie
Eliza Martin
Mary Martin
Delia Mathews
Dorothy Mathews
Jacob Mathews
Elizabeth W. M'Clintock
Mary M'Clintock
Mary Ann M'Clintock
Thomas M'Clintock
Jonathan Metcalf
Nathan J. Milliken

Mary S. Mirror
Pheobe Mosher
Sarah A. Mosher
James Mott
Lucretia Mott
Lydia Mount
Catharine C. Paine
Rhoda Palmer
Saron Phillips
Sally Pitcher
Hannah Plant
Ann Porter
Amy Post
George W. Pryor
Margaret Pryor
Susan Quinn
Rebecca Race
Martha Ridley
Azaliah Schooley
Margaret Schooley
Deborah Scott
Antoinette E. Segur
Henry Seymour
Henry W. Seymour
Malvina Seymour
Catharine Shaw

Stephen Shear
Sarah Sisson
Robert Smallbridge
Elizabeth D. Smith
Sarah Smith
David Spalding
Lucy Spalding
Elizabeth Cady Stanton
Catharine F. Stebbins
Sophronia Taylor
Betsey Tewksbury
Samuel D. Tillman
Edward F. Underhill
Martha Underhill
Mary E. Vail
Isaac Van Tassel
Sarah Whitney
Maria E. Wilbur
Justin Williams
Sarah R. Woods
Charlotte Woodward
S. E. Woodworth
Martha C. Wright

SOURCE: Susan B. Anthony, Elizabeth Cady Stanton, and Matilda Joslyn Gage, eds., *History of Woman Suffrage* (Rochester, NY: S. B. Anthony, 1889).

Major U.S. Supreme Court Decisions Through Women's Eyes

T HE FOLLOWING BRIEF EXCERPTS of Supreme Court decisions, carefully abridged from the full opinions delivered by the Court, have been selected for their particular importance to the history of women in the United States. Not all of them deal solely or primarily with gender discrimination. Those decisions concerning racism and the legacy of slavery, beginning with the 1856 *Dred Scott* case, have profound implications for women. Read one after another, these decisions give evidence of both the continuity of judicial reasoning and the dramatic shifts in judicial conclusions that have characterized the nation's highest court.

Dred Scott v. Sandford involved a couple who claimed they had gained freedom from slavery by virtue of residence for many years on free soil. The case took almost ten years to arrive before the Court, where a seven-to-two majority ruled that the Scotts remained enslaved. In his last major opinion, Chief Justice Roger Taney not only dismissed the Scotts' claims but sought to intervene in the raging national political debate over slavery by declaring that any federal intervention in slavery, including the 1820 Missouri Compromise (which had banned slavery from the territories in which the Scotts had lived), was unconstitutional.

Dred Scott v. Sandford (1856)

It is difficult at this day to realize the state of public opinion in relation to that unfortunate race, which prevailed in the civilized and enlightened portions of the world at the time of the Declaration of Independence, and when the Constitution of the United States was framed and adopted. . . .

They had for more than a century before been regarded as beings of an inferior order, and altogether unfit to associate with the white race, either in social or political relations; and so far inferior, that they had no rights which the white man was bound to respect; and that the negro might justly and lawfully be reduced to slavery for his benefit. . . . We refer to these historical facts for the purpose of showing the fixed opinions concerning that race, upon which the statesmen of that day spoke and acted. It is necessary to do this, in order to determine whether the general terms used in the Constitution of the United States, as to the rights of man and the rights of the people, was intended to include them, or to give to them or their posterity the benefit of any of its provisions.

[T]he right of property in a slave is distinctly and expressly affirmed in the Constitution. . . . This is done in plain words—too plain to be misunderstood. And no word can be found in the Constitution which gives Congress a greater power over slave property, or which entitles property of that kind to less protection than property of any other description. . . .

Upon these considerations, it is the opinion of the court that the act of Congress which prohibited a citizen from holding and owning property of this kind in the territory of the United States north of the line therein mentioned, is not warranted by the Constitution, and is therefore void; and that neither Dred Scott himself, nor any of his family, were made free by being carried into this territory.

T HE FOURTEENTH AMENDMENT, which was designed to overturn the *Dred Scott* decision by defining national citizenship broadly enough to include freedpeople, became the constitutional basis for challenging both race and gender discrimination. Soon after its ratification in 1868, woman suffragists saw the amendment as a potential resource. The National Woman Suffrage Association contended that, inasmuch as women were citizens, their rights as voters were automatically secured. Accordingly, Virginia Minor tried to vote in her hometown of St. Louis, Missouri, and then sued the local election official who refused her ballot. Chief Justice Morrison Waite delivered the Court's unanimous opinion that although the Fourteenth Amendment did indeed grant women equal citizenship with men, it did not make them voters. His contention, that suffrage was not a civil right but a political privilege outside the amendment's intended scope, was underscored by the passage of the Fifteenth Amendment in 1870, which was addressed explicitly to voting. Waite's reasoning applied to all citizens, not just women. After the *Minor* decision, suffragists realized they needed a separate constitutional amendment to secure women's political rights.

Minor v. Happersett (1874)

The argument is, that as a woman, born or naturalized in the United States and subject to the jurisdiction thereof, is a citizen of the United States and of the State in which she resides, she has the right of suffrage as one of the privileges and immunities of her citizenship, which the State cannot by its laws or constitution abridge.

There is no doubt that women may be citizens. They are persons, and by the fourteenth amendment "all persons born or naturalized in the United States and subject to the jurisdiction thereof" are expressly declared to be "citizens of the United States and of the State wherein they reside." . . .

If the right of suffrage is one of the necessary privileges of a citizen of the United States, then the constitution and laws of Missouri confining it to men are in violation of the Constitution of the United States, as amended, and consequently void. . . . It is clear, . . . we think, that the Constitution has not added the right of suffrage to the privileges and immunities of citizenship as they existed at the time it was adopted.

It is true that the United States guarantees to every State a republican form of government. . . . No particular government is designated as republican, neither is the exact form to be guaranteed, in any manner especially designated. . . .

[I]t is certainly now too late to contend that a government is not republican, within the meaning of this guaranty in the Constitution, because women are not made voters.

I NVOKING THE FOURTEENTH AMENDMENT three decades later, Homer Plessy argued that he had been denied equal protection of the law when a Louisiana statute forced him to travel in a separate all-Black railroad car. By a vote of eight to one, the Court ruled against his claims and found the emerging system of state-sponsored racial segregation that was settling on the postslavery South to be fully constitutional. Writing for the majority, Justice Henry Brown argued that because a system of segregation affected both Black and white, it was not discriminatory. The famous phrase by which this argument has come to be known — "separate but equal" — appears in the brave, dissenting opinion of Justice John Harlan. Note how the Court's ruling treats racial distinction and Black inferiority as facts of nature that any legal decision must recognize.

Plessy v. Ferguson (1896)

A statute which implies merely a legal distinction between the white and colored races—a distinction which is founded in the color of the two races, and which must always exist so long as white men are distinguished from the other race by color—has no tendency to destroy the legal equality of the two races. . . .

The object of the [fourteenth] amendment was undoubtedly to enforce the absolute equality of the two races before the law, but, in the nature of things, it could not have been intended to abolish distinctions based upon color, or to enforce social, as distinguished from political, equality, or a commingling of the two races upon terms unsatisfactory to either. Laws permitting, and even requiring, their separation, in places where they are liable to be brought into contact, do not necessarily imply the inferiority of either race to the other. . . .

We consider the underlying fallacy of the plaintiff's argument to consist in the assumption that the enforced separation of the two races stamps the colored race with a badge of inferiority. If this be so, it is not by reason of anything found in the act, but solely because the colored race chooses to put that construction upon it. The argument necessarily assumes that if, as has been more than once the case, and is not unlikely to be so again, the colored race should become the dominant power in the state legislature, and should enact a law in precisely similar terms, it would thereby relegate the white race to an inferior position. We imagine that the white race, at least, would not acquiesce in this assumption. The argument also assumes that social prejudices may be overcome by legislation, and that equal rights cannot be secured to the negro except by an enforced commingling of the two races. We cannot accept this proposition. . . . Legislation is powerless to eradicate racial instincts, or to abolish distinctions based upon physical differences, and the attempt to do so can only result in accentuating the difficulties of the present situation.

I N *MULLER V. OREGON*, Curt Muller challenged the constitutionality of an Oregon law setting a maximum ten-hour working day for women employees. Starting in the 1880s, the Court had turned away from the Fourteenth Amendment's original purposes to emphasize its guarantee of the individual's right of contract in the workplace, free from state regulation. This reading made most laws setting limits on the working day unconstitutional. Arguing on behalf of Oregon, Louis Brandeis, lead counsel for the National Consumers' League, successfully pressed an argument for the law's constitutionality on the ground that it was directed only at women. Brandeis's argument circumvented the Fourteenth Amendment by contending that the federal government's constitutionally authorized police power, which permitted special regulations for the national good, allowed legislation to protect motherhood and through it "the [human] race." The Court ruled unanimously to uphold the Oregon law, with Justice David Brewer delivering the opinion. As in the *Plessy* decision, the Court held that physical difference and even inferiority are facts of nature that the law may accommodate and that are compatible with formal legal equality. Yet the decision here was hailed by many women reformers as a great victory. Brandeis was appointed to the Supreme Court in 1916, the first Jewish member of the Court.

Muller v. Oregon (1908)

We held in *Lochner v. New York* [1903] that a law providing that no laborer shall be required or permitted to work in bakeries more than sixty hours in a week or ten hours in a day was not as to men a legitimate exercise of the police power of the state, but an unreasonable, unnecessary, and arbitrary interference with the right and liberty of the individual to contract in relation to his labor, and as such was in conflict with, and void under, the Federal Constitution. That decision is invoked by plaintiff in error as decisive of the question before us. But this assumes that the difference between the sexes does not justify a different rule respecting a restriction of the hours of labor. . . .

That woman's physical structure and the performance of maternal functions place her at a disadvantage in the struggle for subsistence is obvious. This is especially true when the burdens of motherhood are upon her. Even when they are not, . . . continuance for a long time on her feet at work, repeating this from day to day, tends to injurious effects upon the body, and, as healthy mothers are essential to vigorous offspring, the physical well-being of woman becomes an object of public interest and care in order to preserve the strength and vigor of the race. . . .

Even though all restrictions on political, personal, and contractual rights were taken away, and [woman] stood, so far as statutes are concerned, upon an absolutely equal plane with [man], it would still be true that she is so constituted that she will rest upon and look to him for protection; that her physical structure and a proper discharge of her maternal functions—having in view not merely her own health, but the well-being of the race—justify legislation to protect her from the greed as well as the passion of man. The limitations which this statute places upon her contractual powers, upon her right to agree with her employer as to the time she shall labor, are not imposed solely for her benefit, but also largely for the benefit of all.

T HE IRONY OF THE *MULLER* DECISION in favor of maximum hours laws to benefit women workers on the basis of their maternal dependency is underlined by the *Adkins* case, decided fifteen years later. *Adkins v. Children's Hospital* involved a congressionally authorized procedure for setting minimum wages for women workers in the District of Columbia. Writing for a five-to-three majority (Justice Brandeis had recused himself from the case), Justice George Sutherland found the maximum hours law unconstitutional on two major grounds. First, while maximum hours laws were constitutionally sanctioned public health measures, minimum wage laws were unacceptable restraints on free trade. Second, the ratification of the Nineteenth Amendment granting woman suffrage in the years since the *Muller* decision made protections of women on the basis of their need to be sheltered by men outdated. Thus, whereas in the earlier case the Court used an appeal to nature to sustain special labor laws that benefited women, in *Adkins,* the Court relied on an evolutionary approach to overturn such regulations.

Adkins v. Children's Hospital (1923)

In the *Muller* case, the validity of an Oregon statute, forbidding the employment of any female in certain industries more than ten hours during any one day was upheld. . . . But the ancient inequality of the sexes, otherwise than physical, as suggested in the *Muller* case has continued "with diminishing intensity." In view of the great — not to say revolutionary — changes which have taken place since that utterance, in the contractual, political and civil status of women, culminating in the Nineteenth Amendment, it is not unreasonable to say that these differences have now come almost, if not quite, to the vanishing point. . . .

[W]e cannot accept the doctrine that women of mature age, *sui juris* [able to act on their own behalf legally], require or may be subjected to restrictions upon their liberty of contract which could not lawfully be imposed in the case of men under similar circumstances. To do so would be to ignore all the implications to be drawn from the present day trend of legislation, as well as that of common thought and usage, by which woman is accorded emancipation from the old doctrine that she must be given special protection or be subjected to special restraint in her contractual and civil relationships.

I N THE WATERSHED CASE of *Brown v. Board of Education of Topeka,* the Supreme Court reversed its 1896 *Plessy v. Ferguson* decision to find state-sponsored racial segregation a violation of the Fourteenth Amendment guarantee of equal protection of the laws. The unanimous ruling was written by Earl Warren, newly appointed chief justice. Linda Brown was the plaintiff in one of several cases that the Court consolidated, all of which challenged the constitutionality of racially segregated public schools. The case bears certain similarities to *Muller v. Oregon.* Both made use of sociological evidence, with *Brown* relying on research into the negative impact of segregation on young Black children. Also as in *Muller,* the successful lead counsel in the *Brown* decision, NAACP lawyer Thurgood Marshall, ultimately was appointed to the Supreme Court, where he became the first African American justice.

Brown v. Board of Education of Topeka (1954)

The plaintiffs contend that segregated public schools are not "equal" and cannot be made "equal," and that hence they are deprived of the equal protection of the laws. . . .

Does segregation of children in public schools solely on the basis of race, even though the physical facilities and other "tangible" factors may be equal, deprive the children of the minority group of equal educational opportunities? We believe that it does. . . .

To separate them from others of similar age and qualifications solely because of their race generates a feeling of inferiority as to their status in the community that may affect their hearts and minds in a way unlikely ever to be undone. . . .

We conclude that, in the field of public education, the doctrine of "separate but equal" has no place. Separate educational facilities are inherently unequal. . . .

Because these are class actions, because of the wide applicability of this decision, and because of the great variety of local conditions, the formulation of decrees in these cases presents problems of considerable complexity.

E STELLE GRISWOLD, executive director of the Planned Parenthood Federation of Connecticut, was arrested for providing a married couple with birth control instruction in violation of an 1879 state law forbidding any aid given "for the purpose of preventing conception." Writing for a seven-to-two majority, Justice William O. Douglas held the law unconstitutional, developing an innovative argument for the existence of a "zone of privacy" not specifically enumerated in the Constitution but found in the surrounding "penumbra" of specified rights. Note Douglas's lofty language about the nature of marriage.

Griswold v. Connecticut (1965)

This law . . . operates directly on an intimate relation of husband and wife and their physician's role in one aspect of that relation. . . .

[S]pecific guarantees in the Bill of Rights have penumbras, formed by emanations from those guarantees that help give them life and substance. . . . Various guarantees create zones of privacy. The right of association contained in the penumbra of the First Amendment is one, as we have seen. . . . The Ninth Amendment provides: "The enumeration in the Constitution, of certain rights, shall not be construed to deny or disparage others retained by the people." . . .

The present case, then, concerns a relationship lying within the zone of privacy created by several fundamental constitutional guarantees. And it concerns a law which, in forbidding the use of contraceptives rather than regulating their manufacture or sale, seeks to achieve its goals by means having a maximum destructive impact upon that relationship. Such a law cannot stand in light of the familiar principle, so often applied by this Court, that a "governmental purpose to control or prevent activities constitutionally subject to state regulation may not be achieved by means which sweep unnecessarily broadly and thereby invade the area of protected freedoms." . . .

We deal with a right of privacy older than the Bill of Rights — older than our political parties, older than our school system. Marriage is a coming together for better or for worse, hopefully enduring, and intimate to the degree of being sacred. It is an association that promotes a way of life, not causes; a harmony in living, not political faiths; a bilateral loyalty, not commercial or social projects.

L IKE THE *GRISWOLD* CASE two years earlier, *Loving v. Virginia* concerns the marriage relationship and government intrusion into it. Richard Loving was a white man who married Mildred Jeter, a Black woman, in 1958 in Washington, D.C. When they moved to Virginia a year later, they were found guilty in state court of violating a 1924 Virginia law forbidding white people from marrying outside of their race, a crime known as "miscegenation." They appealed their conviction to the U.S. Supreme Court. Speaking for a unanimous Court, Chief Justice Earl Warren found this and similar laws in fifteen other states unconstitutional under the Fourteenth Amendment. The Court's rejection of the argument that antimiscegenation laws were constitutionally acceptable because they rested equally on all races echoes the logic of its ruling in *Brown v. Board of Education,* in which intent to discriminate is crucial despite the superficially neutral language of the law.

Loving v. Virginia (1967)

This case presents a constitutional question never addressed by this Court: whether a statutory scheme adopted by the State of Virginia to prevent marriages between persons solely on the basis of racial classifications violates the Equal Protection and Due Process Clauses of the Fourteenth Amendment. . . .

In upholding the constitutionality of these provisions, . . . the state court concluded that the State's legitimate purposes were "to preserve the racial integrity of its citizens," and to prevent "the corruption of blood," "a mongrel breed of citizens," and "the obliteration of racial pride," obviously an endorsement of the doctrine of White Supremacy. . . . [T]he fact of equal application does not immunize the statute from the very heavy burden of justification which the Fourteenth Amendment has traditionally required of state statutes drawn according to race. . . .

Over the years, this Court has consistently repudiated "distinctions between citizens solely because of their ancestry" as being "odious to a free people whose institutions are founded upon the doctrine of equality." At the very least, the Equal Protection Clause demands that racial classifications, especially suspect in criminal statutes, be subjected to the "most rigid scrutiny." . . .

Marriage is one of the "basic civil rights of man," fundamental to our very existence and survival. . . . Under our Constitution, the freedom to marry, or not marry, a person of another race resides with the individual and cannot be infringed by the State.

T HE *REED V. REED* CASE involved the mother of a deceased child contesting an Idaho law mandating that preference be given to the father in designating an executor for a dead child's estate. Sally Reed's case was argued by then American Civil Liberties Union lawyer Ruth Bader Ginsburg. Ginsburg revived elements of the argument made in the 1874 *Minor* case, that the Fourteenth Amendment's guarantees of equal protection before the law applied in cases of discrimination against women. The Court found that the distinction here did not withstand "strict scrutiny" and so was discriminatory. The unanimous opinion was written by Chief Justice Warren Burger. Like Brandeis and Marshall, Ginsburg was later a pathbreaking appointee to the Supreme Court, the second woman (after Sandra Day O'Connor) to serve.

Reed v. Reed (1971)

[W]e have concluded that the arbitrary preference established in favor of males by . . . the Idaho Code cannot stand in the face of the Fourteenth Amendment's command that no State deny the equal protection of the laws to any person within its jurisdiction.

In applying that clause, this Court has consistently recognized that the Fourteenth Amendment does not deny to States the power to treat different classes of persons in different ways. . . .

The Equal Protection Clause of that amendment does, however, deny to States the power to legislate that different treatment be accorded to persons placed by a statute into different classes on the basis of criteria wholly unrelated to the objective of that statute. A classification must be reasonable, not arbitrary, and must rest upon some ground of difference having a fair and substantial relation to the object of the legislation, so that all persons similarly circumstanced shall be treated alike.

J ANE ROE WAS THE PSEUDONYM of Norma McCorvey, an unmarried pregnant woman whose name headed up a class action suit challenging an 1879 Texas law criminalizing abortion. In *Roe v. Wade,* the Court ruled seven to two in Roe's favor. Justice Harry Blackmun wrote the lead opinion, relying on the concept of privacy developed in the *Griswold* case. His opinion included a detailed history of laws prohibiting abortion to show that these were of relatively recent vintage, an approach that contrasted with the antihistorical arguments of nineteenth-century cases such as *Dred Scott* and *Minor v. Happersett.* The *Roe* decision very carefully avoids declaring that a woman's right to abortion is absolute. The limits placed on women's choice — consultation with a physician, government interest in fetal life in the third trimester — opened the way for attempts to reinstitute limits on abortion.

Roe v. Wade (1973)

We forthwith acknowledge our awareness of the sensitive and emotional nature of the abortion controversy. . . . One's philosophy, one's experiences, one's exposure to the raw edges of human existence, one's religious training, one's

attitudes toward life and family and their values, and the moral standards one establishes and seeks to observe, are all likely to influence and to color one's thinking and conclusions about abortion.

In addition, population growth, pollution, poverty, and racial overtones tend to complicate and not to simplify the problem. . . .

The Constitution does not explicitly mention any right of privacy. In a line of decisions, however, . . . the Court has recognized that a right of personal privacy, or a guarantee of certain areas or zones of privacy, does exist under the Constitution. . . .

This right of privacy . . . is broad enough to encompass a woman's decision whether or not to terminate her pregnancy. The detriment that the State would impose upon the pregnant woman by denying this choice altogether is apparent. Specific and direct harm medically diagnosable even in early pregnancy may be involved. Maternity, or additional offspring, may force upon the woman a distressful life and future.

Psychological harm may be imminent. Mental and physical health may be taxed by child care. There is also the distress, for all concerned, associated with the unwanted child, and there is the problem of bringing a child into a family already unable, psychologically and otherwise, to care for it. In other cases, as in this one, the additional difficulties and continuing stigma of unwed motherhood may be involved.

[A]ppellant [in this case Jane Roe] . . . [argues] that the woman's right is absolute and that she is entitled to terminate her pregnancy at whatever time, in whatever way, and for whatever reason she alone chooses. With this we do not agree. . . . [A] State may properly assert important interests in safeguarding health, in maintaining medical standards, and in protecting potential life. At some point in pregnancy, these respective interests become sufficiently compelling to sustain regulation of the factors that govern the abortion decision. The privacy right involved, therefore, cannot be said to be absolute. . . .

The appellee . . . argue[s] that the fetus is a "person" within the language and meaning of the Fourteenth Amendment. . . . If this suggestion of personhood is established, the appellant's case, of course, collapses, for the fetus' right to life would then be guaranteed specifically by the Amendment. . . .

The Constitution does not define "person" in so many words. . . . [T]he word "person," as used in the Fourteenth Amendment, does not include the unborn.

In view of all this, we do not agree that, by adopting one theory of life, Texas may override the rights of the pregnant woman that are at stake. We repeat, however, that the State does have an important and legitimate interest in preserving and protecting the health of the pregnant woman, . . . and that it has still *another* important and legitimate interest in protecting the potentiality of human life. . . .

With respect to the State's important and legitimate interest in the health of the mother, the "compelling" point, in the light of present medical knowledge, is at . . . the end of the first trimester. . . . [F]rom and after this point, a State may regulate the abortion procedure to the extent that the regulation reasonably relates to the preservation and protection of maternal health. Examples of permissible state regulation in this area are requirements as to the qualifications of the person who is to perform the abortion; as to the licensure of that person; as to the facility in which the procedure is to be performed. . . .

[T]he attending physician, in consultation with his patient, is free to determine, without regulation by the State, that, in his medical judgment, the patient's pregnancy should be terminated. If that decision is reached, the judgment may be effectuated by an abortion free of interference by the State.

With respect to the State's important and legitimate interest in potential life, the "compelling" point is at viability. This is so because the fetus then presumably has the capability of meaningful life outside the mother's womb. State regulation protective of fetal life after viability thus has both logical and biological justifications.

A SERIES OF CASES followed *Roe v. Wade* that both upheld and limited a woman's right to seek an abortion. The plaintiff in *Webster v. Reproductive Health Services* was attorney general for the State of Missouri, appealing a lower court ruling that found restrictions on a woman's right to abortion unconstitutional, including the requirement that a woman seeking a second- or third-trimester abortion must have a test to make sure that the fetus was not viable (could not live outside the womb). The lower court ruled that the law violated the Supreme Court's *Roe v. Wade* decision. The Supreme Court overturned this ruling. Chief Justice William Rehnquist wrote for the five-to-three majority that, while the *Roe* decision had recognized the state's obligation to protect potential life, it had been too rigid in establishing the point at which this became paramount. From Rehnquist's perspective, it was permissible for the state to act to favor childbirth even while preserving the woman's formal right to abortion.

Webster v. Reproductive Health Services (1989)

In *Roe v. Wade,* the Court recognized that the State has "important and legitimate" interests in protecting maternal health and in the potentiality of human life. During the second trimester, the State "may, if it chooses, regulate the abortion procedure in ways that are reasonably related to maternal health." . . .

[But] the rigid trimester analysis of the course of a pregnancy enunciated in *Roe* has resulted in . . . making constitutional law in this area a virtual Procrustean bed. . . . [T]he rigid *Roe* framework is hardly consistent with the notion of a Constitution cast in general terms, as ours is, and usually speaking in general principles, as ours does. . . .

[W]e do not see why the State's interest in protecting potential human life should come into existence only at the point of viability, and that

there should therefore be a rigid line allowing state regulation after viability but prohibiting it before viability. . . . [W]e are satisfied that the requirement of these tests permissibly furthers the State's interest in protecting potential human life, and we therefore believe [the article] to be constitutional.

Both appellants and the United States as *amicus curiae* [filing a brief sympathetic to the parties that appealed the decision] have urged that we overrule our decision in *Roe v. Wade.* The facts of the present case, however, differ from those at issue in *Roe.* Here, Missouri has determined that viability is the point at which its interest in potential human life must be safeguarded. . . . This case therefore affords us no occasion to revisit the holding of *Roe.*

THE DEFENSE OF MARRIAGE ACT (DOMA) WAS PASSED by a Republican-dominated Congress and signed by President Bill Clinton in 1996. It limited federal conjugal benefits, ranging from income tax deductions to Social Security, to marriages between "a man and a woman." Although gay marriage was not yet legal anywhere in the United States, the political capital poured into the passage of DOMA suggests that antigay marriage forces were beginning to feel themselves on the defensive. Subsequently, states began to formally legalize gay marriages, beginning with Vermont in 2000.

In 2013, a case challenging DOMA, *United States v. Windsor* from New York, came before the U.S. Supreme Court. By this time, the Obama administration's Department of Justice had registered its own objections to DOMA by announcing that it would not defend the law before the courts.

Nonetheless, the Court's decision ruling crucial sections of DOMA unconstitutional was largely unexpected. Indeed, many proponents of gay marriage had been concerned that bringing the law before the Court would give conservative justices the opportunity to rule against them. The five-to-four decision was delivered on June 26, 2013, by Justice Anthony Kennedy, joined by the three female justices — Ruth Bader Ginsburg, Elena Kagan, and Sonia Sotomayor — and by Justice Stephen Breyer.

The constitutional essence of the decision is the assertion that legal regulation of marriage and family life has always been a matter of state rather than federal law. Underlying this, the decision registers a strong moral objection to the use of federal law to visit "indignity" rather than new rights upon a select class of American citizens.

United States v. Windsor (2013)

DOMA is unconstitutional as a deprivation of the equal liberty of persons that is protected by the Fifth Amendment. . . . By history and tradition the definition and regulation of marriage has been treated as being within the authority and realm of the separate States. Congress has enacted discrete statutes to regulate the meaning of marriage in order to further federal policy, but DOMA, with a directive applicable to over 1,000 federal statutes and . . . the whole realm of federal regulations, has a far greater reach. Its operation is also directed to a class of persons that the laws of New York, and of 11 other States, have sought to protect. Assessing the validity of that intervention requires

discussing the historical and traditional extent of state power and authority over marriage.

The State's decision to give this class of persons the right to marry conferred upon them a dignity and status of immense import. But the Federal Government uses the state-defined class for the opposite purpose — to impose restrictions and disabilities. The question is whether the resulting injury and indignity is a deprivation of an essential part of the liberty protected by the Fifth Amendment, since what New York treats as alike the federal law deems unlike by a law designed to injure the same class the State seeks to protect.

O PPONENTS OF THE RIGHT to abortion had, ever since the 1973 *Roe v. Wade* decision, concentrated on getting state laws passed to create new obstacles to the procedure. Their "long game," however, was to overturn the Supreme Court's decision. They achieved this once outgoing President Trump appointed conservative Amy Comey Barrett to Ruth Bader Ginsburg's seat, thus ensuring an anti-abortion majority on the highest court. Justice Samuel Alito wrote the majority opinion in a case brought by the only remaining abortion clinic in Mississippi, which had sued against the enforcement of a new state law banning abortion after the fifteenth week of pregnancy. Alito's argument concentrated, not on the right of privacy implicit in the Ninth Amendment on which *Roe* primarily rested, but on the clause of the Fourteenth Amendment that prohibits interference with "life, liberty, or property, without due process of law." He contended that the right to abortion was not properly understood within women's rights to liberty.

Historians particularly noted that his historical claim, that abortion had been illegal in Anglo-American law for centuries, was incorrect. Traditionally abortion was not criminalized until "quickening," when the pregnant woman felt the fetus move, usually in the fourth month. When state laws against abortions began to be passed in the 1860s and 1870s, they reflected fears that the childbirth rates of white native-born women were falling behind those of newly arrived immigrants. As Theodore Roosevelt put it in 1902, this was tantamount to "race suicide."

Dobbs v. Jackson Women's Health Organization (2022)

We hold that *Roe* and *Casey* must be overruled. The Constitution makes no reference to abortion, and no such right is implicitly protected by any constitutional provision, including the one on which the defenders of *Roe* and *Casey* now chiefly rely—the Due Process Clause of the Fourteenth Amendment. That provision has been held to guarantee some rights that are not mentioned in the Constitution, but any such right must be "deeply rooted in this Nation's history and tradition" and "implicit in the concept of ordered liberty." . . .

The abortion right is also critically different from any other right that this Court has held to fall within the Fourteenth Amendment's protection of "liberty." *Roe*'s defenders characterize the abortion right as similar to the rights recognized in past decisions involving matters such as intimate sexual relations, contraception, and marriage, but abortion is fundamentally different, as both *Roe* and *Casey* acknowledged, because it destroys what those decisions called "fetal life" and what the law now before us describes as an "unborn human being." . . .

Stare decisis, the doctrine on which *Casey*'s controlling opinion was based, does not compel unending adherence to *Roe*'s abuse of judicial authority. *Roe* was egregiously wrong from the start. Its reasoning was exceptionally weak, and the decision has had damaging consequences. And far from bringing about a national settlement of the abortion issue, *Roe* and *Casey* have enflamed debate and deepened division. . . . [P]roper application of *stare decisis* required an assessment of the strength of the grounds on which *Roe* was based. . . .

. . . Interpreting what is meant by the Fourteenth Amendment's reference to "liberty," we must guard against the natural human tendency to confuse what that Amendment protects with our own ardent views about the liberty that Americans should enjoy. That is why the Court has long been "reluctant" to recognize rights that are not mentioned in the Constitution.

We must ask what the *Fourteenth Amendment* means by the term "liberty." When we engage in that inquiry in the present case, the clear answer is that the Fourteenth Amendment does not protect the right to an abortion. . . . Until the latter part of the 20th century, there was no support in American law for a constitutional right to obtain an abortion. No state constitutional provision had recognized such a right. . . .

Not only was there no support for such a constitutional right until shortly before *Roe*, but abortion had long been a *crime* in every single State. At common law, abortion was criminal in at least some stages of pregnancy and was regarded as unlawful and could have very serious consequences at all stages. American law followed the common law until a wave of statutory restrictions in the 1800s expanded criminal liability for abortions. By the time of the adoption of the Fourteenth Amendment, three-quarters of the States had made abortion a crime at any stage of pregnancy, and the remaining States would soon follow.

IN JUNE 2023, the Supreme Court issued a long-awaited decision that found race-based affirmative action programs in public and private universities unconstitutional. Previous decisions reaching back to 1978 had allowed these programs but with restraints. This time, two cases concerning Harvard University and the University of North Carolina, both submitted in 2014 by a nonprofit group representing Asian American students and organized by conservative white activist Edward Blum, were consolidated as *Students for Fair Admissions, Inc. v. President and Fellows of Harvard College*. The decision was 6–3, pitting the Court's conservative majority against its liberal minority. The majority and minority opinions disagreed on whether the original conditions and purpose of the Fourteenth Amendment were meant to remedy Black discrimination or bar all racial distinction before the law (see Chapter 6). Three of the four female justices voted in the minority, with Amy Coney Barrett joining five other conservatives in the majority. The two Black justices, Clarence Thomas and Ketanji Brown Jackson, also took opposing positions.

Students for Fair Admissions, Inc. v. President and Fellows of Harvard College (2023)

Because Harvard's and UNC's admissions programs lack sufficiently focused and measurable objectives warranting the use of race, unavoidably employ race in a negative manner, involve racial stereotyping, and lack meaningful end points, those admissions programs cannot be reconciled with the guarantees of the Equal Protection Clause. . . . In the wake of the Civil War, Congress proposed and the States ratified the Fourteenth Amendment, providing that no State shall "deny to any person . . . the equal protection of the laws." To its proponents, the Equal Protection Clause represented a "foundation[al] principle"— "the absolute equality of all citizens of the United States politically and civilly before their own laws." The constitution, they were determined, "should not permit any distinctions of law based on race or color." . . . Eliminating racial discrimination means eliminating all of it. And the Equal Protection Clause, we have accordingly held, applies "without regard to any differences of race, of color, or of nationality"—it is "universal in [its] application." . . .

The interests that respondents view as compelling cannot be subjected to meaningful judicial review. Those interests include training future leaders, acquiring new knowledge based on diverse outlooks, promoting a robust marketplace of ideas, and preparing engaged and productive citizens. . . . It is unclear how courts are supposed to measure any of these goals, or if they could, to know when they have been reached so that racial preferences can end. . . .

Respondents' race-based admissions systems also fail to comply with the Equal Protection Clause's twin commands that race may never be used as a "negative" and that it may not operate as a stereotype. The First Circuit found that Harvard's consideration of race has resulted in fewer admissions of Asian-American students. Respondents' assertion that race is never a negative factor in their admissions programs cannot withstand scrutiny. . . .

. . . The dissenting opinions resist these conclusions. They would instead uphold respondents' admissions programs based on their view that the Fourteenth Amendment permits state actors to remedy the effects of societal discrimination through explicitly race-based measures. . . . Most troubling of all is what the dissent must make these omissions to defend: a judiciary that picks winners and losers based on the color of their skin. While the dissent would certainly not permit university programs that discriminated against black and Latino applicants, it is perfectly willing to let the programs here continue.

Many universities have for too long . . . concluded, wrongly, that the touchstone of an individual's identity is not challenges bested, skills built, or lessons learned but the color of their skin. Our constitutional history does not tolerate that choice.

APPENDIX

TABLES AND CHARTS

◆ **Chart 1**

U.S. Birthrate, 1820–2020 (Number of Births per 1,000)

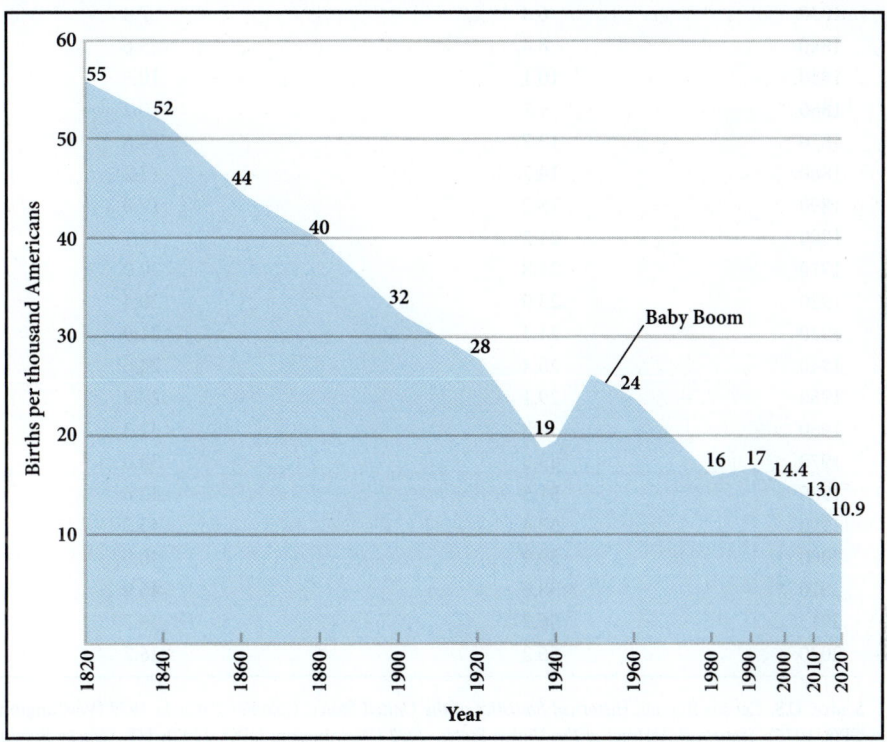

Source: Data from *Historical Statistics of the United States, Colonial Times to 1970* (1975); U.S. Census Bureau, *Statistical Abstract of the United States, 2001* (Washington: GPO, 2001); *U.S. Census Bureau Statistical Abstract* (2011, 2021).

◆ Table 1
U.S. Women and Work, 1820–2020

Year	Percentage of Women in Paid Employment	Percentage of Paid Workers Who Are Women
1820	6.2	7.3
1830	6.4	7.4
1840	8.4	9.6
1850	10.1	10.8
1860	9.7	10.2
1870	13.7	14.8
1880	14.7	15.2
1890	18.2	17.0
1900	21.2	18.1
1910	24.8	20.0
1920	23.9	20.4
1930	24.4	21.9
1940	25.4	24.6
1950	29.1	27.8
1960	34.8	32.3
1970	43.3	38.0
1980	51.5	42.6
1990	57.4	45.2
2000	59.9	46.5
2010	58.6	46.9
2015	56.7	46.7
2020	56.2	46.7

Source: U.S. Census Bureau, *Historical Statistics of the United States, Colonial Times to 1970* (Washington: GPO, 1975); *Statistical Abstract of the United States, 2002* (Washington: GPO, 2002); *U.S. Census Bureau Statistical Abstracts* (2017), table 1; U.S. Bureau of Labor Statistics, Current Population Survey, 2020, table 3.

◆ **Table 2**

Participation Rate in the Female Labor Force, by Family Status, 1890–2020

Year	Single	Widowed/ Divorced	Married	Mothers*
1890	41	30	5	—
1900	41	33	6	—
1910	48	35	11	—
1920	44†	— †	9	—
1930	46	34	12	—
1940	48	32	17	28
1950	51	36	25	33
1960	44	37	32	37
1970	57	40	41	40
1980	64	44	50	56
1990	67	47	58	67
2000	69	49	61	73
2010	63	49	61	71
2015	57.8	44.1	56.3	70
2020	56.3	40.6	53.8	72.5

*Mothers of children under age eighteen.

†Single women counted with widows and divorced women.

Sources: Lynn Weiner, *From Working Girl to Working Mother: The Female Labor Force in the United States, 1820–1980* (Chapel Hill: University of North Carolina Press, 1985), 6; U.S. Bureau of Labor Statistics, "Labor Force Participation Rates of Women by Presence and Age of Children, March 1980–2000"; U.S. Department of Labor, "Women in the Labor Force: A Databook" (2011, 2017, and 2021), tables 1, 4 and 7.

◆ **Table 3**
Immigration to the United States, 1900–2020

Years	Female Immigrants to the United States	Total Immigrants to the United States
1900–1909	2,492,336	8,202,388
1910–1919	2,215,582	6,347,156
1920–1929	1,881,923	4,295,510
1930–1939	386,659	699,375
1940–1949	454,291	856,608
1950–1959	1,341,404	2,499,286
1960–1969	1,786,441	3,213,749
1970–1979	2,299,713	4,366,001
1980–1989	3,224,661	6,332,218
1990–1999	4,740,896	9,782,093
2000–2010	6,227,291	11,351,447
2011–2015	1,659,045	3,084,224
2016–2020	2,777,028	5,146,410

Source: U.S. Census Bureau, *Historical Statistics of the United States, Colonial Times to 1970* (Washington: GPO, 1975), Series C 102–114; U.S. Department of Justice, *1978 Statistical Yearbook of the Immigration and Naturalization Service* (Washington: GPO, 1978), table 10; *1984 Statistical Yearbook of the Immigration and Naturalization Service* (Washington: GPO, 1987), table I M M 4.1; *1988 Statistical Yearbook of the Immigration and Naturalization Service* (Washington: GPO, 1989), table 11; *1994 Statistical Yearbook of the Immigration and Naturalization Service* (Washington: GPO, 2002), table 1; *2003 Statistical Yearbook of the Immigration and Naturalization Service* (Washington: GPO, 2004), table 6; *2004 Statistical Yearbook of the Immigration and Naturalization Service* (Washington: GPO, 2005), table 7; *2005 Statistical Yearbook of the Immigration and Naturalization Service* (Washington: GPO, 2006), table 8; *2006 Statistical Yearbook of the Immigration and Naturalization Service* (Washington: GPO, 2007), table 9; *2007 Statistical Yearbook of the Immigration and Naturalization Service* (Washington: GPO, 2008), table 9; *2011 Statistical Yearbook of the Immigration and Naturalization Service* (Washington: GPO, 2012), table 8; *2012 Statistical Yearbook of the Immigration and Naturalization Service* (Washington: GPO, 2013), table 8; *2013 Statistical Yearbook of the Immigration and Naturalization Service* (Washington: GPO, 2014), table 8; *2014 Statistical Yearbook of the Immigration and Naturalization Service* (Washington: GPO, 2015), table 8; *2015 Statistical Yearbook of the Immigration and Naturalization Service* (Washington: GPO, 2016), table 8; *Yearbook of Immigration Statistics*, Department of Homeland Security, Yearbooks 2016–2020, table 8.

Acknowledgments

Chapter 2: Mrs. Agatha Stubbings (1645). Excerpted from Susie M. Ames, ed., *County Court Records of Accomack-Northampton, Virginia 1640–1645* (Charlottesville: University of Virginia Press, 1973), 433–34. Copyright © 1973 by the Virginia Historical Society. Reprinted by permission of the Virginia Historical Society.

Eliza Lucas Pinckney, letter to Miss Bartlett and excerpt from 1740 letter. From *The Letterbook of Eliza Lucas Pinckney 1739–1762*, ed. Elise Pinckney. Copyright © 1997. Reprinted by permission of the University of South Carolina Press.

Chapter 3: Phillis Wheatley, letter to Arbour Tanner, May 19, 1772. From *The Poems of Phillis Wheatley*, edited and with an introduction by Julian D. Mason Jr. Copyright © 1966 by the University of North Carolina Press, renewed 1989. Used by permission of the publisher; www.uncpress.org.

Phillis Wheatley, letter to Rev. Samson Occom, March 11, 1774. From *The Poems of Phillis Wheatley*, edited and with an introduction by Julian D. Mason Jr. Copyright © 1966 by the University of North Carolina Press, renewed 1989. Used by permission of the publisher; www.uncpress.org.

Chapter 5: "Narrative of Mrs. Rosalia Leese, Who Witnessed the Hoisting of the Bear Flag in Sonoma on the 14th of June 1846," from Rose Marie Beebe and Robert M. Senkewicz, trans. and eds., *Testimonios: Early California through the Eyes of Women, 1815–1848*. Copyright © 2006 by Rose Marie Beebe and Robert M. Senkewicz. Reprinted by permission of the publisher.

Chapter 7: Excerpt from Sarah Winnemucca, "Indian Schools," quoted in *Silver State*, July 9, 1886; excerpt from Sarah Winnemucca, "We are referred . . . ," quoted in *Daily Alta California*, July 24, 1886. Reproduced from *The Newspaper Warrior: Sarah Winnemucca Hopkins's Campaign for American Indian Rights, 1864–1891*, edited by Cari M. Carpenter and Carolyn Sorisio. Copyright © 2015 by the Board of Regents of the University of Nebraska. Reprinted by permission of the University of Nebraska Press.

N O T E S

Chapter 1

1. Mary P. Ryan, *Mysteries of Sex: Tracing Women and Men through American History* (Chapel Hill: University of North Carolina Press, 2006), 21.

2. Karen Kupperman, "International at the Creation," in Thomas Bender, ed., *Rethinking American History in a Global Age* (Berkeley: University of California Press, 2002), 105.

3. Judith K. Brown, "Economic Organization and the Position of Women among the Iroquois," *Ethnohistory* 17, nos. 3–4 (Summer–Fall 1970): 159.

4. Brown, "Economic Organization," 153.

5. Brown, "Economic Organization," 153.

6. Richard White, *The Middle Ground: Indians, Empires, and Republics in the Great Lakes Region, 1650–1815* (Cambridge: Cambridge University Press, 1991), 63.

7. Ramón A. Gutiérrez, *When Jesus Came, the Corn Mothers Went Away: Marriage, Sexuality, and Power in New Mexico, 1500–1846* (Stanford, CA: Stanford University Press, 1991), 34.

8. James Axtell, ed., *The Indian Peoples of Eastern America: A Documentary History of the Sexes* (New York: Oxford University Press, 1981), 142.

9. William Monter, "Protestant Wives, Catholic Saints, and the Devil's Handmaid," in Renate Bridenthal and Claudia Koonz, eds., *Becoming Visible: Women in European History* (Boston: Houghton Mifflin, 1977), 207.

10. John Huxtable Elliott, *Empires of the Atlantic World: Britain and Spain in America 1492–1830* (New Haven: Yale University Press, 2007), 64.

11. Camilla Townsend, *Malintzin's Choices: An Indian Woman in the Conquest of Mexico* (Albuquerque: University of New Mexico Press, 2006).

12. Susan Migden Socolow, *The Women of Colonial Latin America*, 2nd ed. (Cambridge: Cambridge University Press, 2014), 194–95.

13. Clara Sue Kidwell, "Indian Women as Cultural Mediators," *Ethnohistory* 39, no. 2 (Spring 1992): 97.

14. Linda Heywood, *Njinga of Angola: Africa's Warrior Queen* (Cambridge, MA: Harvard University Press, 2017), 210.

15. Kathleen Sheldon, *African Women: Early History to the 21st Century* (Bloomington: Indiana University Press, 2017), 1–34.

16. Elliott, *Empires of the Atlantic World*, 100.

17. *Voyages: The Trans-Atlantic Slave Trade Database*, slavevoyages.org.

18. David Brion Davis, *Inhuman Bondage: The Rise and Fall of Slavery in the New World* (Oxford: Oxford University Press, 2006), 108.

19. David Eltis and David Richardson, *Atlas of the Transatlantic Slave Trade* (New Haven: Yale University Press, 2010), 17.

20. Father Joseph-François Lafitau, *Customs of the American Indians Compared with the Customs of Primitive Times*, ed. and trans. William N. Fenton and Elizabeth L. Moore (1724; Toronto: Champlain Society, 1977), 2:8.

21. Thomas Harriot, *A Briefe and True Report of the New Found Land of Virginia*, reprint of the 1590 de Bry edition (New York: Dover, 1972), 50.

22. John White, *The First Colony*, reprinted in *The Roanoke Voyages, 1584–1590*, vol. 1 (London: The Hakluyt Society, 1955), 430.

23. Joyce E. Chaplin, *Subject Matter: Technology, the Body, and Science on the Anglo-American Frontier, 1500–1676* (Cambridge, MA: Harvard University Press, 2001), 36.

24. Captain John Smith, *The Generall Historie of Virginia, New England & the Summer Isles, Together with the True Travels, Adventures and Observations, and a Sea Grammar*, vol. 1 (1607), Library of Congress, American Memory, "The Capital and the Bay: Narratives of Washington and the Chesapeake Bay Region, ca. 1600–1925," docsouth.unc.edu/southlit/smith/smith.html.

25. Karen Ordahl Kupperman, *Indians and English: Facing Off in Early America* (Ithaca, NY: Cornell University Press, 2000), 199.

26. Camilla Townsend, *Pocahontas and the Powhatan Dilemma* (New York: Hill and Wang, 2005), 152.

Chapter 2

1. Cotton Mather, *A Narrative of Hannah Swarton Containing Wonderful Passages Relating to Her Captivity and Deliverance, in Puritans among the Indians: Accounts of Captivity and Redemption, 1676–1724*, ed. Alden T. Vaughan and Edward W. Clark (Cambridge, MA: Belknap Press, 1981), 153.

2. Juliana Barr, "Borders and Borderlands," in Susan Sleeper-Smith et al., *Why You Can't Teach United States History without American Indians* (Chapel Hill: University of North Carolina Press, 2015), 10.

3. Sophie H. Drinker, "Women Attorneys of Colonial Times," *Maryland Historical Magazine* 56, no. 4 (December 1961): 350.

4. Paula A. Treckel, *To Comfort the Heart: Women in Seventeenth-Century America* (New York: Twayne, 1996), 37.

5. Carol Berkin and Leslie Horowitz, eds., *Women's Voices, Women's Lives: Documents in Early American History* (Boston: Northeastern University Press, 1998), 16.

6. Kathleen M. Brown, *Good Wives, Nasty Wenches, and Anxious Patriarchs* (Chapel Hill: University of North Carolina Press, 1996), 166.

7. James D. Rice, "Rethinking the 'American Paradox,'" in Susan Sleeper-Smith et al., *Why You Can't Teach United States History without American Indians* (Chapel Hill: University of North Carolina Press, 2015), 51.

8. *Voyages: The Trans-Atlantic Slave Trade Database,* slavevoyages.org.

9. Olaudah Equiano, *The Interesting Narrative of the Life of Olaudah Equiano, or Gustavus Vassa, the African. Written by Himself* (London, 1789), Documenting the American South, University Library (University of North Carolina at Chapel Hill, 2001), 79.

10. Peter Kolchin, *American Slavery, 1619–1877* (New York: Hill and Wang, 1993), 51.

11. Philip D. Morgan, *Slave Counterpoint: Black Culture in the Eighteenth-Century Chesapeake and Lowcountry* (Chapel Hill: University of North Carolina Press, 1998), 12.

12. Brown, *Good Wives*, 214.

13. Paul Heinegg and Henry B. Hoff, "Freedom in the Archives: Free African Americans in Colonial America," *Common-Place* 5, no. 1 (October 2004), common-place .org/vol-05/no-01/heinegg-hoff.

14. Morgan, *Slave Counterpoint*, 100.

15. Laurel Thatcher Ulrich, *Good Wives: Image and Reality in the Lives of Women in Northern New England, 1650–1750* (New York: Vintage Books, 1991), 115.

16. Richard Godbeer, *Sexual Revolution in Early America* (Baltimore: Johns Hopkins University Press, 2002), 228.

17. Treckel, *To Comfort the Heart*, 145.

18. Mary Beth Norton, *Founding Mothers and Fathers: Gendered Power and the Forming of American Society* (New York: Alfred A. Knopf, 1996), 351.

19. Lyle Koehler, *A Search for Power: The "Weaker Sex" in Seventeenth-Century New England* (Urbana: University of Illinois Press, 1980), 31.

20. Ann M. Little, *The Many Captivities of Esther Wheelwright* (New Haven: Yale University Press, 2016), 4.

21. Norton, *Founding Mothers and Fathers*, 359.

22. Vivian Bruce Conger, " 'If Widow, Both Housewife and Husband May Be': Widows' Testamentary Freedom in Colonial Massachusetts and Maryland," in Larry D. Eldridge, ed., *Women and Freedom in Early America* (New York: New York University Press, 1997), 249.

23. Treckel, *To Comfort the Heart*, 175.

24. Michael L. Blakey, "The New York African Burial Ground Project: An Examination of Enslaved Lives, a Construction of Ancestral Ties," *Transforming Anthropology* 7, no. 1 (1998), huarchivesnet.howard.edu/0008huarnet/blakey1 .htm.

25. Leo Hershkowitz, "Original Inventories of Early New York Jews (1682–1763)," *American Jewish History* 90 (December 2002): 239–322.

26. Alan Taylor, *American Colonies* (New York: Viking, 2001), 368.

27. Clara Sue Kidwell, "Indian Women as Cultural Mediators," *Ethnohistory* 39, no. 2 (Spring 1992): 97.

28. Richard White, *The Middle Ground: Indians, Empires, and Republics in the Great Lakes Region, 1650–1815* (Cambridge: Cambridge University Press, 1991), 72.

29. Kathleen DuVal, *The Native Ground: Indians and Colonists in the Heart of the Continent* (Philadelphia: University of Pennsylvania Press, 2006), 73, 84.

30. Pekka Hämäläinen, *The Comanche Empire* (New Haven: Yale University Press, 2008), 52.

31. Mary Beth Norton, "Gender and Defamation in Seventeenth-Century Maryland," *William and Mary Quarterly*, 3rd ser., 44 (January 1987): 4–5.

32. Ilona Katzew, "Casta Painting: Identity and Social Stratification in Colonial Mexico," *Laberinto* 1, nos. 1–2 (Fall 1997), acmrs.org/sites/default/files/sites/default/files/ laberinto_v1.pdf.

Chapter 3

1. Mary Beth Norton and Ruth M. Alexander, eds., *Major Problems in American Women's History*, 2nd ed. (Lexington, MA: D. C. Heath, 1996), 81.

2. Mary Beth Norton, *Liberty's Daughters: The Revolutionary Experience of American Women, 1750–1800* (Boston: Little, Brown, 1980), 166.

3. Cynthia Kierner, *Beyond the Household: Women's Place in the Early South, 1700–1835* (Ithaca, NY: Cornell University Press, 1998), 75.

4. Norton, *Liberty's Daughters*, 164.

5. Norton, *Liberty's Daughters*, 168.

6. "Penelope Barker," National Women's History Museum, http://www.nwhm.org/education-resources/biography/ biographies/penelope-barker.

7. Norton, *Liberty's Daughters*, 159.

8. *Virginia Gazette*, September 15, 1774.

9. Marylynn Salmon, *The Limits of Independence: American Women, 1760–1800* (New York: Oxford University Press, 1994), 58.

10. Norton, *Liberty's Daughters*, 169.

11. Colin G. Calloway, *First Peoples: A Documentary Survey of American Indian History* (Boston: Bedford/St. Martin's, 2016), 163.

12. Benjamin Quarles, *The Negro in the American Revolution* (Chapel Hill: University of North Carolina Press, 1961), 135.

13. Quarles, *The Negro in the American Revolution*, 142.

14. Linda K. Kerber, *Women of the Republic: Intellect and Ideology in Revolutionary America* (Chapel Hill: University of North Carolina Press, 1980), 52.

15. Kerber, *Women of the Republic*, 54.

16. Julie Wheelwright, *Amazons and Military Maids: Women Who Dressed as Men in Pursuit of Life, Liberty, and Happiness* (London: Pandora, 1989), 133.

17. Holly A. Mayer, *Belonging to the Army: Camp Followers and Community during the American Revolution* (Columbia: University of South Carolina Press, 1996), 20.

18. Kerber, *Women of the Republic*, 59.

19. Mayer, *Belonging to the Army*, 124.

20. Kerber, *Women of the Republic*, 64.

21. Catherine Van Cortlandt, "Secret Correspondence of a Loyalist Wife," in Robert Marcus and David Burner, eds., *America Firsthand*, 4th ed. (Boston: Bedford, 1997), 2:109–11.

22. Norton, *Liberty's Daughters*, 80.

23. Norton, *Liberty's Daughters*, 184.

24. Norton, *Liberty's Daughters*, 187.

25. Theda Perdue, *Cherokee Women: Gender and Culture Change, 1700–1835* (Lincoln: University of Nebraska Press, 1998), 87, 101.

26. Perdue, *Cherokee Women*, 111.

27. Calloway, *First Peoples*, 226–32.

28. Virginia Scharff, *Twenty Thousand Roads: Women, Movement, and the West* (Berkeley: University of California Press, 2002), 19.

29. Cassandra Pybus, " 'One Militant Saint': The Much Traveled Life of Mary Perth," *Journal of Colonialism and Colonial History* 9, no. 3 (Winter 2008).

30. Peter Kolchin, *American Slavery, 1619–1877* (New York: Hill and Wang, 1993), 78.

31. Salmon, *Limits of Independence*, 111.

32. Jeffrey J. Crow, *The Black Experience in Revolutionary North Carolina* (Raleigh: North Carolina Department of Cultural Resources, 1977), 17.

33. Kierner, *Beyond the Household*, 99.

34. Barbara E. Lacey, "Women in the Era of the American Revolution: The Case of Norwich, Connecticut," *New England Quarterly* 53 (December 1980): 539.

35. Norton, *Liberty's Daughters*, 216.

36. Norton, *Liberty's Daughters*, 223–24.

37. Norton, *Liberty's Daughters*, 171.

38. Kerber, *Women of the Republic*, 226.

39. Kerber, *Women of the Republic*, 163–64.

40. Linda Grant De Pauw, *Founding Mothers: Women in America in the Revolutionary Era* (Boston: Houghton Mifflin, 1975), 211.

41. Norton, *Liberty's Daughters*, 287.

42. Catherine A. Brekus, *Strangers and Pilgrims: Female Preaching in America, 1740–1845* (Chapel Hill: University of North Carolina Press, 1998), 49.

43. Brekus, *Strangers and Pilgrims*, 63–64.

44. Brekus, *Strangers and Pilgrims*, 87.

45. Sylvia R. Frey and Betty Wood, *Come Shouting to Zion: African-American Protestantism in the American South and British Caribbean to 1830* (Chapel Hill: University of North Carolina Press, 1998), 13.

46. Marina Warner, *Monuments and Maidens: The Allegory of the Female Form* (New York: Atheneum, 1985), 12.

47. Stephanie McKellop, "America, the 'Rebellious Slut': Gender & Political Cartoons in the American Revolution," *Common-Place* 17, no. 3 (Spring 2017), http://common-place.org/book/vol-17-no-3-mckellop.

48. Edwin Wolf II and Marie Elena Korey, *Quarter of a Millennium: The Library Company of Philadelphia 1731–1981* (Philadelphia: The Company, 1981), 79.

49. Daniel C. Littlefield, *Revolutionary Citizens: African Americans, 1776–1804* (New York: Oxford University Press, 1997), 14.

50. Phillis Wheatley, *Poems on Various Subjects, Religious and Moral* (1773).

51. Kerber, *Women of the Republic*, 205.

52. Sheila L. Skemp, *First Lady of Letters: Judith Sargent Murray and the Struggle for Female Independence* (Philadelphia: University of Pennsylvania Press, 2009), 227–28.

Chapter 4

1. Lucy Larcom, *A New England Girlhood: Outlined from Memory* (Boston: Houghton Mifflin, 1889), 222.

2. Larcom, *New England Girlhood*, 200.

3. Alexis de Tocqueville, *Democracy in America* (1841; repr., New York: Schocken Books, 1977), 6.

4. Harvey Green, *The Light of the Home: An Intimate View of the Lives of Women in Victorian America* (New York: Pantheon, 1983), 56.

5. Catharine Beecher, *Woman Suffrage and Woman's Profession* (Hartford: Brown and Gross, 1871), 175.

6. Nancy Cott, *The Bonds of Womanhood: "Woman's Sphere" in New England, 1780–1835*, 2nd ed. (New Haven: Yale University Press, 1997), 28.

7. Beecher, *Woman Suffrage and Woman's Profession*, 28.

8. Nancy Cott, "Passionlessness: An Interpretation of Victorian Sexual Ideology, 1790–1850," *Signs* 4 (1978): 219–36.

9. Cott, "Passionlessness."

10. William W. Sanger, M.D., *The History of Prostitution: Its Extent, Causes, and Effects throughout the World* (New York: Harper and Brothers, 1858, 1921), 489.

11. Catharine Beecher, *A Treatise on Domestic Economy* (1841; repr., New York: Schocken Books, 1978), 178.

12. Larcom, *New England Girlhood*, 198.

13. Mrs. A. J. Graves, *Woman in America: Being an Examination into the Moral and Intellectual Condition of American Female Society* (New York: Harper and Brothers, 1841), 58.

14. American Social History Project, *Who Built America? Working People and the Nation's Economy, Politics, Culture and Society* (New York: Pantheon Books, 1989), 1:249.

15. Larcom, *New England Girlhood*, 196.

16. Alice Kessler-Harris, *Out to Work: A History of Wage-Earning Women in the United States* (New York: Oxford University Press, 1982), 47.

17. "Jerusalem," in *William Blake: Selected Poems* (1804; repr., London: Bloomsbury Publishing Ltd., 2004), 114.

18. Cott, *Bonds of Womanhood*, 38.

19. Larcom, *New England Girlhood*, 196.

20. Charles Dickens, *American Notes* (London: Chapman and Hall, 1842), chap. 4.

21. Larcom, *New England Girlhood*, 146.

22. Harriet Hanson Robinson, *Loom and Spindle: Or Life among the Early Mill Girls* (New York: T. Y. Crowell, 1889), 83.

23. Elizabeth Cady Stanton to Paulina Wright Davis, December 6, 1852, in Ann D. Gordon, ed., *The Selected Papers of Elizabeth Cady Stanton and Susan B. Anthony: In the School of Anti-Slavery, 1840 to 1866* (New Brunswick, NJ: Rutgers University Press, 1997), 214.

24. Christine Stansell, *City of Women: Sex and Class in New York, 1789–1860* (New York: Alfred A. Knopf, 1986), 47.

25. Stansell, *City of Women*, 14.

26. Susan Smedes, *Memorials of a Southern Planter* (Baltimore: Cushings and Bailey, 1887), 48.

27. Augusta County, Virginia, 1860 Population Census, *Valley of the Shadow: Two Communities in the American Civil War*, Virginia Center for Digital History, University of Virginia Library, http://valley.vcdh.virginia.edu/govdoc/popcensus.html.

28. Brenda E. Stevenson, *Life in Black and White: Family and Community in the Slave South* (New York: Oxford University Press, 1996), 42.

29. Stephanie McCurry, *Masters of Small Worlds: Yeoman Households, Gender Relations, and the Political Culture of the Antebellum South Carolina Low Country* (New York: Oxford University Press, 1995), 223.

30. Caroline Howard Gilman, *Recollections of a Southern Matron* (New York: Harper and Brothers, 1838), 94.

31. Angelina Grimké, *An Appeal to the Women of the Nominally Free States* (1838), in Nancy Cott, ed., *Root of Bitterness: Documents of the Social History of American Women* (Boston: Northeastern University Press, 1986), 197.

32. Fannie Moore, *Federal Writers' Project: Slave Narrative Project, Vol. 11, North Carolina, Part 2, Jackson-Yellerday*, 1936, p. 128. Manuscript/Mixed Material. Retrieved from the Library of Congress, https://www.loc.gov/item/mesn112.

33. Virginia Clay-Clopton, *A Belle of the Fifties: Memories of Mrs. Clay of Alabama: Covering Social and Political Life in Washington and the South* (New York: Doubleday, 1905), 212.

34. McCurry, *Masters of Small Worlds*, 260.

35. Gerda Lerner, ed., *Black Women in White America: A Documentary History* (New York: Vintage Books, 1992), 34–35.

36. Sharla M. Fett, *Working Cures: Healing, Health, and Power on Southern Slave Plantations* (Chapel Hill: University of North Carolina Press, 2002), 111.

37. Benjamin Drew, ed., *A North-Side View of Slavery: The Refugee; or, The Narratives of Fugitive Slaves in Canada Related by Themselves* (Boston: J. P. Jewett and Co., 1856), 187.

38. Tera W. Hunter, *Bound in Wedlock: Slave and Free Black Marriage in the Nineteenth Century* (Cambridge, MA: Harvard University Press, 2017), 14.

39. Stevenson, *Life in Black and White*, 236.

40. Stevenson, *Life in Black and White*, 232.

41. Deborah Gray White, *Ar'n't I a Woman? Female Slaves in the Plantation South*, rev. ed. (New York: Norton, 1999), 102–3.

42. Mary Boykin Chesnut, *A Diary from Dixie* (1905; repr., Boston: Houghton Mifflin, 1949), 212.

43. Cott, *Bonds of Womanhood*, 68.

44. Lerner, *Black Women in White America*, 38.

45. White, *Ar'n't I a Woman?*, 31.

46. Stephanie M. H. Camp, *Closer to Freedom: Enslaved Women and Everyday Resistance in the Plantation South* (Chapel Hill: University of North Carolina Press, 2004), 66–68.

47. Thomas R. R. Cobb, *An Inquiry into the Law of Negro Slavery in the United States of America. To Which Is Prefixed, an Historical Sketch of Slavery* (Philadelphia: T. & J.W. Johnson/Savannah/W.T. Williams), 39.

48. *Federal Writers' Project: Slave Narrative Project, Vol. 16, Texas, Part 1, Adams-Duhon*. 1936. Manuscript/Mixed Material. Retrieved from the Library of Congress, https://www.loc.gov/item/mesn161/ (accessed July 25, 2017).

49. Stephanie Jones-Rogers, " '[S]he Could . . . Spare One Ample Breast for the Profit of Her Owner': White Mothers and Enslaved Wet Nurses' Invisible Labor in American Slave Markets," *Slavery and Abolition* 38, no. 2 (2017): 348.

50. Susan Conrad, *Perish the Thought: Intellectual Women in Romantic America, 1830–1860* (Secaucus, NJ: Citadel Press, 1978), 20. See Nathaniel Hawthorne, "Witches: A Scene from Main Street," *Godey's Lady's Book* 42 (1851): 192.

51. Sarah Josepha Hale, "Editors' Table," *Godey's Lady's Book* 42 (1851): 65.

52. Alice B. Neal, "The Constant, or the Anniversary Present," *Godey's Lady's Book* 42 (1851): 5.

53. Kate Berry, "How Can an American Woman Serve Her Country?," *Godey's Lady's Book* 43 (1851): 362.

54. Sarah Josepha Hale, "Editor's Table," *Godey's Lady's Book* 47 (1853): 554.

55. Barbara Welter, "The Cult of True Womanhood, 1820–1860," *American Quarterly* 18 (1966): 151–74.

56. John Wood, ed., *America and the Daguerreotype* (Iowa City: University of Iowa Press, 1991), 95.

57. Oliver Jensen et al., *An American Album* (New York: American Heritage Publishers, 1968), 21.

58. Jensen et al., *American Album*.

59. Kenneth E. Nelson, "A Thumbnail History of the Daguerreotype," Daguerreian Society, http://daguerre.org/resource/history/history.html (accessed February 15, 2015).

Chapter 5

1. Martha S. Read to Lorinda Shelton, April 6, 1852, Norwich, NY, http://xroads.virginia.edu/~HYPER/HNS/domwest/read.html (accessed June 16, 2004).

2. Lillian Schlissel, ed., *Women's Diaries of the Westward Journey* (New York: Schocken Books, 1982), 188.

3. Cathy Luchetti, ed., *Women of the West* (St. George, UT: Antelope Island Press, 1982), 145.

4. John Mack Faragher, *Women and Men on the Overland Trail* (New Haven: Yale University Press, 1979), 172.

5. Schlissel, *Women's Diaries of the Westward Journey*, 179–80.

6. Schlissel, *Women's Diaries of the Westward Journey*, 214.

7. Schlissel, *Women's Diaries of the Westward Journey*, 223.

8. Sarah Royce, *A Frontier Lady*, excerpted in Ida Rae Egli, ed., *No Rooms of Their Own: Women Writers of Early California* (Berkeley: Heyday Books, 1992), 15.

9. Egli, *No Rooms of Their Own*, 13.

10. Glenda Riley, *A Place to Grow: Women in the American West* (Arlington Heights, IL: Harlan Davidson, 1982), 127.

11. Sarah Winnemucca Hopkins, *Life among the Piutes: Their Wrongs and Claims* (1883; repr., Bishop, CA: Sierra Media, 1969), 5, 11.

12. J. S. Holliday, *The World Rushed In: The California Gold Rush Experience* (New York: Simon and Schuster, 1981), 164.

13. Susan B. Anthony to Mary Anthony, February 7, 1848, in Ann D. Gordon, ed., *The Selected Papers of Elizabeth Cady Stanton and Susan B. Anthony*, vol. 1, *In the School of Anti-Slavery, 1840–1866* (New Brunswick, NJ: Rutgers University Press, 1996), 134.

14. Anonymous to Catherine D. Oliver, 1850, in Edith Sparks, *Capital Instincts: Female Proprietors in San Francisco, 1850–1920* (Chapel Hill: University of North Carolina Press, 2006), 58.

15. Christiane Fischer, ed., *Let Them Speak for Themselves: Women in the American West* (New York: E. P. Dutton, 1978), 43–45.

16. Holliday, *The World Rushed In*, 165.

17. Nancy Hewitt, *Women's Activism and Social Change: Rochester, New York, 1822–1872* (Ithaca, NY: Cornell University Press, 1984), 40.

18. Constitution of the New York Female Moral Reform Society, 1836, reprinted in Dawn Keetley and John Pettegrew, eds., *Public Women, Public Words: A Documentary History of American Feminism*, vol. 1, *Beginnings to 1900* (Madison, WI: Madison House, 1997), 129.

19. T. L. Nichols, M.D., and Mrs. Mary S. Gove Nichols, *Marriage: Its History, Character and Results; Its Sanctities and Its Profanities; Its Science and Its Facts* (New York: T. L. Nichols, 1854), 202.

20. April Haynes, *Riotous Flesh: Women, Physiology, and the Solitary Vice in Nineteenth-Century America* (Chicago: University of Chicago Press, 2015), 85.

21. Elizabeth Cady Stanton, *Eighty Years and More: Reminiscences, 1815–1897* (1898; repr., Boston: Northeastern University Press, 1993), 284.

22. Georgiana Bruce Kirby, *Years of Experience: An Autobiographical Narrative* (New York: G. P. Putnam's Sons, 1887), 99.

23. Bell Gale Chevigny, *The Woman and the Myth: Margaret Fuller's Life and Writings*, rev. ed. (Boston: Northeastern University Press, 1997), 248.

24. Boston Female Anti-Slavery Address, July 13, 1836, reprinted in *Our Mothers before Us: Women and Democracy, 1789–1920* (Washington, DC: Foundation for the National Archives, 1998), 11–23.

25. Maria Stewart, "Religion and the Pure Principles of Morality," *Liberator*, October 1831.

26. Harriet Beecher Stowe, "Sojourner Truth: The Libyan Sibyl," *Atlantic Monthly*, April 1863, 473–81.

27. Elizabeth Cady Stanton, "Speech to the Anniversary of the American Anti-Slavery Society," *Liberator*, May 18, 1860, 78.

28. Carolyn Williams, "The Female Antislavery Movement: Fighting against Racial Prejudice and Promoting Women's Rights in Antebellum America," in Jean Fagan Yellin and John C. Van Horne, eds., *The Abolitionist Sisterhood: Women's Political Culture in Antebellum America* (Ithaca, NY: Cornell University Press, 1994), 162.

29. Jean R. Soderlund, "Priorities and Power: The Philadelphia Female Anti-Slavery Society," in Yellin and Van Horne, *The Abolitionist Sisterhood*, 73.

30. "Pastoral Letter of the Massachusetts Congregationalist Clergy," 1837, in Aileen Kraditor, ed., *Up from the Pedestal: Selected Writings in the History of American Feminism* (Chicago: Quadrangle Books, 1968), 51.

31. Elizabeth Ann Bartlett et al., eds., *Sarah Grimké: Letters on the Equality of the Sexes and Other Essays* (New Haven: Yale University Press, 1988), 38.

32. Boston Female Anti-Slavery Address, July 13, 1836, 11–23.

33. Quoted in Lori D. Ginzberg, *Women and the Work of Benevolence: Morality, Politics, and Class in the Nineteenth-Century United States* (New Haven: Yale University Press, 1990), 93.

34. Ginzberg, *Women and the Work of Benevolence*, 26.

35. Angelina Grimké Weld to Gerrit and Anne Smith, June 18, 1840, in Gilbert Barnes and Dwight Dumond, eds., *Letters of Theodore Dwight Weld, Angelina Grimké Weld, and Sarah Grimké, 1822–1844* (New York: Appleton-Century, 1934), 2:842.

36. Cady Stanton, *Eighty Years and More*, 83.

37. Cady Stanton, *Eighty Years and More*, 147–48.

38. "Declaration of Sentiments and Resolutions, Seneca Falls Convention," 1848, reprinted in Kraditor, *Up from the Pedestal*, 183–89.

39. Frances Ellen Watkins Harper, letter to John Brown, November 25, 1859, reprinted in James Redpath, *Echoes of Harpers Ferry* (Boston: Thayer and Eldridge, 1860), 418–19.

40. Frances Willard, *Glimpses of Fifty Years: The Autobiography of an American Woman* (Chicago: H. J. Smith, 1889), 155.

41. Mary Chesnut, April 12, 1861, in C. Vann Woodward, ed., *Mary Chesnut's Civil War* (New Haven: Yale University Press, 1981), 46.

42. Mary Livermore, *My Story of the War* (Hartford: A. D. Worthington, 1898), 465.

43. Livermore, *My Story of the War*, 472.

44. Anna Howard Shaw, with the collaboration of Elizabeth Jordan, *The Story of a Pioneer* (New York: Harper & Brothers, 1915), 51.

45. Bell Irvin Wiley, *Confederate Women* (Westport, CT: Greenwood Press, 1975), 177.

46. Elizabeth Cady Stanton to Nancy Smith, July 20, 1863, in Theodore Stanton and Harriot Stanton Blatch, eds., *Elizabeth Cady Stanton as Revealed in Her Letters, Diary, and Reminiscences* (New York: Harper & Brothers, 1922), 95.

47. Dorothy Sterling, ed., *We Are Your Sisters: Black Women in the Nineteenth Century* (New York: W. W. Norton, 1984), 239.

48. Elizabeth Cady Stanton, "To the Women of the Republic," April 24, 1863, reprinted in Gordon, *Selected Papers*, 483.

49. Elizabeth Cady Stanton, Susan B. Anthony, and Matilda J. Gage, eds., *History of Woman Suffrage* (Rochester, NY: Susan B. Anthony, 1881), 1:79.

50. Mary Chesnut, May 7, 1865, in Woodward, *Mary Chesnut's Civil War*, 802.

51. "Mrs. Fannie Berry," interview conducted by Susie Byrd, February 26, 1937, in *Weevils in the Wheat: Interviews with Virginia Ex-Slaves* (Charlottesville: University of Virginia Press, 1976), 38.

52. Sterling, *We Are Your Sisters*, 244.

53. Livermore, *My Story of the War*, 469.

54. Cited in Marilyn Mayer Culpepper, *All Things Altered: Women in the Wake of Civil War and Reconstruction* (Jefferson, NC: McFarland, 2002), 23.

55. Shirley Ann Wilson Moore, *Sweet Freedom's Plains: African Americans on the Overland Trail* (Norman: University of Oklahoma Press, 2016), 160–62.

56. Rose Stremlau, "Witnessing the West: Barbara Longknife and the California Gold Rush," in Tim Alan Garrison and Greg O'Brien, eds., *The Native South* (Lincoln: University of Nebraska Press, 2017), 163.

57. Benjamin Madley, *American Genocide: The United States and the California Indian Catastrophe* (New Haven: Yale University Press, 2016), 54–56.

58. Stacey L. Smith, *Freedom's Frontier: California and the Struggle over Unfree Labor, Emancipation, and Reconstruction* (Chapel Hill: University of North Carolina Press, 2013), 11.

59. The original is in the Elizabeth Cady Stanton Papers, Vassar College, Poughkeepsie, New York. A slightly different transcription can be found in Gordon, *Selected Papers*, 319–21.

60. The original is in the Elizabeth Cady Stanton Papers, Library of Congress, Washington, DC. The version in Gordon, *Selected Papers*, 321–23, is closer to the original in small details of underlining and punctuation.

61. Mary Denis Maher, *To Bind Up the Wounds: Catholic Sister Nurses in the U.S. Civil War* (New York: Greenwood Press, 1989), 51.

62. Maher, *To Bind Up the Wounds*, 53.

63. Louisa May Alcott, *The Journals of Louisa May Alcott*, ed. Joel Myerson, Daniel Sheahy, and Madeleine B. Stern (Boston: Little, Brown, 1989), 110.

64. Drew Gilpin Faust, "Altars of Sacrifice: Confederate Women and the Narratives of War," *Journal of American History* 76 (1990): 1203.

65. Maher, *To Bind Up the Wounds*, 39.

66. *Commonwealth*, July 10, 1863, cited in Earl Conrad, *Harriet Tubman* (Washington, DC: Associated Publishers, 1943), 169.

67. Elizabeth Leonard, *All the Daring of the Soldier: Women of the Civil War Armies* (New York: W. W. Norton, 1999), 94.

68. Stephanie McCurry, *Confederate Reckoning: Power and Politics in the Civil War South* (Cambridge, MA: Harvard University Press, 2010), 103.

69. McCurry, *Confederate Reckoning*, 123.

70. Livermore, *My Story of the War*, 116.

71. Stanton, Anthony, and Gage, *History of Woman Suffrage*, 2:23.

72. Leonard, *All the Daring of the Soldier*, 188–89.

Chapter 6

1. Elizabeth Cady Stanton, "This Is the Negro's Hour," *National Anti-Slavery Standard*, November 26, 1865, reprinted in Elizabeth Cady Stanton, Susan B. Anthony, and Matilda J. Gage, eds., *History of Woman Suffrage* (Rochester, NY: Susan B. Anthony, 1881), 2:94.

2. Ellen Carol DuBois, *Feminism and Suffrage: The Emergence of an Independent Women's Movement in America, 1848–1869* (Ithaca, NY: Cornell University Press, 1999), 63.

3. DuBois, *Feminism and Suffrage*, 60.

4. DuBois, *Feminism and Suffrage*, 175.

5. Elizabeth Cady Stanton to Lucretia Mott, April 1, 1872, in Theodore Stanton and Harriot Stanton Blatch, eds., *Elizabeth Cady Stanton as Revealed in Her Letters, Diary and Reminiscences* (New York: Harper and Brothers, 1922), 137.

6. Susan B. Anthony to Elizabeth Cady Stanton, November 5, 1872, Ida H. Harper Collection, Huntington Library, San Marino, CA.

7. Stanton, Anthony, and Gage, *History of Woman Suffrage*, 3:31.

8. Dorothy Sterling, ed., *We Are Your Sisters: Black Women in the Nineteenth Century* (New York: Norton, 1984), 313.

9. Story told by Lucy Chase of the Freedmen's Aid Society, in a letter to unnamed correspondent, 1868, American Antiquarian Society, Worcester, Massachusetts, excerpted in Nancy Woloch, ed., *Early American Women: A Documentary History, 1600–1900* (Belmont, CA: Wadsworth, 1992), 401.

10. Sterling, *We Are Your Sisters*, 311.

11. Sterling, *We Are Your Sisters*, 314.

12. Charlotte Forten, "Life in the Sea Islands," *Atlantic Monthly*, June 1864, 676.

13. Marilyn Mayer Culpepper, *All Things Altered: Women in the Wake of Civil War and Reconstruction* (Jefferson, NC: McFarland, 2002), 135.

14. Culpepper, *All Things Altered*, 123.

15. Tera W. Hunter, *To 'Joy My Freedom: Southern Black Women's Lives and Labors after the Civil War* (Cambridge, MA: Harvard University Press, 1997), 33.

16. Crystal Feimster, " 'What If I Am a Woman?' Black Women's Campaigns for Sexual Justice and Citizenship," in Gregory Downs and Kate Masur, eds., *The World the Civil War Made* (Chapel Hill: University of North Carolina Press, 2015), 250.

17. Arthur F. Raper, *The Tragedy of Lynching* (Chapel Hill: University of North Carolina Press, 1933), 13–14.

18. "The Race Problem: An Autobiography: A Southern Colored Woman," *The Independent* 56 (1904): 586–89.

19. Nancy Cott et al., eds., *Root of Bitterness: Documents of the Social History of American Women*, 2nd ed. (Boston: Northeastern University Press, 1996), 360.

20. Claudia Goldin, *The Work and Wages of Single Women: 1870 to 1920*, Working Paper 375 (National Bureau of Economic Research, 1979), 1, https://www.nber.org/papers/w0375.

21. Linda Gordon, *The Great Arizona Orphan Abduction* (Cambridge, MA: Harvard University Press, 1999), 8.

22. Nancy Cott, ed., *Root of Bitterness: Documents of the Social History of American Women* (Boston: Northeastern University Press, 1986), 319.

23. Helen Campbell, *Women Wage-Earners: Their Past, Their Present, and Their Future* (Boston: Roberts Brothers, 1893), 190.

24. Campbell, *Women Wage-Earners*, 191.

25. Quoted in Barbara Wertheimer, *We Were There: The Story of Working Women in America* (New York: Pantheon Books, 1977), 178.

26. Gary B. Nash et al., *The American People: Creating a Nation and a Society*, brief 5th ed. (New York: Addison Wesley Longman, 2000), 481.

27. Elizabeth Blackwell, "On Sexual Passion in Men and Women," 1894, reprinted in Cott, *Root of Bitterness* (1986), 302.

28. Women's historians first encountered the De Kay/Hallock romance in Carroll Smith-Rosenberg's pathbreaking essay, "The Female World of Love and Ritual: Relations between Women in Nineteenth Century America," which can be found in her collection of essays, *Disorderly Conduct: Visions of Gender in Victorian America* (New York: Oxford University Press, 1985), 53–76. Their relationship also formed the basis of Wallace Stegner's Pulitzer Prize–winning 1971 novel, *Angle of Repose*. Winslow Homer is thought to have been infatuated with De Kay, and he painted a lovely, haunting portrait of her "in repose." Hallock became an important writer and illustrator of the West. The quote is from Smith-Rosenberg, 57.

29. Karen V. Hansen, " 'No Kisses Is Like Yours': An Erotic Friendship between Two African-American Women during the Mid-Nineteenth Century," *Gender History* 7 (1995): 153.

30. Karen Blair, *The Clubwoman as Feminist: True Womanhood Redefined, 1868–1914* (New York: Holmes and Meier, 1980), 34.

31. Sarah J. Early, "The Organized Efforts of the Colored Women of the South to Improve Their Condition," 1893, reprinted in Dawn Keetley and John Pettegrew, eds., *Public Women, Public Words*, vol. 1 (Madison, WI: Madison House, 1997), 316.

32. Mary Earhart, *Frances Willard: From Prayers to Politics* (Chicago: University of Chicago Press, 1944), 93.

33. Suzanne Marilley, *Woman Suffrage and the Origins of Liberal Feminism in the United States, 1820–1920* (Cambridge, MA: Harvard University Press, 1996), 128–29.

34. Frances E. Willard, *How I Learned to Ride the Bicycle: Reflections of an Influential 19th Century Woman*, ed. Carol O'Hare (1895; repr., Sunnyvale, CA: Fair Oaks, 1991), 17, 75.

35. Ellen Carol DuBois, ed., *The Elizabeth Cady Stanton–Susan B. Anthony Reader: Correspondence, Writings, Speeches*, rev. ed. (Boston: Northeastern University Press, 1992), 176.

36. Charlotte Perkins Gilman, *Women and Economics: A Study of the Economic Relation between Men and Women as a Factor in Social Evolution* (Boston: Small, Maynard & Company, 1898), 156.

37. Elizabeth Cady Stanton, "The Solitude of Self," 1892, http://historymatters.gmu.edu/d/5315 (accessed July 1, 2015).

38. Mia Bay, *To Tell the Truth Freely: The Life of Ida B. Wells* (New York: Macmillan, 2011), 117–18.

39. Patricia Schechter, *Ida B. Wells-Barnett and American Reform, 1880–1930* (Chapel Hill: University of North Carolina Press, 2001), 62–63.

40. Mrs. John Van Vorst and Marie Van Vorst, *The Woman Who Toils: Being the Experiences of Two Ladies as Factory Girls* (New York: Doubleday, Page & Co., 1903), 58.

41. Alice Rossi, ed., *The Feminist Papers from Adams to de Beauvoir* (Boston: Northeastern University Press, 1988), 40.

42. Rosalind Rosenberg, "The Limits of Access," in John Mack Faragher and Florence Howe, eds., *Women and Higher Education: Essays from the Mount Holyoke College Sesquicentennial Symposia* (New York: Norton, 1988), 110.

43. Helen Lefkowitz Horowitz, *Alma Mater: Design and Experience in Women's Colleges from Their Nineteenth-Century Beginnings to the 1930s* (New York: Knopf, 1984), 29.

44. M. F. [Mary Frances] Armstrong and Helen W. Ludlow, *Hampton and Its Students, by Two of Its Teachers, Mrs. M. F. Armstrong and Helen W. Ludlow* (New York: G. P. Putnam, 1874), 89–90.

45. Laura Wexler, *Tender Violence: Domestic Visions in an Age of U.S. Imperialism* (Chapel Hill: University of North Carolina Press, 2000), 168.

46. Martha Patterson, "'Survival of the Best Fitted': Selling the American New Woman as Gibson Girl, 1896–1910," *ATQ: A Journal of American 19th Century Literature and Culture* (June 1995): 73–87.

47. Ida Husted Harper, *The Life and Work of Susan B. Anthony* (Indianapolis: The Hollenbeck Press, 1908), 3:1293.

48. Brooke Kroeger, *Nellie Bly: Daredevil, Reporter, Feminist* (New York: Three Rivers Press, 1994), 167.

49. Dee Garrison, *Mary Heaton Vorse: The Life of an American Insurgent* (Philadelphia: Temple University Press, 1989), 21.

50. Mary Guy Humphreys, "Women Bachelors in New York," *Scribner's Magazine* 20 (November 1896): 633.

Chapter 7

1. Shige Kushida is mentioned in Mei Nakano, *Japanese American Women: Three Generations, 1890–1990* (Berkeley, CA: Mina Press, 1990). Our version of her life differs on the basis of information provided by Rumi Yasutake, Kobe University, author of *Transnational Women's Activism: The United States, Japan, and Japanese Immigrant Communities in California, 1859–1920* (New York: New York University Press, 2004).

2. Laura Jane Moore, "Lozen," in Theda Perdue, ed., *Sifters: Native American Women's Lives* (New York: Oxford University Press, 2001), 93.

3. Mrs. Z. A. Parker's description of a Ghost Dance observed on White Clay Creek at Pine Ridge reservation, Dakota Territory, June 20, 1890, in James Mooney, "The Ghost-Dance Religion and the Sioux Outbreak of 1890," in *14th Annual Report of the Bureau of American Ethnology*, Part 2 (Washington, DC: Bureau of American Ethnology, 1894).

4. Nelson Miles to George Baird, November 20, 1891, Baird Collection, Western Americana Collection, Beinecke Library, Yale University.

5. The term is from Alvin M. Josephy, *500 Nations: An Illustrated History of North American Indians* (New York: Knopf, 1994), 430.

6. Cathleen D. Cahill, *Federal Fathers and Mothers: A Social History of the United States Indian Service, 1869–1933* (Chapel Hill: University of North Carolina Press, 2013), 67.

7. Carolyn J. Marr, "Assimilation through Education: Indian Boarding Schools in the Pacific Northwest," http://content.lib.washington.edu/aipnw/marr.html (accessed June 28, 2004).

8. "A Man Plants the Fields of His Wife," in Ruth Barnes Moynihan, Cynthia Russett, and Laurie Crumpacker, eds., *Second to None: A Documentary History of American Women* (Lincoln: University of Nebraska Press, 1993), 2:82–83.

9. Linda Williams Reese, *Women of Oklahoma, 1890–1920* (Norman: University of Oklahoma Press, 1997), 152–53.

10. Diary of Lucy Hannah White Flake, excerpted in Joan M. Jensen, ed., *With These Hands: Women Working on the Land* (Old Westbury, NY: Feminist Press, 1981), 137–38.

11. Glenda Riley, *A Place to Grow: Women in the American West* (Arlington Heights, IL: Harlan Davidson, 1992), 239.

12. Reese, *Women of Oklahoma*, 38.

13. Michael Lewis Goldberg, *An Army of Women: Gender and Politics in Gilded Age Kansas* (Baltimore: Johns Hopkins University Press, 1997), 40.

14. The term comes from Paula Petrik, *No Step Backward: Women and Family on the Rocky Mountain Mining Frontier, Helena, Montana, 1865–1900* (Helena: Montana Historical Society Press, 1987), 28.

15. Mother Mary Jones, *Autobiography of Mother Jones* (1925; repr., Chicago: C. H. Kerr, 1990), 204.

16. Elizabeth Jameson, "Imperfect Unions: Class and Gender in Cripple Creek, 1894–1904," in Milton Cantor and Bruce Laurie, eds., *Class, Sex, and the Woman Worker* (Westport, CT: Greenwood Press, 1977), 171.

17. Joan Morrison and Charlotte Fox Zabusky, *American Mosaic: The Immigrant Experience in the Words of Those Who Lived It* (New York: E. P. Dutton, 1980), 9.

18. Linda Mack Schloff, *"And Prairie Dogs Weren't Kosher": Jewish Women in the Upper Midwest since 1855* (St. Paul: Minnesota Historical Society Press, 1996), 28.

19. Edith Abbott, *Immigration: Select Documents and Case Records* (Chicago: University of Chicago Press, 1924), 719.

20. Him Mark Lai, Genny Lim, and Judy Yung, *Island: Poetry and History of Chinese Immigrants on Angel Island, 1910–1940* (San Francisco: San Francisco Study Center, 1980), 74.

21. Jane Addams, *Twenty Years at Hull-House*, edited with an introduction by Victoria Bissell Brown (1910; repr., Boston: Bedford/St. Martin's, 1999), 72.

22. "They Enter a Protest," *New York Times*, October 28, 1886, excerpted in Susan Ware, ed., *American Women's Suffrage: Voices from the Long Struggle for the Vote, 1776–1965* (New York: Library of America, 2020), 205.

23. Aileen Kraditor, *Ideas of the Woman Suffrage Movement, 1890–1920* (New York: Columbia University Press, 1965), 128.

24. Theodore Roosevelt, introduction to Mrs. John Van Vorst and Marie Van Vorst, *The Woman Who Toils: Being the Experiences of Two Ladies as Factory Girls* (New York: Doubleday, Page, 1903), vii.

25. Anzia Yezierska, *Bread Givers* (1925; repr., New York: George Braziller, 1975), 135.

26. Addams, *Twenty Years at Hull-House*, 166.

27. Ellen Carol DuBois, *The Elizabeth Cady Stanton–Susan B. Anthony Reader: Correspondence, Writings, Speeches*, rev. ed. (Boston: Northeastern University Press, 1992), 205.

28. Jensen, *With These Hands*, 157–58.

29. Susan B. Anthony and Ida H. Harper, eds., *History of Woman Suffrage* (Rochester, NY: Susan B. Anthony, 1902), 4:519.

30. Jensen, *With These Hands*, 147.

31. Ida H. Harper, ed., *History of Woman Suffrage* (New York: National American Woman Suffrage Association, 1922), 5:518.

32. Anthony and Harper, *History of Woman Suffrage*, 4:647.

33. "Women Keep Up Courage," *San Francisco Chronicle*, November 5, 1896. Thanks to Ann Gordon for the citation.

34. Marion K. Barthelme, ed., *Women in the Texas Populist Movement: Letters to the* Southern Mercury (College Station: Texas A&M Press, 1997), 111.

35. Moynihan, Russett, and Crumpacker, *Second to None*, 2:81.

36. Emma Goldman, *Living My Life*, ed. Richard and Anna Maria Drinnon (New York: New American Library, 1977), 122.

37. Kathryn Kish Sklar, *Florence Kelley and the Nation's Work* (New Haven: Yale University Press, 1995), 272.

38. Alice Miller, "Hull House," *The Charities*, February 1892, 167–73.

39. Sklar, *Florence Kelley*, 215.

40. Sklar, *Florence Kelley*, 283.

41. Ida B. Wells, "Lynch Laws," *The Reason Why the Colored American Is Not in the World's Columbian Exposition*, 1893.

42. Frances Willard, *The Autobiography of an American Woman, Glimpses of Fifty Years* (Chicago: Woman's Temperance Publishing Association, 1892), 431.

43. Kristin Hoganson, *Fighting for American Manhood: How Gender Politics Provoked the Spanish-American and Philippine-American Wars* (New Haven: Yale University Press, 1998), 11.

44. Allen Davis, *An American Heroine: The Life and Legend of Jane Addams* (New York: Oxford University Press, 1973), 140.

45. Allison L. Sneider, *Suffragists in an Imperial Age* (New York: Oxford University Press, 2008), 91.

46. John M. Coward, *Indians Illustrated: The Image of Native Americans in the Pictorial Press* (Urbana: University of Illinois Press, 2012), chap. 3.

47. Leah Dilworth, *Imagining Indians in the Southwest: Persistent Visions of a Primitive Past* (Washington, DC: Smithsonian, 1996), 89–90.

48. Francis Washburn, "Zitkala-Ša: A Bridge between Two Worlds," in Shirley A. Leckie and Nancy J. Parezo, eds., *Their Own Frontier: Women Intellectuals Revisioning the American West* (Lincoln: University of Nebraska Press, 2008), 273.

49. *Harper's New Monthly Magazine* 99 (November 1899): 860.

50. Jane Simonsen, *Making Home Work: Domesticity and Native American Assimilation in the American West, 1860–1919* (Chapel Hill: University of North Carolina Press, 2006), 192.

51. Cited in Cari M. Carpenter and Carolyn Sorisio, eds., *The Newspaper Warrior: Sarah Winnemucca Hopkins's Campaign for American Indian Rights, 1864–1891* (Lincoln: University of Nebraska Press, 2015), 90.

52. Rose Stremlau, "Rape Narratives on the Northern Paiute Frontier: Sarah Winnemucca, Sexual Sovereignty, and Economic Autonomy," in Dee Garceau-Hagen, ed., *Portraits of Women in the American West* (New York: Routledge, 2005), 53.

53. Sally Zanjani, *Sarah Winnemucca* (Lincoln: University of Nebraska Press, 2001), 266–67.

54. Jacob A. Riis, *How the Other Half Lives: Studies among the Tenements of New York*, ed. David Leviatin (1890; repr., Boston: Bedford/St. Martin's, 1996), 61.

55. Riis, *How the Other Half Lives*, 92.

56. Riis, *How the Other Half Lives*, 91.

57. Riis, *How the Other Half Lives*, 95.

58. Riis, *How the Other Half Lives*, 129.

59. Riis, *How the Other Half Lives*, 141.

60. Riis, *How the Other Half Lives*, 140.

61. Riis, *How the Other Half Lives*, 139.

62. Jacob A. Riis, *The Children of the Poor* (New York: Scribner's Sons, 1892), 82.

63. Riis, *Children of the Poor*, 80.

INDEX

Area ceded by
the United States
to Great Britain,
1818

Olympia ★ WASHINGTON

Salem ★

Columbia R.

Helena ★

Missouri R.

MONTANA

NORTH
DAKOTA

Bismarck ★

OREGON COUNTRY
Agreement with Britain,
1846

OREGON

IDAHO

Boise ★

Snake R.

WYOMING

SOUTH
DAKOTA

Pierre ★

L O U I S I A N A
P U R C H A S E
From France, 1803

NEBRASKA

Sacramento R.

Carson City ★

★ Sacramento

San Joaquin R.

NEVADA

★ Salt Lake
City

UTAH

N. Platte R.

Cheyenne ★

Platte R.

S. Platte R.

★ Denver

MEXICAN CESSION
1848

Colorado R.

COLORADO

KANSAS

CALIFORNIA

ARIZONA

★ Santa Fe

NEW
MEXICO

Red R.

T E X A S
Annexed, 1845

PACIFIC
OCEAN

Phoenix ★

TEXAS

ARCTIC OCEAN

RUSSIA

ALASKA
Purchased from
Russia, 1867

CANADA

Yukon R.

GADSDEN PURCHASE
from Mexico, 1853

Rio Grande

Bering
Sea

Gulf of
Alaska

Juneau ★

HAWAII
Annexed,
1898

Honolulu ★

PACIFIC
OCEAN

M E X I C O

0   250   500 miles

0   250   500 kilometers

0   50   100 miles

0   50   100 kilometers

Area ceded by Great Britain, 1818

Areas ceded by Britain, 1842 (Webster-Ashburton Treaty)

CANADA

St. Lawrence R.

MAINE

★ Augusta

Lake Superior

VERMONT

Montpelier ★

Concord ★

N.H.

★ Boston

Connecticut R.

MASS.

Albany ★

NEW YORK

Providence

★ St. Paul

WISCONSIN

Lake Michigan

Lake Huron

Lake Ontario

Hartford ★

RHODE ISLAND

CONNECTICUT

MINNESOTA

MICHIGAN

★ Madison

Lansing ★

Lake Erie

PENN.

Susquehanna R.

Hudson R.

Delaware R.

Trenton ★

NEW JERSEY

Harrisburg ★

Dover ★

DELAWARE

IOWA

★ Des Moines

ILLINOIS

INDIANA

OHIO

Columbus ★

★ Lincoln

★ Springfield

Indianapolis ★

Annapolis ✪

MARYLAND

WASHINGTON, D.C.

Potomac R.

VIRGINIA

Richmond ★

Chesapeake Bay

Missouri R.

★ Topeka

WEST VIRGINIA

Charleston ★

Frankfort ★

Ohio R.

THE ORIGINAL THIRTEEN COLONIES

Jefferson City ★

MISSOURI

KENTUCKY

Gained by treaty with Britain, 1783

James R.

NORTH CAROLINA

★ Raleigh

Cumberland R.

ATLANTIC OCEAN

Oklahoma City

ARKANSAS

TENNESSEE

★ Nashville

Tennessee R.

Proclamation Line of 1763

Cape Fear R.

Arkansas R.

★ Little Rock

SOUTH CAROLINA

★ Columbia

OKLAHOMA

Atlanta ★

Savannah R.

MISSISSIPPI

ALABAMA

GEORGIA

LOUISIANA

★ Jackson

Montgomery ★

Austin

Baton Rouge ★

★ Tallahassee

FLORIDA

Areas taken from Spain, 1810 and 1813

FLORIDA
Treaty with Spain, 1819

BAHAMAS

Gulf of Mexico

U.S. Territories

ATLANTIC OCEAN

San Juan ★

PUERTO RICO
Acquired from Spain, 1898

VIRGIN ISLANDS
Acquired from Denmark, 1916–1917

Caribbean Sea

| 0 | 50 | 100 miles |
| 0 | 50 | 100 kilometers |

| 0 | 150 | 300 miles |
| 0 | 150 | 300 kilometers |

About the Authors

ELLEN CAROL DuBOIS (PhD, Northwestern University) is Distinguished Research Professor of History and Gender Studies at the University of California, Los Angeles. She is the author of *Feminism and Suffrage: The Emergence of an Independent Women's Movement in America, 1848–1869*; *Harriot Stanton Blatch and the Winning of Woman Suffrage* (winner of the 1998 Joan Kelly Memorial Prize in Women's History from the American Historical Association); and *Woman Suffrage and Women's Rights*. With Vicki L. Ruiz, she coedited the influential anthology *Unequal Sisters: A Multicultural Reader in U.S. Women's History*. With Vinay Lal, she is coauthor of *A Passionate Life: Writings By and About Kamaladevi Chattopadhyay*. Her newest book, *Suffrage: Women's Long Road to the Ballot Box* (2020), is the first comprehensive history of the American woman suffrage movement in a half century.

Photo by Scarlett Freund

BRENDA ELAINE STEVENSON (PhD, Yale University) is the inaugural Hillary Rodham Clinton Chair of Women's History at the University of Oxford and the inaugural Nickoll Family Endowed Chair in History at the University of California, Los Angeles. She is the author of the award-winning monographs *Life in Black and White: Family and Community in the Slave South* and *The Contested Murder of Latasha Harlins: Justice, Gender, and the Origins of the L.A. Riots*. She is also the author of *What Is Slavery?*, the editor of the Journals of Charlotte Forten Grimké, and the coauthor of *The Underground Railroad*. Her new monograph, *What Sorrows Labour in My Parent's Breast?: A History of the Enslaved Black Family*, appeared in April 2023. She was appointed by President Biden to serve on the Civil Rights Cold Case Records Review Board in 2022.

John Cairns Photography

LYNN DUMENIL (PhD, University of California, Berkeley) is Robert Glass Cleland Professor of American History, Emerita, at Occidental College. She has written *The Second Line of Defense: American Women and World War I*, *The Modern Temper: American Culture and Society in the 1920s*, *Freemasonry and American Culture: 1880–1930*, and *American Working Women in World War II: A Brief History with Documents*. Her articles and reviews have appeared in the *Journal of American History*, the *Journal of American Ethnic History*, *Reviews in American History*, and the *American Historical Review*.

Lee Brubaker

Key to the Cover Images

Left to right:
Susan B. Anthony
Charlotte Forten Grimké
Sarah Winnemucca
Leung Yee
Elizabeth Freeman ("Mum Bett")

Susan B. Anthony: National Portrait Gallery, Smithsonian Institution; Charlotte Forten Grimké: From The New York Public Library; Sarah Winnemucca: National Portrait Gallery, Smithsonian Institution; Leung Yee: National Archives file no. 12017/37232; Elizabeth Freeman ("Mum Bett"): Massachusetts Historical Society/Bridgeman Images